THE
STRIPED
BASS

THE
STRIPED
BASS

Nick Karas

LYONS & BURFORD
PUBLISHERS

Jointly Published by
KARMAPCO
P.O. Box 194
St. James, N.Y. 11780
and
LYONS & BURFORD, Publishers
31 West 21st Street
New York, N.Y. 10010

Printed in the United States of America

10 9 8 7 6 5 4 3 2 1

Library of Congress Cataloging-in-Publication Data

Karas, Nick.
    The striped bass / Nick Karas.
        p.   cm.
    Rev. ed. of: The complete book of the striped bass. 1974.
    Includes index.
    1. Striped bass fishing. 2. Striped bass. I. Karas, Nick.
Complete book of the striped bass. II. Title.
SH691.S7K37 1993
799.1'758—dc20   93-41437
                                                              CIP

This book is dedicated to
those thousands of lay and
professional men and
women who for untold
years and numerous sce-
narios have unselfishly and
uncompromisingly given of
their time and effort to insure the future of
striped bass.

Acknowledgments

The world of the striped bass cannot be singled out as the realm of any one individual or group of individuals. It belongs to all those people who have ever followed this fish, with rod and reel, with net and trap, or with tags and rulers. It belongs to all those researchers and biologists who have studied, examined, and dissected the striped bass. It belongs to all those fishermen who have chased it for sport, food, and livelihood. It too belongs to all those writers and reporters who have gone before me, extolling the virtues of bass fishing. And it belongs to all those who will seek the striper after you and I are gone.

Therefore, I would like to acknowledge and thank the men who have come to know the striped bass, who have written about its habits, its life cycle, and its needs. And I hope I haven't borrowed too heavily of their ideas. I wish to acknowledge those who have given me guidance, direction, and encouragement to gather as much knowledge, technique, and lore as exists about this fish and then write it down.

Specifically, I would like to my wife, who laboriously typed and helped edit the manuscript, and kept my enthusiasm with in bounds.

Then, there are the researchers with whom I talked bass, primarily Byron Young, whom I first met when he was young Downeaster who has helped to unravel many of the mysteries of the Hudson River striped bass and Phil Briggs, a marine biologist, also with the State of New York who helped me over some of the more profound scientific hurdles in this book.

There are scores of researchers with whom I've met, talked, and corresponded. These include Richard Schaefer of the National Oceanic and Atmospheric Administration; Irwin Alperin, Director of the Atlantic States Marine Fisheries Commission; Bruce Freeman, Stuart Wilkie, and Dr. L. A. Walford of the Middle Atlantic Coastal Research Center, Sandy Hook, N. J.; W. B. Scott, Curator of the Royal Ontario Museum; Fernando Fortier, for her translations; Gerard Beaulieu, Quebec Department of Fisheries; J. W. Baker of St. John, N.B.; Arthur Smith, Fishery Biologist, P. E. I.; Barry Sabean, Fisheries Biologist, N. S.; C. P. Ruggles, Environment Canada; Lewis N. Flagg, Marine Resources Scientist, Maine; Richard Seamans, Chief, Marine Fisheries, N.H.; Bruce Rogers, biologist, and Thomas Wright, R.I. Department of Natural Resources; William Clede, writer, and Cole Wilde, Connecticut Department of Environmental Protection; Paul Hammer, New Jersey Marine Research Center; Arthur Bradford, Chief Pennsylvania Fish Commission; William F. Moore, Fisheries Manager, Delaware; Dr. Ted S. Y. Koo, Chesapeake Biological Lab, Solomans, Md.; William E. Neal, Fish Biologist, Virginia; Michael Street, Marine Biologist, Donald Baker, Chief of Inland Fisheries, and James Tyler, biologist, North Carolina; Dr. Jack D. Bayliss, Marine Resources, Moncks Corners, S. C.; Carl S. Hall, Fisheries Supervisor, Georgia; James Barkuloo and F. G. Banks, Fisheries Division, Florida; W. F. Anderson, Marine Resources, Alabama; Harry Barkley and Larry C. Nicholson, Mississippi Fish Commission and the Gulf Coast Research Laboratory; Bennie J. Fontenot, Jr., Louisiana Fisheries Commission; Harold K. Chadwick, California Delta-Bay Fisheries Project; C. J. Campbell, Fishery Division, and Robert T. Gunsolus, Research Division, State of Oregon; Scott Henderson, Arkansas biologist; Gary Edwards, Fisheries Specialist, Arizona Game & Fish Department; Ron Jarman, Fish Division, Oklahoma Department of Wildlife Conservation: David Bishop, Fisheries Biologist, Tennessee Game and Fish Commission; David L. Pritchard, Texas Parks and Wildlife Department; Charles C. Bowers, Director, Fisheries Division, Kentucky Department of Fish and Wildlife; and Dr. S. I. Doroshev, All-Union Research Institute, USSR, now with the University of California at Davis.

I would also like to acknowledge the great field of researchers whose works influenced, guided, and contributed to my knowledge as well as the world's on the life of the striped bass. They are: A. J. Calhoun, John R. Clark, Albert C. Jensen, D. P. deSylva, William W. Hassler, Edgar H. Hollis, Robert M. Lewis, George C. Maltezos, Romeo Mansueti, W. H. Massman, A. L. Pacheco,

Daniel Merriman, Walter S. Murawski, William C. Nevile, Paul R. Nichols, John C. Pearson, Alfred Perlmutter, John C. Poole, Edward C. Raney, Warren F. Rathjen, Robert E. Stevens, James E. Sykes, R. E. Tiller, Wallace L. Trent, Vadim Vladykov, David H. Wallace, and James R. Westman.

With the second edition of the book, the list grows: Reggie Weaver and Jimmy Evans, Georgia Department of Natural Resources, Fred A. Harris, Inland Fisheries, North Carolina. Mark Trainor, Florida Fish & Game Commission; John Riddle, Tenn. Wildlife Resources Agency; Gary Tilyou, Louisiana Department of Wildlife and Fisheries; Ken Kurzawski, Texas Parks and Wildlife Department, Michael Brainard, Mississippi Department of Wildlife and Fisheries; Ben Kinman, Kentucky Department of Fish and Wildlife; Steven Hawks, Kansas Game and Parks Commission; Ed Enamait, Torrey Brown, Ben Florence and Don Cosden, Maryland Department of Natural Resources; Miller White, South Carolina Wildlife & Marine Resources; Susan Harrell, Virginia Department of Game and Inland Fisheries; Daryl Ellison Nebraska Game and Fish Commission; David Secor, University of Maryland's Chesapeake Biological Laboratory.; Ronald Lukens, Gulf States Marine Fisheries Commission; Thomas D. McIlwain, Gulf Coast Research Laboratory; Donald Stevens, Califirfornia Department of Fish and Game Bay-Delta Project and Glenn Delisle, Inland Fisheries Division, John J. Waldman, Hudson River Foundation; Isaac Wirgin, New York University Medical Center; Bruce R. Friedmann, Hatchery Manager, EA Engineering and David Deuel, National Marine Fisheries Service.

Contents

Foreword

In the introduction to this book, the reader is invited to view the world of the striped bass as the fish sees it. This technique of viewing the life of a fish through its own eyes and feeling its emotions is not wholly my invention. I first discovered the method in a wonderful book called *The Shining Tides*, written by Win Brooks. The book is described as a novel, but it is more a biography of a fish, and all the events occur in a very real way. Brooks was a newspaperman of the first order who wrote for the Boston *American*. Unfortunately, his premature death in 1963 robbed us of more works and this novel was his only book.

His technique so intrigued me that I felt compelled to borrow it. I believe that it is an ideal means of introducing readers to the watery world of this incomparable fish. It is a complicated world that often requires a grasp of scientific concepts and terminology to fully explain and understand. I have not been able totally to relieve the reader of this jargon, and he must bear with me in places where the going might get heavy. But in this new language lie the keys to unraveling the mysteries surrounding this great fish. I hope that the striped bass will be less of a mystery to the angler once he has completed this book.

The striped bass fisher is unique among saltwater anglers. He and she are often endowed with a curiosity that reaches far beyond that of the average angler. The only counterpart they might have of which I know might be the salmon fisherman, found more often in fresh water. Both are interested in their fish and sport in a way that sets them apart from other anglers. To catch the fish is usually not enough: to know how and why it strikes is as compelling a force as the catching.

It is to satisfy this angler's curiosity that I have written this book. The initial intent was not so much to tell readers how or where to fish as it was to inform them about the fish itself, to enlighten them about their adversary. It is my maturing belief that you can tell other anglers very little about how to catch fish. But I believe that if a body of knowledge can be made available to a striped bass angler, he will ingest and assimilate it like a steak or loaf of bread, and it will become part of him.

There is a wealth of knowledge about striped bass buried in the research reports of dozen states and several provinces, and cloaked in terminology that seems like another language to most readers. In effect, this information has been inaccessible to those who might use it best to practice their sport. This information, recast in readable language, constitutes Part One of this book.

How this knowledge can then be applied in practice is the subject of Part Two. The techniques for taking striped bass vary as greatly as the environments in which this great fish is found. They differ from harbor to harbor, beach to bay, as well as between states, provinces, and coast to coast.

The angler who has learned what he is after, and how it can be obtained, can then employ Part Three of this work, a description of the tackle and the mechanical aspects of bringing the fish from the water into the frying pan. This three-part approach to the world of the striped bass—and the striped bass angler—will, I hope, increase both the reader's understanding of the fish and the pleasure the fish can give him.

Since the first edition was published, now nearly 20 years ago, the world of the striped bass has been turned upside down. Environmental forces, not wholly identified, have created a habitat hostile to the production of striped bass, and greatly increased efforts by both recreational and commercial fishermen have brought the fish to a real crisis situation. There has not been a dominant year class of striped bass produced in Chesapeake Bay since 1970.

To determine why these great populations have declined so drastically, a plethora of investigation and research efforts has ensued. They have vastly expanded the horizons of knowledge of this fish, its needs and life cycle, and its expansion into realms it had never naturally experienced or has been missing from for decades. These intense efforts, on both federal and state levels, produce so much new and valuable information that the need for a larger edition of this book and an expanion of its scope was needed. Here you have the result.

Nicholas Karas
Saint James, Long Island, N.Y.
April 1993

THE
STRIPED
BASS

THE STRIPED BASS.
[ROCCUS LINEATUS.]

Introduction

Saxatilis edged closer to the massive granite boulder until its shadow completely hid her body. Along her left side, she could feel the rough edges of barnacles scrape against her scales as she faced into the ebbing tide and settled closer to the rock. Slowly, she let her massive belly touch the rounded pebbles on the bottom. Chasing the blackfish she just swallowed cost her more effort than she had expected. Now, it felt good just to rest, to let the rhythmic motion of the water control her body and lull her.

She was realizing that for the past few seasons, she grew tired more easily when the schools she was with chased after food. That was why she now preferred to feed alone. There weren't many fish remaining with whom she had shared her younger years in Chesapeake Bay, or had made the first trek into the clear, chilly waters of the Atlantic the spring when they were all three-year olds. Now, she liked the solitude of hunting, feeding, and swimming alone. Only when the waters took on a chill at summer's end did she feel a longing to be with others of her kind. They schooled for protection. But she was now large, larger than most other fish she saw; there was very little she feared.

Old Silas had always been a good place to rest and feed. Saxatilis could always depend upon a blackfish or bergall to swim around the corner of the massive boulder, picking at mussels or barnacles encrusted on the huge glacial rock. The submerged ridge connecting Plum and Great Gull islands was a trove of food for striped bass and Old Silas was in the middle of the ridge. Her school discovered it on their very first summer of migration. It had always been a favorite hunting spot for her when she was young; now it was a good place to rest. The summer she found old Silas was now a long time ago. Fifteen years had passed since she left Chesapeake Bay, and only occasionally did she now return. It had been three years since she last spawned. Even though spring was still six months away she could feel the primordial urge again begin to well within her body, to leave the salt and climb the river to where she had been spawned. But that was still months to come. It was autumn in New York, the time to feed heavily, to store food for the months of dormancy off the Virginia Coast.

Saxatilis rested against Old Silas until the tide lost its current and the sky began to darken. It was then that she suddenly realized the blackfish was digested and she again felt the urge to feed. The current direction had shifted and she was ready to move. With only the pectoral fins on her sides, she lifted herself off the rocky bottom. The building current carried her from the boulder and through giant fronds of kelp beating with the pulsating rhythm of the water. The tide was now flooding into Long Island Sound and for a while she let it carry her sideways. Suddenly, Saxatilis resented the will of the current and with a flick of her giant tail set her own course.

She wasn't really hungry, but she knew she must feed often to support her great bulk. She weighed more than 50 pounds. As she worked down tide, the current unexpectedly reversed itself. She was now on the eastern edge of Plum Island, and here the waters separated. Swimming along the north side of the island and against the current, Saxatilis had to use more energy, but she was more powerful than all the other fish of her kind that darted out of her way.

She sensed a taste in the water coming toward her. The tide swiftly carried it to two nostril-like openings on her snout. She couldn't see where it was but turned into the water that carried the flavor and followed it. In the kelp ahead there was a dark, fleeting movement. It was Anguilla. The eel was intent on making headway against the rising force of the tide as it swept around Plum Island and through Plum Gut and didn't notice the approach of the striped bass.

Like a flash of light, Saxatilis overtook Anguilla. Before the eel could respond, she had grabbed it in her mouth, turned it, and gulped it head first. Saxatilis liked eels; they had a flavor that was incomparable to her. The only food she liked better was lobsters, but Homarus and his kind had abandoned most of the coastal waters this summer because they had been too warm. They were in deeper water, too far away from Saxatilis's natural haunts, so she gave up lobster for the summer.

After taking Anguilla, Saxatilis wanted to rest. She found the lee of a large boulder and stemmed the current. But even here the tide moved quickly. To her, it seemed that all the ocean was trying to squeeze itself into The Gut, a watery gap that separates Plum Island from Orient Point on eastern Long Island. As she approached the fast water, the bottom gave way and fell to depths beyond her sight, so she slid back to the respite of the boulder. In the distance, she saw a school of squid swimming with the flooding tide. They were too far away. She would have to leave the sanctity of the back eddy to catch them. There will be more food coming along, closer, she thought to herself all she need do was wait and watch the tide.

Unexpectedly, Saxatilis felt a strange vibration. Almost simultaneously she heard the whine of two high-pitched propellers coming through the water. As she looked up, Saxatilis saw the darkening aspect of the sky broken by a momentary glow that swept over her back. The beacon on Plum Island had been turned on. As she watched the water's surface, the black silhouette of a boat's hull came closer. The vibrations and noise increased in intensity as it approached. She knew she was in no danger and didn't move. There was more than 25 feet of water between her and the surface.

As she had seen many times before after a boat passed, two silvery lines sliced the water behind the craft. She was always concerned with them because she didn't fully understand how they were able to move. Then she saw what looked like a squid, swimming rapidly behind the boat. It moved with irregular, jerking movements and she thought it looked good to eat.

Saxatilis changed her position as the white, pulsating squid-like phenomena came closer. She felt the force of the tide as she moved beyond the protection of the boulder. It discouraged her. The "squid" were moving fast and now were too far away. Besides, there was still Anguilla to digest. Saxatilis was lazy and returned to her lie behind the boulder as darkness flooded Plum Gut. The night held no fear for her. Rather, she preferred this time. The bothersome bluefish would not beat her to food she wanted. Nor did she need light to find squid. They were bountiful in The Gut. All she required was her keen sense of taste.

Near midnight, her satiation wore off as the tide began to lose its direction. In a fit of hunger, Saxatilis moved from behind the rock and drifted into the Sound with the tide, and into deeper and deeper water. Without warning, she suddenly drifted into a school of squid. Through minute sensors along the lateral lines on her sides, she could feel the entire school pulsating, moving in unison. Saxatilis gorged herself until she could eat no more. In a burst of energy, she returned to the rocks under the lighthouse. The current along the shore had already shifted direction. Saxatilis took a new lie on the opposite side of the boulder and let the water ebb as she digested the squid.

The weather above Plum Gut turned cold during the night, colder than any night since spring. Even a dozen feet below the surface Saxatilis was sensitive enough to feel the difference. And, in the morning, the sun rose on the horizon in a slightly different spot than it had the day before. The urge in her to move south became uncontrollable. During the following week, she passed Gardiners Island and turned southeast to Montauk Point. There she felt the bitter sting of sharp hooks in her mouth as she took a plug in the surf at Turtle Cove. But the plug had been too small for her and the line too light. She broke it without effort.

The hook still dangled from the side of her mouth as she worked past Shinnecock Inlet. She tasted the water from the bay and felt it sweep over her skin. It was colder than the water that surrounded her. That changed her mind about entering it to feed. The hook irritated her because she didn't understand it. Why had the fish she thought she had taken suddenly become a part of her jaw? She pouted and refused to eat even though it wasn't in the way. She was losing weight. A striped bass as large as Saxatilis must eat often and in large quantities when she is so active.

Off Moriches Inlet, as she headed farther west along the south shore of Long Island, the hook in her jaw fell victim to the acids in her mouth and stomach. It quickly rusted and fell free. When it happened, it was as if someone had signaled her to eat. She had been tagging behind a school of younger striped bass, fish 20 and 30 pounds in size. They had been feeding on a school of *Brevoortia* and she could taste the oily flavor of these menhaden for miles behind their school. Now it was her turn. The smaller bass forced the bunker into a deep pocket between the beach and an outer bar. Saxatilis wanted her food and charged over the bar as a wave broke. Her belly scraped on the sand and she felt the momentary coldness of the air. The feeding bass parted to let her in and she slashed at the first menhaden that appeared. One, two, then three fish later, she had enough. They were large bunker, 2 to 3 pounds. The big ones were reserved for her and her voracious appetite. She didn't rest after feeding as she had done before. The chill experience of the cold air she felt while crossing the sand bar was a vivid reminder of how cold this part of the Atlantic could become. She must continue to head south.

During all of December, Saxatilis swam. She took a short cut across the New York Bight for Sandy Hook, over deep water, because she no longer feared sharks. She could outswim them in a burst of speed. Off Cape May she was bothered by a school of porpoise, but they let her alone when they spotted the mackerel school. By New Year's Day, Saxatilis was off the mouth of Chesapeake Bay. She tasted the water in which she had spent the first two years of her life.

For a moment she wanted to turn west, slide past Fisherman's Island, swim in the bay's turbid waters, but she hesitated. She had felt the swelling slowly enlarge in her abdomen as the millions of eggs she carried continued grow. But the maternal feeling was still premature; it would be four months more before she would spawn. The coolness of the water from Chesapeake reminded her that winter was overtaking her home. She would find the warmth she needed only in deep water, farther south.

In just a few days, she had passed the numerous piers jutting from the beaches in Virginia and North Carolina and spent a frenzied afternoon feeding on a school of small _Brevoortia_. Saxatilis had arrived at the tumultuous waters off Cape Hatteras. The waters here were cool, but warmer than those off Chesapeake Bay. Another current from the south mixes here with cooler currents from the north and helps temper their sting. Still, the waters continued to cool, and she spent the next week feeding whenever she could. Gradually, the chill was slowing her life. She needed less and less food.

Eventually, Saxatilis drifted a few miles off the beach and joined other large bass. There she met a few with whom she had shared her home river. There were fish from the Roanoke as well, and even a few from the Hudson River. She had never seen very many North Carolina fish go north with the spring migrations. Saxatilis spent February, March, and part of April in the semi-dormant state with thousands of other striped bass. In April she sensed the water beginning to warm, and the bulging in her abdomen had grown larger. It had filled most of the area her empty stomach had lost.

As the water approached 45 degrees, Saxatilis and the other large fish began to move from their winter grounds. It was a short swim into Chesapeake Bay. She felt good. She was eager to spawn. When she was younger she had been an active spawner, every year since she was seven. Only within the past few years did she quit the act. She now did all things more slowly.

The bay's shallow waters were silted because of spring flooding of the numerous rivers that feed this large inland sea and strong March winds riled the waters where they shoaled. Even so, she could separate the tastes of all the rivers that fill the bay and mixed with its slightly saline waters. She especially knew the taste of her river, and at Smith Point turned west and entered the Potomac. She saw schools upon schools of younger bass, fish no larger than 5 or 6 pounds, all males, passing her, racing for the spawning grounds. There were other large females with her, but only one that was larger. There were very few small females. They waited their turn in the bay and would come to the river after the larger fish had spawned. Once past the big bridge near Morgantown, Saxatilis could sense a current in the river that before had been too weak to feel. Gradually, the taste of salt left the water. She could now savor all kinds of exotic sensations. They all reminded her of her youth.

As she continued upstream she could feel the current mount, and old, strange feelings begin to stir within her. The water was still too cool to risk spawning as she passed the narrows at Quantico, but here is where she would drop her eggs. Thousands of small male bass milled around and came close to her. They never would have dared do that in the open bay or ocean. For six days she stemmed the current of the Potomac off Quantico as water temperatures slowly rose. Then one night, up-river, near Hagerstown, it rained heavily. The Potomac was suddenly swollen with warm rainwater. It took two days for it to reach Saxatilis, but when it did she responded.

The young male bass became brazen and began bumping and pushing her as she tried to maintain her position in the current. Some would leap toward the top of the water and splash about until the water was foaming. Even Saxatilis experienced a schoolgirl's delight and began racing about with the males. She turned on her side and slapped her massive tail on the surface and sent a geyser into the air. Males were everywhere about her, pressing on both sides and smothering Saxatilis. Together, they sank to the bottom and she relaxed as millions of tiny eggs flowed into the Potomac. The males about her exuded milt and together they churned the eggs and sperm until they were well fertilized.

Slowly, the eggs swelled in the water and a preordained phenomenon began to unfold within their clear, green envelopes. They drifted slowly down stream with the current, on their way to where Saxatilis, too, had started her life. The cycle of life had come a full turn.

PART ONE

THE FISH

1

Striped Bass and Glaciers

We know that the first animals that had the characteristics of fish developed initially in fresh water. As they multiplied and various species began to evolve from the primordial stock they expanded into all the bioniches available to them in fresh water. Those that could live in brackish water were able to expand their realm and survive over those that couldn't live there. And those that were able to live in salt water had an entirely new environment open to them. Eventually, most of those species that moved into salt water gave up their ability to return fresh water.

Striped bass, however, didn't. They are not a highly specialized fish in either body structure or required habitat conditions. They are very general and adaptable fish and this has been their salvation during challenging periods of climatic change. This non-specialization gave them an advantage over other species when the environment began to alter and other fish couldn't adjust to new conditions. Changes in temperature affect fish rapidly because most are cold-blooded and ambient water temperatures are determined by what happens outside their watery envelope. With a greater tolerance for changes in water temperature, and an ability to use the oceans as travel routes to escape falling temperatures, striped bass, like many anadromous fish species, are able to live in areas ranging from sub-tropical to sub-arctic, with moderate climates in temperate zones their first choice.

But fish do not always have a choice. One example of this is the three glacial epochs that swept the earth for untold years since the Cambrian Period. The last glacial era, the Pleistocene Period, also known as The Great Ice Age, had a strong influence on today's distribution of striped bass populations. During its million-year existence, the period experienced the formation of four great transglobal ice sheets and one or two minor advances. Through geological dating, scientists have pretty much determined that this period reached its height, or the farthest southward advance of ice, about 20,000 years ago. The Wisconsin Glaciation, as it is known, was made up two advances. The farthest advance ended about 75,000 years ago and the last advance in the East, paralleled but didn't quite cover the first terminal moraine it left behind. Evidence is seen on Long Island, off the coast on New York City, where the older glacier formed the South Fork of Long Island and the last glacier the North Fork.

From the geological evidence left behind, it built glaciers that extended farther from the poles toward the equator than any other glaciers. At its greatest, most of Canada, large sections of the northern United States and parts of northern Europe were covered in a mantle of ice .

Along the East Coast, glaciers extended off the shores of Canada, New England, and New York. They stood nearly a mile high at their most southerly terminus, and stretched from what is now Cape Cod, west across Long Island, over the interior of the North America to south of Chicago, then along the northeastern slopes of the Rocky Mountains. The Gulf of Mexico was half its present size, and its waters 300 to 400 feet shallower and temperate, even cool. Glaciers had changed today's temperate seas into an arctic-like environment. At that time, so much of the ocean's water was tied up in glaciers that sea level was more than 600 feet lower than today. Off Connecticut, the ocean was on the edge of the Continental Shelf, 80 miles away. When it began melting, it left in its wake a ridge of sand and glacial debris that on the Shelf eventually became Long Island and formed all the islands east of it, ending in Cape Cod.

But 20,000 years ago, the Gulf of Mexico and the extreme Southeast Coast were the perfect environments for temperate basses *(Percichthyidae)*—striped bass, white bass, white and yellow perch of the Genus *Morone.* Because the glacier's advance southward was so slow, probably over a 10,000-year period, they had been driven there, almost unknowingly. As the glacier moved south-ward over the continent and offshore along the Atlantic coast, it forced the basses and all other wildlife continually, almost imperceptibly, to stay ahead of the arctic-like weather that chilled the land and froze the seas ahead of the glacier's advance. The climate of southern Florida then was probably what New York is like today. Striped bass found the waters along the north side of the Gulf of Mexico and probably as far south as the Yucatan Peninsula to their liking. The temperate basses, unspecialized in their demands, were very adaptable to the changing environment, either marine or fresh water, but they, too, eventually were forced farther and farther southward. They rounded the Florida Peninsula that at the time stood 300 feet above sea level. We know they spread as far west as the Mississippi River, entering and establishing breeding populations all along the way, and even inhabiting the rivers of eastern Texas and Mexico.

The huge continental glacial shield stopped advancing about 20,000 years ago, responding to a gradual summer warming trend as the world's weather again changed. When the annual deposition of snow on the glacier's back was less than what melted at its terminus during the summer, the front began a slow retreat back to the Arctic. Ever the opportunists, striped bass populations pushed farther and farther north, both inland in the Gulf and along the Atlantic coasts, taking advantage of slowly-warming coastal seas and gradually reclaiming, recolonizing the entire coast. At every opportunity, whenever the retreating cell of cold, prohibitive water exposed a new river, some bass would leave the Atlantic and move upstream to re-populate it. As long as late spring tempera-

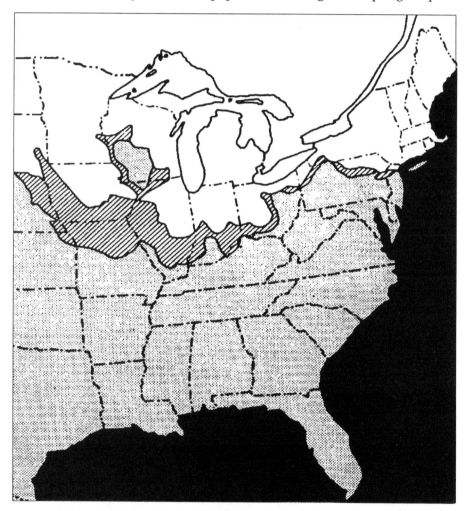

The extent of Pleistocene glaciation in the United States. Diagonal lines represent area covered during pre-Wisconsin stages but not later Wisconsin ice. Gray area is

tures in these expanding riverine environments rose above 64 or so degrees for a short period, to allow striped bass eggs to hatch, the population's advance northward was solidified, and it continued, further expanded the fish's northern frontier.

As the oceans rose, flooding the Continental Shelf, they eventually turned the peaks of the long terminal moraines into islands. Massive rivers, created by the melting glaciers, eroded deeply into the surface of the Shelf until the level of the ocean rose to flood their distal ends. One of the biggest canyons was created by the Hudson River, the glacial waters of which deeply gorged the land as far north as Albany. Today, its bottom is still below sea level and is flooded with brackish water. Temperate lands have been free of glaciers for about 10,000 years though the edges of these massive ice fields, now restricted to the polar caps and several high mountains, continues to melt backwards.

Today, the northern frontier for striped bass is the south shore of the saline/brackish Gulf of St. Lawrence and upstream in the St. Lawrence River as far as Montreal. At one time, these fish even entered the Great Lakes system and inhabited Lake Ontario. The earth is still in the warming trend that began 20,000 years ago. Coastal Nova Scotia and New Brunswick, south of the mouth of the Gulf of St. Lawrence, remained glaciated until about 13,000 years ago. There's no doubt that rivers in this area were eventually repopulated by striped bass that dispersed north along the coast from the United States. There probably were striped bass also ascending streams created on Georges Bank when it was still a highland plateau, then an island as the ocean's waters continued to rise, and then abandoned by the fish as it became submerged. The depth over most of Georges Bank today is about 120 feet.

Though drastically reduced, the striped bass population in the St. Lawrence River system still shows continued signs of expansion. At one time, they probably spawned in most of its tributaries on the Gáspe Peninsula. In reality, striped bass populations are still in a northern dispersal mode, except where they are thwarted by man-made barriers, that is, dams, pollution, and over-harvesting. It's logical that if the present inter-glacial warming period continues, striped bass might eventually move north along the coast of Labrador and Newfoundland to find the type of pristine environments they need to continue their species.

While all this was happening on the northern frontier, another event was unfolding in the south. The waters of the Gulf of Mexico, as all the oceans of the world, were slowly rising because of the melting glaciers. The Continental Shelf was gradually flooded, and the shores were continually inching inward, until the East and Gulf coasts began taking on their current shapes. But as the waters to the north warmed more to the liking of striped bass and other anadromous fishes there, those to the south became almost too warm. Adult striped bass cannot tolerate water temperatures above 70 degrees for too long a period. Younger striped bass can stand water as warm as 80 degrees but only for short periods.

Eventually, those striped bass living in the rivers of the southern and western edges of the Gulf of Mexico found their coastal waters growing too warm. The fish abandoned them, and because of their anadromous capabilities, sought more comfortable temperatures in the upper reaches of the longest rivers in the southern states that emptied into the Gulf of Mexico.

There was probably a portion of the striped bass population that also continued to exist in the rivers and streams of the Southeast Atlantic states even during the glacier's most southerly advance. It is difficult to postulate today what their northern limit might have been but it could have been as far north as Cape Hatteras. Some researchers believe, that at the beginning of the Pleistocene Period (about 1.1 to 1.4 million years ago), there was a direct connection between the Gulf of Mexico and the Atlantic Ocean through what is known as the Suwannee Straits, a channel that made Florida an island and allowed fish to move back and forth between the Gulf of Mexico and the Atlantic Ocean. That the strait existed is a geological fact, however, it was closed several geological periods before striped bass even evolved as a species. At the height of the last glacial period, that area of Florida/Georgia was about 400 feet above sea level. It was not the closing of the Suwannee Straits that isolated striped bass in the Gulf of Mexico from those on the Atlantic side of Florida, but a temperature block that developed, and still continues today, in waters of the southern half of the state.

As the climate continued to change, a portion of this widespread but continuous Gulf-Atlantic coastal stock in the eastern Gulf of Mexico found itself in an intolerable temperature block. Sometime during the last 10,000 years, probably close to the beginning, they found that they could not head south along Florida's west coast and make the turn north at Key West to communicate with the rest of the Atlantic population. Though it's unlikely that these striped bass were seasonal coastal migrants, instead exhibiting the typical riverine-estuarine habits that created isolated stocks indigenous only to rivers with a common estuary, the factors of natural biological drift or dispersion that are always at work to expand any population could not function because the temperature block had isolated these fish . They won't be freed until the next ice age.

The shoal waters along the southern and western edges of the Gulf of Mexico became too warm and striped bass populations became concentrated along the very northern periphery of the Gulf of Mexico. In winter, striped bass sought out the brackish-water bays created behind the developing barrier beaches by wind and wave action. Populations in the Mississippi River and other major rivers that flowed from north to south in Texas, Mississippi, Alabama, Georgia, and Florida moved upstream in these waters seeking cooler, aerated waters for reproduction in the spring and survival in the summer, and some retreated farther upstream to the original habitat and life cycles of their ancestors.

Striped bass here developed riverine as well as coastal populations even though all striped bass spend a part of their lives in freshwater rivers. The saltwater periods, if they had any, were confined to estuaries of the major rivers. Little or no trans-coastal migration took place and these populations became even further isolated. Those small, shallow rivers that became too warm during the height of summer lost their populations. Those with summer respites— springs and deep holes—developed populations that adapted to upstream life and lost the penchant to feed in tidal estuaries during certain times of the year.

There was little or no mixing of individual estuarine stock, and they lived in splendid isolation until the turn of the century. Today, the Gulf strain of striped bass remains isolated, and in much of their original range, eliminated because of industrialization, urbanization, river channelization, and expanded agriculture.

Several families of fishes never lost the ability to change environments and are still able to return at will to fresh water. These anadromous fishes might have been the last group to make the trek to the seas, and never gave up their need to return to fresh water to spawn. But even for some of those today that can make the switch, the adaptation to one environment after living in the other takes a good deal of time. For others, like striped bass, the change can be accomplished quickly. This group includes, along with striped bass, fish like sturgeon, shad, herring, smelt, white perch, salmon, trout, and eels. All these fish, except eels, are classed as anadromous species. An anadromous fish is one that chooses to live most of its life in salt water, but must return to freshwater rivers to spawn. Eels are catadromous, that is, they breed and spawn in salt water but search for fresh water, especially the females, in which to mature.

There are some groups of fish that spend most of their lives in fresh water, but when they are in the proximity of the oceans, they may migrate to the estuaries during summer to feed. A good example of this type of fish is the Eastern brook trout. Brook trout are not really trout but char and are typical of the more numerous char species that live in the north-temperate to sub-arctic regions of the northern hemisphere. These fish make a regular habit of migrating to salt water to feed.

Over most of their northern and western ranges, striped bass are primarily anadromous fish; the greater part of their lives is spent in salt water. When they do head for fresh water, it is only to spawn. Adult striped bass quickly return to salt water after spawning. Even their eggs and young develop within a matter of a few weeks and are swept into brackish water to develop because of the proximity of their spawning sites to saline estuaries. There are, however, some striped bass populations which spend all their lives in fresh water even though they are not blocked from going to the sea. This characteristic, some biologists believe, appears to be a relatively recent development in modern striped bass, somewhat of a reversal to its primordial habits. However, others believe that these fish exhibit the original characteristic life cycle of striped bass and that these interior fish have never trekked to the marine environment. Still in other areas, there are cohabiting populations of both types—estuarine migrants and non-migrants.

2
What Is a Striped Bass?

There is a saying among military strategists that if you can get to know an opponent, he is yours. This holds true for striped bass. If you can get to know the striped bass—its anatomy, life cycle, the numerous forces that motivate it, the environment that surrounds it, and its responses to food, heat, cold, shelter, fear, and love—it is yours.

If you know the anatomy of a striped bass, you then have some idea of where it will swim, how it swims, how it feeds and upon what, and why it inhabits the waters it chooses. If you know its range and distribution, you know where to intercept it, when to be there. If you know where and how it reproduces, you will understand why it is on the Roanoke River in April, why it is in the Cape Cod Canal in June, and why it is resting off Cape Hatteras in January. If you know the foods it prefers, you will know what baits to feed it, what lures to select, and what levels in the ocean at which to present them. If you know what factors control the population of the striper, you can estimate its abundance and your own fishing productivity.

In the Introduction, I attempted to communicate something of the nature of the fish by following a single, typical, sea-wise female through the months leading up to her spring spawning. But, for a true understanding of the striped bass, a more conventional and ordered discussion is necessary. This chapter begins with the basic attributes of the fish, its classification among the fishes, and its physical characteristics.

CLASSIFICATION

The striped bass, *Morone saxatilis,* in one aspect is typical of fish that live in a saltwater environment, possessing all those features it needs to compete successfully in an ocean of other fishes. Until a few years ago, striped bass were grouped with the family of sea basses, true marine species. These fish, of which the grouper is a good example, are warm- or tropic-water fish, and striped bass were thought to be a northern contingent of this large, well-dispersed group. But its preference for cool or even cold water puzzled early taxonomists. Eventually, they decided that it wasn't a sea bass. Its origins in fresh water and a unique kidney that allows it to swim in either fresh or salt water should have been a clue to its classification. Striped bass are freshwater fish that, like salmon, trout, and other anadromous fishes, have the ability to live in salt water. Today, striped bass are considered one of a small group of six temperate-water basses, four of which are anadromous and can inhabit ocean or fresh water. It is itself the best example of its group.

There are nearly 60 different species of fish that are called some kind of bass or another in North America. Even striped bass have been given a number of names ever since the first colonists discovered them swimming alongside Plymouth Rock. They were quick to call it a "basse," because the fish closely resembled the sea bass or common bass (its closest relative) found swimming among the British Isles. There, the origin of the word "basse" is said to be Dutch, meaning perch. Actually, the word "basse" is a Middle English corruption of *Barse* and means perch. The striped bass, and some of its closet relatives in North America (white and yellow perch), certainly are perch-like in appearance.

It was classified with the Family Perca and Dr. Jerome V.C. Smith, in his *History of the Fishes of Massachusetts* called it *Perca labrax*. It was found in several rivers in the Canadian maritime provinces, and early English settlers there called them bass and named several streams "Bass River" after them. The most common name now used is "striped bass," describing the striped appearance of the fish. Where the early settlers were of French origin, they called it *bar raye* (*bar*-bass, *raye*--streak or stripe) because it, too, reminded them of the bass without stripes they knew that were prevalent along the entire French Atlantic Coast.

An offshoot of this same line of thinking is the name "linesider." Bass have also been called "greenheads" because of the head coloring and, because of their penchant for squid, "squid hounds." The second most common name in use today is "rock" or "rockfish," used most in Atlantic waters south of New Jersey. Farther south, in South Carolina and Georgia, and along the Gulf Coast, it is known equally as striped bass and rockfish. But in recent years, because of new introductions of the species to freshwater reservoirs, the name striped bass seemed to be replacing rockfish. On the Pacific Coast, it is almost always called the striped bass.

The name "rockfish" describes more the fish's feeding habits than its outward appearance or fleshy texture. This name evolved because striped bass were often found feeding on foods that dwell around rocks and other obstacles in the water. The aborigines of New England had their own name for the striped bass, *missuckeke*, according to a book by minister Roger Williams, *A Key into the Language of America; or, a Help to the Language of the Natives in that part of America called New England.*

Scientifically, striped bass have had several names over the past few hundred years. The earliest describer of a bass labeled it *Roccus lineatus* (Bloch). Bloch was thought to have been the first person in scientific journals to classify the fish. *Roccus* is New Latin and refers to rock, the environment around which the fish was found. *Lineatus,* also Latin, refers to the lines or stripes on the sides of the fish.

But *Roccus lineatus* wasn't a very appropriate name because it was also applied to a Mediterranean cousin. Sometime around 1880, it was changed to *Roccus saxatilis* (Walbaum). This was accepted by most scientists until 1966 when the name was again changed. *Roccus saxatilis* is a bit redundant because it literally means rock that lives around rocks, or saxatiles. Saxatile is derived from the Latin word *saxum,* meaning rock.

Somewhere in the literature, taxonomists discovered that another person— we don't know his or her name—had classified the fish before Bloch. The convention is always to accept the older name. The genus is *Morone.* Nor has anyone discovered the exact meaning of Morone. It could have been the classifier's own name, which was a common practice first used by researchers, discoverers, and taxonomists. The closest we can come to finding the etymology for *Morone* is the Greek word *moros,* which has two meanings, "death" and "stupid." The latter meaning may have been intended because in colonial times striped bass were so plentiful that they were extremely easy to catch, and if a fish is easy to catch it might be thought of as being an unwise or stupid fish. Take your pick. In any case, since 1966 when the renaming took place, *Morone saxatilis* or "stupid rockfish" is what we must content ourselves with. However, few in the cadre of anglers who chase striped bass would consider it a stupid fish, even during times of plenty.

A taxonomic history of the fish's name includes: *Perca saxatilis* (Walbaum 1792), *Labrax notatus* (Smith 1836), *Perca labrax* then *Labrax Lineatus* (Perley 1852), *Labrax lineatus* (Fortin 1864), *Roccus lineatus* (Adams 1873), *Roccus Lineatus* Gill (Adams 1873), *Roccus lineatus* (Bloch) Gill, Cox 1869, *Morone* (Whitehead and Wheeler 1967), *Roccus saxatilis* (Walbaum) Scott and Crossman 1969, but by 1980 it became know as *Morone saxatilis.*

In relation to other fishes, striped bass are a bony fish (some fish are made of cartilage rather than bone) and belongs to the Order Perciformes and Family Percichthyidae. When striped bass were considered sea bass, to which they bear a strikingly close physical similarity, they were included in the rather large group of sea basses in the Family Serranidae. Fortunately, striped bass have been reclassified. More recent classification has broken the Percichthyidae family into two groups, separating the warm-water sea bass of the south from those preferring slightly cooler water like the striped bass and its near cousins the white bass and white perch. This new family reflects the change of the striped bass's generic name from *Roccus* to *Morone.*

EXTERNAL ANATOMY

Striped bass are fusiform fish. That is, their bodies are shaped much like a torpedo, rather round but a bit deeper in relation to width. Some fish are laterally compressed, from side to side, like a scup, permit, or sunfish and are extremely maneuverable. Others may be dorsally-ventrally compressed like flounder. This shape is best for fish which lie on the bottom much of their time, or fish which "float" through the water hunting, like skates and rays. Neither body form is very swift. Fish almost round in cross-section are the fastest, but they lack real maneuverability. Good examples in salt water are tuna and bonito, and trout and salmon in fresh water. Striped bass fall between the extremes and are a somewhat average, unspecialized fish in shape. This lack of specialization means that while they may not be at their best in certain, unusual situations, they can cope very well with the average conditions they face in daily life. Specialization may make life immediately more successful but it has its drawbacks when one considers the always-changing environemnt of the future.

In all, the striped bass has a generalized fish body, the trunk of which is three-and-one-half to four times as long as the body is thick, from snout to its caudal peduncle (base of tail). The back is only slightly arched, while the bottom of the body has a sway to it, especially in older examples and in adult bass that have lived in strictly freshwater environments. The caudal peduncle is rather stout and gives rise to a large but only slightly forked tail. This large rudder gives the fish the maneuverability it requires for life in fast-flowing rivers, the pounding surf, in strong ocean rips and current, and in placid estuaries.

Striped bass have a large, long head, almost as long as the body is deep. The moderately-pointed snout isn't long enough to cover a slightly projecting lower jaw. The mouth is set on an oblique angle, making surface feeding a bit easier, and extends back under the eyes. Two spines on the posterior margin of each gill cover (operculum) are located on a level even with the eye and seem to make the head extend even farther back. Large eyes are set high on the head, again making surface feeding or seeing from below easier.

Fins

Two dorsal fins on the back are of equal length and just separated from each other. The anterior or forward dorsal fin is triangular in shape, much like a sail. It is supported by nine or ten stiff spines. The posterior or rear dorsal fin is supported by 12 to 14 softer pieces of cartilage called rays. They look as if they had been clipped by scissors because of their even edge. The rays grow smaller in size from front to back. The anal fin, on the underside of the striped bass just behind the anal pore, looks a lot like the reverse of the soft dorsal fin. The fish has three short spines at its head and the remainder is supported by 11 cartilaginous rays.

During the course of the evolutionary development of striped bass and other temperate basses, the paired pelvic fins migrated forward on the underside of the body to a point just behind the pectoral fins. They are of moderate size, similar to the pectorals. The paired pectoral fins are just behind the gill covers, on a line even with the mouth.

Scales and Stripes

Scales on a striped bass are rather large compared to those of most other fish and cover the entire body, on the head, cheeks and operculi. Along the lateral line, they number anywhere from 57 to 67, depending upon where the fish originate. They are ctenoid (toothed) in type and grow rings (annuli) each season—helpful in determining a bass' age.

In general coloration, a striped bass is white on the bottom with a gradual darkening up the sides toward the back. The darkening occurs because the seven or eight, narrow dark stripes come closer together as they approach the back. The color on the back ranges from a dark olive green to a pale blue in some fish, black in others, while the stripes or lines on the sides are more of a black. Three of the stripes are below the lateral line, beginning behind the gill cover and the pectoral fin, tapering but not reaching the caudal peduncle. The longest stripe is that on the lateral line and extends to the very beginning of the tail fin. Three or four stripes above the lateral line extend rearward, merging as the body narrows.

Stripes under the scales are rather uniformly lined with only an occasional interruption. These stripes, as well as the scales on the back, will often take on a brassy, reflective sheen, especially in live fish. The fins and tail are somewhat dusky. Striped bass in a strictly marine environment are often light in color. Those that have been in an estuary for a while, especially an estuary with a dark bottom, tend to deepen in color, and so do striped bass living entirely in fresh water.

INTERNAL ANATOMY

Head

The head is triangular is shape, quite bony, and comprises 24.5 to 27.4 percent of the total body length. There are 24 vertebrae in the spine, not counting the urostylar vertebra at the base of the tail.

Teeth

In the larval stage, striped bass are equipped with huge teeth to catch fish. But as they develop, the teeth regress. Adult striped bass do have numerous small, sharp vomerine (vomer plate in the roof of the mouth) teeth and maxillary teeth along the jaw. They also have a set of small teeth positioned at the base of the tongue in two parallel rows or patches. None of these teeth are used for biting or tearing but only to hold food in the mouth from escaping outward.

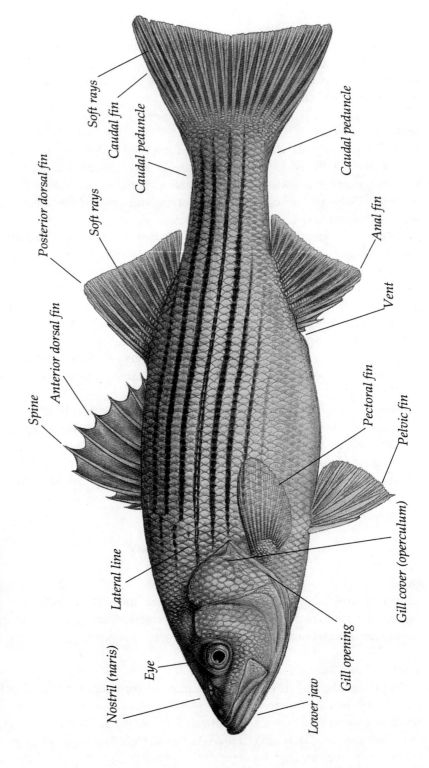

External anatomy of striped bass.

Soft rays

Caudal fin

Caudal peduncle

Caudal peduncle

Posterior dorsal fin

Soft rays

Anal fin

Anterior dorsal fin

Vent

Spine

Pectoral fin

Pelvic fin

Lateral line

Gill cover (operculum)

Nostril (naris)

Eye

Gill opening

Lower jaw

Internal Anatomy of a striped bass.

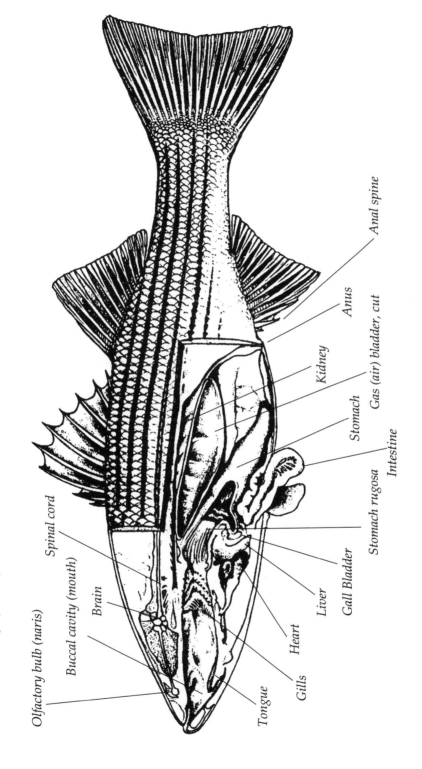

Olfactory bulb (naris)

Buccal cavity (mouth)

Brain

Spinal cord

Tongue

Gills

Heart

Liver

Gall Bladder

Stomach rugosa

Intestine

Stomach

Gas (air) bladder, cut

Kidney

Anus

Anal spine

Anadromy

The ability of fish to live in both fresh and saltwater environments is a function of a specialized kidney. When a striped bass is bent on spawning and enters fresh water, its body is faced with the problem of a salt loss in its bloodstream. There is also a tendency to absorb too much water. In order to make the change, the osmotic pressure—a force created by dissolved salts and minerals in the bloodstream—must be adjustable. Anadromous fish possess glomerular kidneys, which have the ability to respond to differences in urine volume that result from different salinities. These fish also possess gills and membranes in the mouth cavity that can handle the uptake and secretion of ions in the blood and tissue and protect it against undue diffusion. The glomeruli— small masses of capillaries within the kidney—take urinary wastes out of the blood, maintain an isotonic balance, and thus allow striped bass to change environments at will. In many anadromous fish, the change requires a conditioning time, but in striped bass, it seems to be very minimal.

SENSES

Sight

Like all predacious fish striped bass feed by sight. They do this very well and it may be because of its eyes. They are comparatively large, with diameter 16 to 23 percent of its head length. It may use its hearing or sense of smell to find food, but the final approach or attack is made with its eyes. They are well placed and designed for surface feeding or feeding under an object of prey, but still not set so specialized that it cannot see well ahead and below.

The eyes of a striped bass are a lot like human eyes. They can readily adjust to different intensities of light by controlling the size of the iris. Fortunately for a striped bass, its eyes are also constructed with two types of light-sensitive cells in the retina, the area at the back of the eye. These cells, called rods and cones from the general character of their shape, are used for seeing under differing intensities of light in much the same manner as do the rods and cones in the human eye.

Most other fishes have cone cells that are sensitive to color and are used primarily during the day. Those fish with only cone cells become inactive at night. However, the striped bass is an extremely active fish that feeds throughout the night. This is made possible with the rod-shaped cells. The rod-shaped cells are buried behind the cone cells during the day because they are extremely sensitive to light. But as night approaches they rise to the surface and replace the cone cells as the prime light and sensation gatherers.

The striped bass's night-time vision is basically black and white. There's no need for color vision at night. With little light available to illuminate any colored objects, color vision at night would not give the striped bass any great advantage over other fish or escaping prey.

Unlike the lenses in our eyes, the lenses in the eyes of a striped bass are round instead of flattened. The effect of such a lens is to make the striped bass nearsighted. Without muscles to control the shape of the lens, as in our eyes, fish cannot adjust their eyes and focus on far objects. This is one reason why lures and baits presented to the striper must be at close range. Even so, striped bass get

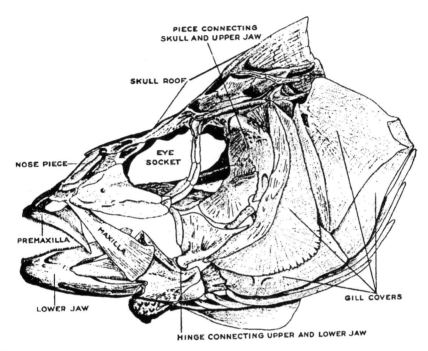

Skull of the striped bass. Reproduced from Fishes of the Vicinity of New York City *by John Treadwell Nichols.*

along rather well with myopic vision because most of the waters in which they swim have poor visibility; even the clearest salt water is filled with suspended particles. To find its prey, initially striped bass rely on the other senses, and eyes become important only when they move in for the kill.

Striped bass lack complete binocular vision because their eyes are placed on the sides of their head rather than in front. Each eye gathers about 180 degrees of scope because the round lens projects slightly beyond the wall of the head. In many fish, there is often a void directly in front of the head because they do not truly gather 180 degrees of vision. It is interrupted by bony structures used to protect the eye. But in striped bass, the eyes are placed slightly forward and above on the head, and so it can watch the action on the surface without undue effort. This even gives the eye a bit of overlap, and a small degree of binocular ability and depth perception. It also explains why striped bass are so fond of surface lures and spend more time looking up than down.

Smell

Like a dog on land, a striped bass in the water really lives in a world of smells. When an odor is water-borne, taste and smell are synonymous and may be used interchangeably. This is probably the most highly developed of a striped bass's senses, followed closely by hearing. One could almost guess that a striped bass can smell better than see just from considering the environments it inhabits. In the large bays and rivers, the waters are turbid. Once in the open, a bass doesn't go far from the beach, and in the wash there is always sand in suspension. Therefore, a striped bass is likely to smell food before it ever sees it. If it's artificial, it had better leave a trail of good vibrations in the water to make up for the lack of taste.

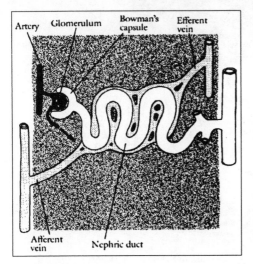

A graphic rendering of a glomerulus that is typical to all anadromous species of fish.

Reasoning in the other direction, we can tell a lot about how a fish feeds from the type of nostrils it has developed. We know from the construction of a striped bass's eyes that it has the ability to feed well after dusk. To go along with this feeding on the dark side of the earth, striped bass need a good sense of smell to locate what they cannot readily see, and evolved one of the best smell/taste systems of any fish.

Instead of one pair of nostrils on its head, such as many fish possess, the striped bass has a double pair—two on each side. The sensation of smell is carried in the water and picked up by olfactory cells in the lining of the nostril. These cells number a half-million to the square inch. The water that enters the nostril of the striped bass doesn't go out the same entrance through which it arrived, but it does not run into the throat as it would in a human nostril. Each nostril has an exit port. This means that the fish is always tasting or smelling a fresh supply of water passing over the olfactory cells. This is extremely important to fish that feed primarily by smell or feed a lot at night, when the sense of smell becomes more important than other of the senses.

A striped bass's ability to smell in the water is hundreds of times better than our ability to smell odors in the air. From miles away it can smell things that we would just be able to perceive from a dozen feet away in the air. Few experiments have been conducted to check the olfactory ability of striped bass, but it is very good—perhaps nearly as good as that of the champion Durante of the fishes, the American eel. Eels have been shown to be able to respond to an alcohol of which one-billionth of a drop was diluted in a large swimming pool. This accounts for the ability of eels to smell the Hudson River from as far away as the Sargasso Sea off Bermuda.

Striped bass possess a homing instinct for natal waters and can find their way back to a parent stream in much the same way a salmon heads home. The homing instinct is probably a highly developed sense of smell that can identify the chemistry of a river immediately at the place where the fish was spawned.

Hearing

Striped bass need a sensory system that will work in the black of night and in waters so polluted that the sense of smell is often disrupted to the degree that it is dysfunctional. Thus a sense of hearing is important, too. And, like the interchangeability of taste and smell in a watery environment, hearing and feeling both have the same effect on the sensory organ that interprets these sensations. The striped bass's auditory system is acute and it can hear sounds well below our own range. One reason is that sound travels more than five times faster in water than in air. The auditory range of a striped bass is also extremely broad, from as low as 15 to as high as 10,000 cycles per second. Some fish can hear far above that. Our range in the air is between 20 and 20,000 cycles.

Sounds in the world of a striped bass are of two types: those that attract and those that make it run in fear. One means food and the other means a predator. Fish have ears, but they don't protrude. Their ears are buried in their skulls, slightly behind and below their eyes. There are no external openings through the skin, but sound is transmitted to the inner ear through the flesh and bone on the skull. In addition to their ears, fish have another organ that functions in pretty much the same manner. After all, sound does nothing for the ear but set up sympathetic vibrations. These are then carried by an electric signal to the brain and recreate sensations of food, danger or the like. So any organ sensitive to vibrations can function pretty much as another ear. In striped bass and in most other fishes this organ is a series of sensitive canals along the lateral line. The sensors in the canals respond to low-frequency vibrations. The lateral line is used by striped bass to pinpoint sources of sound like a directional finder.

Taste

The sensation of taste is closely related to that of smell in both man and fish. Like man, a striped bass can differentiate between sweet, sour, salty, and bitter tastes. The two senses do differ in range. The sensation of smell can be called the long-distance receptor and taste the short-distance receptor. The sensation of taste isn't too important if you are fishing with plugs or other artificial lures. But if you use live bait, the way it tastes to the fish is important, because striped bass discriminate. If the bait is alive, then the taste sensations will take care of themselves and the allure won't be alarming to a striped bass. But if you use dead, frozen, or cut bait, its condition is important. Stripe bass will reject foods that it finds displeasing in taste. There is a diminishing order of preference in baits: live bait first, followed by freshly dead bait, then frozen freshly-dead bait, then frozen old bait, and lastly just plain old bait that has been in the sun without ice. Some fish, like sharks and bottom scavengers, don't mind the state of a bait. But game fish like striped bass prefer live bait to all others.

One of the most effective ways to catch large striped bass is with live menhaden (bunker) as bait. Bass will greedily and readily take them. But fishing a bunker in a heavily-running tide while stemming the flow quickly wears out even the lightest-hooked bunker. The fish develop "lockjaw" and drown. Striped bass immediately shun the dead bunker and pick only those lines with a live fish. It seems that the smell and taste of death can be carried in the water.

Fish taste flavors in much the same manner we do, but their taste buds are not restricted to the tongue alone. A striped bass has taste buds on its tongue, in the throat and around the roof of the mouth. But they don't stop there. They also have a battery of external taste buds on the end of the snout and lips. A bass can taste its food before it opens its mouth, and that may explain why at times they seem to be "mouthing" but not taking a bait. It may only be nosing it to see how fresh it is before it feeds.

Sensitivity to Temperatures

Most fish are cold-blooded animals and have no heat-regulating mechanisms within their body. The temperature of a fish's body is the same as that of the ambient water that surrounds it. When a fish undergoes strenuous exercise, the body temperature may rise a few degrees, but for the most part they have no real control over it. Its life in equilibrium with the environment may be one reason why fish are so sensitive to temperature and temperature changes. Research has shown that fish are sensitive to as small a change in their environment as 1/50th of a degree. This doesn't mean that they must respond to the change, just that they are aware of it and can use this sensitivity when selecting optimum water areas for spawning, migrating, feeding, or resting. Fish feel temperature through minute cells with nerve endings in the skin. These cells then transmit the temperature to the brain.

Outside temperature and thus the inside temperature of a fish affect the body's metabolism, or the vital functions of breaking down food, transporting oxygen, removing excrement, and the like. The higher the temperature, to a point, the more active is our striped bass. As the temperature falls, the body activities slow down. As these activities slow down, so does the demand for food to fuel them.

The active temperature range for striped bass is quite wide when compared to other fishes. Striped bass wintering in the St. Lawrence River and in New England have been observed feeding in water close to the freezing point—that is, the saltwater freezing point, which is even a few degrees colder than fresh water. There's a record on one Connecticut river, while water temperatures were at 35 degrees, of a striped bass that took an artificial lure. However, most striped bass go into a somewhat dormant state once temperatures drop below 40 degrees.

On the high range of the temperature scale, striped bass have been known to tolerate water as high as 80 to 83 degrees, but they become extremely sluggish. The optimal ranges for striped bass are from 55 to 68 or 70 degrees. Adult striped bass cannot tolerate temperatures above 72 degrees for a protracted period. However bass under 18 inches, seem to have no ill effects in temperatures in the low 80s. Their preferred spawning temperature is 64.5 degrees, and this may well be the optimal feeding temperature when they are not preoccupied with spawning.

One researcher found an interesting temperature effect on fish while working with tuna. In a struggle to rid itself of a hook, a tuna's temperature might rise 10 to 15 degrees. The total mass of the fish's body is so great that it cannot cool itself quickly, and it fatigues rapidly. Fish can take changes in temperature, but the adjustment is slow. If the change is too quick, fish will go into shock. Fish with large heads and small bodies can dissipate heat readily, but fish with large body areas, like the striped bass, cannot rid themselves of the heat quickly enough, and they succumb rapidly. Thus a striped bass taken while the waters are still cool (not cold) puts up a good fight because the water helps absorb and dissipate the heat. The same size bass, taken in warm water, during August and early September, is less likely to put up a good fight.

Locomotion

Striped bass are excellent swimmers because of their generalized body shape. A fish swims by undulating its muscles that make its body move in waves. A wave starts behind the head and moves toward the tail. Often another wave is started before the first wave is completed. The real power, however, for sudden bursts in speed and for maneuverability lies in the tail. The tail is supported by a series of bony rays founded on a broad peduncle. When snapped, it pushes the striper ahead.

Striped bass have been known to migrate as much as 12 miles per day, but can move faster with sudden bursts of speed. They can reach 14 miles per hour. A few fish, seen chasing fleeing menhaden, have been clocked at 20 miles per hour. When a burst of power is needed, striped bass derive an immediate energy source from a unique muscle along the lateral line. It separate the dorsal (top) row of muscles from the ventral (bottom) row. If you filet a striped bass, you can easily see this distinct wedge-shaped muscle in cross section, colored darker, and even red in most fish. It also exhibits the distinct oily or fish taste that is associated with marine species.

Sizes of Striped Bass

Striped bass can grow to great sizes. In past years, there have been numerous records of striped bass which weighed over 100 pounds being taken by commercial fishermen. There is a well-substantiated record of the largest striped bass ever hauled ashore from the waters of the Roanoke River. In April 1891, not one but several striped bass over 100 pounds, the largest a 125-pounder, were taken in a seine at in the western end of Albemarle Sound, near Edenton, North Carolina. Another record comes from Nauset Beach, near Orleans, Massachusetts, of a striper weighing 112 pounds that was taken on a handline. And, in 1887 a 100-1/2 pound striper was taken and recorded in Casco Bay, Maine. (See also Chapter 14)

3

Distribution and Migrations
of East Coast Striped Bass

Striped bass are littoral in the marine environment they have selected, though they are capable of swimming wherever they care. Its life is closely associated with the shore front—estuaries, bays, and tidal rivers—and seldom does it stray far offshore. In its early evolutionary history, striped bass were basically riverine fish, but one that eventually learned to go down to the sea and feed in estuaries. The primary motivation for this characteristic was either species crowding or a search for food, probably both. The secondary, more recent motivation in southward-flowing rivers and along the coast, was to escape advancing glaciers. Today, after the retreat of the last glacier that began 20,000 years ago, estuaries and bays near river mouths are still its prime living space.

During the earliest colonial times, striped bass were found in almost every stream that entered the ocean, from the St. Lawrence River south to Florida, and from western Florida to Texas. Every river had its own distinct spawning population of bass that spent their summers at the mouths of the rivers, or in an area along the beaches on each side of the rivers but not too far from the ancestral stream. With the advent of winter, the smaller fish would migrate upstream or winter over in large, deep-water holes in the estuaries and bays. Large fish, however, migrated southward along the Atlantic Coast in late fall. Small groups of this southward migration would often break away from the main body and winter over in a semi-dormant state in deep holes in numerous back bays and deep tidal rivers along the coast, usually behind barrier beaches. These occur from Rhode Island southward to the entrance to Chesapeake Bay. However, the largest part of this migratory body, joined by adult fish from various riverine stocks, would winter over offshore, in 40 to 60 feet of water, along the Virginia-North Carolina coasts. Then, along came man.

After clearing the land and planting crops, the next order of business for our colonist forefathers was to develop a source of power to grind their grains into flour. As in England, in the Northeast they turned to the bountiful number of brooks and small streams, building dams and mills on almost every one. As industrialization spread over New England, during the middle of the 19th Century, the demand for power to turn the wheels of progress increased and eventually even the largest rivers of the Northeast were dammed. In effect, the dams stopped all striped bass in this region from reaching the fresh water necessary in which to spawn. Within a 40-year period, striped bass production and eventually the fish populations that had been spawned on these free-flowing rivers were eliminated from this part of its range.

The only major river in the Northeast, and the country's second largest

Distribution of striped bass in the marine waters of the United States

striped bass nursery that was not dammed was the Hudson River. It provided the only supply of striped bass in the metropolitan New York area and sustained an active fishery in the East River, along Long Island, and northern New Jersey. Rivers south of the Hudson drained a flat, coastal plain and they didn't possess the head of water needed to run a water wheel. In addition, the surrounding lands were primarily agricultural. By the time the Industrial Revolution reached these areas, electricity was available. Industrialization in areas like Chesapeake Bay was a recent event. For the most part, these rivers had the landfall necessary to create mills only in their upper reaches. Fortunately, these areas were far from salt water and far from where striped bass spawned. Today, its is the rivers of Chesapeake Bay and the Hudson which provide the major spawning and nursery grounds for striped bass on the East Coast. There is a third, maturing source, the Delaware River. While there are no dams on the Delaware, except at its headwater branches in New York's Catskill Mountains, municipal pollution from Philadelphia to Delaware Bay acted as a barrier just as effective as a concrete dam. However, with the Clean Waters Act and establishment of sewage treatment plants along the Delaware, striped bass are again making their way upstream and a spawning population was recognized as early as 1989.

DISTRIBUTION

Today, striped bass on the East Coast are found from the St. Lawrence River south to the St. Johns River in Florida, and on the Gulf Coast from the Homosassa River in Florida west to the Brazos River system in Texas, almost on the Mexican border; and on the West Coast from Ensenada, Mexico, north along the United States to several streams in lower British Columbia. Striped bass are still found over much of their original marine range, but in greatly reduced numbers. While they inhabit it, they no longer spawn where they once did. There are token spawnings in the St. Lawrence River in Quebec, that are independent of the rest of the population. There is spawning in several streams in New Brunswick and Nova Scotia, and even occasionally in Maine. But for the most part, spawning is restricted to the Hudson River; a weak effort in Delaware Bay, that at first was composed of fish from the upper rivers in Chesapeake Bay that expanded their breeding sites into the Chesapeake & Delaware Canal; and a great concentration in Chesapeake Bay.

In North Carolina, spawning bass are restricted to streams that flow into Albemarle and Pamlico sounds. These include the Roanoke, Neuse, Tar, and Cape Fear rivers. From South Carolina to the St. Johns River in Florida on the Atlantic side and from streams in western Florida to Louisiana, striped bass are truly endemic fish, living most of the time in the rivers and only occasionally visiting the sea. The farther south along the coast the more prevalent this endemic characteristic becomes.

Striped bass live and travel great distances up freshwater rivers in the United States and Canada. The most distant inland freshwater range on the Atlantic Coast for the striped bass has been recorded in Quebec's St. Lawrence River at Lake St. Pierre, approximately 400 miles inland. However, as late as the early 1800s, striped bass were recorded by New York's Gov. DeWitt Clinton, eminent naturalist as well as politician, and several well-known writers of that era, as being fairly numerous in eastern Lake Ontario, especially in the vicinity of the Thousand Islands, at the head of the St. Lawrence River. Genio C. Scott, a fairly accurate recorder of fishing during the 1840s and 1850s in the United States, noted that he frequently fished for striped bass in the "upper portion of Lake Ontario." This was near the entrance to the St. Lawrence River and long before the first stocking attempt in the lake by New York State. Striped bass there must have been natural migrants.

Other inland limits on the Atlantic include the Hudson River above Albany and to Little Falls, on the Mohawk River, some 75 miles above where it flows into the Hudson. The falls was not insurmountable to striped bass and the fish probably traveled farther west in the Mohawk. However, this ended about 1820 with the completing of the first part of the Erie Canal with its accompanying

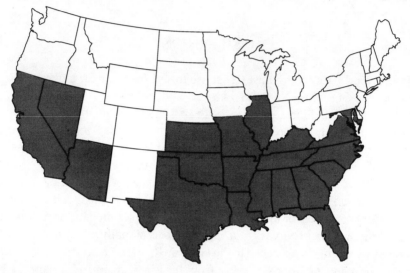

Distribution of striped bass in fresh water, by states.

dames and locks. Fish were also recorded on the Delaware River, at one time as far upstream as Port Jervis; the Susquehanna in past years to the Pennsylvania/ New York border; the Potomac at Great Falls; the Roanoke River to Roanoke Rapids; and the Alabama River to Montgomery and above. On the West Coast, striped bass have been recorded 250 miles up California's Sacramento River.

CANADA

The St. Lawrence River has always held an endemic population of striped bass whose cyclic abundance or scarcity does not seem to be affected by what happens along the remainder of the Atlantic Coast. Head-of-tidewater on the St. Lawrence is a widening of the river midway between Quebec City and Montreal, called Lake St. Pierre. Bass spawn at the rapids at the head of the lake in late June and July, then summer in the tidal river below Quebec City. In the fall, there is a migration out of this estuary and back up the river to the lake. At one time, striped bass were netted through the ice on Lake St. Pierre. Striped bass have occurred regularly up the river as far as Montreal. In 1865, a striped bass was even taken from Lake Ontario at the head of the St. Lawrence River by journalist/angler Robert A. Roosevelt.

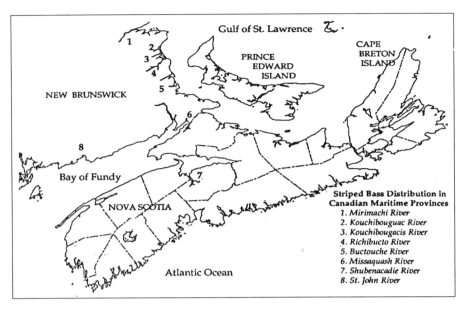

Gulf of St. Lawrence

PRINCE EDWARD ISLAND

CAPE BRETON ISLAND

NEW BRUNSWICK

Bay of Fundy

NOVA SCOTIA

Atlantic Ocean

Striped Bass Distribution in Canadian Maritime Provinces
1. *Mirimachi River*
2. *Kouchibouguac River*
3. *Kouchibougacis River*
4. *Richibucto River*
5. *Buctouche River*
6. *Missaquash River*
7. *Shubenacadie River*
8. *St. John River*

Striped bass are not found north of the Gulf of St. Lawrence, above the Laurentian channel separating Labrador from Newfoundland. In the Gulf of St. Lawrence it is found down river along many of the streams that flow into the bay. In New Brunswick it has been found on the Miramichi River system and estuary, Petitcodiac, Tabusintac, Koucibouguac, Buctouche, Tignisk and Richibucto rivers, all with spawning populations; on Prince Edward Island in Malpeque Bay and Summerside River; and Nova Scotia at Cheticamp, and the estuary of the River Philip. On the outer coast of Nova Scotia it is found on the Canso and in Mira Bay, Chedabucto Bay, and Mahone Bay. In the Bay of Fundy it is found in the Minas Basin area, and along the shores of St. John and Yarmouth counties, as well as in the St. Croix, Digdeguash, St. John, Kennebecasis, Shubenacadie and Annapolis rivers and even in Shubenacadie Lake.

On the St. John River in New Brunswick, striped bass at one time made an extensive up river running spawn to the village of Mactaquac, just above Fredericton. In 1965, the huge Mactaquac Dam was built astride the river, exactly where the fish spawned. The immediate effects were devastating and while striped bass have claimed some of the river section below the dam, spawning there is now only a token of what it once was.

UNITED STATES

From Maine south to the St. Johns River in Florida, striped bass are either seasonal or residential fish in fresh water at one time or another throughout the year. The greatest concentrations in the population of striped bass along the Atlantic Coast is between Cape Hatteras, N. C., and Cape Ann, Mass. During summer months, from June to October, this concentration centers in the north half, between eastern Long Island, N. Y., and Cape Cod. Before the opening of the Cape Cod Canal in 1914, Buzzards Bay and Vineyard Sound were about the northern limit of the migration. Since then, striped bass have readily used the canal to expand their range. One of the most recent users of this short cut have been Hudson River striped bass. Tagging return revealed they have ventured as far north as Nova Scotia. During the colder months of the year, most striped bass are concentrated just off Virginia and North Carolina and in Chesapeake Bay.

Maine

Nowadays, striped bass in Maine are all virtually seasonal migrants with only some slight winter holdover. At one time, there were records of striped bass spawning on the Saco, Kennebec, Androscoggin, Sheepscot, Penobscot, and St. Croix rivers. But barrier dams at the head of the tide or even in tidewater, eliminated these historic spawning sites. In a few instances, rivers have been cleaned, especially of pulp process by-products, and dams even taken apart. On clean rivers, where dams haven't been removed and salmon have been stocked, fish ladders have been built. Striped bass have no difficulty, to the chagrin of salmon-only fisheries managers, in ascending fish ladders. Some spawning has been reoccurring but only in minimal proportions.

The concentration of striped bass in Maine's coastal waters varies from season to season, dependent upon water temperature, the appearance of baitfish upon which striped bass feed and follow, and the size of the coastal migratory stock. Consistently, when the fish do appear, the Saco is one of the best rivers. Generally the fish appear from Kittery to Calais.

New Hampshire

In all of New England, striped bass nowadays are seasonal migrants except for occasional holdover fish that become somewhat dormant and contribute only slightly to the fishery. In New Hampshire, distribution of striped bass is limited to the bays along this state's short coast. At one time, there was a fishery on portions of the Merrimac River in New Hampshire, but this has disappeared.

Massachusetts

During most years, the waters of Massachusetts are the northern limit for the summer migratory stock of striped bass. The fish are distributed at the estuary formed by the Merrimac River and from Plum Island south to the waters surrounding Cape Ann and Gloucester. The greatest concentration appears in waters off Cape Cod, on the north side and in all the bays, inlets, and estuaries along the seaward and southern sides of the hook. During the summer, striped bass are well dispersed about Nantucket, Martha's Vineyard, the Elizabeth Islands, and the numerous bays of Buzzards Bay, as well as inside the Cape Cod Canal.

Rhode Island

Rhode Island has good striped bass distribution in the waters of Narragansett Bay as well as on the outside, along the beaches from Sakonnet Point to Watch Hill. At times of low numbers of Chesapeake migratory bass stocks, the western edge of Rhode Island, near Watch Hill, also appears to be the western limit for summering populations of striped bass. However, despite reduced numbers of Chesapeake stocks, since 1980, Hudson stocks have moved eastward in increasing numbers. Their production has been high and this nursery has become the dominant contributor, in the past three years, to the New England fishery.

Connecticut

Connecticut's waters receive striped bass from two sources. The Atlantic coastal migratory stock expands in late spring and early summer into its eastern waters, in Long Island Sound, when Chesapeake stocks are high. Along the western coast of the state, striped bass are more likely to be summering stock from the Hudson River fishery. From Bridgeport to Old Lyme, there is an overlap in the composition of fish from both the Hudson and Chesapeake Bay. This line has moved eastward in recent years. Striped bass fishing activities are concentrated at the mouths of the Connecticut and Thames rivers, at Bartletts and Hatchett reefs, among the offshore islands in western Long Island Sound, and at the mouth of the Housatonic River. During the last decade, efforts to reestablish runs of Atlantic salmon on the Connecticut River have had an unusual side benefit. As in Maine, the cleaning of waters, along with building fish ladders and removal of a few barriers, has encouraged striped bass to reenter the river with salmon. Fish counters as far as Vermont and New Hampshire have revealed small numbers of striped bass running with salmon. Considering the characteristics of the Connecticut River, before dams were constructed, it had to be a major producer of striped bass. In Colonial Times, and as late as 1850, striped bass regularly migrated up the Connecticut River to the first natural barrier (a falls) just above Hartford.

New York

New York's striped bass fishery is also composed of two differing stocks of fish and hence its distribution varies. The location of striped bass also varies with the season. Striped bass composed of the Atlantic migratory stock appear on the south shore of Long Island from April to November and even as late as December. These fish are on the move, though portions of the school do stay the summer in the eastern bays from Great South Bay to Montauk and in Gardiner's Bay and the Peconics, as well as in Long Island Sound from east of Wading River. Part of this migratory stock becomes residential in the waters around Plum Island, in the Race between Fishers Island and Great and Little Gull islands, and along the coast of Rhode Island during the summer.

The largest resident stock of striped bass in New York waters are produced

Migration routes during the spring from the Hudson River nursery.

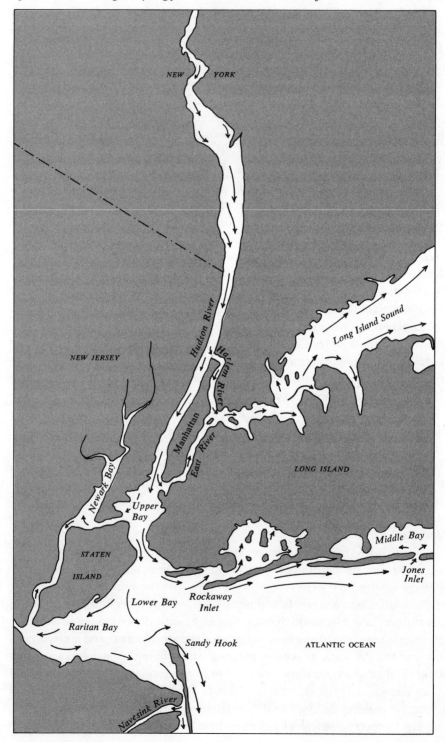

in the Hudson River and dominate the populations in western Long Island Sound. Until recently, the Hudson was thought to be only a minor nursery, but several studies, even before the most recent decline of Chesapeake Bay stock, that began in the early 1970s, revealed that it is far larger than once believed. Striped bass inhabit the Hudson as far north as Poughkeepsie, with some fish present in the river as far north as Albany during the summer. Nursery stock, for the first two years of life, remains in the area around Stony Point before taking part in a local seasonal migration.

When striped bass migrate, they do so for several reasons: food, temperature, reproduction, and environmental pressures or changes. The majority of striped bass in the Hudson are migratory, but only in a local sense with regard to their immediate environment. About mid-April, adult bass and those that have spawned begin a southward migration out of the Hudson. They eventually establish a summer population with its greatest concentration in New York's Upper Bay and Lower Bay and in the bays and estuaries of northern New Jersey, with a few fish moving as far south as Barnegat Inlet. Those fish that do enter the Atlantic move east along the south shore of Long Island and summer in Jamaica Bay. Some fish also enter the western part of Great South Bay.

Another portion of this fishery migrates out of the Hudson through the East River and into the western part of Long Island Sound. It disperses itself across the coast of Westchester County and as far east along the Connecticut shore as Bridgeport. The fish are spread along the north shore of Long Island as far as Port Jefferson. In times of high abundance, they move as far east as Wading River, along Orient Point and even into Fishers Island Sound and the rips off Block Island's North Reef. Bass remain here throughout the summer and fall, the to return to the Hudson River and the Lower and Upper bays as winter approaches. Some fish winter in the deeper rivers and bays of northern New Jersey and western Long Island Sound.

Most recent studies, however, describe two possibly different scenarios for migrations of Hudson River stocks, and what once was true for these fish, prior to 1970, might not be true today. Tag returns came from as far away as Nova Scotia, from bass tagged in the Hudson River, indicate that a substantial number of fish, estimated at several thousand, do take long, migratory jaunts. This has become more evident as the number of highly-migratory Chesapeake Bay stocks have declined. Even more recently, tagging and returns of fish tagged along the oceanside of Long Island's South Fork, along with mitochondrial analysis of the fish sampled over an extended period, revealed that 73 percent of the fish sampled during the fall migration of 1989 were of Hudson River stock. The remaining 27 percent were from Chesapeake Bay.

There are two possible explanations of this phenomenon. One is that there always was a group of highly-migratory Hudson River fish, whose presence wasn't revealed until more extensive stocking occurred, and they were also masked by the huge number of Chesapeake Bay stock that also ranges that far

north along the coast. The second explanation is based more on natural population dynamics that are always in action. With the decline of Chesapeake Bay
stocks along the New England coast, the niche was filled by Hudson River stock
that has been unaffected by the several factors that caused Maryland's and
Virginia's striped bass populations to decline. At the same time, the Hudson
River stock has undergone a rapid population explosion, that has been further
fostered by the elimination of commercial fishing for them in the Hudson River
because of PCB contamination.

New Jersey

Unlike New York, New Jersey's coastal distribution today is composed
almost totally of a migratory stock. The exception might be a limited amount of
juvenile fish that are spawned in the Maurice River and reared along the
southern part of Delaware Bay, and some Delaware River stock that has been
reproducing since 1988. The bulk of New Jersey's coastal fishery is composed of
migrant Chesapeake Bay stock. This is distributed along the beaches from Cape
May to Sandy Hook in the spring as they head northward and again in this same
area in the fall as they return south.

A second contribution of migratory stock, that in recent years has increased
both in its size and the role it plays, comes from the Hudson River. These fish are
spread in New Jersey in waters from Newark Bay south to Barnegat Bay. They
are summer residents here, in Raritan Bay, Navesink, and Shrewsbury rivers.
During their northward migration, some Chesapeake Bay fish will spread in the
large bays of New Jersey and concentrate there for a while. To some degree, they
will occasionally leave pods of summer residential stock. At one time, during
the southward migration, many large bass do not to return to southerly waters,
but winter in Great Egg Harbor and the Mullica River on Great Bay.

Delaware

Most of Delaware's fish are concentrated in Delaware Bay, and striped bass
are distributed at times up the Delaware River only to Wilmington, along the
New Jersey portion of the bay, and about the estuaries near Woodland Beach.
In recent years, as the Delaware River has been cleaned of industrial and
municipal pollution, striped bass have been found farther and farther north in
the river. The Chesapeake & Delaware Canal, near the bay's head, has become
a major migratory shortcut for the itinerant striped bass moving out of Chesapeake Bay. At times, the fish are quite abundant in the canal. In recent years,
studies have shown that the canal also acts as a breeding area for striped bass,
and the waterway has developed an annual spring population of spawning fish.
There's also a limited spawning in Delaware River just below Philadelphia.

Chesapeake Bay

This vast body of water, shared by Maryland and Virginia, was the major nursery for striped bass on the Atlantic. Striped bass are spread throughout the numerous bays and rivers of this area at various times of the year. The coastal portions of Maryland and Virginia receive fish only during the migrations, and there is very little fishing for striped bass in the surf except when migrations are under way. Chesapeake Bay should not be considered as one entity when dealing with the management of striped bass because the individual stocks from all its rivers show great diversity in their biology, distribution and migration. This has been supported by differing policies by Maryland and Virginia, that share the bay. Even the Potomac River is managed separately, because it is shared by the two states, by the Potomac River Fish Commission.

Striped bass in Chesapeake Bay populations can be divided into three groups, roughly based on their rivers of origin at spawning. There is an upper bay group of striped bass that is spawned in the Susquehanna River, the upper bay itself, the Chesapeake & Delaware Canal, and the Northeast, Elk, Bohemia, and Sassafras rivers on the Eastern Shore. The second, Eastern Shore group, is composed of rivers all with the same unique physical characteristics that drain the low-relief Delmarva Peninsula and include three relatively large rivers, the Chester, Choptank, and Nanticoke, and three lesser tidal rivers, the Wicomico, Manokin, and Pocomoke. The third, lower-bay group, all on the Western Shore, consist of bass spawned on Marlyand's Patuxent and Potomac rivers, an in Virginia, the Rappahannock, York, and James rivers. The lowest river in Chesapeake Bay is the James River; its fish are the least migratory of any bass produced in Chesapeake Bay. They more closely resemble the striped bass of Albemarle Sound (North Carolina) in migration characteristics as well as racial features.

The single largest production of striped bass in Chesapeake Bay now occurs on the Potomac River. At one time, before the dam was built, the Susquehanna River might have been the most productive because of its size and length. Before the decline that began in the early 1970s, the Upper Bay was the most productive area of these nursery grounds. Most of the mid and upper bay is essentially fresh water because of the great number of large rivers that empty into it. However, the effect of tides is still felt to the very head of the bay and in the Susquehanna River to the base of the Conowingo Dam, just 10 miles south of the Pennsylvania border. During the summer, the waters of the bay hold large numbers of striped bass. However, the majority of these are small fish, one to two years old, and many of them are only zero-year stock, less than fingerlings. Large fish are present only during spawning.

North Carolina

The distribution of fish in North Carolina varies with the season. During the winter months, there is a large concentration of striped bass located offshore in the Atlantic that does, from time to time, approach the beaches from Cape Fear to Virginia Beach. The greatest catches of fish are in the Cape Hatteras area.

Inside the barrier beaches, in Pamlico and Albemarle sounds, the bays hold a large wintering population of smaller fish, similar to those age classes in Chesapeake Bay. During early spring, striped bass from outside in the Atlantic as well as those wintering in the bays make a spawning migration up the Roanoke, Neus, and Tar rivers and several smaller tidal streams.

North Carolina's striped bass sources are divided into two distinct groups, one composed of fish produced in the Tar and Neuse rivers and associated small tributary streams that empty into Pamlico Sound and another composed of fish produced on the Roanoke River and its associated tributaries that flow into Albemarle Sound. This latter fish stock is the largest in North Carolina and also differs from other North Carolina stock in that it did make minor contributions to the Atlantic migratory coastal population even though it differed substantially from more northerly stocks. In more recent years, however, it has proven to be more similar, with non-migratory tendencies, to Pamlico Sound stock. One reason might be a large decline in its own size, at times mirrored the losses in Chesapeake Bay stocks.

South Carolina

From Cape Fear, N. C., south to Florida and along the Gulf of Mexico, striped bass are more or less confined, of their own volition, to freshwater river systems during most of the year. Only occasionally are they found at the estuaries. The farther south one travels the more this characteristic is an intrinsic part of the fish's habits. In some systems, they are found 150 to 200 miles from salt water.

Estuarine environments conducive to holding striped bass are quite plentiful in South Carolina. However, the fish this far south in their distribution spend more time in freshwater rivers than in estuaries. Each river system in the state has developed a self-sustaining population. From north to south, striped bass are distributed in the Waccamaw and Pee Dee rivers, which share a common estuary, and the Santee, Cooper, Wando, Ashley, Edisto, Ashepoo, and Combahee rivers. South Carolina shares with Georgia the Savannah River, a system which at one time supported a fairly consistent riverine and estuarine striped bass fishery.

Georgia

At one time, Georgia's waters supported an active and extensive fishery for striped bass. Twenty years ago, there was a fair fishery on the Savannah and Ogeechee rivers. Migration runs on the Savannah took fish more than 180 miles up river. The majority of Georgia's striped bass fishing was then done along these coastal streams, with the best angling in the lower estuaries during the cooler fall and winter months.

Over the years, however, rivers here have been polluted by pulp operations, along with the Corps of Engineers, development of Savannah Harbor caused salt water to reach the traditional spawning grounds. Spawning sites were drastically reduced and natural production reached extreme lows. By 1980 the striped bass population had completely collapsed. It wasn't until 1987 that a massive restoration effort was begun. Earlier, in 1974, a striped bass hatchery was established at Richmond Hill, near Savannah, with the idea of further enhancing the coastal fishery. But with the drastically altered environment, all the fish produced at the hatchery have been used to establish striped bass populations in several large impoundments throughout the state. Today, most striped bass fishing is in these fresh waters. (see Chapter 8, The Striped Bass in Fresh Water)

Corps of Engineer projects on the Savannah, that contaminated the back rivers with salt water, were removed, and the fishery has started to make a comeback. All recreational fishing on the river was halted in 1989 to help restore the stocks at a faster pace. Since then, natural reproduction has reoccurred and the young fish are now in their third and fourth years. Eventually, it is the hope of the Georgia Department of Natural Resources to reopen the marine striped bass fishery.

Although Georgia has no actual Gulf Coast striped bass fishery, because it is blocked from the Gulf by the Florida panhandle, it does have stocks of Gulf of Mexico striped bass, glacial anomalies, still active today in several rivers that originate in Georgia and flow south, through Florida, to the Gulf. It has worked closely with Florida to continue, protect, and enhance this fishery.

Florida

To the surprise of most northern anglers, Florida possesses a unique striped bass fishery. The distribution is in two separate populations. One is composed of fish that make up the most southerly limit of the Atlantic Coast population. The second is made up of a Gulf Coast population that either cannot round the Florida Keys and thus has no contact with Atlantic fish.

On the Atlantic Coast, striped bass distribution is limited to three rivers emptying into the ocean in the northeast corner of the state. St. Marys River, shared with Georgia as a border river, contains some striped bass. Within the city limits of Jacksonville and just south of the St. Marys is Nassau River, and in Jacksonville proper there is the St. Johns River, both with striped bass populations. The St. Johns flows north from Washington Lake for about 200 miles before it reaches Jacksonville. At one time or another striped bass have been taken along its entire course. Occasionally, they have been taken along the Atlantic beach as far south along the coast as Ft. Pierce, but biologists consider these as stragglers or wandering fish.

On the west coast of Florida, striped bass appear in all the rivers from the Suwannee west to the Perdido. These include the Aucilla, St. Marks, Ochlockonee, Apalachicola, Chipola, Choctawhatchee, and Yellow rivers. The Apalachicola is the most productive by far, and 40 pound striped bass are not uncommon.

MIGRATIONS OF STRIPED BASS

Migration of fish is a natural phenomenon and all fish, sometime in their lives, move about from place to place. There are several reasons that motivate fish to migrate and they can roughly be divided into three categories: seasonal, spawning, and coastal migrations. The most spectacular are spawning migrations exemplified by the Atlantic salmon or the American eel. Few fish spawn where they live and eat, even fish whose entire lives are contained in one river.

Spawning Migrations

Some fish, like Atlantic salmon, have a well-developed homing instinct and return to the exact site in which they were spawned. To do their own spawning, they will travel hundreds of miles up rivers to reach that location. Pelagic fish species spawn in the open ocean or move inshore to spawn in bays, estuaries, or tidal rivers. Striped bass, however, are endowed with an instinct similar to salmon and return to spawn in their native, natal freshwater rivers. While the specificity of the salmon is uncannily exact, striped bass need only return to the general area where they were spawned to satisfy the same urge.

The actual spawning areas of striped bass are far more limited than those of the salmon. This may result in some way from their lesser degree of exactitude. Also, striped bass larvae and fry that can immediately move into a light saline or brackish environment to grow, when it is available, have a decided survival advantage over those whose eggs are laid and mature entirely in fresh water. In the case of salmon parr, they may spend several years in a small locale learning their environment before they change to smolts and take to the ocean.

For most fish, seasonal migrations are often the shortest. Even a portion of the bass population seems to prefer to winter in fresh or nearly fresh water, often not far from future spawning sites. Others, however, winter in the open ocean and make long pre-spawning migrations to their sites. After spawning, the fish will migrate down river and spend most of the summer and fall in the marine estuaries or along the immediate beaches only to return again in late winter to await another cycle.

Spawning migrations in most fish populations are usually composed only of adult fish. But female striped bass are an exception. A striped bass is considered adult when it is capable of spawning. In male striped bass, this generally occurs when they is two or three years old. In females, it is much later, especially the farther north their nurseries occur along the coast. In rivers south of Cape Hatteras, spawning first occurs in precocious females at three years of age, but in the majority, they are four or five years old. By nine years of age, all female bass are capable of spawning. However, females in certain rivers of Chesapeake Bay usually leave these nursery areas at the beginning of their third year and join the coastal migration north with adult fish of both sexes. These old migrants are striped bass that have wintered offshore and are returning north to spawn or to summer feeding grounds.

Spawning migrations, then, are of several varieties. Bass that live most of their lives in salt water or estuarine environments will move from salt to fresh or nearly fresh water when their time to spawn nears. In river systems that are totally fresh water, striped bass will move from wintering in lower, deeper sections to upper areas with more moving water to spawn. Sometimes they actually seek rapids in which to spawn. In some river systems the migration is over tremendous distances. Striped bass in the San Joaquin River in California will spawn just above tidewater, while other bass in the Sacramento River, which shares the same delta maze of islands and channels, move as much as 250 miles up river, especially when the river is high. One of the longest spawning migrations in the eastern United States is performed by striped bass in North Carolina. The wintering fish will move from the offshore waters on the Outer Banks, migrate inshore over Albemarle Sound, and then up the Roanoke River to Roanoke Rapids, more than 180 miles upstream.

In Chesapeake Bay, a basically brackish body of water, most spawning fish will winter in the deeper parts of the bay, or with a large contingent of old fish mixed with other itinerant bass off Cape Hatteras. Those fish that do stay in the bay take part in a southern migration to lower and deeper parts of the bay as winter nears. As April and May approach, these bass will begin heading for various rivers throughout the bay to spawn. In past times, before the construction of dams, striped bass entered the Susquehanna River and traveled up as far as Berwick, Pa. to spawn. Some fish were even identified as far up this river as Binghamton, N.Y., but it was not determined if they, too, were spawning.

A similar long trek to spawn at one time occurred on the Delaware River. In recent times, spawning occurred in the area between Trenton and Philadelphia, then only as far as Philadelphia. But in colonial times, striped bass were said to have spawned as far upstream as Port Jervis in New York. But industrial and municipal pollution, as the valley became industrialized, made these journeys impossible, and only fish capable of spawning at the head of tidewater, where the salinity is zero or nearly so, were able to continue their strains. Today, confirmed spawning is again taking place in the Philadelphia area, as the pollution has been cleared, and some fish have appeared as far north as the East and West Branches of the river in New York. Other spawnings in Delaware Bay are confined to the Chesapeake & Delaware Canal and a coastal stream on the New Jersey side of the bay.

There is some question as to whether these fish were original Delaware River stock or stock that enlarged its range with the opening of the Chesapeake & Delaware Canal. Today, as pollution has abated, any fish now bent on spawning can move far enough above salt water to spawn. The development of these fish is being closely monitored by the three states involved: Delaware,

Migration Routes—*Illustrated here are the spring or northward migration routes of striped bass. In fall, almost the reverse paths are followed along the Atlantic Coast. Noteworthy, however, is the fact that fall migrations usually take place closer to the*

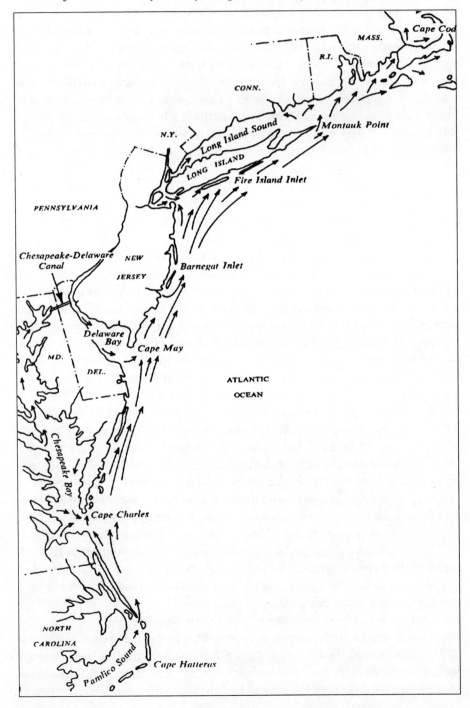

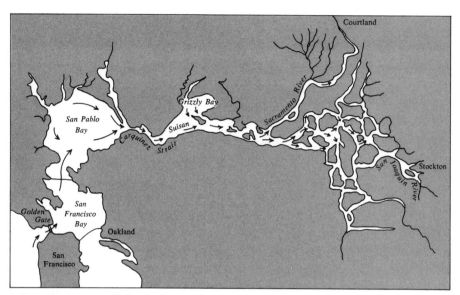

Migration Routes—Fall migration in the San Francisco Bay area. Bass here abandon salt water to winter in fresh or brackish water in the delta formed by the Sacramento and

Pennsylvania and New Jersey.

On the Hudson River in New York, it was believed that all spawning took place in the main river itself but not in side tributaries. More recent studies, however, indicate that while the major spawning effort still takes place in the river, several tributaries—Catskill, Esopus Creek, Wappinger and Roundout creeks, and the Croton River—also act as spawning grounds in their lower reaches. The Hudson is essentially fresh water, or brackish in its lower sections, and spawning in various degrees occurs from Dobbs Ferry, just south of the George Washington Bridge, north to the base of the Troy Dam. However, two major areas have been identified, with the most intensive spawning taking place from Bear Mountain north to Cruger Island, with its center near West Point, in water with no saline content. A second intensive site was discovered farther north in the Hudson, between the towns of Kingston and Catskill.

Striped bass in the Pacific undergo limited migrations within their river-bay-estuary systems. There is no recorded mass coastal migration similar to that on the Atlantic. In the San Francisco Bay area, bass that have spent part of the summer outside the bay reenter and begin a fall migration toward the delta of the Sacramento and San Joaquin rivers. As they move toward the delta, they are joined by fish that have summered in San Pablo, Suisan, and Grizzly bays.

Water along the many channels of the delta and the two rivers proper is fresh, and here the fish feed and wait out the winter until spawning. On the Sacramento River, striped bass spawn in the vicinity above Courtland and as far up stream to Butte City, and on the San Joaquin, between the Antioch Bridge and the mouth of Middle River. A post-spawning migration occurs as fish drop to the lower delta. By the end of spring they are concentrated again in the bays.

In Oregon, striped bass inhabit five rivers and spawn to some degree in all of them. Coos Bay, at one time, probably had the state's greatest concentration of fish, though the Umpqua and Smith rivers also have substantial populations. The fish are concentrated in the bays and near the inlets in the Pacific during the summer and fall and probably winter in the same area because the estuaries are so limited. In the spring, they ascend the rivers for short distances and spawn only to return quickly to their feeding and summer locations.

Coastal Migrations

The model or typical striped bass populations in most areas of the fish's range make only two types of migrations—spring spawning migrations and winter-summer migrations to feeding grounds in the estuaries or lower portions of their river system. Post-spawning migrations are usually to lower parts of these bays or to estuaries only with the intent of feeding throughout the summer. Some of these migrations are also temperature-oriented movements so fish can stay in water best suited to their metabolism and may often be rather short in distance as well as duration. These latter usually take place in the heat of late July and early August and often are short-lived. These migrations are more typical of Gulf Coast populations.

However, there is one unique strain of striped bass on the Atlantic that is atypical of the perfect striped bass model ichthyologists are always trying to build. This group of fish undertakes one of the longest migrations possible for striped bass and was so spectacular in size that for decades it overshadowed other bass populations they encountered and engulfed en route and for a long time had confused the true picture of the typical striped bass life cycle and cyclic migrations. However, their penchant for coastal migration is believed to be a relatively recent phenomenon and appears to have started in the early 1920s. The reason for this belief is substantiated by the fact that there is no evidence documenting these migrations taking place before that time. The contrary is true, based on two prominent ichthyologists of the late 1700s and early 1800s.

> Their greatest run is late in the fall. Instead of going away on the approach of winter, the striped bass seeks refuge in bays, ponds and recesses where he will remain warm and quiet. Here the fishermen find him, and make great hauls during the coldest season, when very great numbers are brought to market [Fulton] in a frozen state.
> — From *Transactions of the [New York] Literary and Philosophical Society*, by Dr. Samuel Latham Mitchill.

Mitchill, a native of North Hempstead, N.Y., whose mother's family dates back to the original founders of Long Island's (N.Y.) North Fork (1639), while trained as a physician in Scotland, became the great American taxonomist. He was first to scientifically described striped bass in North America, and as is the tradition, he added his name to it: *Perca mitchilli.*

Also:

> Striped bass are a sea fish, and principally subsist near the mouths of river, up which the run as high as they can conveniently go. During the approach of winter, instead of striking out into the deep water of the open ocean, like most other anadromous species, the basse finds a residence in ponds, coves, rivers and still arms of the sea, where undisturbed and comfortable, it remains till the following spring. The principal rivers of the state of Maine are places where they now are taken in greatest abundance. In all the rivers, too, of Massachusetts, they are also found, at the inclement season of winter, but the fishery is not so productive as in Maine.
>
> — *The Natural History of the Fishes of Massachusetts,*
> by Dr. Jerome Van Crownin Smith, 1833.

Causes for a change in this strain of striped bass to become coastal migrants can only be guessed at. It could have been a mutation in its genetic make-up or it could have been a response to over-crowding and a search for more food. These fish all stem from Chesapeake Bay stock. There are three, possibly four, definable populations of striped bass in Chesapeake Bay. There are those fish produced in the lower bay, in the James River; then another group in the York and Rappahannock rivers that join with a major contribution from the Potomac River; and a third group from the rivers in the upper bays, Upper Bay itself, and the Eastern Shore. Not all the different stock from these rivers contribute every year to the coastal migration. Some never do.

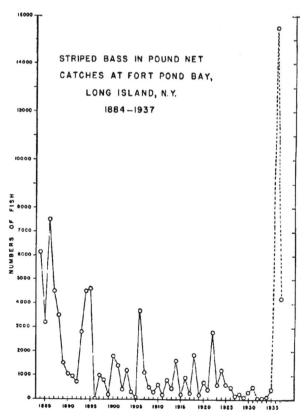

STRIPED BASS IN POUND NET
CATCHES AT FORT POND BAY,
LONG ISLAND, N.Y.
1884–1937

NUMBERS OF FISH

For some not yet totally explained reason, some of the striped bass spawned in the middle bay rivers, principally the Potomac River, and at other times from the Upper Bay, since the early 1920s, suddenly undertook a vast coastal migration. The motivation for this migration has never been fully established. Some biologists speculate that during dominant year classes, the bay is overcrowded and food scarce. Only juveniles stay in the bay throughout summer. These fish typically spend their lives in the bay until they reach two years of age and are beginning their third year, primarily all females, when there is a sudden urge to leave the bay. This is not a spawning run because almost all the females are still sexually immature. In their exodus they now use the Chesapeake & Delaware Canal, at the northern end of Chesapeake Bay, and migrate up the Atlantic Coast.

The first evidence of this great coastal migration didn't manifest itself until the early 1920s. It occurred coincidentally with the enlargement, by the U.S. Corps of Engineers, of the Chesapeake & Delaware Canal, at the northern end of Chesapeake Bay. This work began in 1921. The canal was first opened in 1829 but handled only small, barge traffic. The 1921 enlargement allowed for much larger vessels to traffic the canal between the two bays and a much greater water exchange.

While en route, often at a point near Cape May, N.J., the smaller bass are joined by much larger and older bass, some from Chesapeake Bay that are in a post-spawning migration, and mature striped bass that have wintered offshore in North Carolina or have stayed in deeper bays and estuaries along the coast and are on a pre-spawning migration to their natal streams to the north. The migration begins in April and May and the non-spawning fish continue past New Jersey, eastward along the coast to Long Island, past Montauk Point and on to Cape Cod. During some years, they go as far north as the Gulf of Maine and others swim around Nova Scotia to summers in New Brunswick and Quebec estuaries with local striped bass.

As this group passes north of Long Island it begins to fragment. Some drop off along the way and summer in the bays of eastern Long Island, Long Island Sound to Rhode Island, off the Elizabeth Islands, and on both the coastal and continental sides of Cape Cod. Even a few fish produced in North Carolina waters will take part in the migration, but researchers have shown that this contribution is quite minimal. North Carolina fish, along with those of the James River in Chesapeake Bay, instead take up summer residence in Albemarle and Pamlico sounds or lower Chesapeake Bay.

Bass that are spawned in the Delaware estuaries and those that winter over in Delaware Bay and some of the rivers in New Jersey also take part in this grand trek. A few fish of Chesapeake stock may winter in upper and lower New York Bay, and they too contribute to this migration. All these wintering-over fish are believed, however, to be originally composed of the same Chesapeake Bay population.

The migratory habits of striped bass from the Hudson River nursery at one time exhibited it the more typical migrations that are characteristic of all striped bass populations except the one Chesapeake Bay group. In the Hudson, fish

Summer distribution of Atlantic populations of striped bass. *The ranges of the two strains of striped bass overlap to some degree in Long Island Sound. These areas change in size as both populations expand and decrease in numbers.*

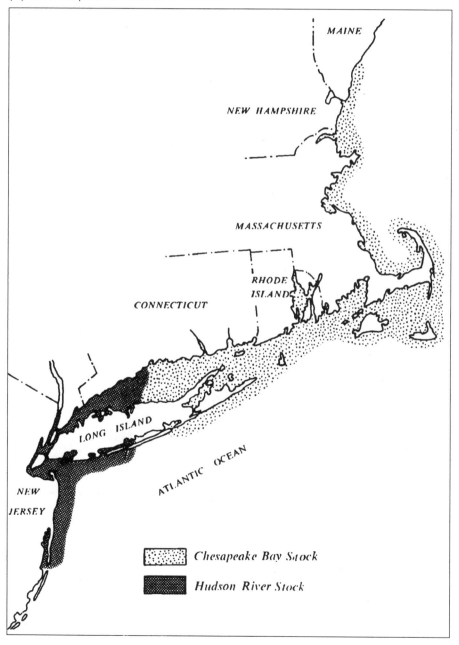

Wintering Grounds—*Primary winter distribution of striped bass along the Atlantic Coast. This does not include the Hudson fishery, which winters in the lower Hudson River, the numerous holdover bass that find wintering spots along the Connecticut, New York, New Jersey, and Delaware coasts. Fish that winter in Chesapeake Bay and Albemarle and Pamlico sounds are mostly immature striped bass.*

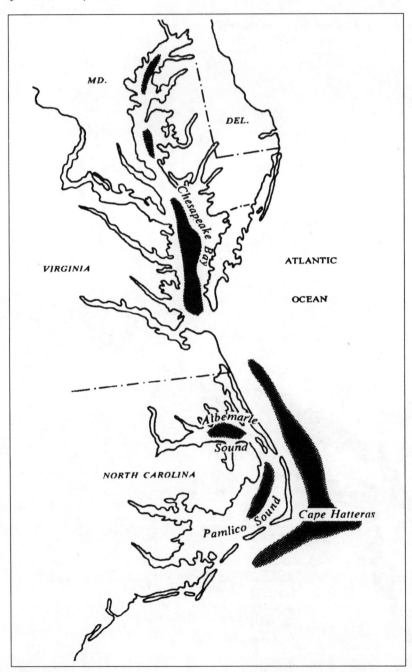

produced in its waters made a relatively short southward migration, spending their summers in lower New York Bay, in several tidal rivers in adjacent New Jersey, and eastward along the Atlantic only as far as Jamaica Bay and western Great South Bay.

In Long Island Sound, Hudson River stock summer on the western end, along the Connecticut shore as far east as Bridgeport and on Long Island's North Shore about as far east as Port Jefferson and Mt. Sinai Harbor. Though this is a coastal migration of sorts, it is still considered a local move when compared to the great journey that is made by fish from Maryland and Virginia. All these waters are part of the grand estuarine system of the Hudson River.

During the recent decline of striped bass populations in Chesapeake Bay, that began in the late 70s, the number of fish from this nursery was diminished sharply, as much as 70 percent according to some estimates. This had a direct effect on the distance traveled during seasonal migrations by Hudson River fish. With a void now left along both north and south shores of Long Island, there was a natural tendency for the Hudson River stock to expand into the unclaimed niche. This expansion was further stimulated by several exceptionally large year classes that produced by the Hudson River population during the late 1980s. They are now contributing more to Long Island's East End fishery than before, and larger numbers, larger than in past years, are showing up with greater regularity in the Massachusetts fishery. In every population, even in rigidly indigenous ones, there are always errant wanderers that for some reason move well beyond their normal limitations. This is true for Hudson River bass. Returns of Hudson River tags now come even from Nova Scotia.

Prior to the Emergency Striped Bass Study, made possible by the 1979 Chafee Amendment to the Anadromous Fish Act, it was believed that of the annual population of striped bass that were produced in the waters of Chesapeake Bay, only about 10 percent were able to escape the heavy commercial and sport fishing pressure and take part in this great coastal migration. Of the total number of fish that did make the coastal migration, nearly 90 percent were believed to have originated in the Chesapeake Bay area. The remaining 10 percent was made up of North Carolina, Delaware, and Hudson River fish. The Hudson River was believed to contribute the least—not because it didn't have the population, but because its fish at that time were believed to be primarily non-migratory in relation to the coast. This is not the case today. However, more recent studies of striped bass population dynamics revealed that more than 10 percent may have actually escaped Chesapeake Bay and that the Hudson River fishery also contributed a far great percentage to the coastal stocks, as much as 30 percent, even during periods of high productivity in Chesapeake Bay.

In late September and October, the coastal stock of migratory fish begins a southward movement, spurred on by falling temperatures, shortened days and shifting food-fish populations. The fish school and move southward along New England, west across Long Island, and south along the coast of New Jersey,

Delaware, and Virginia. Many of the younger fish return to Chesapeake Bay to winter in lower parts of the bay, but large numbers, composed mostly of older bass, choose to winter in deeper coastal rivers and bays or in an area off North Carolina and Virginia, between the mouth of Chesapeake Bay and Cape Hatteras. When they were first discovered in the early 1980s, large numbers fell easy prey to high-speed offshore commercial trawlers because the fish concentrated in such dense schools.

As water temperatures fall below 40 degrees, bass in their various winter locations restrict their movement and enter a somewhat dormant stage. The exception to this are smaller striped bass, fish one to three years old, in Chesapeake Bay. They have been shown to feed actively and move about the bay even under the ice. At this time, their migrations are strictly of a feeding nature. During most of the months of December, January, and February, these fish will feed along the edge of deep water in the lower bay. When temperatures rise during the day they will move into shallower water, only to return when it again falls

The striped bass of North Carolina separate themselves somewhat like the large and small fish of Chesapeake Bay. However, here the separation is even greater geographically. The smaller striped bass will remain in Albemarle Sound during the winter, while larger fish move out the inlets to join other striped bass wintering in the open ocean off the Outer Banks.

4

Reproduction in Striped Bass

All fish are believed to have developed in fresh water. Some fishes, through later physical adaptations, were able to expand their realm into sea water with a saline content of 29 ppt (parts per thousand) content or higher. The evolutionary history of striped bass as a freshwater fish is evident and revealed when they are ready to reproduce. Most marine fishes spawn in salt water because their conversion to this environment is complete. Striped bass, however, have never became an exclusively-saltwater fish and still require a return to its ancestral spawning grounds in fresh water to reproduce its kind.

Where the seasons vary greatly during the year, spawning will usually take place in early spring so that eggs and growing fish have the advantage of the warmer months of the year to begin their lives. Striped bass, throughout most of their range, are influenced by seasonal fluctuations in temperature and the size of annual production varies accordingly. Periods of intense spawning activity are usually triggered by sharp increases in water temperature. Also, dominant year class production on the East Coast has always been preceded by abnormally cold winters. During springs with higher than normal water flows on the West Coast, juvenile production also has been higher than other years.

SPAWNING

Spawning Seasons

Striped bass spawn as early as February in the St. Johns River in Florida and as late as July in Lake St. Pierre on the St. Lawrence River in Quebec. These are the extremes. The bulk of striped bass populations along the Atlantic Coast spawn in April, May, and June. In the Gulf of Mexico, they spawn between March and April. On the Pacific Coast, spawning takes place in California from

April to mid-June, and from April to late June in Oregon and Washington, when it occurs in the latter state. Generally, striped bass in North Carolina's Roanoke River spawn between the middle of April and the middle of May. At the head of Chesapeake Bay, bass have spawned from the middle of May to the middle of June in some years. However, during normal years, spawning begins in April and will last during most of the month of May. On the Hudson River, April and May are the preferred months.

Three factors affect when striped bass will begin moving into freshwater to spawn. They are increased duration of daylight, an increase of water flow, particularly in riverine situations, and rising water temperatures. While all three control the pre-spawning movements of striped bass, the actual triggering of the exact period of spawning is water temperature. During especially cold years, spawning can be retarded by as much as two to three weeks. Duration of spawning is also a factor of the water temperature. As long as it remains in an optimal range, bass will continue to spawn. Any change above or below this range will cause temporary or even permanent cessation.

Water Temperatures

Temperature of the water is the single most critical factor in determining when bass will spawn and also where on a river they will swim to to locate this temperature. Striped bass will carry mature eggs about, but until the reproductive processes are stimulated by the correct temperature, they will remain unshed.

Spawning will occur over a great range of temperatures, from about 57 or 58 degrees to 70 or 71 degrees. However, striped bass have been recorded to initiate spawning in water that was as low as 52 degrees. In an environment where the water temperature is rising rapidly, bass will spawn until it reaches 70 degrees, stop immediately, and will not restart spawning if the temperature continues to rise. The highest recorded temperature at which striped bass will spawn is 73 degrees. However, fertilized eggs exposed to water 70 degrees or higher for any length of time fail to hatch at this high temperature. Thus, maximum water temperatures can be a vital delimiting factor when searching for environments for self-supporting populations of striped bass. It is the mean water temperature, during the time of spawning, that will determine just how far either north or south in latitude a population can establish itself.

Though the preferred spawning temperature does vary over a range of 10 to 12 degrees, optimal spawning temperature, no matter where fish are located over their distribution, seems to be 64.5 degrees. Rivers with slowly rising or steady temperatures at this range will support a complete, continuous spawning of fish in this environment. This is an advantage to the fish because it allows them to spawn completely during the shortest amount of time. Rapidly changing environmental conditions during the spawning process can sharply reduce the number of eggs released and fertilized. This is the first step in developing a dominant year class. A dominant year class is a body of fish produced in one year, that it is so much larger than populations from other year classes, that at any given time their numbers in the overall population dominate those from all other years. There also are times when more than one dominant year class make up the total population migrating along the coast.

In the case of riverine migrations, as soon as spawners reach water temperatures 60 degrees or higher, especially when this occurs near traditional spawning grounds, they will begin to spawn. However, in most instances, the fish will be at the site for a few days before spawning actually takes place. If the spawning population is a large one, as is often the case on streams like the Roanoke River, spawning may last for three or four weeks, all with peak activity. In areas where the stock is small, spawning may be completed in two or three days, as is the case in the St. Lawrence River in Quebec and the St. Johns River in Florida. Temperature variations during the time of spawning also affect the degree of spawning. Cold night temperatures in some cases will stop the activity, and it won't resume until the next time water temperatures rise to the preferred degree. Intermittent or interrupted spawning periods historically produce fewer fertilized eggs than periods with constant water temperatures.

Spawning Sites

Striped bass demand substantially fresh water in which to spawn. However, they will spawn in waters with chloride (salt water) concentrations as high as 10 to 15 ppt. In many instances, the location of this salt block will determine where striped bass spawn. Low salinities, under 8 ppt, have not been demonstrated as being detrimental to the eggs. On the contrary, those eggs deposited in this salinity concentration, or just above it, and are carried into it by water currents, have exhibited better survival than those deposited in pure fresh water.

Today, it's difficult to generalize what an ideal striped bass spawning ground might be like because so much of it has been altered, destroyed, or eliminated by dams and pollution barriers. Now striped bass spawn where they have been able to adapt to existing environmental conditions. In a riverine situation, one with a large head of water and a large watershed, striped bass will still move 150 to 200 miles to spawn. Only the St. Lawrence River in Quebec and the Roanoke River in North Carolina, 100 miles above tidewater on the Atlantic, offer such natural, long-run spawning sites. The spawning run on California's Sacramento River is also a long one. These introduced striped bass would often swim up river as far as Calousa, 120 miles by water, to spawn. In recent years, however, as populations on the Sacramento River have declined, so has the need to swim so far upstream. It's almost certain, that at one time, many of the rivers in Maine, the Connecticut River in New England, and the Delaware and Susquehanna rivers in New York, New Jersey, and Pennsylvania, also offered such long-range spawning sites.

More frequently nowadays, major spawning rivers on the Atlantic are broad tidal streams with a large but slow flow of water. Striped bass select sites just far enough above salt water with sufficient current to allow eggs to be buoyed off the bottom and hatch out before the current carries them into salt water. Hatching time, another function of the water temperature, varies between 48 and 72 hours on the average. The higher the temperature, the shorter the development time. In a preferred situation, eggs should not be carried into an all-saline environment by the current before they have had the opportunity to hatch. However, egg survival has been shown to be greater in an environment into which they're carried that has a slight degree of salinity. The saline solution tends to toughen the outer chorionic and vitelline membranes on the egg.

Thus, current speed and distance between the saline block and the spawning site are two additional delimiting factors that can negatively impinge on the development of a dominant year class. The most successful egg development occurs where the environment is brackish, a mixture of fresh and salt water, for a substantial time. Because of such requirements, spawning on such rivers as the Hudson, Nanticoke, Potomac, Wicominco, York, James, and Rappahannock may take place in an area 10 to 40 miles above salt water. The actual distance is determined by the river current speeds.

Spawning

Male striped bass usually appear on the spawning site days or weeks ahead of females. Large females arrive before smaller females. In the river, the fish congregate in schools around areas that have a gravel or sandy bottom and a substantial current. Some sites are even in the rapids. Pre-spawning rituals, often described as "rock fights," or thrashing about precede the actual spawning act. In the case of a large female, anywhere from 10 to 50 younger males will act as suitors and surround her as she reaches the moment to spawn. The fish will thrash on the surface, often racing on their sides over the top, resembling wounded fish. The splashing may continue for hours until the appropriate time has come, usually in the late afternoon. Generally, most of the activity heightens as the day wears into night and spawning continues through the entire evening if the weather is favorable.

After splashing and gamboling on the surface slows, the female sinks below the surface, and as many as five or six males may press alongside the larger fish, forcing her to exude her eggs. At the same time, milt from the males flows into the water, mixing with the eggs and fertilizing them. As the males become spent new fish take their place, and they continue to nose and bump the female until she has expelled all her eggs.

After spawning, the spent males and females begin dropping back from the spawning area and return to resting areas farther down river. During spawning and immediately thereafter, striped bass do not feed. But as soon as they are well off the spawning site they resume feeding. Fertilized eggs then drift downstream, with the current buoying them off the bottom. The eggs are protected from damage by the perivitelline space—a fluid-filled chamber between the outside membrane (vitelline) and ovum of a fertilized egg. As soon as the eggs are expelled they begin to absorb water through the outside membrane (vitelline and chorionic membranes), and this fluid acts as a buffer to shock. The egg grows from an average size of 1.1-1.35 mm to about 3.63 mm, or from 1/25th to 1/8th of an inch. In about 6-1/2 days the yolk sac is absorbed.

Fecundity of Spawners

As already stated, some female striped bass are capable of spawning at four years of age, though the greater percentage of a year class reach spawning maturity at age five and a few not until eight. Research, especially in the Chesapeake Bay area, during the early 1970s, revealed that the five-year figure is most accurate. However, these studies were conducted during a period of somewhat lower annual temperatures and this could explain the later maturation and the conflict with earlier and more recent research dates. All these data, however, may have to be re-evaluated in the light of special protection given to the 1982 year class from Chesapeake Bay. To ensure that at least 90 percent of the female striped bass produced that year could return to spawn at least once, laws were passed that annually increased the minimum size that fishermen could harvest fish. It rose to 36 inches by 1992, ten years after hatching, when 100 percent of the females had finally attained maturity.

Males are more precocious in their sexual development than females. Records have revealed one-year-old males with mature milt; others may mature at two years of age, but with most, the average age is three years. Female striped bass have the capability of annual spawning. In general, however, it is believed that they do not spawn annually. During the first five or six years of their adult lives, they may do so, but as females grow older they tend to become sporadic in their spawning habits. The number of males above fourteen years of age decreases rapidly in the population. There is evidence of dimorphism—a sex change—in male striped bass, and some researchers believe this might account for the change in sex ratio numbers in older populations. The possibility exists that they may alter their sex as they grow older and the population becomes female-oriented. Because no conclusive studies have been conducted this is little more than a hypothesis.

Hermaphroditism exists in about 4 percent of several Pacific Coast populations (Coos Bay), and some researchers feel that this figure might go considerably higher if a more general study were made of sexual compositions. There are records of bisexual striped bass containing both ovaries and testes and both in perfect spawning condition.

Fecundity (the ability to produce eggs or sperm) varies in differing fishes and changes with the amount of care the parents traditionally provide for their fertilized eggs and offspring. The more care the parent or both parents give the offspring, the fewer eggs are produced. Conversely, the less care parents provide, the more eggs are produced to ensure the survival of that species. It is nature's way of keeping everything within a reasonable balance.

There are three general, though arbitrary, categories of fecundity in fish. A minimal spawner is one that produces less than 50 eggs per individual. A good example is the marine catfish. It produces eggs the size of marbles, and the male carries them around in his mouth until they hatch. The intermediate spawner group produces up to 1,000 eggs, and they provide a degree of post-spawning care. One example is the brook trout, a fish that prepares a gravel redd (nest) for the eggs, and after fertilization, the male continues for a while to guard them.

The third category, the extreme cases of parental carelessness, includes fish like the mackerel, weakfish, and bluefish. Also into this category fall striped bass. Such spawners can broadcast as many as 50,000 eggs, and fertilization takes place almost haphazardly. The eggs are then left to fend for themselves. Because such huge quantities are produced survival of an annual brood stock is almost always guaranteed.

Duration of Spawning Capability

Fecundity of a female striped bass is in direct relationship to her weight. The larger the fish, the more eggs she is capable of producing. The average number of ova increases progressively from 426,000 in a 4-pound female to 4,200,000 in a 55-pound female. On the basis of this information, biologists believe that large striped bass do make substantial contributions in the spawning process and that is why states like Maryland have tried to protect large female bass by limiting, as to size and number, those that may be taken. However, large striped bass are so few compared to the near-astronomical numbers of 4-pound fish in a dominant year class that the overall contribution of younger striped bass is much greater than that of the aggregate number of large fish in the population.

Early regulations in Maryland (1929), followed by similar regulations in Virginia and Delaware, were aimed at protecting large female striped bass because of the great number of eggs they carried. Legislation prohibited the taking of striped bass over 15 pounds in Chesapeake Bay. With the rise in sportfishing the value of a trophy fish began to overshadow the legislation. Not only was the law difficult to enforce and unpopular, but the very concept was challenged by other biologists, who, at that time, believed that the viability of eggs was reduced as fish grew older. They felt that senility was a factor in these fish. Viability tests since on old bass have shown that all their eggs are good.

The 15-pound maximum affects males about nine years old and females about seven to eight years old, and Maryland's biologists reconsidered the restriction. They found no evidence of senility in the large female striped bass collected during the study, even in four females that weighed over 50 pounds and were over fifteen years old. The eggs were artificially fertilized to see if they would develop and hatch. Fish were reared to the larval stage. Therefore, the evidence tends to support the concept that large striped bass are highly productive to the end and are always valuable brood fish.

In 1962, the legislation was amended to allow fishermen to keep one large fish over 15 pounds each day, except during the spawning season, which was bracketed by closed dates beginning March 1 and ending June 15. Since passage of emergency striped bass legislation, these and regulations in other states are in a constant state of change. For the very latest regulations, it is recommended that you check each state's most recent syllabus. In reality, the change didn't have any measurable effect on the brood stock or the striped bass fishery because large fish, 30 pounds or more, enter Chesapeake Bay only to spawn and immediately return to the Atlantic. They do this during the closed season. Outside the closed dates for the trophy fish, striped bass 30 pounds or larger are rather rare in the bay, though a fish estimated to be over 80 pounds was hooked and released in June of 1992.

EGG MATURATION

Mature or ripe striped bass eggs are a transparent green, with a small amber-colored oil globule. In some populations there are occasionally two globules and still in others the lone globule can be slightly larger, enough to change its specific gravity and make it float. In the ovary, they mature at different times, but as spawning approaches, all eggs mature rapidly and are the same size. On the average, the large, mature ovum (egg) is about 1.35 mm in diameter. The eggs remain viable for about one hour after release from the follicles into the lumen.

As soon as they are fertilized, eggs take on a spherical shape and begin to swell and water-harden. They are non-adhesive and just slightly heavier than water (specific gravity of 1.007) and sink to the bottom unless agitated by a slight current. It takes but the slightest movement to keep them buoyed.

After fertilization and exposure to water, the eggs swell rapidly in volume and in 15 minutes attain an average size of 1.84 mm. The size of the yolk sphere and oil globule or globules remain the same, and the chorionic membrane surrounding the egg remains transparent. It is, however, thin and fragile. One strain of fish in the Potomac River unknowingly produced eggs with a slightly larger oil globule than other bass. It wasn't discovered until 1988 when natural reproduction began occurring in Liberty Reservoir without a riverine phase. The eggs, because of the slightly larger oil globule, floated to the top and developed.

At 12 hours after fertilization, the egg shows a greater increase in diameter, reaching 3.2-3.8 mm. Water absorption is just about complete. The blastoderm is in late cleavage and the periblast begins to turn a pale green. During the late blastula stage, striped bass eggs are at their most sensitive to excess temperatures. An increase of 15 degrees, above 67 degrees, would exceed the tempera-ture tolerance of the developing egg by 5 degrees and rapidly increase mortality. The 15-degree increment was used in studies of egg mortality because that was the projected increase in ambient water temperatures from the Indian Point Power Plant on the Hudson River. In the eggs and pre-mobile larval stages, striped bass are most vulnerable to entrainment (the incorporation of small organisms into the cooling water flow at electrical generating stations and transport to water storage reservoirs) and impingement, the physical blockage of larger organisms by mechanisms (barrier screens and louvers) that are designed to reduce entrainment.

The oil globule in the egg stage and its presence in early larval stages is most vulnerable to absorbing chemical pollutants in the environment—PCBs, chlo-rine, copper, zinc, aluminum, cyclohexanes, and aromatic hydrocarbons—that reduce the viability of these eggs. While absorption of pollutants occurs in these stages from the ambient environment, these same pollutants present in the body of the female can also be passed on to the eggs during their development within her body.

All further expansion of the chorion ceases in the egg at 24 hours. By now the embryo has become differentiated and extends about halfway around the circumference of the yolk. Coloring now begins, with small, black dots covering the dorsal or back of the embryo.

Thirty-six hours after fertilization, the embryo is about 1.6 mm in length. The eyes have formed but are colorless, and the tail of the embryo is free from the yolk sac. If the temperature has been an even 64.2 degrees, the egg is about to hatch. Increased embryonic temperatures will hasten the hatching, whereas cooler temperatures will prolong the development of the embryo.

Once the embryo is hatched it is referred to as a larva. There are three sub-stages in the larval period: yolk-sac larva, finfold larva, and postfinfold larva. At 60 hours after fertilization, in the first larval stage, it is about 3.2 mm in length, but the resemblance to a mature striped bass, or even a fish, is still rather distant. The globule of oil in the head of the yolk sac projects beyond the head of the larva. It still lacks mobility, despite a strong swimming action, and it settles to the bottom of its environment unless a current is available to keep it suspended.

Eighty-four hours after fertilization the larval fish has attained a length of about 4.4 mm. The head now extends beyond the oil globule, and a series of black dots begin to appear along the underside of the body behind the anal vent. The eyes still lack coloration.

Pigmentation finally develops in the larval fish at about 120 hours after fertilization. The larval striped bass now is about 5.2 mm long, and the jaws begin to show development. Both the oil globule and yolk sac now show considerable reduction in size, and the beginnings of a digestive tract make its appearance. Pectoral fins now become recognizable.

Mouth parts and the digestive tract are much better developed in the larval fish at age 144 hours after fertilization. The larva is about 5.8 mm long. At 192 hours the oil globule and yolk sac have almost disappeared, and the fish is now in the finfold larval stage. Length increase seems to slow down, 6 mm, in deference to development of body structures. The coloration along the underside of the body is more strongly developed.

A 10-day old postfinfold-larval fish begins strongly to resemble a mature striped bass. The head is still disproportionately large, and the caudal fin is still weak, with remnants extending on both the back and underside connecting it with other fins. The fish now is approximately 9 mm long. The second dorsal and anal fin rays become slightly differentiated, although the first dorsal and ventral fins have yet to begin development. The lateral line has become well defined and the musculature is evident through the thin skin. Mouth parts are well developed, and the pigmented eye seems especially large for the remainder of the fish.

By the 18th day after fertilization our post-larval striped bass is half an inch long and looks like a chubby bass. The two back (dorsal) fins are still connected and the spines are weakly developed in the anterior fin. All traces of the larval fin fold have disappeared.

At a length of about 36 mm and an age of from three to four weeks, the young striped bass assumes the general fusiform shape of a mature fish. The most noticeable characteristics are the well-developed scales that now cover the body, and fully-developed fins and rays.

At 90 days old, our striped bass is a fingerling or fry approximately 80 mm in length. The characteristic lateral black stripes are almost complete, six to nine in number. Also, at this time there appear seven fainter vertical bars (like parr markings in trout and salmon) that extend from the base of the dorsal fins down the sides to the lateral line. After a short period, these bars disappear. Except for the eyes, which are large compared to the body size, the striped bass looks pretty much like an adult. All the development is complete, except the gonads, which will develop when the fish is three years or older.

ONTOGENY AND PHYLOGENY

In the dogma of the biological sciences, especially the field of embryology, there is a saying that ontogeny recapitulates phylogeny. Ontogeny is the biological development of an individual, whereas phylogeny is the evolutionary development of a species. Many animals, in their embryological development, go through several body changes that reflect the different primary steps in the evolutionary development of that animal. These stages disappear before or shortly after birth. Of course, the final, adult forms mask all these levels and they are no longer evident.

In a very real way, the striped bass does this in several respects. Its embryological development gives us a clue to what the striped bass of old might have been like. It reveals a fish model with characteristics adapted to the ecological conditions of life on deltas and in estuaries and reflects characteristics of both freshwater and marine fishes.

These characteristics include a high fecundity (females of 40-50 pounds are capable of shedding 3 million eggs), typical of pelagic marine species of fish. Add to this a short period of embryonic development (forty-eight to seventy-two hours) and a larval animal that is poorly developed, hatched before it is really capable of caring for itself. These are characteristics of a hurried development for life in an unprotected situation without much parental care or protection from predators. To compensate for these shortcomings we then have characteristics that produce sharp fluctuations in abundance under natural conditions, and adaptability to spawning in the lower reaches of rivers and to the variability of ecological conditions in estuarine environments.

The early development of a strong digestive system, the appearance of large teeth in the jaws, the excellently developed eyes, and the positive phototaxis (attraction toward light) all tell us that striped bass were flesh-eating animals from the very beginning, even before they had the mobility to chase their own food. At these stages it is still living off the yolk sac that was a part of the egg stage of the fish.

HATCHERIES

Given the great fecundity of striped bass, there is no way that hatchery efforts can replace natural reproduction in a marine environment. Even during periods when natural production on a body of water is extremely low, the successful spawning and hatching of eggs from just one gravid 10-pound female would far surpass all made-made attempts. However, attempts to establish, or reestablish, a population of striped bass in riverine-marine situations, are well worth the effort and expense and in several instances have proven successful. The criteria that must be met here is that the environment be able supply all the conditions striped bass need for a naturally self-sustaining population.

On the other hand, attempts to supplement or even bolster an existing marine population have never met with any appreciable success. In the late 1970s, there was a cry to supplement poor years of natural reproduction in Maryland rivers with hatchery-reared stock. Maryland biologists J. G. Boone and M. B. Florence had earlier addressed the idea but found it infeasible. They discovered that there is a daily 4 percent mortality among young-of-the year striped bass in a natural environment. At this rate, only one 6-inch fingerling could be expected to survive from each 3,000 fry released. In order to add just one such fingerling per acre to Maryland tidewaters less than 12 feet deep (usual nursery area depth) would require the stocking of 2.5 billion fry. To achieve this number of fry, even with a good 50 percent survival from the egg-to-stocking stage, would require the sacrifice of 2,500 20-pound females, or the equivalent, plus a corresponding number of males. The manpower and material requirements to handle this number of fish and fry would be staggering.

Since the early work by Boone and Florence, most hatcheries have abandoned the physical technique of stripping gravid female and ripe male striped bass to achieve fertilized eggs because the recovery of the donors was so poor. Now, the fish are put in tanks when they are near the spawning stage, the water temperature then elevated, and spawning takes place in the water and there is no survival problem for the adult fish.

However, these earlier hatchery-stocking attempts did produced a wealth of striped bass knowledge, not just in egg production in the hatchery, but the conditions under which stocked fish can successfully compete, survive, and multiply once released into the natural environment. And, with more refined techniques, in recent years Maryland stocked fry in the Choptank, a river the population of which has been severely impacted by the great decline. All factors must have been favorable following the stocking because later testing indicated that stocked fry made up nearly 30 percent of the striped bass population in the river.

Hatchery production is also an excellent source for export of eggs, larvae, fry, and fingerlings for establishing new populations on reservoirs and lakes without striped bass, and maintaining these populations where natural reproduction doesn't occur. In such cases today, use of striped bass fingerlings has proven most successful.

The first attempts ever to hatch striped bass eggs occurred at the federal shad hatchery at Albemarle Sound in North Carolina in 1879. The young were sent to Druid-Hill Park in Baltimore, Md., where they were raised. Maryland eventually established its own shad hatchery at Havre de Grace near the head of Chesapeake Bay and the mouth of the Susquehanna River. In 1886, 20,000 striped bass were cultured there and stocked in Lake Ontario, near the mouth of the Oswego River in New York State. Nothing was ever heard of these fish.

More recently, striped bass were sent across the Atlantic in hopes of planting them in Russian rivers flowing into the Black Sea. Shipments began in 1960. Since 1965, seven shipments of live striped bass were delivered to Russia. Four of the first batches were lost en route before techniques of transportation could be worked out.

The experimental rearing of striped bass larvae and young was carried out at the VIRNO aquarium at Moscow, on the Chernaya River Trout Farm, and at a field point on the mouth of the Don River near where it flows into the Sea of Azov, an arm of the Black Sea. Russian biologists have done some fine original research concerning the development of striped bass eggs, larvae, and fry. However, there is little information now available on how successful the transplants were. In 1972, a two-year-old bass, weighing 1.5 pounds, was caught in the Black Sea. It was the first example of native production and indicates that

Striped bass eggs at fertilization and during embryonic development.

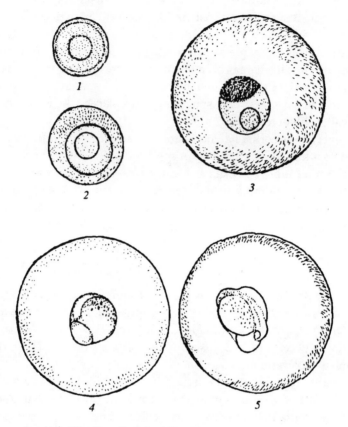

1. *At fertilization, diameter 1.2 mm.*
2. *15 minutes after fertilization, diameter 1.8 mm.*
3. *12 hours after fertilization, diameter 3.7 mm.*
4. *24 hours after fertilization.*
5. *36 hours after fertilization.*

natural spawning took place.

Even though natural spawning became a reality, the program was gradually reduced. It was finally abandoned in the late 1970s when its administrator, Dr. Alexander Doroshev, emigrated to the United States.

The Hudson River Striped Bass Hatchery

An interesting case in an attempt to replace striped bass lost to entrainment and impingement in the egg, larva, and fry stages evolved on the Hudson River. Five massive power-generating facilities, that built plants using Hudson River water, negatively impacted on striped bass in these stages. They were taken to court several times during the early 1960s, by New York's Department of

Striped bass eggs during fertilization and embryonic development.

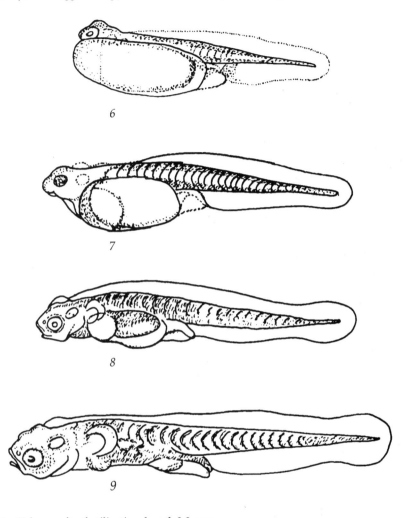

6

7

8

9

6. *60 hours after fertilization, length 3.2 mm.*
7. *84 hours after fertilization, length 4.4 mm.*
8. *144 hours after fertilization, length 5.8 mm.*
9. *288 hours after fertilization, length 6 mm; shows slight atrophy of organs because no food was available to the fish.*

Environmental Conservation, and a judgement was finally handed down in the DEC's favor. It ended a 17-year argument over the impact power plants had on the Hudson River's aquatic life. Allied with this agreement was a concession to allow use of the river's water in lieu of building cooling towers for an atomic fuel plant. The court ruled that these utilities must establish a riverside striped bass hatchery in the vicinity of the nursery grounds and produce and release 600,000 striped bass fingerlings annually, for a 10-year period, to compensate for the loss

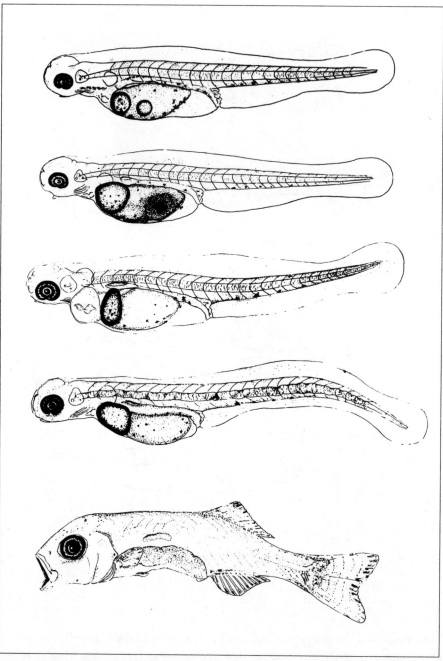

From the perspective of another artist, the above stages represent a striped bass (top) from approximately 140 hours after fertilization to about 28 days (bottom). These were drawn from eggs hatched at a Soviet hatchery in an attempt to establish populations on the Dnieper and Don rivers, flowing into the Sea of Azov and the Black Sea. The attempts were successful but the program was eventually abandoned and only token populations exist today.

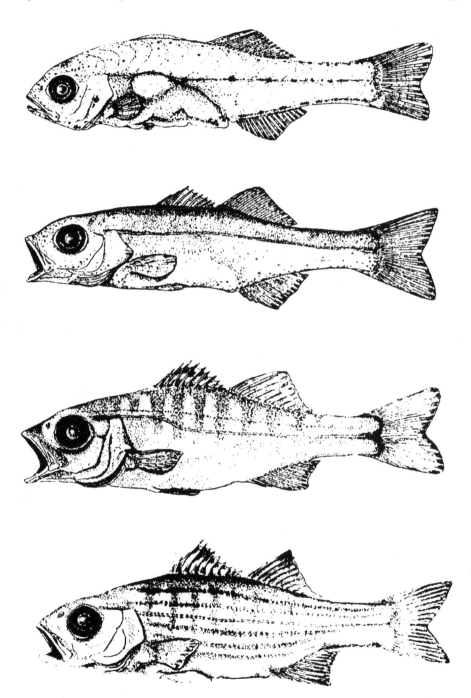

This fish developed from a temperature ranging between 60 and 68 degrees. From top to bottom: age 30 days, length 15.8 mm; age 45 days, length 33 mm; age 60 days, length 46 mm; age 90 days, length 80 mm. (Courtesy of Dr. S.I. Doroshev, VIRNO, USSR, and now the University of California at Davis.)

of striped bass to these facilities. In Verplanck, on the grounds of a ConEdison plant, the $5.8 million Hudson River Striped Bass Hatchery, a unique, totally indoor facility was designed, built, and operated for the utilities by Ecological Analysts. It was the largest intensive culture hatchery of its kind.

Hatchery production during its first year was made more difficult when in October 1982, the state's Health Department closed commercial fishing on the river and throughout the state because striped bass had accumulated more than the federal minimum for PCB levels in their tissue. They could not use the river as a source of hatchery water. The river had been unknowingly contaminated for three decades by two General Electric plants in the vicinity of Troy, near Albany. They had dumped 660,00 pounds of polychlorinated biphenyls, used in the manufacture of condensers, into the river. The practice was ended in the mid-1970s. To avoid PCB contamination, the hatchery used uncontaminated ground water from a quarry on the site.

Fish were to be raised in 100 tanks inside the hatchery and released in mid-summer when they were between Phase I and Phase II fingerlings, either size at which they can be released. Longer retainment in a hatchery has usually been thought of as increasing the survival of the stocked fish. However, in its first ten-year history, that began in 1982, the hatchery has never met its assigned quota. The problem was a chronic infection of presumptive bacterial gill disease in the hatchery's water system that at times vastly reduced the numbers of fish in the hatchery or in some years totally eliminated it.

However, the hatchery did raise a total of 2,612,544 3-inch to 6-inch fingerlings. Eventually, 2,510,640 were tagged and stocked in the Hudson between Yonkers and Stony Point. Not all of the fish raised were stocked as fingerlings, according to Bruce R. Friedman, the hatchery's manager. Striped bass fry and fingerlings also were used to assist other state organizations in their striped bass stocking programs. Some 985,000 were sent to the Maine Department of Marine Resources to restore a striped bass fishery on the Kennebec River. Since 1990, the hatchery has supplied approximately 1,168,000 fry to the Pennsylvania Fish Commission to develop inland stocking programs on Raystown Lake and Lake Wallenpaupack.

Hudson River fry from the hatchery were also shipped in 1991 to the Gulf Coast Research Laboratory's hatchery in Gulf Breeze, Mississippi, to be stocked in riverine estuaries in efforts to reestablish striped bass in several rivers flowing into the Gulf of Mexico. Mississippi had suffered unusually spring floods and was unable to carry out their own hatchery efforts that year, and 500,000 fry were sent to them.

The license to operate the hatchery expires this year. However, the utilities are likely to ask for its renewal, for at least a few years more, because their were never able to meet their annual legal obligation due to extenuating circumstances.

5

Growth and Feeding
in Striped Bass

Striped bass, at every stage of growth and development, are voracious feeders and dine on almost anything edible in their ambient environment. This may help explain that, when compared to other fish species, why striped bass are such rapid growers. However, after about ten years, the rate of growth tapers off rapidly, both in weight and length. Within the sexes, there are also different growth rates. The period from the time of hatching in April or May, depending upon where along the coast this occurs, to the end of the following winter, is considered a single year in the life of a striped bass. During this first year, both sexes grow at the same approximate rate and attain a length of about 4.5 to 5 inches by the year's end. From then on, males grow slightly faster than females until the fourth year. Females then put on a growing spurt, and by the end of their fifth year they have outgrown their male counterparts. Thereafter, throughout their lives, a female is usually larger than a male of the same age. The greatest growth spurt in both sexes takes place during their second year after birth.

These are figures for striped bass in an marine environment. Striped bass in a freshwater environment exhibit slightly different growth characteristics. The growth program between males and females is still relatively the same but when compared to marine examples, freshwater bass exhibit a much faster growth, almost doubled, and are generally larger than their marine counterparts until the age of ten. Thereafter, growth slows considerably and the fish never attain the final sizes of marine fish. They also pay a price for their fast growth and die at ages under the maximum achieved by marine fish.

Male striped bass above the age of ten years are almost nonexistent in California marine waters and rather rare in the Atlantic. Records of old male fish come from the Elk River in Maryland with one 12-year old that weighed 24.5

pounds and was 37.2 inches in length. In 1952, a fish that weighed 16.5 pounds and was 31.5 inches long was thought to be the largest male striped bass ever recorded by 1952.

From 1954 to 1963, Maryland conducted a series of studies of the sexual composition of striped bass that were 15 pounds and larger taken from Maryland waters in Chesapeake Bay. Over that period, 44 males between 15 and 20 pounds were studied; eight between 20 and 25 pounds; six between 25 and 30 pound; and in 1954 one male that weighed 32 pounds and measured 40 inches fork length.

The largest male striped bass eventually recorded was also the longest found during the study. It was a fish measuring 45.2 inches fork length. The bass was tagged and released in the Nanticoke River (Chesapeake Bay) on April 19, 1958. Six weeks later it was captured off Barnegat Inlet, N.J. At the time the fish was tagged on the Nanticoke, its weight was estimated at 40 pounds and the fish was freely exuding milt.

The sex ratio during the Maryland study involved the capture of 672 striped bass that weighed 15 pounds or more; the largest was a 63.2-pound female. Females constituted 91.2 percent of the study. Thus, though male striped bass in the heavyweight class are rare, they do exist. The idea that male striped bass cannot fare the rigors of life as well as females is slowly eroding. Most of the earlier, general studies of striped bass were primarily concerned with habits and life cycles, such as were those in California and the first studies in Maryland. They were not designed, nor had as their main objective, the determination of maximum ages for males. While more recent studies of large fish reveal a preponderance of females, males above 50 pounds have been established. There may be factors other than longevity that seem to reduce the number of old male bass more than females.

Once both sexes reach the age of nine and ten years it becomes progressively more difficult to tell how old they are. There are two methods used by researchers. The first is the length-frequency relationship of a population. In a given haul or collection of mixed age groups of striped bass on their rearing or nursery grounds, they can be grouped rather nicely into specific length groups that contain only a few odd fish with measurements in between the averages. Most fish around 5 inches are part of the one-year group, those near 12 inches are two years old, those 14 to 15 inches are three years old, and those 17 to 18 inches are four years old.

After four years, the growth-rate spread between frequencies is less distinct and this method is less dependable. Another method that supports the diagnosis of age groups determined by the length-frequency method is counting the annuli on the scales, growth marks that are similar to the rings on a tree. Each year, fish have a rapid-growth period during the summer and fall and slow into winter. At the end of winter a ring or annulus is laid down that is darker than the rest of the scale. One annulus is laid down each year, and a fish's age can then be determined under a dissecting microscope, by counting the dark rings on the scale. This works out well until about the tenth year, when the growth rate slows and the dark rings begin to pile one atop another, making accurate age determination impossible. From ten years on, the age-weight-length ratio is extrapo-

This is a graphic summary of the relationship of a striped bass's weight to length, correlated with its age. Striped bass grow so uniformly in a marine environment that if you know a fish's length you can calculate rather closely its weight and age just by comparing it to the chart. Females after age three are slightly larger than males, and in the graph males are shown dark and females light. Recorded males over 11 to 14 years of age are rather rare, but they do exist. Roccus *was the scientific name of striped bass when the drawing was made and has been replaced by* Morone.

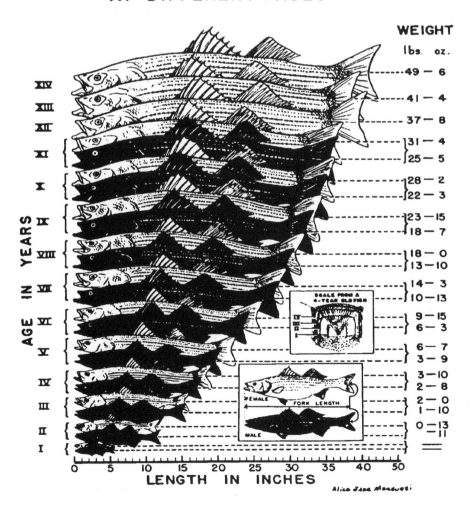

AVERAGE LENGTH AND WEIGHT
OF STRIPED BASS. *Morone saxatilis*
AT DIFFERENT AGES

This is an enlargement of a plastic impression of a striped bass scale. The impression is easier to study than the actual scale. The fish was in its fourth year, weighed 5.5 pounds, and was 60 cm (24 inches) long. At the end of each winter of life a heavy annulus is laid down by the fish and marks one year of growth. Four distinct rings can be seen, similar to rings in a tree.

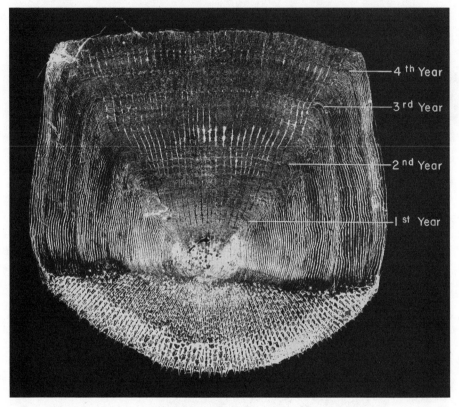

lated to determine the ages of older striped bass.

Female striped bass weighing 25 to 50 pounds are believed to be between 10 and 14 years old. Some researchers feel that a 50-pound female is closer to 18 years old. At these higher weights the length and weight closely approximate each other—that is, a 50-inch bass weighs about 50 pounds. The oldest striped bass on record is a 31-year old fish taken in Maryland's Chesapeake Bay.

Striped bass have grown to enormous sizes, though only a few fish over 100 pounds are known nowadays. In April, 1891, several striped bass were netted in Albermarle Sound, near Edenton, N.C., the largest of which weighed 125 pounds. North Carolina at one time seemed to be an area for larg striped bass, and this may be related to its longer feeding period because of a more southerly latitude. In a haul seine taken off the beach at Avoca, N.C., on May 6, 1876, 840 striped bass were netted that weighed just over 35,000 pounds. Of these fish, 350 averaged 65 pounds each.

AGE AND LENGTH RELATIONSHIP (in inches)

Age	Length, males	Length, females
1	5.3	4.9
2	11.7	11.5
3	15.0	15.3
4	17.0	18.4
5	19.7	21.9
6	23.4	25.4
7	27.7	28.5
8	29.7	30.0
9	32.7	33.7
10	34.5	35.4
11	35.7	36.8

The preceding figures are for fish taken in Maryland's portion of Chesapeake Bay. For California and Gulf Coast striped bass, figures differ only slightly, with males leading until the fourth year. In the Maryland stock, males lead only to the second year. Measurement of striped bass can be taken by three methods: the fork length (FL), already defined; the standard length (SL), from the snout to the base of the peduncle or tail; and the total length (TL), measured from the snout to the end of the tail fin. Most researchers had used the fork length measurement until recently. Now, all measurements in all states are standardized and total length is used.

The following is the approximate growth rate for male and female striped bass produced in the San Francisco Bay area with averages for the first four years:

Year 1	4.0 inches
Year 2	9.8 inches
Year 3	13.4 inches
Year 4	18.5 inches

	Males	Females
Year 5	20.4 inches	21.3 inches
Year 6	22.0 inches	24.0 inches
Year 7	24.0 inches	26.8 inches

FOOD AND FEEDING

If there is one thing that everyone will agree upon it is that the striped bass is a voracious, carnivorous, predacious, mainly piscivorous, and extremely active feeder. A striped bass will eat anything edible that swims, crawls, or floats in its environment, even its own kind. Cannibalism is not rare among these fish.

About the only time striped bass stop feeding is when they begin spawning, and then for only a short period thereafter.

Foods of striped bass can be divided into three groups that correspond with three spans in the fish's life: the larval stages; as an active fry up to one year in age or 5 inches in length; and thereafter. The types of food can further be divided into crustaceans and other invertebrates, and vertebrate or fish foods.

For larval striped bass the principal source of food is zooplankton—microscopic one-celled and multicellular organisms. Small striped bass, from the fry stage to about one year or 5 inches in length, begin aggressively hunting and feeding on marine worms and crustaceans. In some environments the freshwater shrimp *Gammarus*, an invertebrate, composes almost 60 percent of a young bass's diet. The remainder is composed of annelids or sea worms. Even insects are part of the menu when they are available. In freshwater, insects form a large part of the diet in May and June. The average composition, however, is 50 percent marine worms, 48 percent crustaceans, and 2 percent small fishes.

The fish that juvenile striped bass eat are mostly menhaden, along with white perch, a close relative to the striped bass, and spottail shiners. In many freshwater impoundments, where striped bass have been stocked since the early 1960s to control several shad species, they also feed on black bass and crappie. The striped bass's eyes are often larger than their stomachs, and small bass regularly take food that is almost as large as itself. There have been reports of a 6.5-inch striped bass trying to swallow a 3-inch white perch and a 7.25-inch bass having eaten a 4-inch minnow.

While large striped bass will eat almost everything they can find, their favorite foods include such crustaceans as shrimp, crabs, and lobsters. They will eat all kinds of marine worms: sandworms or clamworms as well as blood-worms. Even shellfish aren't safe from bass; they will eat mussels, soft-shelled clams and periwinkles. The range of finfish that bass find to their liking is unlimited. They prefer menhaden, silversides, and anchovies, and at certain times of the year they will feed on spot and croaker. On the West Coast, they have no qualms about feeding on trout and salmon, though these fish do not constitute a measurable part of their diet. Their favorite is the bullhead (sculpin). Other fishes are killifish, shad, sand lance, eels, squid, flounder, blackfish, tomcod, white perch, mullet, catfish, shiners, and blenny. They have even been recorded eating the Portuguese man-of-war, a stinging, toxic jellyfish.

By weight, other fish constitute more than 95 percent of a striped bass's diet. So though a bass may occasionally dine on soft-shelled crab, shrimp, or lobster, the real volume comes in the form of other fishes—most of them species of little or no economic value. This fish diet should be a hint to striped bass anglers who feed their potential fish a strict diet of sandworms. In a study of striped bass in the upper Chesapeake Bay area, around the Susquehanna River, fish as food varied between 46 and 100 percent of the total content in the stomach. Twenty-six kinds of fish were reported eaten by bass in the study.

Anchovy, menhaden, spot, and croaker were the most frequently ingested.

But in another study conducted off the south side of Long Island, where there were plenty of small fish in the surf and offshore, the bass had glutted themselves on sand fleas, mysids, copepods, and isopods while passing up huge schools of silversides (spearing) that existed at the same time.

If you know where and when a striped bass feeds, then your chances of meeting it at the dinner table can be increased. The first place to look for a clue to the kinds of food striped bass eat is within the fish itself, basically the mouth

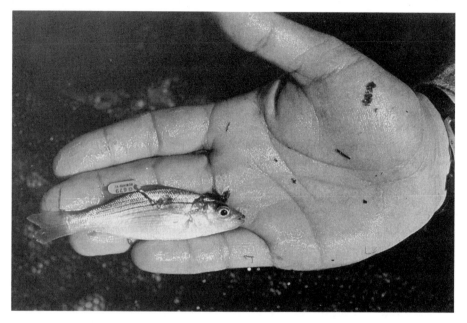

An Age I yearling striped bass tagged and ready to be released.

and the stomach. Striped bass have a fairly large mouth but few real teeth—a double row on the back of the tongue and small rows along the maxillary bones or upper lip. Basically these are used for holding a fish or other food that has been grasped and to keep it from working its way out of the mouth.

Therefore, food fish must be ingested whole, because striped bass cannot bite off pieces—as can such fish as bluefish, which are well supplied with teeth and can feed on any part of a baitfish. Because ingestion in a striped bass must be in its entirety, fish foods must also be taken head first into the mouth. Otherwise the spines and fins on a baitfish would open and the fish would become lodged in the mouth of the striped bass.

The next place to look is in the stomach. The wall is heavily lined with a greatly convoluted lining called the rugosa. It resembles a corrugated washboard. This type of lining increases the stomach's area for absorption of food without increasing its external size. This heavy rugose lining is a hint that digestion is rapid and the digested food large.

Such equipment makes the striped bass a sporadic feeder. That is, when it feeds, it fills itself and stops hunting for more until everything in its stomach has been dissolved. Fish like bluefish , that can bite small pieces, and are hyperactive, must feed all the time and thus are continuous feeders. Studies of striped bass stomachs have supported the contention that striped bass feed in a rather short time, then go off somewhere to digest what they have eaten before they eat again. Nettings at various times of the day have revealed entire schools of bass with empty stomachs. Bass taken on rod and reel have been found with some contents in their stomachs or nothing at all. This indicates that a bass has just started to feed or hasn't completed feeding. Once it has fed, it is not likely to take your lure.

Striped bass are gregarious fish during their younger years; not until they become large "cows" or "bulls" do they become solitary in their feeding and schooling habits. Because striped bass feed most heavily on schooling fish such as menhaden, spearing, and anchovies, they school together when they feed. As a result, a school that feeds together usually spends its digesting time together, and thus the feeding blitz will often stop all at once, over a rather large area of water. This is supported also by seining research. When a school or part of a school has been netted, the stomach condition of all the fish is about the same, either full, empty, or somewhere in between.

Another aspect of striped bass feeding habits is the great specificity for certain foods even though many choices are available at the same time. In other words, though menhaden, anchovies, and spearing may all be at hand for bass to feed upon, they may decide on menhaden and everyone in the school eats menhaden until the fad is over or fish become too scarce to find without a great deal of swimming effort.

When do striped bass feed? During the year, the greatest feeding intensity takes place in the late spring and early summer for adult fish. There is again a flurry of feeding late in the fall. Fish do little feeding during the winter. When water temperatures drop below 39 degrees, the fish not only stop feeding but go into a somewhat dormant state, seeking out the deepest holes or warmest water in which to sulk. Juvenile fish seem to make their big meal in September and even October. One reason for this is that many of the forage fish that young bass may feed upon when they are one, two, and three years old mature to the bite-size stage at this time of year. With a superabundance of food around, young bass put on a feeding spree that lasts until the forage or baitfish have moved on and are no longer available to them.

The time a striped bass feeds is also affected by other factors, including the temperature of the water, whether the fish are in a freshwater or saltwater environment, the time of day, and the physiological condition of the striped bass, as well as its size. Just how much a striped bass will eat varies with the seasons as well as the time of day. From numerous collections of striped bass by biologists at all intervals during the day and studies of their stomach contents, striped bass appear to feed most avidly in the evening, just after dark, and they put on a second flurry just before sunrise.

Striped bass anglers have long known that fishing is far more productive after dark than during the day. This doesn't imply that striped bass don't feed during the day. It does mean that they will feed better and more consistently after sunset and before sunrise. Schooling groups of smaller bass are more apt to feed during the night than the day, while large bass feed equally during the day and night.

While the striped bass's appetite is influenced by the water temperature, the feeding range is wide. The bottom of the range appears to be about the 40-degree mark. At this point, their body metabolism slows. Striped bass are cold-blooded creatures and their life is one big chemical reaction that takes place at a rate directly proportional to the environmental temperature. However, this doesn't mean that you can't catch bass at the low end of the range. Bass, large bass, can be taken on rod and reel, with live bait, and even with plugs. One angler on the Thames River in Connecticut fished successfully one year in January and February. He took fish 4 to 40 pounds from Norwich to the New London Bridge. His efforts were most successful at night with underwater plugs, though he had taken striped bass during the day on live bait.

At low temperatures, those between 40 and 45 degrees, striped bass will feed, but less frequently. In colder water digestion takes much longer. A 4-pound menhaden may take a few hours for a large striped bass to digest when the water temperature is 70 degrees, but at 40 degrees it may take days. Thus, cold-water feeding is a much less frequent event.

The top limit of the feeding temperature range appears to be somewhere between 70 and 75 degrees—higher for young fish and lower for adult fish. Fish will feed in warmer waters out of necessity. If they can't escape it they must still continue to feed. The effects of excessively high temperatures are rather similar to those of low temperatures on striped bass. They begin to move less and feed less. The best examples of this are the doldrums of August in waters along the New York Bight and eastern Long Island. The bass seem to be off their feed and will only strike irresistible baits: live baits and then eels seem the best.

The optimal feeding range of a striped bass is between 55 and 68 degrees. Fish then are most active. The cooler water temperatures are associated with post-spawning temperatures and migratory temperatures. At both these times in the life of a striped bass feeding is intense.

6

Gulf Coast Striped Bass

Despite severe environmental changes in the last 150 years in the Gulf Coast states—Texas, Louisiana, Mississippi, Alabama and Florida—there remained a substantial striped bass fishery, both recreationally and even commercially until the turn of the century in these waters. At this time, striped bass were spread in almost every river system from Texas to the Suwannee in Florida and as far up the Mississippi River as St. Louis, Missouri.

However, these riverine populations suffered a setback when their headwater environments were drastically altered with the construction of dams for flood control, channelization for navigation, and hydroelectric power for rural electrification. This, coupled with the uncontrolled use of insecticides and pesticides after World War II, especially DDT, that is highly toxic to fish, further reduced the remnant Gulf Coast populations. By 1960, coastal populations of striped bass had been eliminated from almost all these south-flowing rivers except for a few in northwestern Florida. The only known indigenous population of the original Gulf Coast stock that exists today is in the Apalachicola-Chattahoochee-Flint river system.

In response to the disappearance of striped bass in their waters, the Gulf States Marine Fisheries Commission, in 1967, with the availability of new but limited federal funds that came with the passage of the Anadromous Fish Conservation Act, now had monies available for research and management of striped bass. Their primary goal was the reestablishment of a coastal population of these fish. But first, they had to enhance the environment for them. All five states began habitat studies that included water quality and ecological evaluations. These led to the enactment of conservation, management, and pollution abatement measures that would create a favorable environment for their striped

Historical ranges and remnant populations (inset) of striped bass in the northern Gulf of Mexico.

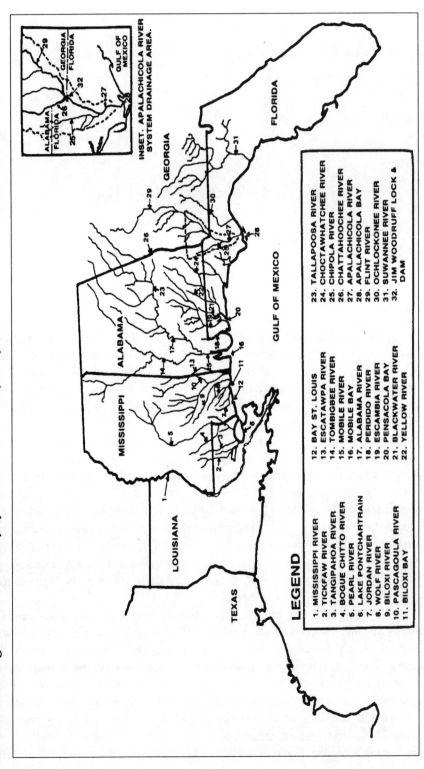

LEGEND

1. MISSISSIPPI RIVER
2. TICKFAW RIVER
3. TANGIPAHOA RIVER
4. BOGUE CHITTO RIVER
5. PEARL RIVER
6. LAKE PONTCHARTRAIN
7. JORDAN RIVER
8. WOLF RIVER
9. BILOXI RIVER
10. PASCAGOULA RIVER
11. BILOXI BAY

12. BAY ST. LOUIS
13. ESCATAWPA RIVER
14. TOMBIGBEE RIVER
15. MOBILE RIVER
16. MOBILE BAY
17. ALABAMA RIVER
18. PERDIDO RIVER
19. ESCAMBIA RIVER
20. PENSACOLA BAY
21. BLACKWATER RIVER
22. YELLOW RIVER

23. TALLAPOOSA RIVER
24. CHOCTAWHATCHEE RIVER
25. CHIPOLA RIVER
26. CHATTAHOOCHEE RIVER
27. APALACHICOLA RIVER
28. APALACHICOLA BAY
29. FLINT RIVER
30. OCHLOCKONEE RIVER
31. SUWANNEE RIVER
32. JIM WOODRUFF LOCK & DAM

INSET: APALACHICOLA RIVER SYSTEM DRAINAGE AREA.

bass restoration efforts. By 1986 some 84 million fry and fingerlings were stocked in the Gulf's coastal waters. As a result, striped bass began to appear within just a few years in the recreational fisheries harvests along the coast.

Florida

In the past, striped bass were present in many rivers along Florida's Gulf Coast. Most populations disappeared because of habitat loss when dam construction blocked their upstream migrations into fresh water. Some of the upstream migrations were to thermal refuges for survival during the hottest times of the year. Not all bass chose to spawn just above the head of tidewater. Many would undertake upstream migrations of a hundred or more miles into the rivers of the Southeast before selecting a spawning site. The only river system today in all the Gulf states with an original spawning Gulf stock is the Apalachicola, that divides into the Flint and Chattahoochee rivers where it enters Georgia.

In 1967, Florida's Game and Fresh Water Fish Commission began its striped bass restoration effort by attempting to culture and stock a limited number of native St. Johns (East Coast) and Apalachicola river fish in fresh water. The next year, striped bass fry were obtained from South Carolina's Moncks Corners Hatchery and met with success when they were reared and stocked in several lakes, including Lake Talquin. Since 1976, Lake Talquin has annually produced sufficient Atlantic striped bass brood stock to meet the demands for hybrid and striped bass production in Florida.

The state also attempted to reestablish striped bass populations, but using Atlantic strains, on several Gulf Coast rivers—Ochlockonee and Choctawhatchee rivers—but had only limited success. In 1976, the Apalachicola received 33,000 Atlantic-strain fingerlings, while from 1965 to 1974, Georgia introduced 124,000 Atlantic-strain fingerlings to Lake Seminole—a large reservoir formed almost on the Georgia-Florida border by damming the Apalachicola, called the Flint and Chattahoochee (ACF) rivers in Georgia after the main river bifurcates at this point. These, too, fared poorly.

It was an expensively learned lesson that stocked fish with the best chances of survival are usually fingerlings derived from brood stock obtained from that same watershed. As result, Georgia then switched to hybrid stockings in Lake Seminole. Since 1980, only "native" striped bass from the ACF have been used as brood stock, spawned, and then these fingerlings used to restock the system. Lake Seminole is a unique impoundment because of its southern latitude and abundance food sources for young bass and is capable of producing brood stock within four years.

The pedigree of striped bass in the ACF watershed system was a hodge-podge of striped bass strains. The Florida Freshwater Game and Fish Commission (GFC), in 1984, enlisted the aid of Dr. Isaac Wirgin of the New York University Medical Center to determine the origins of their stock. Dr. Wirgin

Striped bass anglers at the base of the Jim Woodruff Dam on the Apalachicola River in Florida.

had developed a technique for genetic identification, first using mitochondrial DNA (mtDNA) analysis and then later nuclear DNA fingerprinting to delimit where a striped bass had originated. Wirgin's efforts revealed that half the fish he tested had unique mtDNA genotypes (covert genetic makeup) not found in Atlantic populations and must have been a Gulf strain unique to the ACF. The remaining fish he tested were of Santee-Cooper stock origins.

Because of the poor establishment record of non-ACF stock and a desire to retain the original Gulf strain that was indigenous to the ACF, Alabama, Florida, and Georgia, and the U.S. Fish and Wildlife Service in 1990 agreed to restore only native stocks to the ACF system. Native stocks were better suited for survival. Today, Florida is stocking Apalachicola and Blackwater rivers with Gulf-strain fish.

Before 1976, when Florida began stocking striped bass in the Apalachicola River, the annual 14-week spring survey in the river's tailwater below Jim Woodruff Dam always recorded less than 200 fish. Since supplemental stocking began in 1980, the 1990 survey revealed a record 1,140 fish. Striped bass spawning has been documented in the Flint River in Georgia, the Apalachicola, the lower Ochlockonee River that drains Lake Talquin, and Choctawhatchee River in Florida's western panhandle. In 1985 mtDNA testing of the ACF striped bass fry revealed they were part of the natural strain, while in 1987, fish from the Ochlockonee revealed Atlantic genotypes. Florida is in the process of testing museum examples of past fish to determine if genotypes of today agree with those that are considered to be the original Gulf strain of fish.

Alabama

Two Alabama river watersheds provide one of the longest migration routes taken by striped bass today in the United States. Both Tombigbee and Alabama rivers flow into a common estuary in Mobile Bay. North of Montgomery, the Alabama divides into the Coosa and Tallapoosa rivers. Alabama's record striped bass, a 55-pound fish, was taken on the Tallapoosa. Striped bass are distributed along the entire route of this watershed system. They are rare in the estuarine portion, though in past years they have been taken there by commercial fishermen.

Striped bass were found in all of Alabama's major drainages until the late 1960s. There was an active sportfishery in the Tallapoosa, Coosa, Alabama, Tombigbee, and Mobile rivers until 1962, when the fish suddenly disappeared. Industrial and agricultural pollution were suspected as the culprits for the decline. To combat this, in 1965 Alabama strengthened its pollution standards by upgraded its treatment of municipal and industrial waters from primary to tertiary. In addition, the state stringently regulated oil and gas activities.

Within two years (1967) the water quality had so quickly improved that the Alabama Marine Resources Division (AMRD) began an aggressive stocking program to reestablish striped bass in coastal tributaries and rivers entering the Gulf of Mexico. Between 1967 and 1989 AMRD released 3.8 million Phase I and II fingerlings. Phase II are yearling fish that are kept in the hatchery until the end of summer, and survival is often enhanced.

The AMRD determined that a striped bass sportfishery had been established as early as 1980. In 1981, Alabama, in a joint venture with Mississippi, began releasing tagged fish raised in AMRD's Claude Peetet Mariculture Center. The intent was to gather sorely-needed data on the striped bass's movements, growth, and distribution. Tag returns also convinced these states to increase their minimum size limits of retained fish so that young fish could reach sexual maturity before they were harvested. In 1989, research established that natural reproduction occurred on the Alabama River below Millers Ferry.

Mississippi

Seven rivers in Mississippi have varying concentrations of striped bass in their waters. They are the Pascagoula, Tchouticabouffa, Biloxi, Wolf, and Jordan. Mississippi shares with Louisiana two rivers with striped bass, the Pearl and Tangipahoa. There was little or no marine fishing for striped bass, and even in the estuaries their appearance was only occasional, until 1969. Mississippi inaugurated its Gulf Coast striped bass restoration program in 1969 and since then more than 11 million striped bass fry and fingerlings have been stocked in tributaries leading to Mississippi Sound (that excludes the Mississippi River). By 1980, an highly active recreational sportfishery had evolved and striped bass have now become one of the major species popular in marine fishing contests along the coast.

In 1989, Mississippi's Gulf Coast Research Laboratory ended its agreement with the Alabama Marine Resources Division. It had transferred yolk-sac fry from the Alabama hatchery and raised them in their intensive-culture tanks. Half the fish were stocked in Alabama and the remainder in Mississippi. While successful striped bass reproduction has not been documented, but recent observations indicate that there are spawning activities taking place in the lower Mississippi River.

Louisiana

Until recently, the western limit of striped bass distribution in the Gulf of Mexico was in Louisiana. Even then, their occurrence here was sporadic. Before World War II, a substantial population was recorded in the streams along the Mississippi River delta, but became rare. When they did occur, they were found in the two streams shared with Mississippi—the Pearl and Tangipahoa—and in the Atchafalaya, Tchefuncta, and Mississippi rivers as well as in Lakes Borgne, Rigolets, and Bayou Penchant. At one time, striped bass were present in most of Louisiana's coastal streams. Like neighboring Mississippi, Louisiana's coastal striped bass also suffered a great decline in recent times but it occurred here 10 to 15 years earlier. The decline started in the late 1940s, intensified in the early 1950s, and by 1957 the fish had disappeared. Here, too, poor water quality, because of municipal, industrial, agricultural and contaminants, and channelization and impoundment of rivers were suspected as the causes for the decline.

The recovery of the habitat in Louisiana was slower than in Mississippi and Alabama and this has hindered the pace of reestablishing coastal striped bass populations here. In addition, the effort in the first years relied almost entirely on federal funding that was not nearly sufficient enough to support such a program. Other Gulf states turned to their legislatures for help.

Despite inadequate funding, Louisiana's Department of Wildlife and Fisheries began its program in 1964. From 1965 to the mid 1970s, the Department received Atlantic-strain striped bass fry from South Carolina and stocked them in several impoundments and coastal streams. In the early 1970s, Louisiana received additional shipments of striped bass eggs and fry from Maryland and Virginia, thus further mixing their striped bass strains. Fingerlings raised from these fry were stocked in Calcasieu and Mermentau rivers.

By 1976, Toledo Bend Reservoir had developed enough brood stock to support a Louisiana hatchery program, and the state was no longer dependent upon other sources for its striped bass fry. From 1967 to 1989, Louisiana stocked 3.5 million fingerlings and 2 million fry in coastal waters.

The state conducted a study of Lake Pontchartrain in the late 1960s to determine if any striped bass still existed in the lake and the several small tributaries that flowed into it. The effort didn't reveal any striped bass but it did determine that the water quality had risen and was suitable for stocking. Louisiana's effort to reestablish striped bass in its coastal waters took longer, 10 to 15 years, than other Gulf States, because so few monies were diverted into the effort. Eventually, it paid off and coastal anglers are now taking fish from the Atchafalaya, Mississippi, Sabine, and Pearl rivers as well as their estuaries. Most fish range in size from 12 to 20 pounds, but commercial fishermen have taken striped bass in hoop nets over 25 pounds. Haul seine nettings in these rivers by state biologists indicated large numbers of fingerling striped bass and support the idea that natural reproduction is again occurring.

An important part of striped bass management is genetic strain identification. During the summer and spring of 1990, 24 striped bass from the state's four major river systems were evaluated and it was found that they all were of Atlantic stock origins. The state is looking toward the future to use Gulf-strain stocks in any additional stockings and then to evaluate their adaptability to their waters in comparison to Atlantic strain stocks.

Texas

In light of its recent status, it seems almost impossible to comprehend that in 1890 striped bass was the foremost fish species taken commercially by the bay-seine fishery in the coastal bays of Galveston, Corpus Christ, and Aransas. The original realm of Gulf strain of striped bass stretched from Florida west to the mid-Texas coast. Even today, one can easily visualize how this could evolve as productive striped bass habitat. Almost the entire Texas Gulf coast, from Galveston Pass (inlet), just 60 miles west of the Texas-Louisiana border created by the Sabine River, west and then south to the Rio Grande, is protected almost entirely by an outer, barrier beach. It is similar to beaches, inlets, and back-bays found along the New Jersey and Long Island coasts in the Northeast. These inside bays are fed by numerous rivers, some large and some small, that create an ideal habitat for striped bass, replete with thermal sanctuaries that allowed a place for adult fish to survive during periods of high temperatures and low dissolved oxygen. These include such waters as Trinity, Galveston West, and East Bays; Tres Palacios and Matagorda bays; San Antonio; Aransas and Compano bays; and Corpus Christi Bay behind Padre Island.

The last commercial landings from these bays were recorded in the mid-1940s, with only occasional recreational catches occurring since then. Texas didn't investigate the causes for its population decline but assumed they were the same as those documented elsewhere that eradicated striped bass from all other watersheds emptying into the Gulf of Mexico, except the Apalachicola River—namely insecticides and industrial, municipal, and agricultural pollution.

As early as the late 1960s, planners in the Texas Parks and Wildlife Department realized that demands for improving recreational fishing were growing and that the restoration of striped bass to the coast could solve that problem. As their objective, they set out to produce an adult striped bass population, throughout the original range of the fish along the Texas coast, by 1997. They began by focusing their restoration efforts on stocking fingerlings and fry in Trinity River, north of Galveston, that has Galveston Bay as its tidal estuary. From 1983 to 1988 17.5 million 3 to 10 day old fry were stocked. Lesser numbers of fry (481,000) were also stocked in the waters leading into San Antonio Bay, Corpus Christi Bay (3,000), and Sabine Lake (10,000), an estuary between the city of Beaumont and Sabine Pass. Another 1 million fingerlings were stocked in several coastal bays between 1975 and 1988.

Recent sampling efforts on the Trinity River collected striped bass eggs and larvae, verifying that natural production is occurring here. And, night-time sampling produced juvenile striped bass. However, an adequate natural recruitment into the fishery today is still a problem, and to maintain the sportfishery at its present level requires an active stocking program. To meet this end, the Department has expanded its hatchery capabilities at Possum Kingdom, Dundee, and San Marcos hatcheries.

Striped bass are alive, well, and getting better in the waters of the Gulf of Mexico.

Though not a Gulf Coast state, Georgia be should be because two of its striped bass rivers, the Flint and Chattahoochee, join together just before flowing under the border with Florida to form the Apalachicola River. This is a striped bass that was estimated to weigh more than 80 pounds and was taken by on the Flint River, just below Albany, by federal and state biologists when they were electro-fishing an implanting bass with radio transmitters to follow to their cool water, river retreats in the summer. Though not identified, this fish could possibly be part of the original Gulf Coast strain.

7

Pacific Coast Striped Bass

On the south shore of Carquinez Straits, in the city of Martinez, there should stand a statue of two men holding a milk can. And, at least once a year, preferably in July, all striped bass fishermen in California, and some from Washington and Oregon as well, should walk by the monument and touch it with respect. And each should whisper a quiet thanks to the two men with the milk can.

At the base, the inscription should read: "Livingston Stone, Aquaculturist, U.S. Fish Commission." Under the other figure: "Stephen Rush Throckmorton, Chairman, California Fish Commission." Under the milk can: "132 Navesink Striped Bass." Lastly, the monument should be dated: "July, 1879."

From these 132 striped bass, a part of the Hudson River stock, that in that July were in the Navesink estuary in New Jersey, and a second stocking of 300 bass, three years later from the Shrewsbury River, the entire striped bass fishery on the Pacific Coast had its origin. Most of the original stocking was composed of small fish, between 1.5 and 3 inches, but their potential was great. A recent estimate of the striped bass population in the San Francisco Bay complex placed the population at about three-quarters to one million fish 16 inches or longer. Twenty years ago, it had been as high as three million, but striped bass in the San Francisco Bay area are now on hard times...not too unlike their counterparts on the East Coast.

The latter part of the 19th century was a great time for fish experimentation. Fisheries biologists were introducing new species to waters that had been voided of native stocks throughout the East because of industrialization and severely altered environments, via lumbering and agriculture. It was about this time that the brown trout was brought over from Europe and introduced to American waters. Unfortunately, the European carp also came. It was a field day

San Francisco Bay is the center of abundance of striped bass on the West Coast,
similar in concentration of fish to Chesapeake Bay and the Atlantic Coast.

for any fish culturists with an adventurous spirit.

One such man was Livingston Stone, employed by the U.S. Fish Commission but on loan to California. Stone, long a devotee of the striped bass, believed that San Francisco Bay could support a population, and after netting a catch in the Navesink he nursed the young-of-the-year fish on a long train ride from New York to California. There he made the historic planting. Fortunately, it turned out to be one of the better moves made by fish culturists.

Today, striped bass are established in three areas along the Pacific Coast, the San Francisco Bay area, Coos Bay, and Umpqua River region in Oregon. It is sporadic on the Columbia River system between Oregon and Washington and has been caught as far north as Alberni Inlet in Barkley Sound, on the seaward side of Vancouver Island in British Columbia. From time to time, striped bass have appeared in northern Mexico and southern California, but not with any degree of predictability or dependability.

In just ten years after their planting in San Francisco Bay, striped bass were so well established that further transplantings of striped bass were attempted in other West Coast locations. Humboldt Bay had a stock planted in 1889, and in

1903 the Santa Ana River in Orange County (near San Diego) received striped bass. In 1916 and 1919, Morro Bay in San Luis Obispo County was given a collection of striped bass in hopes of establishing another population. The fish even spanned a big piece of the Pacific and in 1919 were released near Honolulu, Hawaii. All these latter stockings failed to take hold.

Fortunately, striped bass were smarter than fish culturists. In many of these areas, conditions just did not exist that would support a striped bass population, especially one that would reproduce itself. Fast waters were there, with plenty of spawning sites, but most lacked the large estuaries most populations of striped bass need for summer feeding. These big run-outs, before the open ocean, are the kinds of places that house the necessary food supply and offer bass fry a place to grow and mature. Bass on the Pacific Coast exhibited the typical local migratory nature of most striped bass stocks on the Atlantic, and the relatively indigenous attitude of Hudson River fish was carried over into the Pacific fish.

Instead of heading south striped bass exhibited their temperate water penchant and on their own headed north from San Francisco Bay. There is always a natural biological dispersion of fish in any population in the search for more food and less competition, especially from its own kind. This drift northward was not a migration similar to certain Chesapeake Bay fish but a natural tendency of all fishes to spread or scatter into new areas or unoccupied bioniches, a phenomenon always in action in every population.

On their own, these vanguard fish moved into Coos Bay in Oregon. It was to their liking because it contained all the elements necessary to produce a self-sustaining population. They thrived so well that by 1922 a commercial fishery was under way. Eventually, striped bass reached as far as the Columbia River, and here, too, established themselves with a breeding population. However, these eventually disappeared. There were reports of striped bass being taken by commercial fishermen as far north as British Columbia and southern Alaska. Even though these fish may occur annually at the northern limit, they are rare.

CALIFORNIA

Today, despite intentional efforts to reduce its population, striped bass are THE major sport fishery in the San Francisco Bay area, supplanting native species of salmon and trout that had been reduced over the years because of overfishing and changing environmental conditions in the bay and surrounding watershed.

Success of the striped bass transplant is like a Horatio Alger fish story. Ten years after the initial planting, hundreds of striped bass were being taken in the Bay area. By 1899 over 1,200,000 pounds were landed commercially, and from 1916 to 1935, the annual catch by commercial fishermen averaged between 500,000 and 1,000,000 pounds. The commercial take had become so great that it suddenly and unexpectedly threatened the very brood stock needed to sustain a healthy, reproducing population. Before it became depleted, in 1935, progressive fisheries managers, guided by a wise philosophy, as well as pressure from recreational fishermen, halted all commercial fishing. Their goal was to protect the fish for the sport fishery for which they had been intended. Still, thousands of striped bass were killed annually in the gill net fishery for chinook salmon and American shad in San Francisco Bay. They could not be marketed legally and that complicated enforcement of the original closure. Eventually, the salmon and shad fishery declined to the point where it was not economically feasible for commercial fishermen to set for them. In 1957 all gill netting in the bay was ended and striped bass became the prime beneficiary.

Almost all striped bass taken today in California waters come from the San Francisco Bay area. California's striped bass anglers annually caught about 750,000 striped bass during the heyday of fish's population peak in the mid-1960s. Since then, it has steadily declined. In recent times, the sportfishing catch has been reduced to about 150,000 fish each year because of problems generated by water removal from striped bass spawning and nursery rivers for agricultural irrigation demands. By the late 1970s, striped bass catches had fallen to extremely low levels. In order to make their fishing possible these anglers had annually spent an estimated $20,000,000 in pursuit of striped bass. As fish stocks and chances of catching fish fell, so did the interests of striped bass fishermen. Even today, in its diminished state, there are nearly 400,000 dedicated striped bass anglers willing to spend $75 million annually in pursuit of the fish. In 1984, before the decline in fish began taking its toll of anglers, there were 591,180 fishermen and women who bought the required $3.50 Striped Bass Stamp.

*   *   *

Striped bass in California and other West Coast waters differ little in their characteristics and habits when compared to the same species in the Atlantic. The only difference might be their food selection, but that is really governed more by what is available than by what they would like to eat. The Delta area— a broad, freshwater out-wash plane, carved in a lace-work pattern by myriad channels formed by the junction of the Sacramento River from the north and the San Joaquin River from the south, and the adjoining Suisan, San Pablo, and San Francisco bays—sustains California's most important striped bass population.

There is a minor coastal fishery on the San Diego River and its marine estuary Mission Bay, that was created in 1974. It was annually stocked with yearling striped bass from California's Department of Fish and Game striped bass hatchery in Elk Grove until 1985. Because angler use and catches were low, stocking efforts ended in 1986. There were indications that a self-sustaining population might have developed, but there is no evidence of it today. There is also a small spawning population on the Russian River, that enters the Pacific

Ocean at Jenner, about 20 miles north of Tomales Bay. This bay is the apparent northern limit during the summer for striped bass from the Bay area. A 75-pound striped bass was reported to have been taken from the Russian River in 1927. It's difficult to say whether this was a fish produced on the Russian River or was a migrant from the Sacramento-San Joaquin system that was summering in the estuary. This estuary had also produced several 50- and 60-pound striped bass in earlier year.

Spawning

Two major spawning areas and a number of minor sites are used by California striped bass in the Bay area. Spawning sites on the Sacramento River were extensive during years when the number of fish was great, and covered a long section of the river from Isleton on the Delta, upstream more than 125 miles, beyond Sacramento, to Butte City. Spawning fish also moved into the Feather River, a tributary to the Sacramento River, that it joins a few miles north of Sacramento. While some spawning occurs here, it has not made a major contribution to the stock. In recent years, this vast up river area has been reduced as a spawning site and striped bass now concentrate in the section of river between Sacramento and Colusa. From half to two-thirds of the eggs spawned in the combined watersheds are from the Sacramento River.

The amount of water flowing in the rivers affects the exact location of spawning more than the bottom composition or physical stream characteristics. Because spawning time is directly related to water temperature, a great flow of water will cause fish to swim even farther upstream until the correct spawning temperature is reached. During years of high spring water run-offs the fish will spawn farther upstream. During spring seasons of minimal flow they will spawn farther downstream. A correlation has evolved between the amount of water in the rivers and the success of each year class. The more water available has usually produced the better year classes.

The other major arm of the system is the main branch of the San Joaquin River and adjacent sloughs from the community of Antioch up river to Venice Island (Middle River). The situation is somewhat different in the San Joaquin River system, which offers striped bass more of a delta than riverine environment. The San Joaquin-Delta feature produces a greater diffusion of its water than the adjacent Sacramento. In this case, with less of a water flow, the exact location of spawning is determined principally by salinity, or lack of it, as in the Hudson River. Its location can vary greatly from year to year.

Striped bass demand virtually fresh water in which to spawn. However, they will spawn in brackish waters with salinities at 6 to 8 ppt. However, in some systems, they have spawned in waters with salinities as high as 10 ppt. Ocean water salinity ranges from 36 to 39 ppt. In years when there is a high run-off on the San Joaquin, the saline block is pushed down stream and spawning occurs farther down stream. During years of lesser run-off the salt block occurs farther up river and the spawning takes place ahead of it.

Spawning in these rivers begins when the water temperature rises past 60 degrees and peaks out between 63 and 68 degrees, similar to spawning in Atlantic coastal streams. Thus, spawning in the Delta and San Joaquin usually precedes spawning in the Sacramento by about two weeks because of cooler water in the Sacramento River that receives water near its source in several reservoirs just south of Mount Shasta. Approximate spawning times in the Delta range from April 25 to May 25 and in the Sacramento River May 10 to June 12.

Striped bass spawn in large schools; usually several younger adult males will be involved with one, often larger female. Spawning takes place on or near the surface with the fish thrashing about the female. On one occasion, Department of Fish and Game biologists observed several thousand striped bass on the surface along the banks of the Sacramento River above Knights Landing, all spawning. It was similar to the "rock fights" Roanoke River fish demonstrate when they spawn just below Roanoke Rapids in North Carolina. Actual fertilization takes place as females and accompanying males sink toward the bottom.

As eggs are deposited they are fertilized by the male and immediately begin drifting downstream with the current. They are just slightly heavier than fresh water; their specific gravity is 1.005. Moving current is a prerequisite to successful striped bass spawning because the current is needed to buoy the eggs. Otherwise they would sink to the bottom and suffocate under the own numbers or be covered by silt and mud that also would deny them oxygenated water. At the time of fertilization, the milt, composed of microscopic sperms, penetrate the eggs, that are only about 1/25th of an inch in diameter, and cause them to begin developing. In the river, the eggs quickly absorb water and swell to 1/8th-inch eggs that are practically invisible because they are so transparent.

Depending upon the water temperature, eggs hatch between 48 to 72 hours. The young larvae obtain nourishment from the yolk sac still attached to their body, and though they attempt weak swimming movements it is the current that keeps them off the bottom. After a week, the yolk sac is absorbed and disappears. By the seventh or eighth day, their mobility increases and they begin active feeding on microscopic zooplankton. As they grow their food becomes larger.

From four to six weeks after spawning, the young fish are all found down river in the Delta and Suisan Bay, where fresh and salt water mix. By eight weeks, they are two inches long. Through the remainder of their first year, opossum shrimp are the main food for juvenile bass. As winter months come on, young bass begin feeding on smaller fish, which increasingly become the major part of their diet. The fish spend most of their juvenile lives in Suisan, Honker, Grizzly and San Pablo bays. As in the Atlantic, male bass mature sexually during their second and third years, while females mature during their fifth and sixth years. Once they mature they take on the local migratory habits characteristic of adult striped bass.

Migrations

California biologists have intensively studied striped bass and have established migratory patterns for fish in their area. The annual migrations are similar in pattern to fish in the Hudson. In summer, the fish inhabit the lower bay and the Pacific beaches north and south of the Golden Gate. Their environment at this time is basically in salt water. In fall, from September to November, they begin an upstream migration from San Francisco Bay through San Pablo Bay and the Carquinez Straits into Suisan and Grizzly bays. As winter approaches they are in the freshwater delta formed by the San Joaquin and Sacramento rivers. Here they winter over and remain until spring. As spring approaches the fish scatter over the delta, and some head up the Sacramento River to spawn. After spawning, they return to San Pablo Bay and adjacent waters to feed and summer.

Just how many striped bass will trek back to the ocean after spawning varies from year to year. Smaller bass tend to stay within the confines of the bay, while some of the larger bass develop a bit of wanderlust and move outside the Golden Gate. These large fish have been taken, with a fair degree of frequency, as far south as Monterey and north along the coast as far as Tomales Bay, 50 miles above the bridge.

Sportfishing

Prior to 1956, striped bass fishing limits were quite generous in California waters. Anglers were allowed to keep five fish 12 inches or longer. In 1956, it was changed to three fish 16 inches or longer. Since 1982, because of the general decline in striped bass numbers, the limit was reduced to two fish per angler per day. At the same time, the minimum length was increased from 16 to 18 inches, where it stands today. There is no closed season.

Striped bass are caught throughout the year in the Bay area but the quality of fishing improves as weather warms in early March. Fish that have wintered over in the bays begin moving into fresh water to spawn, and good fishing continues throughout the spawning period. By mid-June, the majority of legal-size fish have returned to the estuary and the best part of the summer fishing season then follows.

Most summer fishing involves trolling or drifting natural baits near the mouth of the bay, between Raccoon Strait and the Golden Gate Bridge, and around Alcatraz and Treasure islands. Point Bonita and its lighthouse are to the West Coast what Montauk Point and its lighthouse are to the East Coast. Farther into the bay, trolling is also successful in Carquinez Strait, between San Pablo and Grizzly bays. Earlier in their history, striped bass began their fall migration back to fresh water in August and September but the pattern has shifted in recent years and does not start until October and November. Most fishing is done from private boats. However, there is an active charterboat fishery in the San Francisco-San Pablo Bay area that caters to area fishermen.

The Decline

If you're familiar with striped bass and their various environments along the Gulf and Atlantic coasts—wet, green habitats and rivers filled with water— you might have a bit of trouble visualizing the habitat in which the fish have adapted to prevail on the West Coast, especially in California. Green California has been described as a strip of land 40 miles wide and 900 miles long, and then only in February. Most of California is dry or semi-arid and its 31 million people are crowded into this 4.5 million acres of land that often must be irrigated. Water, enough of it, had never been a problem in this part of California until about 30 years ago. Ground and surface water supplies were adequate to meet the state's needs because most of its water is transported from thinly populated areas in the northern half and is used to green the southern half of the state.

Unfortunately, this involves the watershed for California's major striped bass population, the Sacramento-San Joaquin rivers and their numerous tributaries. These waters have insidiously come under the control of numerous dams and reservoirs operated by federal, state and local water authorities. Over the past three decades, water development has gradually changed the occurrence and magnitude of the watershed's flow both to and through the Delta estuary into San Francisco Bay and the Pacific Ocean. This watershed, because of its location and volume, became the heart of state water development projects.

Like striped bass populations on the Atlantic and Gulf coasts, Pacific Coast striped bass have also undergone a recent decline in their numbers. But unlike the Atlantic, where declines are attributed primarily to overfishing and increasingly hostile environments, and the Gulf Coast, where dams, channelization, and toxic pollution have reduced their numbers, striped bass in the Bay area have all these problems, plus an added one—water diversion.

At first, the demands for these waters were met without jeopardizing striped bass and other fish populations that utilized the watersheds. In the Delta, an area at the watershed's lower end, there are today more than 2,000 small agricultural diversions, two major state and federal diversions and two electricity-generating facilities that take in water and alter the flow. The result is that the Delta and upstream diversions have reduced the mean water flow at the mouth by 50 percent. The decline in the number of striped bass in the Sacramento-San Joaquin water system can be directly attributed to an increase in water diversion that began in 1953, from this system to power-generating plants. These plants utilized water sources on both the breeding and nursery grounds. The shortage of water here was further heightened by natural droughts. The loss-of-water problem has worsened today because the demand to expand farming into more arid areas requires more and more water.

Compounding the loss-of-water problem, that is crucial to successful striped bass spawning, are the numerous agricultural diversions, the intakes of which are unscreened, and while the state and federal diversion are screened, they still cause a considerable amount of lethal entrainment and impingement of striped bass eggs, larvae, and juveniles.

The population has also been negatively affected by other factors: toxicants in the watershed, accidentally introduced species, changes in waste and its treatment, and even increased fishing pressures, both legal and illegal. The long-range effects of past insecticide and herbicide use, though abated 20 years ago, are still appearing in Pacific Coast stocks and creating reproductive problems for striped bass. The more recent introduction of heavy metals is even further compounding their problems in an environment that is growing progressively hostile.

Pollution has not only affected striped bass production directly, but also reduced other organisms in the food chain that provide sustenance for larval, fry, and young-of-the-year fish. Loss of these also reduces the viability of a population, especially juvenile stocks. However, as bad as these factors are, in the aggregate, they are not so overwhelming that striped bass cannot cope with them. Nor is overfishing an uncontrollable problem, because commercial fishing is not allowed and recreational fisherman can readily be manipulated to reduce the harvest of fish. Even without a commercial fishery, a black market in striped bass is still a problem, but not a major factor, and some degree of poaching also exists.

In the last analysis, striped bass abundance in California is delimited by a vast collection of factors, all man-made, none insurmountable, that could be corrected if the desire was there. However, much of the management is based not on the fish's biological needs but on socio-economics.

There is also another factor negatively affecting striped bass populations that is unique to this stock: the annual die-offs near Carquinez Strait. Almost every year, there is a die-off of adult striped bass in this area. The severity and location varies annually, with observed numbers ranging from several hundred to about two thousand. This has been occurring for more than 40 years and may have even been going on before that, undetected since the fish were first stocked (ironically almost in the exact area). Some have suggested that the die-off is genetically influenced, but there is no evidence to support this.

Striped Bass Production

Abundance of young-of-the-year (YOY) striped bass has been monitored annually since 1959, except for 1966. The survey is conducted every second week from late June to late July or early August throughout the nursery habitat. The indices here are somewhat different from those conducted in other states, especially along the East Coast. The fish are measured, and when their mean fork length reaches 38 mm (1.5 inches), a young-of-the-year (YOY) index is calculated on the basis of catch per net tow and the volume of water in the areas where the fish are caught.

Sampling occurs on the nursery grounds, the Delta, and Suisan Bay, so the index has a well-recognized bias. According to Don Stevens, a fisheries management supervisor with the Department of Fish and Game, in high water-flow years when a large proportion of the YOY are washed downstream into San Pablo, which is inadequately sampled by the survey. Hence, in very wet years, the sample is an underestimate of the population.

The indices also show a directly inverse relationship to the amount of water taken out of the Delta watershed for irrigation elsewhere, from the period April to July. The more water diverted, the smaller the surviving year-class. Realizing that this was a problem, screens were tried on diversion intakes but because of the minuscule size of striped bass at this age, none proved effective. Further, young-of-the year striped bass were killed when passing through pumps designed to lift the elevation of the redirected waters. These annual indices, during several years (mid-1960s) before the decline ensued, exceeded more than 100. It reached its lowest in 1990 with an index of 4.3. Indices fluctuations before 1970 were explained by fluctuations of spring outflow and the percent of Delta inflow that was being diverted. When outflows were high and the percent of inflow being diverted was low, the index was high. Conversely, when outflows were low and the percent of inflow being diverted was high, the index was low. Since 1971, the anticipated indices were always lower than expected, and since 1977 they have been very much lower.

The decline in the production of young bass has also been described as the principal cause in the decline of large, adult bass in the population. Part of the reason the annual index has remained low is that since the adult population is now low; fewer eggs have been produced. This reduction in egg production cannot be used to explain fully the decline in young fish but it may have accelerated it and does make recovery more difficult. Nor can this decline be attributed to a change in spawning habits that were investigated with this problem in mind. If this is true, it is the first example of a threatened striped bass population in which sufficient brood stock—needed to produce the minimum number of eggs—has been identified as a problem. In endangered Atlantic migratory coastal stock, egg production has always remained high but larval striped bass are eliminated, from 10 to 14 days of age, by toxic elements in their environment. In California's case, sufficient egg production has occurred. The delimiting factor is physical entrainment and entrapment and thus removal of eggs and larvae by water-diversion equipment.

The solution to the problem in the Bay area would be simplified if all water diversion took place in the rivers upstream of spawning and nursery grounds. Then, only sufficient water-flow volume would be the problem. But because so many diversions take water downstream of spawning and nursery grounds, they physically remove striped bass by entrainment, destroying them en route.

Striped Bass Stamp Project

Frustrated by the Department of Fish and Game's failure to determine at that time why striped bass populations were so low and with no visible change

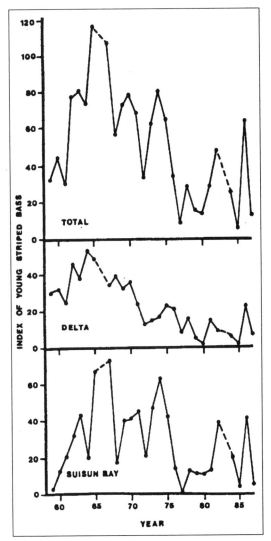

Annual index of young striped bass abundance by area in the Sacramento-San Joaquin Estuary. Young bass suffered unsteady but persistent declines from the mid-1960s to 1985. The decline was most pronounced in the Delta, but also is clearly visible in Suisun Bay despite greater year-to-year fluctuations there. In 1986 young striped bass abundance rebounded to its highest level since 1975. No sampling was conducted in 1966 and the 1983 index was omitted because extremely high flows at the time transported most young bass downstream from the area effectively sampled by the tow net survey.

in the future, California's striped bass anglers gathered together. Led principally by the United Anglers of California and the California Striped Bass Angler's Association, they lobbied successfully for legislation in 1981 to create an annual striped bass fishing stamp, with the caveat that the revenue from its required purchase be used only for the fish's restoration. In September of that year, Gov. Edmund G. Brown, Jr., signed the bill into law requiring all anglers who fish for striped bass to purchase the $3.50 stamp. This was in addition to either a freshwater or saltwater license, dependent upon where they fished. It was to be in effect for four years. However, it was renewed for another four years, 1985 to December 1989, and for a third time in 1990. In the first eight-year period, its sales produced more than $15 million for the Fish and Game Department. The department director established an advisory board on how the money was to be spent.

The greatest number, 591,180, was sold in 1984. Since then it has declined at the rate of about 70,000 stamps per year, roughly paralleling the decline in striped bass populations. Last year, just under 400,000 stamps were sold, reflecting both the loss of striped bass and a decline in fishing interest because they weren't easy to catch and not many were available.

The funds were used to stock 5.5 million young striped bass; to support a hatchery-bass evaluation project that implanted 4.5 million magnetic, coded-wire tags in those stocked bass and conducted a year-round creel census to determine their survival and catch by anglers; to help support annual surveys of distribution and abundance of bass eggs and larvae; to construct and operate an Aquatic Toxicology Laboratory that determines the effects of various pollutants on young bass and their important food, opossum shrimp; to increases overtime law enforcement patrols on bass law violators and purchase boats, night-vision scopes and other patrol equipment; launched and expand more than a dozen scientific investigations to solve the practical problems and to probe biological and environmental requirements of striped bass; and to prepare the Striped Bass Restoration Plan.

Striped Bass Restoration Plan

Striped bass stamp sales helped to underwrite the Striped Bass Restoration and Management Plan for the Sacramento-San Joaquin Estuary. Phase I of the plan was written (primarily by biologist Glenn Delisle) in 1989 by the Inland Fisheries Division of the Department of Fish and Game because this division has the responsibility for management of this public resource. Its goal was to restore the Bay area striped bass fishery to approximate levels it enjoyed in the mid-1960s, when there were some 3 to 4 million adult striped bass, and anglers could expect to harvest about 750,000 fish each season. It hoped to achieve this objective by the year 2,000, by first stabilizing the decline and restoring the fish populations, then improving them and bringing them to the levels it has set for itself.

Phase II of the plan is a highly ambitious Four-Point Program. The four points are: develop public participation in plan preparation and implementation; resolve problems detrimental to striped bass; resolve problems of human use of striped bass; and conduct fishery and environmental investigations. The most ambitious is Point Two because it entails either getting the State Water Project, Central Valley Project, Contra Costa Canal (part of the CVP), Pacific Gas & Electric Company, and the Delta agricultural diversions to drastically reduce their import of water from the Sacramento-San Joaquin River system or find new sources of water for the striped bass fishery. At the same time, the DF&G must also deal with regulatory agencies like the Department of Water Resources and the U.S. Bureau of Reclamation. Attaining either goal is near-impossible.

It has been three years since Part I and II were inaugurated. And, according to Al Petrovitch, assistant director of the California Department of Fish and Game, few if any of the plan's objectives have been reached. Not only has the

1992
CALIFORNIA
STRIPED BASS
STAMP

$3.70

41174507

Expires Dec. 31, 1992
Date Issued
4/4/92

decline in striped bass production and adult numbers not been reversed, it hasn't been halted. The prime reason is that river water in the Sacramento-San Joaquin system is still being diverted to agriculture. In fact, it intensified as California entered the 10th year of a prolonged drought in the fall of 1992. However, exceptional rains during the winter of 1992/93, and a large snow pack in the mountains, caused California's Gov. Pete Wilson, at the end of February, to declare the drought over.

Salmonids versus Striped Bass

However, the rains didn't end the problems for striped bass. The winter-migratory strain of chinook salmon is on the threatened species list of the federal government and on the endangered species list with the State of California. Whether it is justified or not, politicians, and maybe even a few biologists, believed that a further reduction in striped bass stocks would enhance the survival of the winter-run chinooks. They believe that when young salmon in the rivers change from parr to smolts and are then outbound through the series of bays between the Delta and the Golden Gate Bridge, striped bass prey on the smolts and reduce their numbers.

Seemingly to this end, to help further reduce striped bass's population, the DF&G last summer ended production at their striped bass hatchery in Elk Grove. What fish were in the hatchery were sent to Oregon for stocking and some to reservoirs within California where fish couldn't impinge upon salmonids. There's a bit of hypocrisy here. On one hand, the DF&G is still taking all the money it can get from sales of striped bass stamps while on the other hand, it is trying its darndest to reduce striped bass stocks. The decision to close the striped bass hatchery in 1992 and the refusal even to consider increasing the minimum length of striped bass above 18 inches (Oregon three years ago raised its limit to 30 inches) that would insure spawning of more young females in the population, or a season closure while striped bass are spawning, has been the decision of Boyd Gibbons, the director of the California Department of Fish and Game, who said he takes full responsibility for the moves. However, that does not justify it or make it correct. You figure it out.

Nor are striped bass in Oregon waters without their salmon-only advocates. Striped bass in this state's several watersheds are also declining because no dominant year classes have been produced in recent years. A well-devised striped bass recovery plan to establish adult populations at a level of 20,000 to 25,000 fish on the depleted Coos River system had been inaugurated in 1992 but was sharply curtailed. Striped bass are also controversial in Oregon because of their feeding habits and cohabitation with salmonids during certain times of the year, according to the Oregon Department of Fish and Wildlife. The ODFW produced a "White Paper" in 1986 to address the issue of the interaction of the two fish groups. The gist of the paper was: yes, striped bass do eat salmon. But, there is a trade-off: salmonids also eat striped bass in various stages of their lives.

The bottom line was that no one is certain of the degree with which mutual predation occurs or how much it would really increase if striped bass production was enhanced. The final effect was to reduce striped bass stocking numbers.

OREGON

The natural spread of striped bass along the Pacific Coast took longer than might have been expected after the initial 1879 stocking. But they did disperse northward along the West Coast and established themselves in several locations. It might have occurred sooner, but the first striped bass recorded north of San Francisco took 35 years to get there. Most striped bass are real home bodies. In 1914, the first striped bass caught "up the coast" were two fish that had wandered into a gill net set in Coos Bay by Alfred Justrom.

In Oregon, four centers eventually developed that today have varying sizes of reproducing populations. Fisheries evolved on Coos Bay and two tributaries that flow into it; in Winchester Bay where the Umpqua and Smith rivers meet; in Siuslaw Bay and River; and in Coquille Bay and South Fork Coquille River. Occasionally, striped bass are also taken from other small rivers along the Oregon Coast but without consistency. Coos Bay supported an intensive fishery for striped bass that began in 1922, but commercial fishing was allowed only on the Smith, Umpqua, Coquille, and Siuslaw rivers. The largest harvest occurred in 1945 when a total of 250,442 pounds of striped bass were landed. At best, it was really a by-catch fishery for American shad that were taken in gill nets.

Striped bass became a major recreational fishery by 1950 and its followers were legion. Their mecca centered around Bass Harbor Lodge, located on Isthmus and Catching sloughs. The stripe-bass-oriented lodge served as a fishing station with dozens of boats in its livery and all the bass tackle an angler could imagine. In that year, they landed an estimated 5,000 striped bass. By 1978, recreational fishermen brought enough pressure on the state legislature that the commercial fishery for striped bass was closed in all Oregon waters.

The recreational fishing area in Coos Bay reaches from Coos River Bar to the upper tidal reaches of the Coos River, and the Millicoma River, that enters the Coos from the north. At various times of the year, this region has four principal areas that produce striped bass for anglers. Fishing for them takes place on Isthmus Slough; on Coos River-Millicoma River and Catching Slough; in Coos Bay at various tributary mouths and Haynes Inlet; and at the inlet of Coos Bay to the Pacific as well as South Slough. In 1985, a 40-pound 2-ounce striped bass was taken from the Millicoma River. Catches from Coos Bay dominated Oregon's striped bass fishing from the 1940s to 1960, and then began to deteriorate. However, since 1970 the major emphasis has shifted 20 miles farther north along the coast to Winchester Bay and the Umpqua River.

The first regulations to affect the recreational fishery were established in 1946 when the limit was 15 fish per day, but with no minimum size limit. In 1950, it was reduced to five fish. The minimum size limit of 16 inches wasn't set until 1961. In 1978, when commercial fishing was eliminated, anglers in Oregon were restricted to three fish per day 16 inches or longer. However, with a continued overall decline along the entire coast, the limit is now two fish per day, 30 inches or longer. The season is open throughout the year with the exception of Coos Bay and Millicoma River where it is closed while striped bass spawn, in April, May, and June.

While some striped bass fishing in Oregon is done in the actual rivers, most is done in the tidal estuaries, in either all-saline or brackish areas that are still under the influence of a tidal rise and fall. There is no surf fishery because of the rugged nature of the Pacific Coast in the state. Fishing techniques are basically similar to those in San Francisco Bay: baitfishing with cut fish, or live-bait fishing with bullheads (sculpins) and shrimp. It is done either from shore or from boats. Anglers working from boats plug and jig for the fish or troll rigged baits. However, both Umpqua and Coos bays, especially the former, have become centers for fly fishing for striped bass, especially when they are in the rivers. Some of the fly patterns developed on these waters have proven effective wherever striped bass are found.

Migration studies in Coos Bay and Umpqua River were conducted in the early 1960s, but because the number of fish tagged was so small, there was little knowledge gained from the efforts. However, a few patterns were established that are similar to other endemic populations on both Atlantic and Pacific coasts. There are two bass migrations in Coos Bay, a spawning migration upstream in the spring and a second migration to sloughs in the bay in the fall. Two to three weeks after spawning, the adult fish drop down river into the bay and apparently leave the bay for the open ocean, because the bay is almost devoid of big fish until fall. The fall migration sees bass return and winter in the sloughs. Large fish may spend the summer along the outside beaches and take short coastal migrations like large bass in San Francisco Bay. They may even take extended runs, but it is unlikely, because commercial angling with otter trawls, long-lines, shark nets, crab pots, and even salmon trolls have not yielded striped bass off the beach.

Spawning takes place from about the middle of May and lasts until the end of June. Spawning locations in this system are confined to an area where South Fork Coos River meets Millicoma River and about a mile south of this junction on Coos River. As the eggs develop they drift downstream to an area near Enegrin Ferry. Hatching occurs in 48 to 72 hours and young larvae remain in this part of the river for a week to ten days. Young fry and juvenile bass feed in the bay and do not take part in migrations until they have sexually matured.

Like all striped bass fisheries, the size of their populations are often determined by dominant year class production. Records are sparse on annual production of young-of-the year. Historically, such year classes have occurred in Coos Bay in 1940 and again 18 years later, in 1958. The lack of subsequent dominant year classes in juvenile production has caused fishing to deteriorate in Coos Bay, and no dominant year class has occurred since 1958. In 1966, there was an excellent dominant year class of fish produced in Umpqua Bay and was the main reason recreational fishing shifted in the 1970s away from Coos to Umpqua Bay. However, 1966 was also the last time a dominant year class was produced there.

As part of the state's striped bass restoration plan, 50,000 yearlings were released into the Coos River system in 1992. Oregon was also the benefactor in California's change in stocking rationale and received an added 30,000 finger- lings that year. An addition 5,000 yearlings will be released in 1993. The Coos Basin Plan now calls for the annual release of 5,000 fingerlings and 20,000 yearlings beginning in 1994. An analysis of the Coos River habitat revealed that while it had undergone some physical changes, it was still under-utilized by striped bass. The stockings are designed to provide brood stock in a effort to increase the chances of natural reproduction reoccurring. The goal of a popula- tion of 20,000 to 25,000 adults in this system cannot be achieved by stocking alone, and its eventual attainment will rely on natural production.

Catch of yearling striped bass during recruitment surveys in the Coos River system, 1978-1992.

Year	Coos and Millicoma Rivers		S. Coos River.		Combined		
	Seine Hauls	Catch	Seine Hauls	Catch	Seine Hauls	Catch Total	Catch per-effort
1978	47	0	48	0	95	0	0.00
1979	30	1	31	12	61	13	0.21
1980	48	0	53	0	101	0	0.00
1981	35	0	47	0	82	0	0.00
1982	40	6	56	4	96	10	0.10
1983	40	0	70	1	110	1	0.01
1984	44	2	63	1	107	3	0.03
1985	44	13	70	5	114	18	0.16
1986	40	3	56	0	96	3	0.03
1987	40	4	53	0	93	4	0.04
1988	39	0	56	0	95	0	0.00
1989	36	5	57	3	93	8	0.09
1990	27	8	45	0	72	8	0.11
1991	54	66	66	33	120	99	0.83
1992	55	148	66	63	121	211	1.74

It's only natural that the more fish there are available to be caught, the more anglers will be fishing for them. In Oregon, like in California, the fishing effort increases with growing numbers of fish and decreases when they become scarce. A good example was an angler census in 1972 when striped bass fishing dramatically increased on the Umpqua River. Catch per angler effort was estimated from the census. About 31,500 angler-days were expended that year and produced about 6,000 striped bass. The following year, 1973, the number of bass caught dropped to 3,300 because anglers, maybe sensing that the fishing was falling off, spent only 21,700 angler-days on the water. Data on Coos Bay are skimpy. All we do know is that in 1950, about 1,200 anglers caught 2,500 bass. Not bad for a couple of milk cans filled with fry. However, since dominant year classes have been missing in Oregon waters for so long a period, the fishery has been maintained naturally at low levels and no one knows what the future holds in store for both fish and fishermen. A study in 1992 estimated that there are less than 1,000 adult striped bass now on the Coos.

Hermaphroditism in Oregon Striped Bass

As an interesting side note, Oregon research on sexing striped bass taken when commercial fishing was allowed revealed a considerable amount of hermaphroditism in the population in Coos Bay. Almost three percent of the bass samples in a 1950 study were found to possess gonads for both sexes. Occasionally both ovaries and testes were ripe. In all examples, male organs or testes formed the anterior portion of the glands and the ovaries formed the posterior section. In either case, testes and ovaries were both ripe at spawning time. However, more recent sex sampling has revealed that 33 percent of adult striped bass in the Coos were hermaphrodites.

The continued increase in hermaphroditism has been suggested by some Oregon researchers as a possible partial cause for the decline of striped bass in the Coos River system. Their reasoning is that hermaphrodites are usually unsuccessful spawners as females, and when one-third of the stock goes through the machinations of spawning and doesn't succeed, this represents a large reduction in the potential year class even before it is born. Thus, the brood stock is just two-thirds of the total adult female population.

This high degree of hermaphroditism, suggested by some geneticists, may be the result of inbreeding since the initial population probably began with a small number of fish that wandered north from San Francisco Bay. While this may be the case, it doesn't account for the same opportunities that were available to other San Joaquin-Sacramento stock that drifted into Winchester Bay and its Umpqua River system just 25 miles father north. Striped bass there had similar origins and do not exhibit this same problem. The degree of hermaphroditism there is 2 to 3 percent, similar to what it is in California fish as well some in striped bass populations on the East Coast.

While the reason for hermaphroditism may remain obscure on the Coos

River system, the more probable reasons for a decline in year-class numbers are the effects of the lumber industry and its log handling and transport that occurs on the lower river and bay, and the continued deepening and widening of river channels.

WASHINGTON

There is no defined fishery in the state. Occasionally, striped bass are taken near the mouth of the Columbia River or in Willapa Bay, and an occasional fish is caught in Holmes Harbor on Whidbey Island in Puget Sound. At one time, a few juvenile fish were seen on the Columbia, but little else has been noted and the fishery is virtually unexplored and unidentified. Even stray fish along the outside beaches are now a rarity. They were more numerous when production was high in California and Oregon waters but with production levels and populations now depressed in these states, there are almost no striped bass seen along the Washington coast or its marine estuaries.

8

Striped Bass
in Fresh Water

Even early colonists knew from their non-scientific observations that when striped bass ascended the rivers to spawn, they spent a part of their lives in fresh water. Throughout most of the Southeast and Gulf Coast states, biologists as well as anglers have always known that striped bass there lived more of their lives in fresh than in salt water. In several rivers in Alabama and Mississippi, striped bass are only found hundreds of miles from salt water and have never developed the penchant to reach it.

However, many persons in the past, even some biologists, erroneously assumed that at least once a year, or maybe even only once in their lives, striped bass descended from their freshwater environment for a kind of rejuvenation of sorts in salt water. Then they returned to live upstream. Striped bass always had access to salt water but no one even considered the idea that these fish, out of their own volition, had decided to give up the saltwater phase of their lives and return to a more primordial routine. Or maybe those striped bass of our southern waters had never even gone to sea like their brethren along the northern part of the Atlantic range.

It was therefore quite startling to many people when a collection of events began to unfold in a South Carolina reservoir. Quite by accident, a funny thing happened on the way to the ocean. In a vast program of rural electrification of the United States during the 1930s and 1940s, Southern and Central states began harnessing their rivers with hydroelectric dams. South Carolina's needs turned to two rivers not far from the coast, the Santee and Cooper rivers, and here they created a double reservoir. On November 12, 1941, gates of Pinopolis Dam were closed, and reservoir lakes Marion and Moultrie, connected by a 6-mile diversion canal, began to fill.

Lake Moultrie (the lower lake) had been cleared of trees, and Lake Marion would be cleared after the gates were closed because it could take more than a year to fill the reservoirs. But along came the war and the demand for electrical power intensified. The lake was filled as quickly as possible and the timber was left standing. Any fish in the streams became incidental to the urgency.

These two rivers had always produced good largemouth bass fishing, along with some steady panfishing. As always after a reservoir is formed, angling for the first several years is phenomenal and this reservoir was no different. Ironically, striped bass also inhabited the original fresh-water river sections of the new reservoirs and had always traveled farther up their courses to spawn. Unknowingly at first, some striped bass were also trapped behind the dam and also grew large, like the largemouth bass. Though striped bass, or rockfish as they were originally called by local anglers, were few and far between during those first years, the fish caught were huge.

Then, during 1948 and 1949, seven to eight years after the dam was first closed, striped bass fishing also began to pick up in quantity. However, instead of the catch being composed of the behemoths trapped in the reservoirs in the first few years, a great variety of sizes began to show, even fingerling striped bass.

These smaller fish meant that new fish were being produced. But everyone knew that striped bass were anadromous fish and that anadromous fish must spend a part of their life cycle in salt water. How could this be? The single lock on the dam did open occasionally throughout the year for the few boats that traveled up and down the river. However, they weren't open for a duration that would support the large influx of striped bass that would be needed to come up from the ocean and perpetuate the population of the reservoir with young fish. Besides, the bass moved up from the sea, actually the brackish-water estuary, for only two or three weeks in the spring. The chances of the gates being open at the correct time were considered too small to be the explanation.

For all practical purposes, striped bass now behind the dam had been cut off from the ocean and became a puzzlement to fishermen and the state's game managers. South Carolina biologists began to study the phenomenon, beginning with a tagging program. Six hundred striped bass were caught below the dam, tagged, and released in its tailrace. Results showed that the Cooper River supported an endemic group of striped bass that made their home between Charleston Harbor and Pinopolis Dam.

The next study showed that young-of-the-year, that is, striped bass produced in the spring, could be captured by nets along the shore of the reservoir above the dam throughout the summer and fall. From the vast numbers netted, biologists believed that the entire population of the double reservoir could be estimated. They determined that there was no way a sufficient number of striped bass could have come through the locks to spawn and produce this horde of young-of-the-year fish.

The final determination concluded that striped bass on the Santee-Cooper Reservoir had indeed become landlocked and were producing their own young without a need to return to salt water for a part of their life cycle. It did, however, pose another question that may never be answered. How did the landlocked strain of striped bass develop? Had it been the result of the dam, and had these fish spawned on what may have been primordial spawning grounds? Or had these striped bass already eliminated the trek to salt water, for all intents and purposes passing the complete cycle of their lives in an up-river environment? Had this new cycle started now or thousands of years before the dam was built?

About 1950, a sudden increase began in the number of striped bass being caught in the reservoir. The increase turned into an explosion. The fishing was fantastic over the next several years. Anglers were taking striped bass at a rate of better than five fish per trip. It was too good to continue.

The cause of the population explosion was the availability of a great food supply for striped bass in the form of threadfin and gizzard shad and herring. But, while bass were repopulating themselves, these forage fish were not. The dam had also effectively cut off their supply of brood stock. Fishing began to fall, and finally the state's biologists put their fingers on the diminishing food supply as the cause. This was simply corrected by allowing shad and herring spawners to come through the locks during their annual migrations up the river from salt water. During March, the locks at Pinopolis Dam were opened twice a day. This let spawning-bent herring and shad into the lower lake to spawn and created more food for the bass, and in addition the adults themselves were trapped and contributed vastly to the food supply. Since then, the population has risen and annual locking-through of food re-established a balance between predator and food fish.

At the same time Santee-Cooper Reservoir was established, other reservoirs were being built throughout South Carolina. After they became stabilized their indigenous fish populations also increased, but the rough fish overshadowed the game fish, glutting these impoundments with their numbers. The solution was to add striped bass as a fish controller. Gizzard and threadfin shad were the real culprits, and striped bass, because they could feed on the adults of these species as well as fry, loved them.

Adult striped bass that came up the Santee River to spawn in the tail-race of the dam were netted and transplanted to other reservoirs in the state. The bass went to work on the shad. However, self-sustaining populations could not be developed on these reservoir systems. Only Santee-Cooper had the precisely correct water environment above the dam to produce its own supply of new fish. What South Carolina now needed was a steady supply of fish for stocking the newer impoundments. The spawning fish that appeared in the tail-race were not enough to meet the growing demand from other states. An expansive striped bass hatchery was needed.

Before the turn of the century, North Carolina had established a successful striped bass hatchery on the Roanoke River and has since continued to hatch bass taken from Roanoke Rapids as they come up-river to spawn. It employed an armada of fishermen using large landing nets to catch the fish and sell them immediately to the hatchery. South Carolina patterned its Moncks Corners Hatchery, next to the Pinopolis Dam tailrace, after the one at Roanoke Rapids. With a few innovations, it was ready to begin producing striped bass for all its reservoirs that couldn't create their own natural production and for a host of states that were about to begin striped bass introduction but with no source of their own for stocking.

Still another problem crept up in the fishery. South Carolina couldn't obtain many fish in a ripe condition from which to take eggs and milt. North Carolina was lucky because it had such a vast supply of fish on the Roanoke River and anglers were paid to bring ripe fish, netted at the Rapids, immediately to the hatchery where they were stripped.

South Carolina's problem was how to get fish in a ripe state. One researcher, Bob Stevens, had heard of work being done in Alabama with injections of a human hormone—chorionic gonadotropin (HCG)—gathered from urine of pregnant women that caused fish eggs inside a gravid female bass to ripen quickly and ovulate in a matter of days. The technique was then refined at Moncks Corners by Stevens, who used HCG on striped bass, and one of the most successful striped bass hatcheries in the nation was under way.

For years, natural reproduction on Santee-Cooper was able to sustain an extremely active sportfishery. However, it began a slow decline in the early 1980s. Annual natural production in the reservoir varies widely and the state was forced to begin stocking hatchery-reared fingerlings to sustain a sport fishery. Factors causing the reduced natural production have never been isolated with any degree of certainty, but a change of water quality at the spawning sites and agricultural water use have been suggested as possible factors. Nowadays, annual stockings supplement natural reproduction and dominate the fish population.

INTRODUCTION OF STRIPED BASS
TO FRESH WATER IN OTHER STATES

News of success on Santee-Cooper spread throughout the scientific journals, newspapers, and magazines. All states with large impoundments and expanding rough-fish problems began looking toward striped bass as a solution. As a result, striped bass, in the period from 1955 to 1975, were introduced in 36 impoundments from Georgia to California and from Tennessee to Louisiana and Texas. In the 20 states working with striped bass in fresh water reservoirs, 16 have been successful in establishing natural reproduction. However, in several, the volume is not great enough to sustain a recreational fishery must be augmented with stocked fish. These lakes and reservoirs include:

> Santee-Cooper Reservoir, South Carolina
> Kerr (Buggs Island) Reservoir, North Carolina
> Keystone Reservoir, Oklahoma
> Texoma Reservoir, Oklahoma and Texas
> Lake Whiting, Texas
> Lake Possum Kingdom, Texas
> Toledo Bend Reservoir, Texas and Louisiana
> Liberty Reservoir, Maryland
> Piney Run Reservoir, Maryland
> Dardanelle Reservoir, Arkansas
> Seminole Reservoir, Georgia
> New Hogan Lake, California
> Lake Havasu (Colorado River), California and Arizona
> Lake Mohave (Colorado River), Nevada and Arizona
> Lake Meade (Colorado River), Nevada and Arizona
> Lake Powell (Colorado River), Arizona and Utah

Moncks Corner Hatchery, established on the Santee River below Pinopolis Dam, which forms the Santee-Cooper Reservoir. Striped bass migrating up the river to spawn on these ancestral sites are shocked and netted, and the eggs and milt are taken and artifically fertilized. The eggs are hatched out in the jars shown inside the hatchery. Young striped bass produced here are used to establish freshwater fisheries in environments where natural reporduction cannot take place.

Today, nearly 85 lakes and reservoirs, as well as several coastal rivers emptying into the Gulf of Mexico, have established or reestablished striped bass fisheries. States in which freshwater striped bass populations have been established are:

Alabama	Maryland
Arizona-Nevada	Mississippi
Arkansas	Missouri
California	Nebraska
Florida	North Carolina
Georgia	Oklahoma
Illinois	South Carolina
Kansas	Tennessee
Kentucky	Texas
Louisiana	Virginia

ALABAMA

Striped bass existed in the headwaters of several Alabama rivers—similar to streams in Mississippi and Georgia—that flowed south and eventually into the Gulf of Mexico. These populations were composed of the original striped bass strains that some 20,000 years ago were forced southward by the advancing continental glaciers that changed the sub-tropic to temperate waters. As the glaciers retreated north some 10,000 years ago, so did those fish in these rivers. However, their existence, because of being trapped in an environment that was warmer than ideal, was tenuous even before the expansion of hydroelectric facilities began in the 1950s and 1960s.

These impoundments drastically changed the ecologies of the rivers and while some natural reproduction might still be occurring, it has not made any significant or even discernible contribution to striped bass stocks in the reservoirs. The picture is even further clouded by the extensive stocking that has taken place in the reservoirs during the last two decades and even further masked by the activities of hybrids involving white bass, that may overwhelm any natural reproduction.

The first attempt to start a self-sustaining population of striped bass in Alabama occurred in 1965 when 190 coastal (marine) fish were stocked in 40,000-acre Lake Martin, near Alexander City in the east-central part of the state. The reservoir was formed by damming the Tallapoosa River near Red Hill. Biologists hoped that the fish would utilize the Tallapoosa River, upstream of Jay Creek and Erwin Shoals, that appeared to satisfy all the requirements for natural reproduction. Over the next decade, nearly 100,000 addition fingerlings were added, but there was no evidence that natural reproduction ever occurred.

However, fish up to 30 pounds taken by anglers are not uncommon and Lake Martin today is probably the state's best land-locked striped bass fishery.

Four years after the initial Lake Martin stockings began, Alabama expanded its program with fingerlings obtained from South Carolina. They were stocked in Mitchell, Jordan and Jones Bluff reservoirs. Because of ecological changes in Jordan, stocking was halted in 1980, and for the same reasons, in Mitchell in 1984. Jones Bluff, however, proved a successful environment for striped bass and today it supports one of Alabama's best striped bass fisheries.

During the following decade, stockings were made in 27 other impoundments throughout the state. Some were continued for several years, but today, annual stockings take place in only 15 reservoirs and rivers. These are: Big Creek, Claiborne, Coffeeville, Inland, Jones Bluff, Lay, Lewis Smith, Logan Martin, Martin, Millers Ferry, Mobile Delta, Neely Henry, Thurlow, Wheeler, and Yates. The longest stocking and in heaviest numbers occurs on Jones Bluff, Lay, Lewis Smith, Logan Martin, Martin and Millers Ferry reservoirs.

Alabama eventually developed its own hatchery system and today most of its stock is produced in the Marion Fish Hatchery. Striped bass are stocked as fry, advanced fingerlings of Gulf Coast strain striped bass. Gulf Coast strain stocks are unique in that they are derived from breeders obtained from the Apalachicola River in Florida where the original strain of Gulf Coast fish still reproduce naturally. Those designated fry and advanced fingerlings are progeny of stocks originally obtained from South Carolina.

Before reservoir construction began, the largest striped bass landed in Alabama was a 55-pounder taken in 1955 on the Tuscaloosa River and was an old Gulf Coast strain fish. The new record, for a stocked fish, is a 52-pounder, ironically taken near the same spot, on the same river. It was analyzed as a stocked fish that escaped its impoundment. The only true river stocking now taking place is on the Alabama River, below Claiborne, the last downstream dam on the river.

ARIZONA-NEVADA

Colorado River Striped Bass—The Colorado River rises in north-central Colorado, flows west into Utah, then south into Arizona, then west and south again until it forms the border between Arizona and Nevada, then Arizona and California. What water is left eventually flows through a small portion of Mexico and into the Gulf of California. Between 1962 and 1969 both Arizona and California game and fish departments combined their efforts in a program to establish a striped bass fishery on the Colorado River, between Davis and Parker dams. Davis Dam, that forms the reservoir Lake Mohave, is at the up-stream section of this area and was completed in 1953. Parker Dam forms Lake Havasu, and the Colorado River flows 78 miles from Davis Dam to where it enters

Havasu Lake. Lake Mead is the reservoir formed behind Hoover Dam when it was completed in 1935, and while it forms a common border between Arizona and Nevada, a large bay (Overton Arm) extends entirely into Nevada. As a result, the greater part of the reservoir is in Nevada.

Nine stockings of assorted sizes of striped bass fingerlings and yearlings were planted in the flowing part of the Colorado River between Davis Dam and Lake Havasu between August, 1962, and August, 1964. The stock for these fish came from California. In 1969, an additional planting of fish was received from Moncks Corners, S.C. and reared at a hatchery in Page Springs, Ariz.

As early as 1964, striped bass made late spring migrations to the tail-waters of the Davis Dam to spawn. However, there was no evidence of a successful spawn until 1969. Then, in 1970, a strong year-class was produced. The spawning took place from May to mid-June in an area about 10 miles below Davis Dam, now appears to be the primary spawning grounds selected by these Colorado River striped bass.

Catching stripers on the Colorado River was a rarity until 1966 when anglers finally located the fish and figured out how to catch them. In 1974, fishermen switched to whole and cut anchovies, and now almost any angler can catch them with the right bait. The Bullhead City Striped Bass Derby has become an annual affair, and two other derbies in the area have been initiated. And, with the great number of retirees moving to this area, many one-time striped bass anglers from the Northeast have caused the interest to burgeon in striped bass fishing.

Nevada—Striped bass are now in all three reservoirs as well as the Muddy (Maopa) and Virgin River systems, tributaries to the Colorado that flow into the upper end of the Overton Arm in Nevada. The striped bass fishery in Lake Mohave is still quite undeveloped and catches are minimal compared to Lake Mead. There are, however, a few large fish. Successful natural spawning is occurring in the reservoir, probably at the headwaters that begin almost with tail race waters from Lake Mead. The potential for an excellent fishery exists here.

Striped bass have been the dominant game fish in Lake Mead since 1982. In 1986, they made up more than 70 percent of the catch, but dropped in 1988 to just under 60 percent. Heavy stocking of striped bass, along with rainbow trout, took place in 1969. Arizona biologist, erroneously believed that because striped bass were ocean-dwelling fish that needed large rivers with mild temperatures to spawn, their numbers would be limited to those stocked and could thus be controlled if they became a challenge to the trout that selected a deeper, colder environment in the reservoir.

The trout thrived and by 1974 the harvest reached 130,000 fish per year, with some trophy-size fish. The striped bass fishery, however, responded slowly and by 1975 only 2,500 had been caught. Suddenly, there appeared signs that the ocean fish—that wasn't supposed to be reproducing on its own—was doing it, and with great gusto. By 1979, over 576,000 striped bass were landed by anglers.

However, as the bass grew, they consumed the threadfin shad population and then eliminated the trout population. The bass had literally eaten themselves out of house and home. By 1981 the population crashed and only 18,000 fish were caught.

The problem of sufficient food for striped bass was because of the reservoir's low fertility and cold water. Various plans have been suggested to increase water temperatures by diverting incoming water from warm-water reservoirs or by fertilizing the lake. One solution would negatively impacted upon cold-water species in Lake Mead and the other had an expensive price tag. Arizona and Nevada biologist know that Lake Mead has unusual problems and that puts it into the same category as other Colorado River reservoirs.

While the fishery today doesn't produce the numbers it did in the late 1970s, it's still fairly substantial as exhibited by the state-wide 10-fish and 20-fish daily limits on Lake Powell. The state's largest striped bass is a 59-pound 12-ounce fish taken in 1977 in the Colorado River south of Bullhead City

ARKANSAS

Like many other states where the Corps of Engineers has been active since the 1930s, Arkansas is now endowed with a collection of large reservoirs where there once were only river systems. And, as in many reservoir situations after river impoundment, threadfin and gizzard shad multiplied beyond control. To control populations of these fish, Arkansas as early as 1956 began a program to establish striped bass in its waters. The first attempts involved trucking adult fish from South Carolina, but the mortality rate was so high that this method was abandoned.

In 1966, Arkansas sent its biologists to Albemarle Sound in North Carolina, where they netted striped bass and artificially stimulated ovulation with chorionic gonadotropin. They were able to produce a batch of fertilized eggs and raise them to the fry stage. The fry were then flown to a state fish hatchery in Lonoke, Arkansas.

The resulting fingerlings, in the fall of that year, were planted in the Dardanelle Reservoir on the Arkansas River. During subsequent years, Dardanelle, as well as other reservoirs throughout the state, has received additional stockings of striped bass. To date, eight reservoirs—Maumelle, Ouachita, Beaver, Norfolk, Hamilton, Greeson, Alabama-Carbon Hill, and Catherine lakes—provide a striped bass fishery. In 1973, definite natural repro-duction on one system, the Arkansas River, had taken place. The main im-poundment in this fishery is the Dardanelle Reservoir. Other reservoirs are supported by annual stockings of hatchery fish. However, Dardanelle Reservoir has not been stocked since. The largest striped bass landed in Arkansas is a 53-pound fish taken from Bull Shoals in May 1987.

CALIFORNIA

The first striped bass to be stocked in California arrived by train from the Navesink River in New Jersey in 1879. The milk cans filled with fingerlings were planted in the San Joaquin-Sacramento Delta. A few years later, part of an additional shipment did make it into a few nearby reservoirs but nothing was ever heard of the fish. A far more serious reservoir-stocking program took place in the mid-1960s when fish were purposely planted in impoundments where reproduction was unlikely and where continued stocking would be needed to maintain a sport fishery. Today, these include Camp Far West Reservoir on Bear River, a tributary to the Feather River that eventually flows into the Sacramento River, Lake Mendocino on the Russian River, Millerton Lake on the San Joaquin, San Antonio Reservoir and Santa Margarita Lake, the outlets of which flow into the Salinas River.

California has water unique to the state—large temporary "ponds" or reservoirs that hold potential irrigation water stored in them in the spring, then drawn down, redistributed, and used throughout summer and fall as water is needed. Some of these impoundments never really run dry and hold striped bass throughout the year as reservoir and aqueduct fisheries. Striped bass entered these holding waters quite by accident, as fingerlings that migrated upstream from the Delta, as much as 60 miles away. Miraculously, they made it through pumps and turbines and some grew to astonishing sizes.

The most phenomenal of these was a 67.5-pound landlocked striper that was landed May 7, 1992, by Hank Ferguson. He was fishing O'Neil Forebay of the San Luis reservoir. This fish is the largest freshwater striped bass ever landed. These reservoirs and canals are part of the of the Federal Central Valley Project, State Water Project and the Contra Costa Water District Project. The San Luis Reservoir is at the head of California Aqueduct, which also has a population of striped bass; Pyramid Reservoir on the Piru River near Los Angeles; and Silverwood Lake. Of all these reservoirs and lakes, only one has all the unique characteristics to create a self-sustaining population of striped bass and that is New Hogan Lake, the outlet of which empties into that Mokelumme Aqueduct and eventually into the San Joaquin River 60 miles away.

FLORIDA

All of Florida's striped bass, on both, Atlantic and Gulf coasts, are riverine rather than anadromous fish, and no transcoastal migrations are known to have occurred in modern times. This riverine behavior is the result of temperature requirements established by the species. Naturally occurring populations and reproduction take place in three rivers systems on Florida's Atlantic Coast—St. Marys, St. Johns, and Nassau rivers, and on the Gulf of Mexico coast in the

Apalachicola River system. Occasional striped bass spawning occurs in Suwannee, Ochlockonee, Choctawhatchee, Escambia, and Blackwater rivers, also along the Gulf Coast, have been verified. The most productive rivers are the St. Marys and Nassau, but the biggest fish (66 pounds) came from the Apalachicola.

Because Florida is on the extreme southern edge of favorable striped bass habitat, its naturally occurring populations have always been limited by production restrictions incurred this far south. Thermal refuges are required during summer months for adult populations to survive. Young striped bass are more tolerant of high temperatures and can survive them as high as 80 degrees. Larger fish, however, cannot live for long periods in temperatures above 70 degrees. Florida's numerous cold, well-oxygenated springs thus become important striped bass respites in hot weather.

Striped bass spawning requirements in Florida are unique and seldom fully satisfied. Biologists estimate that fewer than 500 striped bass would be taken annually by anglers if the fisheries were not supported by annual stockings. Spawning on the Apalachicola River, though limited, takes place up stream (where its name changes to Flint River) near Bainbridge.

Florida's freshwater striped bass program began in the summer of 1968 when the Fresh Water Game Commission stocked six separate bodies. Even though Florida has some indigenous freshwater striped bass stocks, the source of the initial stock came from South Carolina's Moncks Corners Hatchery. The Division of Fisheries went out of state because during an earlier attempt, striped bass from Florida's two freshwater river populations, St. Johns and Apalachicola, were tried but were unsuccessful. By 1970, its biologists had developed the scientific technology needed for hatchery production of striped bass.

During the first year, Lakes Hollingsworth, Talquin, and Underhil, received young fish. In 1969, Lakes Hunter, Parker, and Bentley were stocked. Growth of the fish in these lakes was rapid and bass were around 11 inches long after the first year. When Florida's hatcheries went into production, large-scale stockings were made in St. Johns and Ochlockonee rivers and Lake Talquin.

The results of stockings, supplementing natural production, now allows anglers to harvest several thousand fish annually. Creel censuses each spring show that over 1,000 striped bass are taken from the Ochlockonee, 1,200 from the Apalachicola and over 2,000 fish from the St. Johns rivers. Because of the demand for thermal refuges most of Florida's freshwater bass are located in rivers with springs and in deeper lakes like Talquin.

GEORGIA

At one time, all of Georgia's coastal streams—Savannah (shared with South Carolina), Ogeechee, Altamaha, Satilla, and St. Marys (shared with Florida)—had some degree of striped bass populations. The only rivers that had substantial populations, however, were Savannah and Ogeechee rivers. But illegal harvesting of striped bass and intense recreational fishing, combined with industrialization, pollution, dam construction and harbor navigation enhancement projects, caused populations to decline on most rivers. Especially affected was the Savannah River, where striped bass population had been falling drastically since the late 1970s, until recently (1989-92).

Today, only the Ogeechee River has retained its breeding population, and has become the primary source of brood stock for the Department of Natural Resources stocking program. However, annual introductions of fingerling striped bass since 1989 to the Savannah River are having a positive impact on the abundance of these fish. The outlook for the population to rebuild, according to Reggie Weaver, a Georgia fisheries biologists involved in the program, is promising though it may take eight to ten more years before riverine striped bass populations can return to pre-decline levels. To insure as rapid a rebuilding of stocks as possible, striped bass are currently being fully protected on the Savannah River.

With the advent of reservoir-building and subsequent demand for a fish to reduce gizzard shad populations, biologists in Georgia also turned to striped bass. Georgia's initial attempts began in 1966 when Lake Nottely, in the northern part of the state, was stocked with 125 (2-3 inch) fingerlings. Lake Blackshear, a reservoir on the Flint River that eventually flows into the Apalachicola in Florida, was stocked the following year with 51 sub-adult and adult striped bass. Some of the fish were 30 pounds in weight and biologists hoped to establish a self-sustaining population. However, natural reproduction never took place because the correct environmental requirements were missing, notably cool, oxygen-rich areas where the fish could escape summer heat. The impoundment's summer temperatures rose too high for striped bass. There was conjecture at one time that some stocked striped bass had escaped the reservoir and lived for a period in the upper Flint River. There was no evidence to support this. Today, there are no striped bass in either the river or the reservoir. The Blackshear appears to be just too shallow and too far south in the fish's range to maintain a year-long fishery.

Next to be stocked was Lake Seminole, on the lower Flint, where it, too, eventually flows out the impoundment into Florida as the Apalachicola River. Here as well, stocking success was made difficult for the same "heated" reasons. However, a moderate population of striped bass exists today on the reservoir and on the Flint River, one of the reservoir's main tributaries, where a limited natural reproduction takes place near Albany.

Lake Burton in northeast Georgia was stocked twice, in 1969 and 1973. Even though it's almost as far north in Georgia as one can get, factors other than summer heat eliminated striped bass in this small reservoir. The most notable of these is the lack of headwater, or stream miles and water flow above this lake and other similar impoundments, in spring to allow sufficient time for egg hatching—normally four to five days in 58-degree water—before the eggs are swept into the currentless reservoirs. There, they eventually settle to the bottom and suffocate because the eggs are heavier than water. Another factor that stopped more stocking of striped bass was that the availability of forage fish (gizzard shad) was being reduced by a large, existing population of predator fishes.

The big boost in Georgia's program to develop a fresh-water striped bass fishery came in 1969 when, in cooperation with the U.S. Fish & Wildlife Service, 111,028 fingerlings were stocked in Lakes Sinclair and Jackson. These reservoirs are in the center of the state. Since then, Georgia has constructed its own striped bass hatchery at Richmond Hill, on the Ogeechee River, close to where adult striped bass can be intercepted on their spawning runs. Here, some fish are raised to fingerling size while other fry are shipped to five other state hatcheries, and at least one federal hatchery, before being stocked into reservoirs. The hatchery annually produces 7-9 million striped bass fry and 13-16 million hybrid bass.

The aim of Georgia's striped bass program has changed, like that of many other states since the mid-1960s when striped bass were introduced into fresh water. Its original goals were to develop cost-free, self-sustaining populations. Today, its efforts are directed to maintain quality fishing in impoundments by stocking striped bass that can be supported by the existing forage base and are compatible with other sport fishes. Limited successful natural spawning has occurred in several Georgia locations but none with the capability of producing self-sustaining populations.

When these initial efforts produced less-than-anticipated fisheries on Jackson, Sinclair and Blackshear, other reservoirs were tried. Many failed, but success did eventually come but only in deeper impoundments in the northern half of the state. Today, Georgia anglers have excellent freshwater striped bass fishing in five reservoirs, and in the others, where striped bass found summer conditions intolerable, substantial striped bass/white bass hybrid populations were established.

Allatoona Reservoir, on the Etowah River in northwest Georgia, is close to the metropolitan Atlanta area. The striped bass population established an equilibrium with its food supply in this nearly 12,000-acre impoundment. Most striped bass in the reservoir are less than 20 pounds, though fish as large as 40 pounds are not uncommon. Better catches of larger fish are made during the winter months, and anglers able to locate cool, oxygenated water during the summer can still take fish. The alternative to deep-water fishing is to move one's activities to the river, above the reservoir, and fish the numerous side creeks.

Samples of striped bass taken in the fall of 1991 showed that striped bass in Clarks Hill (J. Strom Thurmond) Reservoir, on the Savannah River, were doing well and resulted in the second highest catch rate in six years. Angling here has been best in winter and spring and also includes fish populations on the Little

River, near Raysville. Lake Hartwell, also on the Savannah River and above Clarks Hill Reservoir in northeast Georgia, shares the border with South Carolina, and is one of the largest reservoirs in the state with nearly 56,000 surface acres. Striper fishing here was excellent in 1992 due to the increased stocking efforts of the Georgia Department of Natural Resources. Although there are trophy-size striped bass (10- to 40-pounders) on Hartwell, about 95 percent of the 1992 catch weighed less than 2 pounds. The number of big fish is likely to increase in the near future because fishing pressures are so light and this huge reservoir has an abundance of forage fish.

Lake Juliette (Rum Creek Fishing Area) is a relatively small reservoir on Rum Creek in central Georgia, just north of Macon. It has a small watershed, clear water, and though it suffers extensive aquatic plant growth, it is rather infertile when compared to other impoundments. As a result, the stocking rate of striped bass here has been at low levels because of the limited food supply. However, an abundance of cool water, even in the summer, has produced a small but popular fishery. Striped bass as large as 25 pounds have been taken here with some degree of regularity. It is the only lake in central Georgia with big striped bass.

Lake Lanier is a fairly substantial reservoir (38,000 acres) located 50 miles northeast of Atlanta. Stocking levels have been quite high since 1989 and the young bass (3-12 pounds) have not reached their potential in quality, that is, big fish. However, they have provided excellent action throughout 1992 because of their numbers. Some of the 1989 stocked fish reached 15 pounds during 1992 and there are still many fish from earlier stockings to provide the occasional 20- and 30-pounders.

Lake Nottely, a 4,180-acre mountain reservoir on Nottely River, almost on the Georgia-North Carolina border, has produced some of the largest freshwater striped bass in the state. It is just a few miles from the state's highest peak, Brasstown Bald, at 4,784 feet, and consequently cooler temperatures, especially during summer months, might have something to do with the fish's growth. Harvest of striped bass stocked in 1991 was excellent and it should continue as they reach 8 to 10 pounds during the next three years. Fish of 5 to 15 pounds dominated catches in 1992. The number of striped bass over 20 pounds, however, remains low, but the trophy-size fish, including a few 50-pounders, have continued to show up periodically. Two 50-pounders were caught and released by fisheries personnel in 1991. The International Game Fish Association's landlocked striped bass record is a 41-pound 11-ounce fish taken in the Flint River, near Albany, in 1986. The state record, however, is a 63-pounder taken from the Oconee River in 1967.

Recreational catches have been best during the spring when striped bass run up the Nottely River. Observers have witnessed striped bass attempting to spawn here in April; however, there is no evidence to date that spawning has been successful.

ILLINOIS

Illinois began its stocking program with striped bass in 1984 with the release of fingerlings, obtained from Virginia and South Carolina, in Lake Sangchris, Braidwood, and Cedar Lake. These are cooling plant reservoirs with no out-flow. The fish did so well that the state began expanding its stocking sites. Today, the state offers anglers various degrees of striped bass fishing in 15 lakes and reservoirs. It considers its top ten best waters to be: Clinton, Crab Orchard, Glenn Shoals, and Hickory lakes, Lakes Bloomington and LaSalle, Otter, Powerton, Rend, and Sangchris lakes. In addition, striped bass can also be taken from Baldwin, Braidwood Mazonia lakes and ponds, Cedar Lake, Charleston Side Channel Lake, Forbes State Lake, Governor Bond and Heidecke lakes, Lakes Jacksonville and Vandalia, and Pittsfield City, Spring, and Washington County lakes.

Illinois is now in the process of reevaluating its striped bass stocking program and plans to maintain the established fisheries but not expand it to include new waters. The largest striped bass taken in the state is a 31-pounder landed in May, 1991, from Heidecke Lake.

KANSAS

Kansas, like many states in the South and Midwest in the 1960s, saw in striped bass a chance to improve not only the variety of fishing it could offer its anglers, and real trophy-size fish to boot, but a way of controlling the explosive population growths of gizzard and threadfin shad in some of its new reservoirs. Kansas' only problem was that it went into a striped bass program only halfheartedly and thereby turned off many anglers who might have become devotees today.

The first effort in 1965 was in the stocking of Wilson Reservoir located west of Salina, almost in the geographic center of the state, with fish from a Texas hatchery. After Wilson, a half-dozen other waters were stocked. However, the stockings were only "a toe in the water," just to see if striped bass would take to Kansas waters and weather. Until 1974, these stockings were small in number and their success poorly investigated and documented. The following year, the Kansas Fish and Game Commission set up a committee to evaluate striped bass in the state's reservoirs. It recommended selecting target reservoirs, then stocking them at the rate of 10 fingerling bass per acre and then evaluating their success with gill-net sampling. These study waters included Cheney, Glen Elder, Milford, Tuttle Creek, Webster, and Wilson reservoirs.

The study was completed in 1980 and concluded that: "Lack of fishing interest in striped bass and high natural mortality rates for adult fish provided [the] rationale for recommendations to end the present program." The study specifically recommended ending stocking in all reservoirs except Wilson Reservoir and suggested that a creel census be done there to determine if the harvest of striped bass was contributing significantly to the total angler harvest. There were some who criticized the report at the time, saying it was biased, influenced by anglers who saw striped bass as a threat to their coveted walleye and sauger fishery. They even delayed the first creel census that wasn't conducted until 1986.

The state's biologists, however, continued stocking Wilson during the interim, because they felt striped bass were contributing substantially to the sportfishing harvest in the reservoir. The problem with most anglers was that they didn't understand striped bass and didn't know how to catch them, but wouldn't admit it. In 1980, a sonar-tracking study of striped bass movements in Wilson Reservoir was initiated. The study revealed that the fish's migrations were predictable with the seasons and even within the time of day. Fishermen were shown how to locate and follow the fish. Thereafter, anglers were able to find and catch them.

Maybe striped bass were ahead of their time in the 1960s and 1970s in Kansas and catching them had to wait for the development of new equipment—sonar fish locators, marine thermometers, downriggers, and loran. Armed with these devices, anglers began catching striped bass regularly and interest in them expanded rapidly.

On the biological side, striped bass populations peaked on Wilson Reservoir in 1981 and began to decline. Young fish showed what some termed as evidence of overcrowding, so the stocking rate was reduced to five instead of ten fish per acre. In the last decade, striped bass became a controversial issue on Wilson. There were petitions circulated by walleye anglers to stop stocking. On the other hand, there were anglers who discovered how to catch these fish and demanded stocking increase. "Striped bass were stocked in Wilson to provide a trophy fishing experience," said a Kansas biologist. "They did just that and are still doing it."

After the 1981 peak, striped bass in Wilson Reservoir began to decline. There were two reasons: reduced stocking and increased catches. While part of the decreased stocking was planned, most of it wasn't. About 45,000 striped bass fingerlings from the Farlington Hatchery were to be stocked every other year. However, in most years only half that number were stocked, and in two years, floods wiped out the entire hatchery production.

To find out more about striped bass catches and anglers a striped bass diary program was instituted in 1992. It immediately revealed that striped bass that were hooked, fought and released in summer had little chance of survival, especially during very hot weather. Most dedicated striped bass anglers, hoping to improve their fishery, were instituting their own minimum sizes, some at 15 inches and some at 21 inches, in hopes of producing more trophy fish. There is no minimum size limit in Kansas because biologists recognized the mortality caused by catching and releasing a fish during summer months and believe anglers should keep the first two fish they catch. The state-wide limit is two fish per day.

Eight lakes and reservoirs in Kansas today offer some degree of striped bass fishing. The best appears to be Wilson Reservoir, where the state record, a 43.5-pound fish was taken in 1988. The year 1991 also seemed a good year to catch big bass. According to bait-shop trophy certificates and biologist interviews with striped bass guides on Wilson Reservoir, many 20-pound fish were taken that year and at least ten over 30 pounds. Rated almost as good is Cheney Reservoir in south-central Kansas, just west of Wichita. The only other water rated "good" for catching striped bass in 1993 by the Kansas Department of Wildlife and Parks is LaCygne, a small reservoir (2,600 acres) almost on the Kansas-Missouri border south of Kansas City. Others rated "poor" are Webster, Glen Elder, Clinton, and Milford reservoirs. Unrated are Crawford and Malvern River Pond. Striped bass have not been recorded as reproducing naturally in any Kansas waters.

KENTUCKY

Much of Kentucky's striped bass program has been carried out jointly with Tennessee. However, the program has not been as successful as in other states, with fishable populations just on the margin. This is not to say that "rockfish" are not caught in the half-dozen reservoirs in which they have been stocked; it's just that most anglers don't go rockfishing to catch striped bass, and thus most catches are incidental to other kinds of fishing.

Kentucky's program began in 1957 when 12 adult striped bass from Santee-Cooper Reservoir in South Carolina were stocked in Cumberland Lake. Over the years, the program has expanded on Cumberland Lake and now includes Kentucky Lake, shared with Tennessee, and Herrington Lake. Natural production did not occur, though the fish grew, and one 34-pound trophy fish was caught. The latter additions to the system are Lake Malone, Green River, Barren River, and Barkley lakes in western Kentucky, at which the tail-race below the dam is one of the favorite angling spots. Fish up to 20 pounds have been taken from the discharge. In the past 12 years, Lake Cumberland is the only lake in the state that has continued to receive striped bass stockings and the only one that will continue to be developed as a striped bass water.

The state has switched its efforts from establishing striped bass fisheries on lakes and reservoirs to riverine systems. During the last decade, their biologists have regularly stocked the Ohio River and many other navigable rivers with striped bass, where they are stocked at the rate of five fingerlings per acre per year. Kentucky does not produce its own stocking supply but relies on hatcheries in southern states for its source. Fish are received as three-day old fry and

Striped bass have been planted in several large reservoirs in Kentucky. Benny Polston of Jamestown holds a 34.5-pound rockfish that existed for six years as the state record. In 1970 it was broken by a 44.25-pounder taken on a cane pole baited with a 1-pound freshwater drum by Ronald Warner. It was later displaced by a 58.25-pounder. Note the unique, deeper-bellied shape typical of a freshwater striped bass.

reared at the Minor Clark Fish Hatchery in Morehead. The current state-record striped bass is a 58-pound 4-ounce fish taken by Roger Foster from Cumberland Lake on December 1, 1985.

Hybridization is a chance occurrence that happens when striped and white bass inhabit the same environment. Natural hybridization, usually between a female striped bass and a male white bass, occurs in Kentucky Lake, and some of Kentucky's efforts are now going into hatchery production of these hybrids. Kentucky's hybrid-stocked waters include Cumberland Lake, Herrington Lake, Kentucky Lake, Barkley Lake, Green River Reservoir, and Dewey Lake.

LOUISIANA

Like most Gulf Coast states, striped bass in Louisiana are riverine fish and didn't exhibit anadromous characteristics, except in a few, rare occurrences, until recently. At one time, they were present in most of the states coastal streams and rivers. Catch records reveal that the number of striped bass in these waters began a downward trend in the late 1940s and by 1957 had disappeared. Most state fisheries biologists feel that it was poor water quality that caused the collapse of the fishery. The effects of expanding the number of river impoundments may have also contributed to the decline.

Sensing that they had lost a valuable sportfishery, and seeing what other states with hydroelectric impoundments were doing, Louisiana's Department of Wildlife and Fisheries initiated its striped bass recovery program in 1964. For the next ten years, Louisiana imported striped bass fry from South Carolina, stocking them as fingerlings in several coastal rivers—Calcasieu and Mermentau—and impoundments—Toledo Bend on the Louisiana-Texas border and D'Arbonne Lake in north-central Louisiana.

Fisheries biologists had hoped to establish self-reproducing populations in these two reservoirs. By 1977, more than 2.5 million fish (or 14.5 fish per acre) were stocked in Toledo Bend Reservoir and 723,000 (or 48.2 fish per acre) in D'Arbonne Lake. Extensive seining for fry and young-of-the-year fish in both waters in 1975 and '76 revealed natural reproduction hadn't occurred. Biologists believed the cause was insufficient water flow in rivers that fed the impoundments during the time of year when natural spawning would take place.

However, adults in the lake were in excellent condition for artificial spawning and represented a sizable brood stock. This allowed Louisiana to raise its own supply of striped bass. Since then, artificial spawning and rearing in hatcheries has produced a good supply for continued stocking in these two reservoirs. In the years 1967-1989, Louisiana stocked over 3.5 million fingerlings and 2 million fry in its coastal rivers. This has created an active fishery in the Atchafalaya, Mississippi, Sabine (up to 40 pounds) and Pearl rivers, where 20-pounders are not rare. Commercial fishermen have reported striped bass of 25 pounds and heavier in their hoop nets.

Department of Wildlife and Fisheries biologists have conducted small-scale seining operations on the Mississippi, Atchafalaya, and Red rivers and found large numbers of striped bass fingerlings, believe natural reproduction is occurring on these systems. There's the possibility fingerlings may be part of the genetic strain of striped bass that originally inhabited these river, and the state is hoping to start a program to identify the races.

MARYLAND

One would hardly imagine that a state like Maryland, with vast numbers of striped bass available throughout the center of the state, in Chesapeake Bay, would even consider stocking striped bass in freshwater impoundments. But the appeal of a "backyard" fishery to anglers not in the immediate vicinity of this famous bay was enough to start its fish managers developing a freshwater "rockfish" program. As an aside, it seems peculiar that striped bass in the marine environment of Maryland are called rockfish but those in fresh water are known as striped bass.

This abundance may have been one reason why Maryland was comparatively slow in getting into the reservoir-stocking craze that swept our southern states in the mid-60s and western states in the early 70s. Their program began in 1975 with an unauthorized stocking of Piney Run Reservoir. Thereafter, Maryland's Division of Inland Fisheries made stockings in Liberty, Loch Raven, Tridelphia, Rocky Gorge, Bradford Lake, and Pretty Boy reservoirs. The stocked fish came from adult brood stock captured in Chesapeake Bay and artificially spawned in the Joseph R. Manning Hatchery in Brandywine. Though not abundant at first, Liberty Reservoir's stocked bass grew. The biggest, was a 36-inch fish, netted in 1981.

In 1984, Maryland biologist Ed Enamait speculated that because of Liberty Reservoir's steep shoreline, clear water with limited littoral areas, high levels of dissolved oxygen, and relatively low organic content of bottom soils, it was possible for natural reproduction to occur despite the absence of a strong river current. Strong river current is a prerequisite on striped bass spawning grounds because the density of a striped bass egg, with a specific gravity of 1.007, almost the same as fresh water, and with no current it will eventually fall to the bottom and suffocate, either from the mass of other eggs atop it or from being covered by silt and organic debris.

These are also the same characteristics of Lake Powell, located on the Colorado River in northern Arizona and Utah, where reservoir spawning by striped bass and young-of-the-year fish was recorded in 1984. During electro-shocking sampling on the night of September 18, 1986, four young-of-the-year striped bass were collected from Liberty Reservoir. Ever since, natural spawning has been documented each year on the impoundment. In 1988, Enamait also discovered natural reproduction occurring on Piney Run, and Maryland added another reservoir to the short list of impoundments that have reproducing populations of striped bass, and to an even shorter list of bass that reproduce in an impoundment. Piney Run is a small body of water, less than 300 acres, and with only trickle-size feeder streams and springs supplying the bulk of its water. It, too, is now supporting a self-sustaining population of striped bass.

With the discovery of Piney Run's capabilities, Enamait began reevaluating his earlier concept of the requirements for spawning in a contained reservoir. He now feels that it wasn't so much the unique physical characteristics of these two reservoirs and their waters that enabled striped bass to reproduce but an unusual characteristic of the eggs these striped bass possessed. Unlike most striped bass eggs, that sink to the bottom, the fish used to stock these reservoirs produced unique eggs with a slightly larger oil globule. This altered their specific gravity (1.007) so that they were buoyant. Thus, the eggs in these two impoundments were able to float, or remain suspended near the surface long enough (about 48 hours) to allow hatching, and the larvae are moved by water and air currents close to shore to develop into fry and then fingerlings. It was later demonstrated that eggs produced by some Chesapeake Bay females do float. It is this capability of striped bass to adjust continually to changing environments that has made it a unique species.

Striped bass in fresh water got a break from fishing pressure when in January 1985, Maryland made it illegal for anyone to fish for, catch, retain or sell any striped bass in its waters. This included hybrids, that in this instance were considered striped bass because they were used to produce the crosses. The move was made to protect striped bass stocks in the marine waters of Chesapeake Bay because their reproductive abilities had been severely hindered by contaminants. The prohibition was lifted in fall of 1990 and today, striped bass and hybrids can be taken under special regulations established by the Department of Natural Resources.

Striped bass can be caught in several Maryland reservoirs, but only three—Liberty, Piney Run, and Tridelphia—offer anglers any real chance of catching fish. The freshwater striped bass season is always open; minimum size is 18 inches and only two per day are allowed, with only one over 30 inches. The largest freshwater striper landed in Maryland was a 39.5-pounder taken from Liberty Reservoir in 1991.

MISSISSIPPI

Like many states throughout the South, Mississippi, during the late 1960s and early 1970s, tried stocking striped bass in several impoundments. There was little hope that they would establish a self-sustaining population. In most of the impoundments, even survival was questionable because high summer heat would create environments not particularly hospitable to this species. The only exception to the latter fear was Ross Barnett Reservoir, just east of Jackson, where survival was no problem. However, some fish escaped and established themselves, though in small numbers, at the tail-race section of Ross Barnett and several other dams. Historically, striped bass in Mississippi had been a riverine fish, but the state's drive to impound all its major rivers eventually eliminated this strain. So it was no great surprise that a few fish did reestablish themselves in tail-race environments with cool summer waters.

Seeing that striped bass had too many variables influencing their survival, Mississippi fisheries biologists chose instead to stock hybrid bass, a cross between striped bass (*Morone saxatilis*) and its close cousin, white bass (*Morone chrysops*). Because of the popularity of the fast-growing hybrids, Mississippi eventually built a hatchery on Ross Barnett Reservoir to produce large numbers that today constitutes the bulk of their stocking efforts to maintain a put-and-take fishery.

Researchers aren't sure if remnants of the Gulf Strain stock of striped bass exist in the Pearl River, that forms the border between Mississippi and Louisiana. The Pearl River enters the Gulf of Mexico on the eastern limits of the city of New Orleans. Both states have stocked hybrids in the river, and Mississippi, using striped bass from Florida hatcheries, has also had an annual effort to restore striped bass to the river. However, they have found no evidence of reproduction.

MISSOURI

Missouri began its striped bass stocking program in the mid 60s with fingerlings from North and South Carolina and Virginia. The first stocking was made in 1966 when fry were introduced to Taum Sauk Reservoir, a small, pump-back facility operated by Union Electric Company on the East Fork of Black River in Reynolds County. The first large stockings were made the following year in Lake of the Ozarks. The goal of the Missouri Department of Conservation was to put these fish in a series of impoundments of the Osage River, but they concentrated their initial efforts on Lake of the Ozarks. It stocked them annually until 1981. Norfolk and Bull Shoals reservoirs, that traffic back and forth across the Missouri-Arkansas border, were stocked by the Arkansas Game and Fish Department.

One of the early favorite sites with anglers was the tail race on the Osage River behind Bagnell Dam, that created Lake of the Ozarks. Some striped bass stocked in Taum Sauk Reservoir escaped over the dam and were caught as far as 30 miles down river, below Clearwater Dam. There were also reports of striped bass making it as far as the St. Francis and Mississippi rivers. Today, Lake of the Ozarks probably still remains the best water within the state to catch striped bass and Bull Shoals and Norfolk reservoirs that are shared with Arkansas also produce some large striped bass. Montrose Lake, just east of Lake of the Ozarks, into which it empties, also produces some extraordinary catches of striped bass.

There has been no significant evidence that striped bass reproduce naturally in the waters of the Osage River above Lake of the Ozarks which the Department was hoping to establish as a nursery. However, there were several young-of-the-year striped bass taken in the Missouri River; and eggs and larvae were trapped in the water intake of a power generating plant, also on the Missouri, that led to speculation that the source might be the Missouri. However, their source was never determined.

Today, the stocking striped bass by the Conservation Department is a very limited effort that is confined strictly to expansive Lake of the Ozarks. The reduced effort started in 1980, when the department's attention has been directed to stocking hybrids instead of striped bass. Despite this move, there is still a small but dedicated cadre of striped bass fishermen.

NEBRASKA

Introduction of striped bass into the waters of a such a centrally located state as Nebraska typifies the sequence of events that have occurred in several states in the past three decades of striped bass propagation in the Midwest. The first stocking was quite accidental and occurred during the summer of 1873 as a result of a Union Pacific train wreck at the bridge crossing the Elkhorn River near Freemont. The U.S. Fish Commission was shipping a carload of fish from New Hampshire and Massachusetts to California, and striped bass were among the escapees.

The first intentional Nebraska stockings were 10 adult fish, 6 to 10 pounds, obtained from North Carolina, occurred in 1961 on Lake McConaughy, a reservoir created in the west-central part of the state by damming the North Platte River. It was the perfect impoundment for raising striped bass, with plenty of zooplankton to feed stocked fry and fingerlings. In addition to a huge supply of gizzard shad as forage fish, it was deep enough that during the extreme heat of the continental summer, it contained cool, oxygenated water.

During the next few years, additional, inconsequential stockings of fingerlings from California were added to Lake McConaughy. In 1966 and 1967, another 30,000 fingerlings were planted and the first striped bass was caught in 1968. Interest and growth of striped bass fishing in Nebraska is mirrored by the number of entries made each year in its Master Angler awards program, and the annual stockings continued here and in several other impoundments. In 1969, 29 awards were issued. Between 1972 and 1976 nearly 1,800 were awarded with the height in 1975 with 761 awards. The state's largest striped bass taken in the state was a 44-pound 10-ounce fish taken in 1986, but that took place in the midst of the fish's decline.

The primary source of food in the reservoir was gizzard shad and one state biologist calculated that it took 1,500 pounds of them to produce the 44-pound state record. The expanding striped bass population totally consumed these forage fish and the shad population collapsed in 1978; so did the striped bass fishery. Adding to the fish's dilemma were severe winters in 1978 and 1979. Populations of other game fish, walleye and trout, in the reservoir also fell and fishermen blamed striped bass for their decline. Suddenly, the fish had become unpopular with some anglers who demanded the Game and Parks Commission do something.

In 1981, Nebraska discontinued stocking striped bass and switched its efforts to wipers, the hybrid cross between stripers and white bass. However, a hard-core cadre of striped bass fishermen today still longs for the days when striped bass dominated all the fishing in the reservoir. Not many striped bass remain in Nebraska's waters today but the few that are still taken are large. Those anglers fishing for them are sure a new state record is there, still growing, and hoping they will catch it before old age catches up with the fish.

NORTH CAROLINA

Twelve reservoirs on three river systems: Yadkin, Catawba, and Roanoke, in the piedmont and foothills regions of North Carolina are now regularly stocked with striped bass. These lakes, really reservoirs, are: Badin, Norman, Roanoke Rapids, Gaston, High Rock, Tuckertown, Tillery Mountain Island, Blewet Falls, Hickory, Lookout Shoals, Rhodehiss, and Falls of the Neuse. Striped bass do not reproduce naturally in these 12 reservoirs, so they are stocked with 2- to 3-inch fingerlings raised at state and federal hatcheries.

However, North Carolina's first stockings were not in these reservoirs, but in Buggs Island Lake (John H. Kerr Reservoir that is shared with Virginia) in 1953 and 1954, a few years after the impoundment began to fill. Since the early 1960s, the state has used the brood stock on Kerr to spawn striped bass artificially and hatchery-raised the fish for stocking in the reservoirs where non-reproducing populations exist. Because annual hatchery production each year is not sufficient to stock all 12 dependent reservoirs, there is a preferential stocking scheme, the order of which follows the list of reservoirs in the preceding paragraph.

In terms of quality, Kerr Reservoir offers anglers the best fishing, followed closely by Lakes Norman and Badin. However, anglers fishing other reservoirs can take advantage of the migratory spawning urge in striped bass. While they do not reproduce, they still tend to act as if they do and head out of the lakes during the spawning months of April and May and into the various headwaters and tributary streams that feed these reservoirs. Also at this time of the year, fish in rivers below dams tend to run upstream to the dams and concentrate there as if getting ready to spawn.

Ironically, the state's record freshwater striped bass, 52-pounds 2-ounces, landed in 1991, was taken on Hiwassee Reservoir, a small impoundment that hasn't been stocked in more than 15 years because striped bass survival there was considered too poor to sustain a sport fishery.

OKLAHOMA

Even in Oklahoma, with a great diversity of habitat for striped bass, some of the problems of Nebraska's declining fishery are becoming, though to a lesser degree. Popularity, however, is not one of them and striped bass are one of the state's most sought-after fish. A program to introduce striped bass to Oklahoma was initiated in 1965 when 125,000 small fish given the state by North Carolina. However, these fish were lost in the hatchery ponds. In 1966 both North and South Carolina shipped 4 million fry, and eventually 11,000 made it to the fingerling stage. These were stocked in Keystone Reservoir. In 1967, Virginia and South Carolina again supplied Oklahoma hatcheries with 5 million fry. This time 190,000 were raised to fingerlings and stocked in Keystone Reservoir just west of Tulsa.

Good fishing quickly developed in Keystone Reservoir and even below the dam, on the Arkansas River. The big question at the time, however, was that of natural production, something that so far hadn't been achieved on any water except Santee-Cooper Reservoir in South Carolina and Kerr Lake in North Carolina and Virginia. Many states looked toward natural reproduction as a way of avoid, the cost of continued annual stockings. Keystone's two fairly large watershed rivers—Salt Fork of the Arkansas and Cimarron rivers—had the characteristics needed for natural reproduction. On June 18, 1970, seining along the shore of Keystone produced six fingerling striped bass and proved that striped bass had been successfully spawned in Keystone.

Keystone wasn't the only favored body of fresh water for Oklahoma's striped bass program. In May, 1967, 200,000 fry were also planted in Lake Texoma, a reservoir that straddles the Red River between Texas and Oklahoma. Texoma had many characteristics of Keystone's watershed and biologists were hopeful it, too, would develop a self-sustaining population. Biologists in 1973 noted the first evidence of natural production. Since then, Texoma also has developed its own self-sustaining population of striped bass. Today, the state does not stock on either reservoir because each year their nurseries have produced enough fish to maintain the fishery. However, it does actively stock Kerr Reservoir.

The rise and fall of the striped bass fishery on Keystone Lake mirrors many mid-western reservoirs. In the mid-70s, as the fish began reaching maturity, the number of big fish exploded and Keystone developed a reputation as one of the country's best trophy landlocked striped bass waters. However, food for the fish was beginning to be a problem, but before that could manifest itself, there was a larger than usual salt flow from the Cimarron River. This altered the environment and caused a plant as well as fish die-off. Compounding dwindling forage fish in Keystone and other Oklahoma reservoirs is the problem of spring floods. Periodically, entire fisheries have been decimated when filled reservoirs were forced, by heavy rains, to open their gates. In the process many fish are moved into the rivers and often eventually into hostile, overheated summer environments.

Continued successful striped bass fishing in Oklahoma may depend upon its diversity of waters. Today, they are taken in three environments: lakes or reservoirs, tail-races below impoundment dams, and in large rivers. The lakes include Keystone, Texoma and Kerr reservoirs. Tail-race fisheries include the Canadian River below Eufaula Dam on Eufaula Lake, the Kiamichi River tail-race below Lake Hugo, and tail-waters of the Arkansas River Below Keystone Reservoir.

Rivers include: Illinois River, in the northeast corner of the state, where many of Oklahoma's bass records were set with 30- and 40-pounders in an area below Tenkiller Reservoir, and where it meets the Arkansas River near Gore; and Red River below Texoma Reservoir.

Fort Gibson and Kaw Lake tail-waters, as well as Webbers Falls lock and dam near Muskogee offer excellent striped bass fishing at times. Despite rises and fall in the forage fish populations, floods, possible over fishing and the continued harvest of large fish, Texoma is still one of the nation's better striped bass lakes. Oklahoma's largest striped bass was a 46.5-pounder taken April 2, 1991, in the Canadian River, in the tail-waters of Eufuala Dam.

TENNESSEE

Tennessee, during the early 1960s, was one of the earliest inland states to begin developing a striped bass fishery. Like ensuing states, its initial objectives were twofold: to develop a self-sustaining population of trophy-size predators to keep large gizzard shad in check on the expanding reservoir system and at the same time, create a new sportfishery. Initial plantings came from North Carolina and were stocked in Cherokee and Percy Priest lakes (reservoirs). None of these lakes, however, or any other subsequent reservoir stockings, revealed that any natural reproduction of striped bass had taken place in their waters or up-river tributaries.

Since then, the Tennessee Wildlife Resource Agency has resigned itself to put-and-take fishing. Still, the efforts have established a reputation for Tennessee's reservoirs as producing some of the biggest freshwater striped bass in the world. The former world record for striped bass from inland waters was a 60.5-pounder taken from Melton Reservoir in 1988. Three of the eight current International Game Fish Association records for freshwater (land-locked) striped bass come from Tennessee reservoirs.

Hybridization of female striped bass with male white bass at hatcheries in North Carolina and South Carolina produce a fast-growing fish. As a result, Tennessee also began introducing hybrids into several other reservoirs as well as Norris, Watts Bar, and Kentucky lakes. Striped bass fingerlings were also being stocked on a regular basis in these multiple-species lakes and reservoirs. As a result, striped bass were directly introduced to 12 reservoirs and hybrid bass to six reservoirs.

The striped bass reservoirs are: Boone, Cherokee, Cordell Hull, Kentucky, Norris, Old Hickory, Percy Priest, Tims Ford and Watts Bar reservoirs. Striped bass also migrated into several other reservoirs located on the same river system that are not maintained by annual stockings and these include: Barkley, Cheatham, Fort Loudoun, Guntersville, Melton Hill, Nickajack, and Tellico reservoirs.

The ultimate effect of all these efforts over the past 30 years has been the establishment of some level of striped bass or hybrid fishery, or both, in 18 reservoirs. Kentucky Lake had the greatest potential for a self-sustaining population to develop because of the type of watershed feeding the reservoir and its water quality. Efforts were made to bolster stockings in this impoundment in hopes of such a production. Because it never happened, biologists, in retrospect agree that the control of striped bass populations through annual stockings is the best management strategy for a fish that has a tendency to destroy its own food source eventually if propagation remains uncontrolled.

TEXAS

Texas was a land of many rivers but few lakes until the harnessing of its waterways for hydroelectric power began soon after World War II. More recently, rivers were managed by the Corps of Engineers to enhance navigation facilities on these watery roads for commercial vessels. With the addition of locks and dams, the entire character of the land and eventually its fishing changed. Most impoundments, because of their cooler, deeper waters, were initially almost devoid of game fish, but they did produce plenty of rough forage fishes.

To combat their exploding population, striped bass were stocked in Texas as early as 1960. But, the state didn't become really active in their propagation until 1967, with the rearing of small fish obtained from sources in Virginia, Maryland, and North and South Carolina. Today, Texas can boast of having one of the largest striped bass stocking programs in the nation. Striped bass have captured the imagination of Lone Star State anglers, and nearly half of all Texas recreational fishermen on these reservoirs now list striped bass as their first choice, devoting a major effort in pursuit of their fish.

The principal emphasis on initial stockings was in Navarro Mills and Bardwell reservoirs, with other stockings on Lakes Spence, Granbury and Bastrop. These stockings, as fish matured, almost immediately supplied fair catches of striped bass for anglers, but the goal of the Texas Parks & Wildlife Department (TPWD), to establish natural production on these waters, didn't take place. In 1973, they redirected their efforts to establishing a striped bass fishery in Lake Whitney, with additional efforts in Lake Granbury on the Brazos River system. Whitney was stocked heavily with striped bass fingerlings from 1973 to 1976, but it wasn't until 1977, when biologists were seining the shores of the Brazos River, just up-stream of where becomes Lake Whitney, that the first young-of-the-year fish were discovered. Though annual recruitment into the population has been documented on this site, the contribution is minimal at best. To maintain the sportfishery on the reservoir, substantial stocking was resumed in 1984 and has taken place annually since 1986.

Since the program began, Texas Parks & Wildlife Department biologists have stocked striped bass in 34 reservoirs throughout the state. In 1984, it reduced its effort to establish striped bass fisheries in all these reservoirs and instead expanded its stocking effort with hybrid bass. In doing so, it concentrated its striped bass stocking program in nine reservoirs with the intention of improving the quality of catches on these waters.

These include: Amistad, Buchanan, Falcon, Kemp, Livingston, Possum Kingdom, Spence, Texana and Whitney. In addition, Toledo Bend Reservoir is jointly stocked with Louisiana, and Texoma Reservoir with Oklahoma. Other than Whitney, Texoma, and Toledo Bend, where some natural reproduction takes place, all of the preceding nine impoundments with striped bass populations are supported by annual stockings. Many remaining reservoirs, where efforts were curtailed in 1984, receive occasional stocks on an irregular basis.

However, some interesting trends have taken place in Lake Possum Kingdom in the past few years. Since 1987, biologists have confirmed a strong six-year trend in the increase in the number of striped bass there. The average rate of fish taken by gill-net samplings increased from 2.8 in 1987 to 5.5 in 1991 and 13.3 in 1993. Lake Texoma, one of the nation's best landlocked striped bass lakes, has a net-catch rate between 16 to 18 striped bass per net. More dramatic, however, is the evidence that natural production is also took place on Lake Possum King. TPWD did not stock striped bass in 1992, however three one-year-old fish were found in 1993 samplings. Although some degree of natural reproduction has taken place here for several years, this is the first instance where it has been documented.

Texas raises striped bass for stocking in several hatcheries throughout the state but the majority of the effort is concentrated at hatcheries on Possum Kingdom, and Dundee reservoirs. Brood stock fish are taken from two sources: the Trinity River at the tail-race of the Livingston Reservoir Dam and the Red River below the dam on Lake Texoma.

Until just three years ago, the biggest freshwater striped bass in Texas was a 43-pound 8.8-ounce fish caught in 1986 on the Colorado River, below the dam at Lake Travis, just outside of Austin. The record, however, was broken on May 14, 1990, when a 45-pounder taken on the Rio Grande River just below the dam at Amistad Reservoir.

VIRGINIA

The development of Virginia's freshwater striped bass fishery, or landlocked stripers as they are sometimes called, runs somewhat parallel to that of South Carolina. In 1952 the Kerr Reservoir on the Roanoke River was filled and created a vast inland lake over what had once been a rather productive striped bass river, one that may have contained three populations of striped bass with somewhat different migratory characteristics. Postulation suggests that one strain may have been a non-migrant resident riverine population in Roanoke's upper reaches and another population or strain may have annually moved to the estuary in spring and stayed until fall to feed and then return. A third strain, was probably part of the latter group, with a population that used the river only to spawn and as an initial nursery, whose adults occasionally took part in long migrations north along the Atlantic Coast.

Part of the Kerr Reservoir spills over into North Carolina, and during the first two years after impoundment, the North Carolina Wildlife Commission stocked more than 3 million striped bass fry in the body of water. Establishment of a striped bass fishery occurred quickly, and biologists are not certain whether it was a result of the plantings or a natural population that was trapped behind the dam once the gates were closed. In 1957 and 1958, yearling striped bass were taken from the reservoir, the first confirmation that a self-sustaining population had been established in the reservoir.

Before the entrapment, the area at Roanoke Rapids, not more than 30 miles down river from the dam and a major Atlantic Coast spawning site, could have contributed riverine stock. Those fish trapped behind the dam eventually moved from 25 to 42 miles above Kerr Reservoir on the Roanoke (Staunton) River to select spawning sites, and from 24 to 45 miles on the Dan River, another source of reservoir water.

Because natural spawning yields can be highly variable from year to year, the Department of Game and Inland Fisheries has been supplementing the reservoir. Today, the total size of the striped bass population in Kerr Reservoir is probably second only to that in Santee-Cooper and may be even surpassing it because of water quality problems on the latter. In response to a need for more stock for other reservoirs in the state and other states, Virginia in 1962 completed its Brookneal Hatchery on the Roanoke River, 40 miles above Kerr Reservoir. While the demand for its hatchery stock diminished as other states established their own hatchery programs for striped bass, this hatchery has an annual production of 3 million fry and fingerling striped bass. It remains one of the three largest striped bass hatcheries in the world but for a period was unique in that it used only landlocked brood stock for hatchery production. Other hatcheries, like the one at Moncks Corners, S.C., obtain their brood stock from riverine migrant bass which come to the base of the dam to spawn. These latter fish still have access to salt water though they may not use it.

Virginia was active, because of the hatchery, in stocking almost every reservoir in the state with striped bass fry, and it sustains a good put-and-take fishery on most of them. Smith Mountain Lake, near Roanoke, is one of the better lakes maintained on this basis. Other reservoirs in Virginia include Claytor, Carvin's Cove, Prince, Meade, Western Branch, Waller Mill, Gas-ton and Lake Anna. Hardwood Mill was stocked earlier in the program but the poor survival rate here has discouraged further stocking efforts. The state's largest fresh-water striped bass was taken from Smith Mountain Lake in 1992 and weighed 44 pounds 14 ounces.

FRESHWATER VS. SALTWATER STRIPED BASS

For the most part, striped bass in fresh water are the same fish as in salt water. Physically, their appearance might change slightly. Adult freshwater fish, based on current data, do not attain the same length as in salt water. Fresh-water striped bass also have a tendency to grow greater girth dimensions in proportion to length. This produces a fish with a somewhat heavier pouch, often not too unlike a largemouth bass in general body shape.

The only discernible difference between the fish in the two differing environments is the characteristic of growth. Striped bass in fresh water, as substantiated by growth records in Kerr Reservoir in Virginia-North Carolina, Keystone Lake in Oklahoma, and the Colorado River in Arizona-Nevada-California, grow initially at a much faster rate than the same fish in salt water.

The greatest year in growth for marine forms is the second year of their lives. In fresh water, it is their first year. Virginia research established that striped bass in Kerr Reservoir grow twice as fast as fish in Chesapeake Bay. But there is a toll for this accelerated growth—the fish reach old age, seven to nine years, a lot sooner, and begin to die off. Striped bass in salt water are not "old-age" fish until they get beyond fifteen years. Saltwater fish grow more slowly, but live a lot longer.

Similar rapid growth during the first year of life is also a phenomenon of Santee-Cooper fish. One reason for this rapid growth might be greater food supplies in impoundments. A second might be warmer overall water temperature during the first year, allowing fry to feed for ten or eleven months instead of five to eight months as may be the case in saltwater nurseries. To contradict this, however, the growth rate of fry planted in a reservoir was similar to the rate in a marine environment. Under the same growing conditions, as in Santee-Cooper, fry introduced showed a slower growth rate when compared immediately to fry naturally produced in the same environment. As a result, the causes of this faster growth rate are still obscure.

There is one other factor that appears in some but not all freshwater striped bass—the age of maturity. In marine forms, males are mature in the second and third years. In fresh water, they are almost all mature in their second year. However, the greatest differences occur in female striped bass. In a marine environment, they don't reach maturity until five, or often as long as nine years. In fresh water, some females are mature at three, more by four, and all by five years of age.

9

Hybrids, Crosses, and Other Basses

A few years after the introduction of striped bass to many impoundments in the United States, some fisheries managers eventually discovered that maybe striped bass weren't the perfect predator fish that they had been led to believe. Most striped bass were introduced for two reasons, to create a new sportfishery and at the same time reduce vast hordes of gizzard and threadfin shad where they occurred naturally in that system's watershed. Shad became a problem because once the impoundments filled, these fish always experienced a tremendous population growth. Their ensuing annual die-offs created an issue as thousands of dead fish floated to the surface and winds eventually piled their decomposing remains along beaches and shore-front homes.

Predator game fishes—walleye, small- and largemouth bass, northern pike, pickerel, and even trout—were able to reduce shad populations while in juvenile and sub-adult stages. But as adults, the shad were too large to be ingested. Striped bass have big mouths and bigger striped bass have even larger mouths. And, no matter how large a shad might grow, striped bass can always grow larger. However, in many instances, the bass eventually ate all the shad in the reservoir, and at times turned to game fish, sometimes real and sometimes imagined by sportsmen. When this happened, they became unpopular with more traditional warm-water anglers.

HYBRID—STRIPED BASS CROSSES

Man-made hybrid bass, called wipers (**White bass** + str**IPERS**) by some, are a cross between striped bass and white bass, that also can eat big shad. But because a 10-pound hybrid is the top of the line, it never grows so large that it consumes all the forage fish in an impoundment. Also, hybrids seldom have the capability to reproduce and with shorter life spans their numbers can be kept in check by the degree of hybrid stocking that take place.

The development of the first striped bass/white bass cross, in 1964, was the result of a joint effort that involved fisheries biologist Bob Stevens with the South Carolina Division of Wildlife and Freshwater Fisheries and Dave Bishop with the Virginia Commission of Game and Inland Fisheries. For several years, Bishop had been trying to make the cross, but was unsuccessful because he could not get striped bass and white bass to reach peak spawning condition at the same time. However, he learned that Stevens developed a technique, using human chorionic gonadotropin (HCG), an ovulation-stimulating hormone, to artificially induce striped bass to spawn when they were ready for hatchery production. The first use of HCG was in Alabama on largemouth bass. That spring, Bishop rushed six white bass to the South Carolina hatchery in Moncks Corners, where Stevens treated the female striped bass with the spawning-inducing hormone.

The first hybridization involved the crossing of a female striped bass (*Morone saxatilis*) with a male white bass (*Morone chrysops*). The female was forced to ovulate by hormonal injections and the eggs collected. Then a male white bass was stripped and its milt (sperm) mixed with the striped bass eggs. It resulted in the first successful production of the cross. South Carolina kept half of the 80,000 progeny, which did not survive. Bishop's half, however, did extremely well. His larvae were stocked in a pothole adjacent to Cherokee Reservoir in Tennessee. Over 5,000 fingerlings were recovered and then released in Cherokee Reservoir that fall.

The crossing was possible because the two fish belong to the same genus. Of the four-member genus *Morone*, also including *mississippiensis* (yellow bass) and *americana* (white perch) in North America, the white bass is the closest genetically related species to striped bass. A definition of a new species is a strain that has evolved to a point where it can no longer breed successfully with members of the parent stock. Successful breeding isn't only the production of juveniles, but the juvenile progeny must in turn be able to reproduce and duplicate their own kind from among themselves. Non-reproducing hybrids tend to grow fast but their longevity is affected by this characteristic.

Natural Hybridization

It is believed by many biologists, that when hybrids are produced, even though they may take on outward (phenotype) characteristics of both parents, they are unable to produce among themselves. However, biologists conducting beach haul seining in Chesapeake Bay discovered that from 5 to 10 percent of their hauls were composed of juvenile hybrid bass. Pennsylvania has done some extensive stocking of hybrids in the Susquehanna River and several impoundments created on its course. Maryland researchers found hybrids fully developed with roe and milt and are convinced that some strains in thybrid croses do reproduce naturally. Their genetic genotypes show a mixture of both parents.

Characteristics of Hybrids

Wipers exhibit some of the characteristics of both striped bass and white bass, and some that are all their own. They are aggressive surface feeders and most anglers who catch them regularly rate them, pound-for-pound, better fighters than striped bass. This behavior can probably attributed to a biological phenomenon called "hybrid vigor." According to Ben Kinman, who headed the predator research unit for the Kentucky Department. of Fish and Wildlife Resources, hybrids have a faster growing rate than either of their parental species, better survival in a hatchery, and better survival in the wild once they are stocked.

Some anglers also rate them a notch or two higher on the palatability scale than striped bass, especially when the lateral line muscle (typical of all temperate basses) of dark meat is removed before cooking. And, because of, their size, the same amount of forage fish (gizzard and threadfin shad) can produce two or three trophy wipers to one striper.

Biologically, hybrids grow faster during the first 18 to 24 months than striped bass. Males are usually sexually mature at age one or two while striped bass don't reach this level until two. Females are usually sexually mature at age two or three but striped bass females mature at age four to five, and under some conditions as late at eight and nine years. Although hybrid males and females develop sexually, only a limited spawning in the wild has ever been documented. However, in spring, hybrids will often accompany white bass during spawning runs. During the first several months after hybrids are stocked in an impoundment, they spend most of their time in the shallows and don't move into deep water until late summer or fall.

Feeding habits are similar in both fishes, with larvae feeding on zooplankton. In the juvenile stage they feed on invertebrates and fish larvae. As adults, they switch to more substantial foods: primarily shad and invertebrates. Both fish have strong schooling tendencies and feed together in schools on prey species. We can tell from the types of stomachs both fish have that they feed continually, throughout the day and night, but the most intense feeding takes place just before dawn and just after dark.

Reciprocal and Other Crosses

Hybrids produced by crossing a female striped bass and male white bass are now referred to as the original cross. Reports of the successful rearing of hybrids to the fingerling stage and releasing them in Cherokee Reservoir in Tennessee led other biologists to experiment further in hybridization attempts within the genus. The original cross was duplicated by a North Carolina biologist who then succeeded in crossing male white perch (*Morone americana*) with female striped bass. In 1967, working together, Kentucky and Virginia biologists succeeded in crossing a male striped bass with a female white bass and produced the reciprocal of the original hybrid. After these initial successes with other combinations of hybridization, interest declined because neither progeny had characteristics as favorable as the original cross. For a period in the mid 1980s, Nebraska stocked reciprocal hybrids in some of their reservoirs, but anglers found the reciprocal was considerably different in several desirable characteristics—size, fighting ability, and habitat preferences—and opted for the original. Arkansas, with an active hybrid program still stocks reciprocal hybrids in five reservoirs

Differentiating Between Hybrids and Basses

The only negative aspect of hybrids, from a management point of view, is anglers being unable to distinguish readily between striped bass, white bass, and hybrids when all three appear in the same reservoir. This is especially true with fish two to three pounds and under. If it's larger than 10 pounds, it is usually a striped bass, although the largest hybrid is a 24-pound 3- ounce fish taken from Leesville Reservoir in Virginia in 1989. The maximum size white bass reach is four to six pounds but most are much smaller. The management problem has been solved in several states by making a distinction between the three fish unnecessary. They have made regulations—seasons, creel limits, and minimum lengths—the same for all three fish. The mechanism that allows anglers to take different numbers of striped bass or hybrids, as opposed to white bass, is a maximum size limit.

However, even superficially, they can be distinguished without much effort or confusion. Several of the black lateral stripes on the side extend all the way back to the base of the tail only on striped bass. On a hybrid, only one, in the center, reaches that far back. The others are faint and partial. Body shape is another distinguishing method. Striped bass are comparatively slender, with the greatest body depth less than one-third the body length. In hybrids, the body depth is usually more than one-third the body length. In coloration, white bass are really white, almost completely so, with a bit of silvery blue on the belly behind the gills. Striped are a silvery blue all over the back and white on the underside. The same is true for the hybrid.

Anatomically, the separations are more exact. Striped bass have two separate, elongated patches of small teeth on the top centers of their tongues. Hybrids, in this case, took after their mother rather than father and exhibit the same two patches. White bass, however, have only one patch of shallow teeth that is located in the middle of their tongue.

Catching Hybrid Bass

One key reason many anglers prefer hybrids over striped bass is that they are so much easier to catch. Striped bass, in either freshwater or marine environments, have a reputation for being moody and standoffish. The gregarious tendency of hybrids to swim in schools and feed on schools on prey fish can be their undoing. Once you've located such a combination, you're likely to take several fish before you lose the school.

Fishing techniques for hybrids will vary between those used to catch striped bass in fresh water and white bass, that occur only in fresh water. If you're fishing waters where hybrids have been running between four and five pounds, then you should use small baits, e.g., minnows, spinners, spoons, and jigs on light- to medium-size tackle. However, large hybrids are caught on larger baits and lures, and the kind of tackle you'd use for striped bass. There's nothing wrong with using downriggers and electronic fish-finders designed for striped bass on hybrids...of all sizes.

Spring fishing—The best fishing occurs in spring when hybrids school and act as if they're going to spawn. At this time of year they have abandoned the big, open spaces of the reservoirs and headed upstream into the rivers and creeks to hang around the mouths of streams feeding the reservoir, as well as tributaries to the bigger rivers. Don't pass up any shoals or bars near the end of the lake where the river comes in. If you fish strictly with artificials, then shad-pattern lures are your first choice, either surface, medium and deep-running models. Spoons and jigs also work well at this time of year. Hybrids are famous for forcing schools of shad to the surface, where terns and gulls feed feverishly on the remaining tidbits and will often tell you where and when this occurs. Usually, this happens late in the afternoon.

Summer fishing—At this time of year, hybrids are in the big pond and often too deep for easy fishing, seeking cool water and respite from the day's heat. However, they will come to the surface and feed but this usually takes place only just before dawn and again just after sunset. Hybrids, like their parents, are also nocturnal feeders. If you insist on fishing during the heat of the day, your best bet is to drift with live, or recently alive baits deep down or on the bottom.

Fall fishing—In an attempt to escape cooling surface waters and the even cooler waters now at the bottom of a reservoir, schools of threadfin and gizzard shad will often select the mid-range depths to find comfort in their ambient environment. And that's where you will find the wipers. Here's the place where a good depth recorder on your boat will pay off in big dividends. Those that print on paper are far superior to a flasher or LCD type and can even be finely tuned to show developing fall thermoclines in the water column. If you don't have a good depth recorder then the next best way to find a school of bait and hybrids is to drift several rods, at different depths, with light weights and live baits. The next best is to troll at several levels with spoons and small deep- and medium-running plugs. Almost as good a technique is blind jigging as you drift, and changing the depths until you find a school of suspended fish. You can do all this while keeping your eyes peeled for wipers making a commotion on the reservoir's surface.

Winter fishing—This is the toughest time of the year to find hybrids. Like their big cousins, falling water temperatures force wipers to cut down on their metabolism and hence the degree of feeding needed to maintain it. If the weather is really cold, the fish may find the needed relative warmth in the deeper parts of the reservoir. On bright, sunny days, they're likely to climb out of the depths and show up at the mouths of creeks where warmer stream currents enter the reservoir, looking for heat, better oxygenated water, as well as food. If your reservoir acts as a cooling basin for a power generating plant it's sure to have a "hot" water discharge. There are sure to be all kinds of fish in it. Some, which have been there for a while, are actually trapped in the warm water. Under most winter fishing conditions, slowly-worked jigs are often the best producers of hybrids.

RECORD HYBRID BASS
From IGFA Records, 1993 Bass, "Whiterock" (Hybrids)

Line Class	Weight	Place	Date	Angler
2 lb.	10 lb. 6 oz.	Little Red River, AK	9/5/88	Gary L. Evans
4 lb.	18 lb. 1 oz .	Sooner Lake, OK	1/28/88	Neil K. Jackson
8 lb.	17 lb. 11 oz.	Lake Austin, TX	6/21/89	J. Coddington
12 lb.	20 lb. 8 oz.	Osage River, MO	11/22/86	R. Slaybaugh
16 lb.	24 lb. 3 oz.	Leesville Lake, VA	5/12/89	David Lambert
20 lb.	22 lb. 6 oz.	Savannah Dam, GA	7/20/86	Jerry L. Adams

THE OTHER BASSES

In addition to *saxatilis,* the genus *Morone* includes five other species of closely-related fish: *chrysops,* white bass; *mississippiensis,* yellow bass; *americana,* white perch; and two European bass with identical lifestyles, *labrax,* in the eastern Atlantic from Spain to northern Ireland and *punctatus,* from the Mediterranean. The only fish which is really more than just a cousin to the striped bass is *Morone labrax (Dicentrarchus labrax)*, a European fish that looks and acts almost identical to our striped bass.

White Bass *(Morone chrysops)*
White bass look remarkably like striped bass except that the deeper, more laterally compressed body gives them away as being a close cousin, but not a striper. It, too, is a silvery fish with dark, narrow lines both above and below the lateral line. Though distinct, when compared to striped bass, the lines are faint, especially below the lateral line. However, only one extends the full length of the

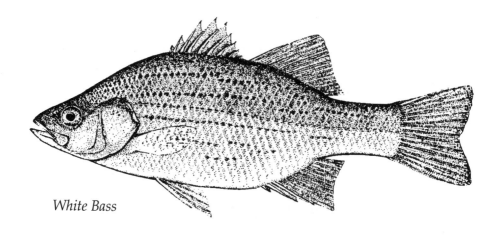

White Bass

body from the operculum (gill cover) to the base of the caudal peduncle (tail). The fish is a dusky silver on the back and shades into all silver on the sides, and the belly is white.

It closely resembles a white perch in shape but white perch lack the longitudinal stripes, and its anal (ventral) fin has nine rays instead of 12 or 13. White bass have two patches of teeth at the base and center of their tongues but they are uneven in length and often so close together that they appear as one. Striped bass have two patches of low teeth in the center of their tongue but these are well separated. The two dorsal fins of a white bass are connected by a low membrane, and early taxonomists used this as a key in separating them from striped bass whose two dorsal fins are separate. Most white bass range from 1 to 2 pounds in weight, or 12 to 18 inches in lenght, with a 3 pounder bass considered an exceptional fish by most anglers. However, the three top white bass listed in the International Game Fish Association's record book are fish of 5 lbs., 6 ozs.; 5 lbs., 9 ozs.; and 6 lbs., 13 ozs. The latter was taken from Lake Orange, Virginia.

This fish's original range was in the vast Great Lakes drainage system and the St. Lawrence River, especially the lower lakes and in the Mississippi River and its tributaries as far south as the Gulf drainages and west to the Rio Grande. It has since been introduced to the Southeast. It was not originally found east of the Alleghenies but the first transplants arrived from the Hudson River with canal barge traffic.

White bass are schooling fish that prefer big waters and this was one reason they took to the numerous newly-created impoundments across the South. They are carnivorous feeders that at night move to the surface to chase foods. They move out of these big lakes and reservoirs to the lower reaches of feeder streams to spawn. Unlike striped bass and other members of the *Morone* genus, white bass are not anadromous and their closest approach to the marine environment is the upper reaches of brackish water.

Yellow Bass *(Morone mississippiensis)*

Yellow bass, in coloration and with its dark, broad longitudinal stripes, more closely resemble striped bass than any other North American members of the genus. Its overall color is a brassy yellow, hence the name yellow bass. The three longitudinal lines below the lateral line are often broken, with one stripe on the lateral line extending from the gill cover to the base of the caudal fin. The broken stripes below the lateral line gave rise to its earlier Latin name *Morone interruptus*. However, taxonomic research revealed that its very first scientific name was *Roccus mississippiensis* so the name was changed to the former. The rule in naming a species is that the first to describe it gets to name it, so in the late 1960s all references to *Roccus* were changed to *Morone*.

The shape of a yellow bass, however, is more closely akin to white bass and white perch than striped bass. The body is oblong-ovate, the back heavily arched, and the forward slope closely resembles that of a yellow perch, ending in a flat head. The fins of all this genus are similar in shape but the two dorsal fins are connected by a thin, low membrane, unlike striped bass and white perch, in which they are separate and distinct. Its anal fin has three spines and

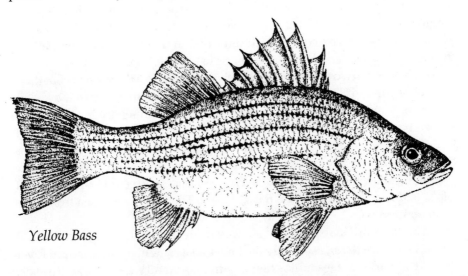

Yellow Bass

9-10 distinct rays. The lack of a connecting membrane between the two dorsal fins is an immediate way to distinguish yellow bass from white perch, with which it is often confused in environments where the dominant brassy color of the yellow bass is less pronounced. However, the best way to separate the two, is that a yellow bass has no teeth on the base of its tongue.

Yellow bass are considerably smaller than white bass and range between one-half to 1.5 pounds. While there are reports of fish as large as 2 pounds, the largest ever recorded was only 2 pounds 4 ounces. However, it is probably the sportiest of all the perch-like members of the genus and readily takes lures, bait, and even artificial flies. Its original range encompassed the lower Mississippi River and its accompanying tributaries as far north as the lower Ohio River. Originally it was a riverine species but impoundment of many of its rivers placed it in lake-like environments where it never adapted as well as white bass. It, too, is a schooling fish, like white bass, but unlike these fish it does little surface feeding at night and instead concentrates its night-time feeding activities in the shallows. During the day, it remains in deep water. They are not anadromous fish.

White Perch *(Morone americana)*

Somewhere along the evolutionary line, white perch either gave up their longitudinal stripes or branched off the family tree before stripes became fashionable in the *Morone* family. They are the only members of the North American temperate basses without stripes. However, they are closer to striped bass in two aspects than other members of the family: the two dorsal fins are separate, but not quite as distinct as in striped bass and the fish are anadromous,

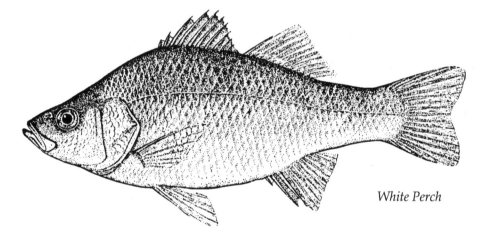

White Perch

trading back and forth between fresh, brackish, and salt water at will. Given a choice, they most often opt for a brackish environment.

A white perch is a bass typical of temperate waters in its distribution, relegated strictly to East Coast waters and rivers emptying into them from the Carolinas north to the Canadian Maritimes, Lake Ontario, and the upper St. Lawrence River and the Hudson-Mohawk river link to Lake Ontario. It never made the leap naturally above Niagara Falls to Lake Erie. It migrates to fresh water to spawn, but populations not necessarily landlocked, have no penchant to seek out saltwater environments.

In shape, it possesses the typical arched back of the basses, but not to the degree of yellow or white bass, with an almost continuous fore-slope from the forward base of the anterior dorsal fin to the pointed snout. There are no teeth on the base of the tongue but there is a band of teeth around its periphery. The tail is weakly forked and contains an average of 15 rays, a half dozen more than yellow or white bass. Its coloration can be highly variable and not necessarily always white. It is described as ranging from olivaceous, dark grayish, green, dark silver-gray, or dark brown to almost black on the dorsal (back) surface, becoming pale olive to silvery green on the sides and silvery white on the belly. The fish is usually darker in fresh than salt water, especially if the impoundment's waters are not clear.

The average weight of white perch is just three-quarters of a pound, but the biggest white perch ever recorded was a 19-inch fish that weighed 4.75 pounds taken from Messalonskee Lake in Maine. It is a popular game fish that will take all sorts of offerings, even dry flies. But when fished in brackish water, small minnows are the prime bait and even earthworms. Its popularity is greatest among anglers fishing estuarine areas of Long Island and Chesapeake Bay, and it's active throughout winter months, often being the only fish able to reduce the effects of cabin fever.

The European Bass

The sea bass, or simply bass, as they are referred to in Great Britain and Ireland, differ only slightly in appearance from striped bass. Of course, the most salient feature missing in the European version is the stripes. Also, the fish is somewhat thinner or longer in the length-to-weight relationship, with less body depth than striped bass. The head is somewhat flatter and snout a bit sharper, but with the same slightly protruding lower jaw and the tail has a greater fork. The back of *Morone labrax* also has a slight arch to it and its lateral line seems more distinct than the North American bass because it is not covered by stripes. Its coloration is more of a silver or silver-blue, and the European bass looks a lot like the Atlantic salmon. Ironically, it is called salmon-bass by some. It, too, is a marine species and frequently inhabits the estuaries and even fresh water, much like our striped bass.

The occurrence of nearly identical fish on the east and west sides of the Atlantic ocean, with a life cycle and habits closely allied, strongly suggests that both had a common ancestor. More than likely, the ancestor was able to move back and forth between continents, across the Arctic, early in the Pleistocene Period (alias the Glacial Period), when the top of the earth was a temperate and a times sub-tropic sea, or probably earlier in pre-Pleistocene times when the continents were considerably closed to each other. The separation of stocks likely occurred before the first great glacier swept down from the Arctic. Each now isolated group further evolved, but not too greatly, from the other. Either the European version lost its lines or the North American version grew lines. It would be interesting to see if these adults could breed, which is probable, and then to see if their progeny, too, were capable of breeding.

This fish is found around most of the British Isles during the summer months but disappears to the south during colder times of the year. Commercial trawlers have located some fish in a state of semi-hibernation, in deeper water off the mouth of British rivers. In summer distribution, it is found in southern Norway and Sweden, and from Denmark to the coast of France and Spain. Little was actually known about the habits of this fish until 1968 when Irish and British ichthyologists began the first of two studies designed to determine its biology. Though the studies were thorough and exacting they raised a series of contradictions that have not been wholly answered, the most pronounced of which, is where do these bass actually spawn. Irish researchers, Drs. Michael Kennedy and Patrick Fitzmaurice, based on the data they gathered, indicated that these bass spawn in salt water.

If this is correct, the European species seems incongruous with the major characteristics of the *Genus Morone*. Of the six members of the genus, two live their lives entirely in fresh water (*mississippiensis* and *chrysops*), two live in either fresh or salt water (*saxatilis* and *americana*) with equal ease, but those strains of the latter two species that spend a part of their lives in salt water return to fresh water to spawn and are considered anadromous fish. And because *labrax* is physically closer to *saxatilis*, than either *americana* or the two strictly freshwater species, it might be assumed that it, too, should have characteristics in common. However, the two differ in three distinct ways: stripes versus no stripes, European bass seldom grow heavier than 20 pounds and, according to Fitzmaurice, they mature in both egg and larval stages in salt water with a concentration as high as 32 ppt. Experimentation here with *saxatilis* eggs in such a high salinity immediately proved toxic; even at concentrations as low as 4 ppt.

On the other hand, there are too many characteristics of *labrax* and *saxatilis* to be discounted. *Labrax* is also anadromous because it is found as much as 40 miles upstream in some Irish and English rivers, it is always in the estuaries and at the edge of freshwater when in physically ripe conditions for spawning. Most of these fish's lives are spent in estuaries or not far from them when at sea. Juveniles of Age I and II are closely associated with brackish waters at the estuary's mouths. They are still there in winter when three-year fish move offshore a few miles to winter-over. This, too, is very characteristic of *saxatilis*. Males mature at three to five years of age and females at five to seven, similar to *saxatilis*. Their way of life is almost identical to striped bass.

While research have not indicated they have found the exact spawning sites or witnessed the spawning act, fertilized eggs found two to three miles in the open ocean were taken to the lab, where they were hatched out and confirmed that they are *labrax* eggs. There obviously is a need for more research to be conducted is to where *labrax* spawns. If it truly is a saline spawner, they this genus has made the irreversible transition from fresh to salt water that scores of other fish species have achieved over the millennia.

Morone labrax, the European version of our striped bass. It is the closest cousin to *Morone saxatilis*. The similarities, even in this archaic-art style of rendering fish, that is still quite valid, are striking. The illustration was reproduced from the 1803 edition of *Natural History of British Fishes*.

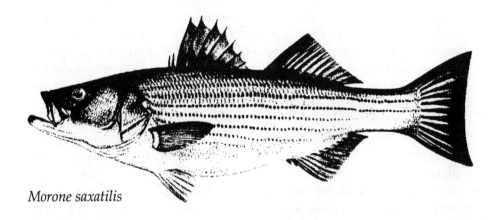

Morone saxatilis

10

Striped Bass
Population Biology

FACTORS AFFECTING POPULATION SIZE

The current size of a population has very little to do with the scope or magnitude of future generations of striped bass. This might seem a statement contrary to everything you've ever believed or learned about fish conservation. But the most important factors that will determine the future populations of striped bass are forces in its ambient environment, especially those surrounding the fish during the very earliest (egg and larval) stages of its life. Because of the great fecundity of a female striped bass, even the smallest number of fish in the brood stock can quickly replenish a striped bass population *if* the environmental factors on the nursery grounds are favorable to a successful hatching.

Striped bass are classed with the free-spawning fishes—that is, species which produce astronomical numbers of eggs, as explained in Chapter 4. If all the factors were always favorable on spawning sites during hatching and rearing of striped bass, from egg to larva to fingerling to adult, soon the oceans would be filled with nothing but striped bass.

But everything does not always go well with striped bass production, so we have what are called dominant year classes of fish. A year class is dominant when the fish produced during that year are so numerous, that when compared to the production of other years, they monopolize the entire population by their numbers.

Because of the immense fecundity of even the youngest, spawning striped bass, it doesn't take many mature fish to create a dominant year class. That's why future populations of striped bass are not so much dependent upon the number of adults that are around as they are upon those conditions which make a successful spawning year. What these conditions are has never been fully defined. In fact, dominant year classes in the past have followed extremely low adult populations. The years from 1965 to 1970 didn't adhere totally to this pattern because bass in Chesapeake Bay produced several dominant year classes in a row. That's why the overall population of striped bass leading up to 1970, the year of the last truly dominant year class, and the greatest in modern times, was so high along the Atlantic Coast until 1974, the start of the great decline that is still in effect today.

The best, almost text-book-like-example of a small population of striped bass in the mature stage capable of producing a great year class or an entire population of striped bass occurred in 1879 and 1881, when 435 small striped bass from New Jersey were transported to the Pacific Ocean at San Francisco Bay. In 20 years, because of the immense fecundity of the fish and with the permission of the environment, a commercial catch of 1,234,000 pounds of striped bass was recorded.

Limiting Environmental Factors

Since it is the environment that controls the success of a year class, we should be able to identify and isolate those environmental factors and modify or control them so that we can guarantee striped bass a future. That sounds ideal, easy, but it doesn't work quite that way. Researchers, during the last 30 years, and especially the last 10 years, have been working feverishly to identify those factors that can limit a striped bass population. Quite a few have been identified, but we don't know all of them. Even more important, we don't know how they interact with each other to produce a habitat hostile to striped bass reproduction.

We do know, however, that the most critical period in the life of a striped bass is during its first two weeks, from fertilization to larval stages. The physical conditions prevailing in the environment at that time control the future of the young fish. More obvious factors that were identified by investigations prior to the start of the Emergency Striped Bass Research Study in 1980 include: water temperature, predation, current, drift, salinity, turbidity, and population equilibrium.

Water temperature at the time of spawning is the first hurdle. It affects the fishery in several ways. First, it controls the time of spawning. Striped bass in a ripened condition over their spawning grounds will release eggs and sperm when the water temperature reaches 58 or 59 degrees and will continue to spawn up to 71 or 72 degrees. These are the outside limits of spawning temperature. The preferred temperature, that at which the bulk of the eggs are deposited, ranges from 61 or 62 degrees to 68 degrees; the optimal temperature is about 64.5 degrees.

Water temperature also affects the duration of spawning. If it falls below the minimum required or rises above the maximum, striped bass will temporarily stop spawning until the temperature returns to the desired levels. If the temperature rises too far and does not return to the optimal range, the fish will not spawn and the eggs will eventually be reabsorbed in the body.

The third effect of water temperature strongly influences the pattern of egg distribution. During a spawning season, when the daily water temperatures rise gradually, the number of eggs spawned steadily increases to a peak and then quickly drops off. This type of action is referred to as a "spawning bloom," and the duration of the bloom can vary from seven to ten days. During a season with vacillating daily temperatures during spawning, bass will lay eggs in several peaks, each corresponding with the rise, fall, and then rise again as temperatures rise. Spawning periods under such conditions can be drawn out over six to eight weeks.

There is a correlation between the number of young produced during two such extreme examples and the temperature. During the gradual buildup of water temperature and a spawning bloom, the number of young striped bass produced is greater than during a season with changeable water temperatures. Whether the correlation is a direct result of this variability cannot be stated with certainty, except that the results are there and though the cause might be something else it does seem to mirror the temperature.

Water temperature also affects the larvae's chances of existence once the eggs hatch. During a three-year study period in Maryland's part of the Chesapeake Bay, researchers checked the viability of eggs spawned and fertilized. During the period studied, their viability each year was approximately 30 percent. The differences were not large enough between years so that the number of eggs was considered a factor. However, during one of the years checked, the daily water temperature fluctuated greatly and during the other two it was steady. The year with a great fluctuation had the smallest production, and this led biologists to speculate that the mortality had to occur *after* the eggs hatched and fish were in the larval stage. Thus, water temperatures appear to be even more critical in the larval stage than the egg stage. As an added footnote, striped bass eggs spawned when the water temperature rises above 70 degrees have a greatly reduced viability, almost nil.

Predation that might affect a year class of striped bass occurs during the egg, larval and fingerling stages of the fish. To analyze predation during spawning, stomach samples were taken by a team of Maryland biologists of all species of fish found on the spawning areas. They included striped bass as well as competitive species. Twenty-seven species of fish were examined during one year at the head of Chesapeake Bay and almost all stomach analyses suggested that striped bass were not subject to measurable amounts of egg predation by other species of fish. The only exception was a few ingested by white catfish. Because of the deep-water egg dispersal characteristic of striped bass and the short incubation period, striped bass eggs were determined to be a minor food for other species of fish.

While striped bass are in the larval stage they are still vulnerable to predation because of their limited locomotion. However, studies indicate that while bass are in this level of development, any other potential predators are also in immature stages or not present on the fish's nursery grounds. Almost the very same is true for striped bass once they all reach the fingerling and juvenile stages. The fish are active and adroit enough in their swimming ability to avoid most would-be predators. In reality, the reverse is true: young striped bass become predators on other species.

There is some degree of cannibalism among striped bass—that is, larger or older year-class fish feed on younger ones—but it has not been proven to be of a major consequence. As a result, young striped bass are in a unique position during the early portions of their lives, with very few predators to affect their numbers. The number of fish and species that share spawning and nursery grounds with striped bass has been reduced over the years because of pollution and siltation, all to the advantage of young striped bass. Striped bass have actually benefited by some forms of pollution, in moderation.

One well known early Maryland researcher, Romeo Mansueti, advanced a rather sound hypothesis that civilization and striped bass populations are compatible in the Chesapeake Bay area because of increased enrichment and turbidity of the rivers. This may have been true, to a point, when pollution first became an environmental characteristic. But this relationship may have changed with the far greater number of people who eventually came to live in the area. Forty years ago, when Mansueti established that pollution-caused enrichment, especially as it concerned foods for larval striped bass, the human population was half of what it is today. Still, this was the only explanation offered at the time for the increase in striped bass populations. While almost every other species of fish along our coast has declined because of changing water qualities and physical alterations of their environment striped bass, had benefited. However, by 1970, these changes went beyond the tolerance capabilities of striped bass and are now considered one of the contributory causes that triggered the great decline that began in 1971, and has not abated 22 years later.

Current on the spawning grounds is also a factor that affects the development of striped bass eggs. The eggs have a specific gravity that is almost the same as fresh water, 1.007. In a body of water with no current the eggs will gradually fall to the bottom. Siltation and a piling of other eggs will cause the bottom eggs to suffocate and not hatch. However, it takes just the slightest degree of current to keep the eggs in motion, off the bottom, and thus well-oxygenated. Even in waters where siltation is quite high, striped bass eggs can survive because of their buoyancy. Eggs of other fish that have a greater specific gravity are likely to be buried by siltation in spring rivers.

Drift, or the distance eggs and larvae will be carried after spawning, becomes a crucial factor if the spawning sites are too close to salt water. With too fast a drift in short rivers, the eggs will be carried into a saline environment too soon and hatch in a lethal environment.

Salinity experiment studies have shown that striped bass eggs can develop in water with as high a concentration of salt as 20 ppt. However, the larvae perished within twenty-four hours after hatching under these conditions. Striped bass eggs are perfectly capable of hatching in a purely freshwater environment and, in some strains, the fish never migrate or even approach salt water. But even here the normal mortality is between 10 and 20 percent. Ironically, the survival of larvae has proved highest in water with a salinity concentration of 2-3 ppt in laboratory tests.

Typically, coastal striped bass stocks pick spawning sites that are totally in fresh water but still under the influence of tides. However, the nature of spawning sites can vary greatly, and fish have been known to travel as little as 20 miles and as much as 200 miles up a river to get away from salt water. Exceptions to the rule happen and fish do spawn in brackish water that can have a salinity range varying from 1.7 to 11 ppt.

Turbidity, that is, murkiness caused by suspended solids in the water—is a characteristic of many alluvial streams where striped bass spawn. Given a choice, striped bass seem to prefer streams with some degree of turbidity over clearer streams. This is evidenced in North Carolina and Maryland where a diversity of watersheds is available. Perhaps turbidity reduces the activity of predators that require sight to feed on striped bass eggs.

One thing most researchers agree upon is that the dominant-year-class concept explains rather well the acyclic nature of striped bass fluctuations. As a species with a population of multi-age fish, an unusually strong year class of striped bass dominates (by numbers) the population for two, three, or more years. Then, as the contribution of the dominant year class wanes, the population drops back to a low level and stays at the low level for two or three years until another dominant year class is born.

Numerous investigators have tried to explain the causes of dominant year classes. One found that dominant year classes were produced only in those years when the preceding winter temperatures were subnormal, but not all the years of low temperatures produced dominant year classes. The conclusion was that there must also be other factors with the subnormal temperature that bring about such production. Some have tried using another variable, like salinity, but couldn't develop a correlation. The only truism agreed upon is that there is no simple, one-reason answer.

Population equilibrium is an interesting side note to be added to the dominant-year-class concept. Each time a dominant year class is produced, it is the result of a parent stock that is in numbers below the equilibrium size. Equilibrium in a population is attained when the recruitment or production is equal to the parent-stock loss; there is no gain or loss in the number of fish in a population. Also, as parent stock increases—that is, as existing fish grow older and larger—the annual recruitment, young fish added to the population, appears to decline slightly. One suggested answer to this is cannibalism by the adult bass. That is, when there are many large bass in a population they eat more of the eggs, larvae, and fry. But as the adult stock falls below the equilibrium level there are just so many young that the big fish cannot possibly eat them all, and thus we have a dominant year class. However, in food studies of striped bass there has been little evidence of cannibalism to support this conclusion. Also, the fact has been established that striped bass stop feeding for a period, maybe only a few days, while they are spawning, and this would certainly reduce the likelihood of spent bass eating their own eggs and larvae. At this point, the question has no answer.

Physical Limiting Factors

The physical limiting factors restricting the future of bass are the most apparent to even the untrained observer. Dams are the most obvious and were the first to affect the great abundance of fish along the northern section of their range. In a few situations, fish ladders similar to those used for salmon were constructed, but their early design was ineffective and striped bass couldn't or wouldn't climb them. The homing instinct, while a functional element in the striped bass, is nowhere as effective or precise as that of salmon. Thus, without a place to spawn and renew their kind, striped bass along the Northeast began to dwindle in numbers.

However, about ten years ago the federal government, along with Connecticut, Massachusetts, Vermont, and New Hampshire, began a massive effort to restore Atlantic salmon to the Connecticut River. In several places, restrictive dams no longer in use were removed, and in others, unique fish ladders were constructed. Some salmon began returning to their natal rivers after the first year, with more in the second and third years. At each fish ladder, observers were stationed during the return migration and through glass windows in the ladders they counted the returning fish. To their surprise, they began seeing striped bass moving up river with salmon. Some striped bass migrated up the Connecticut River as far as Vermont and New Hampshire, where the river forms the state border. The Connecticut River, during colonial times, was a major striped bass nursery.

In some areas of the country, California as a specific example, the demand for irrigation water has lessened the flow over spawning grounds and proved a threat to the survival of the fish population. In other areas, water dammed and used for hydroelectricity has reduced the flow on some streams and caused spawning sites to be changed, reduced, or even abandoned. These factors then affect contribution of new fish to the overall abundance of the population.

Pollution is a different kind of dam that stops migrating fish. Pollution blockages existed on most rivers of the Atlantic Coast; the Delaware River is one of the best examples. At times pollution by chemicals, including industrial and municipal wastes, was so great that it impeded the up river migration of fishes. Shad and striped bass at one time were reported to have spawned as far north on the Delaware River as Port Jervis in New York, but there is no evidence to support this. However, one major historical site was documented in the Philadelphia area of the river. The pollution block in the Philadelphia had eliminated the vast shad runs, and striped bass runs stopped so long ago that they were evident only in history. Pollution here encouraged such a growth of oxygen-absorbing life-forms that fish trying to migrate through it, especially during elevated temperature periods, would suffocate.

About 15 years ago, the City of Philadelphia, the major polluter on the river and creator of the lethal block, began an intense effort, with the aid of federal funds (Clean Waters Act) to clean up its municipal sewage treatment systems, upgrading them from primary to tertiary levels. It took shad but two years to respond and the run up the river into New York quickly reestablished itself. Today, there is a healthy shad fishery on the river reminiscent of the great runs of the late 1800s.

Striped bass, however, did not responded as quickly. Though there are recognizable numbers of striped bass now annually moving from Delaware Bay into the river, and some again as far as north as Port Jervis, there had been no evidence of spawning, even though young-of-the-year fish were netted in the lower, freshwater reaches of the river as well as at the head of Delaware Bay, until 1988. The historical spawning sites were located just below Philadelphia though the head of tidewater reaches up river to Trenton. Most of the old spawning sites on the river were shared by both Pennsylvania and New Jersey. Spawning does occur in the Delaware Bay, in the Chesapeake & Delaware Canal and on the Maurice River, a small stream that empties into the tidal section of Delaware Bay from New Jersey.

At Philadelphia, the pollutants drastically reduced the oxygen content of the rivers and made passage upstream over a long length of river impossible. The situation was heightened during warm springs because of the lessened ability of warmer water to hold oxygen. The last blow to the shad population (before the pollution was cleaned) came when fingerlings, the result of a spawning by the few fish that were able to clear the pollution block, tried to return to the ocean. By this time, it was mid- to late summer. The fingerlings, as they moved downstream, suffocated on their way to sea.

Pollutants also work against the striped bass population in another way, by affecting the biota upon which striped bass depend in their food cycle. While a polluted river may not be directly harmful to the adult striped bass, it can disrupt the delicate food chain. Zooplankton form the bottom link in a long chain that eventually ends with striped bass and man at the other end. Striped bass larvae, as well as young shrimp, upon which bass fry feed, depend on such primary foods as their initial food source. Sulfide pollutants are extremely detrimental to zooplankton and retard their multiplication. This is the chief pollutant in pulp processes and when dumped into rivers can ruin a striped bass nursery. Sulfides can also be airborne, as in acid rain, that has been singled out by recent investigations as a possible major cause of the striped bass decline.

Atomic-energy and fossil fuel power plants, with cooling systems that rely on marine or riverine waters to reduce the great amount of heat generated by their reactors, are another threat. The use of immediate area waters affects the fish in two ways. First, eggs, larvae, and often fry can be sucked into the water intakes and damaged or killed in the process—as was the case with several Con Edison plants on the Hudson River. They were built without regard to location as far as striped bass were concerned and without considering the environmental impact of the plants' operations.

The second threat is from the elevated temperature of the discharge water. Water absorbs the heat in the reactor and comes out several degrees warmer than when it enters. Discharge of water 5 to 10 degrees warmer than the ambient water might not seem great, but in a large marine body of water but it is more crucial than in fresh water. In freshwater environments, fish have learned to survive and adapt to rapidly changing water temperatures because of the relatively small water envelope that surrounds them. The smaller water volume here is more readily affected by outside temperatures and responds to them. So do the fish.

Fish in a marine environment are protected from rapid temperature changes by a large volume of water. Thus, outside changes take a long time to effect great changes of the water's temperature. Saltwater fish have learned to adapt slowly to gradual change. The effect of a 5- or 10-degree change in a warm or cold environment can have immediate results when the plant is in the proximity of the fish's spawning site. This is even more pronounced in the egg, fry, and larval stages, when temperature is a critical factor. Eggs and larval striped bass have no locomotive ability and drift at the whims of tides and currents. They cannot avoid hot-water discharges and can be killed if they drift into it.

Fishing Pressures

Two other factors that can and do affect striped bass populations and their future are commercial and recreational fishing. Until just a few years ago, the sport fishery had negligible effects on the fish population. However, the number of recreational anglers has grown so rapidly in recent years that it now rivals the commercial fishery in many areas of the fish's range. Chesapeake Bay is a typical example.

There was very little sport fishing done during the early history of this nation, and what fishing did occur was to place fish on the table or to barter them for other items. The growth of our sport fishery parallels the availability of recreational time, which has increased enormously since the end of World War II. The number of striped bass taken in the name of sport is quite large, though it is difficult to estimate accurately. During the late 1960s , in Chesapeake Bay and Albemarle Sound, the sport-fishing catch was reported to be just about equal to the commercial catch. Creel censuses during the 1960s at Santee-Cooper reveal that almost 500,000 pounds of bass were taken annually. This decreased sharply in recent years because of a downward change in the reservoir's water quality. On the Pacific Coast, the annual catches in the mid-1960s were estimated at about 3 million pounds, 2 million of which were taken from California waters where no commercial fishing has existed since 1935. Since then, catches there have declined sharply because of a variety of problems threatening striped bass and other fish populations. The annual take from the rest of the nation can only be guessed.

Commercial catching of fish is often described as "harvesting" fish, and is often equated with "farming the sea." I cannot always argue with this term. However, whether a fish is being harvested or exploited (the **full** use of a resource) depends on the size of the population and when in the fish's life it is being removed. Almost all the biological evidence today suggests that harvesting mature striped bass, in a healthy population, when they are on the nursery grounds, is not detrimental to producing fish and little affect future populations. Brood stock is not now, nor has it ever been, the delimiting factor to striped bass populations. However, it could conceivably be. During periods when the nursery environment is hostile, conservation of brood stock fish is considered by some fish managers as a positive hedge against the future. Actually, it is the only hedge they have.

During the colonial period, when commercial or economic netting of fish

Pound traps are fixed along a shore and fish, following the edge of land, are guided by a barrier net into the trap. Confused by baffle nets inside the pound fish cannot usually find their way out. Such pound traps are used in New York, Maryland, Virginia and North Carolina.

meant that one took all the fish possible, with whatever means was available, the effect of this type of pressure was quickly felt. If you continually stretch a gill net or seine across a stream at all times of the year, for several years, quite soon you will effectively stop all the fish from reproducing and will eliminate all fish that would come to that stream.

Numerous netting devices and rigs that would capture great numbers of fish indiscriminately have been outlawed from most of the commercial fishery. However, today haul seines, though recently outlawed in New York, are still permitted in Maryland, Virginia and North Carolina. New York's Department of Environmental Conservation outlawed haul seines when commercial fishing was resumed in 1990. They described it as a "dirty fishery," because it could not discriminate between fish either too small or too large that could not legally be retained by fishermen. The seine, especially the cod end, killed almost all the fish when a haul was completed. It made slot-size management of striped bass impossible.

Other types of commercial gear that are allowed today to harvest striped bass in certain states range from gill nets (staked and floating), fyke and hoop nets, fish pots, floating traps, pound traps, and trawls to pinhooking. Pinhooking, alias hook-and-line fishing, uses rods and reels instead of nets or traps to catch fish. The control of mesh size in gill nets allows for smaller, immature fish and larger fish, too big to enter the mesh, to escape. Pound traps are ideal for size management because only those within the legal length range can be sorted in the pound and the remainder released.

In Massachusetts the only way one can fish commercially for striped bass is with handline or rod and reel, while in Rhode Island pinhooking is allowed, but floating traps take the major portion of bass. Haul seines had produce the most commercial fish in New York, but just prior to the decline, catches by pinhookers surpassed gill netters and pound trappers. Currently, quotas are allotted each gear type and the effectiveness of each is no longer relevant. Otter trawls were used primarily in New Jersey, but that state declared striped bass a game fish in 1991 and all sales of striped bass were prohibited. Fixed gill nets are still the common commercial method in Delaware but hook-and-line catches have increased. Fixed gill nets are also the most popular device in Maryland but the state also allows seine, fyke, hoop, and pound nets as well as fish pots, trawls, and hook-and-line. In the Potomac River, where fishing is governed by the Potomac River Fisheries Commission, composed of Maryland and Virginia, only hook-and-line fishing is allowed. Nor is there a commercial fishery allowed on the Potomac River within the federal District of Columbia. In Virginia, pound nets, haul seines, fyke and fixed gill nets account for about 30 percent of the commercial fish landed. In North Carolina, drift gill nets, pound nets, and haul seines, as well as hook-and-line and trawls, are used in the commercial fishery.

Once, an underrated commercial technique, the hook-and-line or pinhooking method has grown in use and is a very effective method for harvesting striped

Haul-seining striped bass has been a technique used by coastal fishermen since the first colonists landed in Massachusetts. But since 1989, when New York outlawed the technique, only the states of Maryland, Virginia, and North Carolina allow it.

bass. It is growing in popularity because it requires a minimal amount of investment when compared to other gear types, requires only one angler to function and is a very mobile method by which the fisherman can seek out and follow fish over a wide territory, a decided advantage over all other gear types which are fixed or stationary. Massachusetts is a good example of comparing hook-and-line effectiveness to other gear types because the commercial fishery there has been restricted only to the use of hook-and-line since the late 1940s.

In the waning years of the coastal fishery, during the late 1970s, coastal stocks were still relatively high because Chesapeake Bay fish had produced the phenomenally large 1970 year class. Maryland, in 1979, commercially harvested 859,000 pounds of striped bass. Massachusetts was second with 695,000 pounds. The following year, 1980, Maryland was again first with 1,892,000 pounds and Massachusetts again was second with 886,000 pounds. Commercial striped bass catches were still high in 1981 when Maryland accounted for 1,502,000 pounds of fish. However, Massachusetts fell to third place with 708,000 pounds. Its second place was usurped by a growing number of pinhookers in New York, who short-stopped the fish migrating north past Montauk Point on their way to "The Cape" (Cape Cod). Montauk pinhookers, in addition to setting a new world's record for striped bass, taking several fish in the high 60s, and along with other commercial methods, landed 822,000 pounds. But in 1982, the decline finally began to show itself in the coastal commercial fishery. Seemingly to make up for the decline in poundage from the previous year, Massachusetts pinhookers led all other states and hauled 643,000 pounds over their gunwales. Maryland was a distant second with 478,000 pounds, just ahead of New York's 471,000 pounds of striped bass.

Commercial seasons vary from state to state because this harvest coincides with the movement of large schools of striped bass throughout the year, which dictates when bass can be taken commercially. In Massachusetts, the fishery is active primarily during summer—July, August, and September; in New York, from September to late November; in New Jersey it was in winter only; in Maryland and Virginia it is now variable and dependent on the state legislature. In North Carolina, in 1990, it was a week in February and again in late November to late December. Commercial fishing, and sport fishing for that matter, only become a threat to a striped bass population when brood-stock numbers are so low in a given area that fishing can effectively remove all the stock or lower it to a level that would impede the stock's recovery. If enough fish aren't produced to maintain a minimal breeding stock, then the species in that locale is in danger of extinction.

Maryland and Virginia had very similar laws governing the taking of striped bass from Chesapeake Bay. The minimum size limit was 12 inches before the fish declined and an eventual moratorium was instituted. This size limit had allowed the majority of fish to be harvested in their second or third year. If, at that time, the size limit had been raised to 16 inches, similar to the restriction in most other states, it would mean that Chesapeake Bay's commercial fishermen

Pinhook Pete—One of the most effective modern harvesters of striped bass. The term "pinhook-ers" was give them by commercial fishermen who use traditional gear. Since the late 1940s, Massachusetts has allowed commercial fishermen to use only rod, reel, hook, and line to harvest striped bass and in several years has taken more fish than Maryland.

would lose fish to the rest of the Atlantic states.

Prior to 1979, when Chesapeake Bay was still considered healthy, commercial and sport fishermen harvested almost 90 percent of a yearly production of fish. They did not harvest each year class during the first year because of the minimum size restriction. However, when fish were between two years of age and approach, three just before they would migrate, they fell prey to the fishery. Thus two-year-old fish and some at the beginning of their third year, fish 12 to 14 inches long, made up the bulk of the Chesapeake Bay fishery. The 10 percent of those fish that did escape Chesapeake Bay made up almost 90 percent, it was believed, of those fish taken along the coast during their annual migrations. However, more recent analysis of the harvest and re-estimating the contribution by other nursery areas has reduced this contribution figure to between 65 to 75 percent.

This over-harvesting, in a real sense over-exploitation, hastened the decline of the striped bass population in the bay after 1970 and was stopped only after Maryland, in January, 1985, and then Delaware, one week later, declared self-imposed moratoria. When the Food and Drug Administration lowered its allowable PCB levels in fish from 5 to 2 ppm, New York State's Department of Health closed the commercial fishing in all of the state on May 8, 1986, and in effect expanded the moratorium.

In 1986, Rhode Island placed a moratorium on the sale of striped bass caught in its waters, to local consumers, but they could be sold out of state. Commercial striped bass harvests in Virginia's three rivers in Chesapeake Bay fell so low, reflecting the earlier decline in young-of-the-year striped bass production on these waters, that it, too, on the sale of fish on June 1, 1989, declared a moratorium. The Potomac River Fisheries Commission declared a moratorium on the same date. The moratoria were lifted in 1990 when the Atlantic States Marine Fisheries Commission, influenced by Maryland's unique index rise in 1989, produced the triggering mechanism needed and commercial fishing was resumed. However, during this moratoria period, Massachusetts continued to take striped bass commercially.

Strains of Striped Bass

In order to manage a population of fish like striped bass, fisheries personnel must know where they originate, what is the parent stock, and if these various stocks can be differentiated and thus managed to the benefit of the entire fishery. Attempts to distinguish stocks as to their place of origin began as early as the late 1930s. However, it wasn't until the early 1950s that studies were conducted along both coasts as well as the Gulf states to determine if striped bass produced in each area have physically different characteristics, features that are peculiar only to fish in each endemic area, either a river system or an estuary with several rivers entering it. If they do, then the fish populations could then be broken into what might loosely be called races or strains.

Meristics

Researchers today believe race is not an applicable term for striped bass populations because most lack the required temporal as well as spatial isolation to develop true races. Instead, the various groups with somewhat differing characteristics might better be described as stocks. Therefore, stocks are usually differentiated by their morphological meristic features—that is, variations in the number or position of body parts. Groups of meristic features on striped bass were studied, and it was thought that only counts of fin rays and counts of scales on the lateral line proved usable—the scale counts better than the fin-ray counts.

The number of scales on the lateral line do differ, on the average, when compared between stocks from varying locales. Striped bass have been found to contain a number range on the lateral line that varies from a low of 52 to a high of 67 scales. Bass produced in the St. Lawrence River system contained an average of 61.3 scales on the lateral line. Hudson River stocks had 59.6 scales, Chesapeake Bay fish had 60.1, and North Carolina fish had 61.7. As one counts scales of local populations south of North Carolina they progressively diminish to a low of 54.2 scales found on striped bass from the St. Johns River in Florida.

Another meristic method study attempted to separate breeding stocks by counting the number of soft rays in the anal fins of striped bass, but differences were so slight they made a poor tool. Extremes ranged between 10.6 rays for Hudson River to 10.9 rays for Delaware and Chesapeake Bay bass. Most fish south of North Carolina, which had a 10.8 count, all possessed 11 rays except in west Florida and Mississippi with 9.8 rays.

Races were thus established for striped bass in the St. Lawrence River and the Gulf of St. Lawrence, for the Nova Scotia-New Brunswick area, and for the Hudson River. A weak separation exists between Delaware Bay and Chesapeake Bay stocks. Chesapeake Bay further complicated the picture by the discovery of at least three sub-races and possibly a fourth that is more closely related to the distinct race in Albemarle Sound than other Chesapeake Bay fishes. Separate stocks have also been identified for Santee-Cooper fish in South Carolina, and Florida has its own meristically unique striped bass population. In the Pacific, the striped bass stock is the same as Hudson River fish because the transplants that started the Pacific on its way came from northern New Jersey, of stock that had been spawned in the Hudson River.

After all the results of these early studies were coordinated, it was established that striped bass had indeed segregated themselves into strains dependent upon their brood stock or place of origin. However, under more severe scrutiny, the data did not entirely hold up or have the consistency needed in scientific work. There was too great an area overlap and thus margin for discrimination. The use of morphological meristics can be a valid tool when various strains within an animal population have been separated for really long periods of time and no communication occurs between them during this period. At the longest, the current populations of striped bass have been separated by only 20,000 years, a mere blink of the eye in evolutionary time. While meristics is only a weak guideline at best, it did serve to some degree as an early fisheries management tool.

Parasites

Though not devised as an investigative technique for striped bass, examinations of parasites in the stomach and intestine did act as a positive identification in one instance. An investigation in 1984 of intestinal parasites in striped bass caught on the Kouchbougac River in New Brunswick, south of the mouth of the St. Lawrence River, revealed three helminth species found only in Chesapeake Bay, but not in any Canadian-produced striped bass. In a follow-up, 60 striped bass were tagged on the river and later recovered in Delaware and Chesapeake bays. This confirmed the mid-Atlantic contribution to coastal migrants in New Brunswick waters.

Genetic and Biochemical Discrimination

A large number of genetic studies have been conducted to determine striped bass origins, on several historical processes that shape the genetic make-up or genotype of a stock. This is based on the fact that the huge DNA molecule is constantly undergoing chromosomal rearrangements, additions and deletions and point mutations. The longer the fish stocks are separated the greater the chromosomal changes and thus the more accurate this method can be. This is also based on the fact that though stocks do mix in coastal migrations, when it comes time to spawn they all, nearly 92 percent, return to their natal stream and spawn with fish of their own kind. The 8 percent, that can vary, is what makes biological drift work in a population and allows the establishment of new stocks on previous uninhabited waters.

Mitochondrial and Nuclear DNA

In recent years, restriction endonuclease analysis of mitochondrial DNA (mtDNA) has been used to separate striped bass stocks with surprising accuracy. While effective, the use of mtDNA to discriminate between stocks has a few limitations, the greatest of which is that the genetic information it carries is small in comparison to the entire molecule. An alternative approach is to screen the nucleus for a greater number of unique characteristics, e.g., polymorphisms. This technique requires but a small sample of the fish, a piece of fin or scale, and the entire fish does not need to be sacrificed as in mtDNA analysis.

Obviously, the time period needed for isolated stocks to develop detectable genotypic variations is a lot less than the time needed for meristic characteristics to evolve. In striped bass, these modern changes have been underway for about

10,000 years, which has been proven to be a period long enough to develop all the existing strains in the post-glacial era in the Gulf and Atlantic states. And, in what may be a much shorter period is the case between apparent non-mingling stocks, based on tag returns on the Coos River and those 25 miles to the north, on the Umpqua River, both in Oregon. Both riverine stocks originated as Hudson River fish that were used about 150 years ago to establish striped bass populations on the Pacific Coast.

They appear to have already created their genotypes, and their tissue samples will be investigated during the summer of 1993 by Dr. Isaac Wirgin, of the Institute of Environmental Medicine, New York University Medical Center. Dr. Wirgin, along with Dr. John R. Waldman of the Hudson River Foundation for Science and Environmental Research and Dr. Joseph Grossfield of the Biology Department, City College of New York, have greatly advanced these stock-identification techniques. Within the last year, Dr. Wirgin has analyzed fish populations in Canada and confirmed the natural separation of stocks in several rivers in Quebec, New Brunswick, and Nova Scotia. In addition, he has established stock identities for several Gulf Coast rivers as well as those in the Southeast.

Catches of sportfishermen in many areas of the country, especially in New York and Maryland, equal or even exceed those of commercial fishermen in the same area. Here's a trophy catch of striped bass, taken when limits were more generous than today, and became a contributing factor to the decline of Chesapeake Bay fish stocks. Mixed with the bass are bluefish.

11

Management of
Striped Bass Populations

The abundance of striped bass has always been a topic of interest to the public as consumers, to recreational, and commercial fishermen, and biologists. Striped bass were a very abundant species during colonial times, even during natural cyclic lows in their numbers. In those days, maximum sizes of annual populations were determined only by biological and natural physical variables that kept them in check. Today, man, either directly or indirectly, has become another element in the limiting of striped bass abundance along our three ocean coasts, in tidal and freshwater rivers and streams, and in natural and man-made impoundments.

Striped bass played an important role in the early settlements of this country, and our first records of the availability of the fish come from Plymouth and Boston. In 1623, through misfortune, the Plymouth Colony had only one small boat. Yet with the aid of this boat and a net, the colonists were able to take enough striped bass to keep from starving.

Thomas Morton, writing in 1632, tells us:

> The Basse is an excellent Fish, both fresh & salt, one hundred whereof, salted at market, have yielded 5 p. They are so large the head of one will give a good eater a dinner, and for daintiness of diet they excell the Marybones of beefe. There are such multitudes that I have seene stopped into the river close adjoining to my howse, with a sand at one tide, so many as will load a shipe of one hundred tonnes.

The famous Captain John Smith, who was governor of Virginia until that colony failed, then was made admiral of New England, wrote in a book published in London in 1631:

> The seven and thirty passengers, miscarrying twice upon the coast of [New] England, came so ill provided they only relyed upon the poore company they found, they had lived two years by their naked industry and what the country naturally afforded. It is true, there hath beene taken a thousand Bayses at a draught, and more than twelve hogsheads of Herring in one night.

The effects of civilization upon the abundance in nature quickly began to take their toll, even on the seemingly inexhaustible supply of striped bass. Declines were first noticed in New England, where dams were built first to run grain-grinding mills and where excessive netting of fish at times eliminated an entire upriver migration.

Gradually, the decline spread throughout New England and southward into New York, New Jersey, Delaware, and Pennsylvania. The decrease in striped bass numbers was slow until after the end of the Civil War because dams and mills were small. Then, the great American Industrial Revolution began and signaled the rapid deterioration of striped bass numbers. The dams needed to run industry were larger that those for grinding grains and their expansion increased rapidly. Catches of fish along the coast of Maine, Rhode Island, and Massachusetts fell drastically. First, the fisheries in Maine collapsed. Then, fishing clubs—established in the mid-1800s by wealthy sportsmen and dedicated almost exclusively to catching striped bass in southern New England— began to disband as the 20th century approached and striped bass disappeared.

Farther south, in Chesapeake Bay, long one of the oldest and richest fishing grounds along the Atlantic Coast, industrialization was much less pronounced and striped bass populations remained unaffected for a longer time. Its watershed lacks the height of land needed to produce a force of water for running mills, except in the upper reaches, which were beyond the domain of striped bass. Until the end of the Civil War, fishing in Chesapeake Bay had been to supply local markets. The advent of the railroad and dwindling fish food supplies in the Northeast gave impetus to expanding commercial fishing in Chesapeake Bay beyond the immediate socio-economic area.

The original striped bass fishery along the New England and Middle Atlantic coasts was very likely totally self-sustaining, receiving very little or no striped bass from the Chesapeake Bay fishery as it does today. Each river system developed an isolated population that communicated with other riverine populations only if they shared the same tidal estuary. The factors that encouraged one strain of Chesapeake striped bass to develop a great transcoastal migratory characteristic were not in operation at the time. If they were, they did not favor the survival of that particular strain of striped bass until their habitat was altered. If these fish had a migratory characteristic during the 1800s, and were able to move up the coast, they would have continued to fill the growing local void and repopulate the New England coast as they do today.

Very few commercial fish landing records were kept prior to 1880, and during the years from about 1880 to 1930, only sporadic records of commercial landings were maintained by the federal government or many coastal states. While landings and populations of striped bass from Delaware north to Maine were steadily declining, those in Chesapeake Bay remained stable, with only local cyclic fluctuations affecting the size of the population. Landing figures from southern Atlantic Coast states, the endemic populations of which do not contribute to the Atlantic migratory stock, also appeared to remain constant.

Since 1930, however, fairly accurate records of striped bass landings have been maintained by all Atlantic states with striped bass populations. Disregarding local highs and lows in the populations, they reflect a steady increase in the harvest of striped bass. In New England and the Middle Atlantic states, these landings surpassed those of the late 1800s. It is impossible to compare today's striped bass population to what it might have been in colonial times because of the changed environment, greater fishing pressure nowadays, and the lack of records for the first landings.

Even bass landings during the mid-1950s, when a more recent decline in numbers of striped bass being produced in Chesapeake Bay was first detected, were four to five times greater than in the late 1800s. But one cannot use landings in the late 1800s as a population measure, especially when there was no demand for Chesapeake Bay fish because they were plentiful in areas closer to where they were being sold. This was the case in Maryland waters. The fishery in the mid-1970s was being utilized near its maximum but in 1865 it was underfished. We can only speculate at what the actual numbers might have been.

The 1973 striped bass harvest, when nearly 15 million pounds were landed was the greatest in modern times but no one could foresee the calamity that was just around the corner.

STATE LEGISLATION AS A MANAGEMENT CONTROL TOOL

At the General Courte, holden in Boston, the 22nd of the 3rd M., Called May 1639—"And it is forbidden to all men, after the 20th of next month, to imploy any codd or basse fish for manuring the ground, upon paine that every pson, being a fisherman, that shall sell or imploy any such fish for that end, shall loose the said priviledge of exemption from public charges, & that both fisherman, or others who shall use any kind of said fish for that purpose, shall forfet for every

> hundred of such fish so employed for manuring ground
> twenty shillings & portionally for a less or greater number;
> pvided, that it shall be lawful to use the heads and offal of
> such fish for corne, this nothwithstanding."

The preceding act was passed by the Massachusetts Bay Colony in 1639, nineteen years after the initial settlement at Plymouth, so that striped bass could not be used for fertilizer. Thus, it gives us a little insight as to the condition of the striped bass population in just a few years after it was exposed to civilized man. The value and limited supply of these fish were immediately realized. Striped bass and codfish were the first natural resources in the New World to come under conservation measures. Even to this day, striped bass, and legislation to govern its taking, are often topics of heated discussion.

New York was the next colony to pass legislation protecting striped bass, though more than 100 years later. A law prohibited the sale of striped bass during the winter months because of "a great decrease of that kind of fish." At that time, the main source for striped bass was the East River, on the east side of Manhattan. In 1762 the people of Marshfield, Mass., also sought to control the striped bass fishery and preserve a bit of it for future use by passing favorably on a petition to the General Court to enact a bill for the preservation of the fish and to prevent its capture during the winter season.

Little legislation followed for many years as the population of striped bass slowly dwindled along the northern part of its range. Not until the 1930s, and then during the following thirty years, as striped bass suddenly began to reappear along the Northeast coast, was there renewed interest in preserving the species. There then followed a rash of popular legislation, up and down the Atlantic Coast, as well as on the Pacific, to manage striped bass.

Until a decade ago, regulations governing or restricting the taking of striped bass varied widely from state to state. No states considered the migratory nature of the fish. Few, if any, of these laws were based on biological needs of the fish but rather were designed to favor one state over another while the fish were in their domain. Maryland, the producer of most of the Atlantic's migratory coastal stock, continued to harvest vast numbers of immature striped bass while they were still in their waters. They well knew that once the fish matured, they would leave Chesapeake Bay and would then be vulnerable to fishing harvest in other states. Little did they care that they were slowly eliminating the fish's ability to replace the losses they inflicted upon the population. Some of it was just plain ignorance, but most of it was thoughtlessness and greed.

Several biologists from Maryland, in the mid-1970s, even made a statement when other states tried to bring pressure on them to be more restrictive to conserve their stocks: "Maryland anglers and netters would lose and fishermen in other Atlantic seaboard states would gain benefits if the minimum size in the bay were raised from 12 to 16 inches." This is true. At about 14 to 15 inches, when they are in their third year, they leave the bay, often returning only to spawn.

Even though stocks were so badly reduced and fish faced endangered species status, Maryland still wouldn't heed recommendations by the Atlantic States Marine Fisheries Commission, that tried to regulate the taking of striped bass. The Commission was powerless until the federal government stepped in and made adherence to its striped bass management plan compulsory. The federal government threatened to take sanctions against states and declare a fishing moratorium in their waters if they didn't act.

EFFECTS OF PAST LEGISLATION

The answer to how effective past legislation has been in preserving the species for the future is quite simple: it hasn't. Until recently, all legislation affecting striped bass numbers had little or no biological basis but had been rooted in pure socio-economic motivations. Management policies based on the fish's biologically needs are the only approach possible to ensuring a future for striped bass. Current management capabilities deal only with maintaining a viable brood stock, until the brood stock, too, should disappear. But this approach is only effective when all environmental conditions are favorable to the fish. Brood stock currently is the only factor we can immediately manipulate because we can restrict the harvest of fish that would endanger a remnant stock. And because brood stock has never really been in danger, past legislation has never really had an opportunity to be effective. However, there is one theory that supports brood stock management, the "window of opportunity theory," which will be discussed later in this chapter.

Current legislation affects the population of striped bass by controlling the numbers and size of fish anglers and commercial fishermen may take, specifying either maximums or minimums, or both, either by weight or length; and by the time of the year, or even the time of the day during which striped bass may be caught. In general, some state legislation also prevents commercial fisherman from competing with sport fisherman. From a financial and sociological viewpoint, this is fine. However, it has no biological justification as a tool to guard striped bass from total depletion.

Maryland at one time had a 12-inch minimum length limit on the size of striped bass that could be caught and sold. The reason for this limit was to discourage commercial anglers, as well as sport fishermen, from harvesting young-of-the-year fish, or Age I fish, and to give them an opportunity to grow and produce a heavier fishery that would be harvested at Ages II and III. It had nothing to do with allowing the fish to reproduce at least once, which would take place at Age III in males and often as late as Age X in females, at which age would range between 28 to 36 inches. Here, the driving motivation was more pounds of fish, that meant more money. Earlier, Maryland's limit had been 11 inches and a great number of young male striped bass were netted. It was feared that there wouldn't be enough left to migrate to the spawning grounds in their third year to perpetuate the species, so the limit was raised. Though this fear had a biological basis, its ultimate goal was economically motivated.

In 1939, New York established a 16-inch limit, snout-to-fork measurement. Nor was the basis for this rule founded on the biology of the fish but rather to keep 11-inch Maryland-Virginia striped bass from New York fish markets. Maryland's great influx of fish, now iced and shipped by rail from Baltimore, lowered the price of striped bass taken from New Jersey, New York, and New England waters. Maryland had few 16-inch fish left over after it satisfied its local markets, with nothing remaining to send to the New York market.

Since the 1940s, in Massachusetts, it has been illegal to fish commercially for striped bass with anything but a hook and line. This effectively eliminated the larger commercial operations and at the same time allowed a "sport" fisherman to sell his catch without real competition from nets.

An interesting note arises when one reviews past data on where striped bass were caught and not caught and the goal of local legislation that was produced in these states before a federal striped bass management plan was inaugurated in 1981. In the past, those states that produced the fewest number of fish for the commercial market and recreational angling were the only states that attempted to manage the resource through biologically based legislation. They employed the most restrictive size limits and prohibitions. Ironically, none of these states were an important source of coastal migratory stock.

The only state with a major coastal migratory stock, until the end of the 1970s, was Maryland. However, since the drastic decline in Maryland's contribution to this phenomenon, New York's contribution has risen markedly. In addition, but not on a regular basis, striped bass from Virginia and the Roanoke River in North Carolina have made contributions. While these latter states produce substantial numbers of striped bass their contribution was thought to be small, only about 10 percent of the coastal stock. On the other hand, only about 10 percent of the fish produced in Chesapeake Bay escaped the bay but still this number was so large that it constituted the remaining 90 percent of the coastal stock. However, recent studies indicate that the Hudson's contribution may have been grossly underestimated. Today, with Chesapeake stocks in decline, the Hudson is now considered the major contributor to the stocks that migrate as far as Nova Scotia and Quebec in the spring and summer.

The relative size of the Hudson stock was unknown until New York's Department of Environmental Conservation directed state biologist Byron Young to initiate the Hudson River Index in 1969. This thinking is further enhanced today by the fact that while most of the Hudson River stock may not be truly of a coastal migratory nature, with the severe decline in the Chesapeake Bay stock more Hudson fish have become wanderers. Nature abhors a vacuum and by the natural process of biological drift, striped bass are happy to fill the void. This does not hold true for Virginia fish produced in the lower Chesapeake. During certain periods, striped bass from the Roanoke River-Albemarle Sound complex migrated north with other stocks that wintered in the ocean off North Carolina; however, they've made no contribution in the last 10 years.

Before 1984, among the Middle Atlantic and New England states, New York had the least restrictive regulations (no seasons or creel limits, just a 16-inch minimum length) on the taking of striped bass, while supposedly contributing very few fish to the migratory stock in the Atlantic. But unlike other states, which had imposed numerous regulations, New York was also harvesting its own striped bass along its coast.

Most of New York's commercial fishing took place between Jones Inlet and Montauk Point, with the greater concentration from Shinnecock Inlet eastward. It was basically a haul-seine fishery with a few pound traps in the bays and one along the Atlantic shore which did not contribute significantly to the overall commercial catch. However, there was an appreciable gill net and inshore otter-trawler fishery that contributed about 20 percent to the total catch. When all New York's landings were added they amounted to between eight and nine percent of the total striped bass annually caught in the nation.

This figure needed a partial adjustment. New York's otter-trawler fleet may have contributed only 20 percent to the state's landing figures, but the greater number of boats that trawled off Long Island's beaches were from New Jersey. New Jersey had banned all commercial fishing within its 3-mile territorial seas jurisdiction, so its trawlers worked beyond 3 miles and almost on the beaches in New York waters. Their landings, however, were recorded as New Jersey landings even though the bulk of their catch came from New York waters. New Jersey contributes about 1.0 to 1.5 percent to the overall commercial landings. However, with the development of high-speed trawlers needed to take striped bass, New Jersey's landings increased until the Chesapeake stock began its decline. During the 1973 season, a pair of New Jersey trawlers working off southern part of the state, were reported to have run into schools of striped bass so large that they completely filled the trawls and stopped the boats in the water.

The commercial picture has drastically changed in the past few years because of quota limitations and the paucity of fish. In 1990, the first commercial striped bass seasons were allowed in the Atlantic coastal fishery. The Hudson River remained closed to commercial fishing because of PCB contamination. More significantly, however, were gear changes. Haul seines were eliminated in New York because they were considered by biologists as a "dirty fishery." They didn't discriminate as to either species or size of fish, and inevitably anything that was forced to the cod end of the seine was dead and could not be returned. Pound traps and gill netting still function today but the technique commercially producing the most fish, now is hook-and-line fishing.

New York, frustrated in the 1970s and early 1980s by its inability to influence Maryland striped bass management policies, decided to turn to what it could manage, the Hudson River nursery. This fishery is almost totally within the limits of the state and only shared in the summer months with a portion of northern New Jersey and western Connecticut. Ironically, the commercial landings from the Hudson fishery are very low because there was little or no demand for these fish. The main reason was that since the 1940s striped bass there had a tainted, almost diesel flavor because of pollution and were not marketable locally.

Thus a potentially large fishery is being underharvested. In 1985, it was discovered that these fish were also contaminated with PCBs (polychlorinated biphenyl) dumped there by two General Electric plants near Troy on the Hudson River. Striped bass were found to contain more than 5 ppm of the carcinogenic substance, the maximum limit allowed for interstate shipment by the federal government. In response, the N.Y.S. Health Department also banned their sale. In 1987 the federal Food Drug Administration further reduced the allowable health level to 2 ppm.

FEDERAL LEGISLATION and INTERSTATE STUDIES

One role of a marine research biologist is to gather knowledge about fish so that legislators can enact laws that will be effective in guaranteeing the fish's future populations. In the case of striped bass, legislative leaders, before they are asked to make decisions, should be able to rely on scientific facts about the environmental conditions striped bass require to survive, the changes allowable to the environment, and the effects of both commercial and sport fishing as well as industrial activities on these fish,.

During the late 1940s and in the early 1950s, as the abundance of striped bass increased, renewed competition for the fish suddenly became keen among commercial fishermen and between commercial and recreational fishermen. The growing number of recreational anglers now competed with commercial fishermen for striped bass, and immediately a rivalry began. The contests were both immediate and political and made themselves felt in almost every state capital along the Atlantic as well as in Washington. Because of their growing numbers, sport fishermen were now an effective force, and they placed pressure on their legislators help insure the fish's future and regulate how the fishery would be shared.

Because there was a great lack of knowledge about the life history of striped bass, especially its current status, legislators demanded projects from their state fish and game or conservation departments as well as federal agencies. The momentum produced, in 1952, the classic publication on the species: *Striped Bass,* by Edward Raney, Ernest Tresselt, Edgar Hollis, V.D. Vladykov and David Wallace. The 177-page booklet, a compilation of these authors' research works, was published by the Peabody Museum of Natural History at Yale University. Though somewhat dated today, it became the basis for almost all the studies that followed. At the same time, rash of random studies were started by numerous states. Each state, however, concentrated on striped bass as it appeared in their waters. Because of the migratory nature of striped bass, a thorough study and any ensuing meaningful legislation would need a coast-wide scope.

Atlantic States Marine Fisheries Commission

In 1950, the Atlantic States Marine Fisheries Commission tried to coordinate the research and conservation activities of each state by creating the Striped Bass Study Committee. Adherence and participation was strictly voluntary and Massachusetts, Rhode Island, New York, New Jersey, Delaware, Maryland, Virginia, and North and South Carolina became active participants. But because of a lack of real funding, shortages of trained personnel, and no motivative interest by some state legislators, the main objectives were not addressed, let alone achieved.

Georgia, Florida, and California had independent projects underway and contributed their results to the effort. During the 1960s and 1970s, California took a leading role in striped bass research and produced several valuable studies on the fish and its life cycle. The reasons for California's success include the relatively endemic character of its striped bass, so that it could be examined as an entity, the occurrence of the fish in just one major watershed, and the state's willingness to support its projects financially. The fish had also become the California marine fisherman's favorite species.

The ASMFC in 1957 established the Atlantic Coast Cooperative Striped Bass Program. The Department of Interior's U.S. Fish & Wildlife Service acted as the program's coordinator for various state projects. A large part of the funds were supplied to states through the Dingell-Johnson Program. The D-J Program was the result of an act passed by Congress in 1950 for the improvement of the nation's sport fishery and fishery-management programs. The amount of money given each state is based on the number of anglers in the state and comes from a federal excise tax on fishing tackle. For each dollar of its money a state spends on a program, three dollars of federal funds are given.

The intent of the D-J Program was to encourage each state to concentrate on local problems and aspects of striped bass research while the U. S. Fish & Wildlife Service and its personnel investigated aspects that transcended state lines. Federal activities included studies of racial stock differentiation and tagging programs.

However, as an illustration the ASMFC's ineffectiveness in dealing with striped bass strictly on a biological basis, some of its members' motivations were revealed by their actions to end the striped bass moratorium in the late 1980s before the stocks had recovered. But to understand fully what transpired, you need to know how the Commission was established and functions. The ASMFC was formed in 1937, when representatives from several Atlantic states, at New York's behest, gathered in Manhattan to address a fisheries problem—ironically, striped bass. The Commission was formalized by Congress in 1942, with all 15 Atlantic coastal states joining, and eventually the District of Columbia and the Potomac River Fisheries Commission.

"Representing state and industry interests," according to an ASMFC publication, "are 45 commissioners." Either the interests of recreational fishermen were purposely excluded, or they were to be taken care of by state representatives. However, this has seldom been the case when one examines the composition of each state's delegation. Membership in ASMFC had to be approved by each state's legislature because each state was assessed, at varying rates, dues for the Commission's operation. In return, each state was allowed three representatives: one appointed by its legislature, one by the governor, that state's conservation commissioner. However, this latter person is not usually the commissioner but his designee, often chief of its marine bureau.

In reality, all three could be chosen by a governor. If his or her party controls the legislature, the politically elected person, though picked by the legislature, might also reflect the governor's choice. This has been an inherent weakness in the ASMFC, and the political interests of its members are often at odds with the best interests of a fish, in this case, the striped bass.

To fathom just how politically oriented and responsive the ASMFC can be, it was Maryland's governor, William D. Schaefer, who in late August, 1989, and who had been harshly criticized by Maryland's commercial fishermen since the ban was instituted in 1985, seized upon an anomalous an spawning increase in Maryland's young-of-the-year (YOY) index. As relief from his critics, he immediately announced to the press that there would be a commercial striped bass season in his state in 1990, "because [he decided that] the fish had recovered." Then, as an aside, he included recreational fishing and told Torrey Brown, his secretary of the Department of Natural Resources, to see that it occurred.

Also eager to also satisfy the relentless demands by commercial fishermen in New York and Virginia, representatives from these states supported Maryland in the September ,1989, annual meeting of the ASMFC. Even over the objections of the ASMFC's Technical Committee, the troika spearheaded the reopening of a striped bass season. Intimidated, all other states followed suit. After Maryland's use of the site that triggered the YOY index was found in error—because that site alone accounted for nearly 35 percent of all the indices results—was never corrected. There was no basis for reopening the season according to the original requirements set forth by the ASMFC. The Commission failed to take corrective measures and close the season, and in the eyes of many sportfishing groups lost its aura as an infallible, august governing body.

Anadromous Fish Conservation Act

In October 1965, Congress passed the Anadromous Fish Conservation Act. Its purpose was to increase the supply of anadromous fishes in the United States by making $25 million available, on a matching basis for the next five years, to states with anadromous fish . In other words, the federal government would spend one dollar for every dollar a state spent on studies to increase the number of such fish running up their rivers. The U.S. Fish & Wildlife Service again was given the task of managing these monies and coordinating the programs of states that responded. In 1970, the Act was amended to extend it another five years. It has been amended every five years ever since its inception.

Every state that had an anadromous fish, from migrating shad to the Atlantic salmon, took interest in the program. Striped bass projects were started on the Atlantic, Gulf and Pacific coasts. A majority of the early research centered around southern Atlantic coastal states and along the Gulf of Mexico. For the first time, these states began to study the range and distribution of striped bass in their waters, many in environments far from the sea. Monies were used to stock striped bass in reservoir waters and expand the range of this fish.

Striped bass on a migratory binge could cross 12 state and two provincial borders in just one summer. In doing so it would be exposed to 14 different sets of regulations that have its welfare in mind. This is not just conceivable, it actually does happen, every spring, summer, and fall, from the Outer Banks of North Carolina to the rocky shores of New Brunswick and Nova Scotia.

There was such great disparity in these regulations that their total effect on the striped bass population was more irksome than protective. Any rational program for the fish's management had to be of national or international nature in its scope and coordination. Until 1979, when the Chafee Amendment was passed and attached to the Anadromous Fish Conservation Act, we had a regional approach to research and study, a regional approach to minimum-length regulations with little regard to the same problem just across the border, and a regional approach to seasons and limits. While some degree of regionalization was still prevalent in the ASMFC's unamended Striped Bass Management Plan, initiated in 1981, and still is visible in some areas, the over-all effect of the plan was to start the concept of management of the species both on a coastwise basis, on its stock origins, and their distributions.

Two events finally forced states to rethink their management efforts on a cost-wide rather than provincial basis. The most important was a decline in striped bass production in Chesapeake Bay—caused by overfishing in combination with a deteriorating marine environment—that so severely stressed the stocks that commercial fishing was almost unprofitable. Affected states realized how helpless they alone were in reversing the situation. No dominant year class has been produced in Chesapeake Bay waters since 1970. And even when the ASMFC tried to get all the states to cooperate in adopting the plan, there was opposition and hesitation. It wasn't until Congress passed the Atlantic Striped

Bass Conservation Act in 1984, which forced states to comply or experience federal sanctions, that they finally agreed to manage striped bass as a joint effort.

1979 Chafee Amendment

On Nov. 16, 1979, Congress amended the Anadromous Fish Conservation Act with Public Law No. 96-118. It became known as the Chafee Amendment after its sponsor Sen. John Chafee of Rhode Island. It called for the establishment of the Emergency Striped Bass Study (see Chapter 12).

1981 Interstate Fisheries Striped Bass Management Plan

This effort began as the State/Federal Striped Bass Management Project. It was ostensibly prepared in August, 1979, by Michael F. Leverone, and published as a proposal by the ASMFC, for the conservation and management of Atlantic Coast striped bass stocks. It was the first attempt to begin regulation and management of coastal stocks on an interstate level. It was submitted but didn't receive approval until various changes were made by the various state management councils in 1985. Then it was submitted to the National Marine Fisheries Service. However, its recommendations had already become a part of the management scheme in most coastal states when ASMFC officially adopted the plan in October 1981.

1984 The Atlantic Striped Bass Conservation Act

Passed by Congress in 1984, it enabled federal imposition of a moratorium on striped bass harvest in those states that failed to comply with the ASMFC Striped Bass Management Plan. In other words, it put teeth into the Plan.

ASMFC INTERSTATE FISHERIES MANAGEMENT PLAN

The ASMFC's Striped Bass Management Plan needed the Atlantic Striped Bass Conservation Act to give federal backing to The Plan as it was called, and force adherence in 1984 by all those states, districts, and commissions that were signatories to the ASMFC. The Plan and its four amendments have attempted to stimulate the rebuilding of striped bass stocks, according to its authors and supporters, by controlling fishing mortality through a series of management strategies that before 1984 were merely recommendations.

Objectives of the original plan included: maintain a spawning stock and minimize recruitment failure; collect economic, social, and biological data for monitoring and assessment of management efforts; promote research of the specie; promote adoption of standards necessary for natural production; and establish a management coordination effort. The original plan recommended a 14-inch (TL) size limit in striped bass-producing areas of Albemarle Sound, Chesapeake and Delaware bays, their tributaries, and the Hudson River. A 24-

inch size limit was recommended for coastal waters, with retention of any state established maximum size limits. Major spawning areas and rivers were to be closed to fishing during the spawning season.

Amendment 1 was adopted by ASMFC in October, 1984 to provide states with flexibility in meeting objectives of The Plan. Measures other than those in The Plan could be substituted, provided they were quantifiable and reasonably certain of maintaining the same reduction in mortality as those in The Plan. Substitutions for The Plan's minimum size limit were not accepted.

Amendments 2 and 3 were needed to protect the stock further and stimulate rebuilding. Amendment 2, adopted by ASMFC in October, 1984, proposed a 55 percent reduction in fishing on Chesapeake stocks resulting in an equivalent reduction in landings for the first year of implementation. States were encouraged to implement management regimes necessary to achieve this harvest reduction. Continued poor reproduction in Chesapeake Bay spurred the adoption of Amendment 3 in June, 1985. The objective of this amendment was to prevent fishing mortality on 1982- year class females until 95 percent had the chance to spawn at once. Various state options under Amendment 3, included total closure of fisheries, establishment of minimum size limits along with seasonal closures to ensure sub-adult females were not harvested, and elimination of allowable bycatch below minimum size limits. From 1985 to 1990, minimum size limits were progressively increased to 36 inches to protect the 1982 and subsequent year classes.

The Plan's total revision began in 1985 as **Amendment 4**. The original plan and amendments focused on strategies to restore and maintain self-sustaining stocks and minimize recruitment failure. However, little guidance on management of the fishery at the onset of stock recovery was provided. A transition scheme was needed while recovery was underway, and a long-term regime was needed for implementation upon full stock recovery. The revised plan outlined these management regimes, and was adopted by ASMFC in October, 1989. According to provisions of Amendment 3, the transition management regime of Amendment 4 would be instituted once stock recovery was indicated by the Maryland Department of Natural Resources juvenile index. The juvenile index for 1989 increased the three-year average above 8.0 and triggered the implementation of Amendment 4 following its adoption.

The three objectives of Amendment 4 are: to restore and maintain self-sustaining spawning stocks, minimizing the possibility of recruitment failure; to promote fair allocation of any allowable harvest among various components of the fishery; and to adopt standards of environmental quality necessary for the maximum natural reproduction of striped bass and for the utilization of allowable harvest. Over the past few years, Amendment 4 has been modified continually with addenda that have become a bit confusing to the members of the Commission and the direction in which the management plan is heading.

Early in 1993 the **Amendement 5** Outline and Review Committee met to draft Amendment 5. The new amendment would be a comprehensive plan to include the management of all Atlantic Coastal migratory striped bass stocks. This, according to the ASMFC, is a change from the original intention of the Amendment which was to have been a simple rewrite of Amendment 4 and including all its addenda. The format of the new amendment has been promised to be a simple, straightforward statement of principles, goals, and objectives with clear guidelines on how the stocks will be managed.

Game Fish Status

The history of striped bass management reeks with examples of political pressure being brought to bear by various interest groups so that those in positions of control will make more fish available to them. Here, the motivation is usually economic or immediate and often without regard to the welfare of the fish. In other instances these pressures are used to force management to conform to more restrictive measures to ensure striped bass survival. One does not need to be a marine ichthyologist to sense when a fish's future is in danger. One need be but a keen, objective observer. Often a lay person, with a daily relationship with the fish, can make judgements just as valid as a biologist deeply engrossed in some singular aspect of a fish's life.

Dr. Daniel Merriman, noted researcher and director of Yale University's Bingham Oceanographic Laboratory, now deceased, concerned himself primarily with the biological problems of striped bass and occasionally with legislation that affected them. In 1947, he summed up his feelings and those of other biologists at the time in a speech to a gathering of recreational anglers at the Long Beach Fishing Club in Camden, N.J.

"It can perhaps be demonstrated that in certain areas it is sociologically and economically desirable to make striped bass a game fish and hence to eliminate commercial fishing in those places. If that can be done in a democratic fashion, then let the legislation be debated on that basis. But don't let that legislation masquerade under the cloak of conservation."

His statement is as valid today as when it was made. Little did he know that the Jersey Coast Anglers Association, a federation of sportfishermen inspired by his philosophy, initiated a movement that ended February 26, 1991, when Gov. Jim Florio made striped bass a game fish in New Jersey. There's a bit of irony in the fact that the act took place 45 years later and 50 miles away, in Brick, N.J. Now the group is corralling state and federal legislations in uniting to make it a national game fish. So far, 22 legislators in Congress have agreed to support such a bill.

There is no fish species that is more controversial nor has been studied more than striped bass—neither the Atlantic salmon nor the largemouth bass—nor one that has had more legislation proposed, initiated and passed on its behalf. The very first ordinance to protect a fish in North America was a law passed in 1639 by the Massachusetts Bay Colony and forbade the use of striped bass by settlers to fertilize their fields.

Three hundred years later, the first state to see the advantage of making striped bass a game fish, in which status it cannot be sold, was California. Within ten years of initially stocking in San Francisco Bay in 1879 a major striped bass fishery had evolved. But it was eventually so over-exploited by commercial fishermen, who so reduced the stock, that in 1935 the California legislature made it a game fish.

Striped bass are considered game fish and cannot be sold commercially today in the coastal states of Alabama, Arizona, Arkansas, California, Connecticut, Florida, Georgia, Kentucky, Louisiana, Maine, Mississippi, New Hampshire, New Jersey, Oklahoma, Pennsylvania, South Carolina, and Texas. There are organizations active in Delaware and North Carolina pursuing game-fish status for striped bass in their states. In Maryland and Virginia, game-fish bills were recently introduced to the legislatures. In 1993, New York sportsmen began their drive to make it a game fish in the Empire State. On the national level, New Jersey Congressman Frank Pallone, Jr., in January, 1993, reintroduced H. R. Bill 393 to make striped bass a game fish throughout this country.

But why make striped bass a game fish?

The rationale to do so has changed drastically since Merriman addressed the New Jersey fishermen. He was responding to efforts by the League of L.I. Sportsmen and its successor S.O.S. (Save Our Stripers), a New York-based group of recreational fishermen, with an active New Jersey contingent. For more than a decade, S.O.S annually introduced bills in New York's legislature to make striped bass a game fish. However, during most of the 1950s, and especially the 1960s, striped bass populations were sound, in no danger of over-harvesting, and there was no justification for such legislation on a biological basis. They could get no legislative support.

Today, however, there is cause for support on three major bases—biological, sociological, and economical. The most pressing is the biological basis. Since 1970, there has been no dominant year class produced on the nursery grounds of Chesapeake Bay. This area accounts for the majority of the Atlantic coastal stock that replenishes the striped bass lost annually to recreational and commercial fishing and to natural mortality. The decline has been further catalyzed by the deteriorating environment in Chesapeake Bay. It has become progressively hostile, through toxic contaminants produced by intensified agriculture, suburbanization, and industrialization in the bay's watershed, that won't allow the vast horde of eggs produced each spring to develop beyond the larval stage.

The value of the remaining striped bass is far greater to the economy created by recreational fishermen, and industries supporting them, than the commercial value fish is to the economy. James R. Kahn, head of the Economics Department at State University of New York-Binghamton, from the years 1985 to 1987 conducted a survey, "The Economic Value of Long Island's Salt-Water Recreational Fishing," for N.Y. Sea Grant. He discovered that before it was even factored, it amounted to $1.04 billion. During that same period, the value of the commercial fishery was determined to be between $18 and $22 million.

From a sociological perspective, there are 1.1 million saltwater anglers in New York's marine district, according to a Department of Environmental Conservation report. Of course, they are not all striped bass fishers but most would like to be. The intensive style of life in New York's metropolitan area almost demands that recreation be a part of one's mental health. Few activities are better for this than fishing. On the other hand, there are probably less than 50 people today involved in commercial striped bass fishing on a full-time basis.

In 1986, commercial fishermen were reeling from the impact of the new 24-inch minimum limit passed in 1984, and when the N.Y.S. Department of Health closed commercial striped bass fishing because of PCB contamination, Gov. Mario Cuomo formed a task force to aid these fishermen financially. Today, the Fishermen's Assistance Fund combines the Striped Bass Fishermen's Emergency Assistance Program and the Commercial Fishermen's Economic Assistance Program, efforts that for nearly a decade have helped commercial striped bass fishermen develop new means of income. Available to them are loans up to $50,000, with no application and closing fees, at 3 percent interest,

In the days before one-fish limits were impose on recreational fishermen, a good night's fishing was often judged by how many fish were thrown onto the dock. Here, Cuttyhunk striped bass guide "Skip" Tripp cleans the catch after a night fishing over Devil's Bridge, a submerged reef off the northwest corner of Martha's Vineyard Island.

that are supported by the state's taxpayers. The cost per $1,000 per month is but for the commercial fishermen $18.

There is yet one more factor to consider that didn't exist when Merriman made his profound statement. At a meeting in September, 1992, of the leaders of several recreational fishing organizations and the media, called by Gordon Colvin, the head of DEC's Marine Division in Stony Brook, to explain his department's rationale for a September, 1992, expansion of the commercial quota, these leaders told him that because of the DEC's apparent actions over the last decade—that appeared to them to favor summarily the interests of commercial fishermen over the biological interests of striped bass—which they no longer believed that he and his department could manage striped bass strictly along biological considerations.

"It was a time when all the indicators said that the striped bass was still in trouble and that the DEC should consider restricting the harvest for both user groups," said Nicholas Castoro, head of the 40,000-member N.Y. Sportfishing Federation. "But instead, they went the opposite way, loosening the regulations. That was the turning point. It was compounded when the commissioner said he would reconsider the use of haul seines, a method his department excluded from the commercial fishery because it kills all fish."

The results of the DEC's September, 1992, action allowed commercial fishermen to over-harvest their quota. They had been warned this could happen. Though the DEC made an early closure, it couldn't be stopped in time and a large number of striped bass were killed. The quota will be reduce in the coming season to compensate for this over-kill, but the damage to the population has already been done.

Those at the meeting told the DEC they felt it was no longer effective in addressing the biological needs of striped bass because its commissioner and heads of regional offices throughout the state, who were appointed by the governor, were too susceptible to political pressure. They believed that these pressures regularly manifested itself in actions that were not always in the best interest of striped bass.

Commercial fishermen were doing exactly what Merriman had cautioned recreational fishermen not to do. Before the September, 1992, meeting with the DEC, no one there had taken a position totally in favor of making striped bass a game fish. They believed, that at the time, there were still enough fish, even with the spectre of a dwindling population, to allow some degree of commercial harvest. But because that degree was constantly being shifted by the DEC's administration in favor of commercial interest, their only alternative was to form an ad hoc committee, whose goal is eventually to make striped bass a game fish in New York. In a "democratic fashion" legislation has been introduced to both houses of the New York legislature to make striped bass a game fish, on the basis that its future needs continued and permanent protection in our declining environment.

SUMMARY OF REGULATIONS BY STATE AND PROVINCE

Summary of State Harvest Regulations on the Recreational Fishery for Striped Bass for 1991*
(Source: National Marine Fisheries Service)

State/Area	Size	Daily Limits	Quota Bag	Seasons1
Maine	36" min.	1	None	Rivers2
				1 July-30 Nov
New Hampshire	36" min.	1	None	All Year
Massachusetts	36" min.	1	None	All Year
Rhode Island	28" min.	1	None	All Year
Connecticut	36" min.	1	None	1 Apr-14 Dec
New York				
Hudson River	18" min.	1	None	15 Mar-30 Nov
Ocean	36" min.	1	None	8 May-15 Dec
New Jersey				
Delaware Bay	36" min.	1	None	1 Jun-31 Dec
& Tributaries				
Other Rivers	28" min.	1	None	1 Mar-31 Dec
Ocean	28" min.	1	None	All Year
Trophy	38" min.	1	64,800	Area-dependent3
Pennsylvania	36" min.	1	None	Delaware River:
				1 Jan-31 Mar
				1 Jun-31 Dec
Delaware	28" min.	1	None	All Year
				(Spawning
				areas closed
				1 Apr-31 May)
Maryland				
Bay & River	18"-36" slot	2/sea.	455,473	9 Oct-26 Oct
				3 3-day weekends
				in Nov
		2	160,754	9 Oct-27 Oct
		(charter)	(charter)	(charter)
Trophy	36" min.	1/sea.	None	11 May-27 May
Ocean	28" min.	1	None	9 Oct-26 Oct
PRFC4	18"-36" slot		None	11 Oct-27 Oct;
				8 Nov-20 Nov
		2	14,000	11 Oct-30 Oct
		(charter)	(charter)	(charter)

D. C.	18"-36" slot	2	None	5 Oct-16 Nov
Virginia				
Bay & River	18"-36" slot	2	None	11 Oct-27 Oct
				21 Nov-5 Dec
Ocean	28"-36" slot	2	None	Same as Bay
North Carolina				
Ocean	28" min.	1	None	19 Jan-31 Mar
				1 Dec-31 Dec

1 Unless otherwise noted coastal season is year round.

2 Sheepscott, Kennebec and Androscoggin rivers.

3 New Jersey trophy season takes place during seasons for specific areas.
  No trophy fishing in Delaware Bay.

4 PRFC-Potomac River Fisheries Commission

* These regulations were in effect for the 1990-91 season. Because they are evaluated and adjusted annually by the Atlantic States Marine Fisheries Commission, they may change yearly and are dependent upon the overall status of striped bass stock.

Striped bass regulations vary greatly, and within each state or province they can be quite complicated. This listing is not intended to cover every area's regulations completely, but only to summarize the regulations. Before fishing, it is suggested that you obtain a complete syllabus of the state's or province's regulations in which you plan to fish.

New Brunswick—Very little legislation affects the taking of striped bass. A commercial license is required but no sport-fishing license is needed in marine waters. Fish taken by rod and reel without a commercial license cannot be sold. Taking of striped bass from non-marine waters is restricted to April 15 to September 15.

Nova Scotia—No license is required to take striped bass commercially, and striped bass can be sold regardless of the manner in which they are taken. There is a possession limit of 10 per day and the season extends from April 1 to September 30.

Prince Edward Island—No restrictions on the taking of striped bass.

Quebec—A license is required to take striped bass either commercially or by rod and reel. Fish taken by either method can be sold. Season dates for marine fishing extend from June 1 to November 30. In non-marine waters, the date extends from June 15 to freeze-up. The minimum size is 16 inches total length. No other restrictions apply.

Summary of State Harvest Regulations on the Commercial
Fishery for Striped Bass for 1991*
(Source: National Marine Fisheries Service)

State Area	Size Limit	Cap3	Season1
Maine	no fishery		
New Hampshire	no fishery		
Massachusetts	36" min.	238	1 Jul - 28 Aug
Rhode Island	18" - 26" slot (40" max. for gear other than trap net)	35	
Connecticut	no fishery		
New York	24" - 29" slot	128	Sep - 15 Dec1
New Jersey	no fishery		
Pennsylvania	no fishery		
Delaware	18" - 28" slot	23	1 Mar - 30 Apr (spawning areas closed April)
Maryland			
Bay & River	18" - 36" slot	455	2 Sep -18 Oct (haul seine, pound net) 2 Dec - 31 Dec (hook & line) 2 Jan - 28 Feb (drift gill nets)
Ocean	28" min.		25
PRFC2	18" - 36" slot	159	Various days during Feb, Aug, Oct, Nov
District of Columbia	no fishery		
Virginia			
Bay & River	18" - 36" slot	211	5 Nov - 8 Nov (gill nets) 5 Nov - 18 Nov (pound net) 5 Nov - 18 Nov (haul seine)
Ocean	28" - 36" slot		5 Nov - 5 Dec (fyke net)
North Carolina			
Ocean	28" min.	96	4 Feb - 25 Feb 1 Dec - 31 Dec

1 All seasons are calendar year 1990 except for Maryland Bay,
    which extended into 1991.
2 Potomac River Fisheries Commission
3 Commercial cap figures are in thousands of pounds.
* These regulations were in effect during the 1990-91 season. Because they are
evaluated and adjusted annually by the Atlantic States Marine Fisheries Commission,
they may change from year to year and are dependent upon the overall status of striped
bass stocks.

12

The Great Decline

After a long hiatus in the occurrence of striped bass along the Northeast Coast, during the late 1800s early 1900s, striped bass once again, but very slowly, became a part of the recreational and commercial fishery. By the late 1920s and the early 1930s, the fish appeared at irregular annual intervals in the spring and then disappeared in the fall. Between the years 1942 and 1960, they were annual visitors whose numbers rose and fell with an regularity that revealed the cyclic nature in the abundance of coastal migratory striped bass.

However, a strange phenomenon overtook this migratory stock, from 1962 to 1970, as the production of each subsequent year surpassed that of the previous year. In that period, several dominant year classes were produced. Such an occurrence of continuous high production had never been observed in modern times in striped bass. It reached its crescendo in 1970 with the production of still another unusual year class in Chesapeake Bay. This was almost overshadowed by continuous good year classes in previous years. The number of large adult fish, as well as young-of-the year, glutted the East Coast from Virginia to Maine. In that spring, the largest dominant year class in modern times was recorded when the Chesapeake Bay index rose to 30.4.

Then the fishery collapsed!

A sure, steady, almost linear annual decline in production followed. By 1981, it reached a relative production young-of-the-year index of just 1.02, the lowest ever recorded. This decline was not only mirrored in the indices from North Carolina, Virginia, Maryland, and Delaware, but it was also reflected in commercial and recreational catches. There was no similarity to the speed and magnitude of the decline when compared to historical fluctuations. Dr. Ted Koo, a researcher with the University of Maryland, working with striped bass populations in Chesapeake Bay, warned that bass stocks in the bay were being over-exploited, both commercially and recreationally. However, no efforts were made to stem the practice.

Legislative Efforts to Stem the Decline

In 1979, the United States Congress amended (the Chafee Amendment) the Anadromous Fish Conservation Act to provide for the Emergency Striped Bass Study to try to determine why striped bass stocks were declining, to keep track of the size of the available stocks and to determine the economic consequences of the decline.

Also in 1979, the Atlantic States Marine Fisheries Commission, responding to the unfolding phenomenon, prepared a coastwide management plan for the anadromous stocks of striped bass along the Atlantic Coast: the Interstate Fisheries Management Plan for Striped Bass. It was adopted in 1981 by all 15 members of the Commission. However, several states failed to adopt the ASMFC's management recommendations so Congress, in 1984, passed the Atlantic Striped Bass Conservation Act (Studds Bill), which gave the Department of Commerce and its National Marine Fisheries Service power to declare a total moratorium in states that were not in compliance with The Plan. All eventually responded except New Jersey and the District of Columbia, that for this purpose was considered a state. However, at the eleventh hour before any moratoria were to be proclaimed in these states, their legislatures adopted the required restrictions.

The Chafee Amendment gave both the National Marine Fisheries Service and the U.S. Fish & Wildlife Service the mandate as well as the financing needed to begin studying the problem. It also gave them the authority to coordinate the research efforts of all states involved by funding a proportion of their research costs. Finally, instead of the various states studying the problem as it existed only within their realm, the fish were studied on a coastwide basis, without regard to borders and duplication.

THE EMERGENCY STRIPED BASS STUDY

During the 13 years that the Emergency Striped Bass Study (ESBS) has been under way, the horizons of striped bass knowledge have been expanded far beyond what any researcher or administrator could have imagined at the project's onset. While some of it was pure research, with no immediate application to the problem of the striped bass's decline in Chesapeake Bay, most of it has been extremely pertinent to the problem. And, from the beginning, researchers discovered that it wasn't any **one** problem, but the accumulative effects of several that seemed to act as catalysts upon each other, that caused the fish's decline. However, they also must be dealt with in the aggregate.

While the exact causes of the decline may not have been determined, the study did investigate all the areas where problems had arisen, and many were eliminated as contributors to the decline. That, in itself—the narrowing down of the possible causes—was almost as beneficial as if the real causes had been determined. In retrospect, the final analysis was that the problem was caused by two factors—overfishing and an environment that had become hostile to striped bass in the larval stage of their lives.

Before taking to the field, *in situ*, administrators of the study asked those involved in the joint effort which included biologists, chemists, physicists, and engineers from all states involved, as well as federal agencies and from universities and colleges, to develop a collection of probable theories that might account for the decline of striped bass in Chesapeake Bay. Thereafter, these theories could be explored and either discounted if they were not a part of the cause or further pursued if they were.

The study initially identified nine factors or hypotheses: effects of toxic contaminants, inability of newly hatched larvae and fry to obtain food for survival, predation on fry, commercial fishing mortality, recreational fishing mortality, the occurrence of a series of unfavorable natural climatic events, recent changes in water use practices, competition with other species for food and space, and a reduction in water quality due to agricultural and sewage treatment practices. All these were derived from the fact that since the 1950s, the Chesapeake area had experienced phenomenal urban expansion as well as industrialization and great changes in land and water use. This was coupled with an expanding human population and an increased demand for fish as food and recreation. The following is a summary of the study's findings.

Contaminants

Chesapeake Bay is truly a contaminated body of water, and pollution's entry is via an array of sources from the entire watershed of such major drainages as the Susquehanna and Potomac rivers and sources around the periphery of the bay and its many tidal rivers. There is also an unquantifiable amount of contaminants that are airborne, and enter by atmospheric deposition, as in the case of sulphur via acid rain. Aluminum contamination also plays an important role. During periods of low (acidic) pH levels, aluminum toxicity was responsible for the complete death of larval striped bass in some Eastern Shore rivers. Chlorine toxicity was also established to be a lethal factor, again for larval striped bass, and during some years it eliminated entire populations by the end of the second week after hatching.

Even though all the researchers who worked on various contaminants as the causes, both in the field and in the laboratory, discovered that they could be and in some instances were responsible for striped bass mortality, the theories could never be developed to the stage of being a law. The obstacle they all encountered was that they couldn't identify the quantities or amounts needed, or their sources, to draw conclusions or point a finger at the exact cause for the decline.

In reality, it may have been several toxic elements, at times working in concert with each other, at other times independently, such that when environmental conditions were correct, they became lethal to striped bass populations at that time and in that place. The antithesis of this theory is that all these elements are, and may have always been, in the environment of striped bass, but never came together in the combination or concentrations needed to be effective. The catalyst here might have been extremely low pH levels that the bay and its inhabitants had never before experienced.

Predation/Competition

Early studies by various states since the program began reported that while predation and competition could be factors in certain situations, neither was ever the case with the current decline. The same factors that caused the decline in striped bass production seem also to have caused a decline in the species that were competitive with them. In reality, striped bass seemed more resistant to some forms of pollution and actually benefited from it because the competition succumbed. Neither predation nor competition were ever considered significant factors for the decline of striped bass in Chesapeake Bay.

Lack of Appropriate Food

A 1982 study determined that starvation may have played a critical role in the size and strength of the 1981 year class. And because of this, 1981 larvae underwent a greater degree of stress than 1982 progeny. In laboratory tests held at the same time, larvae that were starved for a three-week period recovered with no ill effects after their food source was reestablished. The consensus was that starvation is only a negative factor to affect an entire year class when larvae are denied food over an extended period and over a very large range. And this, as a regular occurrence, was not likely.

Quite to the contrary, many of the pollutants that contaminate Chesapeake Bay often encourage the growth of such larval and fry striped bass foods as zooplankton. This led to Mansueti's 1962 eutrophication hypothesis, that an increase in untreated sewage being added to bay waters because of the rise in human populations in the area in the 1950s provided such a wealth of larval food that it was responsible for several dominant year classes—1956, 1958, and 1961. Nitrogen enrichment from urban pollution might have enriched the bay but it eventually had more harmful than beneficial effects.

In 1982 a team of researchers investigated the effects of eutrophication, organic pollution, on the aquatic grasses, namely eel grass, in the Upper Bay (Susquehanna Flats). The hyper-rich environment caused a reduction in the amount of sunlight and the grasses died. This was coupled with the effects of Hurricane Agnes in 1972, that tore up the aquatic plant life in the Upper Bay.

Upper Bay had been Chesapeake Bay's most productive spawning and nursery grounds, and has never recovered from either of the two effects.

Natural Climatic Events

There's little doubt that physical climatic events like heavy infusions of fresh water from prolonged rains as well as the floods they might cause a sudden rise and fall of temperatures, or the devastating physical effects of a hurricane on a shallow body of water or tidal river, can affect the success of a year class and even adult fish. However, these events did not occur with enough consistency during the period in study, since 1971, to account for the almost methodical decline in striped bass in North Carolina, Virginia, Maryland, and Delaware areas.

Water Use Practices

The U.S. Army Corps of Engineers widened and deepened Chesapeake & Delaware Canal—between the head of Chesapeake Bay and Delaware Bay—in 1973. One aftermath of this action was a net increase in the flow of water moving from Chesapeake into Delaware Bay. It has been suggested that in the flow were striped bass eggs and larvae that had been spawned in the Upper Bay and were carried into the canal and eventually into Delaware Bay. At times, the flow has been enhanced by seasonal winds that blow southwest to northeast, almost the direction of the canal, and increase the spring-time flow of water from the Susquehanna River into the Upper Bay, some continuing through the C&D Canal. As a result, the Corps' construction here may have contributed to the decline in striped bass production. The decline in the Upper Bay has been the most significant of any of the spawning-nursery grounds. Subsequent water flow studies from nearby Elk River showed a net flow, via the C&D Canal, to Delaware Bay.

Diseases

Like all fish, striped bass in all stages in the life cycle are susceptible to certain diseases, especially viral forms. While investigators into this hypothesis, that the decline was caused by an increase or new diseases, did uncover some diseased fish, both in adult and larval stages, they were too insignificant in scope to have contributed to the magnitude of the decline.

Exploitation

Today, some researchers working both in the study and independently believe that the major cause of the decline was over fishing or over-exploitation of striped bass stocks. When over-exploitation occurs in concert with other factors detrimental to expanding a striped bass population, it can produce a decline with speed and intensity characteristics exhibited by Chesapeake Bay in the early 1970s.

None of the management regulations in effect in any coastal state prior to 1970 allowed for the protection of young striped bass. If they had, these would have enhanced the fish's ability to reach maturity unencumbered and contribute to the population by spawning at least once. The result was a continued net loss to the population. Even when striped bass left this bay and were under the more protective regimes of other states, they still were not offered the kind of protection, especially of females, that would ensure they could spawn at least once in their lifetimes.

We know that the demand for fish as a health food, an alternative to beef, began to occur in our population in the early 1970s. It caused the rapid expansion of the commercial fishing industry that had labored for many years just to exist. The value of all fish products rose so quickly that it also encouraged many non-fishermen to enter the industry, either part-time or full-time. Ironically, as fish became scarce, the inadequate supply drove prices higher and higher. Eventually, commercial fishermen didn't have to catch as many fish to maintain the same income.

Recreational fishing also took a greater toll on striped bass and not simply because of the increase in numbers of anglers that reflected a burgeoning population. Benjamin M. Florence, director of the Tidewater (Maryland) Finfish Program, in 1980 argued that the efficiency of recreational fishermen increased manifoldly during the 1970s because of improved technology—depth recorders, loran, radios and electronic thermometers—in fishing and boating equipment, rods, reels, monofilament lines, and effective lures. He demonstrated that striped bass experienced accelerated rates of mortality during the mid-1970s because of recreational fishing.

The inference here might be that if commercial and recreational fishing mortality had not increased in the 1970s, striped bass populations could have dealt with the environmental changes that were taking place. I disagree with this hypothesis because fishing mortality's role only accelerated the process. The factors for decline were already in place in 1971 and could not be compensated for or reversed even if fishing mortality was eliminated. Secondly, overexploitation by both groups affects the available size of the adult brood stock. However, sufficient brood stock was never the problem or even the delimiting factor. The number of eggs produced and successfully fertilized each year has always been sufficient to replenish the populations. The greatest mortality occurs, since 1971, in the larval stages.

If brood stock size is a critical factor in creating a dominant year class, then progeny of Chesapeake Bay's 1970 year class—the greatest year class produced in recent times—should have provided sufficient numbers of males by 1973 and females by 1975 to produce dominant year classes. However, just the opposite was true. Striped bass indices in Chesapeake Bay fell from 1970 to 1982 when the first "normal" production occurred.

The only feasible argument for a large brood stock is the "window of opportunity theory." According to the 1986 report by the Emergency Striped Bass Research Study, survival of eggs and larvae is dependent upon the occurrence of adequate conditions during at least some part of the spawning season. The frequency and duration of an adequate-condition period may vary from year to year, resulting in varying survival rates. Conditions which produced dominant year classes prior to this study are unknown. If conditions for survival occur infrequently and for short-time periods ("windows") during the spawning season, juvenile production would be dependent on the number of eggs produced during the windows. In recent years in Maryland and Virginia waters of Chesapeake Bay, the number of spawning fish was estimated to have been "low" and thus may have been inadequate to produce enough eggs during the occurrence of windows, or windows of opportunity.

If this "window theory" is valid, to increase juvenile production would then require an increase in the number of adults to an adequate level and then maintaining that number of gravid fish on the spawning grounds throughout the highly variable spawning period. This is the only way to insure adequate egg production during the occurrences of these windows. This is especially true since early life-stage mortality of broadcast spawners like striped bass is undoubtedly high even under favorable conditions.

Over-exploitation of the striped bass stocks occurred during two stages in their lives: recruitment exploitation and stock exploitation. Strong circumstantial evidence indicates that the decline during the 1970s was accelerated by overfishing during two stages in a striped bass's life, as large fish, 24 inches or more, and as juveniles, between ages 2 and 4. Recruitment overfishing occurred primarily on the nursery grounds and removed fish before they were able to contribute to the brood stock. This was done by both recreational and commercial fishermen, with the latter group more effective because of the demand in the market for smaller fish.

Stock exploitation, while a part of commercial fishing, was more widespread among recreational fishermen because of the search for trophy fish. Besides, larger fish, especially females, seem more susceptible to fishing tackle and lures and can be discriminatively removed from the population. Recreational fishing took more breeders from the population that did some forms of commercial fishing, excepting the haul seine and pound trap fisheries. Big striped bass are more reluctant to enter
a pound trap than small, schooling fish.

Future of the Emergency Striped Bass Study Play

The Plan was never intended to be an ongoing, continuous study of the problems that faced striped bass. From its inception, it was designed to last but three years. However, the continued reauthorizations of the Plan were necessary and called for at times because the numerous theories for the fish's decline needed time to be studied and evaluated. In a real way, most researchers have achieved their original goals. And, little has been done in the past year or two years that still addresses the original aim of the Plan. Most activities have been quite academic but tangential, and while they have produced valuable information as to the biology of the fish, none have moved us closer to the answers we need to stop the decline and turn it around. The majority of current studies for 1993 have been budgeted and deal more with tagging striped bass and determining the age and sex compositions in a population and the sources of stock origin in the coastal migratory populations. Stocking of hatchery-raised fingerlings is also receiving new emphasis, especially in western Chesapeake Bay rivers.

The Plan's refinancing is up for renewal this year and prospects for its continuation, in the light of current budget cuts on the federal level, don't bode well for an extended future. In any case, its accomplishments have been great and while we may not have isolated the problems, we have removed those from consideration that are not plausibly affecting the fish's future. Unfortunately, the Plan's results point to two major areas: overharvesting, which we can do something about and which is being addressed continuously, and a deteriorating environment over which we have little immediate, and not much, long-range control.

13

Atlantic Coastal
Migratory Stocks

One aspect of the Emergency Striped Bass Study called for the monitoring of striped bass stocks. It's difficult to manage a population if you don't know its population dynamics, such as origins, the number of spawning adults, the number of fish produced at these sites, mortality estimates of both juvenile and adult fish and the migration patterns of the various stocks. At the beginning of the study in 1981, there were believed to be three major and one minor anadromous stock along the Atlantic coast. These included fish from the Roanoke River-Albemarle Sound area in North Carolina, the Virginia and Maryland tributaries in Chesapeake Bay and Hudson River in New York. A minor stock, that has since grown steadily in size and importance but is still relatively small in comparison to other stocks, is one in Delaware Bay and River.

The origins of the latter stock are still in question—whether they are remnants of original Delaware River striped bass strains, or a migration of spawning stock from the Upper Bay of Chesapeake Bay that takes a route through the Chesapeake & Delaware Canal when they migrate north along the coast, or a combination of both. Also, this stock might utilize a minor contribution from the Maurice River in New Jersey, that empties into Delaware Bay. It might be the only remnant stock genetically the same as the historical stock on this system.

It has been established, although there are still some areas of doubt, that the size of the annual production of juvenile fish in these four nurseries can be used as a relative gauge of the eventual overall population of adult fish. And, that when production is down on all or any of these areas, it is reflected eventually in the number of migratory striped bass along the coast. So far, the best method that has evolved to gauge the population's size is to measure the success, or lack

Striped bass landings 1887–1929 (in thousands of pounds). Early records of striped-bass catches, or landings, are spotty and their accuracy is doubtful. However, they do give us a rough indication of the numbers of fish available and taken and their fluctuations. Since 1930, there has been a steady increase in the landings with rather accurate substantiation by the U.S. Bureau of Commercial Fisheries.

TABLE 1. Striped bass landings, earlier records (in thousands of pounds).

Year	New England Region						Middle Atlantic Region					Chesapeake Region			South Atlantic Region				Combined Total
	Maine	N. H.	Mass.	R. I.	Conn.	Total	N. Y.	N. J.	Penn.	Del.	Total	Md.	Va.	Total	N. C.	S. C.	Ga.	Total	
1887	—	—	20	11	46	77	115	615	15	116	861	1,140	505	1,645	500	182	11	693	3,276
1888	—	—	32	13	50	95	98	739	59	116	1,012	1,123	779	1,902	560	251	11	822	3,831
1889	—	—	25	80	39	144	212	306	24	110	652	—	—	—	526	11	13	550	—
1890	—	—	—	—	—	—	208	328	23	107	666	1,366	529	1,895	568	12	9	589	—
1891	—	—	—	—	—	—	205	298	25	95	625	1,265	483	1,748	—	—	—	—	—
1897	25	—	13	102	14	155	116	287	10	129	542	935	576	1,511	845	10	9	864	—
1898	—	—	—	—	—	—	82	274	—	—	—	824	528	1,352	—	—	—	—	—
1901	16	2	28	50	40	136	72	354	13	48	487	721	451	1,172	1,175	10	3	1,188	—
1902	—	—	—	—	—	—	53	66	6	40	165	—	—	—	—	—	—	—	—
1904	—	—	—	—	—	—	—	—	—	—	—	—	—	—	—	—	—	—	—
1905	4	—	21	32	19	76	40	53	7	53	138	—	—	—	—	—	—	—	—
1908	3	1	5	34	2	44	—	—	—	—	—	640	504	1,144	510	5	9	524	—
1920	—	—	—	—	—	—	—	—	—	—	—	1,040	380	1,420	447	—	—	447	1,870
1921	—	—	—	—	—	—	95	70	—	5	170	—	—	—	—	—	—	—	—
1923	—	—	—	—	—	—	—	—	—	—	—	—	—	—	—	—	—	—	—
1925	—	—	—	—	5	—	87	64	—	46	197	—	—	—	—	—	—	—	—
1926	—	—	—	—	5	—	—	—	—	—	—	1,414	821	2,235	—	—	—	—	—
1927	—	—	—	—	4	—	—	—	—	—	—	—	—	—	507	—	1	508	—
1928	—	—	8	44	4	56	—	—	—	—	—	—	—	—	—	—	—	—	—
1929	—	—	19	23	2	44	156	41	—	10	207	1,292	290	1,582	246	—	—	246	2,079

Striped Bass Landings 1930-1970

Year	Mass.	R. I.	Conn.	N. Y.	N. J.	Del.	Md.	Va.	N. C.
1930	27	60	2	66	37	102	1,228	425	457
1931	48	39	4	64	18	52	635	481	327
1932	31	7	4	32	12	8	434	594	507
1933	20	39	2	19	9	12	314	519	–
1934	–	–	–	–	–	–	333	310	362
1935	5	16	+	37	8	17	928	375	–
1936	–	–	–	–	–	27	1,864	520	768
1937	121	317	13	132	241	32	2,011	1,005	713
1938	82	210	9	139	147	25	1,714	1,155	523
1939	63	213	9	184	243	20	1,729	964	339
1940	76	64	8	169	172	41	1,180	659	540
1941	–	–	–	–	–	–	1,223	865	–
1942	98	95	18	266	95	59	2,508	778	–
1943	100	73	25	317	160	37	–	–	–
1944	191	122	17	504	257	39	2,681	1,864	–
1945	186	95	27	301	418	63	1,545	2,119	609
1946	161	217	19	482	–	–	1,615	2,084	–
1947	55	52	11	244	60	109	2,338	1,725	–
1948	78	63	10	356	41	361	2,650	2,452	–
1949	72	81	9	626	21	255	2,629	1,913	–
1950	47	112	7	517	109	271	3,038	2,796	797
1951	132	112	22	626	140	215	2,336	1,804	792
1952	125	51	11	486	536	120	2,172	1,242	647
1953	105	82	6	482	435	106	2,303	803	757
1954	68	116	+	439	51	146	2,108	951	1,122
1955	72	34	+	506	35	88	2,572	894	736
1956	71	26	1	395	50	28	2,150	995	764
1957	56	23	1	553	132	16	1,859	929	597
1958	51	41	3	398	59	22	3,105	1,317	1,096
1959	81	31	8	538	196	12	4,349	2,097	872
1960	129	77	5	731	114	25	4,409	2,278	782
1961	210	167	20	910	276	66	5,408	1,854	550
1962	589	61	32	657	494	108	3,979	1,944	747
1963	480	71	30	673	753	48	3,749	2,747	736
1964	522	75	35	995	996	31	3,300	1,889	714
1965	463	60	–	740	761	32	2,949	2,803	484
1966	585	250	–	1,050	315	64	3,347	2,803	653
1967	662	132	–	1,630	327	66	4,150	1,677	1,817
1968	874	98	–	1,511	459	49	4,532	1,614	1,912
1969	1,038	132	–	1,535	311	42	5,088	2,671	1,568
1970	1,344	84	–	1,338	223	54	3,978	1,782	2,318

of it, in annual young-of-the-year population surveys. Juvenile production is thus estimated annually from surveys conducted in each nursery area. These estimates, or indices, are usually expressed as a total catch divided by the total number of hauls of a seine.

While there is correlation between the annual production of juveniles on three of these nurseries and the overall production, the value of the index figures is relative only to other years of production on the same nursery. Nor is there a real or direct value or relationship between any of the index numbers to the actual number of fish produced annually.

Population Fluctuations

Striped bass catches have been fairly well recorded since 1930 and when graphed show a cyclic rise and fall, but with a general increase in the overall catches. The cycle repeats itself every six, sometimes seven, years. Beginning with 1930, a high year, catches were high again in 1936, 1942, 1948, 1954, 1960, 1966, and 1972. With the exception of 1954, catches during all these years form peaks on the graph.

These peaks in abundance are attributed to the dominant-year-class concept and reflect back to years of good production when spawning success was so great it overshadowed the previous year in the cycle. Therefore, a typical striped bass cycle—when the nursery environment was not hostile to reproduction, as it has been since 1971—represents three somewhat high years of catches and production with one a peak year and three relatively moderate catches and a low year. The spawning peak year predates the year of big catches by three years in each cycle. The reason for this is that it takes striped bass at least three years to mature and take on migrations before they enter either the commercial or sport fishery.

Chesapeake Bay, because it had contributed so heavily to the migratory stock along the northern half of the Atlantic range, became a barometer for the fish's coastal migratory abundance. At one time, the number of fish that would be available along Long Island's South Shore could be predicted quite accurately from the size of each annual production in Chesapeake Bay. The only difference was a three-year lag.

Striped bass populations in Chesapeake Bay are checked from summer to fall by extensive sampling when Maryland biologists then get their first look at how successful the spawning season had been that spring. These fish will stay in the bay until the beginning of their third year and then begin a seasonal migration northward along the Atlantic Coast in late spring with coastal migrants from farther south.

How Indices Are Conducted

Maryland biologists, in 1954, were the first to conduct indices of the young-of-the-year production for striped bass and pioneered the technique. Dr. Edgar

Hollis of Maryland's Department of Chesapeake Bay Affairs helped develop this technique. His experience with the striped bass recruitment survey indicated for the first time that seining could be a very useful tool in determining, rather quickly and inexpensively, the relative success of spawning and annual production. The future availability of striped bass can be estimated from the relative abundance of young fish near shore in late summer and fall. Their investigations employed a beach seine survey of the near-shore estuarine habitat in tidewater and their objective was to provide a relative, annual measure of juvenile striped bass recruitment. While monitoring began in 1954, the present operational format wasn't standardized until 1966.

"Annual monitoring is necessary to detect and document changes and trends in relative abundance in species distribution to better evaluate management options," said Don Cosden a Maryland marine biologist, who has been on

Summary of Methods and Results of
Juvenile Abundance Surveys for Atlantic Coast Striped Bass

Stock	Agency[1]	Time Span	Survey Gear	Index Value			1991 Index
				Min.	Max.	Med.	
Roanoke	Hassler	1957-1987	balloon seine	0.02	26.4	4.6	—
	NCDMF	1982-1991	balloon trawl	0.0	4.3	0.6	0.9
Chesapeake Virginia	VIMS	1967-1973; 1980-1991	beach seine	1.2	15.8	3.7	3.8
Chesapeake Maryland	MDDNR	1954-1991	beach seine	1.2	30.4	6.9	4.4
Delaware	NJBMF	1980-1991	beach seine	0.0	2.7	0.5	1.1
Hudson	NYPA	1969-1991[2]	beach seine	0.0	79.2	21.32	N/A[3]
	NYDEC	1976-1991	beach seine	4.0	60.4	33.9	6.9
	NYDEC	1981-1990	otter trawl	3.9	115.6	22.4	N/A[4]

[1] **NCDMF - North Carolina Division of Marine Fisheries**
VIMS - Virginia Institute of Marine Science
MDDNR - Maryland Department of Natural Resources
NJBMF - New Jersey Bureau of Marine Fisheries
NYPA - New York Power Authority
NYDEC - New York Department of Environmental Conservation
[2] **Survey conducted 1969-1991, but data available only for 1969-1987**
[3] **N/A - Not Available**
[4] **Survey not conducted in 1991 due to equipment failure.**

a team since 1983 and a team leader on the survey for the last five years.

Beach seining is performed at established locations within Chesapeake Bay and its tributaries. Sites are chosen for their beach development, bottom type, and their contribution to spawning and nursery grounds for striped bass. Each separate river, bay or point of land is defined as a system and within each system a series of primary and secondary seining sites are established. Only permanent site samples, however, are used to calculate an index.

Each site is sampled a month in July, August, and September with a 100-by 4-foot seine. Each sample consists of two hauls with a minimum interval time of 30 minutes. The juvenile recruitment index is determined by the total catches of age zero fish, from all samples, divided by the number of hauls. The Maryland annual juvenile index is the pooled average of individual samples taken on the Potomac, Choptank, and Nanticoke rivers and the Upper Bay region

Roanoke River-Albemarle Sound Index

There are three major rivers in North Carolina that are used by striped bass as nursery grounds, the Neuse, Tar, and Roanoke rivers and one minor river, Cape Fear River. Striped bass in the Neuse and Tar are highly endemic in distribution and do not contribute measurable numbers of fish, if any, to the coastal migratory stock. In characteristics, striped bass in the Neuse and Tar rivers are more like fish in the rivers of South Carolina and farther south, riverine fish that utilize marine estuaries primarily as areas to which they make short migrations for additional foods. Even striped bass that move into freshwater sections of the Roanoke River to spawn do not always take part in coastal migrations. Some researchers suspect the Roanoke River may actually harbor two strains of striped bass, one strictly riverine and one that has the capability to make coastal migrations, usually only during years when extremely high or dominant year class production takes place. This hasn't been true for the last two decades on the Roanoke River because of continued stock declines.

Early tagging studies, prior to 1979, painted a somewhat different picture of this stock. It revealed that some of fish, but not necessarily a major portion, did migrate north along the coast in spring with striped bass from other river stocks that wintered over in the open Atlantic off Virginia and North Carolina beaches. However, tagging efforts that began in the early 1980s and continued to the present revealed that almost no contribution to the coastal migratory stock during this period came from the Roanoke River. In 1992, 2,433 striped bass were captured and tagged on the river during the spring spawning run. By the end of the year, 42 tags (1.7%) were returned, 26 from the Roanoke River and 16 from Albemarle Sound. In an earlier tagging effort, all but two tagged fish were recaptured in Albemarle Sound. One of the two was captured off Cape Hatteras and the other from the James River in Virginia.

Juvenile abundance indices in the Roanoke River were highly variable from the period when the indexing started in 1955 to the mid-1970s. These years were marked by several dominant year classes. This pattern changed in 1977 and remained consistently below the long-term average, indicating that there has been no dominant year class since 1976. This suggests that the Roanoke has experienced a stock decline since that time. There was a slight increase in the indices in 1988 and 1989; however, more recent indices still remain below the average level recorded in previous years. The 1990 index fell to 1.4 striped bass per tow and in 1991 slid even farther to an index of 0.86. (See Roanoke Index.)

The juvenile indices have been taken annually from 1956 until 1987 by investigators from North Carolina State University by balloon trawl from seven permanent stations in western Albemarle Sound; and since 1982 by the North Carolina Division of Marine Fisheries. When both groups were sampling, the results were relatively comparable. The highest was a 23.9 index in 1959 to a low of 0.02 in 1984.

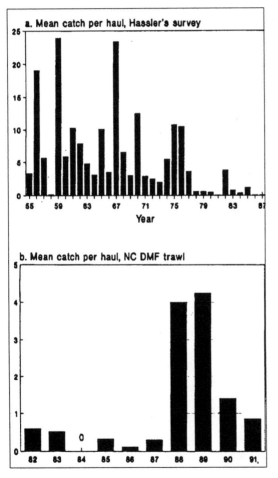

Virginia Index

Tributaries of Chesapeake Bay, in terms of management, should be considered as one biological-geographical entity because all its tidal rivers are contiguous and share the same common tidal estuary. But because the bay is shared politically by Virginia and Maryland each river's contribution of striped bass, in the aggregate, is not always as apparent as it might be. Even though the division is along political boundaries, the tidal rivers in the two states can be separated into three groups because of unique characteristics several of them have in common with each other and those that make them dissimilar from other rivers emptying into the bay.

Three rivers in Virginia, that

Albemarle Sound indices for juvenile abundance for the Roanoke stock of striped bass (a) Survey conducted by North Carolina State University during 1955-87 (Hassler and Maraveylas 1988), and (b) survey conducted by North Carolina Division of Marine Fisheries since 1988.

enter Chesapeake Bay act as major spawning areas for striped bass. They are the James, York, and Rappahannock rivers. The James is the largest, most southerly, and most productive of the three and, on occasion, does contribute some fish to the coastal migratory stock. Some fisheries biologists feel this river actually contributes more fish to the coastal migratory stock than it is credited with. It has also been shown to act as a wintering site for costal migratory bass from other areas that choose not to winter over in the open ocean. The York River is the narrowest of Virginia's tidal rivers and though it acts as a nursery, spawning actually takes place in two tributaries, the Mattaponi and Pamunkey rivers, that come together to form the York. The Rappahannock is the most northerly and longest of the three rivers. At times its fish exhibit characteristics akin to the other two Virginia rivers and at other times more like Potomac River striped bass. During the late 1980s production of juveniles in Virginia increased sharply because of increases on the Rappahannock and James rivers. The trend after 1987's all-time high index of 15.8 has been downward and in 1991 registered 3.8. The Potomac River forms the border between Virginia and Maryland, and while Maryland conducts the annual indices on the river because the border is the Virginia shore, it is managed jointly by the Potomac River Fisheries Commission, an interstate commission formed by Virginia and Maryland.

The annual young-of-the-year survey was conducted from 1967-1973, discontinued from 1974-1979, resumed in 1980, and continued to the present. The discontinuity of Virginia's periodic sampling makes long-term trends difficult to identify; however, recruitment indices from 1987 to 1990 were the highest on record. Since 1987, when the index almost reached 16, the general trend has been a decline. In 1991 it was just under 4. Like Maryland, the early indices were a pooled average of beach seine surveys conducted during the summer. More recently, rather than beach seines, as in Maryland portions of Chesapeake Bay, the juvenile abundance index in Virginia is based on trawl

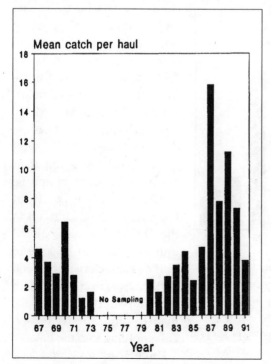

Virginia's index of juvenile abundance for the Chesapeake stock of striped bass, 1967-1991. Samples were not collected during 1974-1979.

samples taken from January to March.

More recent tagging studies have continued to support the idea that the James and York rivers contribute very little to the Atlantic coastal migratory stock. However, this might be more the result of the harvest of these fish before than can migrate rather than a biological characteristic of the strain of fish in these rivers. A number of fish do migrate to the coasts from the Rappahannock River. Coastal migrant stock from Maryland, Delaware, and Hudson rivers historically had wintered over in deep, coastal bays and tidal rivers from Massachusetts south to Virginia, as well as offshore. There is speculation that some of the migratory stock that was believed to be from Virginia waters might actually have been wintering-over fish that originated in other areas and were not really products of that state's three striped bass rivers.

Maryland Index

Striped bass spawn in almost all the rivers that enter Chesapeake Bay. In many, the spawning is slight and does not take place every year. In others, the annual production has been so great that it has overshadowed the production of these smaller streams and made their contribution to the overall population insignificant in comparison. Production in the major rivers, when they were in a healthy condition, had been so vast that the coastal migrant stock it produced even eclipsed the contribution of all other major spawning grounds combined. In its heyday, it was estimated that only 10 percent of the annual production in Chesapeake Bay escaped exploitation in the bay after its second year. And, when at large, it composed nearly 90 percent (more recent analysis of this figure has it reduced) of the striped bass population in the annual spring and fall migrations north and south along the Northeast Coast. That is why when these nurseries began declining in production the entire coastal migratory stock was placed in jeopardy.

For comparison, Maryland's spawning and nursery grounds can be divided into three groups. The Potomac River, on the western side of Chesapeake Bay, constitutes one group. There is natural spawning on the nearby Patuxent River. However, it is so variable, and because in the last few years it annually received large numbers of stocked fish, it is not considered a part of the annual index. The second group is the Upper Bay, where spawning actually takes place in some open areas of the bay itself. It also includes the Susquehanna River, the open Susquehanna Flats, Northeast River, Elk, Bohemia and Sassafras rivers, and the Chesapeake & Delaware Canal. Historically, this area had been the major producer of striped bass in the bay, and its progeny comprised most of the coastal migrants. The third group is the Eastern Shore rivers, where the Choptank and Nanticoke rivers are the dominant waters, but which also include Chester, Wicomico, and Pocomoke rivers.

If one is going to manage a stock of fish properly the first fact one must know is just how many fish are in that group. Getting a handle on the absolute number of an open fish stock you want to deal with is not only impractical but difficult, time-consuming and expensive. The next best thing you can do is take a sample of the population while the young fish are still on their nursery grounds. This **will not** give you an indication of the size of the population. However, if during the next year you take another sample in the same place, using the exact same methods, you can compare the number of fish you caught in the first sample with those of the second sample. This will give you a relative idea of the size of the *increase* or *decrease* of the second year's production. Biologists know it works as a valid management tool, because three years down the line, when fish are vulnerable to harvest, an increase or decrease in the size of the sample is proportionately reflected in the size of the harvest for that year.

The sample is called an index. The more samples you take from a given area, the better will be the accuracy of your index. Maryland has established 22 primary, which are seined three times each season, and 110 auxiliary sites. The final index is the average of all indices that are taken that year. While you may not know just how large the absolute population is, you will know if it is increasing or decreasing in size. In Maryland waters of Chesapeake Bay, the abundance index of juvenile striped bass is based on beach sampling taken during the summer months, and is a pooled average of individual sample taken from the Potomac River on the western shore, the Choptank and Nanticoke rivers on the Eastern Shore, and Upper Bay, that includes Elk River, Chesapeake &Delaware Canal and an open area near the Susquehanna Flats.

Annual sampling of spring spawning production of striped bass has been conducted since 1954. In that period, production showed cyclic highs and lows in a fashion that was believed natural, with several dominant year classes that usually followed a year or two of extreme lows in production. The first inconsistency in this pattern appeared in

Maryland's young-of-the-year index of striped bass production is of interest to all East Coast anglers because it is used as the basis by the ASMFC to determine coast-wide rates of harvest for commercial and recreation fishermen.

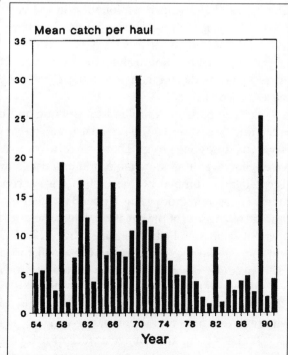

Mean catch per haul / Year

the mid-1960s, when each subsequent year produced more young fish than the preceding year. This increased until 1970 when it reached its zenith. Since then, in the ensuing 23 years, Maryland waters have not produced a dominant year class.

During the decline that began in 1971, the index had ranged from a low of 1.2 in 1982 to a high of 25.2 in 1989. However, the 1989 index is still a source of heated debate, especially among biologists and administrators outside Maryland. Before it was accepted by the Atlantic Marine Fisheries Commission, many believed it should have been thrown out. "The index was valid," said Maryland biologist Don Cosden, whose crew conducted the survey. The controversial site was Hambrooks Bar on the Choptank River, near Cambridge on Maryland's Eastern Shore.

No one challenges the accuracy of Cosden's number; on the second setting, 30 minutes after the first, he and his crew netted more than 1,000 young-of-the-year striped bass. But they did challenge Maryland's use of both the figure and the site. Critics claimed the site was no longer composed of the physical characteristics that had made it valid, and so should not have been used to compare it with other seinings in the past from the site. Because of wave action and tidal erosion, it had changed from a small point of land to a small island with a back eddy that concentrated the fingerlings and their foods. The following year, Cosden reported, the site produced no striped bass. But the damage was already done.

Use of the site data triggered the reopening of the fishery to harvest, both commercially and recreationally. The Striped Bass Management Plan, in 1981, gave the Atlantic States Marine Fisheries Commission authority to close all harvesting of striped bass. In 1985, Amendment 3 to the Plan was passed to give it more control to manage striped bass with added objectives. It also had written into it Objective 1, that would allow for the reopening of the fishery if conditions and production changed in favor of the overall bass population. "Objective 1. That the states reduce fishing mortality on the 1982 year class of females, and females of all subsequent year classes of Chesapeake Bay stocks to zero, until 95 percent of these year-classes have an opportunity to reproduce at least once. This objective is intended to apply to the fishery until the three-year running average of the Maryland young-of-the-young-of-the-year index attains 8.0."

In 1987, the index was 4.8. In 1988 it was 2.7. When added to the 1989 index of 25.2, it amounted to 32.4, that when divided by 3 produced an average of 10.9. This was the triggering mechanism that allowed the ASMFC to reopen the fishery. The governing board of the ASMFC made no effort to interpret, review or correct the anomalous figure. It wasn't until 1991 that its Technical Committee could put forth a more realistic number of 12, because it had to work backwards to derive a more meaningful index from a stock assessment of the 1989 year class when it was Age III. Using the reestimated index for 1989 of 12, it would have produced a three-year running average of 6.5, below the 8.0

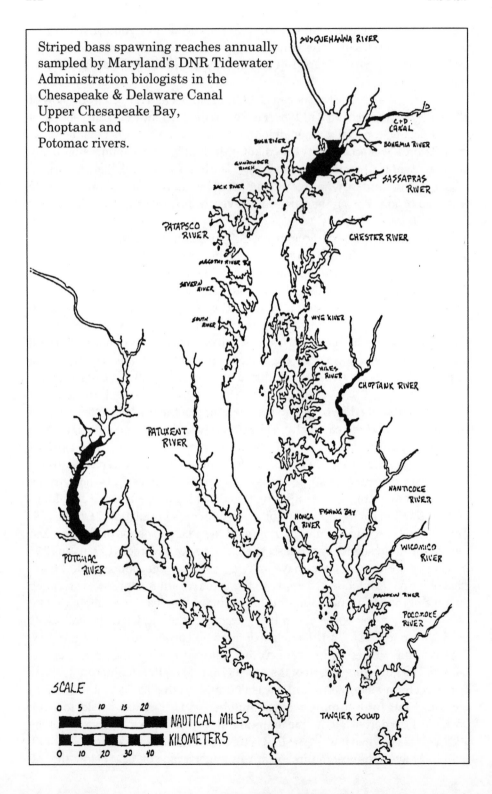

Striped bass spawning reaches annually sampled by Maryland's DNR Tidewater Administration biologists in the Chesapeake & Delaware Canal Upper Chesapeake Bay, Choptank and Potomac rivers.

needed to trigger the opening. The ASMFC was further criticized the following year because it did not respond to the reestimated figure and never closed the season. It had lost its integrity as an administrative body by not acting.

The mistake was even further compounded because the ASMFC continued to use the 25.4 index for the following two years. It was so high that, uncorrected, it continued to influence the average index for 1990, that was 10, based on the 1990 index of just 2.1; and the average index for 1991, that was 10.56, with the 1991 index of 4.4. Even in 1992, when the index was 9.1, again was questionable, and almost apologetically presented to the public in a news release, not by the Department of Natural Resources, but by Gov. William D. Schaefer's office. The thee-year running index, without the influence of the 1989 index, fell to 5.2, again below the index of 8 established by ASMFC, but still the Commission did not respond.

The Commission's credibility to manage striped bass strictly along biological lines has been seriously questioned ever since. The inability of it to respond even to standards it had set for itself, points up the very political aspect of some of its members in thwarting genuine measures that would insure the future of striped bass. There arises a valid, serious question as to their sincerity in attempting to manage striped bass to the betterment of the species. While striped bass management efforts have not had an impact on increasing striped bass production, these efforts have led to a better management and utilization of the existing stocks by allowing more juveniles, that survive the trauma of egg, larval and post-larval stages, to grow to adulthood and be harvested as larger fish.

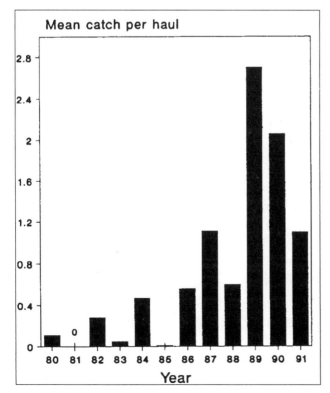

Mean catch per haul

Year

Maryland's young-of-the-year index of striped bass production is of interest to all East Coast anglers because it is used as the basis by the ASMFC to determine rates of harvest for both commercial and recreation fishermen.

Year	Head of Bay	Potomac River	Choptank River	Nanticoke River	Overall Average
1954	0.9	5.2	1.2	25.1	5.2
1955	4.4	5.7	12.5	5.9	5.5
1956	33.9	6.2	9.8	8.2	15.2
1957	5.4	2.5	2.1	1.3	2.9
1958	28.2	8.4	19.5	22.5	19.3
1959	1.9	1.6	0.1	1.8	1.4
1960	9.3	4.3	9.0	4.7	7.1
1961	22.1	25.8	6.0	1.5	17.0
1962	11.4	19.7	6.1	6.6	12.2
1963	6.1	1.1	5.4	4.1	4.0
1964	31.0	29.1	10.6	13.3	23.5
1965	2.2	3.4	9.5	21.6	7.4
1966	32.3	10.5	13.6	3.3	16.7
1967	17.4	1.9	5.3	4.1	7.8
1968	13.1	0.7	6.3	9.-0	7.2
1969	26.6	0.2	4.8	6.2	10.5
1970	33.1	20.1	57.2	17.1	30.4
1971	23.7	8.5	6.3	2.0	11.8
1972	12.1	1.9	11.0	25.0	11.0
1973	24.7	2.1	1.0	1.1	8.9
1974	19.9	1.5	15.3	3.9	10.1
1975	7.6	7.8	4.7	5.2	6.7
1976	9.8	3.2	2.4	1.7	4.9
1977	12.1	1.9	1.2	1.0	4.8
1978	12.5	7.9	6.0	4.8	8.5
1979	8.3	2.2	2.8	0.9	4.0
1980	2.3	2.2	1.0	1.8	2.0
1981	0.3	1.4	1.3	2.4	1.2
1982	5.5	10.0	13.0	6.2	8.4
1983	1.2	2.0	0.9	1.0	1.4
1984	6.1	4.7	2.8	1.5	4.2
1985	0.3	5.6	3.7	2.1	2.9
1986	1.6	9.9	0.5	2.2	4.1
1987	0.3	6.4	12.1	2.5	4.8
1988	7.3	0.4	0.7	0.4	2.7
1989	19.4	2.2	97.8	2.9	25.2
1990	3.8	0.6	3.1	0.9	2.1
1991	3.9	2.5	12.2	1.1	4.4
1992	1.2	22.1	4.1	4.2	9.1
Average (1954-92)	11.9	6.5	9.8	6.0	8.6

The Class of '82

The year class produced in Chesapeake Bay during the spring of 1982 deserves special attention in any lengthy discussion of the biology of striped bass because it is a classic example of what management can do in real life under controlled conditions. This year class became unique only after the initial figures for its index were determined to be 8.4. This wasn't a great index figure, just matching the normal or average of 8.4 for the bay, that spanned the record-keeping years 1954 to 1982. And, it was without the characteristic of being a dominant year class that might stem the steady decline in production. It wasn't even as good as the 1978 index of 8.5 that occurred four years earlier. However, it became prominent because biologist used it to manipulate the fishery.

But at the time, in 1984, biologists involved with the recovery of striped bass populations were becoming desperate because there were no signs of a dominant year class being produced as the overall population continued a steady decline. They decided to make the 1982 year class special because, as managers of the striped bass recovery program, they wanted to protect at least 95 percent of the females (so they could reproduce at least once) produced that spring in four river areas of Chesapeake Bay. They needed to see, when these bass returned as spawners to the Choptank River on the east side of the bay and the Potomac River on the west side, if they could make a difference in production by the sheer enormity of their brood stock numbers. The other two spawning areas, the Upper Bay and Nanticoke River on Maryland's Eastern Shore, had produced only half the number of young bass in 1982 as did the first two rivers.

Before the unique protection afforded all bass by "Objective 1," males of that class would remain in the bay for most of their lives, readily susceptible to over-exploitation by commercial and recreational fishermen. Only later on would some of the surviving males occasionally join the great migration north along the coast at the end of spring. The females of the 1982 year class, at the beginning of their third year, when they are 12-16 inches long and weigh about three-quarters of a pound, would abandon the bay and, because of their numbers, become the major component in the hordes of bass migrating up the coast. They would return to the bay's rivers, it was believed at the time, only when they reached sexual maturity, at age six in 1988. This date was then pushed back to eight years and 1990. However, more immature females did return to the river to winter-over, that were expected. It was believed they wintered else-where with adult fish.

It took Amendment 3 to the 1981 Striped Bass Management Plan, recommended by the Striped Bass Management Board of the Atlantic States Marine Fisheries Commission, to give the females of '82 the special protection they needed from any man-made fishing mortality. The amendment was adopted in 1985 because "it was needed to meet the goals and objectives of the original plan." It would accomplish the protection the fish needed by the use of annual length increments, as the fish grew, keeping the minimum length for all fish caught along the coast just longer than the longest females should be at that time. In January of 1985, Maryland and Delaware even went so far as to declare a total moratorium on all harvesting of striped bass, either recreational or commercial, in waters under their jurisdiction. The waters of the Potomac River, however, were excluded because they were managed under the joint Maryland-Virginia Potomac River Fisheries Commission.

The maximum limit was to have been 33 inches for the year 1988. However, as the program evolved, new light was shed on the maturation rate of female bass from these rivers of Chesapeake Bay. It was assumed that 95 percent of them would have reached maturity by age six in spring of 1988. By 1990, only a few precocious females were mature and the minimum limit was raised to 38 inches. Also, it was revealed that without fishing pressure, many of the young females didn't abandon the bay after three years and some stayed there until they were four, five and even six years old. It wasn't until 1992, ten years later, that continuous monitoring of the year class revealed the bulk of the class of '82 had reached sexual maturity. It succinctly pointed out, that for years we had been harvesting most of the female population before it could spawn at least once and contribute to survival of that species.

The unusual protection for this one year class produced some startling results. From the beginning, based on models they built, biologist were able to estimate that the juvenile 8.4 index would increase the survival to an equivalent index of 18.8 in 1983 with just one year's protection, and to an equivalent of 33.6 by 1984. It further predicted that by 1986, the abundance of the 1982 year class in our waters would rival or exceed the survival size of the 1970-year class, the largest ever produced, that started at an astonishing index of 30.4. Because of the delay in the maturation of female bass, the maximum benefits to the striped bass population weren't seen along the coast in 1988, '89, or '90, but in 1991 and '92. However, there was one caveat biologists also predicted in 1984 that is coming true today and bears heeding. "One likely effect of this increased abundance will be that the fishermen [commercial and recreational] will be

Female striped bass from the Class of '82 rewrote some of the texts on maturation rates. The traditional 3 to 5, maybe 6 years for maturation was found to be substantially short of the real rate. The accompany chart from Rugolo and Jones, 1989, was a projection at that time and there were still first-time straggler spawners from the class returning as late as 1992.

YEAR	AGE	IMMATURE
1985	3	0 %
1986	4	4 %
1987	5	13 %
1988	6	45 %
1989	7	89 %
1990	8	94 %

led to believe that the stock has recovered and that conservation measures should be relaxed. This increase in abundance is a predicted effect of the conservation measures, and one that is expected to eventually lead to increased recruitment. However, it is essential that the conservation measures remain in effect until recruitment increases."

Biologists working the waters of Chesapeake Bay during the spring spawning run in April and May, 1992, discovered that the massive number of 1982 females, while not missing, were no longer the primary driving force among the spawning females that they had been in 1989, '90, and '91. The decline of the 1982 year class had started. Instead, it was females from 1983 and 1984 year classes that had taken over. The results of "Objective 1" illustrated that recruitment was a function controlled, in this case, by factors in the environment and not the size of the returning brook stock because there was no increase in the index. It revealed that the Chesapeake Bay environment continued to remain hostile to the early stages of striped bass maturation.

Delaware River Index

There's little doubt that the Delaware River and its estuary, Delaware Bay, once harbored a major population of striped bass. The river and bay had offered striped bass an environment with all the classic characteristics to produce and sustain a major fishery—a large, long river in an ideal temperate setting, a steady flow of water, a lengthy fresh-water section but under a tidal influence, an extensive, turbulent and hyper-oxygenated area just above salt water for spawning, and a fresh to brackish to saline environment with a large estuary that from a food point of view could support an extensive summer food-migration to the area. And, it had more than sufficient geographical separation from other riverine environments and striped bass stocks to produce a strain indigenous to its waters. In a way, it had a lot in common with the Hudson River.

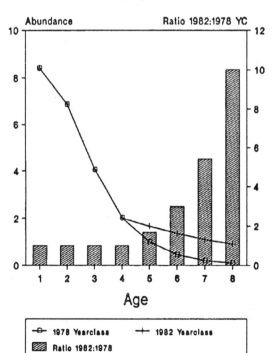

Because historical and recent records of landings from the area are so scant, it is difficult to determine just how large a population it produced. And, because of industrialization and municipal pollution in the area near Philadelphia, and the intensive chemical industry at the head of the bay, striped bass began a decline at the turn of the century that may have totally eliminated the endemic river strain. The pollution area of Philadelphia also happened to be the area where some historic spawning took place. Pollution of the river in the 1950s and 1960s became so heavy that it caused tremendous plankton blooms, and when they died off, decomposing bacteria absorbed all the oxygen available in the water. This created an hypoxic block to the migration of any fish and the survival of any Year 1 striped bass in the nursery area.

With the widening of the Chesapeake & Delaware Canal in the late 1920s, striped bass from the northern portion of Chesapeake Bay suddenly had access to Delaware Bay and stocks from a few Chesapeake Bay rivers used the enlarged short-cut as a new spring/summer coastal migration route. The opening of the canal also led to another phenomenon. Striped bass in the Upper Bay of the Chesapeake began utilizing the canal as a spawning and nursery ground. Most spawning took place where the canal enters the Elk River. The mean direction of water flow in the canal is toward Delaware Bay. In spring, when spawning takes place and rearing begins, the directional flow is further enhanced by flood waters from the nearby Susquehanna River. The result is that some striped bass eggs and juveniles, especially young-of-the-year, are swept into Delaware Bay. Though they are of Chesapeake origin they grow and mature in Delaware Bay.

Juvenile abundance indicies for the Delaware River Stock. 1980-91.

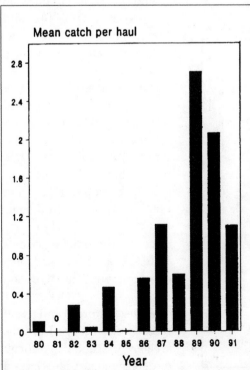

During the last dozen years, efforts to clean the Delaware River and upgrade sewage treatment plants, not only in the Philadelphia area, but from communities upstream in Pennsylvania, New Jersey, and New York that elevated their treatment from primary to tertiary stages, proved quite successful. This, coupled with controlled industrial discharges in the Wilmington area, created a river that was no longer inhospitable to fish migrations. The first to take advantage of the change in

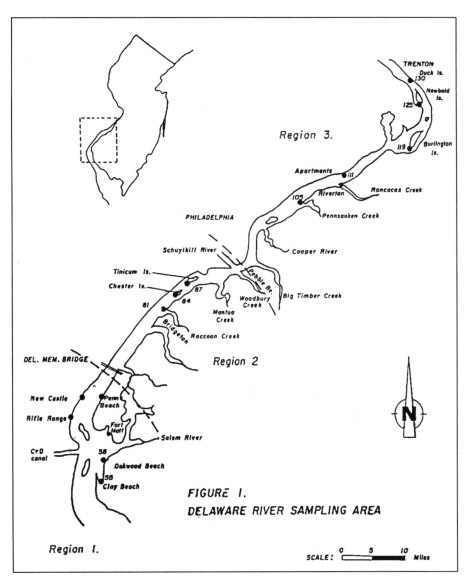

FIGURE 1.
DELAWARE RIVER SAMPLING AREA

the river and the removal of the hypoxia block were shad. Then striped bass responded.

Even during periods of extensive pollution on the river there was one small stream on the New Jersey side of Delaware Bay, about mid-way along the coast, that continued to produce striped bass. The Maurice River is small, nor is it very long, about eight miles. But, it was large enough to produce striped bass. Its strain probably possesses the same characteristics Delaware River fish had because both stocks shared the same estuary. There is even a history of a small commercial fishery just inside the mouth of the Maurice River in the late 1800s. There's no doubt the fishery wasn't large, just enough to maintain a minuscule effort, but because some believe its production has continued uninterrupted to this day, it might eventually become the source of brood stock to restock the Delaware River with its endemic strain.

With the return of improved water quality in the Delaware River, New Jersey biologists began sampling the river in 1980 with haul seines to determine if any striped bass were again using it as a spawning ground. The sampling area extended from where the Chesapeake & Delaware Canal enters Delaware Bay on the west side to the fall line on the Delaware River at Trenton. Juvenile fish were taken in haul seines in the bay ever since exploratory efforts first began but their origins were never exactly determined.

According to Peter Himchak, a New Jersey biologist, analysis of mitochondrial DNA patterns in young-of-the year juveniles and adults captured in the Delaware River system revealed three matriarchal genotypes previous not described for Chesapeake Bay fish. This suggests that a distinct Delaware River stock may still exist. Whether a remnant Delaware River stock exists or not, the presence of young-of-the-year up river of the original oxygen block at Philadelphia suggests that at least some spawning occurs on the Delaware River itself. It wasn't until 1988 that the seines produced the first eggs and larvae in the river proper to substantiate this.

The juvenile index for the Delaware River in 1987 was 1.11 striped bass per haul and was the highest attained at that point since seining began in 1980; this encouraged expanded seining the following year. The sampling format was changed slightly and entailed seining at 16 fixed sites twice a month from mid-July to mid-November, with two hauls made at each site. The index fell slightly in 1988 to 0.58 , but rose to a new high in 1989 to 2.71. In 1990 it was 2.06. The format was again changed in 1991 and reduced the sampling period to August to October, with both fixed and random samples being taken and concentrating half the survey crew's efforts in the brackish-to-fresh tidal water region from the Delaware Memorial Bridge north to the Schuylkill River at the Philadelphia Navy Yard. Indices in 1991 and 1992 were 1.05 and 3.79. Most were caught south of Philadelphia, in nursery areas believed to have historically been the primary striped bass spawning grounds on the lower section of the Delaware River.

Hudson River Index

While the Hudson River has its origins on the highest peak in the Adirondack Mountains, it provides striped bass a hospitable habitat only in its lower reaches. The Hudson from Upper Bay in New York Harbor to the Federal Dam just above Troy is 153 miles long. It varies in width from three miles at Croton-on-Hudson to its narrowest, just below Bear Mountain Bridge, where it squeezes between two mountains and is just a bit less than a half-mile wide. It is its deepest, 180 feet, just a few miles away, but over most of its course it ranges between 12 and 25 feet. It is considered brackish from Upper Bay (New York Harbor) to the Bear Mountain bridge just above Peekskill and is considered fresh from there north. Even so, it experiences a mean tidal change of about four feet throughout its length. The salt block on the river, and separations between brackish and fresh water, varies with the seasons and even within seasons depending upon the amount of fresh water (60 percent from the upper Hudson) it receives from   numerous tributaries along its entire tidal section. The flow sways back and forth with the tide but there is a slow net outflow.

Very few large bass, or even small mature spawners, winter over in the river. The spawning migration from ocean-wintering areas begins about the third week of April and peaks three weeks later, when water temperatures rise above 55 degrees. Spawning takes place anywhere north of Croton Point but is concentrated in two areas, one around West Point and the other near Kingston.

New York's DEC began developing a spawning index of juvenile striped bass in 1976 by shore seining. They seined the Hudson in a 20-mile section from Dobbs Ferry to Indian Point (Miles 22 to 42), from late August through November. In 1981, the Hudson juvenile stock was assessed by an added means, a trawl survey, also conducted by the DEC. However, an earlier haul seine survey, conducted by contractors for Hudson Valley power utilities, had been underway since 1969. This earlier survey sampled by beach haul seines the river shore from Yonkers to Albany (Mile 12 to Mile 150), from July through November.

The DEC instituted its trawl survey in shoal water and river channels as a means to determine the validity of beach seining for developing a truer or more

A healthy haul of yearling striped bass on the Hudson River attests to its ability to produce striped bass while at the same time Cheasapeake Bay nursery areas cannot raise fish beyond the larval stages.

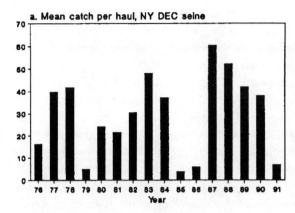

a. Mean catch per haul, NY DEC seine

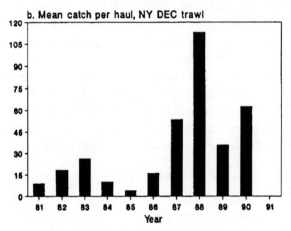

b. Mean catch per haul, NY DEC trawl

comprehensive spawning index, and is still conducted today. In general, when all three indices were being conducted, they showed consistent patterns of juvenile abundance, an indication that the beach seines alone had probably sampled a representative fraction of the juvenile component of the striped bass population present in that region of the river. However, in 1986, the trawl survey index increased sharply while the beach seine index remained low, indicating, according to Andrew Kahnle, a DEC marine biologist on the survey, that a possible shift had occurred in the distribution of young-of-the-year striped bass within that sampling area. Byron Young, head of the DEC's indices program, stated that shore water temperatures (taken as a standard operating procedure in every haul) were higher that year than other years and this may have driven small fish to seek cooler, deeper water in the main channel.

The 1987 index of juvenile abundance for the Hudson River population, based on DEC haul seines, was the highest on record for the time period, 60.7 striped bass per haul. The trawl survey also recorded a high value supporting the shore seining figure. No single fact was identified as being responsible for the high recruitment levels. However, the Hudson River nursery and its striped bass populations are in a unique situation with spawning stocks that now have a relatively broad representation of mature age classes, according to Kahnle. This suggests that protection from recreational fishing and the prohibition of commercial fishing, because of high levels of PCB contamination in striped bass since 1976, has allowed the Hudson stock to maintain a large number of spawning, mature females in its population and thereby increase recruitment. This, along with the added protection of the 1982 year class from Chesapeake Bay stock, gave Hudson River females more protection when, after spawning, they departed the river and joined other coastal migratory stocks.

While still above the long-term average, the annual indices showed a steady five-year decline from a peak in 1987 of 60.7 to a low of 6.9 in 1991. In 1992, however, the index rose to 17.6 This could be explained as a normal, cyclic decline and does exhibit some of a "normal" cycle's characteristics, especially the extreme low in 1985 of 3.9, that usually precedes a high or dominant year class. However, with all the changes in the environment, it's difficult to picture what a normal cycle might be like, especially when we try to compare current characteristics with cyclic characteristics prior to 1970.

In 1991 the DEC switched from determining its indices as a simple arithmetic average or mean to a geometric mean. Maryland has also switched to this method because statisticians believe it gives truer index of the population. In the arithmetic mean, numbers are added and the sum divided by the number of seines to get the average. In the geometric mean, the numbers are multiplied and the mean is the root of the sum. The geometric mean is usually lower than the arithmetic mean. The geometric mean is regarded as a truer average because it gives less weight to extraordinarily large numbers, such as the 1989 index that resulted from the Hambrooks Bar seining in Maryland.

Ever since biologists recognized the decline in Chesapeake Bay production, they have been wondering why striped bass production in the Hudson River has continued, even increased, in apparent independence of the factors that caused declines in Roanoke, Chesapeake, and Delaware bay stocks? Researchers in New York addressed the question in the same way others sought answers to why the Chesapeake was declining. And, like the Chesapeake problem, theories were proposed, a series of factors were isolated, but no one could draw conclusions from them that would answer all of the questions with the same credibility.

There is the possibility that the combined protection afforded both juvenile and adult striped bass by the PCB health restriction and the coastal moratorium offered Hudson River striped bass respite from commercial and recreational fishing mortality and allowed the remaining brood stock to supply the population with large year classes. There might have been enough fish to cloud the effects of any man-made causes, i.e., industrial and municipal pollution and toxic chemical discharges. Nor was the Hudson River watershed immune to acid rain fallout. Most Adirondack lakes, ponds, and streams were devastated by acid rain in the 1960s, '70s, and' 80s. It surely must have also reduced the pH levels in the lower Hudson, which would allow aluminum and copper to become toxic. Still, these had no measured detrimental affect on annual striped bass production.

A group of researchers working under contract to Texas Instruments, that represented several of the involved Hudson Valley power utilities, believed that a large influx of fresh water, carrying nitrogen from the surrounding land, enriched the environment and enhanced zooplankton growth. This made available an exceptional amount of food to larval, fry and fingerling striped bass at a crucial stage in the fish's life cycle and accounted for the large striped bass production numbers.

An true analysis of the reasons why the Hudson River continues to produce young striped bass each year while other areas fail is difficult because of the great number of variables that can create a favorable environment for young fish. They are complex and interact in so many different combinations with each other that no single or even group of causes, has so far been singled out. It is the same problem, but in reverse, that researchers face on Chesapeake Bay waters. The unfortunate aspect about the Chesapeake situation is that there is little or nothing management can do about these factors in the short run to stem or reverse them. And, there are even doubts that long-term changes can be affected. The only tool it has at its disposal is managing what stock the environment allows to survive and either preserving or conserving it, or trying to decide how to distribute it among its demanding user groups.

COMMERCIAL HARVESTS

For years, the size of the commercial harvest was used as a gauge to determine the status of the adult stocks of striped bass along the East Coast. It wasn't a very good gauge for several reasons but it was the only yardstick available. In those years, the size of the harvest didn't depend so much upon to availability of fish as it did upon the sophistication, or lack of it, of the gear that was being used to catch them. In other words, commercial fishermen were hindered by the restrictions of their gear from gathering more fish while they were almost unlimited numbers available to them. In some years, adverse weather was also a problem and this further altered the size of the commercial harvest. In other years, the demand for striped bass and all fish was down. It is difficult today to imagine today, with the great demand for fish, that there were periods in our history when many people just didn't like to eat fish and fisheries industries were not the great money-makers they are now. Even the religious abstinence of eating meat on Fridays had an economic basis in the desire of the Christian church to provide labor and profit for commercial fishermen. In other years, the abundance of fish was affected more by natural cyclic highs and lows rather than environmental factors and the catch was reduced. During war-time years, the availability of manpower, fuel and craft also affected to size of the harvest.

Before the demand became so great for striped bass and other fish as food, and specifically a health food because of their lack of cholesterol, striped bass were annual under-harvested. However, just prior to the great decline, commercial harvests became a fair gauge of the striped bass population because the fishery was being fished at its maximum, that is, they were fully exploited for several years and finally over-exploited for the last decade as the decline set in.

Even during the moratorium instituted on commercial fishing in many states, a commercial fishery, limited only by the number of striped bass available at that time, continued to operate in Massachusetts, Rhode Island, on the Potomac River and in North Carolina. New York had no commercial season for several years, not as a measure to help striped bass stocks recover, but because of a closure by the State Health Department when polychlorinated biphenyl (PCBs) were found in fish from the Hudson River nursery with levels above those that the U.S. Department of Agriculture would allow for interstate commerce. New York set similar limits to protect its resident's health. In an ironic twist of concern Rhode Island officials followed suit and forbade the sale of striped bass to its residents because of PCB contamination, but allowed its commercial fishermen to sell them out-of-state, to unknowing fish consumers.

Since 1990, with the ASMFC's reinstatement of commercial fishing, its harvest numbers have been carefully controlled and scrutinized. These numbers, however, cannot now be used as a gauge of the overall striped bass population because commercial fishermen since have been restricted by quotas established by the ASMFC. While these figures are interesting they serve only to reflect the landings in relation to the cap each state is given. The cap for each state was derived by taking 20 percent of its annual average commercial landings between 1972 and 1979. The 20 percent figure was chosen as a figure that would reduced the new mortality of striped bass because of commercial activities to a value of 0.25 or about 28 percent.

Reported commercial landings of striped bass along the Atlantic Coast reached a record low in 1989 of 285,000 pounds because only three states and the Potomac River Fisheries Commission (considered statistically as a state) were the only states that allowed a commercial fishery. It rose in 1990 to 822, 659 pounds, in 1991 to 1,152,992 pounds, and in 1992 to 1,384,389 pounds. The 1992 data were still incomplete at the time of this printing. The reason the landings increased since 1990 was that eight states again allowed a commercial fishery.

RECREATIONAL HARVEST

Recreational fishing harvests weren't considered significant prior to 1930 because of the small number of sportfishers. However, striped bass have been the Atlantic Coast's most popular game fish since about 1850. Its rise in popularity was the result of, and coincided with, the development of reels and rods, and continued to rise as line and lures, as well as the entire fishing kit, evolved in sophistication, innovation and thus proficiency. There's no doubt that recreational fishermen were harvesting large numbers of fish as early as the 1950s, but in comparison to the commercial harvest, these were still negligible numbers but growing. Fisheries managers, however, were developing a curiosity as to the size of the recreational harvest but there was no easy, inexpensive or accurate way to determine its magnitude because of the individualistic nature of recreational fishing and the fact that these fish were not documented when landed.

Nor is there any doubt that the rapidly growing size of the sportfishery was also a factor in contributing to the decline of the striped bass in Chesapeake Bay, along with commercial harvests. Excessively liberal limits where they occurred, unrealistic minimum lengths that gave no protection to female fish that had not yet spawned for the first time, and no seasons to protect fish before and during spawning, were not the fault of recreational or even commercial fishermen but the inattentiveness of state managers who had been given the mandate to manage these fish and either did not or could not because of political pressures.

In order to manage a resource, you must first know the size of the resource and all the factors that impinge upon its well being. In this case, it is the number of harvesters. When the first serious management plans for striped bass, based partially on their biological needs, were being developed in the late 1970s and early 1980s, the best that could be done initially was to *estimate* the number of fishermen, how often they fished and how many fish they *would* catch. From this raw data a cap based on estimates on what they would be allowed to harvest was established, like the cap on commercial fishermen. The maximum or cap recreational fishermen would be allowed was not defined by actual numbers or poundage, though this was the hoped-for goal, but by seasons, minimum size lengths and daily or seasonal bag limits.

From the onset, the National Marine Fisheries Service had a real problem on their hands because they had no way to determine a real number of marine recreational anglers. One way would be to count saltwater fishing licenses, but not all states required such a license. And where one was required, not all anglers who bought such a licenses were necessarily harvesters of striped bass. The only exact count of striped bass fishermen was accomplished in California where everyone who fishes for striped bass must first purchase a striped bass stamp. The stamp is added to their fishing license, either marine or fresh water.

In 1979, in an attempt to determine the size of the recreational catch, NMFS began conducting its Marine Recreational Fisheries Statistics Survey. However, the survey only ESTIMATES the total recreational harvest as the product of the total angling effort and the average-catch-per-angler. According to NMFS statistics, the recreational survey estimates of total (including fish released alive) of striped bass on the Atlantic coast declined from 2 million fish in 1970 to about 0.6 million during the 1983-1984 period. Between 1985 and 1990 there was a gradual rise in the recreational catch for two reasons, neither of which had anything to do with a resurgence or increase in significant natural production on the Chesapeake nursery grounds. One was the lifting of the self-imposed moratoria in several states. The other was an increase in the number of mature fish from the 1982 year class in Chesapeake Bay, which entered the fishery. They had been given unique protection in several states for a nine-year period following their birth when all of females in that year class were allowed to reach maturity so they could spawn at least once. In 1991, the catch was *estimated* to have reached about 4 million fish.

However, the *estimates* for the total number of fish retained or killed by recreational anglers that year was 332,000 fish, or about 8 percent of their 4 million catch, according to the NMFS report. The remaining 3.6 million fish were released. The statistical error of this number's accuracy is 13 percent. The *estimated* weight of the fish recreational anglers kept was 3.5 million pounds, about three times the harvest of the commercial fishery, according to NMFS. One reason for this heavy weight was because recreational fishermen were restricted to keeping fish 36 inches or longer, and somewhat smaller in Chesapeake Bay and the Hudson River, while commercial fishermen were permitted to take only fish usually between 24 and 28 inches.

The validity of NMFS estimate of the recreational catch has been challenged regularly. When you consider that it is an estimate of the number of fish, with a built-in error of margin of 13 percent, and this estimate is based on an estimate of the number of anglers, the move away from the unknown correct number is multiplied. Even NMFS admits that its finally estimates of the recreational harvest has been traditionally too high, but claims its figures are improving in accuracy. The claim is based on an expanded number of interviews with fishermen. The interviews are of two kinds, on sight where the interviewer actually sees the fish and a larger, expanded telephone interview that depends upon the angler's memory, ability to recall, correctness in evaluation what was caught and a traditional personal ego to be successful among his or her peers. All this makes for a pretty sandy foundation upon which to build a house as important as ascribing a figure to the recreational catch.

Too often groups interested in down-playing the commercial take and exaggerating the recreational catch will use NMFS statistics to their advantage by comparing commercial fishing numbers, that are derived at by a census, with recreational catch numbers, that are attained by a survey. It's like comparing apples and oranges. To further compound the exaggeration, the data base gathered by NMFS for the commercial fishery is a census, that is, an exact count of the fish, while the other is a survey based on estimates that are given in weight or poundages. They cannot be compared, exactly, though they are by some. One can statistically, but again with a slight built-in error, convert pounds of fish into numbers of fish by taking an average-weight calculation, then dividing the estimated total weight to get number of fish. This is another manipulable figure that moves the derived-at number still one step farther from the correct number.

Since 1979, the proportion of fish released alive by recreational anglers, according to NMFS, has generally increased to 90 percent or more in the late 1980s and early 1990s. Though there is an increasing trend, recreational anglers are keeping fewer striped bass, even though they may be legal size. The reason the release number increased was not because of this trend but because the minimum size at which striped bass could legally be kept annually was increased over that period. The release was not so much legal-sized fish but sublegal striped bass.

Estimated total recreational catch (1,000 fish) of striped bass, including both harvested and released fish, by state, Maine to North Carolina, 1979-1991

State	1979	1980	1981	1982	1983	1984	1985	1986	1987	1988	1989	1900	1991
Maine	-	-	-	-	-	177	-	-	-	-	-	16	69
N.H.	0	0	-	0	-	0	-	0	-	-	-	15	7
Mass.	66	-	-	129	68	132	123	655	113	302	236	453	582
R.I.	31	-	-	-	-	72	50	-	98	31	47	82	46
Conn.	81	42	-	555	45	41	41	-	80	30	111	159	371
N.Y.	733	59	37	-	36	101	95	149	219	146	376	286	800
N.J.	-	-	40	151	210	84	-	43	63	95	287	246	222
Del.	-	0	0	0	-	-	-	0	-	-	-	18	39
Md.	1,005	377	174	40	155	148	102	502	145	182	152	631	1,422
Virg.	-	0	0	0	-	-	-	-	-	36	98	60	344
PRFC	prior to 1990, PFRC catch was included with Maryland and Virginia											64	55
N.C.	57	-	576	0	-	-	-	-	0	-	-	0	-
Total	2,005	548	892	911	568	626	618	1,399	761	840	1,334	2,030	3,957

PART TWO

FISHING TECHNIQUES

14

Early Striped Bass
Fishing and Fishermen

The Basse is one of the best fishes in the country....the way to catch
them is with hooke and line: the Fishermen taking a great codline,
to which he fasteneth a piece of Lobster, and throws it into the sea,
the fish biting at it pulls her to him, and knocks her on the head with
a stick....the English at the top of an high water doe crosse the creeks
with long seanes or Basse netts, which stop the fish; and the water
ebbing from them are left on dry ground, sometimes two or three
thousand at a set....
—William Wood, New England's Prospects (1635)

Our earliest striped bass fishermen weren't very sporting by today's standards.
They weren't fishing for sport, but for food that would see them through the year
in a land everyone thought hostile. Early settlers along our New England coast
created very efficient traps for taking striped bass during the summer months
as they stretched long seines and weirs across the coastal streams at high tide.

As the water ebbed from the creeks the stranded fish were obtained in far
greater quantities than the fisherman could haul to land. The fish were used
either fresh, salted, pickled, or smoked. Pickled bass, along with salted codfish,
even became a medium for trade in the West Indies. The earliest colonial record
of the smoking of striped bass as a means of preservation is also by wood:

They drie them to keepe for Winter, erecting scaffolds in the hot
sunshine, making fires likewise underneath them, by whose smoake
the flies are expelled till the substance remaine hard and drie. In this

manner they drie Basse and other fishes without salt, cutting them very thin to dry suddenly, before the flies spoyle them, or the raine moist them having speciall care to hang them in their smoaky houses, in the night or dankish weather.

Of course, Indians had been fishing for striped bass long before the colonists arrived. The earliest accounts of their methods are re-latively late and come from Canada. In the St. John River, New Brunswick, according to Joshua Adams (1873), Indians captured striped bass at spawning time:

A few canoes would drop down-river, each with an Indian in the bow, spear in hand, and another in the stern gently paddling. A sudden splash close by would indicate a spawning bass on the surface and like an arrow, the birchbark skiff shot toward the spot while the man in the front, resting on his knees, with much force and dexterity sent the three-pronged harpoon into the fish.

The art of fishing for striped bass as we know it today rested on the development of fishing equipment. Though rods and reels had been around since the 14th century, few if any found their way to salt water where striped bass could be caught. The first rods and reels were designed more for light baits and flies with which to catch trout and salmon. They made their way toward salt waters as an alternative method only after the bait-casting reel was invented and perfected.

Most anglers, up until about 1825 or 1830, would take bass by handlines from boats and the surf. The accepted method had changed little since Wood's description. From the surf, a cotton or linen line was uncoiled in the sand and a large piece of bait—crab, shrimp, or cut fish—was secured on the hook. The fisherman swung the line around his head and then flung it into the surf. A fish was played on the hands or by running along the beach.

One of the most complete descriptions of this technique for fishing striped bass in the surf comes from a rather definitive work written in 1845 entitled *The American Angler's Guide; or Complete Fisher's Manual for The United States: Containing the Opinions and Practices of Experienced Anglers of Both Hemispheres* by John J. Brown. The title of the short chapter is *Basse Fishing on the Shores of Long Island*, written for Brown by T.D. Lowther, Esq.

Off the south-east shore of Long Island, during the fall months, Basse are taken in considerable numbers. About the middle of August, fish from four to ten pounds begin to make along the coast from Montauk to Fire Island Inlet, and enter the Inlets, where they are generally taken upon the bar, or just beyond the surf, either by trolling, or by "heaving and hauling" from shore. The latter is a favorite mode of fishing, but laborious, requiring both physical strength and practiced skill. The squid for this purpose should be of block tin, full six ounces in weight, with large hook (no kirb), size Number 1 for Cod. This is attached to a cotton line, full twenty fathoms long, light and close twist, is made to gyrate around the head [the angler's] until it acquires sufficient velocity and momentum, when it is cast, with the full swing of the arm, into the breakers, carrying after it the line that is held loosely coiled in the left hand. The moment the squid strikes the water, it is hauled swiftly ashore that it may not sink, but play on the surf, and imitate the motion of a natural fish. At Montauk, they wind around a long squid-lead, a strip of fresh skin from the belly of the basse, or draw and tie up over the lead the tail-skin of an eel. But hungry fish will snap at anything moving. I have seen taken a basse of twenty-five pounds that bit at a rag.

Even after the development of rods and simple reels that could throw a hooked bait into the waves, many anglers were still forced to use handlines because of the high cost of fishing equipment. For years, a piece of squid on a cotton line (squid line) was the standard striped bass outfit even after tackle costs were reduced and within everyone's financial reach. Squidding lines remained popular until monofilament came onto the market and totally displaced them.

Striped bass fishing as a casting-trolling sport began to develop with the invention of the first bait-casting reel in the early 1800s. Between 1800 and 1810—no one is sure of the exact date—George Snyder of Paris, Ky., developed a reel composed of a spool to spin and pay out line when cast and a handle on the spool to retrieve it. The lure had to be heavy to pull the line. Snyder, who had the background and inclination to develop such an idea, was a watchmaker and a silversmith, as well as president of the Bourbon Angling Club. Others picked up the idea and by 1840 the reel was being mass produced.

At first, most reels had a direct or 1:1 ratio. It was a simple trick next to add gears to the reel handle and spool. This created a multiplying reel, one with a ratio of 2:1 or more. Still, these reels had no clutch to disengage the gears nor drag—other than maybe a click—but nothing else to slow down the spool when cast or when a fish was running, except one's thumb. Therefore, surf fishing was not as popular as it is today.

The nature and scope of striped bass fishing and fishermen is rather difficult to determine for the first half of the 19th century. We had to wait for the development of the American outdoors press as a keeper of records and teller of tales. From about 1850, the lights begin to go on.

One of the first writers of note was Frank Forrester, whose real name was Henry William Herbert. Herbert was a transplanted Englishman who condescended to make his living in America by telling us what was wrong with the way we practiced our sports. He was a decided Anglophile and assumed a rather snobbish position throughout much of his work. Despite his prejudice, his descriptions of our early times and techniques are invaluable, though often inaccurate. His principal work was a pair of books on field sports and another volume on fishing. He wrote several other books that were more novels than factual descriptions.

Squidding. *The original technique for fishing the surf was with a live squid as bait, tossed on a handline into the surf. The original sketch appeared in the* Fifth Annual (1899) Report of the Commissioners of Fisheries, Game and Forests of the State of New York. *The caption identifies the fish as a bluefish, but it is obviously a striped bass, and this was the technique used for bass.*

Herbert was a dedicated salmon and trout fisherman, but he also held the striped bass in great esteem. He considered it second only to the salmon as the most desirable fish along the coasts. His knowledge of the fish was less than he would have us believe, but still he tells us a lot about how the art of angling was practiced in the mid-1800s.

Herbert lived at "The Cedars" in New Jersey, and much of his striped bass knowledge is about the fish in the area of the New York bays. During his time, there was great striped bass fishing around Manhattan, in the East and Harlem rivers, and in the meadows of New Jersey, as well as in the Hudson and around Staten Island. The New York *Sun*, at one time, ran a daily account of the striped bass catches from the Battery Bridge, on Manhattan's southern tip which was this nation's first fishing forecast.

A far better account of the status of the striped bass fishing in America during the 1800s is supplied by Genio C. Scott in his authoritative book *Fishing in American Waters*. There is little doubt that during his forty years of fishing for striped bass, Scott had become addicted to the fish. In an opening statement to his book of 1869 he apologized for putting a picture of the fish on the frontispiece and asked for "pardon in placing this beauty first on the list" of fishes he describes.

During Scott's day most striped bass angling for sport was either done from boats—trolling and some "still-bait" fishing—or by a weak attempt at casting off rickety platforms that were built above surf and rock areas where striped bass had been known to frequent. At this time, the hot spots were on the western end of Long Island in Hell Gate (though occasionally even then someone trekked to Montauk), among the Elizabeth Islands, from such renowned clubs as the Cuttyhunk Club, Pasque Island Club, the Squibnocket Club on Martha's Vineyard, the West Island Club off Sakonnet Point, and a few other choice spots off Point Judith, Newport, and Cohasset Narrows.

Scott even traveled north in New York State to Lake Ontario, and while fishing for salmon (landlocked) he also caught striped bass "in the upper part of Lake Ontario" on several occasions.

In a brief summary of the methods of the day, Scott tells us:

> The angler pursues many methods for capturing this beauty of the estuary, the chief of which is still-baiting from an anchored boat along the edge of the tide, trolling with live squid (small cuttle-fish), and casting with menhaden bait—but without sinker—into the surf off a rocky beach, along the shores and islands from New York to Martha's Vineyard.

It is also interesting to note the equipment of the day that Scott suggests. The accompanying illustrations are taken from his original book. The first rig is intended for taking of small bass, fish probably no larger than 10 pounds, that were fairly common in the lower Hudson during the season from June until October. The bait was often crab or shrimp. The rod was from 9 to 11 feet long, "bearing in mind that a short, stiff rod is best to cast with, but not so good to play a fish on light running tackle. The reel should be a multiplier type, without any stop, check, or drag; it should be of brass, German silver, or bell-metal, run on steel or agate pivots, and with a balance crank."

Corks were of solid construction and tied to swivel sinkers. Rods in those days were of wood that would take a set or warp and therefore had guides back-to-back so that you could reverse your line every other time you went fishing and discourage warping. Hooks were of two styles: one with an O'Shaughnessy bend that held shrimp best, while the other had an Aberdeen bend that was more suited to a shedder crab.

The second illustration is of a very elaborate set of gear for the day, more appropriate for fishing on the end of a bass stand, for larger fish in a boat, for angling from a bridge, or for venturing into big waters. Here, Scott recommends a rod 8 to 9 feet long, with butt and second sections of ash and the top section of lancewood. This would enable you to do battle with striped bass in Hell Gate, a part of the East River on the sunny side of Manhattan, that was a favorite during Scott's time.

No one at the time could tell it better than Scott himself. I've borrowed a few pages from his book so you can capture the flavor of saltwater angling as it was once practiced in New York more than a century ago.

When you decide to troll for a day over tumultuously-seething and hissing waters of Hell Gate, where an oarsman must know the tides and shoals to keep his boat right side up, you will require heavier tackle.

Those who employ a man to row and gaff the fish would do well to direct him to squid half a dozen hooks before starting, and lay them aside in the boat under some wet rock-weed before leaving shore. If you have ever been trolling—as I have—when large bass were biting generously, you will realize the force of this advice. It is unpleasant to be trolling in rough waters, and, when a bass strikes the back of your hook and takes your bait without fastening, to be obliged to stop and squid a hook before proceeding.

Now for the fray!

Our boats are made by Hughes, fellow-apprentice of George Steers: and with Sile Wright and Sandy Gibson as guides and gaffers, we shall be sculled over all the favorite trolling grounds from the ferry below to the Drowned Marsh above Ward's Island. Our first move will be toward Tide Rock, swinging Big and Little Mill Rocks on the way; then we shall glide over the Hen and Chickens, swing * Holt's Rock on the Hog's Back, round Nigger Point, and, stopping at John Hilliker's to rest, enjoy a piece of incomparable apple-pie and a glass of milk served by two charming ladies. While indulging these ruminations one day, as my friend was swinging Holt's Rock, he hooked a large bass and played it all the way round the east end of Ward's Island to Chowder Eddy. Where, on landing, it weighed twenty pounds.

I was not so fortunate as my friend; for, as my squid was struck by a large bass, Sile said he heard the rod crack; but the fish made

Swinging a rock is done by the oarsman holding the boat sixty feet from the rock and swinging it so that the troll will move about the rock on all tides and play as if alive. This art was possessed in perfection by Hell Gate oarsmen.

Genio C. Scott recommended this striped bass outfit for small fish in his classic book: Fishing in American Waters (1869).

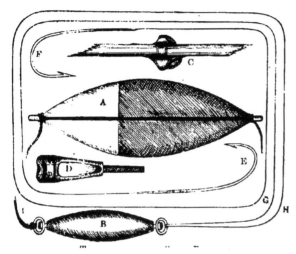

Tackle for Taking Small Bass.

A. Solid Cork-float. B.Swivel Sinker. C.Piece of the top of Rod, showing the double guides; on one side bell-metal, and on the other agate. D. Agate or Cornelian tip to screw into the top of the rod. E. Upper Hook, rigged a foot above the other hook for a shrimp. F. Lower Hook, for baiting with shedder crab. G & H. Single-gut Leader, I. Line; either of linen twisted or silk braided; very small, no larger than for trout, but from 300 to 400 feet in length.

such a long, vigorous run, that I scarcely realized what he said, and, after turning the fish and reeling him in gradually, he broke water with a leap, clearing the surface, and revealing a forty-pounder. While turning and bringing him toward the boat for the third time, he darted down and snapped the middle joint of my rod in two, when I threw the broken rod down at my feet and took hold of the line; the fish made but feeble resistance, and I towed him alongside the boat and shouted to Sile for the gaff, but he had thoughtlessly placed it in the other boat. I then endeavored to put my hand in his mouth, and, while in the act, the fish turned over, breaking the hook and bleeding profusely as he settled off into the tide, leaving us astonished and almost desperate. On examination, I learned that a flaw in the hook had been the cause of our loss of the fish; but had we rowed ashore and towed the fish after the rod broke, we should probably have landed him.

Well, with broken rod and tangled line, I ordered Sile to row away from the scene of our misfortune. I found my friend at Hammock Rocks, his fish laid out in state on rock-grass, and he mutely bending over it with a face radiant with pleasurable satisfaction at his achievement. Trolling, to him, was a new-born pleasure, and his first capture a trophy of which a slayer of lions might he justly proud. It would be superfluous to add, we drank to the study for a Stearns or a Bracket as it lay shining on the pallet of sea-grass. Sandy commiserated Sile's misfortune at losing the large bass. In

Scott's recommendation for bigger striped bass in the surf.

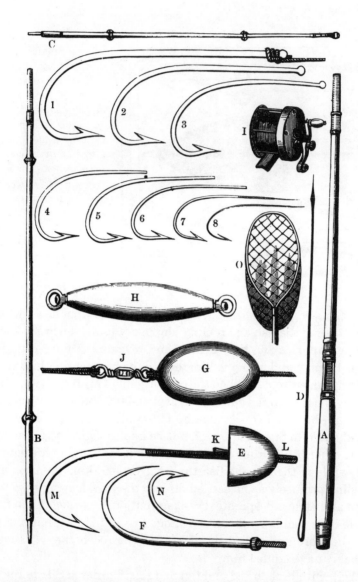

the centre of a radius containing the most picturesque landscape near the metropolis, we rested, wondered, and admired.

Having toasted the health and appetite of bass in that neighborhood in a glass of sherry, and replaced the broken joint of my rod with a sound one, we again seated ourselves in our boats, and commenced trolling the Little Gate, the Kills, and all about Randall's and Ward's Islands, and, after the usual alternatives of hopes, fears, and moments of ecstasy, we finished up a mess of seven bass between us, the largest nearly thirty, and the smallest four pounds in weight.

Well, having given you a taste of the sport on the waters bounding Manhattan Island on the north and east, let us anchor our boat near the lower hedges of New York Bay, and learn how different bottom fishing with a tracing sinker is from both trolling and angling with a float.

Just on a historical note, the George Steers to whom Scott refers to is the same man instrumental in building the schooner America that went on to become famous, inaugurating the America's Cup Races and was a major figure in America's burgeoning nautical prominence.

The other accepted form of striped bass fishing of the day was casting, probably better described as heaving a bait into the water and waiting for something to happen. It was done mostly from rocks and from bass-casting platforms that sprang up over almost every rocky promontory from Long Island to the Elizabeth Islands. There were platforms built at Montauk, along the Rhode Island and Connecticut coasts, and on Block Island, Martha's Vineyard, and Nantucket. The more famous ones were on West Island, off Sakonnet Point, and on Cuttyhunk and Pasque islands in the Elizabeth Chain, that parallels Buzzards Bay. The holes drilled in the granite rocks are still evident today on Cuttyhunk Island and some even sport a bit or rust from a hundred years ago.

Scott felt that casting a "menhaden bait" for striped bass from the rocky shores of bays, estuaries, and islands along the Atlantic Coast constituted the

Scott and guide Silas Wright fished the tumultuous waters of Hell Gate in New York's East River.

This print from Alfred Mayer's Sport with Rod and Gun *(1883) depicts the clubhouse at the famous Cuttyhunk Striped Bass Club as it appeared in 1882.*

The same clubhouse today, now in private hands.

highest branch of American angling. He says, "It is indeed questionable—when considering all the elements which contribute toward the sum total of sporting angling—whether this method of striped bass fishing is not superior to dry-fly fishing for salmon, and if so, it outranks any angling in the world. This style is eminently American."

Surfcasting is indeed a purely American invention and Scott's statement might well serve as the credo for the modern surfcaster. However, the surf today is a little different from the surf of Scott's day or the surf at Cuttyhunk and West islands. The water was usually below the angler— the platforms saw to that— and only on a big comber did he become a part of it as is so frequent in modern surf fishing.

It was only natural that this type of surf fishing should encourage the development of clubs. However, striped bass clubs in the past were considerably different from today's clubs. They were an extension of the polo fields, the race track, and the leisure life of the late 1800s that only the wealthy could afford. Maintaining a bass stand was costly and involved a good deal of work. And, only if you were wealthy could you afford to play at fishing in this era.

First, the boulders leading to the point were drilled and iron pipes placed in them to form the foundation of a catwalk. Then a wooden walk was built atop the frame to the distal end. The end of the stand was often equipped with a chair in which the sport sat while a chummer employed by the club fed cut menhaden, crabs, clams, and even lobsters into the surf. If a fish was taken, the chummer did the gaffing. Even the best of fishing areas would provide only spotty catches if the bass were not tolled to where a fisherman waited with baited hook. Netting fish to be used for chum, digging clams and maintaining a clubhouse provided a lot of employment for the islanders and baymen, and clubs were welcomed along the coast.

The oldest was the West Island Club, founded about 1862. The most famous was the Cuttyhunk Club on Cuttyhunk Island, the westernmost of the Elizabeth Islands. This latter club was formed on May 31, 1865, by a group of men at the St. James Hotel in New York City. It was composed of well known businessmen, politicians, and industrialists from Philadelphia, New York, and Boston, who wanted a fishing retreat close to home and fitted out in the grand manner of their day.

Striped bass clubs existed as long as striped bass were plentiful. However, during the latter half of the 19th century, the industrialization of northeastern America began to affect the striped bass population. Diligently kept records by many of these bass clubs are our only accurate sampling of the striped bass population for this period. The decline is evident in all their catches. The sizes of the bass caught were getting larger, but their numbers fell off. Eventually, fishing became so poor that in 1907, the Cuttyhunk Club sold its holdings on the island and the organization was disbanded. Today, the clubhouse is a private residence. You can still walk the spacious lawn in front and look out over the rocks and beaches, all named and hallowed. You can even find remnant bore holes in the granite boulders where the foundations for the platforms stood.

When a fish population is in danger, there are few or no young fish, and only large or extra-large fish begin making up the catches. It would have seemed almost predictable that a large striped bass should be caught about the time the Cuttyhunk Club called it quits. In 1913, six years after the closing, the world's largest authenticated striped bass caught on rod and reel was taken almost within the shadow of the clubhouse.

During the bright of day, Capt. Charles B. Church rowed through the
Canapitsit Channel, which separates Cuttyhunk from nearby Nashawena
Island, trailing a rigged eel behind his boat. He hooked and landed a 73-pound

*"A Fine Game—Sea Bass" is another reproduction from the 1899 New York State
Commissioners' Report. This supposedly illustrates a bass stand somewhere in New York
waters, but because of the rocky coastline, it cannot be Long Island and is more likely
somewhere along the Rhode Island or Massachusetts coast.*

Bass stands were extremely popular at Cuttyhunk during the latter part of the 19th century. Reproduced from Angling *by Leroy M. Yale et al.*

striped bass that stood as the world's record fish for 56 years. Though no longer considered an official record by International Game Fish Association IGFA) standards, Church's fish measured 5 feet in length and 30-1/2 inches in girth. The date was August 17, 1913.

Large striped bass seemed to disappear from the fishing scene and almost from the Northeast coast, until the resurgence of the population in the 1930s and 1940s. Four large striped bass were taken between 1958 and 1967. After a 54-year hiatus, the record set by Church was challenged by Charles Cinto of Mansfield, Mass. In 1967, while fishing with Captain Frank Sabatowski aboard the *June Bug*, Cinto caught the fish while trolling on the west end of Cuttyhunk. Ironically, the fish exactly equaled the weight of Church's fish, though it was weighed several hours after being caught. But because the bass was hooked while trolling wire line and with a plug having multiple treble hooks, it could be not considered for an official record by the IGFA, the sanctioning body for such feats.

Cinto's striped bass measured 56 inches in length and 35 inches in girth. It was gaffed after a 20-minute battle at 3 a.m. in the morning while Sabatowski trolled over the Sow and Pigs Reef. Incidentally, Sabatowski was no stranger to big bass. In June 1963, he had boated a 67-pound 1 2-ounce fish in the same area.

The next challenger to Church's record was Edward J. Kirker. Even more unique is that Kirker boated a 72-pound striped bass from almost the exact same spot where Church had found his fish. Angling late in the afternoon on October 10, 1969, he took the big bass from Canapitsit Channel. Kirker had been casting live eels in the channel when the striped bass hit. It made five powerful runs before he could beach it and get it to the scales at Cuttyhunk. The fish measured 51 inches in length and 31 inches in girth.

EARLY RECORDS OF THE LARGEST
STRIPED BASS TAKEN ON ROD AND REEL

Weight	Angler	Date	Place	Length	Girth
86.0	Francis W. Miner	7/?/87*	Block Island, RI	*	*
73.0	Charles B. Church	8/17/13	Cuttyhunk MA	60	30.5
73.0	Charles Cinto	6/16/67	Cuttyhunk, MA	56	35.0
72.0	Edward J. Kirker	10/10/69	Cuttyhunk, MA	51	31.0
68.8	Ralph Gray	1/1/58	N. Truro, MA	50	34.0
68.8	John J. Solonis	9/5/67	N. Truro, MA	54	32.5

* The exact date, length and girth measurements on this fish were recorded and the fish photographed. However, the documentation was lost and thus Miner's striped bass was never an official record.

For a 56-year period, Charles B. Church's striped bass was the rod-and-reel record. Prior to Church, there was a well substantiated but unofficial record of an 85-pounder taken in 1887 by Col. Francis W. Miner. Church's official record finally fell to Edward Kirker's 72-pounder caught in October, 1969. In 1974, the IGFA reviewed its records, especially the older entries. All those fish taken on untested lines were dropped from the official standings. Twenty-four records were affected, and Charles B. Church's was among them.

Another of Mayer's illustrations. The club kept accurate records of all fish taken, and in 1876 to 1882 the largest annual bass weighed 51, 51-1/2, 51, 49, 50-1/4, 44 and 64 pounds.

It wasn't until July 17, 1981, when Bob Rocchetta of East Setauket Long Island, N.Y. boated a 76-pounder while drifting in a boat at night off Great Eastern Rock, just a long cast from Montauk Point, that a bigger fish than Church's was caught. However, the record wasn't to last long. Just a few minutes before midnight on Sept. 21, 1982, an Atlantic City lifeguard, Albert McReynolds, tossed a small plug off a beach jetty and was pulled into the wash twice by a 78-1/2 pound striper before it was landed.

Nor are big bass restricted to the East Coast. Fish in the 60-pound class were not difficult to find during the early years of the fish's introduction to the Pacific Coast, nor in later years as the populations began a gradual decline...as long as there was the occasional dominant year class produced. In 1910, a San Francisco fish dealer was supposed to have displayed in his counter a 78-pounder that was

taken in a net. It is "well-established" that several decades ago, a 90-pounder was netted in Suisun Bay. Emil Cherski is supposed to have landed on rod and reel a 72-pounder taken from Georgiana Slough in 1926. Though never documented, but disclosed in an interview with Ed Crawford in 1971, a resident of the lower Russian River, he recounted the feat of his friend Frank Leppo of Santa Rosa, who caught a 75-pounder in 1927 in the Russian River. Leppo was quoted as saying, "It tasted just as good as a small bass." A commercial salmon fisherman using nets off Decker Island, in June 1949 was alleged to have caught and released—because only sportfishermen were allowed at that time to keep striped bass—a fish that weighed 83 pounds.

Once the unofficial world's record striped bass, a 73-pound fish caught by Charles Cinto on June 16, 1967, while fishing off the western end of Cuttyhunk Island.

Nor are big bass the strictly the realm of the saltwater angler. In Georgia's Flint River, in the spring of 1985, four biologists were electro-shocking a pool in the river about a mile downstream from Albany, sampling for fish. They "rolled over a striped bass that was humongus," according to Lee Kieffer, one of the crew. "We were awed by the fish even though we had already weighed one bass at 65 pounds. Our scale ended at 70 pounds and this bass pulled it down so hard it 'thunked' when it bottomed out. In our collective opinion, we 'guesstimated' that the fish weighed 85 pounds."

According to Frank Paruka, another biologist on the scene, "The big bass took quite a jolt and it took us almost an hour before the fish was fully resuscitated and took off." In the meantime, they rigged her with a radio transmitter. She carried it about for several weeks and then the signal ended. No one is sure of the cause for the signal's cessation. Georgia biologists have tracked big striped bass that have been at large with transmitters for up to 11 months. That is how they discovered the thermal refuges, deep, spring fed holes, in the Flint River that striped bass need to make it through the hot times of the year. If the fish had died somewhere in the river, the radio would have continued to send. If its location didn't change they could assume that the fish died. Probably, the transmitter, that was imbedded internally in the fish, lost power.

Catches of big striped bass from Massachusetts waters dominated the record books until the late 1970s and early 1980s for two reasons. The first was that the waters inside Buzzards Bay, with the mainland to the north and the picket-like chain of Elizabeth Islands to the south, and then Martha's Vineyard and Nantucket Island beyond them, were in the center of the summer feeding grounds for the bulk of the Atlantic's coastal migratory stock. The northern terminus in most years was Cape Cod, and the southern/western limit, the waters off the east end of Long Island—Orient and Montauk points, and encompassing Block Island Sound. The second reason was that there were large numbers of people living on the New England coast in the center of the summering fish population and this summering striped bass population was heavily fish by local anglers and recreational fishermen at numerous seaside resorts that specialized in bass fishing.

Aside from recreational anglers, there was another group that fished the striped bass schools most intensively, the "pinhookers." The term is used by commercial fishermen who use nets and traps to describe those who fish commercially for striped bass using rod, reel, and hooks. The Massachusetts Legislature created this commercial group in the late 1940s when it restricted commercial fishing for striped bass to rod and reel. These men were then fishing for a living. If they caught a large bass, it could be submitted as a record as well as sold to the markets.

This same type of commercial fisherman also evolved on Long Island's East End. Like their Massachusetts counterparts, few were full-time commercial fishermen. Their ranks were composed of policeman, firemen, teachers, and

*Left—Bob Rocchetta of East Setauket, L.I., N.Y. with his 76-pound striped bass taken in 1981. It lasted as the IGFA All-Tackle record for little more than a year. **Right**—John Alberda of Bayville, L.I., N.Y. with a 69-lb. 3-oz. striped bass he landed in 1983. It would have made the record book except that the line over-tested in its class. Both were taken off Montauk Point.*

shift workers who often had lots of extra time for themselves. The motivation was the increasing prices paid by seafood dealers for striped bass. As the fish's numbers declined throughout the 1970s, because of the failure of Chesapeake Bay to produce a dominant year class, the value of the remaining fish escalated as fewer and fewer striped bass entered the market.

There was every reason to believe that big striped bass and even a new record could be taken off Orient or Montauk points, on Long Island's East End, especially at Montauk Point. All the fish that migrate to Massachusetts waters in spring must first pass Montauk Point, that juts 120 miles into the Atlantic Ocean. Striped bass are strictly littoral in the migration routes, closely paralleling the beach and often no more than a long cast from its sands. But, if you had a boat, you could follow them and fish where they swam.

Al McReynolds, current IGFA World Record holder with the 78-pound, 8-ounce striped bass he landed at Atlantic Beach Sept. 21, 1982.

About two dozen regular pinhookers, all part-timers, formed the nucleus of this cadre. They fished day and night and in every kind of weather. Their boats were fast and radio communication allowed them to work in groups and as partners. In a given night—because night was when striped bass fishing was most productive—they could fish Montauk, Orient, The Race, or Block Island, or all four locations. It was only a matter of time until a new record was set.

There were many fish in the 60-pound range that were taken in the late 1970s as the "Class of 1970" fish, the largest number ever spawned in Chesapeake Bay in recent times, were maturing. But there were also good year classes produced in the late 1960s and many of these fish were 15 years and older and 60 pounds and larger. It started with Glen Dennis's 64-pounder, taken in Plum Gut, between Orient Point and Plum Island, in 1980. It was followed by Dennis Kelly's 66-pounder a year later and from the same place. Almost at the moment Kelly was landing his 66-pounder off Orient Point on July 17, Bob Rocchetta was hauling his big fish over the gunwale 15 miles away, at Montauk Point. Rocchetta's bass was big, so big it set a new world record at 76 pounds. Almost an entire year latter, on July 9, 1982, Kelly bettered his own record by a half pound, again off Orient Point, at the eastern tip of Long Island's North Fork.

With the pace big bass were being taken, it was almost expected that Rocchetta's record would be challenged. Little more than a year later, one-time lifeguard Al McReynolds was tossing a plug off a rock jetty near Atlantic City and hooked into the current world record, a 78-1/2 pound fish. Alone, Reynolds was twice pulled off the rocks and into the water before he beach the bass.

During the period 1980 to 1983, Long Island pinhookers didn't stop all the big bass from swimming to Cape Cod. Two big fish got past them, a 73-pounder taken by Anton Stezko from the surf on Nauset Beach and a 69-1/2-pounder taken just 200 yards from the same spot a few weeks earlier by 17-year old Stephen Petri, Jr., of Lindenhurst, Long Island. The same night Stetzko caught his fish, the young Petri also beached fish of 66 and 59 pounds. The youngster was on his way into the record book but Stezko, who was also using 20-pound class line, never let him get there because his bass was bigger.

Today, few if any fish above the rod-and-reel record are taken commercially because of restricted fishing methods and the growing move to make striped bass a game fish. Today, 17 coastal states prohibit its sale. Recreationally, there are plenty of large striped bass in the 50- and 60-pound class caught each year but the majority caught by sportfishermen range from 6 to 10 pounds. There still are new record-class striped bass available. On May 25, 1992, fishing in Long Island Sound, just outside New Haven Harbor, Steve Franco landed a 75.4-pounder. That's getting close. During early May in 1992, Maryland charterboat captain Ed Darwin, while fishing during that state's special trophy season, hooked and boated a striped bass estimated by the experienced skipper to weigh at least 80 pounds. Because the fish was gravid with a huge amount of eggs, he tenderly resuscitated and released her. Of course, it was all captured on video.

DOCUMENTED STRIPED BASS CATCHES, 60-POUNDS AND HEAVIER

Weight	*Angler*	*Date*	*Place*
78 lbs. 8 oz.*	Albert R. McReynolds	Sept. 21, 1982	Atlantic City, N.J.
76.0 lbs.*	Robert A. Rocchetta	July 17, 1981	Montauk Pt., N.Y.
75.4 lb.	Steven Franco	May 25, 1992	New Haven, Conn.
73.0 lbs.	Charles B. Church	Aug. 17, 1913	Cuttyhunk, Mass.
73.0 lbs.	Charles E. Cinto	June 16, 1967	Cuttyhunk, Mass.
73.0 lbs.	Anton Stezko	Nov. 2, 1981	Nauset, Mass. (S)
72.0 lbs.	Edward J. Kirker	Oct. 10, 1969	Cuttyhunk, Mass.
71.0 lbs.*	John Baldino	July 14, 1980	Norwalk, Conn.
70.0 lbs.*	Chester A. Berry	Sept. 5, 1987	Orient Point, N.Y.
69 lbs. 8 oz.	Stephen Petri, Jr.	Aug. 24, 1981	Nauset, Mass. (S)
69 lbs.*	Thomas J. Russell.	Nov. 18, 1982	Sandy Hook, N.J.
69 lb. 3 oz.	John Alberda	July 26, 1983	Montauk Pt., N.Y.
68 lbs. 8 oz.	Ralph Gray	Oct. 1, 1958	N. Truro, Mass.
67 lbs.12 oz.	Harold Hussey	June 8,1963	Cuttyhunk, Mass.
67.0 lbs.	Jack Ryan	May 31,1963	Block Island, R.I.
66 lbs. 12 oz.*	Steven R. Thomas	Nov. 1, 1979	Bradley Beach, N.J.
66 lbs. 8 oz.	Tom Parker	June 29, 1963	Nauset, Mass.
66 lbs. 8 oz.	Donald Nee	June 14, 1962	Gay Head, Mass.
66 lbs. 8 oz.	Dennis Kelly	July 9, 1982	Orient Pt, N.Y.
66 lbs. 4 oz.	Frank Mularczyk	June 4 ,1954	Gay Head, Mass.
66 lbs. 4 oz.	Jim Paterson	June 10, 1964	Narragansett, R.I.
66.0 lbs.	Harold Slater	Oct. 15, 1964	Weekapague, R.I.
66.0 lbs.	Frank Hunsinger	Nov. 12, 1961	Montauk Pt., N.Y.
66.0 lbs.*	Dennis Kelly	July 17, 1981	Orient Pt., N.Y.
66.0 lbs.	Stephen Petri, Jr.	Nov. 2, 1981	Nauset, Mass. (S)
64.70 lbs.	Allan Sosslau	May 14, 1992	Chesap'ke Bch, Md.
64 lbs. 8 oz. *	Rosa O. Webb	Aug. 14, 1960	North Truro, Mass.
64.0 lbs.*	Mrs. Asie Espenak	June 27, 1971	Sea Bright, N.J.
64.0 lbs.	Glen Dennis	June 6, 1980	Orient Pt., N.Y.
61.0 lbs.	Al Ristori	July 25, 1966	Cape Cod. Mass.

(S) From the surf
* IGFA Record Fish (3/93)

15

From the Surf

There's a certain mystique about fishing for striped bass in the surf. Surf fishing has a strong attraction for many thousands of anglers. Ironically, while it is one of the more pleasant ways to fish, and the rewards seem the greatest when a fish is landed, it is also the least efficient and least productive of all the techniques available for taking striped bass. However, surfcasters are legion on the beaches, and perhaps it is not necessarily from the end that they derive such great satisfaction, but from the means by which they seek this end.

Certainly, it is one form of the sport in which the fisher actually meets the fish on its own level, or in its environment. The surfcaster spends a great deal of time in the water, and maybe here, too, there is some explanation of the fascination. There is a masochistic ruggedness about surfcasting. Nothing delights the typical surfcaster more than to be immersed in cold water up to the top of his chest-high, insulated waders, with a wind howling off his back and a comber threatening him. With seeming impunity, he lashes back at the elements with a long rod that is often too heavy for comfort. Sometimes shivering even in his insulated waders, a thermal sweatshirt and a hooded rain coat tightly buckled around his waist by an outside belt, he will tell you "this is great fun!"

Quite often, I think surfcasting is more of a social exercise than a serious attempt at fishing. True, the cold water does eventually steal away one's body heat, and true, the rods are usually long and heavy and the baits are even heavier, and therefore the surfcaster has good cause to take numerous breaks out of the suds. The upper beach will always see a score of anglers, rod butts in the sand and encircled, trying to determine why the fish aren't there, or when they will strike again. Truly, surfcasting has something in common with the coffee break as an American institution.

The striped bass is, however, a creature of the surf, and surfcasters do catch them. In their migrations north and south the fish are seldom more than a mile off the beach and more often are only a long cast away. Too often, however, they seem always to be just beyond the reach of the longest cast. Striped bass inhabit a more varied watery environment than any other fish, though they are truly a littoral fish. They can be taken in deep water, rivers, estuaries, and bays. They can be taken by casting, trolling, spinning, and even fly casting. Bass will hit almost every kind of lure imaginable. But of all these conditions and variables, the classic form of striped bass angling is still from the surf. Probably, because it was the first technique—fishing with line and squid—that fathered everything else we today know as surf fishing.

THE NATURE OF SURF

The surf is that region where water and land meet. An angler once described it as that place between a point on the beach where the highest tide reaches, out to where the farthest cast can be made. In a very real sense, he just about covered the entire realm of the surf and the surfcaster. Generally, the surf falls on two types of land, that made up of sand and graded and that composed of rocks and irregular. The greater majority of angling is done from sandy beaches, but along our Northeast, in Connecticut, Rhode Island, parts of Massachusetts, and

Dr. Ernest Raphael, a devoted surfcaster, lifts a small bass from the waters of Moriches Inlet, Long Island, N.Y.

Maine, there is a fair amount of rocky beach that has not yet been sanded. Like the East Coast, the West Coast also has a range of surf-casting environments, from long, flat beaches to rocky, treacherous cliffs.

A surf is created by moving water, and four phenomena can make the water move: wind, tide, ocean currents, and ground swells. At times, two or more of these phenomena work together and can create a huge surf. At other times, they may oppose each other and can cancel out some of their effects. And, at other times, they can work from different directions and the surf can be confused or mixed. When each phenomenon works independently, it can develop a surf with different characteristics. And each one can be counted upon

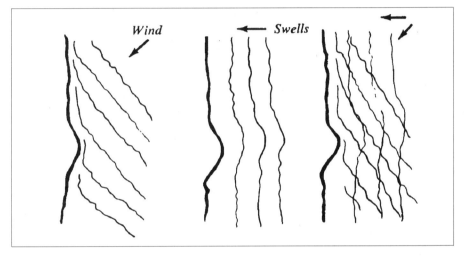

WAVE PATTERNS: *Three situations are shown. The first reveals the pattern of waves striking a beach on an angle and pushed only by the force of the wind. The middle pattern shows waves created by swells as they approach the beach parallel to its shape. The figure on the right depicts the combined effect of wind and swells that produces a mixed surf.*

to affect, either for the better or worse, the state of fishing at the time.

Most anglers approach the beach with little heed to the actual way the waves are formed. Seldom are waves parallel to the beach, but strike it at various angles, sometimes evenly at all points when the waves land at right angles. When a wave approaches the beach at an off angle, it can then be seen running along the beach as the leading edge touches and the remainder follows. At other times, the waves can be at direct right angles to the beach. This is best seen at a point of land. We even have situations where two sets of waves, from different angles, can be working onto the bars and beaches. One can be the result of ground swells far out at sea, created by large storms often hundreds of miles away. These waves may be approaching the beach in a parallel fashion, but the wind might be on a quarter off the swells and create a secondary pattern. We then have two sets of waves, together striking the beach.

The result is a lot of white water, and white water means that striped bass are more than likely to be feeding. A confused sea has its effect on the baitfish, and the big fish are there to take advantage of such factors. If you watch the wind and weather, you, too, can figure where such a situation might occur. You should probably be there.

Slope

Not all sandy beaches are the same, nor are they a simple meeting place of water and land. If you have some knowledge of the factors at work in shaping a beach, then your chances of predicting where bass might be are substantially increased.

The steeper the slope of a sand beach, the greater will be the drop-off formed under the breaking water. Moving water approaching the beach is lifted over the outer bar and begins to break, losing some of its force. Over the inner bar it again breaks, losing more force, and then dissipates its energy as it rushes up the beach to the top of the tide line. The spent water then returns to the surf. However, a second wave or force of water is immediately behind the first. As it approaches the beach, it overrides the returning water. The returning water is then forced to turn, circulate, and tumble against the force of the incoming water. This circulation has a digging or routing effect just under the surf. It creates the drop-off or trough.

The drop-off or trough area created by scouring is an ideal location for finding small fish. Here, they become confused by the stronger water currents, and the water-forced concentration of baitfish forms a feeding area for striped bass. This unique biozone is also full of other food for striped bass. In this constantly changing and forceful environment, many life forms have learned to survive by burrowing and boring into the sand. As the wave action disturbs the sand, sand fleas, crabs, sea worms, and clams are often disrupted.

On a gently-sloping beach, it is far more difficult to locate where striped bass might be feeding without external signs. A gentle beach does not form such evident drop-offs or troughs and bars. There is a reduced wave action, and as a result, these are often the least likely spots along a coastline for finding feeding bass. Any fish taken here are usually en route to somewhere else to feed. At low tide, the water may move far off the beach and many areas may not provide sufficient water for fish. Only at the higher tides is there a chance of catching fish on a slow or gentle slope.

Bars

Wave action on a sandy beach usually produces a series of ridges or bars along the bottom. More often than not, these bars are formed parallel to the contour of the beach. Their numbers vary anywhere from two or three to half a dozen, depending upon the depth of the water off the beach and the force of the wind, tides, and currents in the immediate area. Because of their distribution, a fisherman usually worries only about the first and second bar. That is about the limit of his casting range.

An average surf fisherman can expect to cast between 60 and 80 yards. If he can throw beyond 100 yards, he's in a select class. Bars can build as close as 3 yards from the beach or as far away as 65 yards. Each bar is formed parallel to the others as well as the beach, making a corduroy pattern. I's the inner and outer bars (second) that are frequently fished, because here is where waves most disturb the sand and frees bait, and here is where bass are likely to come hunting.

The outer bar is usually the larger or higher and stops the initial force of an

SCOURING: The force of a wave rushing up the beach and then back to sea has a scouring or digging effect on the area immediately in the wash. How much of a hole it will dig depends upon the angle or slope of the beach and the depth of the water coming over the first and second bars.

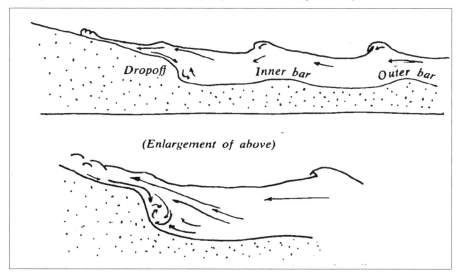

incoming wave. It can reduce it in size so that only a smaller wave or a flood of suds washes over the inner bar and the beach. Bars are not continuous along their entire length but are breached by channels and cuts of deeper water. The force of the water returning from the beach gradually builds up, and the bars act as temporary dams. This water is affected on top by the incoming waves and must eventually find its way back to more open water. It does so by cutting through a bar and developing channels.

These channels are hot spots for surfcasters. A pair of Polaroid glasses is indispensable for looking into the water. Deep holes, pools, and cuts can often be spotted by a somewhat different color of water. Channels are thoroughfares for fish and they enter the inner slough through such openings. Larger bass are more likely to stay in such channels while smaller bass come closer to the beach. Big bass are notoriously lazy and prefer to take a lie here, waiting for baitfish and loosened shore life to come streaming out to sea.

Winds

Winds have a direct effect on the size of the surf and can also contribute to keeping currents along the beach in motion. Onshore winds will increase the agitation and scouring effect of waves. Thus, when a good wind is blowing onto the beach, the chances for catching fish are improved. Wind also has the effect of creating turbid water. In most cases, the turbidity is sand in suspension and unfortunately many anglers quit the beach, thinking that striped bass won't feed in such turmoil. I believe that a good, muddy surf is more productive than a clear surf. Striped bass depend upon their sense of smell for locating food and they can feed equally well in the riled water. Riled water means more loose food, so don't stop fishing or decrease your efforts just because the water looks bad. Instead, consider the picture from the view of a striped bass.

Wind is probably the single variable that has the greatest effect on the surf. On windless days, there is often very little action in the surf. Baitfish, and hence the striped bass, are farther offshore. An offshore wind has an even greater detrimental effect on the catch than days with no wind at all. It has a tendency to scatter fish farther off the beach. Baitfish seek protection in riled water, and if no riled water exists along the sand, there is no reason for baitfish and hence, predator fish to come ashore. There is little confusion at work on a school of bait when there is no wind.

Swells

Ground swells can create a surf that is often as large as that produced by immediate winds. I have worked the surf on days when there was no wind at all but combers 4 and 5 feet high came rolling ashore. These waves are created by offshore storms, or by local storms that have passed and left the seas seething and falling. Their effect on the animal life in the surf is less than that of wind-formed waves, but still creates similar situations.

Currents

Local water currents can be created by wind, heated sea water expanding, movement of the tide, and water flowing through inlets and rivers. The temperature of shallow water over dark bottoms on sunny days can also create currents. Water on the surface is stimulated to expand and move. This movement is further enhanced by colder water rising and pushing to take its place. Effects along the beaches are minimal and are felt more as massive thermal currents spawned farther offshore.

Many parts of our coasts have local currents generated by larger offshore currents. Along the Atlantic Coast the main current in the world of the striped bass is the Gulf Stream. This massive river within the sea originates because heated water expanding in the Caribbean moves northward along the coast from Florida, scrapes Cape Hatteras, and then follows the Continental Shelf past Long Island and off Cape Cod. Past Cape Hatteras, it creates a small back eddy that comes down from the north, with another coastal offshoot following it from the south which meets it at Hatteras and collides, forming a massive rip that extends more than 15 miles offshore. The fishing here is fantastic and attracts baitfish and game fish during all times of the year. It provides some excellent striped bass fishing during the winter months.

On the Pacific Coast, the currents head in a direction opposite to that on the Atlantic. Two streams, the Alaska Current and the Subarctic Current, flow east and then south after striking the continent. They spawn a California Current that then sweeps down the coast from British Columbia, hugging the land until it touches Baja California. Here it abruptly turns west. While off Oregon and California, this current brings the cold arctic water in touch with the coast and creates the fog that is so typical of northern California fishing. It may also be the reason that striped bass here prefer to winter in fresh water rather than in the cold Pacific.

Tides

Tides move only slightly, from off the beach onto the beach, but work in a rather local way, moving in one direction up or along a beach and then reversing. The tide is actually only the vertical rise and fall of the water but this does generate a current, often erroneously but popularly called tidal currents. The direction tidal currents take are independent from the action and direction of waves. However, tides and waves have a canceling or additive effect on each other, depending upon their direction.

Tidal flow runs parallel to the bars, creating small rivers running up and down the beach. Striped bass will usually face up tide, the direction from which the tide is flowing. This should be a clue as to the presentation of bait and lures. Also, lures when they are retrieved against the force of the tide's current, work better than with it.

Tides also have a secondary effect on the beach and the water immediately adjacent to it: they vary its depth. The environment in the surf is constantly changing as the tide floods and ebbs. Parts of a beach at times may be devoid of feeding striped bass because of insufficient water. However, as the tide floods, bass will move in with it to search the newly covered sand and feed in the protection of the deeper water. The inner and outer bars also affect the possible location of striped bass. A bar with little or no water at low tide doesn't look inviting to a hungry striper. But two or three hours later, when there is more water over the bar, bass may feed at it if it contains food.

The direction or state of a tide also affects where striped bass feed on a bar. On a flooding tide, the fish are more likely to be on inside of a bar, often between the inner and outer bar foraging for food. On a falling tide, they are more often located on the outside of the outer bar, and there is where you should concentrate your fishing efforts.

The state of the tide also affects the wave sizes and eroding action. A surf at low or mid-tide can be monstrous, rolling up the beach with great crashing and force. But as the tide rises and more water appears over the bars and bottom, the waves diminish and lose some of their ferocity. High tide, with a reduced wave and scouring activity, can be a poor time to fish for striped bass.

Low tide along a beach is also a time to make notes, either mental or actual. It is a great time to study the shape of bars and sloughs, locating the cuts and channels and examining the bottom texture of the sand. Then you can return four or five hours later and cast where you think is best over a flat-surfaced ocean and have a fair idea of what lies beneath the waves.

Low tide is also a good time to study the composition of the bottom as a source of potential striped bass food. If the beach and bottom are finely textured sand, then you will have to depend a lot on migrating food and boring animals like marine worms, copepods, sand fleas, crabs, and clams. If the bottom has a muddy texture, sandworms will constitute a lot of the smells let loose in the water. If the beach is made of coarse sand and large pieces of stone, almost a shingle beach, then the food in the area is likely to be only passing fishes and drifting varieties of animal life.

Not far from Montauk Point on Long Island's South Shore is one the prettiest sections of beach one could imagine. However, it is constructed of glacial stones and boulders, millions of stones that were transported by the glacier and released from the sand and mud by the action of sea on the towering cliffs. The stones are all of a size, between golf and tennis balls, and make walking impossible. With each wave, they shift into the sea and then come out with it. No matter how hard I have fished this section, or how inviting the environment looks, it has yet to yield a bass for me. There is nothing in this life zone that can take the pounding of the shifting gravel.

Also typical of this beach and the beaches east, as far as Nantucket, are large boulders deposited as the headlands weather and wear away. At low tide many are exposed, and if you read them, plant them on your visual map, they can be productive sites when the tides return.

HOW TO FIND FISH

Now that you know what creates the surf, how do you find striped bass that might inhabit it? There are natural fishing locations along each beach, and these are where you begin. Fish will concentrate in an area if attracted to it for some reason. These attracting devices can be a collection of rocks on a normally barren beach, a bed of mussels, a point of land that juts into the ocean and will narrow the fish's passage to within casting distance. It might also be an inlet in the beach between the open ocean and back bays. Equally good are places where freshwater streams or rivers flow into salt water, either first as an estuary or directly into the briny. Piers and jetties are also places that will attract baitfish as well as weed and kelp beds. Baitfish have little protection from striped bass except to hide, and if any of these natural or man-made affairs can provide a sanctuary for them, then striped bass won't be too far away.

Rips—where two different tidal currents pass, where a river flows into the bay or ocean, or where back eddies are formed as the tide passes a point of land—are some of the best places to search for striped bass in the surf. Points of land, either off the main beach or on parts of islands, often have natural shoals extending from them. These natural shoals are likely to be rocky and provide excellent small-fish habitat. The best example of such a natural shoal is Sow and Pigs Reef off the western end of Cuttyhunk Island. It has been a surfcaster's delight. Facing the opposite direction, but quite similar in composition, are Long Island's shoals off Montauk and Orient points.

Immediate signs

One of the most immediate signs revealing the location of striped bass is the activity of gulls and terns. Birds have been called the eyes and ears of the fisherman's fleet, and even beginning anglers quickly come to realize that a flock of screaming, reeling, diving birds are advertising the fact that they have found a school of feeding striped bass and are getting in on the leftover tidbits.

Gulls and terns have an ability to communicate with their kind that has baffled investigators. Through some unknown means, gulls and terns miles away know when their brethren have found food and come streaming the spot. A surfcaster who keeps one eye on the skies watching the activity of birds can usually also cash in on the bonanza. If the birds around you suddenly get up and join other birds on the move, there is some reason for the action. And if you are not catching fish, there's no reason why you, too, shouldn't join them.

There is a difference, however, between the credibility of terns and that of gulls. I have seen terns make a real ruckus over a single small piece of menhaden and have too often been left holding nothing when chasing terns. Years of bird watching over the water have proven to me that gulls are better fishfinders for anglers than terns. However, don't totally discount the terns, because on some days they are all you have to watch or chase and they might just be telling the truth...this time.

Hunting Versus Sedentary Surf Fishermen

What signs you look for will also be determined by which school of surf fishermen you belong to. One group firmly believes that it is best to stay put once you have located a natural area that should draw bass. If the fish aren't there when you arrive, then the chances are good that if you can wait long enough, the bass will eventually be there. There's nothing wrong with this. If you don't have a beach vehicle, then you may be forced to join this school of thought.

On the other hand, there is another group that is more active or aggressive in hunting feeding striped bass. This group seldom fishes unless they spot the genuine article or imminent action. They are usually quite mobile and in 4-wheel-drive vehicles will cruise miles of the beach looking for bird activity. In addition to the birds, they look for "oil slicks" on the water. These are places where striped bass feed on schools of menhaden, spearing, or anchovies, after which something is released in the water that breaks its surface tension. It appears as a wind or oil slick on the surface. It doesn't really look oily, only the wind-ripple is lessened or flat in the area.

Smaller hints, as you cruise the beach, are sudden swirls or boils in the water where a fish breaks near the surface as it chases bait. More evident are fish breaking water or a school of small baitfish suddenly leaping clear of the water. I have seen striped bass force schools of smaller fish into the wash and even out

Bird life along the beach can be the fisherman's eyes and ears. They indicate baitfish and hence feeding striped bass, giving the alert angler a chance to get in on the action.

of the water. Striped bass, when in large schools, can be as vicious a feeder as bluefish, and everything in their way runs.

Two modern aids that are now aboard almost every beach vehicle that regularly hunts striped bass are a good pair of binoculars and a Citizen Band radio. Surfcasters who regularly fish together approach the problem of finding feeding fish with some forethought. They will set up watching stations at likely natural areas, combing the surf and offshore waters with their glasses. If the fish are spotted or actively feeding birds appear, the word goes out over their radios—in a code, of course. The other vehicles come running. If you can't figure out the code, just follow the crowd; a traffic jam is hard to hide.

WORKING THE SURF

This section might better be titled "Fishing Blind," because that is what the majority of your surfcasting techniques will involve. Even if you do find signs of fish you will still be fishing in the dark unless bass are actually breaking water. Your best weapon is a state of mind that will give you the determination to continue fishing when you don't see fish.

Every angler should fish a section of water just as if he was sure that fish lay beneath its hiding surface. It's surprising how often this approach does pay off. Some call this concentration, and in the long run it pays dividends. It keeps the above-average fisherman longer in the surf, it gets him there earlier in the day, and it keeps him there into the night. It gets him out on rainy, cold days. Only by being in the water can you hope to catch fish.

Where to Cast

I'm sure you've heard the statement that more fish are cast over than are cast to by surf fishermen. I agree with it and it bears repeating once more. For some reason, beginning surfcasters, and numerous" regulars" who don't consistently take fish, feel that they have to cast as far as possible each time they decide it is time to throw bait or a lure. There is a time for long casts, and if you are a long caster you will have a decided edge over the angler who has a case of the shorts. Long casts pay off by increasing the territory you can reach. They also give you the edge when the ocean is flat and the fish are wandering off, with no natural reason to be at your feet or within your scope. But these days are rather rare in the surf—it is always seething or in motion. And it is that very motion that stirs the sand at your feet and tolls bass onto the beach.

I'm a firm believer of casting in a radius of 50 to 60 feet about the beach even before I wade into the suds. I don't want to stir or cast beyond any fish that might be in the immediate area. Gradually, I work away from the shore, but never more than 10 or 15 feet unless I want to reach the other side of the outer bar. It doesn't take much water to float even a 50-pound striper. If the water is up to my waist, the bass can be behind me.

Nor are all my casts always away from the beach. To cover the area adequately, you should sweep casts in every direction, up and down the beach as well as over the bars. The cast down tide is my favorite because the lures always work better. Once I have covered a 50-foot radius, I extend my casts by 10 feet and again sweep the area. Then I extend my casts again, and keep doing so until I have cast to all the water in my range.

Working Downtide

Once you feel that you have exhausted an area, how and where do you move? The most productive direction is down tide. Cast on a quarter direction off the beach and let your lures sweep below you. Then haul them directly back. Take a few steps and cast out again on a quartering angle shot. With this technique you eventually sweep the beach of all possible areas. If there is a bass in the water, your presentation will be natural.

Walking downtide also stirs the bottom. In a way, the drifting sand is like a slight chum line. Fish face up tide in a running slough. In a freshwater situation, the sudden appearance of muddy water might signal danger. But in the surf, riled water is a way of life and can only help you. When you see a change in the water's surface, like a submerged rock or log, take your time working casts around the cause of the change. Might even be a big bass.

Retrieve

The speed of retrieves will depend on the equipment you use, the lure, and water movement. There is a certain minimal speed necessary to deliver action to the lure. You can also override the action with too great a retrieval speed and have an unnatural effect. However, no natural bait swims at a steady pace unless something is chasing it. You should vary the speed of your retrieve as you work an area.

Occasionally, really highballing a lure through the water does pay off, especially with bass. The action is unnatural but it is an attention-getter or an irritant, and many striped bass will fall for just such a trick. Floating surface lures have no minimal speed, and sometimes a plug left floating dead in the water has been hit by a striped bass that couldn't stand the tension. Popping plugs and surface lures have their own characteristics, and a little experience with each type will tell you how best to work the lure.

When to Fish

The best time to fish for striped bass is any time that you can get away to fish. As long as striped bass are around—that is, as long as you are fishing for them in season—then, there are going to be some striped bass available at all times. There are times that are better than others, but somewhere there is always a bass that is hungry.

One group of anglers believes that the tide is more important than the time of day. Striped bass, like other game fish, use the current and movement of the water to help them feed. A moving tide carries more bait, and striped bass, being basically lazy fish, would rather wait and let the bait come to them than go actively after it, unless they haven't eaten for a long time.

We know that striped bass are spotty or sporadic feeders and that they might all feed at one time. If the tide is the controlling factor, then it should be best when the tide is moving best—that is, an hour or so after it turns until an hour or so before it stops to reverse itself. This means that you have about four hours of prime fishing time on each tide and two hours of not-so-productive time. These not-so productive times are an hour on each side of flood and ebb tides. However, don't tell the bass that. I have had some great bass fishing when it was dead low and the fish didn't know they weren't supposed to be feeding.

Another school of striped bass anglers believes that time of day is more important than the state of tide. The reasoning here—and there is some biological support—is that striped bass are more nocturnal than diurnal feeders. Best times, then, are from just after sunset for a few hours and then an hour or so just before sunrise. I know from experience that summer and early fall fishing is best during the night. I have taken three or four fish at night for every one I caught during the day. I have fished throughout a night, taken fish regularly, and then felt the action slow at daybreak and almost stop at sunrise. Raising a fish after that was all work, with strikes few and far between.

I think that the real answer is far more complex than what any one of these schools of thought offers. I believe that each factor has an effect, the tide and its speed, as well as the time of day. Both have an interaction, and each affects the other in varying degrees at different times of the year.

Then, you must add such variables as the wind direction, water temperature, and fishing pressure in an area to develop a complete picture. Even more important is the availability of natural food in the spot where you might be fishing. All these factors must be considered, because they create so many possibilities that predicting the feeding habits of a striped bass becomes an art and not an exact science unless you carry a portable computer in your 4 X 4. Now, maybe you won't think my first recommendation—that you should fish for bass whenever you have the time—is so flip or far-fetched.

Fishing From Rocks

A "rock hound" in striped bass terminology is not a collector of stones, but an angler who fishes the surf from the tops of rocks, boulder rip-rap located along the beach or some way out in the water. Very little rock fishing is available to anglers from North Carolina northward until they reach the eastern end of Long Island. Here, glacial boulders appear for the first time on the beaches, but they are transported rocks. The real stuff is just a bit farther north, along the coast of Connecticut, and then east and north past Rhode Island, parts of Massachusetts, and into Maine, as well as along most of the West Coast. Along their shores, the bedrock of the earth is exposed to the marine environment. Here is where the striped bass should be called a rock or rockfish, because it is here where they truly inhabit the rocky ledges, outcroppings, and boulders dropped along the shore by glaciers.

Rocks are ideal areas in which to go bass hunting because kelp, wrack, marine weeds, and other growth like to attach themselves to rocky surfaces to perpetuate their kind. It is here that smaller baitfish will come to hide from the marauding striped bass, and it is here, too, where the striped bass angler will wade into the surf among the boulders.

Using the wave action in a rocky environment to help you determine where the striped bass should be lying won't work. You need to read the water at low tide, and through Polaroid glasses, to get your first hints of what the

In the fishing sense, "rock hounds" are collectors of striped bass who use rocks and boulders to get above the splash and force of the waves or to be able to reach farther into the surf. Here, Montauk Point bristles with rods during the daylight hours as a fall migration of fish passes The Point.

bottom is really like when the rocks are covered. Real predictions can be made only based on fishing success in the past. If you are near natural-attraction sites for bass you can cut down on some of the odds.

SAFETY IN THE SURF

When an angler walks into the surf wearing cumbersome waders that come up under the arms and fights an undertow from each wave that tries to take him or her to the sea, there exists some degree of danger. Danger also creeps up when a surfcaster doesn't pay attention to a rising tide and walks out too far, climbs a rise, and forgets about the now deeper water behind.

The garb of a striped bass fisherman in the surf is primarily a high pair of chest waders and the top half of a rain suit. The rain suit is worn over the waders and a web belt is cinched tightly around the waist. Surf fishermen have leaned that this technique is effective in keeping water out of their waders when they are unexpectedly swamped by a large wave. Overlapping the rain suit will prevent water fill his waders and carry him off. Even if a person so clad falls in the surf, he or she can right himself quickly without taking on too much water. But the belt must be snugly secured.

Not all the surf is on a sandy bottom. If rocks are around they are sure to carry moss, and that means poor foot traction. At one time, fishermen could buy chest waders with spikes in the soles of their shoes, much like golf shoes. Today, you can also keep from slipping off rocks with felt-soled waders. They are good, but not as good as the spiked waders. Some diehards will use ice-creepers or will glue on secondary soles that have had the spikes added. Some even place a pair of spiked golf rubbers over their waders if they can get them large enough. If you're really in slippery territory, however, the best bet nowadays is to strap on a pair of corkers. These are sandal-like shoes developed by trout and salmon fishermen with various cleat patterns that are almost slip-proof. They are a spin-off of the kind of cleats used by loggers prone to walking on rolling timber.

There is a new breed of surfcaster now on the scene who wears neoprene scuba wet suits. These anglers walk into the surf, at all times of the year, well beyond the wading range of many others and even beyond casting range. The neoprene makes them buoyant. They take waves over their heads with little concern. If they get knocked down they just get up again. About the only safety device they need is an anchor, so that they won't get knocked off a rock and pulled out with the current. If you like to fish like this but don't wear neoprene, you should wear an inflatable life jacket.

Not all surf fishermen wait for the surf to lie down enough so that they can wade out to reach an outer bar. During recent years, a cadre has formed of dedicated surfcasters who don wet suits and walk into the surf during any of the seasons that the bass are there.

A nice bass and two weaks.

16

From Bank, Pier, Jetty, and Bridge

To the land-bound striped bass fisherman standing on the beach, fishing from a pier or jetty is almost comparable to wading to the outer bar for that first cast. These natural and man-made features—banks, piers and jetties, and bridges—all have the effect of bringing the fisherman closer to deep water and closer to the fish he seeks. While they offer the angler certain advantages over fishing from the beach they have a few inherent disadvantages.

When compared to a boat fisherman, these fishing situations restrict the angler's mobility. He can move only as far as the edge of the sod bank will allow him, or the limit of the jetty and groin as it thrusts into the ocean. On the plus side, these situations provide a stable platform from which an angler can fish in almost any kind of weather. There are numerous occasions during foul weather when the boat fisherman cannot get out of port or past the breakwalls. But it is seldom that the bass angler cannot walk along a sod bank, fish from a pounding jetty, cast off the end of a pier high above the waves, or troll back and forth along a bridge as he walks his lure. Being land-bound at times can be an advantage and forces the angler to better scrutinize the options available. At times, the concentration is vastly improved when the only worry is how far one can cast or where to cast and the more contemplative anglers often catch the most fish.

BANK FISHING

Fishing from the bank in a marine environment is somewhat different from the picture you might conjure up of a bank-fishing situation in fresh water. Most marine banks are found in estuarine situations, lining open bays and marshes where tidal rivers flow twice a day, to flood the grasses and then drain back into

The more contemplative techniques of striped bass fishing is that used by bank fishermen.

the sea. Banks are formed at the end of freshwater streams or rivers where they finally meet the sea. They also appear in large bays and along inlets, where the bottom might he too deep for sod formation, but where the shore is steep and chopped by constant wave and current action.

Many fishermen naturally shy away from the sod bank found in a marine estuary, and with good reason. It is a part of the ever-changing scene of the tidal zone. The sod bank, like the barrier beach, is in a constant state of flux. Walking on it can be tricky and only those familiar with an area at low tide should begin walking the banks when they are covered with water, or when the tide is rising.

To those willing to spend the time to learn the intricacies of the channels and streams of a tidal marsh, walking and casting along the edge of the sod banks can be a highly productive and rewarding way to fish. Striped bass are especially fond of feeding along a sod bank, because it is an area rich in food. The bank with its covering of salt grasses provides protective habitat for killifish and spearing, as well as a home for fiddler and green crabs. Barnacles and mussels line the bank from high to low tide marks, and numerous crustaceans swarm over the shell beds. It is a perfect banquet for the hungry striper.

Sod banks are usually in relatively shallow water and for the most part they attract school-sized striped bass, fish 2 to 3 pounds and up to 10 pounds. However, really large stripers only occasionally enter shallow estuaries in search of food. The tendency for smaller fish to frequent such an environment means that the angler can use rather light tackle. Sod banks provide the perfect situation for light spinning gear with plugs, buck-tailed jigs, and spoons. It is also an ideal situation for the fly-rodder.

Unlike freshwater bank fishing, marine bank fishing is not sedentary. The fisherman moves along the bank line, casting and searching the water as he walks. Most sod banks are built as they stop the current and collect the sediment from the estuarine waters. As their holdings pile up sod banks build and grow. That's how banks are form and are constantly building, shaping and shifting. Their composition is not the best for easy walking. Mud is the basic element, held together by the root systems of the marine plants that grow in it. As they mature, they are rather solid but can give way without warning. The wise sod-hopper is always sure of his next step before he lifts his back foot.

A good bit of sod-bank fishing is done during the mid part of the tide. At high tide, the water may be too deep, even for waders. In a mid-tide situation, hip boots rather than waders are the preferred footwear. With hip boots you are not likely to be tempted into water deeper than you can handle. If you do find yourself on the edge of a collapsing bank, your maneuverability is better in hip boots than in waders. An inflatable life vest or flotation jacket is an even better bet when cruising sod banks.

The only time you may want to heave a lure or bait across the channel when fishing in bank situations is when you want to reach the water at the foot of the opposite bank. For the most part, you should be fishing the water adjacent to the bank you are on. The action of a current passing back and forth across and alongside a sod bank is to undermine the foot of the bank. As a result, most banks overhang slightly, and here is where you are more than likely to find striped bass foraging for food or resting in the current.

The most effective cast is one on a quartering angle down current and then retrieved slowly as it swings under the bank. This means that you might need a 7- to 8-foot spinning rod to help you keep the lure away from the bank without walking too close to its edge. The line test might also be a bit on the heavy side—10-pound, for most situations—because you can't always follow a fish if it insists on going out with the tide. Too many sod banks are interrupted by side channels, some with deep water and others with mud bottoms too deep to navigate.

Sod banks can also provide a good place from which to chum if you cannot cast to an area where striped bass naturally congregate. All the elements are there for successful chumming—a current, water not too deep, a stationary chumming location, and in all likelihood striped bass on the other end to be tolled to the bank.

PIER FISHING

At one time, striped bass stands that dotted the rocky sections of our coast in striped bass country represented the height of pier development. They were individual piers placed where the chances of taking striped bass were at the maximum. Today, the bass stands are gone, an element of the past. The only comparable structures we have are the numerous large commercial fishing piers built along the East Coast, intended to let you reach out to any fish that pass.

Some states have very active fishing-pier construction programs. But in the major range of coastal migrant striped bass, they are rather few. Fishing piers exist in North Carolina, Virginia, Maryland, Delaware, and New Jersey. From time to time, some good catches of striped bass are made off piers, especially when the fish are migrating along the beaches in the spring and fall of the year.

The pier is the land-bound angler's greatest extension into the ocean. It is a safe extension of the land onto the water and brings the caster closer to the fish. Some piers extend several hundred yards off the beach and give the fisherman a real cross-section of water in which to angle. A good many bass will be found between the end of the pier and the beach.

There are, however, several negative aspects of fishing for striped bass from a pier. The foremost is the height above the water level at which most piers are built. The caster will find that only the outer half or two-thirds of his cast is really fishable when using plugs or spoons. The elevation of his position begins to draw the lure higher in the water as it approaches the pier and angler.

Another drawback is the landing of a hooked fish. If the bass is large, the angler can be in a real bind. If the fish decides to head for the pilings instead of the open ocean, its chances of anchoring and breaking the line are good. If the bass is played to exhaustion, getting it into your hands can be another problem. If the fish cannot be lifted by the line and rod, it must be walked off the pier and onto the beach. However, most commercial piers, at their beginnings, have gates or fences extending out of their sides so that no one can fish the pier without passing through the tollgate. Getting around these devices with a fish on the line

Angling from bulkheads and fishing piers gets you farther over the water without getting wet, and it is far more communal than most other techniques. Usually, it's a family trip.

can be next to impossible. A few piers have ladders and catwalks on the lower level down to which you can climb or on which a gaffer can wait.

Another negative note is the great number of anglers who may be on the pier with you. At times, the pier may become so crowded that serious fishing is impossible. Not only is it impossible, it can also be dangerous when 6-ounce lead sinkers are being cast about. But if you don't like fishing alone and are willing to put up with a few inconveniences, then maybe angling for striped bass off a high pier is your cup of tea.

Not all piers extend off the beaches and into the ocean. There are far more piers that are on the backsides of the barrier beaches and many that parallel, rather than project off a beach. These inside piers are productive when striped bass move into the bays and estuaries to feed. Most are on the edge of the current that floods and exits from the bay, and this brings striped bass to the piers where the lie in wait for food to pass. It is these inside piers that are the most productive for taking striped bass.

Areas around a pier are natural places for fish to congregate, and the pier itself does a lot to enhance the fishing on what might otherwise be a barren coastal beach. Pilings that support a pier quickly become encrusted with barnacles and marine plants, and these attract small fish. The small fish attract larger bass, and the bass in turn pull in the fishermen. The collection of pilings in the path of wandering bass are natural attractors to migrating fish. Striped bass on the move over a barren bottom are likely to spend a bit of time investigating the pilings after a long trek with no food.

Most pier fishermen work two rods at one time. Both rods are on the stiff side, and the line is usually 30- or 40-pound test, capable of hoisting a fairly large fish out of the water. One rod is often finished off with a bottom rig, usually a 3- to 4-ounce sinker and a spreader with two or more baited hooks on it. The second rod can be equipped with a fish-finder or a float and a bait that doesn't rest on the bottom. Fishing off the downtide or downwind side, the pier fisherman can let the float drift as far as he wants and expand the range of his fishing from under the shadow of the pier. Bait is fished more often from ocean piers than plugs or spoons because of the height of the structure. Pier fishing can be comfortable. Often, the pier operator runs a restaurant or concession on the pier, provides bait and tackle, and also has the latest fishing information. You can even fish in your own chair and set up a windbreaker on gusty days.

JETTY FISHING

Too often, novice anglers equate jetty fishing with a modified form of surfcasting. I must admit, it does look like a similar situation, but jockeying around on a slippery jetty in a storm is a far cry from fishing the surf with your feet firmly planted in the sand. The entire approach is considerably different, from fishing lore down to the tackle you use.

Jetties and groins are rather new concepts on the marine scene and until the last few decades were rare along Atlantic beaches. Jetties and groins are constructed to control the flow and erosion of sand along the beach and prolong the life of the sandy barrier. Most jetties are built on long, sweeping sand beaches, and their purpose is to interrupt the flow of current, slowing it down and forcing it to deposit its sand load. They also are intended to keep the water from sweeping down the beach fast enough that the sand is picked up and transported elsewhere.

Beach jetties were built to protect beaches and the houses built on them during the last forty or fifty years. More recently, jetty construction to stabilize beaches has been halted in many areas. One factor for the move is the high cost of transporting the needed rip-rap. More important, however, is the ineffectiveness of groins to do what they were constructed to do. Sanding-in also negates their effectiveness. Before such house-building began, the beaches were left to shift and move on their own. Other jetties were built to protect inlets to bays and harbors and keep the sand from silting in or filling up the passageway. Jetties paralleling an inlet or harbor are there strictly as aids to navigation, prolonging the period that it remains open and free of siltation. However, while doing this, it also provides protection for many baitfishes.

In a sense, jetties are low-level piers, but they do not have the disadvantage of being too high, and as a result they appeal to the plug caster as well as to the bait fisherman. Construction of jetties and groins varies greatly, and so does their attraction to fish. The best fishing jetties are those constructed of large boulders or rip-rap. Huge boulders are placed in position with a crane, leaving innumerable pockets and spaces in between that eventually become havens for small fish and crustaceans that inhabit a shore. These boulders are quickly covered with barnacles and marine plants and at their lower levels are extremely slippery for anglers.

Solid concrete jetties are nice to walk upon, but do little to attract or hold passing fish. They do get you out to deeper water, however. In many areas of the nation where rocks are not immediately available, jetties have been constructed of poured concrete blocks. These are piled together much like the natural boulders but leave plenty of space and openings in between which encourage fish to set up housekeeping among them.

The jetty jockey is a more stationary breed of angler than the surfcaster or pier fisherman. He picks out his rock and climbs onto it while other anglers take up other positions. A rock isn't the best surface from which to cast, and long rods and big reels for the surf are out of place in the jetty fisherman's precariously balanced world. Nor are long, reaching casts needed. As a result, the rods are somewhat shorter for this type of fishing, from 6 to 9 feet in length and usually with more build-up of the butt section so that the angler can persuade a large bass to stay on his side of the groin.

A pounding surf can make a rock jetty a rather hazardous place to fish if one comes ill-equipped. The most important item is on the jetty fisherman's feet. Steel or aluminum spikes on his shoes or waders are a must so that he can safely stand on the slippery rocks. Felt soles work, but the metal points work better. A few fishermen wear waders, but most wear knee-high boots because they don't intend to wade into the water. The angler is often swamped by a wave or spray, and a good rain suit with hood can protect him from that. Even hip boots can be dangerous if an angler falls off a rock while hopping from one to another.

The jetty fisherman is fishing on the edge of deep water, and his casts needn't be great. If he's fishing the rock pile by himself, his most productive casts are likely to be up and down the length of the jetty rather than away from it. Fishermen here read the water currents much the same as those on the beach. Water moves at right angles to the jetty, and a back eddy is formed on one side or the other of the construction, depending on the current direction. It is fished much like a natural rip off a point of land.

Most beach jetties and groins are built in New Jersey and Long Island in New York, where beaches are being protected from erosion. Throughout most of the other sections of the striped bass's range, jetty fishermen must content themselves with rock piles protecting the mouths of harbors and inlets. These are often more productive sections than beach jetties because they appear in natural areas where striped bass would normally be feeding or waiting to feed. When the weather is too rough on the outside to fish from a boat, jetties offer the striped bass angler still another area from which to practice his sport.

BRIDGE FISHING

Fishing for striped bass from and around bridges has become a way of life for some anglers. Bridges spanning saltwater streams and estuaries are favorite haunts for striped bass. They mean deeper holes for resting and natural collecting sites for food. Any obstruction in salt water means a place for smaller fish to hide, and if grass can grow there, so much the better. Bridges, with their pilings and stanchions, provide such areas.

Fishing around bridges is accomplished either out of a boat or from the bridge itself. There are a few bridges in Pamlico and Albemarle sounds in North Carolina that are used for bass fishing; and the Chesapeake Bay Tunnel-Bridge is one of the largest in Virginia waters, and a popular "rockfish" attractor. But for the most part, bridges that really attract striped bass and bass fishermen are the causeway-and-bridge situations found crossing many bays from the mainland to the outer barrier beaches. They number in the hundreds from Cape May in New Jersey north to the Atlantic Highlands, and along both shores of Long Island. From New Rochelle in New York, east along the north shore of Long Island Sound through Connecticut, Rhode Island, and Massachusetts, spanning

Jetties can be extremely productive. A jetty that protects a river channel or a harbor with moving currents creates an ideal location for catching striped bass.

the great number of streams and rivers flowing to the sea, we have another great addition to the world of bridges and striped bass. All along the Massachusetts coast and on several offshore islands there are more bridges. And, each bridge has its resident striped bass pro.

Before you try fishing from a bridge, however, you should know a little about bridge features and how they affect striped bass. There are two sides to a bridge, the front and the back. The front of a bridge is the side facing the current, and the back is on the lee side. In tidal situations, of course, front and back switch twice a day. Most still-fishing with live bait is done off the back of a bridge. Casting can be done off the front or the back, with the front having somewhat of an edge. Bridge experts have found that striped bass will lie in two positions in relation to a bridge. Some take up a stand in front of the bridge, while others take one behind the bridge. Few bass hold under a bridge; they move in only to feed or chase bait.

Water being forced between the abutments of a bridge will move faster because the pressures increase as the cross-section of the channel is reduced. This faster current under a bridge will dig or scour out holes deeper than the bottom level surrounding the outer area of the structure. These deeper holes naturally attract bass and baitfish, especially during the day when there is no other protection except the depth of water in which to hide. Striped bass have come to associate bridges with food and will lie in wait near these holes because they are aware that all the food must pass through some sections of the bridge, usually the one with the greatest current.

Tackle for bridge fishing can be spinning or bait-casting with a level-wind reel. The latter is preferred for working bait because line control is so much better, and the line rides atop the rod so there is less risk of its chafing on the railing of the bridge. Spinning outfit are better suited for casting light lures and bait off the front of the bridge. The best retrieve is not in line with the current but on an angle, sweeping the lure in front of pilings or abutments before they can foul on the bridge supports.

Heavier lines are also in order because the abutments, pilings, and stanchions are often encrusted with barnacles and they are murder on monofilament line. Then again, a bass may decide to head under another section of the bridge and you may have to let it run. Longer-than-normal rods also play an important role in bridge fishing. The longer tip helps the line clear any obstructions under the bridge while the fish is being played, and many of the casts will be lobs under the bridge or to one side, with little room for back-casting because of bridge traffic. The longer rod makes snap-casts much easier and puts a lot more distance on the cast.

When trying to land a fish from atop a bridge, you are up against much the same situation as when fishing from a pier. Some bridges are not high off the water, and an extra-long-handled gaff can work. On others, especially those connected to a long causeway, there is no place to land a fish. I once watched one angler who solved the problem with a large treble hook, the size you might use for grappling or shark fishing. Around the shank of the hook he had poured about 10 ounces of lead, and he had attached the hook to a stout line. He simply lowered this rig under the hooked fish and used it as a sort of flying gaff. It worked, and he hauled his large fish over the railing with no trouble.

If you believe that bridge fishing during the day is good, then you should try it at night. The fish are spread out over a larger area around the bridge and are more cooperative when it comes to feeding. On a lighted bridge, the fish take up positions just inside the shadow cast by the bridge and here is where you must concentrate your casting efforts.

Trolling from a bridge is not as far-fetched as it might sound. The best action on a plug or spoon is when it is retrieved across the direction of the current flow, not with or against it. I have seen anglers walk their plugs back and forth across a long bridge and score well. This technique is fine as long as there aren't other anglers on the bridge. And, like trolling from a boat, it is a good way to sample where the fish might be holding and which span of the bridge has the greatest potential. Then you can concentrate all your efforts in that particular section of the bridge.

Chumming is also very productive from a bridge. It can be done effectively from a boat or from the bridge itself. Of course, the bridge can't be too high above the water: you won't be able to create a fine, concentrated chum line that will lead the fish right to your baited hook. I have watched a bridge-load of anglers trying for striped bass, and only one older gentleman seemed to have all the luck. I concentrated on watching him, hoping to spot what he was doing correctly and what I was doing wrong. About every half hour, he would set the rod in a portable holder and walk back to his car. In a minute he was back again. It wasn't a chilly evening, but still he wore a jacket and kept one hand in his pocket. Then I spotted him taking out several grass shrimp, slowly, one at a time, dropped them unobtrusively into the water. Bridge fishing is a crafty sport.

There are two ways to fish a bridge, from the top or from the water in a boat. The latter technique gives bass fishermen a bit more mobility but requires more gear.

17

From Boats

Boats freed beach-bound and bank-bound striped bass fishers. Boats freed them from the land and gave them a mobility on the water to chase their prey wherever it went. No longer must surfcasters or jetty jockeys watch a school of feeding bass chase menhaden beyond the reach of their casts—they could follow. No longer must they sit bound to their beach vehicles watching birds dive and feed over a school of fish—they could go after them. Not only did the boat free them from the land, it also opened up an entire new realm of fishing techniques that increased their prowess. It wasn't only boats that became affordable and gave them this freedom but outboard engines. Anglers, beginning in the mid-1930s could now troll for bass, or anchor and take them by presenting baits in areas they could never reach from the beach. They could chum for them and bring the fish right to the boat, or they could seek out striped bass in rips, holes, and eddies far from the pounding surf and desolate beaches.

BOAT HANDLING IN
SURF, RIPS, AND OPEN WATER

One of the most productive areas to fish when striped bass are migrating is the surf. Most surfcasters, bound to the beach, can reach only a small percentage of the fish because they may be just beyond the range of their best casts. Striped bass make two migrations a year along the Atlantic beaches from Chesapeake Bay to Maine. On the northward migration, there is a tendency to range a bit farther off the beach, sometimes never showing unless the angler can move out in a boat. The fish may not actually be farther off the beach when they migrate

north, but closer to the bottom. Migration studies centered along the South
Shore of Long Island disclosed that migrating fish will seek the bottom water
when moving north for two reasons: that is the direction in which many near-
shore currents are moving, and the are swim north is easier, and bottom waters
at this time are warmer than surface waters exposed to a still-chilled atmo-
sphere.

During the fall migration, bass habitually take a course closer to the beach
and more often than not are actually in the surf. This may be for the same reasons
as in the spring, but with the physical conditions along the beach having
reversed themselves. In fall, surface currents tend to "be going their way" and
bottom temperatures may be a bit too warm for their liking, fish then prefer the
aerated surface waters.

Surf fishing or inshore fishing from a boat can be the most rewarding of all
techniques for taking striped bass. However, it requires a fisherman and boat
skipper with a good knowledge of boat handling and a certain cool when the
combers suddenly break on the gunwale. It also takes a good boat and a
dependable motor, or two motors. Lastly, because the bottom rises and falls so
quickly under a boat in the surf, a large, easy-to-read digital fathometer is
indispensable.

The surf is worked either by trolling parallel to the beach or by using the boat
as a casting platform and drifting with the tidal currents. Either way, the
fisherman must read the waters as if he were still linked to the beach so that he
can take his lures in and out of the channels and over the bars into the deeper

*The small boat revolutionized surf fishing. It allows the angler to fish the same waters as shore-
bound fishers but from the outside in. Now an angler is better able to work the flooded bars and
then move with the fish when they decide to move. The boat also makes an ideal casting platform.*

sloughs. Trolling is the easier of the two methods because the boat is always under power and always under control. If a wave suddenly makes up too closely, the fisherman can quickly turn the boat's bow, directly into it if it isn't large, or taken the oncoming wave on a quarter angler to avoid being swamped.

If a fish is hooked, an experienced skipper usually turns out to sea and fights the fish in deeper water, beyond the origin of the breakers. Needless to say, fishing in the surf is a lot easier with two anglers, but a lone boatman can do the job if he has his wits about him. The rewards are usually worth a bit of daring.

Fishing the surf by boat requires that the boatman develop a sense of timing for the waves and a knowledge of where they will break. He should be familiar with how much his boat can take along the side and when he must turn into the waves to avoid shipping water. Most boatmen will work the surf up to the back of the big wave. A wave moving toward the beach will lift a boat and pass under, breaking on the beach side. Waves consistently break at about the same point on the beach. If you watch them for a few minutes before you move in you can readily define this point. You can fish just to the outside and not worry about capsizing.

When the boat is used as a floating casting platform, the same ability to read the waves and note where they break is just as important, if not more so. Once the wave pattern is established, the angler can let the boat drift as close to the breakers as the pattern allows so that he can cast over holes and channels around the bars. The engine is put into neutral. There is little evidence that an idling engine will spook fish unless the water really becomes shallow. And then, the hulking shadow of the boat above them probably scares the fish more than vibrations in the water.

Fishing the surf in this manner requires a good sense of balance and a pair of swivel hips. The boat is in constant motion and the angler is always in danger of falling out. Two fishermen can nicely work such a situation, one casting from the bow and the other from the stern. Together, they can sweep a large section of the surf.

Rips and rivers develop where tidal currents flow strongly over a shallow bar, about a point of land, or around an island where the tide on one side has not yet completely turned. Thus a rip is created by two current flows, meeting and working their edges against each other. A rip can also develop on a tidal river, in the estuary where the tide is flooding out of a bay or at some constriction that meets the relatively motionless water of the open bay or ocean. Tide is the rise and fall of the water level in a marine situation. There is even a tide on some extremely large lakes. The current or flow is created as the tide rises and water moves in or out of an area.

These are all good locations to fish from a boat, and several techniques can be used. The first is to troll. Lures are trolled up-current as well as down-current. The down-current troll may require greater speed to keep the lures in action and is the less productive of the two directions. Lures are also trolled cross-current, sweeping back and forth on angles to the moving water. This is the most effective way to troll over a body of moving water.

There is a third trolling technique, called stemming the tide, that is also quite effective. The skipper slows the boat's forward motion to a point where it just equals the force of the current. The boat is almost standing still relative to the bottom. The angler can then sweep the lures back and forth over the rip and rocks by slight turns of the wheel, giving it a precise presentation. He can push the engine throttles ahead to move it slowly up-current, throttle back enough to hold him on a new position, and begin sweeping again over a new area.

Tidal currents and rips can also be fished with the boat at anchor. The hook is dropped well ahead of where you intend to fish, and enough line is paid out to provide the scope needed by which the anchor can make fast to the bottom. You can locate yourself exactly over the spot you want to fish by paying out enough line until you are there. Obviously, you must anchor the boat near where you intend to fish or you'll need a lot of anchor line.

This technique has advantages over trolling or stemming because you can shut down the engines, fish quietly, and save fuel. It also frees your hands to work the rods and chum pot if you are chumming; this is a good technique when you are fishing alone or in shallow water. However, there are also disadvantages. You have no mobility and can fish only the area the length of anchor line allows. It can also be hazardous to anchor in too swift a current. Caution and common sense are important when anchoring.

The next technique is similar to fishing the surf from a boat but involves a lot less chance of swamping the craft. The current in the area provides mobility. Here, the skipper may believe that the noise of the engines is alarming the striped bass, especially if the water is shallow. He runs the boat to the head of the water he wants to fish, turns off the engine, and drifts back with the current. He can use the boat as a fishing platform and cast to each side as the boat moves over new bottom, or he can even use cut bait and sinkers and drift the bait over the bottom.

If the current is too strong, live-bait fishing will not be as effective because the bait is apt to ride too high off the bottom. Casting lures will also be less productive because the retrieve will be affected by the force of the moving water. Some lures work so strongly or have so much action that an up-current retrieve is impossible and only down-current casts work. Your best bet in a situation like this is to cast across the direction of the current and fish it on a quarter. However, if the current is not moving fast then the distance you can cover is limited.

In open-ocean and bay situations, where there is little or no effect by tides and currents, most anglers will spend their time trolling potential areas and keeping an eye on the birds for a sign of action. Here is where the boat comes into its own. However, chasing birds can be frustrating. Too often, once you arrive the birds disappear. Also, the skipper horsing around a boat must be careful not to put down the bait and fish.

The best approach to a school of feeding fish is from an upwind or up-current direction, whichever might be the strongest. If you are casting, then skirt the birds and feeding fish and come in again ahead of them. Cut your engine and drift down onto the fish. This is the safest approach. You can cast ahead of the boat and get several tries at the fish before they go down or move away from your line of drift.

If you are trolling, a similar approach should be used. Do not set a course through the birds and school of fish. Rather, swing wide around the school and then come in after you have passed them. The lures will swing in closer than the boat traveled, and you will pick fish off the edge and not put down the entire school.

FISHING TECHNIQUES IN A BOAT

There are four basic fishing techniques possible while using a boat for striped bass fishing. The first is casting or spinning, that uses the boat primarily as a mobile platform from which to cast. The second is trolling, that eliminates casting; the third is jigging, that utilizes the drifting boat; and the fourth is bottom or still-fishing. Each method is discussed in the following.

Casting

Casting and trolling are both widely used, but casting from a boat is held in higher esteem by many anglers. It is much like surfcasting but with mobility, and the type of equipment the complete striped bass angler might need is different. Instead of the long and heavy rods of the surf, boat sticks are modified and vary in size from 6 to 8 or 9 feet. Spinning reels are by far the most popular reel; they allow the angler to throw lighter artificial lures than if he were beach-bound. This also means that lures can be more lifelike and respond better in the water, since weight and distance are not prime factors. Casting ability and distance are not nearly as important in a boat as on the beach. Boat fishermen can move closer to fish if distance is a problem. This general, all-around lightening of tackle gives the boat fisherman more sport than he could have if he had his feet stuck in the sand.

No matter how large your boat, there is basically only enough room for two casters. I have seen three and four anglers working closely and effectively from a boat, but it cramped their styles. The reason is obvious. One person can nicely fish, even when alone, only about 180 degrees around his station. If he is on one side of the boat, then he is working an area from the bow to the stern. That leaves only enough room for another angler to fish the opposite side of the craft. If he is in the bow, his sweep is approximately the same, but from beam to beam. There is also a certain amount of room needed for the back cast and this becomes very evident when you get more than two people working from a boat. It is even more complicated when one is not especially skilled in spinning.

Trolling

The word "trolling" is derived from the French word *trôler,* which means to lead or drag something about, like a dog on a leash or a lure on a line. That is exactly what you are doing when trolling. After you pay out a lure into the water with your line, you lead or drag it about until something comes along that is interested in what you have to offer.

Trolling lures and bait is not an especially new technique and was employed by fishermen even before engines were installed on boats. In the early days of striped bass fishing, a favorite technique was to set a single line with sandworms as bait in the water and troll about a bay by rowing. It was a slow affair. However, unlike bluefish or tuna, which can be trolled successfully for at high speeds, striped bass are caught more often on the slowest possible troll. Trolling as a technique for striped bass becomes important when you don't know where the fish are or when there is no bird activity or other signs to tell you where to fish.

Like the two positions on a boat used as casting platforms, there are really only two positions for trolling—at the edges of the transom or the corners of the boat. This is even true on big-game fishing craft with especially wide transoms when used for striped bass fishing. Even though outriggers are used to add lateral lines, and as many as seven rods can be used at once, it is the two sides of the boat that determine the actual number of efficiently played rods when trolling for striped bass.

One of the most effective uses of a boat is trolling. The anglers can cover a great deal of water in exploratory fishing and can present baits too large or heavy to be cast. Here three "old time" charterboats work the seething waters off Montauk Point.

Trolling for striped bass is an important technique when you cannot see fish activity on the surface or when the fish are at depths that never bring them to the top. The depth at which lures or bait travel can be determined by the speed at which you move relative to the water, not the bottom. A slow trolling speed will drop lures deeper and fast speeds keep them on top.

There is a maximum depth at which a lure pulled through the water will ride. To get it deeper, you must change its shape, add lead weights to the line, add diving planes or use down-riggers, or fish with lead-core or wire lines. A second factor that controls the depth at which the lure rides is the amount of line you have in the water. The more line you pay out into the water, the deeper the lure will travel, but only to a certain point. However, this does not work in a direct ratio. Beyond 100 yards, additional line may only drop your lure by inches.

The reason is that resistance on the line, as it is dragged through the water, lifts the line and affects its depth. The more line astern, the more the resistance increases. Eventually, a point is reached where the deepening effect of letting more line out is cancelled by the line's resistance in the water and no additional depth is achieved. This point varies with the speed at which you are moving through the water, with the diameter of the line, and with the texture of the line's surface—that is, braided nylon, copper, lead-core, and wire surfaces all offer different resistances to the water.

Not all baits or lures can be trolled effectively. When it comes to striped bass fishing, they are limited almost to artificial lures. Those natural baits that can be rigged must also meet the requirements of being dragged through the water. A good example of the latter is the efficiency rigged eel versus a whole bunker (menhaden).

How deeply you want to troll is then a function of the amount of line. Most trollers have their lines marked with different-colored tape or swivels every 100 feet. Then they coordinate their speed or engine RPMs with the amount of line in the water to achieve a certain depth. An accurate determination of your real fishing depth requires knowing the depth of water over a certain point. This is best achieved with the use of a fathometer. Pick a shoal that comes up, as an example, to 20 feet. Make several passes over the shoal with different amounts of line in the water but keeping the RPMs of the boat constant. When your lures begin bumping bottom, you will then be able to match up the depth, in feet, with the RPMs, say 700, and you can note that you have 200 feet of line astern with that particular lure.

At first, this might sound a bit complicated, but it isn't. After a while you will be able to judge quickly how much line you need to take a 3- or 4-ounce lure to 20 or 30 feet. Usually, your trolling RPMs are constant for striped bass, between 500 and 1000, depending upon the type of engine and size and hull shape of the craft. The lures will vary somewhat, between 1 and 4 ounces, and this weight will affect the depth between 2 and 3 feet. The remaining variable is the length of line, your most easily controlled factor. Also, don't forget that if you troll up-current the resistance is greater on the lure and line and will lift it off the bottom. At the same RPMs, when you are trolling down-current your lures will be hanging up. And, the direction of the wind on you and your boat has the same effect as water current. To troll successfully, you must be able to compensate for these differences.

Trolling's great advantage over other techniques for taking striped bass is its ability to cover large amounts of open water with lures. This makes trolling essentially an exploratory process, but it isn't all blind. You can read the surface of the water in much the same way you read the water outside the surf. Rocks and dips on the bottom will cause a current moving over them to rise up and boil. From the change in color between shallow and deep water you can tell where the bottom gives way. Striped bass love to hang around such a drop-off. Rips manifest themselves on the surface and tell you what to expect.

Trolling is a methodical technique for working an area to determine if striped bass it holds fish. Most successful skippers develop trolling patterns when covering new or even familiar areas. They do not aimlessly wander back and forth. In effect, they take a piece of water and begin slicing it, almost as if they mentally placed a grid over it and were searching out each square. They slice it back and forth, each time moving slightly into a new untrolled, unsampled area. Each run should be taken in two directions. If the area is exhausted it is then

A very efficient way to troll deep without weights is to use downriggers.
Here are a pair of electric downriggers on the boat that produced a striped bass

crisscrossed at right angles until the correct presentation to the striped bass is determined.

After a strike, the skipper knows that there might be more bass there because of the schooling nature of these fish. It's not always practical to put a marker in the water if there are other boats also working the same area, and a marker with its line and sinker are apt to foul a trolled lure. The next best thing is to take a range on where the fish was struck. Taking a range involves finding two points, one on the horizon directly on the bow of the boat and a second off the stern. That gives you only one line and you need a point on that line. You pick another line at right angles to place your position on the first line, and here maybe only one position on the horizon is needed. Most skippers take a set of range points each time they start a trolling course maybe it's no more than a mental note, but they know roughly where they were headed when the strike occurred. After a strike happens there isn't much time to take a reading and fight a bass at the same time.

In water where there are natural rips and boils forming, ranges are not quite as important. But as the tide shifts, these rips and boils will make up differently, so a few ranges in the back of the mind are never wasted.

Jigging

The synonym for jigging is jerking, a word that describes the swimming patterns of the squid, one of the striped bass's favorite foods. The action is an abrupt up-and-down jerking, and this pattern of movement has come to mean food to every striped bass that has ever seen a squid. To imitate this, bait fishermen have devised two jigging techniques, both involving a moving boat as a fishing platform.

Drift jigging is the older of the two and accounts for a lot of striped bass over the course of a season. The elements necessary here are a favorite stopping place for fish, like the edge of an island or a bend in a tidal river, and a body of water in motion. In some typical constricted areas, like Plum Gut between Orient Point on Long Island and Plum Island, or The Race, between Fishers Island and Great Gull Island, jigging is fairly popular because of the fast flowing tide. It is the prime method used for taking big striped bass at Great Eastern Rock, off Montauk Point, where a world's record fish was taken in 1982.

The lure for drift-jigging is usually a tin squid or heavy metal spoon like a Hopkins lure. It is allowed to fall to the bottom and then jigged a few feet up and down as the boat moves over the shoals. At the end of the drift, the lure is retrieved and angler runs up-current to begin anew.

Jigging while trolling is the classic approach to striped bass fishing in deep water and is probably one of the oldest effective techniques. It can be worked by either large or small boat and is the favorite method for producing striped bass on charterboats. The jigging rod is a bit more limber than the average trolling rod and gives the lure an additional jerking action. The

Drift-jigging probably accounts for more striped bass than any other technique. Here, the anglers is fishing in Plum Gut, with a bottom that varies from 25 to 190 feet is the span of just 100 yards. Note the short jigging rod and large-spooled reel.

preferred lure is a black-tailed jig, composed of a lead head poured onto a large hook. Behind the head, the hook is dressed with dyed deer or polar bear hairs. The hairs pulsate as the lure is jigged or jerked through the water, opening and closing, closely resembling the movement of a squid as well as the jerked swimming style.

Some jigs are made with an additional band of bucktail or marabou feathers tied facing the eye of the hook. This enhances the pulsating swimming action. Bucktails are jigged at a steady pace as the boat is moved rather slowly over a possible striped bass area. The rod is jigged by the arms, it is or held steady by the arms and the entire body, from the waist up, is jerked sideways, back and forth, to relieve the strain on the arms. Jigging while trolling is a tiring activity but it is a good producer of fish. And, when all modern methods of drumming up bass fail, skippers will inevitably fall back to the jig. Jigging is still in wide use today off Long Island's East End and called the "Montauk Jig" a play on the dancing connotation of the word.

Bottom Fishing

Striped bass do more of their feeding along the bottom than at any other level. It's only natural when you consider that the bottom houses so much food. The goal of many anglers who cast baits and lures, as well as troll lures, is to get the lure as close to the bottom as possible. However, none works as effectively as bottom fishing from a drifting or anchored boat. In a sense, the anchored boat represents an extension of bank or pier fishing except that the fisherman has the mobility to move about, either closer to deeper water or up and down the beach. Another term for bottom fishing is still-fishing, because the boat is usually stationary and the bait is held in one place by a lead sinker.

There are many situations in which an anchored boat is the only way to fish for striped bass. One is where shallow water, a distance away from shore, suddenly gives way to a deep hole or trough in a tidal river or along a bar marking a connecting point with land. Striped bass naturally congregate along such drop-off areas, and a boat anchored in the shallows with lure or bait trailing off into a deep spot is a sure producer. The proper depth, in the moving current can be attained by changing the weights of lead used with the bait; the bait can even be kept directly on the bottom but striped bass have problems when their food is underneath them unless they are specifically rooting in the sand for worms.

Still-fishing from an anchored boat requires patience and it is not the most aggressive form of striped bass fishing, but to many anglers it is an enjoyable technique. Some baits can be effectively fished only from an anchored or slowly drifting boat. The live eel is a good example. The stationary boat over a potential striped bass hole provides the best technique for chumming, one of the deadliest methods for taking striped bass. Chum can be accurately distributed from an anchored boat and the fish tolled to the baited hook. Chumming, a very effective way to take striped bass, will be discussed in greater detail in Chapter 19.

BOATING A BASS

Boating a bass from a trolling boat is approached differently by different skippers. At one time, I ran a boat with two outboard engines. When I fished alone, trolling two rods, and had a strike, I'd slip one engine into neutral and drop the other to its lowest RPMs. This kept a light tension on the line and fish. If I trolled up-current or stemmed the current, I didn't change direction until the fish was alongside and ready to be gaffed, or the fish was so large that water resistance on the fish became a factor in getting the bass into the boat.

Most fish taken on a trolled lure will hook themselves—or rather, the boat moving through the water does the hooking. I usually set the drag lightly but with the click on, to contribute some pressure and also act as an alarm to tell me a fish is on. Immediately after picking up the rod, I disengage the click and only slightly adjust the drag, letting the fish run. A bass, even the largest bass, will not run more than 100 yards. If it does, you can always follow it with the boat if you are fearful of running out of line.

An experienced fisherman can land a bass with the engine in neutral, taking up the slack with a charge by the fish toward the boat or giving line when it is needed. If you are not familiar with the speed of the charge of a big bass, let the engine remain in gear, turn the wheel, with rod in hand, and drift away from the current on a quarter course. This will slightly reduce the drag created by the current. If the fish is really large and might test my tackle, I make sure the engines are out of the water when the fight reaches the see-saw stage along the side or stern of the craft.

Whether taking bass casting or trolling, the place to gaff it and bring it aboard is along the rear quarter of the boat. The lower gunwale here makes the job a lot easier. You should also fight the fish from this same area and be ready to stick the rod in the water if the bass should suddenly decide to head for the other side of the boat. The tip under the boat will guide the lines past the engine skegs or any obstructions on the boat's hull.

Gaffing a fish is best done by someone else in the boat with you. When the fish is ready to be gaffed, don't reel in all the line, down to the leader and snaps, but leave enough so that you can slowly work your way to the bow of the boat and bring the bass abreast the side where the gaffer can easily get to it. You must get away from the transom or you will hinder his ability to swing easily after the fish.

Getting a large striped bass into the boat can be a problem, but if it is boated along the after-gunwale with a gaff of the proper size, then there isn't much chance for a mishap.

18

Fly-Rodding for Striped Bass

Fishing for striped bass with a fly rod is not the most efficient method available for taking large numbers of fish. However, it makes up in quality what it might not offer in the way of quantity. The thrill of even a small bass surging, rolling near the surface, or bulldogging along the bottom is difficult to duplicate on any other type of equipment.

Fishermen who seek striped bass with a fly rod are probably the elite among saltwater anglers, though few who have attained this ability consider themselves elitist. There's no doubt that a few who flail the willowy wand may make a practice of looking down at surfcasters or plug-tossers. There's no justification for this attitude and it is snobbish. It's the mark of a beginner. However, those who begin to take striped bass regularly with a fly and fly rod seem to move to another plane, not that of a snob, but that of a person who has discovered the real joys of fishing. They become proselytizers of their newly found faith and are eager to share their discovery with others. They become teachers.

I like to catch striped bass by all methods and derive pleasure from each, but fly-fishing is a sport relative to your own tastes. It can be the most frustrating of all the techniques. But when you do take a striped bass on a fly rod, you know there are few other methods with such great rewards.

Fly-rodding for striped bass is something easiest practiced by the experienced saltwater angler because he doesn't have to start with learning to read the waters but can concentrate on developing the technique. Not that a freshwater fisherman can't take his fly rod into the briny, but success is more certain and comes sooner if he also has a store of salty lore to his credit.

To the angler who is already accomplished in catching striped bass under all conditions and uses the numerous other methods and techniques available, the fly rod offers still another challenging method. At times it will even work better than others. Fly-rodding for striped bass should thus be one of the several techniques of the complete striped bass fisherman.

For the great majority of anglers, there is, however, an inherent limitation built into fly-fishing: the maximum size of the fish you are apt to catch. Fly-fishing equipment is great for small- and medium-sized fish—that is, schoolies from 2 to 9 or 10 pounds and lone striped bass from 10 to 30 pounds. But prospects of catching larger bass are in an inverse ratio to the size of the fish. There's no doubt that a 70-pound striped bass could be caught on a fly rod, but the equipment, the well-tuned tackle, and the capability of casting heavy rods, heavy lines, and big flies is beyond the regimen of all but the very most dedicated of striped bass fly fishers.

The basic reason is that bigger fish demand bigger baits. Really large bass look for a mouthful of food, and though they may nibble on shrimp and sandfleas during part of their daily search for food, they'd rather expend just the

energy needed to catch a few 3- or 4-pound bunker. We approach the limiting factor when we try to make a fly or bucktail large enough to entice a big striper. There is just so much hackle and marabou that most casters can effectively or efficiently wield on the end of a fly line with a 9-1/2-foot fly rod for hour after hour. Beyond an 8-inch fly, it becomes nearly impossible. I don't mean to imply that a good caster can never take a 50- or 60-pound striped bass; it's just that the odds fall off so sharply as to make it a fluke. But there's nothing wrong with resolving one's self to catching 20- or even 25-pound striped bass with some expected degree of regularity.

Big striped bass can be taken on a fly rod. Here, Lou Tabory of Ridgefield, Conn. offers the proof. However, Tabory is an experienced striped bass fly-rodder and author of the authoritative book Inshore Fly Fishing *(Lyons & Burford, 1992).*

FLY-RODDING WATERS

Of course, you can take a fly rod after striped bass anywhere the fish swim. But the fly rod is most effective under controlled fishing conditions, those which you are more likely to find in a salt creek, a tidal river, along the edges of a salt marsh in an estuary, along the borders of great stands of grasses, or under the heavy sod banks cut by river channels in a large, shallow tidal bay. You can fly-cast to striped bass in the open bays or on the outside of barrier beaches when they show on top, under the birds, or along the outer tips of groins and jetties. But for the most part, the ocean is a big piece of water and you are too often fishing waters without fish concentrations. Your chances for success are lessened by the breadth of these waters.

In a tidal creek, however, when the water floods into the marsh grass, you can feel pretty certain that if any striped bass are around, they will be poking their snouts into the banks, looking for shedder and fiddler crabs, killifish that are seeking the protection of the grasses, and mussels, and that they will be beginning to feed as the beds are covered with water.

My favorite striped bass haunt for fly-rodding is in my own back yard, on the Nissequogue River. The Nissequogue is a typical Long Island tidal stream beginning first as a small, spring-fed creek that opens into a fairly large tidal estuary before passing through a narrow inlet to salt water and Long Island Sound. As the tide rushes in to fill a large, thatch-island-filled estuary, schools of small striped bass flood in with the rising water. First, the tide fills the channels, guzzles, and drains, as if working backwards in an intricate freshwater watershed. It then overrides these waterways, spreading over the mud and sod banks. The fish follow it over acres of salt hay, *Spartina alterniflora*, and higher in the tidal zone *Spartina patens*. When the tide has risen to its greatest height, the river and its estuary have disappeared, transformed into a huge salty lake. Only the tall phragmites plants, in the zone between mean high tide and dry land, are free of the all- encompassing flood.

Striped bass move in with the tide, often so close to the front of the tidal bore that you can occasionally see their dorsal fins and square tails break the surface of the water. They seem more like a pack of hounds on the scent of a rabbit than fish as they move with the flooding waters. This is the best time to cast for them because they are actively feeding on anything that gets swept before them. Almost any kind of fly streaking just inside their myopic world is deadly. This is especially true if several others in the school are close at hand. Mob instinct operates even within a school of striped bass, though it reaches its greatest frenzy in bluefish, as competition becomes keen, catching a fish becomes easier.

Fly-fishing here is most productive on a flooding tide. However, it isn't really much more difficult to catch them on the ebbing tide. The only prerequisite is that you must know the river's bottom configuration so you know where to intercept fish falling back with the tide. As the tide falls, striped bass work from the drains and guzzles into the rivulets and eventually return to the main channels. They are much like a retreating army, constantly falling back but taking up new positions where the terrain is in their favor, turning and facing into the current wherever and whenever they stop. In a few places, the ebbing current forms rapids-like situations and pulling a bass out of here is akin to hooking an Atlantic salmon, but without the jumping. Striped bass don't jump.

On a falling tide, I like to don a pair of waders and work the edges of the river much like a freshwater stream. The river is always changing character, and as the water rushes back to the Sound, bass take up new positions. I prefer working down current, with the tide, casting along sod banks, searching edges of the rapids formed just below a sand bar and letting a streamer or bucktail sweep through the pool, fathoming its depth, searching among its fish.

There are two ways to get into a position to fly-cast to striped bass in such an environment. If the bottoms are firm and the tide-rise is no more than a foot or two, you can cover the changing scene in chest waders. This is the most preferred technique. Or, you can following the flooding tide in a small boat and use it as a mobile casting platform. This is an excellent way if you have a second person to row the boat, maneuver it into position, and stop or anchor it and then release it as you cover water. The compromise is to take turns with the person on the oars. The third method to fish a tidal stream with uncertain bottoms and larger tidal exchanges is a combination of wearing waders and using a boat to get you off the bottom when the water gets too deep. It's not the ideal method, but having a boat nearby when the tide gets near the top of the waders gives you areal feeling of security and safety.

I believe that this type of striped bass fishing is even more challenging than salmon fishing because you must learn the river and its moods in four dimensions. Not only must you know its width, depth, and length, but you must learn these through a span of time as the tide rises and falls, keeping the other three dimensions in a constant state of flux. Time and tide affect the river as well as the fish. The successful angler must comprehend each in the numerous combinations created in a saltwater stream.

Fly-fishing for striped bass is not something new or recently discovered, though during the last decade advances in equipment and technique have been so great that you might imagine that it is a brand-new sport. Fly-casting for striped bass has been done for more than 150 years. However, it was always performed with freshwater or salmon tackle. During the last decade, maybe a little longer, the refinements of the fly rod and matching equipment have put saltwater fly-fishing into a category all by itself. In addition, the sport has become organized, and there are now clubs and associations dedicated strictly to the taking of striped bass by fly. The International Game Fish Association has a category dedicated to this method, and it sets the requirements and maintains the records.

A saltwater estuary, especially along its banks and channels, is a nursery area for many bait-fish upon which striped bass feed and, the imitations thrown by saltwater fly-rodders, duplicate many of these small food-fishes. The sport is as enjoyable and rewarding as freshwater fly-casting.

FLY-RODDING TECHNIQUES

All the techniques of handling a fly rod in fresh water can be useful in salt water when after striped bass. One difficulty that a saltwater fly rodder does not have, which often plagues his freshwater counterpart, is limited space for back-casting. The openness of the marine estuary gives the caster great freedom. But at the same time, he must also cover a greater area of water than must the freshwater angler who works in relatively confined river or stream situations.

Wind can be a constant problem to the saltwater fly caster, and there is very little lee found on an open marsh and less on a open bay. Most casters can work in a wind up to 10 knots, but above that only the better men and women are afield, and they, too, are hard put to make a fly rod work. This might be the time to lay aside the fly rod and pick up another type of equipment. There are few days on the marine scene when wind is not a factor, so light-weight fly-casting equipment is seldom seen in salt water.

Unless you are fishing a moving body of water, a tidal creek, or the edge of a rip, there is very little movement in salt water when compared to that found in freshwater situations. As a result, most of the action imparted to the fly must come from the caster. Stripping line becomes the most important technique for the saltwater fly-fisherman.

Stripping line, sometimes at a rapid pace, is simply the pulling or retrieving of line by one hand, while the other holds the rod parallel to the water's surface, after the line and fly have been cast. The line is stripped by the left hand (if you are right-handed) while it is guided by hooking the line over the first of the right hand near the reel. The length of each strip varies. Some fishermen prefer to haul their lures through the water at great speeds and feel this is essential to getting a striped bass to strike. Others prefer to work it with short hauls, 6 to 12 inches at a time, with a lull between each pull or strip. Whether you prefer the full length of your arm, 18 inches or so, or the short strips will be determined by the water, its depth, the type of fly on your line, and how the fish are responding. Don't make up your mind too hastily about any one technique; variety is the spice of life in fishing and the successful angler is always willing to accommodate to changing demands and conditions.

FLY RODS AND FLY TACKLE

The first rods used in salt water for striped bass on the East Coast were often long salmon "sticks," or steelhead rods on the West Coast. Some anglers simply took their longest freshwater rods and adjusted them to saltwater fishing. Bass-bugging rods and popper rods are also adaptable, and one of my favorites is still a 9-foot bugging rod that works beautifully on schoolie bass up to 10 pounds.

During the last decade, basic innovations in new saltwater rods have put them in an altogether separate class of fly rods. And, within just the short span of the last two years, the class has evolved some of the best rod designs and space-age construction technologies and materials to make them some of the best of all fly rods. They often possess more backbone or power in the lower or butt section than standard freshwater rods. This is needed to set the hook on hard-mouthed bass and to fight the larger fish. Guides are constructed of noncorrosive metals, which are a real must in salt water. Normally, freshwater guides have a 1/4-inch diameter, but to handle the heavier lines typical of a balanced saltwater outfit, and to make stripping an easier chore, guides on saltwater rods, especially the first few have been opened to 1/2 and 3/4 inches. This also reduces the amount of friction and makes casts travel a bit farther.

Metal ferrules that joined rod sections gave early salty fly rodders a fit. Once the rod was put together, it was often left together for the life of the rod. The perfect rod has no ferrules, but this is impractical if you want to take your rod traveling. The next best thing is glass-to-glass ferrules, which have been perfected to the point where they have little negative effect on the action and curvature of the rod. Today, they are about the only type you'll find used in both fresh and saltwater rods.

On the butt end, the reel seats now are almost all constructed of anodized aluminum, which is highly noncorrosive and is also a weight-saver. A butt extension, a 2- to 3-inch extension beyond the butt, helps to balance the rod and gives the angler added leverage under the elbow when needed to fight big fish for extended periods. It also extends the rod down to the angler's elbow and reduces fatigue.

The saltwater fly rod comes in a range of sizes—weights and lengths. The typical saltwater fly rod used on striped bass is probably a 9-weight rod. If the chances of a bigger bass are good, you might prefer a 10-weight rod. A dozen years ago, a 9-weight rod was usually termed a "man-killer" by many fly rodders because of its weight and clumsiness, especially by those fishers accustomed only to freshwater fishing or an occasional salmon trip. But the evolution of rods today, from fiberglass, through boron, carbon and graphite materials and occasionally combinations of two, have produced 9-weight rods that are light in comparison to older rods and possess the kind of backbone needed, all the way to the tip, to give the angler great control. Most are on the long side, between 8-1/2 and 10 feet in length. The average is in the middle, about 9 feet, that can be matched with a No. 9 or No. 10 fly line. The actual length of rod should be determined by your handling ability and personal casting idiosyncrasies.

Fly Lines

Like their freshwater counterparts, saltwater fly lines come in two basic types: floating and sinking. However, because more line is usually on the water in a saltwater cast, this means more must be lifted each time a cast is initiated. It's nearly impossible to lift a long cast laid out on the water with a sinking line, and as a result most saltwater lines that are not all floating lines are combination lines with a floating body and a sinking tip. Even in an outfit built around a floating line, sinking leader-to-tippet connectors will take the fly deep enough to avoid using a sinking tip. Lines for salt water tend to be on the heavy side, 8-, 9-, 10- and even 12-weight, because large flies, streamers, and poppers are used. Still another reason heavier lines are used in salt water is because they can allow the angler to make casts into the wind, conditions typical of most days on the water, with greater accuracy.

AFTMA FLY-LINE STANDARDS

Line No.	Weight (grains)	Line No.	Weight (grains)
1	60	7	185
2	80	8	210
3	100	9	240
4	120	10	280
5	140	11	330
6	160	12	380

Both the sinking and floating lines are most often tapered lines rather than level lines that can be used in fresh water. The realm a saltwater caster must cover is so much greater that every advantage that can be squeezed into an outfit makes that much more water can be swept. The weight-forward (WF) fly line gives him an added edge. A WF10F line is a weight-forward, 10-weight floating line. Such lines would typically be used with a 10-weight rod to toss large streamers or bucktails or when using poppers and floating bugs that are strictly surface lures.

In deeper water, where an angler wants to haul a bucktail or streamer through the depths, a WF10S line can be used. This is a weight-forward, 10-weight sinking line. In mid-depth situations, where the angler doesn't want a lot of line to pick off the water, he might select a WF10FS. This is a weight-forward, 10-weight line with a sinking head and floating body. The front half of the line sinks and can reach water depths greater than a floating line. Some floater-sinker lines are double-tapered—that is, reversible—so that you can switch them around.

To achieve even greater distances over salt water, some anglers have gone to specialized "shooting heads," to reach out for fantastic distances. A shooting head is no more than a short section of fly line spliced to a light running line made of Dacron or monofilament. The latter is used more often because it creates less resistance in the guides and thus travels somewhat farther. The fly, lure, or even bait is cast with the fly line still in the guides, and as it escapes, the weightier fly line shoots forward, carrying the running line out of the guides. In false-casting, the caster should never work on his running line; it adds little or no appreciable distance and dampens the action of the tip. The weight of the shooting section should be heavy enough to bring out the action of the rod and is the same weight line that would be used to match the rod, regardless of the weight of the running line.

Leaders

A good rule of thumb for leader length is that it should be approximately the length of the rod. Tapered leaders are heavy in the butt section and taper down to the tip to meet the eye of the fly. Or, a tippet, made of level monofilament line, is used between the end of the tapered leader and the eye of the fly. The length of the tippet can vary and its test strength is usually that of the end of the tapered leader...but not always necessarily so. Using a tippet allows a length of lighter line before the fly that is an advantage in the case when fish are leader-shy or the water is exceptionally clear, and it helps preserve the distal end of tapered leader because most of the wear and tear usually takes place there.

Tapers can vary in test from 50 pounds at the butt to 10 at the tip, and many lesser combinations exist. Some tapered leaders are constructed with a double tape: a second, much shorter taper at the butt section where it meets the fly line. This is not only preferred but necessary when you use a metal eye on the proximal end of the running line because the smaller diameter at the butt allows you to tie a knot in the metal eye. Casters who don't use metal eyes generally tie a nail knot when fixing the line to the leader.

I prefer the metal eye "splice." This device is an eye the size of a small hook with a shaft about 1/2 inch long. The shaft has minute barbs on it that keep it from pulling out of the line. The shaft is skewered into the usually hollow center of the fly line. I have used these for years and have never had one pull out if it was properly inserted. I first use a small needle to open the center core of the fly line before forcing the barbed shaft into its center. Most eyes come in iron or stainless steel for saltwater use. But even the stainless-steel eyes corrode after a while when exposed to salt water, and they should be replaced regularly, depending upon how much use they get.

Leader material is usually made of monofilament and should be stiff enough to turn over the fly at the end of the cast. This isn't quite as necessary when fishing with streamers and bucktails on a sinking line. In fact, I often shorten the leader to 3 or 4 feet so that the fly is closer to the bulk of the sinking line and thus gets deeper into the water. Under such conditions, a tapered leader doesn't offer any advantages and I often substitute a piece of level monofilament.

Also available nowadays are braided, tapered leader-connectors. Today, many fly lines come with a loop on their distal end, and instead of adding a tapered monofilament leader to the loop, some fly casters employ a 3- or 4-foot length of braided connecting-leader. To the distal end of the connecting-leader is a connecting loop. Attached to the end of this you can add either a regular tapered leader, or a short-length tapered leader, or the tippet. Some braided leader-connectors are made of high-density monofilament and actually sink. They were initially designed for nymph fishing in fresh water where the use of lead encumbered the cast or where it was prohibited. They are ideal for use in situations where you still want to use a floating line but want to get the fly down a bit deeper.

Shock-leaders are pieces of heavy monofilament or fine, braided wire line that are placed just ahead of the weakest part of a leader system, that is, between the distal end of the tippet and the fly. They are often heavy, cumbersome, create

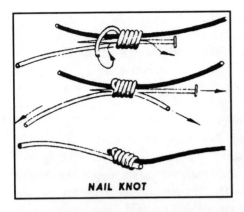

NAIL KNOT

difficulty in turning over the fly at the end of the cast, and shorten the distance of the cast because they increase wind resistance. So why use them if they have so many drawbacks?

Because you might want to when bluefish are mixed with striped bass, as is often the case, to ensure the longevity of your fly. However, I never use them, even when bluefish are mixed with striped bass. Striped bass take a fly or bait by the head because, like most fish, they have few teeth in their mouths designed for biting. Bluefish, however, have the best chopping dentures in fishdom. Because of this, they have evolved a different technique for eating their prey. They almost always bite by the tail: actually biting, cutting off the tail, and immobilizing the prey. On the second pass, they take a bigger gulp or the entire fish, but head first. Because of this feeding technique, bluefish I have caught were almost always hooked in the front of the jaw or roof of the mouth. When their choppers came down, it was usually upon the shank of the hook. While bluefish mess up many flies I've lost very few. When a fly is lost, and I have seen them do it, it was because another was bluefish trying to take the fly out of the hooked fish's mouth.

Reels

The first reels used for striped bass fly-fishing were salmon reels. But salmon in river situations don't have the wide-water prospects that a striped bass has, and the reel's capacity often limited the fighting abilities of the fisherman. A saltwater reel on a striped bass outfit today should be about 4 inches in diameter and capable of holding 40 yards of 9-weight fly line and approximately 200 yards of 15- to 20-pound test braided Dacron or nylon line as a backing.

The basic reel should be single action—that is, one turn of the reel handle equals one turn of the spool. Also available are anti-reverse reels with drag systems that allow the spool to unwind, without the handle turning, when the pull reaches a certain force. There is also a third category of reel, the multiplying reel, which through a system of gears turns the spool more than once when you turn the handle at least once when retrieving the line. The spool should be capable of being removed so that the insides can be rinsed of salt water, or so that other spools with different lines can be added without changing the entire reel.

There are several ways to slow down the force of a striped bass hauling line off the reel's spool. A good reel will usually employ two of these, an exposed spool rim and an internal drag system. The reel should be of such construction that the rim of the reel is outside the frame and pressure with the palm of the hand can be used as a drag to slow down the run of a fish. All reels for striped bass should have an anti-reverse device that won't allow the spool to revolve freely in a direction that would let line go out. In the simplest reels, with no anti-reverse device, putting on the click and the resistance it offers is one way to slow down a charging fish. The clicker's original use was simply to keep the spool from over-running when a fish suddenly stopped its charge. On better reels, the drag system in anti-reverse, along with a clicker, does allow the spool to unwind but it takes the fish's force to accomplish this. In most such drag systems, the amount of drag is variable and how much you use depends on the size and strength of the fish.

Weight in a reel is an important feature when you consider that you already are using big rods, heavy lines, leaders, and flies. This becomes evident after wielding such an outfit for an hour or more. Earlier reels were rather heavy, and when added to a large saltwater rod and a heavy line capable of carrying large flies, the overall weight was a man-killer. This did turn off some anglers to saltwater fly fishing. The stamina required was excessive for many fishers, especially women. Today, aluminum and space-age metals and alloys have made reels a lot lighter, stronger, and often saltwater-proof.

In summary, when you begin looking for a reel for a striped bass outfit, there are three things you should consider in your selection—the drag system, the line capacity and the weight of the reel—in that order. The drag should be smooth, adjustable, and preferably easy to take apart, with replaceable elements for when they become worn. The reel should be able to hold 200 yards of Dacron backing, another 125 to 150 feet of 25- or 30-pound-test monofilament if you're using a shooting head system, and the fly line. Care should be used in selecting

Saltwater fly-rodding gear is like freshwater gear, but heavier and the reels are corrosion-proof. Note the butt extensions on two or the three rods.

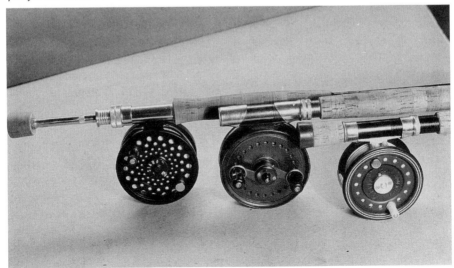

the monofilament line because while all may test at 25 or 30 pounds, whichever you use, they do not all have the same diameter at comparable tests. Get the smallest diameter in that test and you have more storage space on the spool. While looking for a light-weight reel with the two preceding characteristics, the reel must be totally corrosion-proof and easy to disassemble for cleaning.

The primary purpose of a fly reel is store line. In other kinds of tackle, the reel, in conjunction with the rod, is used to fight the fish. In the majority of freshwater fly fishing situations, the reel has also become adapted to fighting the fish. You can fight a fish from the reel, even a very large fish, in streams and rivers because the force of the river, as well as the strength of the fish, always keeps some degree of pressure on reel and spool. However, in salt water, there is no constant pressure on the fish from the water, and when the fish stops fighting, you may not be able to reel the line in fast enough to maintain pressure on the hook to keep it engaged unless you are using a multiplying reel. Or, in a very real situation, when a striped bass charges you, you may not be able to turn the spool handle fast enough to maintain pressure and any slack in the line could free the fish. In such situations, you may have to hand-strip the line until the fish again starts to take it out.

In freshwater situations, most fish are played by stripping the line on the water or beach. Fly-rodders after striped bass who fish from boats will often find a lot of line off the reel and in the boat or on the water. This can cause immediate problems. Your immediate goal is to get the line back on the reel but it may mean that you first start by keeping tension on the departing line with your fingers and guiding the coils into the water. Small fish can be tackled by stripping, but a large bass that has practically cleaned the line from a spool is best handled by putting line back onto the spool and fighting the fish off the reel.

FLIES FOR SALT WATER

Flies for striped bass originally were large freshwater flies: bucktails and streamers used for salmon or other freshwater species. The two most popular were the Gray Ghost and the Mickey Finn. The latter is still on the top of the list today. But we will probably never know for sure who tied the first fly with the idea of using it to catch a striped bass. Probably, that credit should go to Tom Loving of Baltimore, Maryland. When in 1928, Loving took a 20-year-old named Joe Brooks fishing for brackish-water largemouths on Frog Mortar, a small stream that flows into Chesapeake Bay, he had already been catching striped bass on a fly he designed. He and a small following had developed a reputation on Maryland's tidal river for taking striped bass up to 20 pounds on their flies.

Loving designed the prototype as pattern for catching shad on the Susquehanna River, near where it flows into Chesapeake Bay and must have discovered that striped bass liked it as well as shad. He changed it a bit, catering to the

This replica of Tom Loving's Feathered Minnow Fly, first fly tied specifically to catch striped bass, was dressed by Howard Eskin of Stony Brook, N.Y., using turkey quill for hackle as did Loving.

fancy of striped bass, developed it a bit further and called it the Loving Feathered Minnow. He fished it on a 5-ounce, 9-foot fly rod. The fly was nothing more than a tuft of 3-inch white bucktail hairs, with a quill (hackle) head. The exact components are not known, but the fly, when tied today, is called the Loving Bass Fly and tied on a straight eye, standard length hook with white bucktail wings, a red hackle and a black head.

"Other fly fishing activities [according to O.H.P. Rodman in *Striped Bass*, Barnes and Co., 1943] for striped bass go back to the good old days, according to Boston's Dana Chapman, experienced tackle merchant and angler in his own right, when, if the fishing in spring got a little slow in the famed Bangor Pool (Maille) for salmon, the boys used to bend (fasten) on a red and white bucktail fly that was tied fairly full and take themselves a mess of striped bass. These flies had a joint about half an inch back from the eye so that the hook was free to swing—not such a bad idea, either."

The next record we have of an effort to design a fly strictly for catching striped bass comes from Rhode Island. In the spring of 1940, Harold L. Gibbs of Barrington, a long-time fly fisherman for Atlantic salmon, tied a 5/0 bucktail-wing streamer that imitated a small silversides (spearing), a bait fish, and used it successfully one afternoon on the Warren and Barrington rivers behind his house. That year, Narragansett Bay had an unusually large number of small striped bass in its waters. The story goes, according to George X. Sand, author of *Salt-Water Fly Fishing* (Knopf, 1969) who knew Gibbs, that he was so happy with his concoction that he phoned his brother Frank and that evening they experimented with more patterns.

The original fly, however, produced the best. In the following year, the Gibbs brothers were able to catch some 800 striped bass with it. Frank's fly was known as the Frank Gibbs Streamer, but today, Harold's is still the better-known pattern, the Gibbs Striper Fly. Harvey Flint, a fishing companion of the Gibbs brothers, tied a variation on Harold's fly, with the addition of red and blue bucktails (Harold's was white with a thin streak of blue) and it became known as the Palmer Diller. These three fly patterns dominated early striped bass flies.

In Ken Bay's classic *Salt Water Flies*, published in 1972, of the 50 most popular saltwater flies he selected, that ranged from tuna to tarpon, 31 patterns were devoted to catching striped bass. And of these most seemed to be variations on the Gibbs Striper.

They are tied as follows:

The Harold Gibbs Fly:
#4 long shanked hook with turned down eye
Silver body, no tag, 3-inch white bucktail fairly full
1-1/2" bright blue feather as cheek, tapering to a
    point, each side
Shorter cheek (tied over blue feather) of brown feather
    with white rib (1/4-inch long)
Painted yellow eyes, with small black dot for pupil.

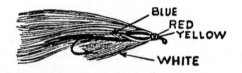

The Frank Gibbs Fly:
#4 Sproat hook, turned down eye
Silver body
 4-inch white impali tied full
Atop the white impali, 3-inch red bucktail
    3-inch barred rock hackle feather on each side
Shorter cheek (tied over hackle feather) of brown
    feather with white rib (1/4-inch long)
Painted white eyes, with red dot for pupil.

Early saltwater fly rodders abandoned the idea that look-alikes were the most effective flies for saltwater fish. They de-emphasized the idea that an effective fly should look like the real thing in the fly patterns they created for striped bass, believing instead that attraction was paramount to preciseness and that pattern and color were more important. Regardless of the motivation, there's no doubt that these early flies proved very effective for striped bass. Catches supported this thinking because their concoctions didn't duplicate a bass's food so much as they acted to get its attention.

Colors now were important, but not for the original reason, and shape and action of the fly were distorted. In fact, they exaggerated colors to enhance a fly's attention-getting abilities. For the most part, saltwater flies duplicate the shape and size of small food fish—spearing, killies, herring, menhaden, mullet, even snapper bluefish and sand eels. Effective striped bass flies were built and shaped like these foods, or something with no comparison in real life except that it grabbed the attention of the bass. Today, the variety of flies in use and offered by striped bass anglers shows some degree of return to the original concept of duplicating color and pattern as closely as possible the real thing. Much of this has been made possible by a great variety of new synthetic material and adhesives. Both types of fly produce fish and the choice is yours. If a natural won't work, switch to an exotic, or visa versa. They both can be found in the three basic styles of saltwater flies: popper or popping bugs, bucktails, and streamers.

Poppers

Popping bugs are surface lures made with either cork or balsa bodies and adorned with either feathers or bucktails on the backsides. The face of the popper can be cupped and angled, and performs as a true popping bug, making a thrashing noise as it is intermittently hauled over the top of the water. Other surface poppers have a flat but slanting face, one that lifts the popper onto the surface. This type really skitters or slides across the top of the water and doesn't set up quite the commotion a regular popper does. It is used when a fast retrieve is desirable. A third type of popper has a pointed or bullet head. This form is retrieved over the surface with a greater speed. It is the favorite of the fast fisherman with a full stripping arm. Each type can effectively take striped bass on the surface.

There are a great variety of poppers constructed. One of the more famous poppers is the Kah-Boom-Boom, tied by "Cap" Colvin of Seaside Park, N.J., one of the founders of the first chapter of the Salt Water Fly Rodders of America. This, is a slim, cup-faced edition, with a few bucktails, either red or white, on a red or white cork body, mounted on a 1/0 to 3/0 hook.

Bucktails

As the name implies, these lures are made of bucktail deer hairs. They are similar to freshwater bucktails except that they are tied on long-shanked, stainless-steel hooks, anywhere from 2/0 to 4/0 in size, though the majority of other saltwater flies are tied on 1/0 hooks. Because striped bass take all their bait and food by the head, short-shanked hooks are equally in order and bass hit them as effectively as flies tied on longer hooks. Longer hooks are used primarily when making bucktails to increase the size of the fly and create a larger area for mounting the materials.

Patterns or colors on bucktails are extremely simple. Most flies are two-color combinations with white dominating in almost all patterns. Black and white, red and white, and even red and yellow, semblances of a Mickey Finn, are all effective. Since bucktails imitate small baitfish, the basic light-and-dark patterns require a lure with a light underside and a dark topside, like the shade patterns in live fish. Additional features are added to the sides of the flies to suggest stripes or bars.

A collection of traditional patterns would include a Palmer Diller, (Harold) Gibbs Striper, (Frank) Gibbs Bucktail, Black Nosed Dace, and several of the Joe Brooks double-tied bucktails, including the Strawberry Blonde (red-orange), Platinum Blonde (white), Honey Blonde (yellow), and Black Blonde. These double-tied bucktails are constructed on a long-shanked hook. The first bucktail is tied just behind the eye as in a standard pattern and then a second tuft is tied on the shank just before the bend. In effect, it extends the bucktail, making it longer than would be possible with a single tuft. The double tie gives the fly more action and the forward tuft even imparts a breathing action. In addition, these flies are large and will appeal to larger striped bass.

Streamers

Streamers are much like bucktails in construction, but made with feathers rather than hairs. However, this doesn't mean that hairs, tinsel, and artificial materials cannot be used in their construction. They are often of multiple-wing construction, either on long- or short-shanked hooks. They include four to six

Poppers for saltwater fishing are generally larger than for fresh water and the hooks are made of nickel or steel. They can range greatly in size for presentations to either small or large bass.

angled feathers that, when compressed by the action of water as they are drawn through the medium, bulk at the front to look like the shoulders or body of a baitfish. Most streamers, as well as bucktails and poppers, have large painted eyes to further simulate the small baitfish striped bass feed upon. Eyes are extremely important in getting the attention of striped bass and are used effectively in all but the smallest streamers.

Marabou feathers find their way into many streamers because of their pulsating effect when pulled through the water with an uneven haul. Newer concoctions are the series of shrimp flies that have blossomed during the past years. Because striped bass do a considerable amount of feeding on grass shrimp, as well as larger shrimp, these flies have become especially popular and productive.

Fry flies are another group. They are composed of eyes, hackles about the hook, and long chenille or Mylar and Saran bodies to imitate long, slinky baitfish, especially small elvers (eels). Some have a tail tuft, and an example of this group was tied by Fred Schrier of Toms River, N.J., long an advocate of fly-fishing for striped bass.

Modern Patterns

More recent fly pattern innovations make ready use of numerous new synthetic materials using which early fly tiers could only dream of using. Here's a partial list from a vast array that are available to Atlantic and Gulf Coast striped bass anglers who wield a willowy rod in salt water. They include: David Olson's Deer Hair Deceiver, Don Avondola's Epoxy Silversides, Eric Peterson's

Bucktails are among the most effective flies used in salt water for striped bass because they can so effectively imitate a bass's natural food and a lure can be large enough to get the attention of a big striper. From left to right, these bucktails are: Mickey Finn, Loving Bass Yellow, Lyman's Terror, Brooks' Blonde, and Grizzly and Yellow.

Baby Bunker, Floating Sand Eel, and Sand Eel, Chico Fernandez' Glass Minnow,
Bob Popovic's Keel Eel and Surf Candy, Farrow Allen's Lefty's Big-Eye De-
ceiver, Lefty Kreh's Lefty Deceiver Olive, Dick Stewart's Loving Bass Fly, Tom
McNally's McNally Smelt, Jim DiGregorio's Pick Fly Herring, Bill Peabody's
Rhody Flat Wing, Jack Gartside's Sand Lance and Soft Hackle Streamer, Bruce
Dorn's Sea Snapper, Don Brown's Silversides, Lou Tabory's Tabory's Slab Side,
Tabory's Snake Fly, and Tabory's Surfboard Foam Fly, Tom Piccolo's Tom's
Blue Back Herring and Tom's Bunker Fly, Charley Waterman's Waterman's
Silver Outcast, Ray Smith's White Water Witch, and Dick Wolf's Wolf's An-
chovy.

West Coast innovators have also created a host of flies that take striped bass
and work equally well on either coast. A partial list of these includes: Dan
Blanton's Blanton's Bay-Delta Eelet, Deep-Water and Chartreuse Flattail, White
Whistlers, Fatal Attraction, Lime Punch, Sar-Mul-Mac Blue Mackerel, Steve
Probaco's Froggy Tandem Herring, Joe Butorac's Krystal Flasher Candlefish,
Farrow Allen's Lambuth Candlefish, and John Shewey's Polar Bear Candlefish

Streamers can be in bizarre patterns that don't imitate anything living but they sure catch striped
bass. Most of these concoctions came from Fred Schrier of Tom's River, N.J. From left to right they
are: marabou streamer, marabou with peacock hackles, eelet with Mylar body, spearing with a good
dose of Mylar, and a hackle streamer.

and Polar Bear Herring.

FLY-FISHING FROM BOATS

Not all fly-fishing for striped bass is done from shore or in the water. A great amount is performed from small fishing boats, 12- to 14-foot car-toppers with flat-bottomed hulls that can drift with the wind across the tops of the grasses at high tide. The 13- and 16-foot Boston Whalers are ideal boats for fly-rodding because of their hull configuration and lateral stability. These boats are so stable and the bow so clear of obstructions that they act as perfect mobile casting platforms.

The prime requirement of a boat that is to be used for fly casting is that it be clear or free of any possible projections or obstructions in or on the bow. If there is the slightest thing that can catch the line, especially when it is coiled on the deck or foredeck, you can be sure that it will eventually foul. All hardware and guard rails should be smooth and unobtrusive. All nails, screws and bolts should be flush with the deck. If it has a removable bow light, so much the better. The ideal deck is a 3-foot square casting platform that projects slightly beyond the boat and is covered with indoor-outdoor carpeting so that the angler has maximum stability when standing there. Of course, the two outside corners are well-rounded.

Water depth in a tidal estuary can vary greatly, and a wading fisherman's reach is limited by the tops of his waders. A small boat becomes invaluable in making the correct approach and presentation to feeding striped bass as well as increasing the area which the angler can cover. It also makes up for short casters. The 80- to 100-foot casters loose their advantage over short casters when the latter is casting from a boat.

Most fly-casting from a boat is done drifting, either with the tidal current in a salt creek and marsh or with the current caused by a wind on the water. This movement is desired and constantly presents fresh, new water to the fly-caster. In one drift, he can cover a surprising amount of water. In the case of a fast drift or too much wind, the boat be slowed down by tying a bucket to a line and tossing it over the side, or by dragging a cinder block or pair of sash weights that won't hang up on the bottom or totally eliminate the boat's drift. In such shallow circumstances, it is best not to use an engine to put you onto the fish. Instead, pole to the spot or run upwind or uptide so that you can drift down onto the spot you'd like to fish.

You can also use a boat at anchor if you want to work a spot that is a consistent bass-producer. With a lot of anchor line, you can pay out a few feet after every cast and cover a lot of territory. In a similar situation, you can also use a boat to chum fish within casting range of your flies. I have chummed with grass shrimp at the edge of a tidal creek and tolled bass to my Mickey Finn. Shrimp patterns can be used in the chum instead of bucktails or streamers.

International Game Fish Association
Striped Bass Records as of 1993

Bass, striped (Salt Water) *Morone saxatilis*

TIPPET CLASS	WEIGHT	PLACE	DATE	ANGLER
2 lb	6 lb 11 oz	Rappahannock R., VA	Nov. 23, 1991	Norman Bartlett
4 lb	8 lb 13 oz	Chesapeake Bay, MD	Oct. 20, 1990	Randy Hunton
8 lb	42 lb	Sacramento R., CA	May 30 1986	Ronald S. Hayashi
12 lb	64 lb 8 oz	Smith River, OR	July 28 1973	Beryl E. Bliss
16 lb	51 lb 8 oz	Smith River, OR	May 18, 1974	Gary L. Dyer
20 lb	Vacant			

Bass, striped (landlocked) *Morone saxatilis*

TIPPET CLASS	WEIGHT	PLACE	DATE	ANGLER
2 lb	19 lb 4 oz	All Amer. Canal, CA	May 15, 1982	Edward J. Cramer
4 lb	22 lb 7 oz	San Luis Res., CA	April 18, 1991	A. L. Whitehurst
8 lb	38 lb	San Luis Rese., CA	May 4, 1991	L. B. Bearden, Jr.
12 lb	40 lb 4 oz	O'Neill Forebay, CA	Dec. 10, 1989	A. L. Whitehurst
16 lb	54 lb 8 oz	O'Neill Forebay, CA	Sept. 17, 1989	A. L. Whitehurst
20 lb	39 lb	O'Neill Forebay, CA	June 1, 1992	A. L. Whitehurst

Bass, whiterock (Hybrid-Fresh Water) *Morone saxatilis* X *Morone chrysops*

TIPPET CLASS	WEIGHT	PLACE	DATE	ANGLER
2 lb	8 lb 8 oz	Anna Res., OR	Oct. 28, 1989	James A. Crofoot
4 lb	9 lb 13 oz	Anna Res., OR	Aug. 12, 1988	James A. Crofoot
8 lb	6 lb 15 oz	L.Wallenpaupak, PA	May 12, 1991	J. Rappenglueck
12 lb	12 lb	Nockamixon L., PA	Oct. 14, 1990	Jonathan Greasor
16 lb	11 lb	Percy Priest, TN	April 7, 1992	Charles Moeling

19

Chumming for Striped Bass

Chumming is an especially effective and highly efficient aid in taking both small and large striped bass. It is something of an art because of the great number of variables involved, and it takes certain skills. However, even the novice or beginning fisherman will have a better than average chance for putting more striped bass into his cooler if he chums. To become really expert at chumming requires only time, an alert mind and of course, chum.

Some anglers object to using chum. One reason is understandable: they dislike the smell, the method of handling, and often the messy boat that results. But chumming does produce fish when other methods fail, and if your goal to catch fish consistently then you may be forced to chum.

The second objection is that chumming isn't sporting. That couldn't be farther from the truth. When it comes to saltwater fishing such a contrived sense of what is sporting and what isn't is snobbish. Chumming isn't always fatal to a striped bass nor does it make catching one a sure thing. It certainly does help— a good chummer could fill the boat with bass when the fish won't strike on plugs or trolled lures if that was his goal. When it comes to catching really big bass, sometimes chumming is the only way to get them to develop an interest in the bait. For the complete bass angler, one who wants to consistently catch fish, chumming must be added to his bag of tricks.

Striped bass normally are very wary fish. In shallow water, their wariness increase as the depth decreases. The chum line in effect helps subdue some of this wariness, enabling you to bring bass closer to the boat and bait. Prospects of a free meal are just too much for a striper to pass up, and when they are in schools they compete among themselves and become even more foolhardy.

Chumming is both old and new to the striped bass scene. A hundred years and more ago, it was the standard procedure when fishing for bass among the Elizabeth Islands and off the bass stands along Buzzards Bay. The numerous striped bass clubs in Massachusetts and Rhode Island practiced bass fishing in a much different manner than we know it today. Typically, the wealthy sportsmen would sleep until the sun rose before taking their allotted places on the bass stands. However, hours before, their guides would have been on the stand starting a chum line going, doling out bushels of cut menhaden, eels, and lobster tails and parts. It seems inconceivable that someone would chum with lobster, but in those days, at $1.50 per hundred, lobster were mere chum. By the time the sports were on the stands, the bass were well tolled and boiling in the surf waiting for tidbits. All the fisherman had to do was select a whole lobster tail, put his hook into it, and toss it into the melee. It may not always have been that simple but often it was.

During the same period, chumming striped bass with soft-shelled clams was practiced on Chesapeake Bay. Without lobsters, Chesapeake Bay fishermen doled out what they had the most of, oysters and clams. This technique of clam chumming in Chesapeake Bay has never waned and for the past century has been among the standard techniques for taking rockfish. Today, most of the bay's 600,000 striped bass fishermen use the clam-chumming technique during at least some part of the year to take striped bass.

Until just a few years ago, one popular chumming technique along the coast from New Jersey to Long Island, Connecticut, and Massachusetts involved the use of grass shrimp. There are several varieties of grass shrimp along our coast and probably all are used at one time or another. Grass shrimp were the preferred bait because striped bass like them and large quantities are readily come by. Grass shrimp, small crustaceans about 1 to 1-1/2 inches in length, closely resemble the shrimp you pick out of a shrimp cocktail. They are easy to find and net in the grass along a tidal creek or marsh. But grass shrimp have been cyclic in abundance, their numbers seeming to parallel the availability of eelgrass along the estuaries.

During the late 1940s and early 1950s, a blight struck the eelgrass beds and they quickly disappeared along the coast, along with brant, weakfish, and grass shrimp. During the blight, chum was difficult to find. However, some enterprising Long Island bass chummers turned to the sea and found skimmer clams and clam bellies, the by-product of the chowder business, an equal if not superior substitute for grass shrimp. Eventually, grass shrimp returned when the eelgrass blight was over, but many chummers stayed with the clams.

Clam bellies are the discard product of skimmer clams. The offshore dragging industry on Long Island produces a great amount of clams that go into canned chowder or deep-fried clams. The discard is the softer parts and the lining of the clam, parts that cannot be used in the chowders. At one time it was thrown away or ground for bluefish chum. However, unground, and along with

Grass shrimp are kept in a bait car off the transom of the boat and doled out at a steady rate to chum bass to a baited hook.

all their juices, the bellies provide a great striped bass enticer. Nowhere has the art of chumming with clam bellies been developed so highly as under the numerous parkway bridges, crossing the bays to the barrier islands, along Long Island's South Shore. It is so popular with striped bass anglers that it comes packed, frozen in 3-gallon tins and selling from $5 to $10 a can, depending upon the season and the demand.

The purpose of chumming is to bring striped bass within the scope of your baited hooks. It is a tease or attraction that, in the water, works something like a smoke signal. A chum line appeals to the striped bass's greatest sense, that of smell, and a chum line can extend a mile or so away from the place where you are waiting, enticing any striped bass which enters the zone of smell and taste you are offering to come on up for more.

CURRENT AND CHUMMING

Aside from the availability of bass, there are several factors that will affect success while chumming. The most important is water current because it is your communications vehicle with the fish. There vehicle a moving tide that will be used to carry your message to the fish, or it can be a current in an estuary where a freshwater river or stream enters the briny. Whichever, you cannot chum effectively without it. Nor can you chum very well at the top of the tide or at dead low when the water flow has stopped. And, too much current can reduce your effectiveness. It thins out the chum, interfering with its continuity, that fish will have a difficult time following it to its source or pinpointing the baited hook.

The amount of tide or current, then, is a factor you must consider above all others when selecting a site to chum. The current should be strong enough to carry your chum away from the boat so that you can fish a minimum of 50 feet down tide.

As the tide rises and falls, the degree or speed of the current will change. You must alter your chumming to meet these variables. In a fast current you may have to use more chum to keep the chum line connected. In a slow current, your chum should be reduced so that all the tidbits don't pile up under the boat and provide a competing mouthful of chum rather than the baited hook for your bass. A good current is necessary to increase the length of your chum line. The longer the line, the more fish you are likely to intercept and attract. If you are fishing a defined area, like a deep hole in a shallow flat or the space under a bridge or along a sod bank, then you might not want an especially long chum line. In such cases, you already have some idea where your bass might be. But in an open bay or along a beach, where you are chumming blind, the longer the chum line, the better your chances are for success.

WATER DEPTH

The next variable to consider is the water's depth. There is a minimum as well as a maximum. I have effectively chummed striped bass while anchored in 3 feet of water. It was tricky and required real silence in the boat and a current so that I was taking fish 100 to 150 feet away. If I had to try to take them closer to the boat in a slow current at that depth, I'm afraid the boat might have spooked the fish.

It's difficult to say what might be the maximum depth. I don't like to chum in water more than 20 or 25 feet deep, but it can be done. The problem here is chum dispersal. The deeper the water in which you chum, the wider will be the spectrum the chum develops, both in depth as well as width. This places your baited hook in too large an area in which striped bass must hunt to find it. I believe the ideal chumming depth is somewhere between 10 and 15 feet of water, and the ideal current is one moving at 1 or 2 knots.

WHERE TO CHUM

Deciding where to chum can be a big problem if you are working a new body of water or at a stage of the tide during which you have not regularly fished. The best place to chum is where you know stripers can be found. Chum in natural areas that have something to attract bass. You can chum along a barren beach

One of the best sites to chum for striped bass with clam bellies is under a bridge. Bass seek the bridge's protection during the day and its abutments cause scouring and deepen holes that add to this sense of protection. When day-time fishing is good, night-time fishing is usually even better.

if the current is running parallel to it. You can chum off a point, off the end of a jetty or groin, or along the edge of a sod bank where the water will eventually feed a hole. You can chum under bridges where striped bass come to feed on the life around the barnacles and grass, or along the edges of a rip where bass wait for feed to come their way. You can chum just about anywhere there is a current and a natural reason for striped bass to congregate.

Most chumming today is done from an anchored boat. However, in the past, most chumming was done from a point of land. Today, an angler can effectively chum from a bridge when he is land-bound. Some of the best catches of striped bass along the south shore of Long Island are around the numerous bridges and causeways that crisscross the several bays. In New Jersey, some of the better chumming sites are off the ends of the numerous jetties or groins, long, finger-shaped piles of rock and riprap designed to keep beaches from eroding.

The anchored boat, however, makes the presentation of the chum and bait easier. The angler can more precisely pick the place in the current where the chum line can flow most effectively to the striped bass.

HOW MUCH, HOW OFTEN, AND HOW LONG?

The rate of chumming will be determined by the speed of the current and the depth of the water over which you are anchored. Chumming for bluefish is easily figured out. The chum line must be continuous, and you ladle the chum into the water at a regular rate. However, when it comes to striped bass, chumming is a miserly operation, and the danger here is to chum too freely. The object of chumming striped bass is to get them to your hook, teasing them with just enough tidbits to keep them moving up the chum line. If you feed them too much, then they'll lie back, waiting for the food to come, and never get to that morsel with the hook. In such cases, you may never know if the bass were there or not.

It is far better to under chum than to over chum. Chumming for stripers is an intermittent affair. You toss a few shrimp into the water, breaking the backs on some so that they will die and sink to the bottom. Others will swim slowly with the tide. I once fished with an angler who doled out one small shrimp every minute, and we did quite well. The rate is something that is determined by practice, and no one can tell you exactly how much to dole off the side of your boat.

In the case of clam bellies, chumming is a combination of their juices and body parts. The technique is to stick your hand into the can of chum, grab a fistful, and then stick your fist into the water alongside the boat. You don't release it, at least not at first. You hold it there for a few minutes, letting the current wash off your hand and accompanying clam juices. Then, you gently squeeze—only once—the contents of your fist. A minute later, you squeeze it again. After five or six squeezing intervals, you open your fist, just a bit, letting some of the body parts drift out. Slowly, it is all washed away. Needless to say, the best time to chum is on a warm July or August evening...when the water is warm.

How long to chum can vary greatly. Most chummers will give a spot they know, which has produced bass in the past, half an hour to an hour of time, if the current is moving well, before deciding that the fish just aren't in this hole. If the tide is slow at making up, they may stretch it to an hour and a half or two hours before finding another location. Once you have laid down a streak of prime bass chum, giving it up too soon can be a waste of money as well as fishing effort. To move means that you must start all over again, and at best it will take half an hour if the bass are somewhere within the scope of your chum line before you can expect one to take a baited hook. The fish have, however, occasionally made a liar out of me and moved into a chum line less than ten minutes after anchoring the boat.

TYPES OF CHUM

Chum can be made up of anything on the menu of a striped bass, and that constitutes just about everything that lives in a marine environment, and some things that don't. The three most popular types of chum are grass shrimp, clam bellies, and clamworms. Grass shrimp are obtainable by netting along most creeks and tidal marshes, almost anywhere that good beds of eelgrass or other aquatic grasses are available for protection.

At high tide, the shrimp are up into the grass and may be difficult to locate. At low tide, they may be out of the creeks and into deeper channels waiting for the water to return. Mid-tide will find them at a wadable depth, and two anglers, stretching a small-gauge net across a creek and walking against the current, should be able to fill their shrimp car in a few minutes.

Once the shrimp are caught, they are kept in a floating wooden box (car) with screened sides to allow fresh seawater to flow through and a lid on top for retrieving shrimp when needed. The shrimp car is tethered off the stern of the boat. Shrimp held in a pail inside the boat need a lot of fresh seawater added to keep them alive. Two to three quarts of shrimp should be more than adequate to fish one tide. One tide involves about four hours of actual fishing time.

Shrimp are liable to swim away from your chum line if the current is not strong enough to keep them in line. In such cases, and even when there is plenty of current around, shrimp should be fed slowly into the water and every second or third shrimp should be pinched to kill or wound it. If the current is swift, the shrimp should be tossed ahead of the boat so that they land on the bottom closer to the stern of your craft. In slower water, they can be broadcast off the back. Some anglers like to throw a handful of shrimp at a time and then not chum again for five or ten minutes. Others keep shrimp going over the side at a regular rate, with a few extra added every third or fourth time.

In many areas where sandworms or clamworms are plentiful, successful anglers chum with them. They are a natural bait, and striped bass are especially fond of worms during the spring and early summer months. The technique is much the same as when chumming with shrimp. A sandworm is cut into six or eight pieces and then one or two pieces are dropped into the water every minute or so. One school of clamworm chummers prefers to cut up an entire sandworm and toss all the pieces in at once, then wait about five minutes before giving the water another dose of the same amount of worms.

Bloodworms or marine tapeworms work just as well as sandworms. With sandworms approaching $5 a dozen today, this technique may become too expensive, much the same as chumming with lobster tails. However, if you are willing to dig your own worms and have a sand or mud flat at low tide nearby where you can do it, you can still chum with these baits.

Clam bellies as chum are increasing rapidly in popularity. One reason has been the increased cost in other baits and the ready availability of frozen clam bellies. Almost every coastal bait shop now has them available. Frozen clams are as good as those that have been thawed out the night before.

Mix the clam bellies with equal amounts of seawater to form a clam broth. This clam broth is just as valuable as the bellies, maybe even more so. And the broth gives clams an advantage over shrimp. It is so full of flavor, like a concentrated bouillon, that it is a great fish attractor with very little food or calories in it. Another clam-belly technique, a variation on the one described earlier, is to scoop out a ladle of broth and bits and spread it over the water, then grab a belly or two in your hands and squeeze the juices out and into the water before letting the clam fall into the current. This is repeated about every five or ten minutes, depending upon how well the current is moving and how well the bass are responding.

To make the chum go even farther, some anglers mix in a bit of sand. The sand takes on some of the chum flavor and in the water it drops first and paves a chum line on the bottom. You can even mix broken shells bits and some anglers even pulverize them for added effect.

Soft clams can be used as well as clam bellies that come from ocean and skimmer clams found farther offshore. Soft clams and bank mussels are pounded to a pulp with a potato masher or the end of a 2x4 to form a stew of meat and shells. This is ladled into the water every few minutes, and the shells do for these clams what the sand does for the clam bellies.

In the Chesapeake Bay area, where crabs are especially plentiful, a considerable amount of chumming is done with blue crabs, fiddlers, hermits, or any crab form available. Crabs are cut or chopped into small pieces and dispersed at intervals into the water. Large pieces are likely to fall too quickly and often pile just behind the boat. The smaller pieces are more likely to be carried farther astern and increase the length of your chum line.

Fish can also be used for chum and was the preferred material at the Elizabeth Island bass clubs. The oilier the better, and menhaden or mossbunker were the favorite. Mackerel also found their way into the chum slick, and these oily fish broadcast far and wide that there is a free meal to be had. These fish are cut into small pieces, some even ground, then mixed with seawater and doled off the boat or into the surf. The only drawback with this type of chum is that it also attracts bluefish and is best used early and late in the season, when the water is too cold for the blues.

Small baitfish are also used to chum bass. Spearing and small bunker are favorites. The small fish can be chopped up or just cut in two, with scatterings of whole fish mixed with the pieces. Securing this kind of chum can be a problem unless you have a fine meshed net with you or you set traps for the young fish in a tidal creek when hunting for grass shrimp. Don't toss away any small fish; they can be used as bait if not chum.

FISHING TECHNIQUES WITH CHUM

The thoughtful chummer will quietly approach the place he intends to begin chumming, often drifting to the area after cutting his boat's engine, and then anchoring. In a steady current with little or no wind, one anchor off the bow will be enough to keep the boat in place in the current. But with a variable current and a wind on the surface, you can be swaying back and forth over 15 or 20 feet and produce a sloppy chum line, one difficult for the fish to follow toward your baited hook. In this situation, you will have to double-anchor your boat or straddle the current. The double-anchor technique here is to drop one hook and see that it takes a bite, then motor uptide, off the first anchor, and drop the second. By adjusting the length of the lines, the boat can be brought to any position in the current. Straddling the current—that is, with the boat at right angles to the current and an anchor off the bow and a second off the transom— is an especially effective way to anchor when you have two or more anglers in the boat. All can get an even chance at the chum slick. However, a word of caution here is in order: don't anchor cross-current if the tide moves with any great speed; you might capsize.

Another variation on anchoring with two anchors but still having the bow heading into the current is to drop your first hook and pay out enough line until you are well anchored and approximately where you want to chum. Then pay out an additional 30 feet and drop a navy-type anchor. Ease up on your stern line and take up on the bow anchor line and when you are back to your original location you can then snub up both lines. The navy anchor should be to either side, just off the current line and not directly down current of the boat. The bit of side current on the boat keeps it from swinging. The navy-type anchor will hold because of its bulk and weight, and while it won't keep you exactly in place you will not swing so wide of your chum as to lose its effectiveness.

Tackle in a chum slick can be either spinning gear or a conventional reel and rod. I prefer the latter because it is easier to handle the line, and line-handling is an important part of the fishing technique in chumming. If you select a spinning outfit, it should consist of fairly stiff rod, one between 7 and 8 feet long, with an equally stiff tip so that you can set the hook firmly on large striped bass. You can chum up almost any size bass, from 3-pound schoolies to behemoths of 50 and 60 pounds. However, if you are working a school of strictly small fish, you might better match the tackle to the size of the fish.

If you are chumming near obstructions like docks, bridge pilings, and bulkheads, you will want a fairly strong line, and 20-pound test monofilament should be your minimum. This should be piled onto a spinning reel capable of holding 200-300 yards and with a good drag in case you nail a large striped bass. With a spinning outfit, the line is paid into the current and chum slick with the bail open. After the current begins pulling it out, the bait is allowed to drift back at a pace just about that of the current. If it moves too fast, you can slow it down by forcing the line between your finger and the housing of the reel.

Retrieval is not with a steady, upstream pull. Instead the bait is jerked like a shrimp or squid swimming through the water. This gives any bass around the impression that the bait is swimming against the current. This action is more likely to catch the attention of a striped bass than a steady pull back to the boat. It can be imparted by reeling, but is better done with the tip of the rod.

I prefer to chum using a heavy freshwater bait-casting outfit or a medium saltwater outfit. I like a level-wind reel, equipped with a star drag and fished on a 6- to 7-foot rod. I have even chummed with a light trolling outfit when I knew that 40- and 50-pound striped bass were in the hole I was feeding. But even here, for the size of the bass, the rod was light, a balanced 20-pound outfit.

I think the trolling or level-wind reel is the better choice in a chumming situation because a fisherman can better work his line on the down-drift of the bait. The reel can be put into free spool with a thumb on the spool in case of an unexpected strike and the line can be hand-pulled off the spool and fed into the current. I like to fish either 20- or 30-pound test Dacron with a 10-foot monofilament leader of approximately the same test. The Dacron can easily be marked with a waterproof pen at 10-foot intervals. Knowing exactly how far your bait is astern the boat is invaluable after the first strike. With a marked line, you know just how far back the bass are lying and when you can anticipate a strike. Also, if you know that you are anchored 60 feet above a hole you can pay out the correct amount of line and be in the right place, rather than hoping you are there and maybe always being too short or too long. Line measurements are just as valuable for the serious chummer as for the successful troller.

I don't like to fish more than 200 or 250 feet of line off the end of a boat in a chum slick. Beyond that distance, I feel out of touch. I let the current pull the line off the reel and occasionally slow it up to let the current lift the bait off the bottom. Otherwise, it is liable to lodge on something and nothing but a belly in the line will go out.

The baited hook should always drift just a slight bit slower than a free-floating or drifting piece of chum. This difference in drift rate within the chum line is likely to attract a striper that otherwise might be hesitant. The line is paid out until about 200 feet of it is in the water, then begin the slow, sporadic, and jerking retrieve until the bait is again back to the boat. After a quick inspection of the bait, let the current pull it out again after stripping off enough footage for

To keep the source of chum coming from one point, so the bass don't become confused, this shrimp chummer has double-anchored his boat off a thatch bed.

the effect of the current to begin its task. After three or four such retrievals, the bait is liable to be waterlogged and lost most of its taste and smell. Bait should be changed frequently. Add the old bait to the chum slick and put on a new one; you can't afford to be frugal when it comes to the bait on your hook.

Hooking bass in a chum slick can be a ticklish task. Live bait, or bait that once was alive, is approached differently by striped bass when compared to the strike of a lure or trolled bait. They may taste it externally before ever mouthing it. Often, striped bass will swallow clam bellies before you have any idea that they have taken in the food. Other times, they may gently mouth the shrimp or cut bait and you can only tell they have it if you always have the line between your fingers.

When striking clam bellies or cut bait, bass may only take it into their mouths and swim off. It is important that there be little or no drag on the line. This can easily be accomplished with a conventional reel set on free spool but with the slight drag of a click left engaged. As soon as the bass stops or makes a telltale rush, the drag can be engaged and the fish hooked.

More often than not, striped bass feeding in a chum slick will hook themselves if the hooks are sharp and of the proper shape. I use a variety of sizes, ranging from a 1/0 for grass shrimp to 4/0 or 5/0 on cut bait, with clam bellies on a 3/0 hook. I also prefer the Eagle Claw shape and the bait-holding barbs on its shaft. These are also especially good when stringing on several sandworms or several clam bellies when they are used as the bait.

Which bait to use on your hook can be a matter of personal choice. The generally accepted rule is to bait up with a glob of the firmer parts of clam belly when chumming with clams, to use two or three shrimp on a hook when chumming with shrimp, or a of couple sandworms, whole, when chumming with worms. The hooks and barbs are left exposed so that the fish can more readily hook itself.

However, there is no reason why you cannot chum with grass shrimp and bait your hook with worms, or mix any other combination. They have all worked at times. When I chum with clam bellies, I will also dig or buy a couple of dozen skimmer clams, use the muscles on the hooks, and add the bellies to the rest of the chum. Clam bellies are nearly impossible to keep on the hook, and you are likely to find only small bits of muscle left over in the chum you buy. If you work the bait up-current properly, the bellies are likely to slip off.

When using crabs, half or even a quarter of a crab can be enough to bait a hook. The crab is hooked and then tied onto the shaft. Many anglers use a piece of Dacron line, but I carry a small spool of soft wire in my tackle box to save making knots with slippery fingers.

Most striped bass in a chum slick are likely to be found near the bottom at the end of your chum line, but they work progressively toward the surface as they approach the source. A good technique, especially when two or three anglers are fishing out of the same boat, is to fish a line on the bottom, one somewhere near the middle, and the third, a high line, often just under the surface. A line with just hook and bait is likely to float just under the top, buoyed up by the current. To get your line deeper won't normally require a lot of weight. I prefer split shot, 2 or 3 feet ahead of the hook.

In a really fast current, trying to keep the bait on the bottom while in close to the boat may require a 1- or 2-ounce bank sinker. But if you fish 100 or more feet behind your boat in 10 to 15 feet of water, all you will need is two or three large split shot.

Striped bass must feed and if anything can get them to move for food it is a well laid chum line. Chumming is also a contemplative method for taking striped bass, and if anything ever impresses you on the first trip you take with an experienced chummer, it is the silence that is an integral part of his fishing method.

20

Striped Bass Fishing At Night

When the sun goes down and the stars come out, the view is just as different for striped bass as it is for the striped bass fisherman. This nighttime world, however, is completely familiar to the fish. To most fishermen, it often seems a perpetual first-time experience, a kind of fishing to which one never really becomes adjusted. It is totally unlike striped bass fishing under the sun. But to the truly dedicated striped bass angler, the night is the only time to fish.

Night fishing can often be the most productive in terms of striped bass caught, for the angler willing to master an entirely different set of fishing techniques. The differences aren't caused simply by the lack of light. The entire approach and attitude of the angler must come about 180 degrees. Usually, for those who are willing to make this adjustment and to put up with the various inconveniences of fishing in the dark, the rewards are worth the extra effort.

The most obvious reason for fishing at night is that the striped bass is a nocturnal as well as a diurnal fish, with perhaps more emphasis on the nocturnal aspects than most fishermen realize. The anatomical make-up of the striped bass—the rod development in the eyes for night vision, its great eye size, and its exceptionally well developed olfactory system—indicates a creature highly organized for living and feeding in the dark. Feeding studies conducted by biologists also point to this same conclusion: the most likely time striped bass will be on the move looking for food is from dusk to midnight and again just before daybreak. If for no other reasons than these, you should fish striped bass at night.

There are other reasons. In some of the areas where striped bass are known to concentrate, fishing pressures during the day can be so great that it is impossible to fish effectively. Sandy Hook, Montauk Point, Watch Hill, Sow and Pigs Reef, Point Bonita, and many more such areas along our coasts get such great fishing pressure, both from private anglers and from charterboat skippers, that effective and enjoyable fishing can be near to impossible. These conditions are compounded on warm, windless weekends during the summer months when the boating horde all but drives the fish off these natural feeding grounds.

But come sunset, the stream of boats heading back to port is like a traffic jam on the Long Island Expressway. The traffic in the other direction is almost nil, or so minimal that you occasionally like to see another red and green light bobbing next to yours just to assure you that you aren't on the River Styx.

Aside from the aesthetic disadvantages of crowded fishing, there are practical disadvantages. A lot of boat traffic, especially in shallow water, will alter the feeding habits of striped bass. One of the best examples comes from my own back yard on Long Island Sound. A few miles west of where the Nissequogue River empties into Smithtown Bay is an area known locally as The Brickyards. Near the turn of the century a barge loaded with bricks capsized in a midwinter storm and the bricks settled to the bottom in 10 to 15 feet of water, just 100 yards off the beach. A freshwater stream from a small pond behind a barrier beach also seeps through in this area. This combines with the brick-strewn bottom to produce some pretty good bass fishing during the summer months.

When I first began fishing the Brickyards, it wasn't too difficult a chore to take an occasional bass from the area throughout the day. But over the year, as more and more people moved from New York City to suburban Long Island,

Striped bass are extremely active during the dark hours, and the nighttime angler is apt to get both more fish and bigger fish. Here the author battles a striped bass that fell to a live eel.

they bought boats, began fishing or else and the daily fishing pressure as well as boat traffic increased greatly. The bass almost entirely abandoned the area during the daylight hours. During a typical August, I like to anchor my boat over the bricks and drift live eels with the current off the transom. I take fish continuously, with steady success, until a powerboat approaches and whizzes over the area and the fish stop biting. An hour or so later, they begin again, if no more boats streak over the spot. During recent years, the traffic has been so steady that the fish refuse to come into the shallows, even for the best-looking eels fresh from the pot. But as the day wanes and night approaches, boat traffic all but dies, and the fish are less wary about approaching the shallows. Fortunately, they still feed there throughout the night and fishing is less complicated.

Another reason to fish at night is the day-to-night migration that striped bass often make from deep to shallow water. Striped bass feel more at ease in the protection of deep water and as long as they are not feeding will more than likely stay put. But the protection of deep water becomes less of a factor as night approaches. Striped bass will abandon it to feed in water often so skimpy that their backs are in the air. At night, bass are more likely to haunt the beaches looking for food that normally wouldn't tempt them during the day, following bait into shallower water. Nighttime trolling in the shallows, or casting while your boat is drifting along the beach bumping into the bottom, will produce more bass than the same techniques during the day.

Even for the surf fisherman, nighttime bass fishing is far more productive, and he needn't try to reach the outer comber or bar for bass. Often the fish will be swimming around his feet or close thereby. The best surf catches are consistently made at night during June, July, August and September. But come October and November, while night fishing still reigns supreme, at times, it can be almost as good during the day when the migration is at its peak. This might be one reason one sees so many surfcasters who make a several-day jaunt of a fishing trip, and sleep in their campers during the day, only to come out at night to fish.

Another factor that can justify fishing at night is the routine of many striped bass foods. One of the favorite foods along the New Jersey, Long Island, and New England coasts is the sandworm or clamworm. This salty annelid burrows into the mud during the day and leaves its hole to feed and find other sandworms only once the sun goes down. Striped bass are more active feeders at night because more sandworms are then available, and the fish adjusts its feeding habits to those of its food. Likewise, striped bass anglers must adjust their fishing habits to the feeding habits of the bass.

Still another reason to fish during the night might be the occurrence of the right tide. Some bass anglers fish strictly by the tides, regardless of the time of day. A flooding or falling tide may be the only time striped bass will feed at a particular rip. And if that tide occurs during the dark, then this is **the** time that you, too, should be there.

Lastly, during especially hot summers, in late July and August, the water in certain bays and estuaries can rise above 75 and 80 degrees and put the fish off their feeding routine during the day. The 70-degree mark is a temperature barrier that most adult striped bass will not cross. They avoid water this warm and seek cooler depths. Until the hot spells are over they will be active only at night. During the late night and just before daybreak, temperatures along the shallows and in the surf can cool enough that striped bass will come inshore to feed. Under these conditions, this means that night fishing is the only approach to success .

FISHING TECHNIQUES AT NIGHT

All the methods used to take striped bass during the day will work effectively at night, but of these, three are even more productive in the dark: surfcasting, trolling, and drift-fishing. It's difficult to say which is the more popular or more effective, and after a while, it becomes a matter of personal choice.

Surf Fishing

Surf fishing is even more effective during the night than during the day, as I have said. At night, striped bass abandon the deeper haunts and chase fish into the surf and among the rocks and suds. This is the time when the jetty jockeys really come into their own, and striped bass are taken where none could even be chummed during the brighter hours of the day.

Needless to say, fishing the surf and jetties and among the boulders at night can be hazardous if not approached with some degree of caution. It is safest to fish in pairs and to keep a constant chatter flowing. Lights are taboo except when gaffing a fish, so you can't keep shining a searchlight about to see where your buddy is or how he is doing.

Spinning rods and reels are less popular at night because of the greater possibility of fouling. Level-wind baitcasting reels are better suited to fishing in the dark, and even the larger closed-face spin-casting reels are better because they are almost foul-proof. But they aren't made large enough for big surf fishing and not too many find their way onto the marine scene.

At night, striped bass are apt to approach the top of the water as well as come closer to the shore. Thus swimming surface plugs and poppers work well. On a quiet night, without wind and with little wave action, you can hear striped bass feeding and splashing about on the surface as they chase baitfish. A popper plug is at its most effective under such circumstances. But to cast at night requires some skill on the part of the angler. It is difficult to cast into the dark, not knowing where or when your plug hits the water—or who it hits if you are a wild caster.

If you're fishing an established hotspot for striped bass you'd better also come prepared with a large dose of patience, because everything that can go wrong during the day will go wrong in the dark. And, there are sometimes other anglers in the surf who can help it come to such an end. A tangle of lines and lures, especially with a bass on the end that decides to run up and down the beach in the dark rather than out to sea, can put a score of surf fishermen out of action for hours. It requires the wisdom of Solomon to untangle such messed lines with everyone claiming the fish. It might be a good idea to scratch your name onto the plug before you go casting it into the dark.

Trolling

Some anglers consider trolling the most effective nighttime method, but it requires a good bit of boat-handling savvy. The first prerequisite is an intimate knowledge of the waters you plan to fish. You must know how to get out of the harbor, inlet, or port in the dark, and even more important, how to return in the dark. You must be familiar with the buoys and lighthouses as well as prominent land features. Street and shore lights will appear during the night that you never knew existed during the day. If you learn where they are, you can put them to valuable navigational use. Further, you need a lighted compass by which to travel and a fathometer that lights up enough that you can read its figures.

You should be able to handle your boat in pitch darkness. Be thankful for moonlit nights—they are added bonuses. Lights for night fishing are taboo, except those boat lights required for navigation by the Coast Guard. You can beat the problem of light shining on the water by mounting inside deck lights that shine down on the deck, from under the gunwale and not over it. Running lights are required, but if yours are too bright, they will turn off the bass and even annoy other nearby anglers.

So much for navigation.

Trolling at night should usually be done over areas with which you have become familiar during the day. You should know, or should have developed, a set of ranges or trolling patterns over these home waters. The fathometer will help you keep these same patterns, and you can check them as well against lighted landmarks on the beach. More than likely, you will be fishing closer to the beach at night than during the day, so you'd better be familiar with the bumps on the bottom and those that stick out of the water at all tides. The best way to learn about them is to spend some time at low tide, during the daylight hours, mentally or actually plotting the locations of boulders, shallow bars, sunken obstructions, natural cuts in the bars, and kelp beds.

When trolling during the day, you can get some idea of the depth of your lure from the angle the line makes with the water. At night, this is difficult to do, so you must have measured and marked your line to let you know how much of it is in the water. A tachometer on the boat also comes into greater play. You judge your speed during the day by watching objects in the water pass the hull of your boat or landmarks slowly march past. At night, you have only the tachometer as your traveling friend.

Choice of bait and lures also changes somewhat at night. Eels are more active then and are thus preferred. Eels can be live, hooked through the lip, or rigged with lead heads for trolling. Eel skins and plugs with eel skins are also widely used. Sandworms and large spinner combinations trolled especially slowly are also standard favorites in protected areas and places with little or no current. In areas where water moves and rips, or where the tide piles over shoals, the white bucktail jig and white or yellow pork rind are established winner. Night and day jigging techniques are the same.

"Fire in the water," or phosphorescence, can put the jinx on your nighttime trolling or casting. During the warmer months of the summer in northern seas, the waters are filled with uncountable billions of one-celled microscopic plants and animals collectively called plankton. These drifting organisms provide the initial food for many crustaceans and fishes as the first link in a long food chain, often ending with man.

Fish, if they don't swim too fast, do not disturb the zooplankton enough to make it glow. But metallic lines, lures, boats, or almost anything else that moves at a rapid rate will irritate the little critters and cause the plankton to glow. The hull of a boat can set up such a glow that the rig looks like a meteor crashing through the water. The cause of all this firewater is a microscopic protozoan called *Noctiluca milaris*. Compared to other plankton forms, *Noctiluca* is rather large, with a swollen, bladdery appearance. It has one flagellum (tail hair), and is colored a faint red under the microscope. It feeds only on living organisms. This protozoan is capable of an intense glow, but only when physically or chemically stimulated. It floats in our seas and is the chief cause of marine phosphorescence.

Striped bass naturally refuse such an apparition. On moonlit nights, the phosphorescence is greatly reduced or totally eliminated. When the sun is on the moon's other side, the minute animals glow with any disturbance of the water. There's nothing you can do about it. This usually occurs from July and August into September, even October in more northern parts of the striped bass's range, from New Jersey north to the Gulf of St. Lawrence.

Trolling speeds at night should be conducted just as slowly as possible. The fish have lost the use of most of their sense of sight, but smell and hearing take over except on brightly lit full-moon nights. Coupled with slow trolling is the use of small boats. It is far better to use a small boat—a car-topper, flat-bottomed skiff, or something like the 16-foot Boston Whaler—to duck in and out among the rocks than a large sportfisherman. Smaller boats also require less power and you can hang a smaller engine on the transom, one that will create less noise than the big mill used to push you about during the day. You are in no hurry while night fishing. If you do have a large, immovable unit on your transom, you can augment it with a bracket and small engine alongside for night trolling and getting close to the beach.

Better yet, go with a really small boat and use your muscles for some rowing power. This is best conducted in a protected cove or bay, with a small engine for emergencies and getting to and from your fishing waters. With a pair of oars you can troll slowly enough for the laziest of bass.

Still- and Drift-Fishing

Fishing at anchor or while drifting at night are thoroughly enjoyable ways to spend an evening. In addition, they can produce some especially large striped bass. Drifting, in a sense, is like slow-trolling. If you aren't especially familiar with your waters at night, still-fishing is a gradual approach to learning what they are like. You can pretty well plot your way to a spot and back, and rest without fear of running aground while you are at anchor. You can learn the landmarks and coastal lights better from a sitting position and make them a part of your night-fishing lore.

Most still-fishing involves live bait, and again the eel is one of the preferred baits. It can be fished at anchor or while drifting. But you must know your bottom. Still-fishing with eels is best done around rocks or over a smooth bottom with some degree of running tide. The eel is left to swim and drift on its own. If there is a lot of kelp or grass in the area, the eel will bury itself in the safety of the grass and won't be working for you or any potential bass that might come your way. Chumming is also very effective at night, and is easily practiced without boat traffic running across your chum line or someone else fishing the tail end of it for you.

Noise is kept at minimum while night fishing at anchor because bass are relying more on their ears than eyes as danger receptors. You can also anchor closer to the rocks and beach at night because the bass are more likely to approach your boat under night conditions. The only time you are allowed to turn on the lights while still-fishing is when you are boating or gaffing a bass. The only other exception is when you must flash your beacon to warn an approaching boat. Usually your running lights are turned off while at anchor, and the signal is needed to warn other boats of your presence and position.

In addition to live eels, live mackerel and bunker can be fished at night. The technique of drifting is as effective as working from an anchored craft. These baits can be fished by a boat underway, or while stemming a tide. When striped bass approach live bait, like eels or bunker, the bait becomes especially active, a warning that a strike might happen at any moment.

Fish taken on live bait usually hook themselves and you can let them run. In the case of eels or bunker, striped bass will take them by the head almost every time. If they don't, they run, stop, and turn the baitfish around to swallow it head first, and hook themselves. The barb is usually left exposed with such baits, making the self-hooking that much easier.

As a rule, heavier lines are used when fishing at night because of the obscurity of the waters. Hooked fish may head for deeper water or run along the shore, among the boulders and pilings, and the heavier line acts as a slight safety margin against fraying. It is also a plus when you hook an unexpectedly large fish. Even the largest bass move in close to the beach to chase foods, and you can never tell what has struck your bait until it heads the opposite way.

For an entire night's fishing, it might be a good idea to combine techniques. I like to troll for the first few hours after sunset. When it really gets dark, I head for a spot that has proved productive and anchor, or drift live bait into the area. As daybreak approaches and I get itchy to move about again, I'll switch back to trolling if the action has been slow. However, if either method continues to pay off, there is little sense in switching. There's no need to.

Nighttime is not too far away

21

Striped Bass Fishing
in Fresh Water

The freshwater environment is considerably different from the marine habitat in which striped bass live, and it is not just loss of salt. The entire interdependency of the food chain is structured differently and striped bass in turn respond differently. The differing environments pose no problem for this fish, it's often the angler who must readjust his or her thinking to get back on the track of catching fish. The first experience of chasing striped bass in fresh water is likely to be disappointing to the long-time saltwater angler if he does it strictly on his own. His cherished fish has suddenly become a stranger to him and he must learn a whole new set of tactics.

But to the experienced freshwater fisherman who suddenly finds that a reservoir or lake at home has been stocked with striped bass, the learning of how to catch them is often little more than an extension of fishing lore he already possesses. Nevertheless, even the knowledgeable freshwater angler, in a new environment and after a new species of fish, must do some homework before he can expect to take striped bass with any degree of regularity.

Many freshwater anglers now find themselves in this position because of the great expansion in the man-made distribution striped bass have had in the last several years. Striper bass were planted in almost every newly created, and several well established, impoundments as techniques for transfer and hatchery reproduction became refined and enlarged. Impoundments that for years yielded black bass, sauger, crappie, and several species of perch, suddenly began producing cane-pole-busting fish, the striped bass.

There is no great mystery about how to catch striped bass in fresh water if you can develop a bit of knowledge about the fish as well as the impoundments in which you are fishing. Striped bass in freshwater environments act neither like a saltwater striper nor like a freshwater largemouth or smallmouth bass. Instead they act a lot more like the walleyed pike, sauger, or even the white bass, a close and kissin' cousin. Striped bass in fresh water are a tighter-schooling fish than when found in salt water and are not as apt to spend a lot of time in shallow water except when their food is chased there. In fresh water, striped bass feed more often than in salt water, and thus are more likely to be found where their food is swimming.

FRESHWATER SEASONS

There are good and poor seasons for catching striped bass in fresh water just as there are in salt water, but they are not as closely tied to migrations as in the ocean. Striped bass can be caught in landlocked situations throughout the entire year, with the slowest period during the warm days from mid-July to late September.

Much of our early freshwater stripe bass lore was developed on Santee-Cooper, the fabulous impoundment in South Carolina which is responsible for most of the striped bass populations now stocked throughout the Southern states, from the Carolinas to California. But here the fishing season gets its annual rejuvenation or revival about the end of March, when the blueback herring migrate from the Atlantic and pass through the locks on the Pinopolis Dam. They are allowed in to replenish herring populations in the reservoirs.

Striped bass begin feeding on the bluebacks as they spawn and after they themselves take part in their own annual ritual. Striped bass in most freshwater impoundments, because of the latitude at which most are located, spawn from late February through May. After this act, they put on a feeding frenzy that is matched again only in the fall.

From about the first of March until near the end of April, striped bass are not as grouped or schooled as they are during other times of the year. At this season, they also prefer, especially in Santee-Cooper, to feed near or on the bottom, and cut bait, especially herring, has proved to be the best striper producer. After spawning, however, they go for more wiggle in their food, and from the end of April to the end of May, live herring, or gizzard and threadfin shad where herring are missing, are the preferred baits. This baitfishing falls off about the beginning of July because the bass have eaten most of the adults and those that remain are difficult to find, even for stripers.

July usually heralds a slowdown in striped bass activity. The fish have followed their forage fish to deeper water and stay there throughout the summer. The best fishing technique to use until late September is trolling. And though it is difficult to troll in many impoundments, with their loads of stumps and brush piles, large plugs that swim and dive deeply are now the best producers of fish. If you've located a school in deep water, jigging is then the

A fine mess o' bass. You can tell these fish were taken in fresh water because no marine angler worth his salt would string up his catch like a bunch of black bass.

most effective method. When striped bass were first stocked in many reservoirs, especially those in the Midwest, anglers had difficulty finding them in the huge impoundments during summer months. Most had never used depth recorders or didn't know how to use the ones they had. However, the development of paper graph recorders made finding striped bass in a big reservoir much easier.

With the first hint of fall, the numerous herring and shad that were spawned in the spring are now bite-size baits for striped bass. The fish seem to come out of their doldrums as well as deep water and begin to feed ravenously on schools of these baitfish. At these times of the year, gull-watching really pays off. Gulls in fresh water are as helpful to striped bass anglers as those found in salt water. Gulls have an uncanny ability to spot schools of feeding stripers, follow them to take advantage of the bass's sloppy feeding habits, and pick up anything that floats to the top.

Now is the time of year when a pair of binoculars and a fast boat pay off. Follow the birds and approach the feeding school slowly for the last 100 yards. If the fish are breaking on top, surface plugs will work nicely. If the birds are milling about and you can't see the bass, begin tossing buck-tailed jigs and bouncing them along the bottom. The bass are down deep and the bucktail is the lure that will entice them. If you still don't connect, run the boat along the edge of the activity with your depth recorder working, on the widest cone available, to locate the school of striped bass or their baitfish. They might be suspended somewhere between top and bottom. Only a depth recorder can tell you where the lures should be.

The author with a 22-pounder that fell for a large, saltwater plug trolled in the gin-clear waters of Lake Mead in Nevada.

Another technique that pays off at this time of year, from mid-fall and throughout the winter, is drift-fishing. If you run into a school of bass, you can stay with them until you limit out. In most parts of Santee-Cooper and on Keystone Reservoir (Oklahoma), anglers drift large, live shiners. When they get a strike, a marker float is dropped over the side and the boat returned upwind for another drift. The advantage of drifting live bait over other techniques is that you can cover a lot of water when you have wind and the opportunities of locating the bass are quite good.

Equally profitable for the striped bass fisherman during the fall months is vertical jigging. During spring and summer, you should make note of all brush piles on the bottom which you have snagged. Mark them on your topographical map or use any other means, but be sure you can return to them in the fall. At this time, the numerous small baitfish are tightly schooled and they seek protection from the marauding striped bass in the cover that old brush piles or submerged brush rows along creek beds afford. Stripers are likely to lie alongside such fish havens and wait for the smaller fish to come out. Brush piles are difficult to fish other than from a vertical position. The technique is to drop a metal spoon or jig into it and bounce it around. The lure most often used by Roland Martin, a striped bass guide for years on Santee-Cooper and later on Keystone Reservoir, is a Hopkins hammered spoon called the Shorty.

FRESHWATER TACKLE

Much of the light tackle used for striped bass in salt water, while fishing from boats, docks, or bridges, can be used in fresh water. The conventional reel seems to be the preferred reel in most bait situations and is used almost exclusively except when casting with surface plugs. Reels are loaded with 10- to 15-pound test monofilament or Dacron when fishing cut or live bait or when drifting live shiners. When fishing over obstructions, the line test is increased to 25 or 30 pounds because any striped bass that are hooked must be hauled out before they retreat to the safety and tangles of the brush. And, they will head there immediately if its near.

Live herring are fixed on a 6/0 to 8/0 O'Shaughnessy hook and fished either with a barrel sinker on the bottom or off a three-way swivel with a bank sinker on a 2- to 3-foot leader. The herring is hooked its dorsal fin, and the hook passes only through the skin so that a minimal amount of injury occurs to the fish.

Rods for live or cut bait are about 7 feet long with a medium-action tip. The bait is fished in free spool with just the click on to keep the reel from unwinding. When drift-fishing with live shiners, the click is not enough to hold the spool and the drag is set very lightly to help. When striking a fish, the thumb is momentarily used to keep the spool from rotating, and after the strike, as the fish runs, the drag can be adjusted.

For vertical jigging, a somewhat stiffer and shorter rod is preferred. The stiffer tip is likely to give you a faster recovery when the lure is jigged. The technique is to drop the lure, with the reel in free spool, to the bottom, engage the reel, and retrieve it 2 to 4 feet off the bottom with the rod tip in a jerking manner. Then let the lure fall again to the bottom and jerk it again a few feet from the bottom. Most bass will strike the lure on the free fall between jerks. You won't be aware that a fish is on unless you keep a slight degree of tension on it as the rod tip is lowered to let the lure fall. Too slow a dropping of the tip will ruin the fluttering action of the lure. Too fast, and you will lose touch with it until you retrieve it. The correct rate takes a little practice and know-how that comes only with experience.

FRESHWATER LOCATIONS

Finding striped bass in a large reservoir might at first seem like looking for needles in a haystack, an insurmountable task. But if you know a bit about the fish's living requirements—and we have already discussed the seasons—then you can begin eliminating a lot of the water by eliminating the other variables. Striped bass quickly fall into recognizable habits in a landlocked situation. They are schooling fish, even in fresh water, and they do like to move around a bit. However, there are certain environments which they prefer.

The drop-off is a typical striped bass cruising area. Here they can keep an eye on what is happening on the flats and watch out for any bait or larger fish that take off for the protection of deep water. Bass themselves feel skittish in shallow water and like to venture onto it only when they know that deep water is near at fin. The preferred depths seem to vary between 6 and 10 feet on a slope with water on the deeper side going down from 20 to 30 feet or more. Follow such contours with a boat, mapping them on your chart or topographical map with the use of a fathometer. Drop a bucktailed-jig and bounce it along such slopes, or troll a deep-running plug that can hug the bottom in 15 or more feet of water. As already stated, trolling a plug can be a problem in some reservoirs because of the submerged trees and brush.

The other preferred bass residence is around old brush piles. From a topographical map that shows the bottom the way it was before the floods came, you can almost pick good striped bass sites before you get there. Mark several that look good on a map: where old creek beds entered the main river, around old house and barn foundations, or along the edges of country roads that were lined with trees and shrubs. There are two simple methods for locating these spots you have marked on your chart and confirming that the brush is still there. The first is to have a sensitive fathometer on your boat that will record these, either on a paper graph or by flashing on a screen. The other is to make casts in the area with a heavy spoon or jig and sweep them until you snag or hang up.

Ease your boat to the snag until you are directly over it and confirm it with your fathometer, then mark it on your map. Keep fishing snags or brush piles while exploring and you're likely to get a striper.

During colder times of the year, from December to the end of February, striped bass are likely to be off their feed and will not normally chase a lure far or run after a jig. For the most part, they have abandoned the shallows and are not around the brush piles. Instead, they have taken to deeper water where their body metabolism isn't affected quite as much as by the chilled upper waters. Below 45 degrees, the world of a striped bass, even in fresh water, hasn't much activity going on in it.

Bass will feed, however, during these times of the year but are on a modified dining plan and feed almost exclusively on bait. The best bait is cut herring or other baitfish that is fed slowly into the deeper spots of the reservoir. Search out old riverbeds, and more often than not, the closer you are to the dam that impounds the reservoir, the better will be your chances.

Another idiosyncrasy of freshwater striped bass is their preference for a certain depth in a particular reservoir when they are schooled and on the move. Of course, the depth they choose will first be determined by what is available there to eat, and deep reservoirs give them a wider range and more variables for you to solve. Roland Martin, who has fished both Santee-Cooper and Keystone reservoirs, has found that striped bass will cruise between 15 and 25 feet searching for schools of baitfish. The prime zone appears to be between 20 and 25 feet but can vary, lower in deeper water and higher in shallower. In large, deep-water reservoirs, the development of thermoclines also acts to trap bait and bass within their limits.

STRIPED BASS IN RIVERS

Striped bass throughout much of their distribution in Georgia, Florida, and the Gulf states often spend very little if any time in salt water. They have become landlocked, but of their own choice, though we'll never know if they ever really did go to sea in these sections of the nation. The striper here is a freshwater riverine fish and has been as long as Europeans have been in this land. And here they react like most riverine species, similar in habits and haunts to white bass, white perch, and sauger. The difference is that they are bigger and go where and when they want to go.

There are two seasons for riverine striper fishing, in the early spring, from February to April, and then again in the late fall, from November into December. The better of these is in spring, soon after they have spawned. The location of the spawning sites is known and the angling is concentrated on them or just down river. In Alabama, Mississippi, and Louisiana rivers, striped bass are seldom fished for specifically but are taken incidentally while fishing for other species.

The rapids on the Roanoke River near Weldon, N.C., have been a favorite river location for catching striped bass since earliest colonial times. Striped bass migrate nearly 100 miles up stream from Albemarle Sound to spawn in the spring in the rapids just above Weldon.

In several Georgia, South Carolina, and North Carolina rivers, striped bass do constitute a major part of the spring fishery. Most of these fish, however, are not the pure freshwater form. They have ready access to the sea and spend a part if not most of their lives in the estuary and along the shore. As one heads north from Georgia to South Carolina, this is even more true. Striped bass migrate up these streams when the time to spawn approaches. In South Carolina, these are basically estuary bass that migrate up the Santee and Cooper rivers and a few lesser streams to spawn at the sites below constrictive dams and return after their task is completed.

In North Carolina, this run is even more spectacular. Striped bass spend almost no time in the freshwater river except when they are about ready to spawn. Many spend summer, fall, and winter in the large bays—Albemarle and Pamlico sounds—as well as offshore. But as April approaches, these bass begin entering the rivers and will swim more than 100 miles to their primordial spawning sites. One of the best examples is the bass run on the Roanoke River, near Roanoke Rapids at Weldon, N.C. When the striper, or "rock," run is on, there is little parking room at the surrounding ramps, and the many river channels are filled with boats and fishermen.

The best bait at this time is live minnows. Bass arrive a few weeks prior to spawning, especially younger males, and feed up to the day they spawn. While are spawning, they stop eating, but after a few days or even less, they resume feeding. After spawning takes place, the bass slowly drop down-river and by the middle of June they have abandoned the river to their fry.

There is a protracted spring run of striped bass on the Sacramento River in California, but this, too, is associated with a spawning migration. However, there are several large rivers throughout the South, that produce excellent striped bass catches during all seasons of the year. But even in a strictly riverine environment, striped bass do make migrations based on spawning, food and temperature requirements. One of the most productive areas to fish on these Southern striped bass rivers are their tail-race sections, just below the numerous dams. These dams have drastically altered the original riverine environments.

All the south-flowing rivers that empty into the Gulf of Mexico had indigenous populations of striped bass. However, only one today has a major population—the Apalachicola and its watershed. This river changes its name at the Florida-Georgia border to the Flint and Chattahoochee rivers. The confluence today is flooded by the Jim Woodruff Dam and Reservoir and is collectively known as Lake Seminole. Spring River also flows into the reservoir. While all three Georgia rivers offer some degree of fishing for resident striped bass, the Flint River, especially in an area downstream of Albany, produces some of the largest examples of indigenous riverine striped bass in the country. Several fish in the 60-pound range have been landed on rod and reel from the river. One behemoth, estimated at more than 80 pounds was taken a few years ago by elctrofishing, had a radio transmitter implanted, and released into the river.

Another favorite freshwater river for striped bass is the Santee River. The Pinopolis Dam at Moncks Corners stops farther upriver migration of bass. They spawn here in the spring and are taken by anglers fishing the discharges of the dam.

International Game Fish Association
Fresh Water Line Class World Records, 1993

Bass, striped (landlocked) *Morone saxatilis*

CLASS	WEIGHT	PLACE	DATE	ANGLER
2 lb	22 lb 11 oz	Lake Norris, TN	July 16, 1988	Michael J. Pack
4 lb	44 lbs	Watts Bar Lake, TN	Feb. 2, 1987	Rufus S. Morgan
8 lb	53 lbs	Bull Shoals, ARK	May 1, 1987	William G. Sligar
12 lb	67 lbs 8 oz	O'Neil Forebay, CA	May 7, 1992	Hank Ferguson
16 lb	66 lbs	O'Neil Forebay, CA	June 29, 1988	Theo. H. Furnish
20 lb	60 lb 8 oz	Melton Hill Lake, TN	Feb. 13, 1988	Gary E. Helms
30 lb	47 lb 11 oz	Flint R., Albany, GA	Mar. 7, 1986	Don A. Fowler
50 lb	52 lb 8 oz	Elephant Butte, NM	Jan. 16, 1991	J. C. Dickerson

PART THREE

TACKLE
FOR
STRIPED BASS

22

Rods, Reels, Lines, and Hooks

In 1869, Genio C. Scott's recommendation for a typical surfcasting outfit was a 9- to 9-1/2-foot, rather stiff bamboo pole. And that is what was used on both East and West coast beaches until the late 1940s. I suspect, however, that anglers were always hoping better materials would come along, and when fiberglass appeared on the sporting scene, it completely revolutionized rod-building and the thinking of a good many fishermen. At roughly the same time another important development took place: the introduction of the spinning reel and rod.

Though spinning reels of various kinds had been around for a few decades, their development lagged until they were introduced into the United States in the late 1940s and early 1950s. Most were brought over by returning GIs who found them in use in France, and to some degree in Germany. However, the reels they packed in their duffel bags were hardly recognizable compared to those that were developed here in the 1960s and 1970s, even though many brands were still made in Europe. Today, they are made in Japan, except for one American manufacturer.

Even with fiberglass rods and spinning reels, it took still another event to make all three advance together. It was the development of monofilament fishing line by E. I. Du Pont. With its introduction fishing and fishing tackle entered the modern era.

RODS

Rods can be classified either according to type of fishing (surfcasting, boat fishing, etc.) or according to design (spinning, conventional, etc.). In the following discussion, they will be covered from both points of view.

The long "sticks" at Montauk Point, N.Y. waiting for the action to start.

Surf Rods

Today, surf rods have grown in length, some to as long as 15 feet, though most are a lot less. But big "sticks" are cumbersome to use, require big men to handle properly, and are difficult to travel with. In the last few years, new materials—boron, carbon, and now graphite—have pretty much replaced fiberglass in all but the least expensive rods. With these new plastic materials, the creation of shorter rods that are stiffer and lighter but with the same capabilities as the big sticks, make 15-footers impractical in all but special situations. Surf rods can be divided into two general forms, depending upon the reels used: the spinning rod and the conventional surf rod. Spinning today has captured the imagination of almost every angler, especially the beginner because it is so easy to master. Anyone beginning in the surf is more than likely to pick a spinning outfit, and most of the older beach regulars now tote one or more spinning rods along with their more conventional sticks.

Spin-casting or spin-fishing or just plain spinning has grown rapidly because this system of reel, rod, and line is so easy to learn. After just half an hour of instruction, a beginner can walk into the surf and seriously fish for striped bass—it is that easy. On the other hand, the conventional reel (also referred to as the free-spool reel, level-wind reel or baitcasting reel) takes weeks or months of practice before a fisherman can cast any great distance without fear of creating a bird's nest on the reel. Both types will be discussed separately.

Surf rods, both spinning and conventional styles, can further be roughly divided into three classes—the lightweights, medium rods, and the heavy stuff for big fish, big lures and big baits. Light rods range from 7 to 8-7/2 feet long, are easily worked with one or two hands, and are capable of tossing lures weighing 1-1/2 to 2 ounces. They are equipped with lines ranging from 6 to 17 pounds in breaking strength.

Medium rods are a bit longer, between 9 and 9-1/2 feet, with more power in the butt and with a somewhat stiffer tip so that the power imparted by the caster is not dissipated or lost in the whip of the tip. Such rods easily handle lures between 2 and 3 ounces on line between 12 and 24 pounds in breaking strength.

Heavy rods are between 10 and 12 feet long. A few specialized rods are longer, but all in this class can be loaded with line up to 36 or 45 pounds in breaking strength. The lures they can toss range between 3 and 5 ounces. As you might imagine, some of these rods are real man-killers, used only under certain conditions, and by skilled fishermen.

Spinning and conventional rods differ in several ways. Most apparent is the size of the eyes or guides used for leading the line off the spool. On a spinning rod, the first eye should be as large as the diameter of the fixed spool on the reel. This is a standard construction principle. Then, there may be five to ten additional guides, diminishing in size as they approach the last or tip-top guide. In a spinning rod with a soft tip, more guides are needed so that the bent tip won't allow the line to slap. Slapping increases line friction and reduces the length of the cast. Too many guides, however, will ruin the action of the tip because of increased weight in that section of the rod. Everything in fishing is a compromise.

On a conventional surf rod, the first eye or guide may have a diameter of one-half inch and the remaining three or four guides are all the same size but slightly less in diameter. More guides are not needed because of the somewhat stiffer nature of the conventional rod and the fact that the line comes off the reel from a relatively fixed position. As a result, a large first guide is not as important.

The butt section of either a spinning or conventional surf rod in the medium and heavier classifications is a two-handled affair. If the reel seat is fixed, the foregrip is then separated from the rear grip. In the better spinning rods, there is almost always a fixed reel seat, in the upper third of a 30- to 35-inch butt. On conventional butts, the reel seat may be no more than a pair of rings, or the reel may be simply taped into the position that best fits the arm-length of the fisherman. This lack of a ring seat makes tailoring the reel's location to the angler's arm a good deal easier.

Butt lengths average 31 to 32 inches. They must be fitted or picked for proper length when being selected, like the stock of a gun. A man with short arms will have difficulty casting a rod with a 34- or 35-inch butt. It is likely to stick him in the ribs with each cast. A good rule of thumb to remember when picking a new type rod is to match it to your sleeve size and you won't be too far off base.

Not only must a rod be matched to the bait or lures you are planning to cast, to the line size, and to the reel, but it must also be matched to your physical specifications and casting ability. A 5-foot 6-inch person will have a tough time with a 12-foot rod, and a large man can overpower a 9-foot stick. Experience will be your best guide.

Almost all surf rods, either spinning or conventional, are constructed of tubular or hollow fiberglass, boron, carbon, graphite, or a combination of these. These materials, given a modicum of protection and consideration, are almost indestructible. Butts are covered with specie cork or neoprene and come with chrome-plated brass or anodized aluminum reel seats. The first deterioration in a spinning rod is likely to be with the lines used to wrap the guides to the rod, because the rods flex, even within half-inch lengths. If you coat the wraps periodically with epoxy rod varnish, they will serve you a lot longer before the rod's guides need to be completely rewrapped.

The ideal surf rod is a one-piece stick. However, because long rods are difficult to travel with or store at home, they are generally made in two sections. The butt section runs entirely through the handle and is an integral part of the grip. In two-piece construction, the ferrule was formerly always constructed of chrome-plated materials, but more recently glass-to-glass connections have become popular. All-glass connections produce an almost perfect rod curvature; ferrule interference is so slight that it can be discounted.

Bank, Pier, and Jetty Rods

The jetty rod can be either a spinning or a conventional rod, and it is nothing more than a shorter version of the type of rods used in surfcasting. Because adequate casting room is often a problem on jetties, shorter, snappier casts are called for. The typical jetty rod is shorter than a surf stick. The jetty stick ranges between 6 and 7-1/2 feet in length for a conventional rod and between 6-1/2 and 8 feet long for a spinning rod. Butt sections are shorter because of the tighter elbow room, and range between 21 and 25 inches. The number of guides is likely to be reduced correspondingly, and the entire rod is somewhat stiffer, right to the tip, where the snap for such casts receives most of its impetus after it leaves the wrists.

Most conventional rods for bank, pier, bridge, and dock-side fishing are also fairly stiff, short rods because they are not called upon to great castings. They are the typical bay or popping rods, 5 to 6 or even 7 feet long and equipped with a baitcasting or bay reel. They are used primarily for fishing live or cut bait and are as at home off the dock, pier, or bridge as over the gunwale of a rental rowboat by a fishing station.

Great action or response isn't a built-in characteristic of most popping rods or rods designed for still-fishing from a boat. Sturdiness and an ability to handle a 4- or 5-ounce bank sinker and a big chunk of cut bait are requirements. These rods are equipped with four or five guides with eyes made of chrome or stainless steel. The tip-top is made of tough tungsten carbide to withstand the cutting action of monofilament line. Most are designed for line classifications between 8 and 30 pounds.

The butt section is divided into grips, a smaller foregrip ahead of the fixed reel seat and a larger aftergrip. The butt is covered either with specie cork or neoprene. In less expensive models the butt is wood, either oak or hickory.

Spinning Rods for Boat-Fishing

Rods for use in a boat vary greatly, from spinning rods and conventional rods, also found in the surf, to the large trolling rods designed to handle large striped bass on 60-pound tackle. Between these extremes, we have specialized jigging and boat rods that are modified slightly from bank, pier, and bridge rods uses in a slightly more confined fishing situations.

The spinning rod reaches the height of its development when used for casting plugs and spoons from a boat because it is not required to cast maximum distances. The typical spinning rod used in a boat is considerably shorter than one used in the surf. Most noticeable is the reduced size of the butt—it may extend only 15 to 18 inches under the arm. Often it is also one-handed. Its overall length can vary between 7 and 9 feet, but most are about 8-1/2 feet long. The butt is equipped with a fixed reel seat and fore and aft butt grips of cork or rubber. In one-piece rods, the butt section is often removable, but a rod with the blade extending through and becoming a part of the handle has a better overall action.

A spinning rod used in a boat should be capable of throwing rather heavy striped bass plugs, lures weighing as much as 4 and 5 ounces. It is impossible to find one rod that can toss both small and large plugs equally well, so the properly equipped boat angler often will have two or three rods of different lengths and actions.

A boat-spinning rod should have a stout tip if it is used primarily for casting plugs. The added snap of the tip can put extra feet on every cast, whereas a willowy rod that is better suited for casting live bait will absorb some of the snap. Most spinning rods come with fixed reel seats of either anodized aluminum or chrome-plated steel or brass. The eyes are large wire or ceramic ring guides which match the spool of the reel being used.

Spinning rods for boats can be roughly divided into two classes according to length. The lighter group is composed of rods between 6 and 7-1/2 feet long, and the heavier group of rods from 7-1/2 to 8-1/2 or even 9 feet long. Butt lengths vary from a minimum of 20 inches to a maximum of 25 inches. Smaller butts, even on longer rods, are somewhat preferred because of the limited space aboard a boat. Smaller rods are often constructed with one grip section, with the after-butt construction typically that of a one-handed, heavy, freshwater rod.

Trolling Rods

Trolling rods for striped bass generally fall into three classifications closely based on IGFA regulations for line-class distinctions. The lightest are 20-pound class rods, and these, obviously, are equipped with reels loaded with 20-pound test, or 20-pound class line when you're not fishing for records. Mid-range rods for striped bass fishing are 30-pound rods, and the heaviest are 50-pound rods. The last group is heavier than most sportfishing dictates. However, some charterboat captains fish in crowded waters where tides run heavy and are forced into using heavy tackle to pull bass out of the rips and keep fighting time to a minimum. Rods in the 20- and 30-pound classes are nicely suited for trolling under most other conditions.

Most trolling rods are approximately 6-1/4 to 6-1/2 feet long. A few may reach 7 feet. The butt section constitutes nearly 24 inches of the overall length and is built with a rather large foregrip, equal to or exceeding the after-grip section. The chrome-plated reel seats are fixed, and the butt is often detachable from the blade. The aftergrip section is exposed hardwood, and the foregrip is covered in specie cork or neoprene. The end of the butt is finished off with a cross-slotted gimbal nock.

The guide on a trolling rod closest to the reel (called the stripping guide) is usually equipped with double rollers through which the line is fed and controlled. Four hand-chromed stainless-steel ring guides run up the rod, and the tip-top guide is a roller guide to reduce wear on the line as it angles off the end of the rod. Not all bass fishermen like to use such regulation rods. Some feel that the rollers occasionally jam the line at the most inappropriate times, though

The strain of heavier lures maintains a constant arc in trolling rods. The mate aboard Capt. John Wadsworth's sportfisherman Sunbeam, *out of Waterford, Conn., adjusts the third rod so that a full party can work the transom of his large boat.*

I have never had problems with them. Instead, they prefer rods with all eye guides, even on the tiptop.

A variation of the regular trolling rod—which handles either monofilament, Dacron, nylon, or lead-core lines—is the wire-line rod. This rod is used specifically for trolling with Monel, stainless-steel, or braided-wire lines. It is quite similar in construction to the standard trolling rod except that the roller guides are replaced with eye guides and all the guides are constructed of tungsten carbide, which is so tough that wire line cannot cut grooves into it.

A special kind of trolling rod has evolved for use with bucktail jigs. This rod is worked with a jigging action from a moving boat. It has an extra resiliency that adds a bit of snap to the jigger's dance. Such a rod responds quickly to a pull and returns quickly to a straight position. It usually is equipped only with eye guides, though it may have a roller tiptop. Not many manufacturers carry or produce these rods, but nevertheless they bristle along the docks at Montauk. Most were made at one time by a local maker, Johnny Kronuch, specifically for the charterboat skippers in the area, before he retired to Key West.

There is another type of rod often used for vertical jigging in waters like Plum Gut and The Race between Fishers and Little Gull islands, off the eastern end of Long Island. The rods are similar in construction to the trolled jigging rod but are often a bit shorter, 5 to 6-1/2 feet long, and capable of working 30- or 40-pound-test lines.

REELS

Four types of reels are used in pursuit of the striped bass in addition to the fly reels previously in Chapter 18. By far the most popular seems to be the spinning reel, though actually trolling reels might run a close second if someone were capable of conducting an accurate survey. Reels for saltwater fishing differ from freshwater reels in but a few respects. Foremost among these are the materials used in their construction. A good saltwater reel must be resistant to the corrosive effects of salt. If it isn't, it is unlikely to last a season even with constant washing and care. Second, saltwater reels are generally larger than freshwater reels, both because the fish have more area in which to run when hooked and so require more line, and because saltwater fish are larger.

Spinning Reels

The real value of a spinning reel lies in its ability to let a rod cast very light lures. On a conventional reel, the spool must revolve to let the line off, and thus drag is increased on the line and the casting distance is reduced. On a spinning reel, the spool is fixed and the line spills off the end and out of the guides, reducing friction considerably.

Not only can lighter lures be used with spinning reels but lighter lines as well. And the lighter the line, the longer the cast. Another feature of the spinning reel is that there is no strain on the line once the forward pull of the lure has stopped. This means that the line will not continue to spill off, as it will with conventional reels. This has a secondary application. The beginning caster need not learn that fine point where he must apply pressure to stop the line and yet not cut short his cast, as he must with conventional equipment.

Since the spool on a spinning reel is fixed, another device must do the work of putting or laying line back onto the spool. This device is a bail, an arm that is flipped into place when the handle is cranked forward and guides the line onto the spool as it revolves about the outside of the spool.

A drag mechanism holds the spool rigid and keeps it fixed or lets it revolve only under designated pressures. Though the spool is fixed when compared to the conventional reel, it can slip or revolve when intense pressure is applied to it—pressure that is greater than that exerted by the brake shoe or the spring-loaded mechanism that keeps it from revolving. These drags can be set extremely fine and release in a very smooth operation, giving the spinning reel an exceptional drag for fighting fish on light tackle. This has helped beginning anglers catch fish that they might have lost with other types of equipment.

The amount of drag is controlled by a knurled knob on the spool with an indicator as to the degree of drag. This setting controls the drag tension only for that spool and is set at a slipping point under the breaking strength of the line. With push-button removable spools, the drag need not be reset each time; the setting stays intact with the transfer. In other spinning reels, the drag is set in the

Spinning Reels—*Five size classes of spinning reels are generally available to striped bass anglers. From left to right: an ultralight reel, basically freshwater in design but* corrosion-resistant *and suitable for small or schoolie striped bass; a reel that is about the size of a standard freshwater reel and will work in many boat and bank situations; a special saltwater-size reel used for spinning from boats and light surfcasting; a standard surfcasting reel, for rods 8 to 10 feet long, also found in use in many jetty situations; and finally a large reel used primarily with the longest saltwater rods and heavy lines and lures.*

back of the reel and pressure is applied via a shoe to the gears or the shaft upon which the spool will be allowed to rotate. Both are effective.

The rate of retrieve—that is, how much line is added back onto the spool with one turn of the handle—is fixed in spinning reels and is determined by the ratio of the gears inside the reel. Larger reels usually have a smaller ratio because they deal in heavier strains. A 2.5:1 or a 2:1 ratio is rather standard. In medium and smaller spinning reels a faster retrieve is often desired because the spool diameter and the reel handle are smaller. In order to make lures work at normal speeds through the water, a higher gear ratio is often needed, anywhere from 3:1 to 5.5:1. But what you gain in speed, you lose in power, and so the higher ratios require more effort from the angler.

Spinning reels can be divided into five classifications based on overall size and the diameter of the spool. The smallest group is composed of the ultralight reels that match ultralight rods designed for freshwater fishing or school-sized striped bass under controlled conditions.

A slightly larger spool and reel characterizes the next class. This size is the standard found on most well balanced freshwater spinning outfits. This size is readily adaptable to saltwater fishing. If the reel is made of corrosion-resistant materials it can be used in either environment. In salt water, this size reel is typically used in bank and pier situations when fishing with bait and light lures, especially small bucktails, and in boats on small striped bass.

The third class is the standard size found in most saltwater spinning situations. It is often the same model as the freshwater reel we just described but one size or slightly larger. The bigger reel is needed to provide the extra line required for saltwater species, as well as a large spool to match the larger eyes on a somewhat larger rod that is the typical plugging rod used on boats and in some bank and pier situations. This reel has a spool that will take 300 yards of 12-pound test line. The spool is typically released by a push button so that it can easily be replaced with a spool loaded with lighter or heavier lines.

Almost all models and sizes of reels, except the large surfcasting varieties, come with both shallow and deep spools. The shallow spools are used with lighter-test line which would not fill a deep spool properly unless hundreds of unneeded yards of line were laid on. On reel models without shallow spools, a false arbor is often provided—one that slips over the axle of the spool and partially fills it. The line is then laid upon this filler device.

For the moment, let us skip the fourth class of spinning reels and go on to the largest class, the big spinning reels that are found in the surf. This class is almost exclusively for surfcasting because it matches the 10- to 12-foot rods, some even larger, that are used in a high surf to toss a large lure or chunk of bait to the outer bar. There is little place and little need for such a large reel on a boat. But in a big surf, when heavy lines are used, the reel must be large enough that an adequate amount of line can be spooled. The reel is heavy, even when constructed of the lighter materials, and when it is coupled to a big rod, the total outfit can be a lot to maneuver.

The fourth class of reels are often the same model as the fifth class, the large surf reels, but are reduced in size and can be matched to intermediate surf rods. The largest stick is not always the most appropriate stick for the surf. In many plug-casting situations, you don't need to reach the outer bar, and a smaller rod and a smaller reel are called for. In addition, a smaller outfit is often better for shorter men and women. In a jetty situation, where the overall spinning outfit should be reduced in size, class-four reels and intermediate rods are perfect.

This last class constitutes the largest number of reels found in the surf. Like most reels below it in size, it contains a push-button spool, while class-five reels often lack this device. This means that you must switch reels when you want to change to a different line test.

Conventional Surf Reels

The conventional reel for the surf is a specialized form of the baitcasting reel, which has a revolving spool. It has been called the free-spool reel, the multiplying reel, and the level-wind reel, all descriptions of one of the reel's characteristics. The original surf reel was nothing more than a larger version of the freshwater baitcasting reel. It possessed no gears between the spool and the reel handle that would increase the retrieve ratio and had no drag but the thumb applied to the spool. The first innovation was to add gears so that for each turn of the reel handle, the spool might turn two or three times. Today, most conventional surf reels are built with a 4:1 or 3:1 ratio of retrieve.

On a cast, gears that are engaged with the spool will slow down the revolution of the spool, and thus some device was needed to disengage the gears

Conventional Reels—The one on the right is for surfcasting and the other three for bay fishing. Bay-fishing reels are also called popping reels and used with popping rods for fishing from boats, bridges, piers, and banks where very little casting is needed. The conventional surfcasting reel has an adjustable anti-backlash device, but an educated thumb is also required to get the maximum distance from every cast.

while casting. On most freshwater baitcasting reels the handle still spins while the gears are engaged. In the modern surf reel, the gears are disengaged by throwing the handle of a clutch, and the reel is in free-spool. But a reel with no pressure on it can create a lot of backlashing, and the caster's thumb had to apply pressure at the correct time to stop the spool the instant the forward momentum of the lure and line fell to zero.

Built-in drags have been developed—counterbalances in some reels, magnetic devices in others, even air brakes in the form of fins on still others. For the most part, they are all quite effective. Backlashes, however, still happen, and the reels must be finely adjusted at all times to make their anti-backlash mechanisms function properly.

The better designed squidding reel—as a conventional reel was once called (a carry-over from days when fishing in the surf began with squid and the lines were called squidding lines)—is shallow and wide. This design allows line on the spool to spread and not pile or bury itself when a big fish runs. The line is laid back and forth with the thumb or by a level-wind device that moves back and forth across the spool, distributing line as it moves.

Drag on these reels is controlled by a star-shaped lever on the side and a part of the reel handle. The drag works only when the clutch is engaged and when line is pulled out, not when it is reeled in. There can be an infinite number of settings with the star drag, and over the years it has proved to be an extremely hardy and functional drag in the surf.

A well designed conventional reel should also have a quick and easy take-down so that it can be cleaned when out of the surf. One-screw designs are almost standard. The anti-reverse mechanism should be controllable by the caster so he can switch it on or off. Ball bearings have become standard and add smoothness to the spools. Spools can be constructed of either plastic or metal.

Plastic spools work best with monofilament lines, which when tightly wrapped on a reel can exert fantastic pressures on the spools. Metal spools under such strain can actually break or become warped. When using braided Dacron or nylon lines, metal spools are sufficient.

Baitcasting Reels

The freshwater baitcasting reel has easy application in salt water if the reel is constructed of materials that can withstand the effects of salt. The simplest reels, used in boat- and bank-fishing situations, possess an uncomplicated star drag that is easy to operate, have an anti-reverse mechanism have a click that warns the fisherman that the line is going out when the reel is in free-spool. They are capable of holding from 100 to 200 yards of 15-pound-test line.

Most saltwater versions of the baitcasting reel don't have level-wind devices because they must revolve with the spool, and they add friction to the cast, slow it down, and shorten its length. Instead, saltwater fishermen have learned to thumb their line, as a matter of course, as it is retrieved, thereby spreading it evenly over the surface of the spool. Also, level-wind features add to the cost of the reel and increase the number of parts which could be affected by corrosion.

Often called the bay reel, this unpretentious version of bigger trolling reels is fished off short rods, 5 to 6, or 6-1/2 feet long. They are designed for boat, or bank fishing, from a somewhat sedentary stand. In free spool, the line falls to the bottom with the weight of the sinker pulling it. The free fall is controlled with pressure from the thumb on the spool. To stop it one just presses harder with the thumb once the sinker reaches its destination. The clutch is then engaged, which connects the reel handle, via gears, to the axle of the spool, and the drag set light enough that a fleeing striped bass can strip out line without experiencing too much resistance until the angler is ready to pick up the rod.

Within the baitcasting or bay-reel group is another form of reel designed almost entirely for use with monofilament lines. Monofilament is a little more difficult to spool evenly with a thumb on a small reel, so the need for a level-wind mechanism is greater. This reel contains all the features of the squidder, the bay, and even the larger trolling reels. It includes a gear ratio of 2.5:1 or 3:1, a clutch for engaging or disengaging the spool, a star drag for uniform resistance, and large handles for easy grasping and winding in wet situations. However, instead of a wide spool it has a narrow but deep spool. This allows the fisherman to add line quickly to the spool and build up a diameter at a fast pace. The increasing diameter of line on the spool as it is retrieved has the effect of changing the mechanical ratio and makes retrieving quicker.

Still another variation of this reel is the jigging reel. It has all the same characteristics as other saltwater conventional reels but also has a narrow spool, an increased gear ratio of 4:1, and an increased handle length to increase the fisherman's mechanical advantage and compensate for the high gear ratio. Such a reel is matched to a special jigging rod. This form of jigging does not involve the use of tackle to work a bucktail jig from a moving boat. Instead, it has become specialized for the vertical-jigging technique. This style typically employs a heavy diamond jig that is fished off the bottom while the boat is drifting over deep water. The diamond jig is free-spooled to the bottom and then quickly retrieved for the first 15 or 20 feet. It is jigged with a fast retrieve of the reel rather than with the lifting and dropping of the rod tip, making several rapid or quick turns of the handle, then slipping into free-spool. The lure is again allowed to drop to the bottom, then again quickly retrieved when it hits bottom. This constant up-and-down motion, at a fast retrieve, attracts striped bass. The larger gear ratio and the long handle on the reel makes this form of jigging easier.

Trolling Reels

Reels used for trolling are modified versions of the simple conventional reel. Many features have been added but the basic design and principles are still the same as when the reels first appeared over a hundred years ago. The big difference, when compared to a bay or boat reel, is their added weight, that is not just a function of the increased size. Because they are not held for long periods of time, but fished from a rod-holder on the boat and handled only when retrieving the line, they can be made heavier in their construction and selection of materials. The bigger trolling reels have been modified to handle larger fish, stronger lines, and heavier lures. There are more than a dozen different sizes of trolling reels, ranging from 1/0 to 16/0. For the most part they vary only in size and line capacity.

Not all of the numerous sizes of trolling reels are practical for striped bass fishing. The small reels, from 1/0 to 3/0, are extremely light, designed for small fish or for record fishing, and probably only the 3/0 finds any extended use by striped bass fishermen. The 3/0 is capable of holding approximately 350 yards of 30-pound test Dacron or 375 yards of 30-pound test monofilament.

The more popular sizes for striped bass are the 4/0 and 6/0 reels. They are better suited because of their larger size, heavier drags that can withstand the powerful rush of a big bass in a roaring rip, and larger line capacity. Both 4/0 and 6/0 are considered light reels with respect to big-game fishing but they are the top of the line for the striped bass angler. A 4/0 will load approximately 450 yards of 30-pound-test Dacron, 800 yards of 20-pound-test monofilament or 500 yards of 30-pound-test monofilament. The larger 6/0 reel is capable of holding 400 yards of 50-pound-test Dacron, and 1,050 yards of 20-pound-test, 650 yards of 30-pound-test, or 415 yards of 50-pound-test monofilament.

Seldom, however, is all this line used when trolling for striped bass. On a typical wire-line (Monel) outfit, 100 or 200 yards of 30-, 40-, or 60-pound-test wire is spooled onto 200 or 300 yards of 30- or 50-pound-test Dacron. The Dacron acts more as backing, to bulk up the spool, and only in rare instances is it ever in the water fighting a striped bass.

Trolling Reels—*Trolling reels are essentially baitcasting reels modified to handle more line and heavier fish. For striped bass, they vary in size from 3/0 to 6/0. Illustrated here from left to right: 4/0 Penn 209 with a level-wind device and used primarily with monofilament, 4/0 Mitchell 624 and a 6/0 Penn Senator. The preferred size for smaller bass boats is 4/0; the larger reels are for big game, heavy water and heavy lines.*

On most trolling reels, the star drag control is still on the axle of the reel handle. In a few more costly trolling reels, the drag is a separate lever, located along the wall of the reel, and calibrated with settings that don't always seem to hold true after being exposed to salt water for a period. About ten years ago, Penn Reels introduced trolling reels with an added set of gears that could be selected or shifted at will that would change the rate of retrieve. These reels are invaluable to big-game anglers when they suddenly finds themselves with a strong fish and unable to retrieve line. By lowering the ratio, the turn of a handle suddenly may not bring in as much line but the effort is made a bit easier. This gear-shifting was then adapted to reels used in stand-up outfits for tuna fishing. It had to be matched with a an entirely new concept in rod-making because the reels were so powerful an angler could easily exert enough pressure to break the conventional rods. While there might be some application of a dual-geared reel in striped bass fishing, the reel's added cost isn't really justified by the expense.

LINES

At one time, the saltwater fisherman was restricted to the use of cotton and linen lines, and these were his only connection between hook and reel. The famous Cuttyhunk linen lines were standard for years. But linen lines had a tendency to rot when not properly dried, were inconsistent in strength, and changed in strength when wet or dry. Not until the development of synthetic fibers, like nylon, Dacron, and eventually monofilament, was the fisherman freed from the woe of such troubles. Heavy lines and undependable breaking strengths were all but eliminated with these fibers. Nylon lines were the first on the scene. Braided nylon made a strong line with a fairly small diameter. It was quickly put to use by surfcasters using conventional reels. But nylon has a great amount of elasticity or stretch, and sometimes it was difficult to feel a fish or set the hook if you had a lot of line in the surf.

After nylon came Dacron, another synthetic fiber. It was an improvement with even greater strength in relation to the diameter and less stretch than nylon. Dacron today is the preferred fiber for braided line. It is as popular as monofilament, a single strand of plastic line that has all but revolutionized casting and trolling. Today, both braided Dacron and monofilament lines are widely used in specific areas. Though they have somewhat different characteristics, neither is truly superior to the other. It becomes a matter of personal choice and line use.

Monofilament Lines

Monofilament lines are formed by drawing the fluid plastic material through a series of dies, each diminishing in diameter until the correct size and corresponding strength test is reached. The result is a fiber with a smooth surface, one that offers little resistance to guides and has an extremely small diameter but great strength. Because of all these features it today has become almost the universal line and the only one used in spinning and spin-casting. Monofilament lines have characteristics—stretch, diameter, tensile strength, knot-breaking strength, knotting ability, limpness, recovery, abrasion resistance—all of which can be controlled: enhanced or reduced. However, they cannot all be incorporated into one line. Instead, monofilament lines are now designed for uses where one or more of these characteristics are desired.

When trolled, monofilament lines offer less resistance in the water than braided nylon or Dacron lines, and where a deeper-running line is desired it has an advantage over other materials. There's an inherent elasticity in all monofilament lines. When first produced, stretch was so great that they were shunned by many trollers. But as the manufacturers brought stretch under reasonable control, the line was quickly adapted to casting and later even to trolling.

A certain amount of stretch is desirable in a trolling line, especially when a big fish strikes a lure that is going in the opposite direction. The stretch acts as a shock absorber and softens the force before the line approaches its breaking point or the drag comes into play. Too much stretch, however, will prevent the fisherman from feeling what the fish on the other end of the line is doing. It will make him strike a fish too late and in some cases make the setting of the hook difficult if not impossible.

Monofilament lines also have a "memory." If they are wound under pressure on a reel and allowed to stand, they uncoil with large loops that may foul if constant pressure is not always maintained. This memory also acts in the direction of the circumference of the line and will cause twisting if tension is not regularly relieved. Most anglers who troll a lot use high-quality, all-bearing swivels that allow a lure to swim freely and not twist the line while doing so.

One would think that monofilament is the perfect material, and it almost is. But its only natural enemy is sunlight. The ultra-violet rays in the sun affect the plastic and shorten its life. That's why most boat fishermen never leave their reels exposed to the sun any longer than is needed.

Monofilament lines are produced in the greatest variety of tests available, 13 classifications in all: line tests of 2, 4, 6, 8, 10, 12, 15, 20, 25, 30, 40, 50, and 60 pounds. There are even greater strengths used in special situations but the striped bass angler seldom finds use for them. Occasionally some odd strengths creep into the market, like 17- or 27-pound test These are usually lines that were designed for a higher or lower test but worn dies or other variable factors during production altered the specific diameter, and rather than destroy the lines, the manufacturer labels them correctly and places them on the market.

Dacron Lines

While stretch can be controlled in monofilament lines, it is better controlled in braided-Dacron lines. Many dedicated trollers still believe that a Dacron line is better suited to setting the hook and that the feel is maintained down to the mouth of the fish. On the other hand, because it is braided, Dacron will fray more easily than monofilament and thus will not last as long. Dacron line is also more expensive than monofilament. However, it is easier to work, and many big-game fishermen prefer it for tournament fishing. Braided-Dacron lines usually correspond to the IGFA line groupings or classifications and come spooled in 50- to 1,200-yard quantities. There are eight classes of strength: 6, 12, 20, 30, 50, 80, 130, and 162 pounds.

Nylon Lines

Nylon lines, still in production today, are often called squidding lines, replacing the cotton and linen first used in the surf. They are made of high-tenacity nylon that creates a smooth, flat, and supple line. The line's stretch can be controlled and then set with special heat devices during the winding. At the same time, special braided-in silicone lubricants are added to help eliminate internal friction in a line, and a special water-proofing reduces water absorption. Squidding lines come in numerous test strengths: 12, 18, 27, 36, 54, 63, 72, 90, and 110 pounds.

Lead-Core Lines

When you must go deeper than Dacron, nylon, or monofilament lines allow, and still don't want to adorn your terminal end with sinkers and drails, you can switch to a lead-core line. The line is a hollow braided-nylon outer shell that surrounds a supple lead wire or strand in the center. It handles easily on trolling reels. Most lead-core lines are marked every 10 yards by color-coding with which the manufacturer has impregnated the nylon sheath. Lead-core lines are produced in coils of 100 or 200 yards and come in four strength classifications: 18, 25, 40, and 60 pounds.

Wire Lines

Wire lines for trolling are used when the bass are deep and no other lines can get down without the addition of cumbersome lead weights. Wire has less stretch than any other type of line, and the feel you get is immediately transferred along the length of the line. The first wire lines were copper and were used for freshwater fishing, but because copper's tensile strength is low it had to be braided. Today, copper wire is rarely used in salt water, but a steel version of braided line is available. Braided steel line is especially strong for its small diameter size. However, the braiding increases resistance in the water, a drawback when trolling, and the lines do not sink as deeply as single strands of stainless steel or Monel (an alloy).

Both stainless-steel and Monel wire are popular among striped bass fishermen, and it is difficult to state which might be the more favored. Stainless-steel wire is a bit more difficult to handle than Monel because it possesses a stronger "memory." Its tendency to coil is less pronounced in the lighter-test wires, and it is used more often on these levels. Heavier tests are more apt to be Monel, a somewhat more supple wire.

Twist is not allowable with wire lines, and therefore they must be used with the best swivels or the line will fatigue and part unexpectedly. Wear spots in wire cannot be spotted as they can in monofilament or Dacron. If uncoiled improperly, wire will kink and the breaking strength of the line will be reduced by as much as 90 percent where these kinks occur. If a kink is unwound in the same direction it was created, it can be eliminated. This is easier to accomplish in Monel than in stainless steel.

A constant strain or pressure must be kept at all times on wire line when getting it into the water or when retrieving it to keep unwanted coils from forming. This is especially true of the more springy stainless-steel lines. Few reels are spooled entirely with wire; a heavy backing line, like 30- or 50-pound-test Dacron, is used to build up the diameter and then 100 or 200 yards of wire are added. I like to add small, high-quality swivels to my wire trolling lines. They serve two functions: to eliminate twisting and to serve as length indicators. I place them at 100-, 200-, and 250-foot intervals and can immediately tell how much wire is in the water simply by counting the swivels as they pass off the rod tip. I have tried painting each swivel with red, white, and blue enamel paints but it seems to wear too quickly. At night, swivels make the task of marking the line easier than colored tapes. Feel alone is enough to tell you how much line is in the water, and they can be heard as they rattle going through the guides.

Many anglers use colored plastic tape to mark different lengths on the wire but I have difficulty keeping them in position. With swivels in the line, you know the measurements haven't changed. There's the added feature of the swivels eliminating any twist a bad lure or spinning fish might put in the line. Seldom does kinking or coiling become a problem when swivels are used in the line.

The International Game Fish Association still will not recognize as records

In many instances, wire line is preferred when fishing for striped bass. The top illustrations show how to attach the line to the backing with a barrel swivel. The closeup shows a barrel swivel connecting two lengths of wire line. The proper knot, the haywire twist, begins by equally and evenly wrapping one line around the other. Swivels not only reduce kinking and eliminate twist, but also serve as permanent length-markers to tell you how much line you are trolling. It's a good idea to mark the test strength of the line and its length on the side of the reel with plastic labels.

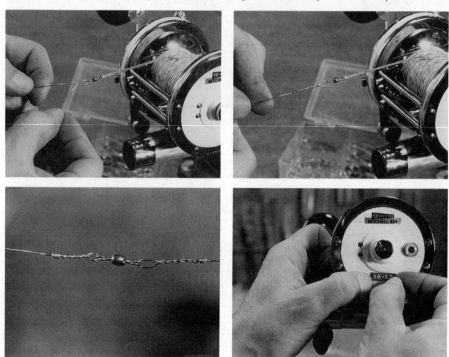

fish that are taken on wire lines. I fail to see the reasoning for this. A wire line is just as sporting as a Dacron or monofilament line. It works better to get lines down deep than the addition of drails or diving planes. A 40-pound test wire line will break at 40 pounds of pressure just as a 40-pound test nylon, Dacron, or monofilament line breaks.

In many crowded fishing situations, where you must troll close to the boat as well as deeply behind it, wire line is the only answer to catching fish. In areas where striped bass seldom come to the surface, few other lines can be used, and here again, wire line is the answer. In areas where rocks and barnacles make the landing of a hooked-bass difficult, wire line again is the only answer. It's not unsporting, and is sound in conservation to use lines which won't fray, leaving a fish to struggle with hooks in its mouth.

Test Lines Versus Class Lines

There are two ways to measure and classify the tensile strength of a line, class strengths and test strengths. The best way to explain their differences is by example. A manufacture will label a line as "12-pound- test." This means that as a consumer you can expect that this line will withstand a pull of it of at least 12 pounds and probably more. Here, the maker is guaranteeing you that it is at least that strong but makes no indication of its upper limit; the force at which it will break. This makes it more economical to produce and it covers non-uniformity in line diameter.

In a competition, where everyone must use a line of a certain strength, otherwise one angler would have an advantage over another, the line is manufactured so that it will break if the force of the pull exceeds, in our example, 12 pounds. These are called class lines and are the only ones recognized by the IGFA for records. You can use a test line, but if you use a 12-pound-test line, its maximum strength might be 16 or 17 pounds and that would put you into the next class above 12 pounds.

Simply put, class lines break under the weight printed on the packaging spools and test lines break somewhere above the number on their packages. Because control is much more exacting in the production of class lines, they are usually more expensive than test lines. IGFA line classes are 2, 4, 8, 12, 16, 20, 30, 50, 80, and 130 pounds.

Leaders

Leaders are terminal lengths of line used between the main body of line and the snap, swivel, and hook, on the very end. Leaders are use either to place the heavy- bodied line farther from the bait or lure so it won't scare the fish or to save the lure from loss through abrasion, excessive force, or fish biting through the main body of line. At times, a leader is no more than a doubling of the body line, as in the case of monofilament, or it can be of different materials.

Leader material may consist of either wire or monofilament, and it is used for one of two reasons. In the case of Dacron, nylon, and wire line, the terminal leader is usually a strand of clear monofilament. It is used where the sight of the main line might alarm fish or make them suspicious of the lure or bait. In this case, the leader is a level piece of monofilament, often considerably heavier in breaking strength than the main line so that it can resist abrasion or cutting by fish other than striped bass. When monofilament is used as the main line, the leader is simply another piece of much heavier monofilament. However, some bass become leader-shy. In this instance, the leader is still monofilament but is either colored, e.g., coffee-stained or lighter test monofilament.

In other situations, where bluefish and other fishes equipped with sharp teeth are apt to occur with the striped bass, and when fishing and trolling around rocky areas and those encrusted with barnacles, a 2- to 10-foot piece of stainless-steel wire is used as the terminal section of a line. It can be smaller in diameter than the main body of line and still be stronger than the rest of the rig. Wire resists abrasion better than much heavier monofilament, and where the presence of the wire will not alarm bass, it is the preferred leader material.

Shock leaders can also be used, as in fly-casting lines, to save the lure from being cut off by other fish. In this case, it is usually monofilament that's heavier than the main leader and often but a foot or two in length.

KNOTS

There are hundreds of knots that a fisherman may use at one time or another in maintaining his tackle. But for the most part, he can get by with six or seven. The form of knot to use is first determined by the line material. Some knots in monofilament won't always hold in Dacron, and vice-versa. A knot is the weakest part in your line; if the line tests out at 20 pounds then you know that any knot tied in it will break at less than that. There are no 100- percent knots, though some have breaking points close to just a few percent less than the line strength. The fewer knots in your line the better. How and where you tie them can measurably affect the maximum size of the fish you can land, so it pays to know the right knots and their best application.

The most efficient knot which can be used when tying monofilament to hooks and swivels, and in some cases to other lines, is a simple jam-type knot called the clinch knot. There are a few variations, including the improved and the double clinch knot, and all work well. This group of knots is one of the strongest you can tie and lessens the line's breaking strength by the least amount.

The blood knot is a variation of the clinch knot, a clinch tied on a clinch, and works well when tying two pieces of monofilament together and when tying one of slightly larger diameter to another. In tying two monofilament lines of greatly different diameter, the lighter line can be doubled for added knot strength and clinching ability. When their respective diameters are still too great, then you can switch to a surgeon's knot. This is the knot often used when tying lead-core line to a leader.

With Dacron or nylon lines, the last 15 feet are usually doubled for strength and wear resistance and the swivel is attached to the end by a Bimini hitch. In cases where wire and monofilament and Dacron must be joined, a swivel is a better bet than a knot. The backing is attached to one side of the swivel with the Bimini hitch and the wire to the other eye of the swivel with a haywire twist. The haywire twist must be evenly twisted by both strands of the wire and not simply be one wire wrapped around a standing wire. The bitter end is finished off by twisting it with a cranking action. The cranking action fatigues the wire immediately next to the standing line and does not leave sharp edges on which to cut your fingers.

When finishing off monofilament knots, especially when using a clinch knot on heavy lines, the line should be cut fairly close to the knot to avoid "Irish pennants." However, the line might pull through if the knot was not jammed

Useful knots for the striped bass fisherman.

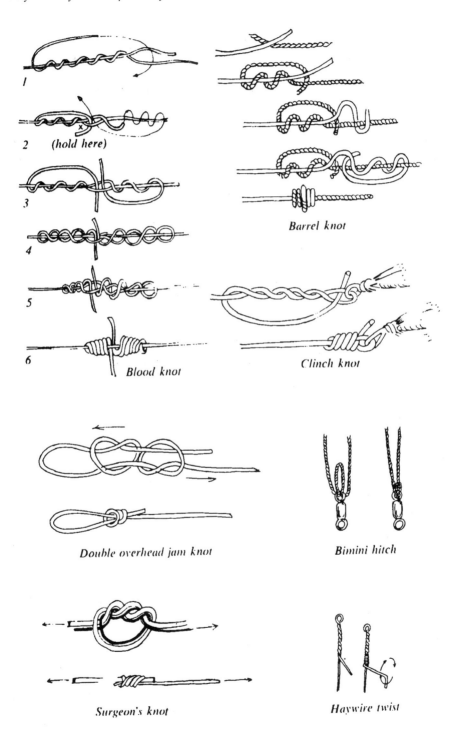

Barrel knot

Blood knot

Clinch knot

Double overhead jam knot

Bimini hitch

Surgeon's knot

Haywire twist

Snaps and Swivels

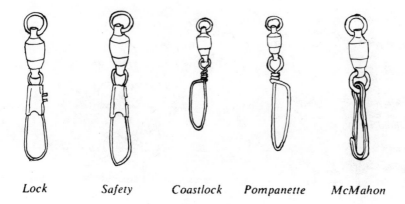

| Lock | Safety | Coastlock | Pompanette | McMahon |

SIZE AND TEST

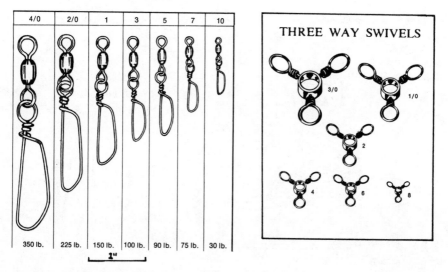

completely or was cut too short. This can be avoided by taking a match and melting the tip of the free line to form a small ball of monofilament. This will harden, increase the size of the line on the tip, and never pull through the jam. Keep the flame away from the rest of the knot or it will be weakened.

Some lures, especially plugs, will have their action hindered if the knot does not allow the eye to swing freely. In this case, a double overhand knot is jammed together to form a sliding loop. This knot is not as strong as the clinch knot, but if a clinch knot will affect the swimming action of a plug, it must be substituted for by the double overhand loop knot.

SNAPS AND SWIVELS

Terminal tackle is often the weakest link between line and fish. Other than knots, it should receive the closest attention. The connection between line and lure or hook can be made directly. But often some lures are likely to twist and thus weaken the line. In other cases, you may want to change lures quickly without a lot of knot-tying, and the snap is your answer. Snaps and swivels come in combination or separately and in a great variety of shapes as well as sizes.

Snaps and swivels can influence the action of your lure if they are too large. Too often, I have seen snaps and swivels used for striped bass that would have held a giant tuna with ease. Don't use snaps or swivels any larger than the anticipated fish require. They should be kept small and unobtrusive. If they aren't they can scare off a fish that is looking for an excuse no to take you enticing offering. Even the smallest snaps and swivels test out at great strengths, often far greater than the lines used.

For heavy trolling lures, the ordinary barrel swivel should not be used. Instead, small swivels with minute ball bearings are available, and though they are expensive, they will ensure that your lure swims properly and will protect your line from excessive twisting. Other swivels are simply eyes with expanded ends encased inside a barrel housing. The two eyes are separate and revolve against the inside walls of the barrel. Snaps come in several shapes: lock snaps, safety snaps, Pompanette snaps, Coast Lock, and McMahon snaps.

Swivels range in size from 12, the smallest to 10, 7, 5, 3, 1, 2/0, and 4/0 the largest—and vary from 20 to 350 pounds in breaking strengths. Thus, even the No. 10 swivel is large enough to handle the needs of most striped-bass outfits. The size of swivel should slightly exceed the strength test of the line.

In cases where a lure and sinker must have separate leaders, then a three-way swivel is in order. These, too, vary greatly in size and strength and are available from No. X, the smallest, through 6, 4, 2, 1/0, and 3/0, the largest. Even larger snap-swivels are made for specialized fishing—marlin, tuna, and swordfish and constitute still another class of swivels and sizes.

LEAD AND SINKERS

Even the most sophisticated striped bass fisherman must at one time or another resort to fishing with lead if he wants to catch fish. If he is dedicated to using nothing but a spinning rod and lures, he may never reach this point, but then he may not be able to catch bass whenever he wants. To the versatile angler, there are times to fish on the bottom and times to troll. To get you into these situations effectively, you may have to use lead, the universal weight. Lead sinkers are seldom pure lead—rather a combination of lead and tin, with occasional other metals added that help it flow into molds and maintain its shape. Shapes are quite important in sinkers because they can affect a sinker's holding power.

The surfcaster appreciates the value of a lead sinker while fishing bait in a running surf. Here a pyramid sinker is about the only way he can hold bottom and put his rod in a holder for a time to rest his arms. Pyramid sinkers come in 1- to 6-ounce weights. The line or snap is attached to a wire eye molded into the sinker's base. This means that any pull applied at right angles to the square base causes its edges to dig in and resist the pull. Pyramid sinkers are ideal when used with a fish-finder that allows the bait and line to run through the eye while the line is tethered by the sinker and guided to the bottom until the strike occurs.

For anchoring by virtue of sheer weight, a bank or dipsey sinker is best. Because of their smooth shape and form, they are also good bets when trying to hold bottom among rocks and offer less opportunity for the lead to lodge in a crack or crevice. Ball- or egg-shaped sinkers with holes through their centers can be used in the surf when it isn't moving quickly or in the bay and quiet areas where it won't be rolled about by a current. This type of sinker functions a lot like a pyramid sinker except that the line is allowed to pass freely through the sinker, and be carried off by a fish. The weight of the sinker isn't noticed by the fish until the angler sets the hook.

Drails are torpedo-shaped weights mounted on bead-chains and used in-line when trolling. The beads allow the line or drail to rotate independently of each other and thus the line is not twisted. The front of the drail is usually equipped with an eye and the end with a snap. Some drails have slight keels on one side so that they will not twist when trolled. Other drails are even kidney-shaped to achieve this same no-spin feature. Drails come in weights from 1/2 ounce to 6 and 7 ounces, with intermediate weights in 1/2-ounce increments.

HOOKS

The final link between fisherman and fish is the hook, and they deserve the angler's utmost attention. There are scores of hook shapes and sizes from which to choose. Each is designed for a special task and each suited to the mouth of a

Sinker styles—Left to right: dipsey, bank, pyramid, barrel, and two trolling drails with beaded chains a. One drail has a keel to further discourage it from twisting while trolled.

particular species of fish or a type of bait. Not only is shape important, but size is vital to a successful hookup. There are 30 to 40 hook sizes, ranging from No. 22, the smallest, up to 16/0. There are larger hooks beyond the 16/0. Unfortunately, hook manufacturers don't all agree on the code number and hook sizes and so those used are often relative suggestions. A No. 3/0 by one manufacturer might be two or three sizes larger on the scale of another.

There are almost as many patterns for hook shapes as there are hook sizes, but here the striped bass angler is rather fortunate because only about three are ideally suited for striped bass fishing. These include the Siwash hook, best suited for trolling and hooking a following striped bass; the O'Shaughnessy hook, well suited to a striped bass's underslung jaw and used on plugs and spoons; and the Eagle Claw or beak bend, used with bait, both live and cut. This latter is often equipped with minute barbs on the shaft to hold bait.

Bass hook sizes range from a small of 2/0 or 3/0, for school-sized stripers (fish up to 8 or 10 pounds), to the 10/0 and 12/0 hooks found on bunker spoons and large trolled lures. In a fairly medium position are hooks in the 6/0 to 8/0 range. You should vary or adjust the hook size to the size of the fish you are taking. A complete bass angler is equipped with a collection of hooks in various sizes and shapes, a sharpening stone and small, fine-tooth file in his tackle box.

Treble hooks also find their way into the striped bass fisherman's box and are often the hooks adorning his plugs and spoons. Some live bait is better hooked on a treble than a single point, and every angler should be equipped with a variety of sizes. Shape is not as important in treble as in single hooks. The great majority of plugs come equipped with Eagle Claw or Sprout treble hooks.

Hooks are made in bronze, stainless steel, and annealed iron, and plated with gold, nickel, cadmium, and tin. Cadmium plating is the best protection on large hooks. Insist on hooks be stainless steel, nickel, or cadmium-plated. Otherwise, the lures won't be worth using more than once. Hooks that go into salt water, even if you wash them, eventually rust away unless they are made of the best anti-corrosive materials.

Hook styles—Left to right: Eagle Claw or beak-type with bait-holding barb; same style but without bait barbs; Siwash; and O'Shaughnessy. At far right, fish-finder snap and swivel.

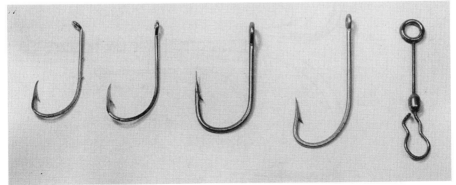

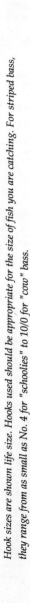

Hook sizes are shown life size. Hooks used should be appropriate for the size of fish you are catching. For striped bass, they range from as small as No. 4 for "schoolies" to 10/0 for "cow" bass.

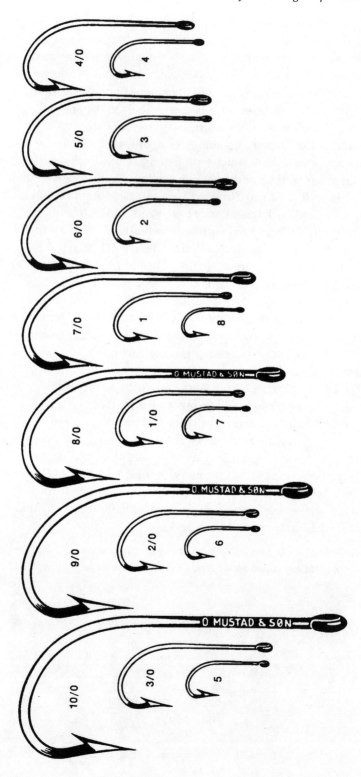

23

Live and Natural Baits
for Striped Bass

Natural marine baits account for taking a great number of striped bass, from small, school-sized fish to those behemoths affectionately called "bulls and cows" by many anglers. Natural bait is an important part of fishing for striped bass and the angler who masters its use and presentation can take striped bass while purists are left fretting with their tackle. Every well rounded bass fisher should be as familiar with the great variety of natural marine baits as he is with the great variety of artificial lures that take bass.

There is a certain snobbishness about some anglers who swear by the plug and the spinning rod and never seem to condescend to the use of live bait. I'm sure that part of this attitude is the result of ignorance with natural baits and how to use them. Too often, live- or cut-bait fishermen are referred to as sinker bouncers. But presenting a live bunker or mackerel to a bass waiting behind a boulder while stemming a 5-knot tide requires just as much skill as balancing on a boulder in the surf or fighting a head wind while on the distal end of a fly rod.

The really serious striped bass angler who employs live bait when it is appropriate often knows as much about the bait he is using as the fish he is after. He should, because the lives of striped bass and the foods they eat are intimately entwined. To study one without any knowledge of the other is like wearing a set of blinders through life.

Thus fishing with live bait can be extremely challenging both physically and mentally, and often produces more striped bass than artificial lures. And if it is large striped bass you are after, just check the records. Almost all the big bass have been taken on natural marine baits, alive or rigged. There are certain times of the year when striped bass are vulnerable only to big baits, and many of the artificial lures just aren't large enough and do not swim well enough to entice a striped bass.

The striped bass is an omnivorous feeder. It will eat almost anything alive in the ocean that it can. As a result, there is a vast array of baits that can be threaded onto a hook or added to the water that will bring a striped bass to feed. These baits can roughly be divided into four biological divisions: marine worms; mollusks, or clams, mussels, and squid; crustaceans, or shrimp, crabs, and lobsters; and the vertebrate fishes, including killifish, spearing, sand eels, real eels, menhaden, sculpins (bullheads on the West Coast), and a list of game fish in small or large sizes that includes mackerel, whiting, flounder, blackfish, bluefish, and weakfish.

Most of these baits can be found in our bays and estuaries or in the inshore seas. They are found in the sand, over mud beaches, along the banks of tidal streams, and in the marine grasses from deep water to the intertidal zone. Some are in the swift water of the estuary outlet, while others are true pelagic fishes and you must seek them in deeper water beyond the barrier beaches and tidal rips. Most you can buy from a seafood store or a coastal bait shop. But for the most part, you can dig or net them yourself or set traps to collect them in large enough numbers to begin fishing. Sometimes, catching the bait can be almost fun as catching the bass.

WORMS

The three worms that most interest striped bass are strictly marine in their habitat: sandworms, bloodworms, and "tapeworms." The first two are annelids—members of a phylum of segmented animals generally called worms by most people and including the famous "garden hackle;" true tapeworms, and a host of marine worms. The "tapeworm" is really a ribbonworm and belongs to another phylum. Marine worms are more popular than any other bait and take a great percentage of striped bass. One reason is that they are so easy to dig or nowadays easy to buy, are easy to fish with, and are extremely well-thought-of by striped bass.

Sandworms

The sandworm or clamworm is by far the most popular of the marine worms. *Nereis virens* is a polychaete annelid—that is, each segment contains several bristles. (The garden worm, a close relative, is an oligochaete, because it lacks the bristles.) In range, the common sandworm is distributed from Cape Hatteras north along all of the coast to Labrador. It is spread in the mud across the Arctic even to Europe and is found along the coast of Great Britain and Norway. Most North American specimens reach 12 and 18 inches when fully grown, but European varieties are considerably longer, up to 3 feet long and as much as 1-3/4 inches wide. Wouldn't that excite a bass in Cape Cod Canal?

The other common name, clamworm, gives us an indication of where the worm can often be found. Clam and mussel beds, especially if they are founded on a clay or mud base between the mid- and low tide marks, are the kinds of environment sandworms call home. Their homes are often temporary, built between the ranges of tide, and are mucus-lined burrows which they inhabit during the day. During the night, sandworms take to wandering, swimming by undulations much like an eel or any other fish. That is one reason why striped bass are such avid night feeders.

The sandworm is carnivorous, eating other worms and little fishes. Its pharynx can be thrown out of a mouth located at the very front end and is armed with two black pincers that grasp food and help it down the gullet. Sandworms vary in color, and many anglers believe it is a characteristic associated with the surrounding mud or sand. This isn't true. Sandworms are sexually color-coded. Males range in dark colors from steel blue to green while females are olive-green with reddish or orange appendages that are used as side feet. When sandworms are in a healthy, fresh condition, their skin reflects with an iridescent sheen.

The best time and place to dig sandworms are on a falling tide on exposed mud flats. Usually below the half-tide mark, you can dig them with a spade or fork. You must be fast, however, because they can disappear before your very eyes. Don't place them in a galvanized bucket or it will kill them. A wooden car or plastic bucket is your best bet. To keep them alive for any length of time, don't fill the bucket with water. Instead, drain the worms and add marine weeds like bladderwort or strands of kelp cut to form layers like a lasagna. Heat will quickly turn them into a stinking mess, so store them in a cool spot out of the sun. If you won't use them until the next day, better put them in a cooler or refrigerator, and don't let fresh water from ice get on them.

Sandworms as striped bass bait can be used in several situations. One of the more pleasant ways to take striped bass is by trolling for them in a small rowboat late in the day or early in the evening. The technique is carried out in shallow water, along the edges of bays and tidal estuaries, and in protected areas where the current isn't so great as to challenge your rowing ability.

The worms are fished on a spinning or popping rod, 100 or more feet astern of the boat, on 15- or 20-pound test line. Small split shot can be used but aren't necessary in such shallow water. One or two large sandworms are placed on a 2/0 to 4/0 Eagle Claw or beak-type hook. The barb of the hook is pushed through the mouth of the sandworm and then immediately brought out the side. The worm is then slipped up the shaft of the hook and kept from returning by small barbs. The second worm is fastened in the same manner and left on the bend of the hook. Sandworms hooked only by their heads have the best natural appearance and look like they are swimming along when trolled slowly. Between the hook and the end of the leader, a small willow-leaf spinner can be added for extra attraction. The contemplative bass fisherman can usually handle two such rigs off the transom of his boat. Of course, the rod tips should be separated as greatly as possible, by rod-holders in the boat, placed at right

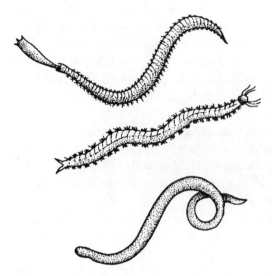

The favorite three baits of saltwater fishermen are (left to right) the sandworm, bloodworm, and ribbonworm, all marine worms found naturally in the world of the striped bass.

angles to its length, allow you to accomplish this.

In areas where a fair current moves and an angler can get to its edge from a point of land, a jetty, or a pier, he can use sandworms effectively to take striped bass. The rig here differs slightly, with the use of a three-way swivel in the line and a dropper leader of less strength than that of the main line tied to a 1- to 3-ounce bank or dipsey sinker. The rig is gently cast into the current and the slack in the line is taken up until the fisherman can feel the sinker bouncing along the bottom.

To keep the sandworm from becoming hidden in the grass, a 1- to 2-foot leader is placed on the sinker and the festooned hook usually sails downstream on a 2- to 3-foot strand of monofilament. A few inches before the hook, many fishermen add a small, torpedo-shaped cork or balsa float. It should just be large enough to cancel out some of the weight of the worm and hook but not so large as to lift it toward the surface.

Sandworms are often used in conjunction with artificial lures. I couldn't believe it the first time I saw it, but one day at Cuttyhunk (Massachusetts), on the famous Sow and Pigs Reef striped bass ground, I watched the charterboat skippers trolling with long surgical tubes. To the hook ends of 2- to 3-foot long tubes, they would add small pieces of sandworm, maybe no more than 2 or 3 inches long. At first I laughed (to myself), but they caught fish and I didn't, because I didn't have sandworms for my surgical tubes. The sandworms must have provided that small bit of food odor that the lure needed to make the bass come up and strike.

Sandworms are also effective baits in the surf for striped bass when they are used in conjunction with a fish-finder rig and a pyramid sinker. The size of sinker, 1 to 6 ounces, will depend on the state of the surf and running tidal current. One or two sandworms are skewered onto a hook and gently heaved out to sea. The slack in the line is taken up with the rod in a surf spike (holder) and the drag adjusted to just as light a setting as possible to keep the surf from taking out the line or lure. The click is left on, and when a bass picks up the sandworms, it can run, taking the monofilament or Dacron line through the large eye on the fish-finder without feeling the weight of the sinker. In many instances, a float is also used with the fish-finder rig to keep the sandworms just off the bottom of the surf and away from sand sharks and sea robins.

Bloodworms

Bloodworms are used almost as much as sandworms for striped bass bait. *Glycera dibranchiata,* as it is known in scientific circles, has a somewhat less extensive range than its close cousin the sandworm. It is found along our Atlantic Coast from North Carolina to the Gulf of St. Lawrence and on the Pacific side from California to Mexico. It has been reduced in abundance and today can be found in commercial numbers only in the land surrounding the Gulf of Maine, in Maine, New Brunswick, and Nova Scotia.

The bloodworm is somewhat smaller than the sandworm, about 12 to 15 inches in maximum length, and is rounder, and more closely resembling an earthworm than the flatter sandworm. It has a darker red color than the earthworm and a pointed head with a tail that diminishes rapidly in size. The bloodworm has no true system of blood vessels like other worms and the body fluids are filled with hemoglobin in corpuscles that slosh around its cavities and account for the purple-to-pinkish body color.

This open circulatory system also accounts for the profuse bleeding when a bloodworm is cut. Often after it stops and the blood is gone, there is little left in the area but the outside skin. It takes several bloodworms to adorn a hook the way one sandworm can.

Like the sandworm, bloodworms have a pharynx that can be flipped out, and they have a similar proboscis, but armed with four pincers or sharp jaws that can bite. The bite can be painful as well as slightly poisonous. Unlike the aggressive sandworm, the bloodworm is not a meat-eater but instead finds sustenance in organic debris in the soft, dark-colored mud it likes to call home. The strong jaws and the stinging bite are really defensive structures.

Unlike the wandering nocturnal sandworms, bloodworms are real home-bodies and don't take to spending much time outside of their muck. Because of their softer body construction they can be found only around rather soft muds, away from well packed sands, rocks, and gravel which are occasionally the home of sandworms. In some cases, both can be found together in the same spade full of mud.

Though the bloodworm is found almost the length of our Atlantic and Pacific coasts and most that are dug come from its northern range, it is used as a striped bass bait more commonly in the southern part of its range. Long Island seems to be an arbitrary dividing point, with anglers on the South Shore and from New Jersey to the Carolinas seeming to prefer the bloodworm to the sandworm. From the North Shore of Long Island to Maine and New Brunswick, the sandworm seems the first choice in baits.

Bloodworms can be fished in each of the situations described for the sandworms. They are just as readily taken by stripers as any other worm. But because of their smaller size, you may have to add more. Also, because of a weaker skin, they have a tendency to break apart, and smaller and thinner hooks make it easier to use them as bait. They are hooked like sandworms—that is, through the mouth and out the side. Often, however, because they stretch and break so easily, they must be hooked a second time near the tail. Because of this double hooking, they do not present as natural a picture when trolled as sandworms. Given a choice, pick the sandworm for trolling situations and the bloodworm when you are fishing with lead, in the surf, or from a fixed position.

Also, bloodworms are more difficult to keep on the shank of a hook than sandworms. In addition to the hooks with barbs on their shafts as bait-holders, some companies manufacture a special "sea-worm hook." This hook has a sharp wire point in the eye to which the first worm can be skewered if you are using more than one and if will hold its position.

When bloodworms are drifted in a current with no weight attached to the line they can prove a deadly bait for striped bass. The action of one or two head-hooked worms looks like the pair are wrestling with each other, and bass don't make good bystanders. Drifted off a low-lying bridge or pier, or off the end of a jetty or sod bank into a bass hole, bloodworms are one of the best baits available. If the current is too great for the worm to be live-lined, then one or two split shot, 2 or 3 feet away from the worms, will get them deeper and still not influence their swimming.

Ribbonworms

Commonly and erroneously called tapeworms, ribbonworms are the third group of marine worms used by fishermen to take striped bass. The ribbon-worm is not an annelid, because it lacks the body segmentation. Instead, it belongs to another phylum called the nemertean worms, a group that are not segmented and have a long, tube-like proboscis that is extremely muscular. Nor are the ribbonworms parasitic as are most tapeworms.

Ribbonworms, as their name implies, are extremely flat or dorsal-ventrally compressed, and closely resemble a ribbon. They are long worms, and seldom do you see both ends at one time. A 5-foot ribbonworm can stretch itself to about 20 feet and maintain a width of about an inch. There are several nemertean worms, but *Cerebratulus lacteus* is the one most often used by fishermen. It is widely distributed along the Atlantic, from Maine to Florida, but is concentrated from New Jersey to southern Maine and likes either sand or mud beaches as a place to burrow a home, and it is an active burrower. It has a mucous covering over its body and is colored an ivory or creamy white with hints of pink. Ribbonworms are highly carnivorous and are active swimmers, leaving their burrows at night to hunt mainly other worms. They attack by rapidly everting the slender proboscis. The proboscis is not armed with teeth but simply wraps itself around the prey, e.g. a clamworm or bloodworm, and in effect squeezes it

Worms can be fished in a variety of ways. The top two illustrations are of terminal rigs for worms in the surf. A pyramid sinker anchors the rig and a fish-finder allows a bass to run with the bait. The second rig has a cork or balsa float added to it so that the worm is not directly on the sand, but on the bass's eye level. The third rig is a typical trolling rig, with a Cape Cod spinner added for attraction. Bottom illustration shows two worms on the same hook.

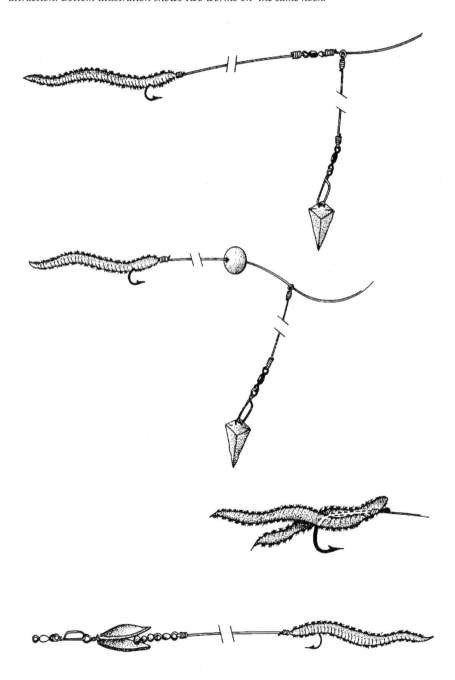

and works the food back into its mouth by retracting the organ.

Ribbonworms are difficult to buy because most fishermen are repulsed at the sight and only a small group are aware of what great striped bass baits they make. The common name, "tapeworm," also turns off a lot of fishermen. If you want your own, more than likely you will have to dig them, and it can often be a two- or three-man job. The worms are extremely fast burrowers, and once they have been discovered can rapidly move through the mud. To get one out intact requires fast work and often more than one shovel.

An entire ribbonworm would be too much to troll, even though striped bass are known to be head-hitters. Instead, the ribbonworm should be cut into 8- or 10-inch strips and hooked on the leading end several times to ensure it won't slip off. The other end is left trailing free. Small striped bass may often hit a long bait like the ribbonworm, or even long sandworms, on the tail or short side. This can be remedied by tying a second hook onto a piece of clear monofilament and then attaching it to the eye of the first hook. The length of mono leader should be a little shorter than the length of the worm. The second hook is just slightly passed through the trailering bait and should not appreciably affect its action. The leader material must be rather light and supple or it will override the undulations of the bait.

MOLLUSKS

Mollusks are soft-bodied animals that in many cases have developed external skeletons to protect them from the ravages of other animals and the elements. They include several classes, two of which are extremely important natural foods for striped bass. One class is composed of clams and mussels, and the second class is the Cephalopoda or squids, a closely related form.

Clams, mussels, and squid are high on the menu of striper bass, and the linesider's penchant for squid has even earned it the name "squidhound" in some angling quarters. The striped bass is unable to do much damage to hard-shelled clams when they are inside their element, but after a storm, when they have been smashed about by combers on the beach, bass readily take advantage of the situation and gorge themselves. Some soft-shelled clams and some mussels are another story; bass can break their shells with their strong jaws. In other situations, bass catch mussels and clams traveling—that is, with their best (and only) foot forward—and strike the mollusk before it can get its body back into the protection of the two valves.

Clams and mussels are used in two ways to catch bass: either impaled on a hook, or as chum to get them to a hook with more clams or other baits on it. The broadcasting ability of clam odor in the water is terrific and one reason clams are used so frequently in bass fishing. Squid are almost always used as the bait itself, either as an entire morsel or stripped and a part of artificial lures.

Skimmer Clams

The skimmer clam, *Spisula solidissima,* is the most popular of all the clams and mussels used. It is locally known as a sea clam or surf clam and often commercially sought for chowders and packaged seafoods. As a marine bait, the skimmer is unsurpassed. When freshly shucked, it has a large muscle that holds well on a hook, and is full of juices that entice a striped bass to come looking.

A great abundance of skimmers also makes them the preferred bait over other clams, the smaller hard clams, soft clams, and razor clams. They can readily be purchased at seafood stores or bait shops along the coast, and at reasonable prices. They are easy to open, and if you walk the beach after a storm, they are more than likely to be in an open state. Pack a bagful and store it away in your freezer while they are still fresh and you have the cheapest bait available.

Spisula solidissima is widely distributed along the North Atlantic Coast, from Cape Hatteras to Labrador on the north side of the Gulf of St. Lawrence. Its greatest abundance occurs in the New York Bight, between mid-New Jersey and as far east as Montauk on Long Island. Concentrations of skimmers are particularly large off the south shore of Long Island. This may explain the great popularity of chumming and fishing in this area with clams and clam bellies, the by-product of the clam-dragging industry.

Skimmers also are our largest clams, measuring up to 4 or 5 inches across their widest part. They also produce large meats, and half a dozen big clams is usually enough for one man and an afternoon's fishing. They are great baits to use in the surf for bass because, if hooked properly, they will take a lot of heaving and casting and stay together in the pounding melee. The clam is strung onto the hook, preferably a long-shanked Eagle Claw or Siwash, between 3/0 and 5/0 in size. The soft parts are strung on first, if you can find them, and the muscle is then the last part over the hook and barb to keep the remainder of the clam from slipping off. If hooked in this manner, it is likely to stay on for a while. Such an affair is best fished off the end of a fish-finder rig.

In other angling situations, clams are fished from a boat while chumming under a bridge, along a tidal creek, or in a river channel. The greater bulk of sea clams is ground or pulverized and fed methodically into the water. The bigger clam pieces or whole clams (without the shell, naturally) are hooked and drifted into the chum. A weight is seldom needed; the weight of the hook and mass of clams is enough to take it slowly to the bottom and keep it in the region of the chum. If the current is moving too fast, then a sinker is added in the line, 4 to 5 feet ahead of the bait. Clamp-on, in-line type sinkers with rubber cushions work well without pinching or weakening the line.

Most other baits for striped bass are fished with the hook and barb exposed. But because of the soft body of the clam, even its tougher muscle, the hook and barbs should be hidden whenever possible. The bite of a bass will force the hook through the muscle. With the barb covered while fishing, the hook is less likely to collect drifting eelgrass or other debris.

Hard Clams

There is only one hard clam, *Mercenaria mercenaria,* that is favored by bass and bass fishermen. It has three different names, and these are not colloquial handles, but instead are market terms that refer to their sizes. The hard clam was known to the coastal Indians of the Northeast as the quahog. Today, this clam in the larger sizes is used mainly for chowder and is often called the chowder clam as well as the quahog. Littlenecks are the smallest hard clams, and cherrystone are the size between littlenecks and quahogs.

Hard clams are not frequently used for striped bass bait unless you have a surplus of quahogs, because they taste as good to the fisherman as to the fish. They can be used in much the same manner as skimmer clams, but because of their smaller size, several might be needed in the place of one skimmer. Hard clams are dug or raked at the edge of low tide along the beaches or tonged up in shallow water in protected bays and estuaries. In many states where they occur, there are seasons and regulations affecting their taking and use and restriction, on taking them from polluted waters, whether for bait or human consumption. You should be familiar with local regulations before you go clamming for bait.

Soft Clams

The soft clam, *Mya arenaria,* is also locally known as the steamer clam. Steamers also are as palatable to man as hard clams, but because they are far more numerous and it's easier to rake a bushel, they are more practical to use as a striped bass bait. Soft clams range from the warm, shallow protected bays of North Carolina to the frigid, ice-covered waters of the Arctic. They are most often found in soft, muddy bottoms between high and low tide, and more often nearer the bottom reaches of the tide.

Steamers group together more closely than hard clams, and when you discover a bed you can fill your bucket in a matter of minutes or a few shovelfuls of muck. They burrow just under the surface and their siphon holes can be seen pock-marking the beach. These clams are characterized by a long maneuverable siphon which can be extended beyond the shell to take in fresh seawater or hunt for food. Also, steamers have a softer, whitish shell that can easily be crushed between the fingers. The shell of a soft clam is more elongated in shape than the oval hard clam and has more pronounced ridges.

The meat of the soft-shelled clam is not as firm as that of the hard or skimmer clam, but the siphon, a tough, rubbery appendage, can be hooked on last, like the muscle of a skimmer clam, and will stay on for quite a degree of abuse. Soft-shelled clams are also used for chum. They are smashed or ground up, shells and all, and mixed with seawater to form a soup or broth. The gruel is ladled into the water, and the hook is adorned with several soft steamers, minus their shells.

Razor Clams

Like other species of clams, the razor clam, *Ensis directus*, can also be used as bait because they are everywhere found in the environment of the striped bass. The razor clam does a lot more wandering on the bottom, instead of in it like soft clams and quahogs, and thus is a more familiar food to striped bass. However, their numbers are few compared to those of other clams and anglers are not as apt to use them.

Their long, curved shells, closely resembling the handle of a straight razor, can grow to 7 or 8 inches in length. And though narrow, they do provide a lot of meat for the hook. They are swift burrowers, and if you spot one in shallow water you might be hard-pressed to catch it. They are distributed from the southern tip of Florida to Labrador and are more fond of sand beaches than strictly mud environments.

Striped bass like clams as much as people do. Here is an assortment of the striper's favorites.

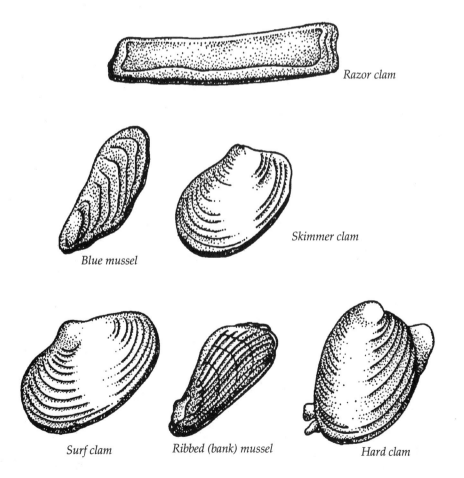

Razor clam

Blue mussel

Skimmer clam

Surf clam

Ribbed (bank) mussel

Hard clam

Blue Mussels

The blue mussel, or edible mussel, *Mytilus edulis,* is extremely plentiful along our coasts and distributed on both sides of the Atlantic, from North Carolina to Spain. In Europe, it is a favorite seafood, but in America it is seldom eaten by anyone except transplanted Europeans who aren't keen on spreading the word. Striped bass are also fond of blue mussels, but because their bodies are so soft, they are seldom used for bait. Instead, they are often pounded or ground into chum by bass fishermen and other baits are then used on the hook.

The elongated blue-colored shells are up to 2-1/2 inches long. Blue mussels are extremely colonial and sedentary, binding themselves into huge mussel beds by strong, yellow byssus threads that each mussel secretes. These beds are great hunting grounds for striped bass and clamworms alike and are good areas over which to fish and chum. The mussels do not burrow in the mud but live on its surface and pile colonies upon themselves. Their beds are located in the intertidal zone, in the lower portion, and mussels shut their shells while the water is gone so that they do not dehydrate. Collecting a pailful is simply a matter of breaking them away from the mass. A fork works better than a spade.

Ribbed Mussels

The ribbed or bank mussel, *Brachiodontes demissus,* is a close cousin to the blue mussel. It is quite similar in shape but is colored a soft brown to a yellow, or even an olive drab tinge, instead of blue, and the shell is heavily fluted or ribbed along its longer axis. Bank mussels also prefer to live in vertical situations rather than build horizontally on the beach or flats. Banks cut by tidal creeks and streams meandering through marshes are the forte of the bank mussel. Unlike blue mussels, the bank mussel is not edible. As a bait for striped bass it is difficult to place on a hook because of the extremely soft and fluid body. But as a chum ingredient, it is supreme for stripers, surpassed only by clam bellies.

Nor are bank mussels as colonial in their living habits as blue mussels. You may have to hunt along the sides of a creek for a distance before you get enough to fill a bucket for chum. If you do insist on using them for bait, and they can fill this requirement, they need a little help staying on the hook. The mass must be supported by twisting a soft wire around it or tying it on with a piece of thread.

Squid

It is difficult for anyone but a biologist to believe that a squid, that fast-swimming denizen of our inshore and offshore waters, is actually a mollusk. This extremely mobile creature has all but freed itself of its shell but still uses jets to get around like more sedentary clams. The squid is an aggressive carnivore, a highly organized animal that swims about in schools similar to those of real fishes.

Because of its pelagic distribution, the squid has become a real favorite of striped bass and ranks high on its menu of preferred foods. Squid move about the waters by jet propulsion, squeezing water out of their bodies through a restrictive port that shoots them backward as they travel. The size of their schools can be extremely large and their only protection is sheer numbers so that some are always left to maintain the schools. Their prime source of food is small fishes, and a school of squid can decimate a school of sand eels or small menhaden with the rapidity of ravenous bluefish.

The most common squid, *Loligo pealii*, can shade its appearance with tints of blue, purple, red, and yellow. It sports a spindle-shaped body, tapering in the back to an arrowhead point and trailing ten octopus-like tentacles from what is its front. To see where it is going, squid have taken the light-sensitive eye area of a clam and developed it into an organ comparable to eyes in vertebrates. The arrowhead backside, which glides through the water first, has its edges modified into fins or diving planes similar to those of a submarine.

The range of this squid is from South Carolina northward to Cape Cod and occasionally into the Gulf of Maine. Its distribution covers both inshore and offshore waters. Most are caught by draggers traveling at high speeds or pound traps planted along the shore.

As bait for striped bass, squid can be fished on the bottom, rigged in a somewhat free-swimming form for the surf, or trolled. The last is the best technique and the one employed by the majority of anglers. The squid is used whole in most instances, though some anglers prefer to use only the head when casting or still-fishing. In this case, the head is pulled off the rest of the body and skewered onto a 3/0 claw-type hook, with barbs on the shank to keep the squid from slipping down. It can be cast into the surf, eased out of an anchored boat, or fished in shallow water with no weights. With a three-way swivel and snelled to a sinker it can be fished when the water is too deep or the current too strong to let the squid fall to where bass might be cruising.

The whole squid can also be rigged in several ways. One of the easiest is to hook three or four (depending upon the length of the squid) O'Shaughnessy hooks in tandem to each other—that is, through the eye of one and then the eye of the next to form sort of a chain. The last hook is passed beyond the barb, into the space between the eyes of the squid. The second goes into the bulk of the body and the third is planted not far from the pointed tail. If the squid is fresh and the meat firm, this may be enough to hold it on the hook, and it can be cast into the surf, fished off a three-way swivel in fast water, or trolled behind a boat. If the trolling is against a strong current, the squid can be further secured to the hooks by several pieces of light line or thread wound around the body of the squid and passed through the eyes of each hook.

Still another technique when trolling is to fix an 8/0 Siwash or O'Shaughnessy hook to a 12-inch length of wire leader. The tip of the leader can be cut at a sharp angle and the wire then needled up through the base of the tentacles and out the tip of the pointed posterior. If you want to troll the squid at deeper levels, then a small barrel sinker can be slipped onto the leader before

The squid today is one of the most overlooked striped bass baits, though it was one of the first baits used by early sportfishers. Illustrated here are four possible squid rigs. The top rig is a whole squid with the tail cut square and then skewered onto a lead-headed hook. The tail is then sewn or threaded through holes in the lead head. The second rig is similar but the squid is tied to the head. The hook is attached inside to an eye and swings more freely with the body of the squid. The third rig is a series of hooks attached to each other and then imbedded into the squid. The bottom rig, the simplest, is primarily a surf rig, while the three others are used when trolling.

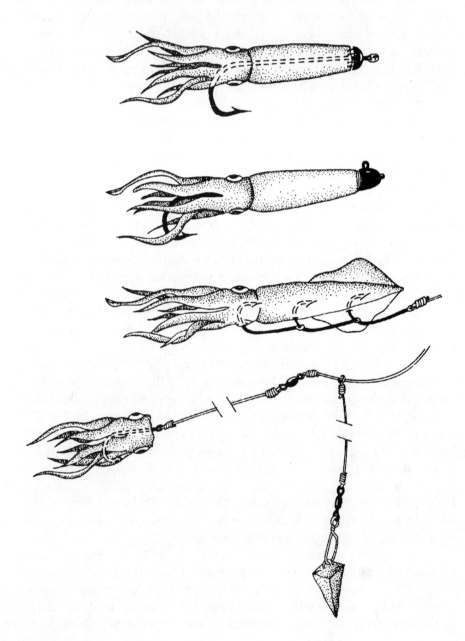

the squid is pierced. The hook and sinker are drawn into the squid and covered by its tentacles and head. The wire is then fastened to the eye of a swivel and the free end cut loose. The softness of a squid's flesh is difficult to handle and extreme care must be taken because the body is very likely to give way at the point with excessive trolling. It is best kept in shape by sewing the tougher tip to the eye of the swivel.

Still another effective technique, though not widely used because of a lack of materials, is the use of a lead head for squid. This is nothing more than a half-round ball of lead poured around the shank of a long-shafted 9/0 or 10/0 hook just below the eye. The pointed back end of the squid is cut off at a right angle and the squid worked on the hook through the center of the cut until the bend of the hook comes out near the mouth or eyes of the animal. To keep the squid from slipping down on the hook, a series of holes are drilled around the edge of the head and the squid sewn against its base.

This type of rigged squid can be trolled at good depths, or cast into the surf and slowly retrieved, or trolled with a jigging motion to simulate the manner in which a live squid swims. The jerky action also is a better attractor of striped bass than a steady, even pull.

Squid can also be cut into long strips for trolling, either by itself or at the end of a bucktail jig, spoon, or other comparable lure. In this case, the head is cut off and the body sliced open. The outer covering is skinned off and the firm, white meat sliced into longitudinal strips that taper at their distal ends. The larger part of a strip of squid is always attached to the hook to give the tapered end a better swimming action. If you are drifting or still-fishing the squid strips, you can change their shape to add more meat to the morsel, with shorter but chunkier slices.

CRUSTACEANS

Lobsters, shrimp, and crabs are crustaceans familiar to all of us, but striped bass are on more intimate terms with these ten-legged creatures that swim and crawl in the marine world of the striped bass. They are favorite foods, and, wherever they can easily be obtained in fair quantities, are good selections for bait. I doubt today that there is much fishing done with lobster tails as bait, as once was the accepted custom at Montauk and Cuttyhunk. But the lobster's close cousins are still in use, and even the famous blue crab, that is equally satisfying to striped bass and striped bass fisherman is used in many areas of our country to subdue an old linesider.

Grass and Sand Shrimp

The grass shrimp, *Palaeomonetes vulgaris*, is the most popular of the shrimp used to catch striped bass. It can be used as the bait itself, with several strung on a hook, or as chum to entice striped bass to come to other baits. These small, 1-to 1-1/2-inch crustaceans are liked by both large and small bass, though smaller bass are more regularly taken with them as bait.

Grass shrimp have a translucent body, delicate and sharp-pointed, with a saw-edged spine that extends forward between the eyes to discourage diners. Grass shrimp are found in shallow bays, creeks, and marine estuaries, where they are netted or out in deeper water, off the barrier beaches, and in deep sounds and bays. Given a choice, they prefer to live and feed over soft bottoms with good stands of eelgrass and other forms of marine vegetation. The grass shrimp's distribution ranges from the lower Gulf of Maine south to Florida, and its abundance in many years has been regulated by the available amount of eelgrass or other protection offered by the marine environment. During years when eelgrass underwent a decline because of a coast-wide blight, grass shrimp also declined and all but disappeared from their natural range.

Shrimp can be used both as a bait and in a chum line. Both grass and sand shrimp are good chum material, while the common edible shrimp is more often used on the hook because of its larger size.

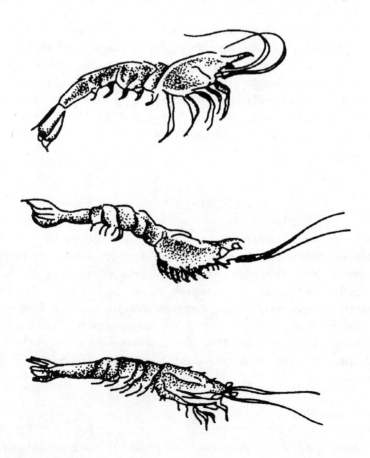

The sand shrimp, *Crangon septemspinosa*, is more abundant than the grass shrimp but not quite as desirable. It can be distinguished from its close cousin by broad, fanlike expansions at the base of the antennae on the shrimp's head. Sand shrimp grow slightly larger, up to 2 inches, and are more abundant along sandy beaches and open environments than grass shrimp. They are distributed from the Carolinas north to Labrador, with the greatest concentrations located from Cape May, N.J., north to the southern Massachusetts coast. It is not quite as transparent as the grass shrimp but its pale-gray color and mottling make it well camouflaged and nearly invisible until it moves. The color adapts within a range to that of the bottom over which it is found.

Sand shrimp can easily be caught by sweeping the beach with a small-meshed haul seine, and a bucket can be filled in minutes. Grass shrimp are taken by seining the creeks and tidal bays at mid-tide by two men sweeping through with a roller-type net and moving down tide swiftly with the bend of the grasses. Both shrimp are stored best in a floating car attached to the transom of the boat and always exposed to a fresh supply of sea water.

Grass and sand shrimp, because of their small size, are often employed as chum for striped bass. When they are also used as bait, it takes several of them to fill a 2/0 beak-type hook to provide a mouthful for even a small striped bass. They can be frozen in plastic milk cartons, mixed with water so that all air is sealed from their surface. Freshly thawed, they are as effective as live shrimp except that swimming shrimp are not a part of such a chum line.

Edible Shrimp

The shrimp you find swimming around in your shrimp cocktail cup belong to the genus *Penaeus,* and though they are generally native to the waters from Cape Hatteras south, they are found naturally from time to time as far north as Long Island. About the only way you can get them on your hook is by fishing around a seafood market, and if you are willing to use them without a sauce, the striped bass will feed on them. They are best used when chumming with grass or sand shrimp, the hook, baited with *Penaeus*. But, like lobster, shrimp may be strictly a rich man's bait.

Blue Crabs

The well known blue crab, or blue claw, *Callinectus sapidus*, is common to the marine waters from southern Massachusetts to Cape Hatteras and is a denizen of the intertidal shore zone. When its summer migration brings it out of the deeper bays and estuaries, the crab is fair game in either its hard, soft, shedder, or paper stages. The greatest center of abundance for the blue crab is in Chesapeake Bay, in Maryland and Virginia waters. It isn't difficult to tell a blue crab from other crabs in marine waters because of its large size (up to 7 inches), sharply pointed, dark green top shell (called a carapace), bright blue trim, and dangling red-and-scarlet legs.

Like many clams and lobsters, blue crabs are protected by laws in several states, with seasons and size limitations. You might also be called upon to return female crabs, but they are easy to sex, with massive, bright orange egg sacs attached to their undersides.

As bait, the crab is excellent and can be used in any of its stages, though soft crabs are preferred by bass. Crabs, like other crustaceans, have an exoskeleton. Man has an endoskeleton. As we grow, the muscles are added to the outside of our skeleton, but crustaceans, crabs, and lobsters grow from the inside and soon fill their outer hard shell or skeleton. To grow larger this skeleton from time to time is split, and the crab emerges with a new shell but in a somewhat softer state and unable to swim. It is most vulnerable to striped bass at this time and it takes several days before the new and larger exoskeleton is hard enough to protect it. Crabs shed or molt several times during a summer, depending upon how fast they grow.

One of the favorite methods for fishing a crab while seeking striped bass is to float it. The soft crab is somewhat buoyant, and when its fixed to a 4/0 to 6/0 O'Shaughnessy hook will float long distances with the tide or current. The pull of the current against a fixed line helps buoy up the crab. It is almost impossible to hook a crab, nor should you while it is in the soft state. It can be fixed to the hook by two soft rubber bands, crossed over the back with the hook laid across the short axis of the crab, allowing its feet to be free and wiggle as an added attraction for bass.

Floating crabs is best done at night, from an anchored boat or off a point of land. At this time, bass will not hesitate to come near the surface for a crab feast. The hook is best laid on the underside of the crab, and when the fish runs with the bait, some time must be allowed before setting the hook to ensure that the bass has taken the crab deeply enough for the hook to find a spot to lodge.

Hard crabs can be fished live or by passing a hook between both shells. They are better fished on the bottom with a three-way swivel with enough line on the sinker so the crab is about 18 inches off the sand or mud. Nor need crabs be fished whole to be effective bass baits. A cut crab advertises its presence in the current of things in a striped bass's world by the odors and juices it exudes.

A crab can be cut in half or quartered and the pieces placed on a hook with the bend and barb hidden. If you have plenty of crabs, the legs and other materials can also be used to set up a small chum line. Don't waste anything that might entice a striped bass. Half and quarter pieces are difficult to hold on a hook. They can be fastened with the help of a rubber band or light sewing thread.

Crabs can be fished from an anchored boat, off a pier, dock, or bridge, or fished while drifting. When floated, the crab is allowed to be pulled away from the boat by the force of the current. The bail is open on a spinning reel or the reel left in free spool on a conventional-type reel. The line is first pulled out by hand to get the crab into the current, and then its downtide drift is controlled by pressure on the spool from the thumb. When a bass strikes—usually a rather soft strike with crabs—it should be allowed to run until you think you dare not let out any more line. Then, the clutch is engaged on the reel and hook firmly set.

Calico Crabs

The common calico crab, *Ovalipes ocellatus*, is also known as the lady or sand crab. It is a brightly colored crab with a yellow to lavender back and purple spots. Calicos can be used when blue crabs are scarce or you'd rather cook the blue claw crabs for yourself. The calico crab is found on the outer beaches and sandy areas—more so than the blue crab—and is frequently in the surf trying to race the water back into the ocean.

Its distribution is broader than that of the blue crab, from Cape Cod to the Gulf of Mexico, and it can be collected on the beaches by a rake equipped with a basket on its trailing edge. The calico will bury itself in the sand until only its eyes are exposed, but a rake drawn through the first inch or two of sand will easily pull it from its hiding spot.

Though smaller than the blue crab, the calico can be used in the exact same manner when trying for striped bass. Small ones can be doubled on the hook, and if you rake in a bushel the others can be cut into small pieces and used as a chum. Because it is more often found in the surf than the blue crab, the calico is preferred by some surfcasters who want to match the bait to the environment, and striped bass are less likely to be startled by an injured calico in the suds.

Green and Fiddler Crabs

The green crab, *Carcinides maenas*, and the fiddler crab, three species within the genus *Uca*, often share the same environment. All can be used for striped bass baits. The green crab is a darker, mottled crab, medium in size, and is common from New Jersey to Maine. Bigger specimens, up to 3 inches, can be cut in two or used whole on a 2/0 hook.

Fiddler crabs are more gregarious than green crabs and set up housekeeping in colonies along the banks of salt creeks and tidal marshes. As the tide floods in, striped bass are fond of searching all fiddler holes to catch one too far out and make a meal of it. The pale-colored Uca minax, called "china back" by many anglers, is the species used most often for bait.

Hermit Crabs

This rather specialized crustacean, *Pagurus pollicaris*, has given up its protective carapace or shell for a life of mobility but feels so insecure that it seldom wanders far from its makeshift home. Without a shell to call its own, the hermit crab, not really a true crab, will set up housekeeping in the abandoned shells of large moon snails or whelks. When the shells are crushed the soft, helpless hermit crab makes an ideal bait for striped bass. But because they're not often available in quantity, they are not too often used. If you are out of bait and spot a hermit slip into a whelk shell, don't pass it up—it may mean a bass for you.

Crabs are some of the striped bass's favorite foods.

Two methods of hooking, directly or with a rubber band.

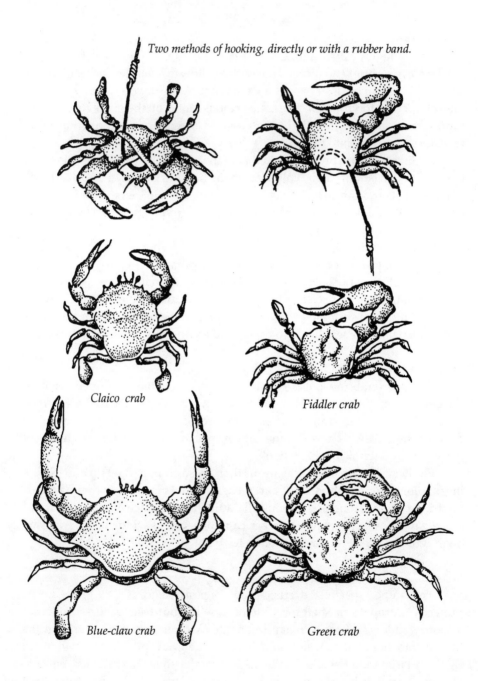

Claico crab

Fiddler crab

Blue-claw crab

Green crab

Sand Bugs

Not bugs in even the widest meaning of the word, this specialized crustacean burrows into the intertidal zone of a sandy beach and when knocked loose by pounding surf is eagerly sought by striped bass. At times, the sand bug, *Emertia talpoida*, is all that striped bass will seek out for food. During the striped bass's spring migration north along the Atlantic's sand beaches, from Virginia to Cape Cod, aside from bunker, sand bugs are about the only bait upon which they will readily strike.

I've never seen them for sale at a bait shop so the only way to get them is to catch them yourself. The bugs inhabit the tidal zone of sandy beaches from Massachusetts to the Yucatan. They rush up the beach with the waves and then race it back into the wash. They are best taken with a wire scoop, because they move so quickly that the hands are neither large enough nor fast enough. They can burrow rapidly and disappear as you watch them. Sand bugs are rather large as far as beach life goes—up to 2-1/2 inches long, with a curved or arched back that is covered by a smooth, tough carapace colored tan or yellowish-white. Most, however, are under an inch and sport a pair of "feathered" antennae that are half as long as the bug's body. Because of their small size, it takes more than one average bug to make a tempting meal for a bass in the surf. Fishermen prefer to string two on a hook and hide the barbs.

Not really a crab, the hermit crab finds a home in the shells abandoned by mollusks while the sand bug or sand flea finds a home in the sand beneath the surf by burrowing.

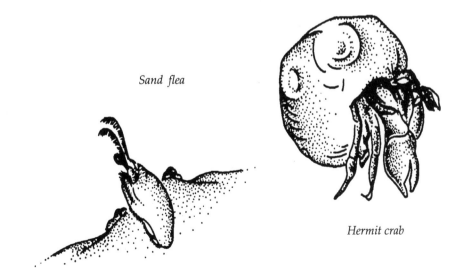

Sand flea

Hermit crab

FISH AS BAIT

Striped bass are primarily piscivorous feeders—that is, the bulk of the food in their diet, by weight, is composed of other fishes. Though there is a great variety of foods bass will feed upon, once they grow to fry or fingerling stages, they begin shifting from small crustaceans to small fish as their main food source. There are two general groups of fishes that appear on the striper's menu. The first are primarily food or forage fishes, those that seldom grow large and are not sought after by fishermen as game fish. With regard to the striped bass's likings, these include the killifish, spearing, sand eels, butterfish, and menhaden, the last being the largest of this group.

The second group of food fishes for striped bass constitutes the young stage of many game fish or even the adult forms when these fish are not especially large. This group includes mackerel, whiting, blackfish, bluefish, weakfish, sculpins, and eels. Of all these species, the eel and menhaden or bunker are by far the most effective baits. Sophisticated and complicated angling rigs and techniques have evolved around them. Further, there appears to be a real correlation between the size of the bait and the size of the striped bass caught. Generally, the larger the bait, the bigger the bass.

Killifish

The common killifish or mummichog, as it is called along the New England part of its distribution, is a plentiful forage fish and constitutes a fair share of the striped bass's diet when bass are in estuarine and river environments. The killie, *Fundulus heteroclitus,* is a tough little fish, inhabiting some rather polluted waters along our coasts, in places other species have long abandoned. These fish prefer moving water and are often swept in and out with the tide, flooding creeks and marshes, and often dallying too late and becoming stranded in potholes without water until the next tide. Remarkably, they survive.

There are several related species and subspecies, and most of their range covers the coastal waters from the Gulf of St. Lawrence south to Texas. *F. heteroclitus,* has a rather stout body, heavy caudal peduncle, and rounded caudal fin. Males are dark green with white and yellow spots and silver vertical bars and yellow bellies. The girls of the species are rather drab, uniformly a pale to medium olive.

Killies are extremely hardy and take a lot of punishment while being cast about. They survive being hooked for long periods. If they grew a bit longer, they would be the perfect striped bass bait. The maximum is up to 6 inches but most are between 2 and 4 inches; they appeal more to small bass and even then must be doubled on a hook.

They are almost always fished whole, hooked by No. 1 or 2 O'Shaughnessy hooks, skewered through the lower lip or just ahead of the dorsal fin. They must be fished—that is, hooked so that their action and swimming appears natural.

When caught and frozen, then fished, they can be used for chum either whole or cut, and account for plenty of bass.

Spearing

In the more open bays and larger estuaries, striped bass will herd and corral whole schools of spearing or silversides, *Menida menida*, and harass these little food fish to the point where they literally jump from the water by the hundreds. Unfortunately, spearing are rather fragile fish and won't take a lot of abuse or wear on a hook. They are a slender, translucent species, with a forked tail, pale green above a bright white or silver stripe that extends along the lateral line from the gills to the tail.

The fish is distributed from Maine to Chesapeake Bay and in lesser numbers farther south. During summer months, they concentrate in numerous bays that surround Long Island, especially Long Island Sound. They have a habit of sweeping in and out of these bays with the tides and are as much at home in *Spartina* grasses as in deep bays and kelp beds.

Because of their fragile nature, spearing are seldom used as live bait. More often, they're caught and frozen in blocks and diluted for use as chum, ground or cut into small pieces and fed into the slick of a boat. When baiting, several are fitted onto a hook at a time and allowed to drift in the chum line.

Sand Eels

The sand eel or sand lance, *Ammodytes americanus*, is a more hardy food and forage fish and can take punishment almost as well as the killifish. It grows somewhat longer than the spearing or the killifish, up to 8 inches, and can play a more important role as a baitfish. It is the greatest forage fish for other fishes and mammals in the Atlantic. They are fed upon by everything from whales down to snapper bluefish. However, it is thin, elongated for its length, and doesn't fill a hook, so several must be used at one time. It has a pointed snout— hence the "lance"—and a long slender dorsal fin. The body gives off an iridescent luster that is a bluish-green sheen above the lateral line and silver and white on the underside and belly.

These fish move in dense schools both inshore and offshore and are distributed along the Atlantic from Cape Hatteras northward to Canada, across Greenland and Iceland to northern Europe. They can best be used for striped bass when hooked through both lips, with a light hook and behind a small willowleaf spinner, and trolled from a rowed or slowly motored boat. In mass, they can be used as chum, ground or cut in pieces.

Menhaden

The menhaden, mossbunker, or just plain bunker, *Brevoortia tyrannus,* has more than thirty common names. It might more appropriately be placed with latter rather than the former group of fish used as bait for striped bass because

The sand eel (top) and the killifish form a large part of the diet of a growing bass.

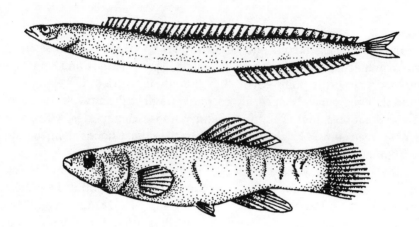

of its size. But because it has no sporting value, or fish food value other than to be reduced to fish meal, it is associated with the smaller baitfish. Migration times and routes for striped bass are often heavily influenced by what the bunker decide to do. Within bounds, menhaden play a vital role in the life and times of the striped bass because the linesiders feed so heavily and consistently on these fish. From the time bunker are small fingerlings to the time they are 3- and 4-pound adults, striped bass chase and follow them. When bunker head north in the spring along the coast of the Atlantic, striped bass are usually immediately behind, following their dinner as it swims.

It is also a widely used bait fish by anglers because it is readily available from pound traps and caught easily by commercial draggers and purse seiners, who are after the rich oil it possesses. Bunker are members of the herring family, and like other herring are pelagic swimmers that work their way from Florida to Nova Scotia and back again during the course of a year.

Menhaden are deep-bodied fish, somewhat straight across their backs, with deeply forked tails, a rather thin caudal peduncle, and a large head that is almost a third of the size of the body. The mouthparts are somewhat transparent and delicate, with an underhung jaw that extends well beyond the top lip. Coloration in a bunker is quite variable, but generally it has a blue back with an ivory or silvery cast and a strong, brassy luster along the sides. The sides are marked with various-sized spots that grow smaller as they pass caudally to form weak rows. One large dark spot is usually located just above the lateral line and behind the gill cover on each side.

Younger menhaden spend the greater part of their growing years in the numerous bays and estuaries of the Carolinas, Maryland, and Virginia, and migrate north during the spring to summer and grow in the bays of New Jersey and Long Island.

Bunker are almost the universal striped bass food and are used extensively ground up in chum, cut in halves and strips, and fished dead or alive. Because of their deep bodies they don't troll very well when dead but are excellent live baits when trolled at a snail's pace or stemmed against the tidal currents.

As a cut bait, the bunker's best portion is its head, sliced on a bias just behind the gills, or long slabs cut out from each side. When used as head bait, a 5/0 to 10/0 Siwash or O'Shaughnessy is buried from the back and curved back through the bottom jaw, keeping the hook hidden at all times. As a bait strip, it is sliced into a wedge-shaped filet and the hook pinned into the wider section. In these two hooking techniques, the bunker is best fished in the surf or off a boat or bridge with a three-way swivel or a fish-finder rig. This cut-form can withstand a lot of casting if correctly hooked and can be tossed into the suds or fed off a bridge with a light sinker and bounced out with the tide and away from the fisherman.

Whole bunker are fished dead along many parts of northern New Jersey, from Barnegat Inlet to Sandy Hook, and along western Long Island's South Shore, from Lower New York Bay east to Jones Inlet. Big bunker, 1 to 2 pounds, are best when freshly dead or fresh-frozen. Their effectiveness after dying diminishes rapidly with age. Here, two variations of the technique are practiced. The first method, basically that employed in New Jersey, is to drift the dead bunker. This requires a minimal amount of wind or a moving part of the tide. The bunker is hooked through the eyes on an 8/0 Siwash hook and lowered over the side. If there is a fair amount of current or wind, the bait is liable to rise to the top. It is kept down by adding a sinker in the line. This is often a 1- to 4-ounce drail, depending upon the speed of the drift, or a dipsey sinker on the end of a three-way swivel. The first is the preferred terminal rig because a bass can't use the dropper-sinker to help open the hook-hole and free itself in a fight.

On the drift, 100 to 200 feet of line is paid out in free-spool and then the click put on. The line is kept from going out farther with thumb pressure. Once a bass picks up the dead bunker it will move off, and the click alone will not offer enough resistance to frighten a fish. Bass pick up live bunker by the head, but a dead bunker can be picked up in several ways, so an unimpaired run is necessary before throwing the clutch and setting the hook. Needless to say, the drag should be set to the correct tension, then tested before the bait is lowered into the water.

Off the beaches of western Long Island, the technique is somewhat different but still with enough similarities to be lumped together. Here, menhaden are hooked in the same manner and weighted similarly. But instead of fishing the dead bunker on a drift, the boat is slowly run almost onto the beach or alongside a groin and turned seaward. Then, the bait is lowered over the transom. With the reel in free spool, the boat is slowly run away from the beach and the bunker stays approximately where it was dropped. When the skipper has run out as much line as he thinks possible, sometimes 200 or 300 yards, the boat is stopped, the engine(s) shut down and the angler slowly retrieves the bunker in a series of stops and starts.

Both techniques catch a lot of bass during the spring and again while the fall migrations are on. A few fishermen in these areas also fish with live bunker, and they, too, are quite successful. In areas where striped bass won't hit dead bunker or where there is too much current, only live-lining pays off. Live-lining is far more effective, but requires more gear and sophistication on the part of the fisherman.

Before a fisherman ever thinks of fishing with live menhaden he must equip his boat with a live-bait tank. Bunker are extremely active swimming fish and must swim all the time to move sufficient water over their gills to obtain

One of the favorite foods of bass, as well as baits for fisherman, is the plentiful mossbunker, or bunker. The top figure illustrates one method of hooking dead bunker. Occasionally, the head alone is a good bait, and the hook is passed through the back and down to come out near the bottom of the gills. Live or dead bunker can be fished from the surf by hooking the fish in the tough flesh just ahead of the pectoral fins.

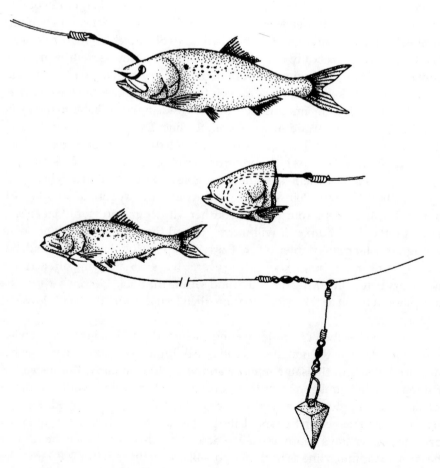

enough oxygen to stay alive. A tank must be large enough to hold from one to two dozen bunker, 10 to 15 inches in length. This means that the tank should be 3 to 4 feet long, 18 to 24 inches wide, and about 18 inches deep. Water can be aerated in two ways. You can buy a large aquarium pump or build a two-pistoned affair that shoots a steady stream of air into your water. Or, you can modify a bilge pump or similar pump and pour fresh seawater into your tank. This latter is the better system and will maintain more fish for a longer period of time. It also demands that you have some hosework to take in the water and an overflow or pipe stem in the tank to take off the excess water.

Bunker are peculiar fish and if you build your tank with corners in it, they will stick their snouts into them and suffocate without swimming. But if you have rounded sides, no corners, they will swim continually and stay alive. The direction they swim is almost always the same; they swim in a counterclockwise course. All pools, sinks, and toilets drain in a clockwise direction north of the equator and in a counterclockwise direction south of that line (because of the Coriolis force). Fish swim always against a current, and so should the fish in your man-made current. This is important and must be taken into consideration when you construct a tank and fix the direction of the inflow pipe. It should enter the fish box in such a manner that it sends the water circulating in a clockwise direction. If it does, you won't lose current or pressure trying to overcome the Coriolis effect.

Such a live-bait system works equally well with other forms of large baitfish used for striped bass—mackerel, blackfish, whiting, weakfish, sculpins, or even hyperactive bluefish. This form of the art is practiced to some extent by fishermen on western Long Island and northern New Jersey, but it is more highly developed by anglers on eastern Long Island, at Montauk Point, on Gardiners Island and Shelter Island, off Orient Point, and east along Great Island and Little Gull Island, across the Race in New York to Fishers Island, and up to Watch Hill, R.I.

Obtaining live bunker can be achieved by one of two ways: by snagging your own, or by making friends with a pound-trap fisherman. If the latter, be there every morning, often before daybreak, to get them from him when he lifts his nets. Live bunker must be gently handled to keep them alive. They bruise easily and develop red blood spots on their flesh if hurt in the transfer. They are best transferred with a long-handled net and kept in the water whenever possible. Fresh seawater should fill the tank before the bunker are added and it should be capped with a lid when not withdrawing fish. I have had bunker leap out of the tank when they panicked and jump more than 15 feet into the water.

Many species of fish that are live-lined, like mackerel, herring, and whiting, are hooked by a single large hook through the flesh just ahead of the dorsal fin. However, they cannot be trolled in this hooking position. Bunker, however, are best hooked through the nostrils with a treble hook no larger than 6/0 and can thus be trolled. The larger hooks open the nostrils too greatly and break the thin

Live bunker or menhaden is a devastating striped bass bait. Illustrated here is a treble hook in the nostrils, with a free hook and wire leader for short bluefish strikes, a flexible braided-wire leader leading to a trolling drail, and a short wire leader just before the line.

piece of cartilage that bridges the two openings. Once this wears through, the bunker is free. Hooking a bunker through the nostrils doesn't damage the fish. Nostrils on fish are used only for smelling or tasting water, not breathing. With both jaws able to function, the bunker can breathe and easily swim. From this anterior hook position on the fish's head, bunker can easily be trolled...but very slowly because it is likely to twist and turn and challenge the very best swivels you might have.

I have found that the treble hook is better than a single hook for live-lining striped bass. The single hook too often lies alongside the fish and if a bass strikes there are times when it misses the hook and doesn't hook itself. With live, moving bait, striped bass invariably hit it at the front, the head. A treble hook ensures that at least one hook is in the right position. Nor would I use smaller hooks, because I have had 40- and 50-pound bass bend open very good hooks. I prefer to use an 8/0 or 10/0 treble hook, and do when I get an exceptionally large bunker. But because of the nostrils, I don't regularly use larger hooks.

Seldom do striped bass strike the rear of a bunker. But bluefish in the same waters are equally fond of bunker and when they strike there is no question about it. They leave a cleanly cut fish with no tail. To solve this problem, I attach a second treble hook, about 4/0, to the eye of the first hook by a piece of wire leader. This second hook can swing freely in the current and will usually lie alongside the tail of the bunker. Or, it can be held along the side of the fish with a small rubber band.

Bunker hooked in the nostrils can be trolled, but at very slow speeds. My favorite method is to find a point of land where large boulders are sunken off the shoal in 15 to 20 feet of water and where the tidal current passes over at a fair speed. This is a natural spot for big striped bass and such locations can be adequately fished at a snail's pace. I stem the tide in such situations, letting the bunker, or two if someone else is fishing with me in the boat, slide back and forth across the tops of the submerged boulders. I can work ahead ever so slowly and present the bunker to new spots or drop back and sweep again over the area repeatedly until the lethagic striped bass suddenly come to the top fighting for the bunker.

It is an awesome sight to watch three or four large striped bass, fish over 40 or 50 pounds, chase a live bunker to the surface and eventually strike it. This to me is one of the real highlights of striped bass fishing: to watch the actual strike. Live bait or not, it is a rewarding thrill.

In areas of running water the current's speed will gradually change as the stages of the tide change and the current floods or ebbs. In water with some depth to it, or where the current is fast and keeps the bunker high, a live bunker may have to be weighted. This is done with in-line drails. I continually change them as the current speeds up and falls off, from as little as 1 up to 6 ounces.

The standard outfit for such fishing is usually a trolling rod and reel loaded with 20-pound test Dacron line. In trickier situations, with a lot of boats around and the boulders closer to the top, I use a similar combination but switch to a 30-pound test outfit. This strength line is all you need to handle a 50-pound bass with little or no worry about its breaking the rod or line.

The terminal end of the Dacron is finished off with 15 feet of 50- or 60-pound-test monofilament, and if bluefish are around, the last 2 feet are wire. It is amazing how little line is fished in such stemming or trolling situations. Bunker may hold about 5 feet below the surface, but striped bass will quickly rise to them if they are alive and swimming properly. Often, I fish with as little as 40 feet of line astern of the boat and seldom more than 100 feet, and bass show little or no fear of the boat or running engines. The water averages between 20 and 30 feet.

Bunker will last a long time swimming by themselves, and the only casualties come when the tide moves exceptionally fast. In this case, the fish develop what anglers normally call "lockjaw." The constant fight against the current weakens them and their lower jaw drops open. Eventually it cannot be retracted and the fish drown and die. Dead bunker never seem to catch fish in these situations and they are returned to a fish box alongside the live-bait tank.

Butterfish

Butterfish, *Poronotus triacantus,* are baitfish rather than game fish. It has a very small mouth and takes only the smallest of lures. It is a relatively small fish with a real value as cut bait for some species and whole bait for others. It is seldom fished alive, but caught by commercial netters and frozen, only to be sold to tuna fishermen or chummers for striped bass, who use the butterfish as the hook bait. Butterfish have a deep body with a small, sharply forked tail and reach a maximum length of 12 inches, though 6 or 7 inches is generally considered large. From time to time, butterfish move into the estuaries, bays, and rivers along our coasts, especially when small, but for the most part they frequent the near-offshore waters and find protection in its depths and expansiveness. They range from South Carolina to Newfoundland and Nova Scotia, prime tuna grounds in the summer.

American Eel

I would be hard pressed to choose between the bunker and the eel as the best striped bass bait. Both produce a lot of big fish and both require a somewhat skilled and sophisticated angler to fish them properly. I think that more eels are used to fish striped bass than bunker, only because they are more easily obtained, are easier to maintain, and can be used in a greater number of ways.

The common or American eel, *Anguilla rostrata*, is catadromous, the opposite of striped bass, which are anadromous fish. It is spawned and hatched in the Sargasso Sea, in the middle of the Atlantic Ocean in an area north and east of Bermuda. While eels are still in the juvenile stage, one group begins swimming for North America and the remainder to Europe. It may take some of these little fish more than a year to make land, then several years more to grow to maturity. They do so along our coastal estuaries, bays, and tidal rivers. Not all are confined to the coasts, however; large numbers (usually females) begin an upriver trek and will swim hundreds of miles upstream to spend one or more years in a strictly freshwater environment. When the urge to reproduce creeps into them, they head back for the ocean, meet the males at the estuaries, and make that long crossing back to the Sargasso Sea. There they mate, reproduce, and the mature fish die.

While along our coasts, eels have a special place in the diets of striped bass and esteemed as well by fishermen. Striped bass are great feeders on eels and will readily strike at them. By the time the juveniles reach the Continental Shelf, many are 6 to 10 inches long. These "shoestring" eels are great baits for smaller bass. Adult eels grow as large as 3 or 4 feet and some reach 15 pounds, but most range between 2-1/2 and 3 feet. Bass feed on eels regardless of size.

Many fishermen prefer smaller eels for striped bass, thinking that the

The American Eel

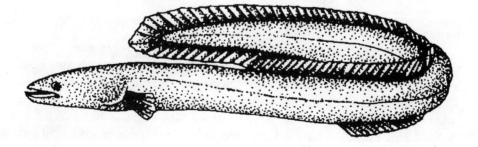

longer eels discourage smaller fish from striking. I don't believe this is so. I have fished with eels of every size that happened to swim into my lobster pots and have taken small bass, fish 7 and 8 pounds, on eels that were twice as long as they were. Bass are gluttonous as well as omnivorous.

Eels spend a great deal of time in mud and burrow into it just before winter. There they remain in a state of semi-hibernation. During the warmer days of the year, they spend their daylight hours in the safety of the mud and come out at night to feed. That is one reason why striped bass are such avid night hunters, seeking eels on the move. Eels are basically scavenger fish and are easily lured into an eel pot or trap by just about anything dead.

One of the most effective ways to fish an eel is while it is alive. Eels will take considerable punishment and handling. An eel hooked through the lower and upper jaws will last through hours of casting. The fish is best hooked with a 4/0 Eagle Claw or beak-type hook, one with a substantial barb and curve to keep the eel from squirming off the hook. Handling a live eel to get a hook in it can be a chore. Most bass fishermen use a terry-cloth towel to grab the eel, and with the head protruding slightly from the towel, give it a gentle rap on the head on the transom of the boat. This temporarily stuns them and allows you to implant the hook. They are quickly revived when added to the water.

Eels can be fished from a drifting or anchored boat, under a bridge or from the edge of a jetty or dock, off a bulkhead and in the surf. The bottom where you fish should be fairly free of cover so that the eel won't dig into it and hide, or swimming striped bass are likely to pass it by unnoticed unless the eel is directly up current. Eels can also be cast and then slowly retrieved or trolled while rowing or being pushed by a small, quiet engine...or better an electric motor. In the use of an outboard in shallow water, a lot more line must be used to separate the noise from the food.

Rigged eels are one of the most effective baits that can be trolled for striped bass. Here is all the equipment needed to rig and eel: a spool of waxed line, weighted head with hook, threading needle, second hook on a sash chain, and, of course, an eel.

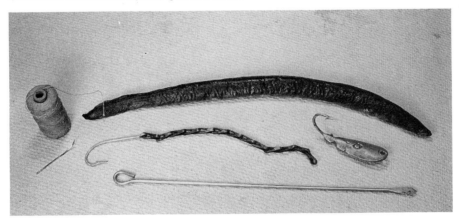

The threading needle is passed through the eel's mouth and forced through its body and out the vent.

At the vent, a length of waxed line is tied to the slot in the needle. Then it is pulled through the body and out the mouth

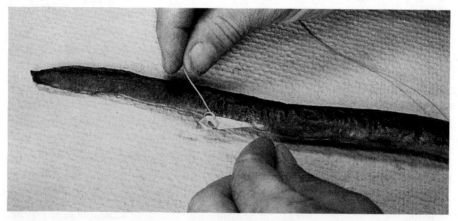

The line is attached to the sash chain after it has been measured to the eel's length and the hook is fastened to one end. Then, the free end is drawn through the eel until the rear hook just shows out the vent.

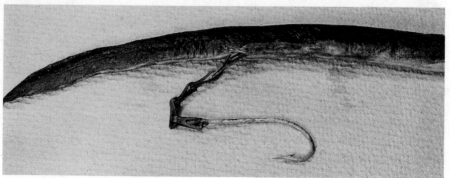

The front hook is threaded through a link in the chain.

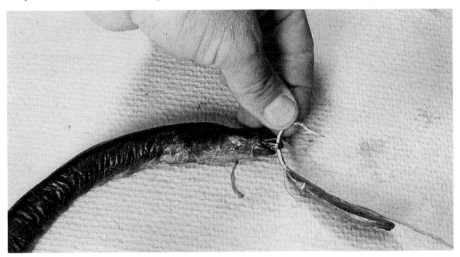

The hook is pushed through the mouth of the eel until it comes out between the gills. The mouth of the eel is wrapped tightly shut around the lead head. A notch is cut into each side of the lead head, as a small groove, to give the thread a gripping area. The eel's mouth must be completely secured so that no water will flow into it and affect its swimming action.

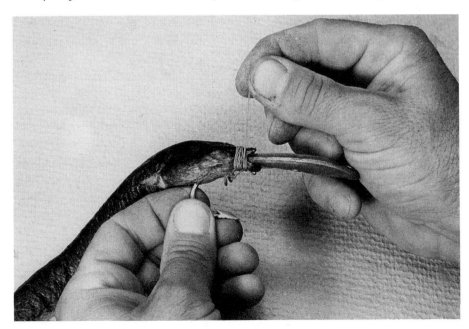

One of the most versatile lures for striped bass is the eel, either in parts, skinned, or whole. Illustrated here are several versions, and for each one here there are at least a dozen variations in use. 1. Eel skin attached to a metal squid or tin spoon, a rig that swims well in the surf. 2. Whole eel attached to a sash chain. 3. Rigged eel attached to a chain and lead head designed to make the eel body swim when trolled. 4. Eel with head removed but replaced with a lead head to make the rig sink when trolled. 5. Trolling rig for an eel skin. 6. Short eel skin attached to a swimming plug after its rear hooks were removed.

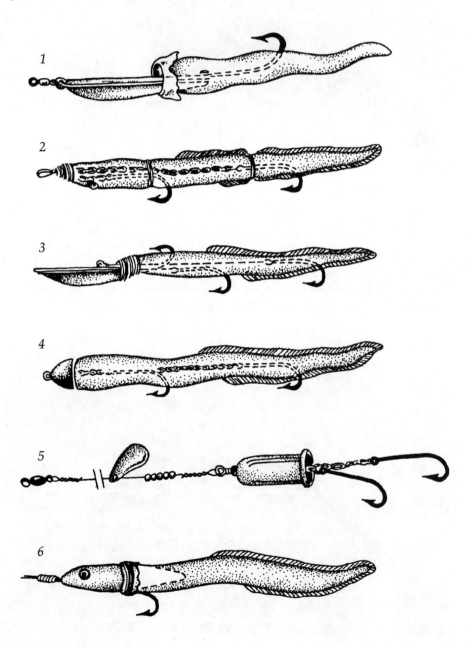

Because of their shape, eels can be trolled at higher speeds and fished with wire line, or rigged on lead heads that provide weight. The right shape of the lead head should give a dead eel realistic swimming action as it is pulled along by the boat. One technique for rigging an eel is illustrated here; there are several others. One that is popular among the islands of Massachusetts is the eel skin. The first step is to cut a ring in the skin behind the head of the eel and pull off the skin. The skin is then added to the back of a large plug that has had its tail hook removed. The eel skin is secured to the plug (stapled, nailed, or sewn) and a few slits are cut in the skin near the head to let in water. While trolled, the plug and its diving plane give the eel skin an exceptionally lifelike action. Water fills the eel skin and it undulates almost as well as the real thing.

Other variations on rigging eels are similar to the leaded hook used for squid. An eel, minus its head, is impaled on the hook and the skin sewn to the holes on the lead head. Almost all forms of fishing with a dead eel require that a lead of some sort be added to the head to control the depth at which the eel settles and to give it a lifelike action when trolled.

Pieces of cut eel are also used for striped bass. The eel is sliced into 3- or 4-inch lengths and then halved. The half pieces are then hooked as you would any other piece of cut bait. Eels make especially good bait because of the great oiliness of their flesh which sends out odor messages as it lies on the bottom of the surf. They can be used with a fish-finder rig or a three-way swivel. But because the cut eel is such a great bass attractor, it also calls other fish often the bottom scavengers, sand sharks and sea robins, will get to the cut eel before a striped bass.

Atlantic Mackerel

The common mackerel, *Scomber scombrus,* makes a great live bait as well as cut bait for striped bass. Early migrations of mackerel up and down the Atlantic Coast make them harbingers of spring and winter. In most parts of their range they are transients, but off Massachusetts and in the Gulf of Maine, mackerel take up summer residence and are used through the fishing season as a bass bait.

Mackerel are not used as often when trolling for bass as is the live bunker. Instead, mackerel are fished on a live-line, or free-swimming. Though not totally free-swimming—it has a hook and line attached to it—the mackerel is still able to swim about tethered on the line. This free-swimming method is used in an area striped bass frequent and mackerel usually avoid, and can cause pandemonium among a pod of bass.

Mackerel fishing is a lot simpler than angling with bunker. The requirements for catching mackerel also are simple, and they are easily obtained by attaching half a dozen small tube-hooks, off dropper lines or directly to a main line, and finishing off with a large diamond jig or Hopkins lure on the terminal end. Keeping them alive requires the same technique as for bunker. Once you have solved these problems, fishing with them is easy. Unlike bunker, mackerel are usually hooked just under the skin and through only a small part of the flesh, just ahead of the dorsal fin. Some anglers use single hooks, 4/0 O'Shaughnessy, while others swear by treble hooks. I prefer the first for mackerel.

Large spinning rods are used with live mackerel, and with caution, they can be cast away from the boat. The accepted technique is to use a fairly stiff spinning rod, about 8 to 8-1/2 feet long, a light surf reel, and about 250 yards of 20 to 30-pound-test monofilament. The line is attached directly to the hook without sinkers and the live fish is allowed to swim away from the boat with the bail open on the reel. Once the fish has taken 100 to 200 yards of line, the bail is closed and the drag set especially light on the reel. After striking a fish, the drag is readjusted. This takes a bit of skill so that you don't tighten it too greatly. Instead of putting too much pressure on a drag, many anglers develop the habit of fingering the spool, applying pressure to its edge with the index finger to add more drag without adjusting the reel.

The highly-effective technique of live-lining mackerel is best done from an anchored boat, a bridge, or a point of land. It is a lot easier, however, and somewhat more effective to perform from a drifting boat. This slow movement of the boat over the bottom keeps the fish off the bottom and exposes your bait to new water and potentially more striped bass.

Bullheads

There is another forage fish that often finds its way into the stomachs of the striped bass, but only rarely do anglers on the East Coast use them for bait. These are the sea robins or sculpin, belonging to the families *Cottidae* and *Hemitripteridae*. Their species are so numerous and varied that a listing would thrill only the taxonomist. The fisherman is interested in them only as bait, and they reach their

The sculpin (sea robin) or bullhead of the Pacific Coast is a favorite striped bass bait. Here are two methods for rigging the spiny fish:

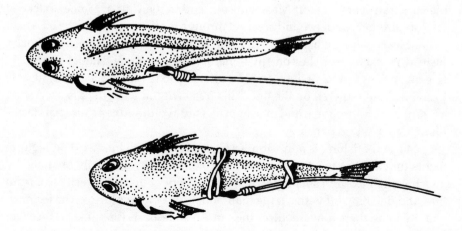

highest perfection as bait in the hands of West Coast striped bass anglers. In San Francisco Bay and the surrounding area, fishing with bullheads (sculpin) is a finely tuned art and is used most when the bass are off the estuaries and in the bays during the summer. One reason they are not popular on the East Coast might be that most sea robins that show in shoal waters there are too big, some as large as 15 inches.

Bullheads are fished dead and backwards. The hook is forced into the fish behind the head and in a forward direction. It is brought out through the gills and laid alongside the bait with the tip and barb exposed. The hook eye is tied against the body with a half-hitch and the thread passed back to the tail, where another half-hitch is wrapped, keeping the fishing line close to the body and the tail of the fish and giving it a directional pull off the tail end. Otherwise, any pressure on the line would make the fish turn sideways and offer a lot of unmangeable resistance.

Hook sizes are 5/0 or 6/0, depending upon the size of the bullhead, and usually O'Shaughnessy or Siwash in style. The terminal end is finished off in a 5- to 10-foot heavy monofilament leader. A barrel sinker is used with such a rig so that any soft-mouthed bass won't flinch at the first hint of resistance. The bait is taken head first and because of the exposed position and direction of the hook, there are very few missed fish.

Sardines

The California sardine, *Clupanodon caeruleus,* is a close relative of the common herring found on the East Coast. But California fishermen make better use of the bait and it is fished on the West Coast as much as bunker are fished by Atlantic anglers. The sardine is seldom used in the live state; it is more often

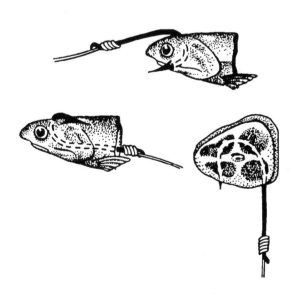

cut and fileted. The side of a sardine is sliced free of the bone and when the entire piece is used, it is skewered onto the hook in much the same manner as a worm. Really large pieces are pushed on the hook and up the leader. Smaller chunk baits are made by slicing the sardine filet into pieces. The hook is run completely through the

Three methods of rigging the sardine, another West Coast favorite.

piece, out the other side and the point and barb are brought back into the meat to be hidden.

The sardine head is a valuable piece of bait, and after the filets are removed, the remainder is cut squarely, a little behind the gills. The head can be hooked through the eyes and out the side, or from the open cut into the head, and the hook then turned up to come out just behind the eye. Slabs or steak cuts are also popular and are cross-sections of the entire fish with the filets intact. This is a valuable cut because the hook can be pushed in from one side, guided around the backbone, and brought to the surface on the next side, and most of the hook, except for the very tip, is well hidden in the flesh. Hooks for cut sardine range in size from 2/0 to 3/0 for small pieces to 8/0 for the bigger slices. The Eagle Claw, with its bait barbs is an extremely popular pattern with live-bait fishermen and the O'Shaughnessy a close second.

Other Fishes

There are several other species of fish, often younger stages of game fishes, that make excellent bait for striped bass. These include other herrings in addition to the menhaden, the occasional mullet that works its way north in the summer, blackfish (tautog), black sea bass, weakfish (squeteague), bluefish, winter flounder, and whiting. Most are fished like mackerel when alive and like bunker when dead.

The typical hooking of a dead bait is through the eyes if it is not to be trolled. Dead baits, unless adorned with lead heads and special rigs, are poor choices for trolling. Fish like black sea bass and blackfish are especially hardy and will last a long time in the live condition. In this case, hooking just ahead of the dorsal fin or through the nostrils is the best method for keeping them alive and active.

24

Artificial Lures for Striped Bass

It's difficult to determine just when the first artificial lures were introduced to salt water. Though flies made of cloth and feathers had been used to lure trout and grayling to the hook in ancient Salonika and later, even before the Romans came to Britain, to catch salmon, their application to salt water and other species of fish was extremely tardy. Actually, the general use of plugs, spoons, and other lures in salt water, or even fresh water, had to wait for the development of rods, lines and especially reels. In the meantime, saltwater fish were fed real foods as bait until this development took place. It was the ubiquitous squid that was most often tossed into the surf with a hook in it to entice striped bass to feed.

Squidding, as the technique was called, was strictly a handline operation for many generations. Even after rods and reels for saline fishermen became cheap and common, handlines were still favored by local beach bums and bayrats. The use of artificial lures for striped bass even predates the development of rod-and-reel fishing. Bass were taken from the surf by bones and feathers fastened to hooks, spun over the head, and then flung into the water.

The retrieve was determined by how fast an angler could pull in the line, hand-over-fist, or how quickly he could race up the beach to keep the lure moving. If a striped bass hit, it was a tug-of-war. If the hook held, the bass usually lost.

The first bait used to catch striped bass were squid. It was only natural that the first artificial lures to be cast in salt water (by hand) for these fish were probably metal jigs or "tins," as they then were called, and designed to imitate a squid. The tin squid, poured from tin mixed with lead and other metal, and often adorned with feathers or bucktails, was strictly a saltwater lure with no freshwater ancestry. The earliest plugs for saltwater fishing were adaptations of freshwater varieties, designed for black bass and northern pike. The development of the saltwater plug came only after the development and diversity of tin squids was almost complete.

The tin squid worked well for several reasons. The first was its weight. A wet linen or cotton line, after a few casts, created a lot of resistance in the guides and along the rod. A heavy tin squid could overcome this drag and still be sent a nautical mile to the beginning of the comber. Eventually, large saltwater plugs replaced the freshwater versions and with their added weight, they, too, could be tossed quite well with a conventional reel.

Even with these modifications in lures, and conventional reels with built-in anti-backlash devices, the artificial lure still lagged far behind live or cut bait in popularity when it came to saltwater fishing. What the sport needed was the development of new equipment. The spinning reel was the answer. It came to the United States shortly after World War II. In just a few years, it was introduced to salt water and the boom in artificial lures was underway.

Today, the saltwater angler has a great selection of artificial lures from which to choose. Their variety is even greater than the natural animals they intend to imitate. Each group of lures is also expanded by color variations, finish, and specific actions. To a beginning saltwater bass fisherman, the world of artificial lures might seem a hodgepodge. But it can easily be put into order.

Lures are effective and work because they are based on several principles that make them inviting to fish. If they weren't, fish wouldn't strike. Lures are most often designed to imitate small fish upon which larger fish feed, or to stimulate the fish's senses of smell, sound, and sight. Lures are colored either like the real bait or with vivid combinations that do more to attract a fish's attention than its appetite. Color combinations and patterns need not necessarily resemble the real thing to make a fish bite. Some of the best plugs are colored red and white, and I haven't found a striped bass food colored red and white.

Other lures appeal to the receptors on a striped bass that respond to sound or vibration. This can mean food to the bass or just act as an irritant, making it angry or excited or goading it into hitting the lure. Some lures have hollow bodies and contain weights that rattle, others make popping or gurgling noises that appeal to a bass's curiosity.

Another class of lures possess a smell or have an odor about them that can attract striped bass. The sense of smell is far more keenly developed in striped bass than the ability to hear or see. This area has long been overlooked by lure manufacturers. At one time the Woodstream Corporation of Lititz, Pa., produced lures coated with a Hydron spray, a highly concentrated bait scent that is supposed to attract fish. I have used it on freshwater fish and found that it outfished non-coated lures. When I tried it on striped bass it didn't seem to make a difference; they still didn't bite.

Artificial lures for striped bass can be divided roughly into several categories—plugs, spoons, jigs, tubes, and copy-cat lures. Plugs for striped bass can be further divided into classifications determined by the zone in the water column within which they work. First, there are surface lures, including poppers, chuggers, darters, and propeller lures whose basic function is one of noise and attraction. Then there are medium-running lures. Some are subsurface lures that swim rapidly just under the top of the water. Others are floating-diving lures. These lures will float when at rest, and the pressure of being pulled through the water on a uniquely shaped face forces them to dive.

The last category is the deep-running or diving lures. Many of these lures achieve their depth because they are heavy and sink in the water. Others have large diving planes in the front that when pulled through the water force the lure to head down. Others are combinations of sinking lures with diving lips, and they search out the deepest waters when cast or trolled.

Spoons in salt water are not as numerous or as variable as plugs. There are small, solid, rather heavy spoons and chunks of metal or else larger spoons that are thinner in build and imitate large baitfish. Jigs are of two basic types, the all-metal or diamond jig, which is a hybrid between heavy spoon and jig, and the feathered or bucktail jig, with a lead head that can be made in numerous shapes and sizes.

Tube lures are rather new, though earlier turkey- and chicken-bone lures are quite old. Today, the tube lures are designed to imitate everything from a school of baitfish to a long sandworm. The final classification of lures is the look-alikes or the copy-cats, and their development paralleled the development of soft, plastic materials that could be molded into bait shapes and adorned with action heads and hooks.

PLUGS

The plug came into its own with the development of efficient conventional reels and then spinning reels. A plug in either system provides the weight which takes out the line and makes a cast possible. Lures are measured in two manners. The first is by their weight, which can vary from fractions of an ounce up to 6 and 7 ounces. The other measurement is length, and plugs for striped bass can vary from 2 to 9 inches. Some larger plugs can be cast, but most are designed to be trolled rather than heaved.

Top-Water Plugs

Quite naturally, these plugs are designed to float on the surface and are built of wood, hollow plastic, or molded condensed plastic materials that are lighter than water. The first requirement of a top-water plug is that it be able to attract fish by one of several methods. One is the creation of sound by popping or chugging. Many top-water plugs or poppers have faces cut on various angles to the water. If they are cupped, they will make a popping plug, and this noisy

Top-water plugs. *Top row, left to right: Gibbs Satellite Darter, Heddon Big Chugg, Raja Goo-Goo Eyes. Second row: Old Pal "817," Rebel Popper, Rebel Popper-Bucktail. Third row: Odap Bullet Popper, Old Pal Hydron Popper. Bottom: Arbogast Dasher.*

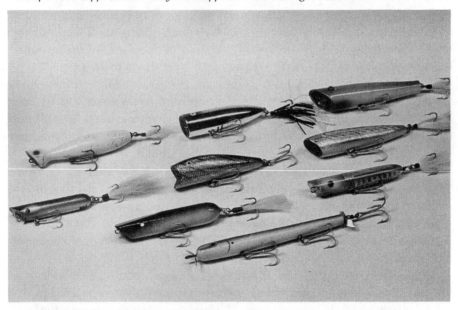

nature is used in several situations. The most common is when a school of surface-feeding bass has been spotted. The commotion on top puts the popper right into the action and striped bass readily strike it. In shallow-water situations, along a beach or river bank, poppers will catch the immediate attention of any nearby bass and usually bring on a strike. Poppers can also be used effectively when fishing blind, over deep water. A popper working frantically over the surface can cause a deeply lying bass to rise and strike.

A second group of surface plugs are called darters or swimmers. These two styles are closely allied. Darters have a face or control plane on the head that causes the lure to dash off to one side or the other when pulled against the waters. This simulates the erratic swimming of an injured baitfish and is a real bass attractor. The swimming surface plug sets up a heavy vibration pattern that is transmitted through the depths and attracts interested bass. A modification of this is a swimmer with propellers on the head and tail of the plug. These not only set up vibrations in the water when retrieved, but the metal rattles and has an added noise attraction. These plugs can be just as effective on striped bass as on freshwater fish.

Medium-Depth Plugs

These plugs can also be classed as subsurface and floating-diving plugs. Some are designed with shallow lips at the head so that they do not run very deeply into the water. This is a desired feature when fishing in water 2 to 4 feet deep and filled with weeds that do not quite reach the surface. A popper plug might cause too much noise or action, but a shallow-swimming plug nicely fills the bill for attracting any hiding striped bass that might be too hesitant to come out and feed.

Also part of this group are the floater-diver plugs. When at rest, these plugs float on the surface of the water, but because of a slight diving plane on the front, they will descend when pulled through the water. This type of plug has a special fishing action that, with several fast turns of the handle, will make the plug dive. Then the retrieve is stopped. In the stopped position, the plug rapidly floats to the surface and that attaction can also attract a striped bass. Then the retrieve is resumed. This dive and float, dive and float resembles an injured minnow and is a real bass seducer.

Still a third type of plug that works in this zone of the water is a slight variation on the floater-diver plug. It has a density just slightly less than that of the water and will float when first cast and allowed to rest. It is faster to dive, however, and does not recover as rapidly to float back to the surface. This is a true medium-running plug, a lure that is controlled more by the shape of the diving lip rather than the density of the plug or the speed at which it is retrieved through the water.

The lip on a diving plug provides all the swimming action, as well as the rate of dive. The angle the lip makes with the horizontal line of the body will determine how deeply it travels. The width of the lip determines how well and how often it undulates. A lip that is close to the angle of the horizontal will dive deepest. The lip that is steeply sloped spends more time wiggling than diving.

Subsurface Plugs—Medium-running minnows. Top row: Raja Goo-Goo Eyes "Big Daddy." Second row, left to right: Old Pal Raposa, Rebel Super Minnow. Third row: Cordell's Big Red Fin, Cordell's Red Fin, Rapala Salt Water Minnow. Last row: Rapala Magnum Minnow, Boone Bait Minnow.

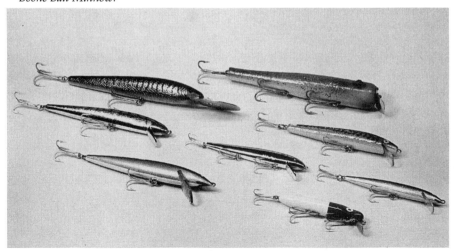

The length of the lip also controls how fast it dives as well as its wiggle. A long, wide lip on a slight angle means that the lure dives deeply and shimmers wildly. Lip angles vary with manufacturers but fall into three ranges: shallow, medium, and deep divers.

Deep-Diving Plugs

Deep-diving plugs achieve their goal by using one of two construction techniques. The diving plane is the first and we have discussed it rather thoroughly. The second technique is to weight the lure—that is, make it heavier than water so it will sink. Some lures are weighted and provided with a shallow lip. The weight takes the lure deep while the lip makes it swim. Medium-running lures, when equipped with big, slow-angled lips become deep-diving lures.

The ultimate in deep-running plugs are the big-lipped lures with a sinking bodies. These are often large lures, far too heavy for easy casting, and are designed primarily to be trolled. A large lip, one big enough to take a lure deeply into the water, can be cumbersome and collect weeds. That is why the sinking lure, with a modified lip, is used in combination to achieve almost the same effect. The eye or ring to which the line or snap is attached on some plugs can also affect whether it dives, runs on top, or is a deep-diver. The position of the eye has its effect on the direction of the pull and controls the angle the diving lip makes with the surface. Actual lure choice is determined by where the fish are feeding, with your sole objective to place the plug as close to these striped bass as possible.

Deep-running plugs—*Top row: Rebel's "Reb" 2 Shorty. Second row, left to right: Rapala Blue Mullet, Rapala's Magnum Minnow. Third row: Rebel's Diving Minnow, Rebel Diving Minnow (medium). Bottom: Old Pal's Flash Raposa Deep Troller.*

SPOONS

The first spoon-type lure was just that—a spoon, cut off at the handle. A hole was drilled on one end for the ring or line and another drilled on the other end for a ring and hook. A school of baitfish swimming through the water, or even an individual fish, will flash or reflect sun regularly. This flashing gets the attention of game fish. The action of a spoon is produced by its wobbling effect. It sets up a flashing sequence which bass can follow. The wobbling motion imitates the side-to-side undulations of a swimming fish and is quite effective in its duplication.

Light Spoons

Light-weight spoons rely more on their shape to produce the desired action than on other factors. As a result, weight will kill the action in this type of spoon and for the most part they are thin and large. The reduced weight allows them to flutter better against the force of the water and at slower speeds, and the large sides increase their surface area so that this action can be exaggerated.

Most spoons used for striped bass in saltwater situations are chrome-plated and metallic in appearance. Painted spoons can be effective, but the metal finish endures longer. Spoons of this nature are attention-getters in proportion to their light-flashing abilities. Some magnify their effectiveness with real

Spoons, heavy and light: Top row, left to right: Hopkins Red and White 550, Hopkins Hammered Spoon 550, Hopkins Hammered Spoon 388, Hopkins Hammered Spoon 3-1/2 No-EQL, Hopkins Hammered Spoon Shorty 150, Hopkins Hammered Spoon S-1. Bottom row: JAG Mooselock Wobbler (1-1/4 oz.), Spearing Spoon, Luhr Jensen Krocodile (5 oz.), Abu Toby (5/8 oz.), Abu Toby (1/2 oz.), Tony Acceta Pet 15, Tony Acceta Pet 13, Squid Spoon 2.

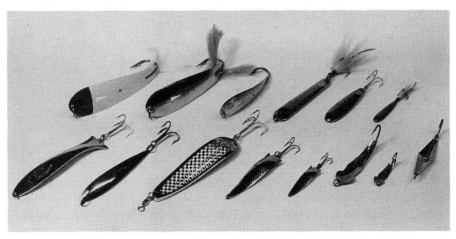

swimming action. One of these is the large bunker spoon. It is designed to imitate one of the striped bass's favorite foods. It is made in either chrome or painted versions and as an adult bunker and a "Baby" bunker in size. Smaller spoons are often adorned on their hooks with feathers or bucktails to add a swimming action, while still others are finished with strips of pork rind that extend the length of the lure and create a tail for added interest.

Heavy Spoons

These striped bass lures might not be considered spoons by some, but for the want of a better classification or name, they are referred to as spoons. These include the famous tin squids, castings of lead that must be periodically brightened by polishing, and the famous Hopkins collection of pounded or hammered metal lures.

Both lures have some action in the water when retrieved or trolled at an even pace, but it is minimal when compared to lighter, hydrodynamically responsive spoons. The reason is their weight versus exposed area. They are just too heavy to be retrieved smoothly. They were made heavy so that they could be small in size yet cast a long distance.

The secret to working these lures is to vary their retrieve, and the action is imparted more by the fisherman than the design of the lure. A jerking retrieve, simulating the swimming pattern of a squid, is a surefire bass-producer. These are favored lures when fishing blind because you can cover great amounts of water and set up an enticing swimming pattern.

The tin (really lead) squid is seldom fished without a bucktail or set of

The Bunker Spoon—one of the best artificial lures used in the fall during the southward migration of striped bass along the South Shore of Long Island, N.Y. and the New Jersey Shore. It is trolled parallel to the outside surf. It comes in two sizes: standard and Baby Bunker Spoon and in two finishes, either chrome or painted white with a red head.

feathers attached to the hook. This increases the illusion of a swimming fish. Hopkins lures can be fished without a tail dressing, but when the hook is covered in feathers or adorned with a pork rind, it stands a better chance of catching the eye of a striped bass.

In addition to being retrieved like other lures, the hammered metal spoon can also be fished as a jig, because of its weight. Striped bass in freshwater impoundments are regularly taken by vertical jigging of a small hammered spoon, and the action is carried on in a vertical rather than horizontal plane.

JIGS

Two widely used but totally dissimilar striped bass lures fall under the heading of jigs, not so much because of their construction or shape, but in accordance with the way they are fished.

Bucktail Jigs

The bucktail jig is one of the oldest and probably still one of the most effective striped bass lures available to an angler. Its design is still rather basic, composed of a hook that when fished is turned toward the surface, a lead head on the shank near the eye, and a dressing of bucktail deer hairs around the trailing edge of the lead head, covering the hook. There are some variations to the dressing. Recently, synthetic filaments have been used when bucktails are scarce. They can be made in any length whereas bucktails are rather fixed. Marabou feathers are also used and give the jig a pulsating effect similar to the squid they are trying to imitate and are very effective.

There is also a reverse bucktail that works quite effectively at times. Some anglers have just discovered it, but John Naimoli of Amityville, Long Island, has been tying and fishing the reverse bucktail since the early 1930s. This lure is dressed similarly to the standard bucktail jig but with somewhat fewer hairs. Then, a second mass of hairs or artificial fibers is tied with their tapered ends in a forward direction, all but burying the eye. This also produces a pulsating effect similar to the marabou feathers.

Bucktails can be fished just as they are but they are far more effective when used in combination with a pork rind. The pork rind/bucktail combination is a standard lure in most Northeast bass waters and is fished best on wire while trolling and jigging. At one time, the bucktail was built with a swinging hook. The head was molded onto a shank with eyes on each end and the hook was attached to the rear trailing eye. When coupled with a 4- or 5-inch split pork rind, the action was so great that it could be fished without being jigged. For some reason, this type of jig, with the swinging hook, is near impossible to purchase nowadays.

Jig heads come in a variety of patterns and shapes, from blunt-headed

Buck-tailed jigs. Left to right: Beri-Jig, Reverse Bucktail by Sea King, No-Alibi Jig (4 oz.), Boone King Jig (4 oz.), Boone Bean Head (4 oz.) and Nickelure (1 oz.)

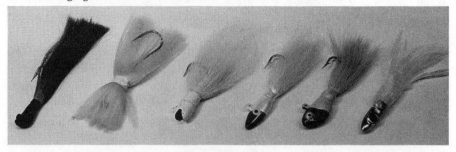

chunks of lead designed for bouncing along the bottom to bean- and bullet-shaped heads used in faster trolling situations. The weight of jigs also varies greatly according to the size of bass you are after and the depth and speed at which you are trolling. They range from 1/2 and 1 ounce to 4 and 5 ounces. Colors also are used, with white the favorite. Matching colored pork rinds are used or switched for red or yellow versions.

Diamond Jigs

Diamond jigs are quite similar to tin squids and hammered spoons in their use, weight, and hydrodynamic reaction. Basically, the diamond jig is shaped like an elongated diamond, often 1/2 to 3/4 inches at its widest and 5 to 7 inches at its longest. The jigs are made of cast metal and then chrome-plated so that they reflect light. They act like a baitfish and are jerked up and down off the bottom to look like a squid. The jig is finished with a treble hook on the business end and

Diamond jigs. Left to right: Abu Egon (2-1/8 oz.), Bridgeport Diamond Jig (10 oz.), Bridgeport Diamond Jig (2 oz.), Bridgeport Diamond Jig with imbedded hook (1/2 oz.).

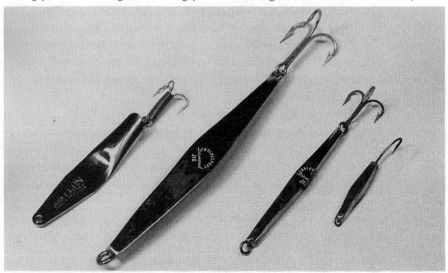

a fixed eye on the other end. However, a large number of anglers prefer to replace the treble hook with a single hook that makes unhooking fish easier.

Diamond jigs can be fished alone, with pork rind, or with strips of cut squid. In some cases, the treble hook is replaced with a single O'Shaughnessy or Siwash. Diamond jigs range greatly in size, from 1/2-ounce jigs for mackerel to 2-pound jigs for small cod and up to 16-ounce for big cod. Diamond jigs for striped bass range between 4 and 8 ounces. The speed of the water in which you are jigging and its depth will determine the weight of the jig you should use more than the size of the fish you hope to catch.

Most jigs are finished in metallic chrome. However, one year in Plum Gut, off eastern Long Island, fishing had come to a temporary standstill for everyone but one charterboat skipper. A close look through a pair of binoculars proved that he had painted his jigs a fluorescent red, and the bass liked it.

TUBE LURES

The striped bass fisherman is usually an innovative person and can readily adapt materials outside the world of the striped bass to the fishing scene. One of these innovations is the use of surgical tubing. This tubing, in its natural state, is a tan or translucent brown and doesn't look very appetizing, nor would one imagine that it could catch fish. But when cut into 1-foot lengths, with a lead head added, with or without eyes, and a pair of hooks, one on a wire leader inside the tube that comes near the head and a second hook a few inches from

Original surgical-tube lures (eft to right). Classic lures no longer manufactured: TriFin Eel (10 oz.), Tube Alou (3 oz.), simple surgical tube, Raja Tube (3 oz.) and TriFin (2 oz.)

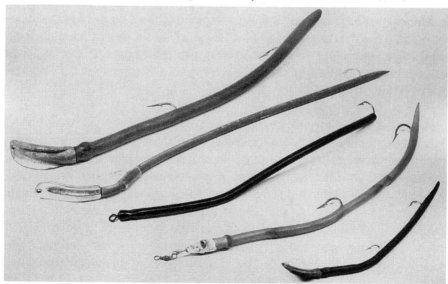

Roland Martin, well-known bass (largemouth black bass) fisherman started as a professional striped bass guide on Santee-Cooper Reservoir in South Carolina. This, however, is a Plum Gut (New York) striped bass that fell for a bucktailed-jig and a pork rind combination,.

a split in the tail, you have what closely approximates the action of an eel or long sandworm moving through the water.

For added effect, some of the early forms that actually used surgical tubing were dyed red to simulate a healthy sandworm or black to imitate an eel. They all took plenty of bass. The surgical tube now ranks in the number two spot, close behind bucktail/pork rind jigs as a bass-getter.

In early editions, the head was little more than a bullet-shaped piece of lead. Eyes were added for extra effect and planing heads were added to make it swim in the water. Later, some of the long tail hooks with exceptionally long shanks were bent slightly and the action was further increased. Today, surgical-tube lures are a favorite with charterboat skippers who cannot get their fares to jig a bucktail.

Umbrella Lures

Large pieces of surgical tubing worked so well that some fishermen, mostly innovative charterboat captains, began using smaller diameter tubes to imitate smaller baitfish. A single-plane spreader was used to catch striped bass as long ago as the 1930s. In this rig, two or more lures were strung together on a trolling plane and used to simulate several baitfish swimming together in a small school. Usually they all had hooks and a striped bass could get caught on any lure. When surgical tubes became available about the middle 1960s, one Montauk charter skipper switched the plugs to tubes and strung them on what looked like a coat hanger. It really caught striped bass and he kept it a well

This is one example of an umbrella rig that is collapsible. The arms are opened and locked into place by a nut and bolt imbedded in a grooved lead head that also acts to weight the lure.

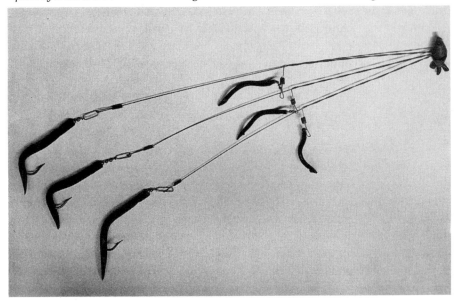

guarded secret lure for months. He so outfished other skippers that they finally went out of their way to snag his trolled lures and that was how they discovered his secret. The resulting umbrella rigs that evolved from this lure have, for the last 20 years, been the top bass-producer at this famous point of land.

But the single plane of the lures gave him trouble. The lures and coat hanger spun too much, twisting his line, overriding the swivels, and there weren't enough tubes. Also, the coat hanger wire wasn't heavy enough and collapsed when trolled against the heavy rips off Montauk. If one plane is good, then two must be better, he reasoned to himself, and set two at right angles to each other. Thus, he had four spreader arms, each trailering a tube lure. Then he poured a lead head at the point where they came together and a swivel to which the line could be added. He further modified the lure by adding small, hookless teasers halfway down the spreader arms. He also now used brass welding rod because it was tougher and springier, and fished four hooked lures on each rib or arm of the umbrella rig. It began closely to resemble an umbrella's ribs and a school of small, whirling baitfish. Then he added a larger tube on a leader that emanated from the center. He made this the hook-tube and cut off hooks on the others. Now they wouldn't foul and the larger lure almost always got the strike.

The umbrella rig now truly looked like a school of baitfish and the striped bass fell for it in such record numbers that there was a lot of talk about it being unsportsmanlike, or even illegal. But the rig got so elaborate, as each skipper tried to outdo one another, and so expensive to produce, that if you hung one on the bottom and couldn't break it loose, you could leave $15 to $20, even if you made your own lure. The umbrella rig is still in use today, but is not the "hot" lure it once was. It is still effective, but like many lures, if you don't use it, it can't catch fish in the tackle box. Often anglers seriously believe that a fish changes its preference for a lure. If the food upon which fish feed happens to change, then lures can change. But too often a lure loses popularity not because the fish have switched, but because fishermen have lost faith in their artificial bait.

COPY-CAT LURES

This group of lures was made possible because of advances in technology. Plastics that are lifelike in both texture and coloration have produced a host of lures good enough that they regularly fool striped bass. They are modified with lead or metallic heads that enable them to be fished at various depths and give them the action to make the plastic look like the real thing. Foremost among these lures are imitations of eels. It is only natural that the eel be duplicated so often; it is a prime striped bass food. The Alou Eel was one of the first, designed by Al Rinefelder and Lou Palma, and made in varying lengths to please both fisherman and fish. They swim effectively because the head for the plastic body has been well designed.

An offshoot by the same designers is the Bait-Tail, a cross between a jig and a plastic lure. The head is similar to that used on bucktail jigs but modified in shape and weight so that it can be fitted with a plastic tail or body. It is fished similarly to the jig and probably should be classed with that type of lure.

Along lines similar to the Bait-Tail are the numerous shrimp-like baits. These too have a jig-type head, a hook that is fished up, and soft, pliable tails that respond to the water's force. They are actually jigs with plastic bodies and were introduced to striped bass fishing after the great success plastic worms had in fresh water. Many imitate shrimp in size, shape, and coloration and are quite effective in taking striped bass.

The plastic squid was an engineering breakthrough. To duplicate the many curves and folds of a squid took an engineer with some degree of artistry. The look-alikes are quite effective when trolled and jigged. The problem is to weight them properly. Barrel sinkers inside seem to work, and the action comes not from the shape of the lure or the sinkers but the way the lure is worked by fisherman and rod tip.

There are a variety of lures that seem to rise and fall in popularity with fishermen. Some are based on sound principles; others are bizarre in concept, are accepted for a while, and then fade away. One that seems to rise and fall is the Eelet, a small, thin, French lure made of hard plastic. It is probably better classified as a plug, if you can make a plug look like an eel. It is basically a freshwater lure, jointed in the center and with a small plastic plane in the front designed to give it a swimming action rather than depth. The depth is controlled

Copycat or look-alike lures. These are only a few of the many that were once available to bass fisherman. Top to bottom: Alou Bait-Tail, Alou ShoeString (1-1/2 oz.), Alou Eel, Sevenstrand Squid, Boone Shrimptail, Beri-Eel, TriFin Whip-Tail, Cordell Tattle-Tale and Garcia Eelet.

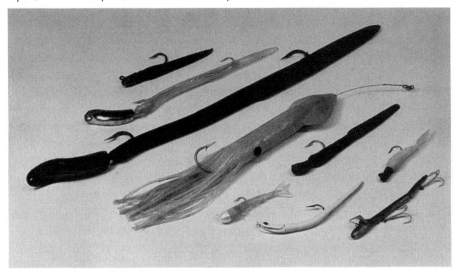

by the lure's weight, which is heavier than water, and it will sink rapidly unless pulled against the resistance of the water.

There are several other freshwater lures that make good plugs for striped bass. One is the large minnow made by Creek Chub for northern pike and muskellunge. Both solid and jointed minnows are good and work well either trolled or cast. The bigger lures are better trolled slowly. Some of these lures are modified by removing the tail treble hook and adding an eel skin. Most of these plugs are floaters and dive because of the shape of the forward lip. The lip can be easily adjusted to modify the degree of dive if it is a metal lip. However, some good lures are made with plastic lips that are molded right into the body of the plug and cannot be adjusted.

SELECTING YOUR LURES

Some lures are constructed so that you can get all the action you need simply by steadily retrieving them through the waters. They are hydrodynamically de-signed to react to the force of water flowing over their lips and heads, or against the sides of the body. These are good lures for beginning striped bass fishermen to choose. It takes the guesswork out of how to fish or retrieve them.

Other lures have no inherent action in them and are designed so a fisherman can make them work in the exact manner he likes. These lures are almost always retrieved at variable speeds so that their depth can be controlled by the angler. Lures of this nature often require rods with educated tips to help the fisherman in the task and reels with higher retrieve ratios so that he can vary the speeds easily.

Whichever lures you choose, make sure you give them the care and maintenance necessary so they are always ready to work for you. Bent diving planes ruin the action of your plug. Weak rings, rusted or partially sprung, can give way when you are fighting a fish. Dulled hooks can make it impossible to set the hook on a tough-mouthed bass. Even the best quality saltwater hooks eventually fall victim to the effects of corrosion. You can retard this effect by rinsing the lure and hooks in warm, soapy fresh water before storing them after each trip and definitely after each season. Rusted, battered, and bent hooks should all be replaced.

The Bucktailed-Jig Pork Rind Combination

There's little doubt among most experienced striped bass anglers that the most effective lure ever devised is the bucktailed-jig. When used in conjunction with a long pork rind, its ability to catch striped bass is even further enhanced. The traditional combination is a 3-ounce, white bucktail and a 5- to 7-inch pork rind. However, the pork rind color is varied at times and either yellow or red are the alternate colors of choice. Even the color of the bucktail is varied and anglers

at Montauk or off Orient Point, both on Long Island's (New York) East End, switch to yellow or even chartreuse when they feel the bass are being picky about their food. However, the choice might be more that of the fisher than fish when one realizes that there is very little color in the watery world of a striped bass. At 10 feet of depth, red disappears, a 20 and 30 feet, orange and yellow become bland and below 50 feet green looks a bluish-white. Under 70 feet, the fish's world is all blue.

25

Accessory Fishing Equipment

The serious bass angler cannot go fishing armed with rod and reel alone and hope for consistent success. He needs more gear—accessory equipment—to take striped bass under all the varied conditions he may encounter. Weather alone requires him to pay heed to his personal gear so that he can be out whenever bass are running. Because of the great variety of fishing techniques by which striped bass can be taken, the duffel of the bass angler must be more complete than that of any other saltwater fisherman. Striped bass can be taken day or night, from boats, from bridges, from jetties, and from the beach. They can be taken by casting, trolling, chumming, jigging, spinning, and drifting. To facilitate all these methods, a great array of equipment has evolved over the past few decades that makes this task a bit easier for the fisherman.

Accessory equipment for the complete striped bass fisherman can roughly be divided into two groups, that designed to help you catch fish or get you into a position to catch fish, and that needed to make you safe, comfortable, and warm while you are doing the fishing. Of course, you can catch striped bass without any accessory gear, but good equipment lets you concentrate longer on your fishing, allows you to be out longer when the weather is miserable, and makes those good times just so much more enjoyable.

CLOTHING AND PERSONAL GEAR

Foul-weather clothing starts with insulated underwear. If you plan to fish the surf, even during early summer months the water can still be cold enough that you get chilled after standing in it, in waders or hip boots, for even a short time. Insulated underwear, tops and bottoms, are also a must when it comes to night fishing on all but the warmest August evenings.

Closely associated with thermal underwear is the thermal or insulated sweatshirt. This heavy hooded shirt has almost become part of the standard uniform of the surfcaster, and with drawstrings around the hood it neatly fits under the hood of your rain jacket or foul-weather gear. CPO or chamois shirts are almost as popular as the hooded sweatshirt and are worn to keep the chill from getting you around the neck. If you wear waders or neoprene outerwear you should take advantage of new innerwear materials that not only breathe but allow the moisture to only flow one way, away from your body, and trap it on the garment's exterior. It gives you a dry feeling all the time.

Foul-Weather Gear

Foul-weather gear is usually of the two-piece suit type. In the surf, if you have waders that come up to your chest, only the top half of the suit is worn. It is tied around the bottom and then further secured with a web or leather belt to keep out the ocean if you happen to fall. If you ride a jetty or don't plan to get into the surf, the suit with top and pants is sufficient. This combination is also used by boat fishermen, even on dry days. Rain gear is good protection against wind, too, and there are wet times in heavy seas when the boat sets up a spray as you run through it.

Some forms of foul-weather gear don't "breathe" and can get you as wet inside as having no gear on a rainy day. Your body gives off a lot of moisture, even during the most routine activity. If there are no vents in your foul-weather suit, or if it is made of sealed nylon or plastic, then the suit will not let this moisture pass through. It condenses on the inside and in an hour or so, you are just as wet and chilled as if you hadn't worn a suit. Good rain suits are loose-fitting and allow moisture to escape through sleeves, collar, and front. Trousers should be of the bib type with supporting straps over the shoulders. Rain pants with elastic in the waist hold well but they don't let the heat rise and moisture dissipate out the top. In a boat, if you wear knee-high boots and a finger-length top parka, you can get away without wearing rain trousers.

The ultimate in wet-weather fishing are neoprene suits. They started with anglers who were also scuba divers who donned their diving gear to fish the rock jetties and boulders that line the points of land in many fishing areas. In foul weather they were impervious to the waves. And, if they fell in, they just floated back to the beach because of the buoyancy inherent in the closed-cell neoprene material. Today, you can get just the neoprene jacket and that's all you need if you wear waders.

Waders

There are numerous brands and styles of waders on the market and those that are good are not very cheap, except the light plastic type that are designed for a single day's fishing and intended to save you on the day you forgot to bring your real waders. They are worn over the shoes, weigh almost nothing, and cost

The well dressed surf fisherman dons a pair of chest-high waders, pulls over a hooded rain jacket, straps a web belt around his waist, and puts on felt or metal-studded sandals. On his hip he sports a short hand-gaff and over his shoulder a lure bag. If he's lucky, he'll walk out of the surf with a 34-pound striped bass as did this angler who happens to be famed jazz bassist Percy Heath. Seems unique that Heath is both a bass master and a master at bass.

Surf casting equipment. Shoulder-bag lure carrier and headlight with belt battery pack, web belt, sand spike, felt-soled sandals, Bimini belt, leather rod holder for belt, and ice creepers for the rocks.

between $1 and $2.

Most surfcasters have two pairs of waders. Both have built-in bootshoes. The first is a heavy-duty type with insulated feet. If you fish early in the season or very late, then this type of wader is a must. It is built of somewhat heavier-gauge material than lighter summer gear, and the foot, from about the knee down, is finished in double layers with a slight air space between which acts as insulation.

Most waders should have a pocket on the inside to keep important items near and handy; a ring or grommet well attached to the outside is there in case you want to add a stringer of fish; and belt hoops to help you thread your belt around the waist. Wader fit can be a problem. During recent years, there has been a tendency on the part of many manufacturers to reduce the number of sizes they produce, for economical reasons, and this may make it difficult for you to find the perfect size. The wader is measured by the boot size, and it is usually about one size larger than your street shoe of the same size number. Very few manufacturers make half-sizes.

The other important measurement is the leg length. At one time you could order them almost as you do trousers, by length in inches. Today, you have only long, medium, and short from which to choose. Don't pick a wader if it fits you just right while you are standing up. It is too short. Bend the knees and sit down. If you are not pinched in the knees when you do this, then you have enough room and the waders fit. They may look a bit sloppy when you stand up, but you will be able to move around easily and sit down on the tailgate of your vehicle when you want to.

In recent years, form-fitting neoprene waders, that first evolved for the trout and salmon fisherman, have made their way into the surf. Some come with a boot attached to the waders while others are "stocking feet" — you must also buy a wading shoe. Both styles have advantages. Neoprene waders come in different weights that range in thickness from 1 to 4 mill.

Hats

Hats have become another symbol of the surfcaster and boat fisherman. Typically long-visored, the hat plays an important role in a fisherman's ability to see what's happening on and in the water. When picking a hat to wear in the surf or on a boat, make sure that the underside of the visor is colored black or a dark green. This reduces the amount of light reflecting off the water and hitting your eyes.

The boat fisherman has a somewhat modified surf hat, with a hard, plastic visor, not transparent, but proof against rain and spray. Some fishing hats also come with flip-down cloth panels that shade the back of the neck and sides of your head from excessive sun. A good hat costs a little more but will often last a lot longer. Some of these hats, especially those with extra-long visors, occasionally come equipped with flip-down sunglasses attached to the underside of the visor. These are great, and when they have Polaroid filters they are even greater. If you'd rather not have them attached, then Polaroid sunglasses are your best bet. If you wear prescription glasses, then Polaroid snap-ons can meet your needs, or you can have prescription Polaroids made.

Polaroid lenses help you fish better in two ways. First, they filter out the stray rays of light and let you see deeper into the water. You can spot moving bass or read the bottom for signs of navigation obstacles. Second, they reduce the glare on the water during a warm, summer day, and this can make fishing much less fatiguing. Glare can have a negative effect on your fishing attitude if you can't escape it.

Shoes

The best shoes to wear in a boat have bottoms that grip wet or slippery surfaces, do not carry sand and dirt into the boat with each step, and do not mark the fiberglass decks. Some boat shoes fill one or more parts of these requirements, but it doesn't take much more effort or money to find the proper boat shoe. Getting chewed out just once by a boat skipper or a fisherman who has invited you on board for the day because your shoes have left black scuff marks on his boat's deck is embarrassing enough to make you wish you'd given more thought to footgear. Or, he might say nothing but you'll never get a return invitation.

Most boat shoes have canvas tops, can readily be washed when dirty, and dry quickly if they become wet. But early in the season, wet canvas shoes never seem to dry, and they become especially cold after they are wet. You can get boat shoes with the same gripping soles found on canvas shoes but with leather uppers. I don't know how wet feet affect you, but as long as my feet feel dry and warm, the rest of my body can be wet and I won't mind it too much. If my feet are wet, I'm unhappy.

FISHING ACCESSORIES

There are numerous accessories for fisherman both on the beach and in the boat. Some he can do without, others are more of a necessity than an accessory. Listed below are just a few that are important. Other skippers can always add their own personal necessities to the list to make it complete for them.

Bimini Belt

Most spinning rods can be worked standing up and held in both hands. But a 20- or 30-pound class trolling outfit, loaded with wire and worked from a moving boat, makes a portable gimbal or Bimini belt a real necessity. Reeling in often to check for weeds has a tendency to enlarge your belly button if you don't have a belt or rod pocket handy. When it comes to the actual fighting of a fish, you'll find it is much easier to handle a big bass from a belt. You can then use your legs and back to take the strain off the arms.

Gaffs

Freshwater anglers often seem shocked when they first see a gaff used on a fish. They prefer the idea of a net. But adequately sized nets are often too big to handle when it comes to boating a big fish. Lures or rigs with multiple hooks foul a net so badly that very soon even the most considerate angler switches to a gaff. A gaff is an efficient, effective device to get a fish quickly into the boat. Gaffs for boat use come in several lengths and sizes. I'm a firm believer that every boat should have two on board, one a large, double-handled affair for really large fish, and a second somewhat smaller, but still with a handle at least 2 feet long so that you don't have to double over on the gunwale to gaff a bass.

In the surf, long-handled gaffs are out of the question if you are doing your own gaffing. A short-handled gaff, often with just enough wood on it to hold the hook, is used. Many come with tip covers or holders that attach to the belt to hide the tip so that the surfcaster won't gaff himself. Some come with coiled line, much like a telephone cord, attached to the handle so that the gaff isn't left behind or dropped in the water.

One thing that should be common to all gaffs, regardless of their size or where they are used, is a sharp point. A dull gaff can help you lose a fish more quickly than someone crossing your line with a boat. The point should be sharpened with a file and then finished off on a stone.

The concept of gaffing a striped bass versus netting is getting considerable attention today....and rightly so. In two states, it is illegal to have one on board while striped bass fishing, and legislation is pending in other states to the same effect. The reason is that a gaff is not a striped bass management tool. A fish that is gaffed is usually mortally wounded. Today, all states have minimum sizes for striped bass some have maximum sizes as well, and often just one or two fish is the daily limit. Chances are that you might gaff an undersized bass and not be able to return it alive, and this is a waste of the resource when striped bass populations everywhere are in trouble.

Today, every boat should carry a large landing net and, where legal, a gaff. If there is even the slightest doubt that a fish is sublegal or just legal, or even legal by only a short amount, the fish should be netted. But in the case where the fish is obviously well above the minimum length, a gaff works better. I'd sure hate to find myself in a situation, alone in the boat, as I often fish, bring a bass alongside that was 70 pounds or bigger and being forced to net it. I'd never forgive myself if I lost it. But then again, I would probably unhook it while it was still in the water and let it swim away. But, I probably won't ever have to make that decision.

Sand Spikes

Sand spikes come in assorted shapes, sizes, and constructions. Basically, they are designed to do for the surf fisherman what a rod holder does for the bass angler in a boat—hold his rod. The rod can be set in a sand spike when you stop fishing, when you're mending your terminal tackle, or it can be used while fishing in conjunction with a pyramid sinker and fish-finder rig. This is the still-fishing aspect of surfcasting.

The sand spike is nothing more than a tube in which to set the butt of the rod and a spike on the tube to pierce the sand. The spike should be long enough to give the tube firm support and at the same time hold the butt above the sand and incoming water. In some models, the tube is pointed on one end and becomes the spike. In others, a piece of angle iron is bolted to a tube of aluminum or plastic pipe. Needless to say, materials that won't rust should be used for the tube. The spike material is not quite as important.

Pliers

I just don't feel dressed properly when I go fishing if I don't have a pair of pliers strapped onto my belt. One of the most important pieces of equipment that a fisherman in salt water can have is a good set of marine pliers. There are several models from which to choose, and there are two sizes. The best pliers are geared or levered so that the two faces move and meet in a parallel plane, rather than scissoring like simple hinged pliers. This makes them more useful when something must be evenly crimped or squeezed together. Most pliers of this type have indentations on their faces so that they can hold split shot without slipping.

Also, on the back of the face, they should have a device for cutting wire, hooks, and other materials. They should also have a good gripping surface on their handles, because your hands are likely to be wet whenever you use them. Lastly, they should be impervious to salt water and its corrosive effects. If not, they aren't worth much because they will rust shut the first time you set them aside. Even the best pliers should be given some care, and regular doses of silicone spray or oil are a must.

Knives

On the hip opposite the pliers, I always carry a knife, and I'm ready to fish. Most anglers carry a fileting knife on their belts. The knife can clean fish as well as do a host of other tasks. It should be made of metal that holds its edge, because a dull knife is worse than no knife at all. It goes almost without saying that it should be impervious to salt water. Large knives are not needed in the boat or in the surf; a blade of 4 to 6 inches is more than enough. If the knife has accessory blades, so much the better. But too many may bulk the knife holster and hang up whenever you're in a tight passageway.

Billy Club

Both the well equipped boat and the well equipped surfcaster or bank fisherman should have a short club, with leather strap for ease of handling, to put away big and ferocious fish. If the club is made of hickory, oak, or other heavy woods, it may be heavy enough to pacify even the largest bass. If it is made of a lighter wood, it should have a core of lead to give it oomph. A hard blow isn't always needed to kill the biggest bass. A well-placed blow is more desirable. A fish's brain is located just behind a line drawn between the two eyes. A light tap in this spot is enough to do in most bass. You can tell when you have hit correctly—a bass will stiffen and the tail and fins will vibrate quickly for just a short time. It is the most merciful way to finish the job.

Creepers and Felt Soles

Rocks, jetties, and extremely gravelly beaches are most safely and easily fished when you are wearing metal creepers or felt soles on your boots or waders. Manufacturers make felt sandals that slip over your wader foot and can be taken off when you are in the sand. Creepers are spike-laden frames that also strap onto your foot and were originally designed for walking on ice or mountain climbing. Once, you could buy waders with built-in metal spikes.

Today, you can achieve much the same effect by buying a pair of golfer's rubbers and pulling them over your wader shoes. They come equipped with spikes, can be fitted snugly over your wader boots, and won't get lost in the wash. They can be removed to save the points when you aren't teetering on a slippery rock. However, you can order replacement felt soles for your waders that also come equipped with Carborundum spikes.

Still other fishermen have devised their own felt soles, added spikes, and then glued this affair to the soles of their boots. These also provide the ultimate in traction and can be replaced when the spikes wear or the felt becomes solid with debris. Almost as good are corkers, studded sandals that can be slipped over your boots, made in a style used by loggermen when rafting logs.

Flashlights

If you walk the surf at night your hands are usually filled with other equipment, and when you begin fishing there isn't a hand left to hold a light. Surfcasters have taken an idea from spelunkers and adopted a headlight with headband for fishing the surf. It frees their hands to tie on lures or to gaff a bass when it is ready to come ashore. Lights worn below one's head in elevation are too often turned green by the effects of salt water splashing or flooding them.

Lure Carriers

Most fishermen who wade out into the surf find it difficult and dangerous to carry lures in their pockets. It's too long a walk back to the beach vehicle to get a new lure if one is lost, and early in the game many small side packs were

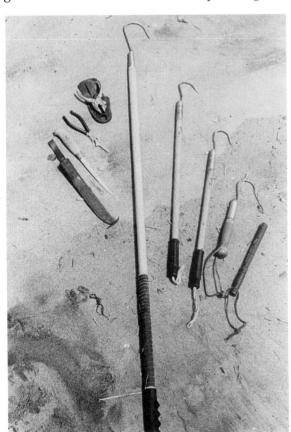

improvised that would carry lures, snaps and swivels, and any other gear. But such packs were regularly washed by the surf. With the introduction of plastics, the entire kit was molded to hold lures, and equipped with a shoulder strap. Today, there are several sizes bag and lure carriers available, some made of plastic, others of aluminum with canvas covers. All do the job and you can't go too far wrong with either variety.

More surfcasting equipment. Fileting knife and belt case, long-nosed pliers, parallel pliers and cutters, long-handled gaff, two smaller boat gaffs, surf fisherman's gaff, and lead-core billy club.

Where all the accessories are put to work.

26

The Bass Boat

Almost any boat will do for striped bass fishing, but some boats do a lot better than others. For a long time in the search for striped bass, it was the rowboat that accounted for the angler's getting to sea. During most of these early years, striped bass fishing from boats was restricted to bays and harbors, especially those that contained a minimum of current, and to anglers with a strong back and light oars.

Striped bass fishing as a sport in small boats was well practiced during subsequent years (late 1800s and early 1900s) in Cuttyhunk, along the Massachusetts coast, and as far west as New Jersey. It was a great occupation, at the turn of the century, for the boat houses and the numerous bass guides who knew how to stem the rocks in Hell Gate in New York's East River. The boats were large seaworthy dories that took a lot of row power to move. More often than not, they were manned by guides and fished by sports. Not until after the turn of the century, and the installation of small gasoline engines in dories, did boats specifically designed to catch striped bass begin to evolve.

THE MONTAUK BASS BOAT

There were only two boats built during the early years on the eastern end of Long Island that can be termed Montauk bass boats. They both carried the same name, *Pun'kinseed*. They were the end product of an earlier type of skiff first in use around Sandy Hook, N.J. The daddy of all of today's striped bass boats was a man named Otto Scheer. Originally from New Jersey, Scheer grew up with fishing deeply entrenched in his background, and striped bass above all other kinds of fishes. His father, William Scheer, has been credited with being one of the first anglers in the New York Bight to practice inshore fishing. He pioneered fishing the Mud Hole for giant tuna before anyone found the big fish were there.

Otto Scheer, while still a youth, regularly rowed the waters on both sides of Long Island Sound. One summer, he and a companion devoted three weeks to rowing a double-oared boat from New Rochelle to New London, trolling for striped bass all the way. As he grew older and wiser, Scheer became a leading international jeweler. His first love, however, remained striped bass fishing. Eventually, he headed east, spending more and more of his life at Montauk while it was still a primitive part of Long Island.

Otto was as rabid a striped bass angler as God ever made. In the beginning, he joined the early surfmen who had been hurling "tins" for years at bass off Montauk. Sometimes he fished from the water, at other times from bass stands that dotted the Point. Scheer knew there had to be a better way, so he planned and executed a careful scientific campaign for the demise of striped bass.

His greatest discovery was that bass were lying inside the surf, and that when disturbed, they ran inshore, not off. The only way to get to them was by boat, but no one in those days, during the early 1920s, fished Montauk by boat. There weren't any, excepting maybe a few that were launched into the surf and took part in "pleasure fishing" as an early history described it. After years of studying the Jersey boats like the Jersey skiff and Seabright dory, and after gaining a lot of experience in small boats, he built or had a hand in building a boat he designed. It had a special purpose in mind— fishing between the breakers and among the large boulders that surrounded Montauk Point. The boat was finished in the early 1920s. It was 18 feet long and had an 8-foot beam. It was only natural that she be named *Pun'kinseed* because of her overall appearance.

This first boat did a lot of inshore as well as offshore fishing during the late 1920s. On one trip, John Sweeting captained the *Pun'kinseed* for Scheer and guided Otto to the first white marlin ever taken on rod and reel off Montauk. They are also credited with the first broadbill swordfish, taken in the little *Pun'kinseed*.

In 1929, Scheer built another version of the first boat which was destined to become the most famous small open fishing boat on the Atlantic Coast. The boat was completely open, with a coaming around the cockpit that came up to the hip of the average man. Like the first boat, it was 18 feet long but 8 feet 4 inches wide. It was powered by a 91-horsepower, six-cylinder Gray engine—a lot of power in those days even for a large boat. In addition, it was extra-heavily planked so that the hull could withstand a pounding on the rocks if the boat was steered in too tightly. Steering was accomplished from two positions, with long-handled tillers both fore and aft on her port side. A locker was also fitted at the bow position to increase the height for the helmsman. The bow tiller gave the skipper immediate view of the rocks ahead and he could man the craft from that position while fishing.

For many years thereafter, the *Pun'kinseed*, with Otto Scheer on the rod and Capt. Bill Bassett at the helm, accounted for thousands of striped bass under

The Pun'kinseed *at work. This is Otto Scheer's boat working the inshore waters under the light at Montauk. The painting was done by Lynn Bogue Hunt, the angler on the port side of the boat. It was the cover for the March, 1936, issue of* Field & Stream Magazine, *which carried a story by Hunt on striped-bass fishing in the combers off this famous landmark.*

Montauk Point's famous lighthouse, that stands atop Turtle Hill. Gradually, the boat was copied by others who joined the growing cadre of boats fishing striped bass in the surf.

During the big blow in the fall of 1935, while tied to her mooring in Great Pond (Lake Montauk), the *Pun'kinseed* sank. Scheer immediately raised her, and after installing a new engine, she was again fit for duty on the Point. But three years later, on September 21, the 1938 hurricane hit the village of Montauk with full force. Bill Bassett tried to pull her ashore, next to Jack Well's gasoline docks. There was no one else to help him, and he was in water up to his neck. The *Pun'kinseed* finally broke away from Bassett and the huge seas swept her away. They towered 6 feet over Well's dock, and the *Pun'kinseed* was last seen heading out to sea, battling the waves.

THE CUTTYHUNK BOATS

But before the *Pun'kinseed* was lost to the world a wise old Cuttyhunk skipper had been west to pay a visit to Montauk. He was especially impressed by the way the few boats there pursued striped bass in on the shore and among the rocks. Capt. "Coot" Hall brought the idea back to Cuttyhunk Island. The design was modified slightly and emerged as the Cuttyhunk bass boat. Hall had three or four guides working for him, all out of this style of boat, and for a while they dominated bass fishing on Sow and Pigs Reef, an area just west of Cuttyhunk's shore with shoal and boulder conditions similar to Montauk Point.

There's little difference today in the basic design of Cuttyhunk boats from those 40 years ago, or even from Scheer's boat. They are between 18 and 22 feet long with a beam somewhat less than the 8 feet 4 inches of the *Pun'kinseed*. The sides are rather vertical, with a fairly hard chine. The bow still carries sem-

blances of the straight, almost knife-like bow of the *Pun'kinseed.*

The coaming is still an integral part of these open boats, and a fore-and-aft tiller is standard. The engine housing, an inboard, is amidships, and a pair of chairs, sometimes light fighting chairs, are placed along each side of the housing or near the clear transom. There are no obstructions across the back, and rods are stored upright near a little cuddy cabin that is hidden under a bow deck. The boats are quite fast; 25 knots is a beginning speed.

At one time, most of the Cuttyhunk boats were of stripped-plank construction, but lapstrake quickly took over. Today, the boats are about evenly divided between lapstrake and

Though a bit difficult to make out, the last boat in this row of "Cuttyhunkers" is the boat "Coot" Hall had built when he returned with the Punkin'seed's specs by Lyman Boat Works, New Bedford, Mass. It sports a beautifully fared coaming around the entire gunwale except at the transom and is appropriately named "Coot."

plywood hulls, with a few fiberglass hulls now breaking through as "accepted" boats. There is a lot less care involved. Most of the older boats are Dodges, Prigs, and Lymans, with several custom jobs made by the South Dartmouth Yards in Massachusetts.

THE MODERN BASS BOAT

Distribution of specialized boats like the Cuttyhunk bass boat was rather limited. They were ideally suited for the specific kinds of water in which they were designed to operate. They appeared in northern New Jersey, along eastern Long Island, and in parts of Connecticut and Rhode Island, as well as the Elizabeth Islands, of which Cuttyhunk is the westernmost. The boat was fine for the turbulent waters off Montauk Point but lacked the versatility to fish other areas and wasn't especially trailerable.

In 1963, Richard Fischer of Rockland, Mass., designed and introduced a boat that would become the mobile bass fisherman's dream, the Boston Whaler. It was a small boat, as far as boats designed for fishing tricky waters was concerned. It was only 16 feet long, but had a 4-foot width, a ratio rather close to that of the old *Pun'kinseed*. And like the *Pun'kinseed* it had a tremendous amount of lift. It would not sink deeply into heavy seas or incoming waves. The hull design was basically that of a sled, or scow, and was quite close in appearance to the Chincoteague scows of Virginia's coastal waters. Unlike other scows, it had a trihedral hull, with sponsons on the chine that gave the boat exceptional lateral stability. There are better boats for specific seas than the Boston Whaler but there aren't any that can do as many jobs as well. It was designed as a general all-around boat, but striped bass fishermen took it to their hearts and it became the classic boat for years.

The Whaler was seaworthy beyond its dimensions. It was so buoyant that it rode above most rough seas. It was notorious for catching water with its sponsons, but in a following sea it would handle better than any boat afloat and it was great for working in close to the beach. The gunwales were shallow, but with the lift the boat afforded, deep gunwales would be a detriment and only catch cross winds.

Its unique feature, however, was a stand-up console, located just aft of center and used for steering the boat. It was a compromise with the Cuttyhunk boats with their dual steering. Because the boat was relatively small, it could easily be guided by a man in the middle. This basic configuration or style then spawned a series of new boats that extended the fishing prowess of the boat-equipped striped bass angler. The most pressing need for advancement in the 16-foot Whaler was a longer hull so that it could work in larger seas.

Mako and Aquasport produced the next innovations in the bass boat. They retained the center-console concept of the Whaler but built their boats more on

A "modern" Cuttyhunk boat fishing the famous Sow and
Pigs Reef on the west end of Cuttyhunk Island in the early 1970s.

the deep-vee principle with hulls 17, 19, 22, and up to 23 feet long. This modern bass boat can handle a lot of water. Boston Whaler eventually produced the extended Whaler, a 22-foot model called the Outrage, which even today has never been surpassed as a striped bass boat. The hull was modified in front to form a modified-vee. The sponsons on the sides were reduced and the bow raised to give it a greater sheer and produce a dry-running craft. Its only drawback was that because of its still relatively flat- bottom hull, it pounded when one attempted to go fast in heavy seas. This drawback was modified in subsequent models and the center of the trihedral hull design was changed, as more and more vee was added.

Another feature that is unique to this class of boats is that they are all self-bailing. This is achieved by building a double bottom in the boat with the top of the inner deck above the waterline. They work beautifully when underway but when loaded with gasoline and all the paraphernalia needed to do battle with striped bass, many will slosh water on their decks. However, the self-bailing concept is a needed feature for a boat that follows the fish in all kinds of weather. The water intake is corrected by plugs or scupper guards.

HOW TO RIG A BASS BOAT

Generally, this breed of inshore fishing boat is between 17 and 22 feet long, of an open construction, with steering and control console designed for stand-up operation from near the middle of the craft. The boat is powered by one or two outboards and toted about from place to place on a tandem-wheeled trailer. The last item has not only freed the roving bass fisherman from working out of a single port but has also reduced the cost and gas consumption by allowing him to drive closer to his fishing, with a minimum of on-water running.

Nowadays, there is a wide range of hulls from which an angler can make a selection when it comes to choosing a boat to turn into a bass-fishing machine. The choice, however, can be a mind-muddling experience unless he first comes to terms with himself as to what kind of boat he wants. Before ever looking for the correct hull, he must first decide, truthfully, just what he wants the boat to be able to do. That's easy; the second part is the toughest, and that is setting an honest maximum limit of what the pocketbook will allow. Prices of fiberglass hulls can vary from as little as $3,000 for a minimally equipped boat to $20,000 for a rig with all the extras you'll ever need loaded onto it. This great disparity is one of the nice features of this class of boat; you can manipulate the variables and really tailor-make a super bass boat.

There's no such thing as the perfect bass boat. Everything in a boat is a compromise of features. We all are individuals, and our boats and their characteristics are likely to reflect this individualism. What equipment you feel you might need or its arrangement on a specific hull might be just great for you but to another angler it might feel all wrong. This is even evident in selecting the basic hull. That's why there is such a choice available. Your boat should match the fishing conditions of the water over which you spend the greatest amount of time. After you pick the hull, then there is more room for us to agree and we can go on and build the near-perfect bass boat. After the initial decision about which hull and then which length to buy, the next most pressing question to be solved is the power plant or propulsion. You have three possible selections: inboards, inboard/outboards, or outboards. All possess advantages, but a quick comparison will show that outboards are preferred by most operators of such rigs. The reasons given are: low initial cost, fuel economy, power selection, size, weight, location in a craft, ease of replacement, and dependability.

A second consideration at this time is the use of dual power. A single unit is easier to handle, less complicated as far as installation is concerned, and more

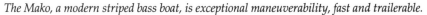
The Mako, a modern striped bass boat, is exceptional maneuverability, fast and trailerable.

economical to run. With two units, you can figure that your troubles have doubled. However, when you are working in close to the surf or when you are making those long reaches between islands you have the assurance that if one engine should go down there is always a second. The two engines should be large enough in horsepower, that one of them alone is capable of putting the boat on plane and you'll be able to limp back at least at half speed. Many bass boats are equipped with double engines, so there must be a need for them.

What size power? I believe that most outboard boats are overpowered. The majority of craft in this class are capable of handling a maximum of 200 to 250 horsepower. This doesn't mean that you must put the maximum on your transom. The actual engine ratings will be a factor of the size and weight of your craft. For a single installation, the choice can range from 85 to 135 horsepower. For dual installation, they can range from a pair of 50-horsepower outboards on the smallest boats in this category to pair of 100s. The final choice will depend on your budget, the speed you feel is necessary, the gas consumption, and possibly the weight of the engines.

ACCESSORIES

One man's necessities can be another man's frivolity, and when it comes to accessories, this can also be true. However, I've included what I feel is important to me when I go hunting for striped bass. I first got serious about catching striped bass long before I was really able to get the kind of boat I wanted. When I finally could, I choose a 22-foot Boston Whaler Outrage because its general features suited what I like in a boat. While it has been 20 years since I rigged this boat, the principles and equipment I chose are just as valid now as then.

The place I began rigging the craft was at the console, the heart of any such stand-up machine. Mine eventually looked like it might be from the inside of a jet airplane's cockpit, but at one time or another, everything was called into use. More often than not, most of the gear was in daily use. I like to go fishing all the time, whenever I can and often whenever I shouldn't. The instrumentation on the boat helped me get there and back every time.

The most important item, especially when you get out of sight of land, or run long distances in the dark, or suddenly find yourself engulfed in fog, is a compass. A long and established name in things that always point north is Ritchie. I picked the Ritchie Navigator model, though even Ritchie has less expensive models. This one works well at almost all angles of heave, the card has a rather quick return, it is adjustable so that the compass can be swung (for correction), and most important of all, it is lighted by two (red) bulbs so that it can be seen while running at night. Even if you don't think you'll ever run at night, it is a good idea to have internal-lighted compass for unplanned times.

A boat's trim, both hull and engine, is controlled by the location of the center of the load within a craft and by engine tilt. The first can be adjusted, to a degree, simply by shifting about the heavy movable gear. Greater or more minute adjustments can be made by adjusting the angle of the engine with relation to the boat and water. Trim tabs located on the transom of a boat at the level of the bottom work well for big boats, but power tilt on the engine, actually adjusting the angle of the entire outboard, is an easier way to achieve the most accurate trim. Not only does power trim or tilt adjust the engine while under way, but when you are alone launching and retrieving a boat, the power trim lifts the engines out of the water while you still have one hand on the wheel.

Checking trim while the boat is underway can be done by eye, watching how the spray is thrown, and by feel. However, a much more accurate method is with the use of a tachometer. If a boat isn't trimmed properly, it will be pushing a head of water before the hull and the engine will be overtaxed for the given amount of speed. By playing with the power trim and keeping one eye on the tachometer you can see when engine speed picks up without touching the throttle, and when engine and boat achieve their most efficient trim.

A tachometer's first job, however, is not so much to be a check on the boat's trim but to indicate the speed at which your engines are turning over. Dual engines work best when their speeds are exactly the same. You can tune them fairly well just by your ears alone, but you can be exact with a pair of tachometers. Tuned engines are a must because they help stretch fuel, make steering easier, and keep one engine from working harder than the other.

A tachometer is also a fuel-saver when used in conjunction with a speedometer. After getting a boat onto plane, by using the full or almost full force of the engines, you can often cut back several notches on the throttle and still maintain the same forward speed if the boat has a planing hull. Once a boat is stepped onto plane it takes less power to keep it there than it took to get it there. As you pull back on the throttle or throttles, the tachometer(s) will slowly fall, telling you that the engines are turning over at a slower speed and that you are using less gas. However, the speedometer will hold constant. If you continue to pull back, the speedometer will eventually begin a slow fall. At one point, it will drop off abruptly. Put it back to the point just before it started the nose dive and you'll squeeze the maximum possible range and gas economy out of both the engine and boat.

It's foolhardy to run out of sight of land or far away from your home port without some sort of radio equipment. A goodly number of today's traveling bass boats are still equipped with Citizen Band radios (CB), but Very High Frequency (VHF) marine radios are used more in certain areas. CB was great until it was abused, and today, even though they are quite inexpensive when compared to VHF radios, their popularity has sharply waned. The safety reasons are obvious, and that is why some skippers even have both types. VHF equipment has a greater range. Its wattage is now limited to 25 and this restricts its broadcasting scope. In the past, marine radios could reach anywhere from

Here is a the author's first, dedicated striped bass boat, the 21-foot Boston Whaler Outrage, that was rigged in the early 1970's. Because of its unique hull construction, it is still considered one of the most versatile craft every made for fishing shallow, inshore waters and even between the combers. It can be used as a model for outfitting other craft intended for striped bass fishing.

100 miles to halfway around the world, depending upon how much you paid for the increase in wattage. But the few number of frequencies available were so jammed because of this range that it was nearly impossible to get a call through or talk with someone even a few miles away. The Federal Communications Commission (FCC), the overseeing governmental agency, phased out all marine radios of this high-wattage type.

VHF radios, under good transmitting conditions, can span 25 miles over water. On a radio with a good ground, it might even be doubled. There are nearly sixty possible channels or frequencies from which to choose. Most VHF radio, have all channels but older sets had room only for six to a dozen channels. While all channels are not working frequencies available to the public, there are still many more for the bass skipper to use than in the past. Quite a few are assigned to specific users like the Coast Guard, commercial vessels, bridge masters, and gate tenders at the locks.

VHF radio sets today are made non-tunable. That is, each frequency is controlled by a crystal and picked up on a selector. FCC regulations also require manufacturers to place certain channels on every set for distress calls. Channel 16 is used specifically for such messages. The U.S. Coast Guard monitors Channel 16 but can also be reached on Channels 12, 21, 22, 23, and 83. Until just recently, Channel 16 was also the hailing frequency. Everyone was required to monitor this frequency so when you wanted to communicate with other boats or land-based stations, you called them on 16, and when you made contact you switched to another channel you designated at that time. But because of the vast increase in usage and proliferation of sets, the hailing channel now is 9.

Your local marine radio-telephone operators are also there if you need their help to call home, or anywhere else for that matter. There is a service charge for marine hook-up calls and then the regular cost of telephone service. There is no place at sea to put your nickels, so out of necessity your call must be made collect or charged to a credit card number. Marine operators usually monitor Channels 25, 26, 27, and 28. Most of your ship-to-ship communications should be done over Channel 6.

At the end of the choices of channel selection are WE-1 (162.55 MHz) and WE-2 (162.4 MHz). With these channels, the set only has receiving crystals and all you can do on these is listen. They continually broadcast weather forecasts produced by the U.S. Dept. of Commerce's National Weather Service Office. In the last 15 years, National Oceanic and Atmospheric Administration (NOAA), a part of the Commerce Department, has completed establishing weather antennae along all three coasts, as well as the Great Lakes. Even coverage in the interior of the country is almost complete. Today, unless you're in a very remote area, you can receive continuous weather updates. These stations are strategically strung along our coasts so that you can always reach one. The slightly different frequencies are necessary because one station may have a range that overlaps the next. The stations' frequencies thus alternate up and down the coast. The set should have both frequencies so that you can always keep tabs on weather conditions to come and marine surveys of existing conditions.

Your craft or "ship" will need to be licensed, and the agency that handles this is the Federal Communications Commission office. For an application you should request FCC Form 502 directly from the Secretary, FCC, Washington, D.C. 20554. The ship's license is valid only for that craft, and if you move your radio to another boat, you will need a new license. Licensing involves filling out the form and sending in your money. As an operator of a VHF radio, you ,too, must be licensed. Like the station license, there is little effort except a short waiting period and paying the fees. The form needed is FCC Form 753A .

Citizen Band radios can also extremely helpful and in a few areas of the country are still in greater use than VHF, especially by small- boat fishermen and anglers concentrating on inshore waters. Most fishermen would prefer to use CB because it has a shorter broadcasting range and therefore affords channels that are less crowded. The average range can vary, depending upon the quality of your set, the antenna, how well it and the radio are grounded, and atmospheric conditions at the time. A good set should generally be able to reach between 10 and 25 miles. On exceptionally good days, they can broadcast up to 50 and 60 miles without skip, but these are exceptions.

The broadcasting range of CB is, like VHF, now limited by its input wattage. CB sets are regulated to a maximum of 5 watts by the FCC. Other

Accessories: This close-up of the console of the author's current small, striped bass boat shows the location of recording fathometer, loran, tachometer, speedometer, bilge pump switch, gasoline tank gauge, light switches, power trim controls, gas and shift levers, and compass.

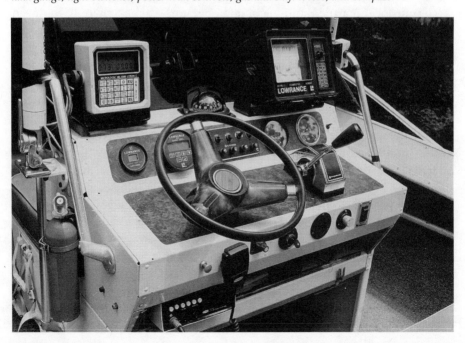

reasons striped bass fishermen in certain areas still seem to prefer CB over VHF radios are because CB sets are more compact, cost about half as much, and now offer a maximum of 40 stations or channels, all usable by the operator. Less expensive CB sets have fewer crystals, five to a dozen, instead of 40, but the cost saving is so slight it's worth getting a full set of channels.

VHF radio used to communicate between other boats, the Coast Guard and the marine radio operator. They also carries NOAA marine weather forecasts.

Unfortunately, the Coast Guard does not monitor CB frequencies the way it does VHF radio, even though it has CB capabilities. However, most CB operators reserve Channel 13 (REACT), or in other areas Channel 8, as their distress channels. Here, the word is likely to be passed along quickly. It is seldom that you cannot raise another boat, possibly one with VHF, or a beach vehicle, or even a shore station with a telephone nearby to call for help and the Coast Guard. You might even get a return call from the Coast Guard station on their more powerful CB radio if you are within their range.

In 1975, the FCC ruled that CB Channel 9 be reserved for emergency communications involving the immediate hazards to life or to property. This channel is also reserved for rendering assistance to motorists. This FCC ruling applies to both AM and SSB Citizen Band radios. However, it hasn't found wide acceptance because no one will monitor it. That is, no one talks on it unless it is an emergency, and a service like the Coast Guard must monitor Channel 9 before calling on it can have any practical effect.

Unlike VHF, the CB station is not licensed. However, the operator is, and he must apply on FCC Form 505 for a Class D license to operate a CB set. These can be obtained from local FCC offices or from Washington, D.C.

Most charterboat skippers fishing on a daily basis out of New Jersey, New York, and New England ports at one time made greater use of CB than VHF. However, that has changed drastically in the last decade and VHF is now their choice because they operate over greater stretches of water than do most sportfishing boats. Still, when you hear a charter- or partyboat skipper say "go to the other channel" when he's talking with another skipper, he may well mean, because of prior indication, to "go to the other (CB) radio." They're tricky at times. If you keep tuned to them for a while, you can actually develop some idea where and when the fishing is great. Some skippers, like beach-buggy clubs, have developed their own code for fishing action and locations, and maybe you too can get in on it. Of course, a scanner can help you locate the local radio traffic a lot faster than manipulating the dials.

Next to the compass, the second most important navigational as well as fishing piece of equipment on your boat should be a fathometer, or depth meter. This device tells you how much water you have between the boat and the bottom. The simplest fathometer operates by sending a signal via a transducer through the water. The signal bounces off the bottom and is picked up by the transducer and recorded as a flash on the dial of your machine. The signal is constantly emitted and thus you know, by looking on the screen, exactly the depth on the scale. This is the basic form. Other forms will translate the transducer signal into a number and read out on a digital screen. Many flasher-type fathometers are also capable of reading any obstructions that might swim between you and the bottom. They are so sensitive that they can read individual fish or schools of smaller fish. Thus, many are fish-finders as well as bottom locators. The depth range of fathometers varies considerably but most can work between 50 and 300 feet.

In the evolution of fathometers, early models that printed the signal on an advancing strip of paper, also include a flasher. In subsequent models, the flashers were discontinued. In scale, the chart eventually prints a facsimile of the bottom profile and frees the angler from continuously monitoring the screen. The paper graph allows him to watch what is going on about the boat. The chart also records any fish that appeared on the screen and at the correct depth. It might be just that moment that you turn your head away from the screen that a fish appears. It also gives you some idea of the shape and distribution of the school. Recording fathometers cost more because of the added service. A flasher-type fathometer will cost between $100 and $250 while the recording type begins at about $300 and has almost no limit. Most commercial models start at around $1,000.

Striped bass are especially sensitive to water temperature. They are almost dormant when the water falls below 40 degrees. But between 50 and 65 degrees they are on the move. In water over 70 degrees, they start to panic, and you won't find bass in water over 80 degrees unless they are traveling real fast or dead.

There are two types of thermometers available for bass fishermen. The first is a surface meter that has its sensory unit mounted to the hull of the boat and measures the temperature of the top of the water. At times, this may be all you need to fish successfully. But at other times, when the water temperature is not uniform at all depths or you are fishing over great depths, then a meter that can go down is in order. There are two types that do that easily. One is a mercury or alcohol thermometer that can be lowered on a string and measures the temperature at a prescribed depth, and the other is an electric thermometer that can be unwound off its holder. On the latter, the temperature change is noted on a dial as the sensor descends and the depth measured on the calibrated cord.

A variation of this last unit is an electric thermometer mounted on a downrigger. The downrigger is a heavy weight lowered on a cable from a large wheel to a depth that is read off on a meter attached to the reel. The line used to lower the weight has an electric wire in it, and at the end to which the weight is attached it is connected to a temperature sensing device. The downrigger is usually trolled at a specific depth and a constant reading of the temperature can be made to find the layer at which striped bass are apt to be located.

Since I rigged this boat about 20 years ago, one extremely important navigational item has appeared on the marine scene and I rank it equal to a fathometer in importance as an accessory on a boat; this is a loran set. Loran stands for **Long Range Navigation**. A loran set is nothing more than a radio receiver, but a very sophisticated receiver capable of receiving multiple signals at one time. The signals it receives are transmitted from a series of federally operated radio stations placed strategically along all three coasts, the Great Lakes, and the interior.

The loran unit measures the time it takes for the signal to travel from the station to the receiver on the boat and translates the time differential, in microseconds, into a number. The farther the receiver is from the transmitting tower, the larger is the lapsed time or time differential (TD). But, it takes two straight lines, or in this case, two signals, to define a point on a line. That's why the unit is cable of receiving signals from multiple stations. The closer the lines cross each other on a right angle, the more precise is the position's location. The set displays two signals at one time, and you can choose from several signals those that cross on the best angle.

With a loran set on your boat, and knowing the two loran numbers (coordinates) that define your home port, you can get home in the thickest fog or darkest night with a precision that at times is closer than 50 feet. You can determine or remember where your best bass fishing location is by entering the coordinate numbers in the set. The set's internal computer will not only give you the correct heading, it will also tell you how far away it is, how fast you're traveling to the spot, how long it will take you to get there at that speed and how long you have been under way. It's a fantastic machine and prices now have fallen so that you can get a good set for under $500 and sometimes $400.

There is a great variety of optional equipment that can be added to a boat. The following is what I had on my 22-foot boat. You might want to add or subtract to suit your particular needs.

Anchor

The type and weight will depend a lot on the type of bottom in your area. A Danforth is one of the best all-round anchors and is great in the sand, about the only one that will hold on this type of bottom. A navy anchor is a compromise, with its weight doing a lot of the holding and the flukes making a slight contribution. It will not foul as much among rocks as a Danforth. The grapple-type anchor has little or no holding power except in rocks and can be retrieved when a Danforth or navy anchor might stay lodged.

Anchor, Line and Chain

For a boat between 16 and 24 feet in length you will need a fairly sturdy line of substantial length. The amount of line you carry will be determined by the depth of the water over which you normally fish. The scope is the amount of rode or anchor line you will have to pay into the water to get your anchor to take a bite, or hold, at that depth without letting the boat drift. There is a minimum ratio of depth of water to length of line needed that will let the anchor hold in fairly calm seas. It is 1:3. That is, for every 10 feet of water over which you anchor, you will have to let out 30 feet of line. If you hope to anchor in 100 feet of water you will have to carry 100 yards of line on your craft. This is the minimum ratio. The Coast Guard recommends a 1:5 ratio. The more you increase the ratio, the greater will be the holding power of the anchor.

The best lines are made of nylon or other synthetic materials, but hemp and other natural fibers are cheaper. The diameter will vary between 3/8 and 1-1/2 inch for easy handling and sufficient holding strength. You should have at least 5 feet of chain between the anchor and the line. Chain helps lay the shaft of the anchor parallel to the bottom, which allows the flukes to take a better bite with less rode.

If you find that you will be traveling or fishing in water deeper than you normally fish, you may have to increase the rode of your anchor line by stowing away an extra hank. It is discouraging to try to anchor a boat in deep water while your engines are down and to have the anchor dangling under the boat as you drift. The extra line is a safety factor and it will more than likely come in for a hundred and one other uses.

Bilge Pump, Automatic/ Manual

An automatic bilge pump is motor-driven and works off the boat's battery (ies). It is operated automatically by a switch that is controlled by a mercury float. When the water level in the bilge rises to a certain point, lifting the float, mercury inside the float flows to a pair of internally exposed terminals and closes the circuit. The pump is turned on until the water level drops and the float returns to the low level. Or, it can be turned on manually by a toggle switch. An automatic bilge pump is ideal if the boat is left at a mooring or dock, to remove rainwater or leaked water. The automatic device is also handy when you are running steadily in rough seas and taking on spray. The spray builds up in the bilge if you don't remember to pump it out, and the trim of the craft will change with the added weight.

A manual bilge pump is a handy device to have aboard in case the electric pump fails or the batteries run low. It is a simple tube-and-piston affair that moves a surprising amount of water in a short stroke.

Billy Club

This might also be called a pacifier. If the core is made of lead it carries a bit more weight. Big and even small fish should be tapped on the head to kill them after they are in the boat. This is especially true if you are trying to remove a plug with a gang of extra hooks on it. A sudden lunge by the fish could bury the hooks in your hand. The pacifier is also great on bluefish that get in the way while you are trying to concentrate on striped bass fishing and allow you to get back to catching the fish you have targeted for the day.

Bimini Belt

A Bimini belt is a must if you are working a trolling rod with a lot of line or wire, even without a fish. The butt of the rod sits in a portable rodholder mounted on a small platform that fits against your groin. The platform attaches around the waist with a belt. It is an inexpensive item and saves a lot of wear and tear on the belly button.

Bulbs, Spare

Before you take your boat on the water you should go over the entire craft, making a list of every bulb's number in use. Check the running lights, as well as those for your instrumentation and your auxiliary or accessory equipment. Buy duplicates and store them aboard your craft in a tool kit. Be sure also to include a few spare bulbs for the boat's trailer and any flashlights you might have on board.

Bumper or Fenders

If you plan to pull alongside a dock for gas or leave it docked for an extended time, bumpers or fenders are a must. This is especially true if the wind is blowing. They are indispensable for use between boats and bulkheads.

Canvas, Navy Top

The navy top canvas, sometimes called Bimini top, illustrated here comes into its own in either hot or cold weather. During early-season fishing, the top can be zippered to a plastic windshield to keep out the wind. It works equally well in rain. But it really pays off during the hot days of July and August, when, even out on the water, the noonday sun is just too much. Sun exposure can really wear you down and shorten a fishing day.

Canvas, Mooring Cover

Whether your boat is tied to a mooring or rides on a trailer, a mooring cover over the entire works is a must if you like to keep a clean boat and protect the instruments. Most instruments are waterproof, and weatherproof but if you've ever been caught in a rainstorm while trailering your boat down a highway, you know how dirty it can get. You'll swear you'll never do it again without a cover.

Cleaning Gear

A clean boat is an efficient boat. Every craft should have aboard an assortment of rags for wiping your hands or wiping salt water off the rods, reels, and other equipment as well as the boat. An old-fashioned scrub brush is a must on the deck, and if it comes on a long handle, so much the better. Cleansers are needed on fish blood and other grime that builds up but don't use them on the fiberglass's gel coat; it's thin enough. Sponges and paper towels are useful.

Cooler (for Food)

Food coolers, with enough room for ice, are a real must during an entire day of fishing. During cold weather, when they aren't used for their primary purpose, they can double as a watertight box for your binoculars, cameras, and clothing that must stay dry. A big cooler, 90 quarts or larger, should be mandatory, on very striped bass boat. If you keep a fish, it should be held in a cooler filled with ice. And because minimum limits nowadays are so large, it takes a big cooler to handle a 36-inch bass.

Deck Shoes and Boots

Traction on a fiberglass deck is increased if you wear rubber-soled deck shoes. When the going gets wet, they grip all the better. And more, they don't leave black marks on your deck. One step better is short boots with a deck-shoe sole. These are indispensable in wet weather or rough seas and keep your feet dry beneath your foul-weather trousers.

Distress-Signal Kit

Like a first-aid kit, a distress-signal kit should be aboard every boat, no matter how large or how small, and whether or not it is required by law. Most come sealed in a plastic bag ready for use and contain a few road-type flares, a smoke flare or two, and some even have flares that are fired into the air for help. Most have an expiration date, and, while they may work after that date, the Coast Guard won't take that as an excuse.

Recording fathometer. This device frees you from constantly monitoring the screen and draws a profile of the bottom's contour by recording soundings on a unscrolling piece of graph paper.

Fish Boxes

These can be portable or fixed, but should be large enough to hold several big bass when you have more than one angler in the boat. They should also be self-draining, out the transom and not onto the deck. Many are constructed of only one skin of fiberglass. Those with double skins and foam insulation between are better and can have ice added to them to preserve fish during especially warm weather. If they are insulated, they can also act as a second cooler for food.

Fog Horn or Whistle

Most states as well as the federal government require that every boat have aboard a sounding device that can be used to signal at night or in the fog. You might not think you'll ever need one until the first time you find yourself broken down and in the fog, unable to move. Then you hear another boat bearing down upon you and there is no way to yell above the sound. Fog horns and whistles can be manually operated, run off the battery in your boat, or can have refillable compressed-air cans that blow a toot as big as a tugboat's.

Funnel, Gas

Every craft should have a gas funnel aboard, equipped with a screen that will filter out water. The bucket-type funnel is the best and aids in getting gas into your tank when it is poured from another can or tank. Nozzles are hard to find at sea when you are out of gas.

Fuses

Like light bulbs, you should make a list of all the fuses you have on your craft and then duplicate them with spares, set aside in your tool box or elsewhere aboard the boat.

Gaffs, Small and Large

The only sure way to bring a big striped bass aboard your boat, especially when it has hit a lure loaded with hooks, is to gaff it. Every boat should be equipped with a small gaff that will work on most bass. But what about the time when you nail a 50-pounder and all you have is that little hook? I've seen few striped bass fishermen who can leave the dock in the morning and predict what size fish they'll be getting. Bring along both gaffs. Because gaffs on striped bass are illegal now in several states, and more states may be joining them, bring along a big landing net.

Gas Cans, Auxiliary

If the tank won't hold enough gas for a full day's running then you might have to take along spare cans. They should be stored out of your fighting area and used first. After they are empty, you can place them out of the way and somewhere where their weight will no longer affect the boat's trim. Some anglers use collapsible plastic containers that can be folded and stored out of the way. If you use metal cans, the bottoms should have rubber liners or they should be placed on rubber mats so that they stay put while you are underway and do not harm your deck.

Life Jackets

Now that they are mandatory and new regulations limit them to only the approved type, everyone carries life jackets aboard a craft. But too often, they are not readily accessible. Stow them where you can get to them in a hurry. The area should be one that is light, dry, airy, and easy to reach. If you carry a youngster on board, remember, adults jackets don't fit them too well. Get one for every youngster in the boat, and your wife or lady-friend if she's petite and a fisherwoman.

Lights

Every boat nowadays comes equipped with running lights, but there are several auxiliary lights that come in quite handy, especially if you spend many evenings fishing for bass . . . and you should. The most valuable are a set of deck lights. I installed a pair under the gunwale on each side of the afterdeck. They flood only onto the deck and the lights don't shine in my eyes or in the water. A spotlight is dandy if you are running into a strange port or in the fog. The intense beam can be more effective than a fog horn that might not be heard by another skipper because of his own engine's noise. A hand flashlight is also a must in the dark, not only for finding your way around or locating equipment, but also for signaling.

Live-Bait Boxes

These items have become integral parts of this new class of boat. But I have found few that are really functional or can handle enough live baitfish for a trip. I designed the one illustrated here. It has its own pump for pulling in fresh seawater and circulating it. I let gravity, through a high standpipe, take care of getting the water out. Fresh seawater is much better than an aerator. The purpose of the aerator is to saturate the water with oxygen. Fresh seawater is it at the saturation point, so why not use the real thing?

A portable live-bait box or bait-well, like the one illustrated here, is also a smart item to have because when you aren't fishing with live bait, the box can be left at the dock or at home and the cockpit space used for other gear or fighting room.

Marker Floats

These are handy little devices that can be purchased at a marine store or made yourself from a flat chunk of Styrofoam and 100 feet (or more if needed) of 30-pound test Dacron or nylon line. Add to the end of the line a 4- or 5-ounce lead sinker. The heavy lead will flip the Styrofoam, unwinding the line, until it reaches the bottom. All you need do is toss it over the side when you strike a fish and return on another pass to pick up another bass.

Maps (Charts), Navigational

Even if you are fishing in your backyard, a good coastal navigational chart, with all the contours and points of land as well as man-made landmarks, is invaluable and will always come into use. One of the times they did for me was almost in my backyard when a fog suddenly formed and I needed a course for home. Nautical charts can be purchased at most marinas, tackle shops, or book shops or ordered directly from the federal government in Washington.

Outriggers

You shouldn't find much use for outriggers when striped bass fishing unless you like to fish live bait. I believe that live bunker, hooked and stemmed against the tide over a rocky shoal, are one of the most devastating baits for taking large striped bass. But live bunker or mackerel have minds of their own and if you want to fish more than one line at a time you will have to spread the baits. Too often, the transom isn't wide enough for two bunker to be live-lined. The only way I know how is with outriggers usually a single pole version without structural supports or braces will do for any striped bass fishing situation.

Radio, Weather

If you don't have a VHF radio on your boat with the weather channels you can still take advantage of the continuous weather broadcasts by the National Weather Service. Small portable FM radios, with only the weather band on them, are produced by several companies and for under $25 you can have all the weather you want. Most have crystals capable of tuning in on the two dominant frequencies and a third that may even be able to hopscotch to the next transmitter along the coast.

Rodholders

Every well equipped bass boat should have aboard a minimum of four rodholders. They should be placed as sets, two on each gunwale—one pair near the transom and the second about amidships. Many anglers add additional pairs to their boats, on the backs of fighting chairs and even a series ahead of the console. Those on the console serve only as upright storage racks for rods when they are not in use rather than holders while fishing or trolling. Rods in these storage racks, at-the-ready and rigged with plus, can be grabbed an immediately cast when the line on another rod breaks and bass are boiling on top.

The angle at which the holders are set is quite important for the security of the rods, and for them to function while trolling. Those on the gunwale closest the transom are usually slanted aft. Those amidships or on your console or seat should be tilted outboard of the gunwales. This will give you the ability to troll four lines separated as far apart as possible. *If* you use outriggers, then two sets amidships on the gunwale, though in line with those astern, can have their lines running off to the side of the stern rods.

Rod Storage Racks

No boat should be without a permanent place to store rods. This is even more necessary when you are under way or when trailering the craft. Most are stored on each bulkhead against the gunwale of the boat. These horizontal racks can accommodate from three to five rods on each side. They are hole-and-hook devices that keep the rods from bouncing out because of the boat's action. The butt fits into the hole portion and the tip is put over the hook. They alternate hooks and holes on the same side to allow you to alternate tips and butts because the reels take so much more room than the rods.

Storage Lockers

Some boats come equipped with storage lockers. Most storage space on the center-console-type boat is either under the bow or in the console itself. On a few boat models the bow is enclosed to form a small cuddy with doors and woodwork so that the elements don't ruin the gear inside and all your more valuable gear can be left onboard. Most such doors can even be locked. Storage space is always at a premium aboard a boat because there's never enough. It can be extended if you add shelves or mount some of your equipment, like radios, to the top of the storage area and leave the bottom free for loose gear.

Tackle Boxes

These are portable items that will usually be carried on and off the craft. I set mine on a pair of heavy rubber gasoline mats and they seem to last longer, resisting the pounding that comes while running in heavy seas, and, stay in position. To keep them from bouncing about, I also secure them to the bulkhead with elastic cords and hooks. My tackle boxes are always too heavy and affect the trim of a boat, so I make sure that I place one on each side to balance it out.

Tool Boxes

I have established a separate tool box for the boat and it always stays aboard. There are a host of items that can be added to it but there is a minimum amount for unexpected repairs. A pair of screwdrivers, both Phillips and slot type, are standard. Mine includes a pair of pliers, a plug wrench, an adjustable wrench, a roll of electrical wire, wire trimmers and terminal posts, a set of box wrenches, and almost everything that is emptied, from time to time, from my pockets.

Water Jug

If you don't have a fresh-water supply on board then you should carry a plastic gallon jug of water. Store it away in a compartment and forget about it. Though it may never be used season, you'll know it's there when the need arises, like dry batteries, when you become thirsty, and coffee or Coke just won't do, when your eye glasses need washing, or, most important, when you find yourself unavoidably drifting at sea with nothing to drink. This might never happen, but it could.

THE TIN BASS BOAT

They just don't make many tin boats today but surf fishermen still refer to the aluminum craft they use as a "tin boat." The tin boat is used primarily by surfcasters who can't stand to see the birds and fish breaking just beyond their casting range. But the surf is no place to try to launch a regular striped bass boat, so the best means of transportation from the beach to the fish has been a lightweight aluminum car-top boat. Not all are carried on cars nowadays—some fishermen use small trailers that are pulled over the sands by 4-wheel-drive vehicles.

The primary element of this type of boat is lightness, and the small, round-bottomed craft vary in length between 12 and 14 feet. They are easily pushed by a light 6- to 10-horsepower outboard. There is little else in such a craft, other than the gas supply—maybe an anchor and the rods for a pair of fishermen, all strapped down in case the launch fails and is swept back onto the beach.

The scene in a tin-boat launching is reminiscent of the days when lifesaving stations existed every few miles along the coast. The service went out to rescue ships and persons foundering in the water. The time boat is launched by two anglers, on each gunwale, with the outboard running and sputtering in the shallow water. As a wave dissipates on the beach they rush into the next one, hoping to get the engine in gear and under way before the next wave can turn them sideways and swamp the boat. If the weather and water are warm, the entire effort can be a lot of fun, but striped bass have a peculiar way of appearing at times of the year when swimming isn't healthy and swamping is dangerous.

Getting the boat back ashore isn't too difficult is the engine is fast enough to outrun a tumbling wave. The skipper just runs it full throttle on and up the beach, the momentum carrying it out of the water. Of course, the engine, as well as everything inside needs a good rinsing in fresh water. Then engine is run in a tub or garbage can to flush the sand out of the water pump's impeller or the life of the pump will be short.

Not really tin today, but lightweight marine aluminum, tin boats can be carried on top of a 4-wheel-drive vehicle or towed on a trailer equipped with "fat" tires and launched into the surf to follow the moving schools of fish.

27

The Beach Vehicle

The beach vehicle is the primary tool of the surf fisherman. Without it he might never fish the surf, or if he did, the number of times would be greatly reduced. Walking in sand with all the necessary gear is a chore most anglers would not do more than once. Then, think how tough it would be hauling back on your shoulder a 50-pound cow late in an August morning. The beach vehicle provides surfcasters with a speedy way to cross miles of sand without effort and usually in comfort. It allows him to take along all the paraphernalia necessary for him to practice his sport in the manner he likes. The beach vehicle has opened hundreds of miles of striped bass waters that would normally be out of the reach of fishermen if the buggy hadn't evolved into the vehicle we now know.

Before the advent of the beach vehicle there was very little surf fishing except at access points where you could drive with a horse and buggy or where the pavement was close to the surf. To take a car onto the sand was unheard of. First of all, automobiles cost too much and were put to better use. Secondly, the early automobiles wouldn't hold up very long to the corrosive effect of salt water. Nor do some later models.

The angler had to wait until the first automobile became old or well used. It was the used car, one with very little resale value, that could be considered for beach use. The first automobiles to become old that might be used in the surf were the first ones mass produced in the United States, Henry Ford's Model T and Model A. Not only was the Ford a good used car, with many miles of use left to it, but it was well suited for going over the sand. The front end was relatively light (as was most of the car) with a small but powerful engine, and the entire car didn't sink very deeply into the sand. With oversized tires, it could literally float over the softest sand. And float became an integral part of the beach buggy. Not only that, if anything went wrong on an isolated beach, it was

A collection of beach vehicles gathers at the mouth of Oregon Inlet, N.C.,
as anglers try their waters for migrating striped bass.

usually easy to fix because there wasn't much that could go wrong with Ford's automobile.

The first appearance of the Model A as a beach vehicle was just before World War II, during the late 1930s and into the '40s. It coincided with the rediscovery by the average American of saltwater fishing, that had begun during the Depression. World War II had a great effect on the development of the beach vehicle. Most of it began with the attitude of the fishermen, ex-servicemen who knew what they wanted and figured out every means to serve their ends. The war also spawned a number of all-terrain vehicles, but the only one that amounted to much, as far as the coastal fisherman was concerned, was the universal jeep. Many ex-servicemen had come to know it intimately, and it was only natural that they should turn to the jeep when the going (in the sand) got tough.

Another factor encouraging the use of the jeep and other vehicles for beach use was the great supply of war-surplus materials. The jeep was sought everywhere as a vehicle to get the sportsman where he wanted to go. If a jeep couldn't be had, then the surfmen would use other vehicles. The beach buggy was born. In most instances, the beach buggy was a Model A or early-vintage Chevrolet or Plymouth, cars lighter than the average. The surfmen stripped all excess weight from them and added oversized tires that were run at low pressures. It took a bit of learning to drive in the sand, and the fact that these vehicles could move over sand amazes modern beach vehicle owners, who rely almost entirely on 4-wheel drive.

Because most of these vehicles had seen a lot of use, it didn't matter much what you did in the way of alterations or innovations. A buggy's real value lay in how well it moved along the sand and not what it might bring when resold. The beach vehicle was terminal, used until so much was wrong with it that it was beyond repair. Most eventually finished up behind some gas station near the beach.

Today, the main purpose of most beach vehicles is to get an angler to the fishing and back again, all within a day. But the earlier anglers took more time with their sport, and a fishing trip usually lasted for two or more days. This meant that his vehicle had to provide the basics for food, shelter, and comfort. The innovators went to work and the early beach buggies acquired bunks, sinks, and stoves. At first, the gear was just carried inside, and the stoves were set up on the beach and the bunks set alongside the shady side of the vehicle. The heater was no more than a pair of blankets.

As the demand for more and more facilities in a buggy grew, the thinking surf fishermen discovered the old bread vans and delivery wagons were just what they needed. By the 1950s, there were enough "old" or "used" vans of this nature to make them perfect targets for surfmen, and their conversions began to sprout along the beaches. The sport of building or rebuilding beach buggies had spread up and down our Atlantic Coast. Where there once had been but a handful of vehicles parked on a point, there were now thousands leaving their tracks from Florida to Maine.

Along with this explosion of beach vehicles came a new problem. These vehicles could pose a serious threat to the stability of fragile marine flora along the beaches, and unthinking fishermen often left heaps of refuse and litter at their favorite meeting spots. Local municipalities began to pass restrictive ordinances and caught many of the buggy operators by surprise.

However, the Massachusetts group that rode the sands of Cape Cod and adjacent beaches saw the future through dark glasses. They organized into an association to police their own members and adopted a code of ethics. The code was written by an ex-GI named Francis W. Sargent, who later become governor of Massachusetts. For years he sported MBBA No. 1 (Massachusetts Beach Buggy Association) on his vehicle. The secretary/treasurer picked Number 13 for good luck. He is Frank Woolner, who was editor of *Salt Water Sportsman* magazine for many years.

Similar beach-buggy associations sprang up in New Jersey, Virginia, and Long Island, and today they exist along most of our Atlantic Coast states. They have, in part, adopted the code of ethics of the MBBA and together pay more heed to the condition of the beaches than many local parks and recreation departments.

Walk-in vans heralded a new aspect in the life of a surf fisherman. He no longer had to rough it in tents or sleep stretched across the seats of his vehicle. Inside bunks, a sink with running water, a propane heater, and a table gave him most of the comforts of home. But a van with all this extra weight meant that the tires had to grow larger and softer and 4-wheel drive was needed. Very few vans had 4-wheel drives, and those which did were so expensive as to be beyond the reach of most surfmen.

The panel truck began to appear on the beaches as these commercial vehicles also became old or too worn for efficient use in business. Many, like the Dodge trucks, came with 4-wheel drive and when modified inside, could sleep a pair of fishermen and carry all their gear for a few days of life on the sands.

The affluence of the American surfcaster grew during the 1950s and his leisure time increased correspondingly into the 1960s. Fishermen were now capable of affording a new unit to take onto the beach. Besides, most of the Model As and early Chevies and Plymouths were now too far gone for the beach or had become collector's items that were far too valuable to run in salt water. The need was still there, and in the late 1940s and early '50s Kaiser-Jeep developed its Jeepster and then the Wagoneer, a Jeep station wagon, both with 4-wheel drive. Though there is today a rash of similar vehicles on the beach, I don't think I would be too far wrong if I said that the Wagoneer was still the most popular vehicle. Some of the worst sand on the East Coast for 4-wheeled driving is at Cape Hatteras. If you did a survey there, you'd find that most of the North Carolina license places are on Wagoneers.

It was finally taken out of production by Chrysler, that today owns the Jeep line. It had become an anachronism, a dinosaur in its own time—too heavy, too

The modern beach vehicle cannot really be called a buggy. But during the beginning and developmental years of vehicles in the surf, old buggies were converted for service on the sand by the use of oversized and deflated tires. This early Model A Ford was converted by Dick Woolner.

expensive, and too costly to operate. In its early days, it was a compromise vehicle for fisherman. It was both a beach buggy and a station wagon for the wife. It worked as effectively on sand as in the suburbs and in shopping centers. Its early success in the 1960s encouraged other manufacturers to produce more such multiple-use vehicles, and Jeep today shares the beach with Chevrolet, Dodge, Ford, GMC, International, and a host of foreign manufacturers.

TYPES OF VEHICLES

Beach vehicles today can roughly be divided into five classes based on size and expected performance. Old beach buggies are, for the most part, a thing of the past. Very few 2-wheel-drive vehicles now appear on the beaches.

Day Vehicles

For want of a better name, the smallest beach vehicles are grouped as day vehicles, intended mainly for transportation and carrying only the equipment needed to fish and make the angler comfortable while he is on the beach. The classic example is the Jeep Universal, a somewhat enlarged version of the old Army jeep. It has been increased in size so that the rear compartment can handle most of the angler's gear, or even tote two additional fishermen. Other similar units are the Bronco by Ford and the Scout by International that now, too, is history, though enough still survive. Toyota and Land-Rover also produce smaller units comparable in size and performance.

Mid-Range Vehicles

Only one unit can be classified in this group: the Jeepster by American Motors. More recently, the Jeepster has been supplanted by the Commando by American Motors, but when American Motors went out of business, so did the Commando. This is still a day vehicle in the real sense because it isn't large enough for sleeping or eating quarters and its carrying space is still somewhat limited. Also, it is less adaptable to general use and thus isn't practical for the family which can afford but one car. The Jeep Cherokee is a down-sized version of the Wagoneer and doesn't quite fit into this group nor the next largest group. In 1991 Jeep introduced a new version of the Wagoneer that was really a slightly expanded Cherokee, but still not big enough to make the old station wagon class. Besides, it's too posh and too expensive, at $30,000, to run in salt water.

Station Wagons

This group, the largest, has burgeoned during the last decade. At one time it was the almost exclusive realm of the Jeep Wagoneer. The beach station wagon is a multiple-use vehicle that can double as the family car when not on the beach. In addition to the Wagoneer, there are the GMC and Chevrolet Blazers, somewhat similar in construction to the modified panel trucks and not quite as

The Jeep Wagoneer, more recently called the Grand Wagoneer to distinguish it from Jeep's Cherokee model, was so popular that it inspired other auto manufacturers to produce multiple-use beach vehicles. It is at home at the shopping center as well as alongside the surf. Here, two Wagoneers line up for the ferry from Hatteras to Ocracoke Island, N.C.

adaptable a family car as the Wagoneer, and International's Travelall wagon. New to this class and similar to the Blazer are the Dodge and Plymouth Ramchargers with either soft or hard tops. The latter two have been downplayed ever since Chrysler bought Jeep from American Motors. Toyota and Nissan have a cruiser in this class and Land-Rover has a larger version of its smallest all-terrain vehicle, but it is not as adaptable to the one-car family as the Travelall and Wagoneer. Chevy introduced its Pioneer, their answer to the Wagoneer, but it's a tad smaller than the Grand Wagoneer.

Pickup Trucks

A large number of surf fishermen who require a pickup truck in their work purchase them equipped with 4-wheel drive so that they can be used in the sand or off a hard road. An empty pickup truck, however, has extremely poor rear-end traction and will spin out on a wet or muddy surface. But if the box is loaded and weight is placed on the rear wheels, it will go much better. However, a loaded pickup without 4-wheel drive will not make much headway on the beach. A 4-wheel-drive pickup, even when empty, has the bulk of its weight on the front drive system and has no problem on the beach.

Camper-Pickups

The ultimate beach vehicle should provide a surf fisherman with transportation over the sand, a place for him to sleep comfortably, a kitchen in which he can prepare his meals when a long stay is in mind, all the space needed to carry his unmanageable equipment and maybe even a boat, and communications equipment. In reality, the complete beach vehicle is much like the complete boat and does for the surf fisherman what a boat does for the floating angler.

The only beach unit capable of approaching this ideal and meeting the demands of such an angler is the pickup truck equipped with a camper unit on its bed. The normal quarter-ton pickup is often too small except for the lightest of box units. Instead, most fishermen who intend to take it all with them select a half-ton or even three-quarter-ton pickup, and always with 4-wheel drive. To help spread the load over a wider surface of sand, extra-large, often balloon tires are used on such units. These tires are not well suited for hard roads, and camper-truck owners often have a set of regular tires to use when prolonged hard-surface travel is in order. Running the beach does get expensive and if you want to be a turtle you have to pay the price.

The majority of camper units slide onto the box so that the pickup truck can be used for other jobs. The unit can be taken off and stored in the driveway when not in use. However, a considerable number of units nowadays are chassis-mounts. This gives the camper-surf fisherman a lot more room in the camper, but at the same time means that its only use will be on the beach or in other camping situations. This requires a considerable outlay of money but apparently enough anglers are willing and able to spend it because there are quite a few on the beaches.

HOW TO RIG A BEACH VEHICLE

Outfitting a beach vehicle used to be a very personal affair because the unit itself had little value other than its ability to travel over sand. Today, however, with new vehicles going into the saline world, a lot of care is taken of such units, with a thought to second sales, and therefore modifications that won't please a potential buyer are not made. Also, many modifications can be factory-made or purchased; not all improvements are left to the art or skill of the surf fisherman.

Factory Options

Before you ever take delivery of your vehicle, you can have it half-designed for the beach. The first consideration is the 4-wheel-drive aspect. Of course you are getting 4-wheel drive. How it goes into 4-wheel is another matter. Some 4 X 4s are built with full-time 4-wheel traction. In others, as the load on the engine and traction on the rear end demand it, the vehicle is automatically shifted in and out of 4-wheel drive. In other models, you have the option of automatic 4-wheel drive that is engaged from inside the unit, or manual 4-wheel drive which is engaged by getting outside and locking the front hubs for 4-wheel operation.

Locking hubs engage the axle to the wheel and they spin together. Unlocked, the axle doesn't move and there is less wear on it. With the hubs

Everywhere on the beaches as well as in inland camping areas are campers on pickup-truck bodies, either the slide-on or box mount, illustrated here, or the chassis mount that can provide the surf fisherman with all the comforts of a boat or home away from home.

locked the axle spins with the turning of the wheel. However, not until you shift it into 4-wheel drive do you have power turning the front axle. Thus, you have an option of three methods for achieving 4-wheel drive. The manual-locking hubs were once the more popular type, but as 4 X 4 technology advanced, most system in use today abandoned manual- locking hubs.

In addition to front-axle drive, you can get a positive form of traction for the rear wheels. If one wheel is spinning, the other won't stop but will turn to help pull out the spinning wheel. This is done automatically without your having to think or act and is a handy option in most vehicles.

Cooling systems found in most beach vehicles are adequate for fall, winter, and spring driving. However, if you are on the beach during the summer, driving in soft sand and forced to stay in low gear, the engine is working hard and overheating. The fan and water pump are not capable of keeping your coolant cool at slow speeds. An oversized radiator is a must, even if you don't intend to get into hot situations. And if you can get along without an air conditioner, do it. The air-conditioner radiator or cooler sits in front of your engine's radiator and not only stops the cool air from hitting it but adds its own heat load to the car's radiator. An oil cooler is also handy when you do a lot of beach traveling during the summer months. If you are driving a pickup-camper unit, it is a must. It prolongs the life of your oil as well as that of your engine. It is easy to install and not expensive. Also available are transmission coolers and they are as important as oil coolers.

The electrical system is also being taxed on the beach. Start out by selecting a heavy-duty battery, of 90 or more amps, and get a heavy-duty alternator to help keep it up to snuff. At slow beach speeds, an old generator or normal alternator may not be able to keep it fully charged. When you add a CB radio, extra lights, and electricity for a camper if you are carrying one, the heavy-duty electrical system is not an accessory but a real necessity so opt for the heavy-duty battery with all the amps you can possibly get.

If you can get a larger gas tank on your unit, do it. It will save you a lot of future headaches. There are few gas stations near the beach and on some really isolated strands, you might even have to tote along jerry cans. Also, the gas is always more expensive at the first station from the beach than at home. The bottom of the unit should be protected in two ways. On many, you can get skid pans to protect the oil pan and gas tank when trafficking over a lot of debris washed onto the beach and you need the bottom protection. Undercoating is another must if you run in the surf or anywhere near it. If you can get it done locally rather than at the factory, you can talk the man into an extra-heavy coat.

Most beach traffic is over bouncy rut situations and your vehicle is sure to need heavier shocks and springs. Adjustable shocks are a great idea and a little more expensive. If you have a camper unit, you will automatically be encouraged to get the heavy-duty equipment by the auto salesman. Don't argue with him on these items. They really are needed.

At one time, beach-buggy addicts shunned automatic transmissions. However, experience has shown that they produce a smooth, even start, get the operator stuck less often, and hold up better than a standard transmission. Power brakes are good, but most braking on the sand is done by engine compression or just taking your foot off the gas pedal. Power steering, however, is another story. When you try to follow a wheel-set wider than yours, you need full-time power steering. When running on soft sand, power steering takes some of the constant strain off your arms. If the wife will be doing some of the driving, get her power steering. It pays for itself in your own well-being.

The engine should be able to run over the sands without over-exerting itself. It is therefore far wiser to have more engine than you think you need and allow it to work at a more leisurely pace rather than to get a smaller engine and make it work at its maximum all the time. Going through sand is tough work, even for something as impersonal as a car engine. But give it a break and you'll have less to worry about in new parts and repairs. A V-8 is almost standard on most vehicles, but smaller units can get by with a straight 4 or a V-6.

Tires

The rubber on your vehicle is the main link between you and the outer world, or the sand on the beach. Tires can make you go or stop you dead in your tracks. Tires, their treads, shape, pressure and construction, are crucial to your mobility. The more tire surface you have spread over the sand, the less you will

One of the most efficient methods of temporarily carrying rods is to attach a series of rod holders on a large plank mounted on the bumper of your vehicle.

sink and the less will be your friction per square inch . . . all letting you move more easily over the beach and your engine work at a reasonable stride.

Snow or mud treads with their knobs have no place on the sand. They have a tendency to dig and bury the wheels. Regular suburban tires on all four wheels are all that you need in the sand. In fact, less tread on them, as they wear, will provide you with better go-power.

To have four wheels turning is not always enough to get you through the sand. You may not have sufficient flotation if your package is exceptionally heavy. Flotation is achieved in two ways: by purchasing and equipping your vehicle with as wide a tire as possible and by deflating the tire so that its profile changes and more of it appears flattened at the bottom, increasing your contact area. A disheartening sight is the owner of a new 4 x 4 taking his vehicle onto the sand, slipping it into 4-wheel drive, and getting stuck 10 feet off the hardtop.

Most tires are rated to a maximum air pressure of 32 pounds per square inch (psi). At this pressure, the tires are hard as wood and last a long time. But on the beach, they should be deflated down to 18 or 20 pounds for normal going and you can get away from bad sand with as little as 12 pounds of pressure. Your biggest worry at lower pressures is breaking the tire seal and pressures this light are used only in emergencies. If the engine's temperature gauge begins climbing, you know the engine is working too hard and the needed flotation just isn't there. Then deflate your tires to 10 or 12 pounds and the vehicle will travel with a lot less strain. You can even deflate them to 8 pounds in special situations but you must be careful.

This is the minimum deflation pressure for most tires. The reason involves the sidewall of a tire. This portion isn't designed to take the flexing that the bottom can withstand. At low pressures, the sides of the tire bulge and work constantly. As they do, the rubber begins to heat. Eventually this leads to cracking and short tire life. That is why, as soon as you are off the sand and onto a hard surface, you should inflate your tires before traveling at high speeds.

Sidewall bulge is desired on the beach and necessary. This is more difficult to obtain with tires with six or more plies, and as a result, most vehicles should be equipped with the four-ply versions suitable for the majority of automobiles. The six-ply, that is typical of balloon and over sized tires, is designed for mud, dirt, and snow, but not sand operation. They're just too stiff and you don't get the deflation advantage with it that you do in a four-ply tire.

Wheel size should be as large as possible, and 15-inch is what most vehicles can handle. This gives the car a higher lift above the sand with its chassis. In addition, it also means more tire surface on the tread in contact with the sand and hence more flotation. Width of tread is still another tire variable, and the widest most rims can handle is the L-70 designation. Tire-width terminology has changed a couple of times during the last decade, and if you aren't sure of what you want and are getting, don't feel lonely. Here you'll have to trust to the experience of your tire dealer.

For large beach vehicles and truck-camper units, special tires, some verging on balloons, are necessary. These call for extra-wide rims that must be specially ordered, and they increase the cost of a beach vehicle. But if you want to take your home with you, that's the price you must pay.

Fishing Accessories

The first accessory equipment you must add to your new beach vehicle are holders for your rods. There are two types and you'll need both in most cases. The first are permanent or traveling rod holders to hold the wands when they are not in use. A series of holders over the top of the unit, similar to a ski rack, will do and are the type often used. The rods are held parallel to the length of your vehicle and across its top. If you plan to tote a box on the top, then you can install rod holders along each rain gutter. On camper vehicles, where it's a chore to reach the roof unless you have a ladder built into the cab, most rods are carried on the sides of the vehicle.

Some units come equipped with inside holders, mounted to the inside roof of the vehicle, while still others have holders along one side of the window. However, because most surf rods are so long and often are produced in one piece, the inside holders don't work with the back window closed.

The second type of needed holder is the temporary holder for use while you are fishing. A few fishermen take actual boat holders and secure them to the sides of their vehicle, but most go for a bumper-type holder. This holder is basically a 2-inch x 12-inch x 4-foot piece of wood, bolted across the front of the bumper, to which any number of plastic or aluminum tubes or holders are secured. The rods are carried upright across the front of the vehicle. Short lengths of 2- or 3-inch PVC tubing will do as well as the regular holders and cost a lot less. Or you can take the easy but expensive way out and buy a bumper rod holder—but I doubt if you can get a good one for less than $100.

The next item needed is a cooler to carry fish. After a while, you'll become tired of fish flopping around on the floor of the unit or in the back and you'll get a fish box. Some boxes are no more than a wooden box bolted to the front or the back of the vehicle on a special frame. Others are large, insulated coolers that can hold ice and keep your fish from spoiling during warm weather. If you carry the big cooler inside the vehicle, it eats up valuable space.

Most dedicated beach fishermen eventually build a platform on the roof of their vehicle and box it in so that they can carry a lot of the bulky gear—waders, hip boots, lanterns, rain gear, sand spikes, and the like—on top. There may even be enough room to add your fish cooler to this box.

A number of such vehicles have top boxes constructed with collapsing sides. When the sides are down, they expose a pair of crossbars on which a light, car-top boat can be carried. If you regularly carry a cartopper you will need an engine bracket welded to the side or back of your vehicle so that the small outboard can be carried upright, outside, and always ready for use.

If everything that can possibly be carried on the side is out there, you then have room for a few collapsing bunks. These can fold against the side when not in use. A small propane heater is a must if you aren't carrying a camper. Propane bottles can be mounted on top or in the back. If you use a lot of fuel or have a camper, select a unit that has two bottles rather than one. Not that their capacity might be greater; it's just that you can use one until it runs out and then switch to another.

Miscellaneous Accessories

Most beach vehicles keep in touch with other units and keep tabs on what the boats are doing offshore by installing a Citizen Band radio. Not only are they great as information gatherers but if you bury your rig below the high-water mark and the tide's flooding in, you might be able to get help from other vehicles if there's a CB set in your cab. Most beach vehicle clubs designate a channel they monitor. If you know what it is, you can reach them when you're in trouble.

If you do a lot of beach riding during the off season, when few other vehicles are out, or work in areas where very few other fishermen frequent, then a power winch on the front of your unit can be the only insurance against getting stuck. Most beaches where there is enough sand to require a beach vehicle have few boulders to tie onto to let your winch pull you out. A large Danforth anchor and a stout cable or line will get you out of a hole.

If you plan to fish the surf from a small boat carried on a trailer, then a ball and hitch is a necessity. A factory hitch is usually best because it is either welded or bolted directly to the chassis's frame while the unit is being built. Even if you don't plan to use a boat, the hitch is a great place to attach a towing cable.

Emergency Kit

You may be beach-wise enough so that you never need your own emergency kit, but too often you are likely to come across someone who isn't, and if you want to give him a hand, you'll need some added items. Foremost among these is a towing chain or heavy line. You will need to know how to tie a bowline in the line or you'll never get loose without cutting it after you're free. Next, add a shovel. A collapsing army shovel is great, but it won't carry a lot of sand. Though this smaller shovel may take longer to dig you out, it doesn't require a lot of storage space.

If you are traveling into isolated country, a pair of planks or some carpeting can help you out of tight situations. An extra bumper jack is also a great help. If you really bog down in rotten sand, one of the best techniques is to jack both rear tires off the ground and then push the vehicle forward, off the jacks. Stand clear when it's falling. If you can fill the hole with sand before you let go, or add a few planks, you'll get out sooner and more easily.

During really hot weather, it's a good idea to carry a few plastic gallon jugs of water for the radiator. If you do boil over, you can use salt water in an emergency, but you'll have to flush the cooling system thoroughly.

Inflating your tires can be a problem in some areas, and if you don't need gas, the service-station operator may give you a hard time. Some unscrupulous entrepreneurs even take advantage of your deflated state and charge for air. Spark-plug pumps are available if you want to pump your own air. With these, one plug is removed and the device placed in the head of your engine. The other end, via a long tube, goes to your tire's valve stem. If you don't like this method, there are several small, compact air pumps you can buy that derive their power from your cigar lighter. They do take a long time to pump the tires to 30 pounds of pressure, but you don't have to inflate them to road-running psi's until you can find a garage. Of course, you should have a good tire-pressure gauge in the glove compartment of your vehicle, but we'll say it anyway.

An extra fan belt, maybe a spare water hose, and assorted bits of wire and tools should also find their way into your emergency kit. In addition, you should always have a first-aid kit and a fire-extinguisher stored under the seat or in an outside holder. You might also want to add an emergency tire repair kit and a pair of heavy work gloves to the kit.

DRIVING THE TRACK

There's only one way to develop the knack of handling a vehicle in sand, and that is by driving it in sand. There are a few tricks you can pick up immediately by imitating other drivers. The first is to overcome the feeling that your adventurous spirit is being stifled if you follow a rut rather than make your own marks in the sand. A vehicle that has gone on before you has already knocked down the sand and partially compressed it for you. It will be easier driving and you can go somewhat faster if you stay in the track. Make new tracks only if there aren't any where you want to go. If there are hazards on the beach or in the sand, then the guy before you has probably experienced them and cleared the path for you. Learn by his tracks.

Next, learn to read the sand. Not all sands are created equal, or the same. Sometimes the color can be a key to its consistency. Some sand will pack easily under weight and this makes for easier going in your vehicle. Other sand won't pack at all, particularly if it is fine and without moisture. Understandably, this type is called "rotten" sand and all you can do is slowly plow through it. Maintain a constant speed and forward motion and you'll stay on top. If you drive too slowly, you are making the car's engine overwork and giving the vehicle time to sink into the sand.

When you turn out of someone's tracks, do it quickly and then return the wheels to a parallel course. It will make breaking out of the rut easier. Otherwise, you can have your wheel partially turned and still be stuck in the rut. Don't use your brakes to stop unless you are too close to what you want to avoid. Heavy braking causes the tires to dig into the sand and you may not be able to get going again easily. The best way out of this situation is first to back in your tracks, then make a running start over holes you just made.

Running the beach below the high tide can be tricky and it takes some experience. The sand left behind by a falling tide is usually better packed than that above high tide and your car can run easier and faster on it. But never stop or lose your forward momentum while traveling below the high-tide mark unless you are certain you can get out again. There's nothing that will make a man cry harder than watching the tide come into his cab.

Don't cross barrier beaches or sand dunes where vegetation is growing. In many states and federal parks it's illegal as well as thoughtless. These wild grasses hold the dunes together and keep the beach in place. If ramps are not available over such areas, then cross only where tracks have previously been made. This means that you won't always be able to get on or off the beach where you want, without some extra running, but it won't make you unpopular with local officials or other beach buggy operators. It means that you and they will be able to continue to use the beach in a vehicle. It's better than walking.

Many municipalities and parks have placed restrictions on the use of the beach by vehicles, especially during the months when bathers swarm into the surf. Become familiar with these regulations, abide by them, and obtain a beach permit when necessary. You might get all the information you need by contacting the beach-buggy association in your area. If you can't find one, then write United Mobile Sportfishermen, Inc., P.O. Box 74, Forestville, Conn. 06010, and ask for help.

28

Striped Bass Cookery

The proof of the pudding is in the tasting, and the taste of striped bass, properly served, makes all those early reveilles and rain-soaked, wind-swept days worth the effort. Cooking and eating a striped bass you caught seems to make the catching so much more pleasurable. If you haven't tried it, you've missed one of the better parts of striped bass fishing. Nor is there any fish comparable to a freshly caught bass, packed on ice as it is rushed to the frying pan and then served almost while there's a little wiggle still left. You'll never visit a fish market again.

STORAGE

Striped bass are firm-fleshed fish with flaky, white meat that will take some abuse before it begins to deteriorate. But it's still best to take care of the bass immediately after it has been unhooked. During the early and later part of the striped bass season, outside temperatures are usually cool enough so that you don't have to worry about bacteria immediately attacking your fish. But during the warmer months of the year, you'd better pay attention or most of the flavor will be lost in the first hour.

If the weather is warm, striped bass should be immediately placed in a cooler or ice chest. The fish shouldn't be allowed to soak in their own blood and salt water, even in a cooler. The cooler's drain plug should be left open. A wooden grid placed in the bottom of the cooler will guarantee that the striped bass doesn't soak. Water, warm or even cold, will immediately begin to soften the fish's firm meat. Empty the cooler regularly if it doesn't have a drain hole.

If the boat doesn't have a cooler, store the fish out of the direct rays of the sun and in an area where it is exposed to the air. You can cool it further by covering the bass with a burlap bag and regularly splashing it with water. Air passing over the burlap will evaporate the water and slightly lower the temperature of the fish. If you are on the beach, you can bury your bass in the sand. But make sure that you dig deep enough to reach cool, wet sand and that it isn't too far below the high tide mark or you may have a difficult time finding it. Mark it with a stick, just to be sure.

CLEANING

If you plan to scale your fish, it is most easily done as soon as the fish is caught. The longer you wait, the more difficulty you will encounter, especially if the scales are given the chance to dry. However, even the driest striped bass scales aren't especially difficult to scrape off. You can do it with a scaling device, or simply use a sharp knife with a rather stiff blade. Hold the tail firmly and start just behind the head and work your way toward the tail, against the grain of the scales.

If you are going to filet the fish and don't need the skin, you can forget about scaling. They will all come off with the skin. To filet a fish, you need a sharp pointed knife, often known as a fileting knife. The spine on the knife is rather thin and the blade somewhat flexible to help you cut around the curves and get all the meat possible. The first step is to cut a line parallel down each side of the dorsal spine or fin, from head to tail. The incisions should not be deep, at first—just under the skin. After the skin is pulled off, the cuts, first on one side, then later on the other, should be deepened. The next incision, also just skin deep, is just behind the head, from the back, over the sides of the bass, behind the pectoral fin, and then across the belly toward the vent. The line is then extended to the base of the tail. The cut across the sides of the belly shouldn't be deep enough to cut into that cavity. If you do it correctly, you'll miss spilling the insides.

With your fileting knife, pry the skin from the muscle near the head, against the back. When you have freed enough to grasp the skin with a pair of pliers, hold the head of the fish firmly against the table and quickly strip back the skin. Once you get the hang of it, all the skin will come off with one stroke. Pull the skin off the meat all the way to the tail and cut it free. Now separate the filet on one side by deepening the first incision along the dorsal fins and spines, all the way from the head to the tail, as deep as the backbone.

Much of it can be freed by slipping your finger down along the spine. Next, cut the filet away from the head and follow closely the contour of the ribs that bulge out to protect the stomach. Don't try to save the belly meat unless you like striped bass sushi—it is thin and tough. Work the tip of your knife over the lateral side of the spinal column and then down the side to the ventral line. The filet is almost free except for the tail, and that is cut at right angles. Follow the same procedure for the other side. You have almost 95 percent of the bass's flesh, and without any bones.

Fileting works best for small bass, 3 to 10 pounds. You can also filet larger bass, but the pieces of meat are so thick that to cook evenly they must be sliced into thinner filets or cut across to make strips or fingers of fish. Fish for baking are also best selected from bass about 3 to 10 pounds in weight. They are first prepared by scaling. Then remove the dorsal fins by incisions on each side and one cut on an angle to sever the spiny bones from the vertebral column. The anal and caudal fins are cut at their bases and the pectoral fins are usually removed with the head and stomach.

The head is cut on an angle from the top, behind the pectoral fin, in much the same manner as in preparing for skinning. The knife is forced through the backbone of the spine or is broken by hand. The fish is cut along the bottom to the vent and the entire head and entrails can be pulled free in one piece.

Almost every bit of the bass filet is good to eat. The only exception is a small strip along the sides in the area of the lateral line. This can be distinguished by its dark, liver-like color. It is rich in oils and gives the bass an excessively fishy flavor if cooked while still on. It is easily removed, rather shallow in depth, and doesn't leave much of a hole.

If you plan to use the fish immediately, don't wash it in water, but clean it with a paper towel and dry out the inside. If it is to sit awhile, sprinkle the inside with salt and let it stand. If your striped bass is to be frozen, separate the filets into whatever size portions you want and freeze them separately. If you thaw it too much, you cannot refreeze it. A great way to ensure almost perfect freshness is to place your filets in a plastic bag and then fill the bag with water. The bag should be placed in a milk carton or something similar to give it shape, and then when frozen it can be removed and stored. The water freezing ensures that no air will ever get to the meat and give it freezer burn. Also, the ice seems to lock in the bass's flavor.

Really large bass can be treated as filets, as we mentioned earlier, or they can be steaked. If they are to be steaked, they should be cleaned like a bass to be baked, scaled and with the skin in place. The steaks are cut at right angles to the body, going from head to tail in parallel slices. The thickness will depend a lot upon your personal preferences, but a bass steak 1 or 1-1/2 inches thick is easily cooked and handles well in the broiler or frying pan. Smaller sections are apt to fall apart because the flesh is rather flaky. Slices too thick might not be sufficiently cooked in their centers.

COOKING

The striped bass is a gourmet's delight. The flesh of a striper can be prepared in a great variety of ways. Bass can be fried, broiled, boiled, poached, and baked,

Fileting a striped bass. The first incision is made, just skin deep, along the back, from the base of the head to the base of the tail. The cut is made on each side of the dorsal spine.

Then another incision is made over the side of the bass, just behind the head, from the cut on the line to a spot just past the ventral fin.

The incision is then followed along the bottom of the belly, just breaking the skin, all the way back to the base of the tail.

With a fileting knife, cut away the skin from the flesh as shown in the photograph.

When you have freed enough skin from the flesh to grasp with a pair of pliers, hold down the head and flesh with one hand and quickly pull the skin off the flesh with the pliers. Pull it all the way to the base of the tail.

With the fileting knife, deepen the incision on the back, following the long spines downward to the backbone. Free the filet from head to tail along the backbone.

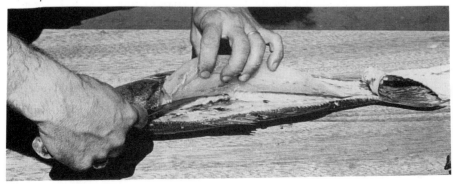

Cut over the rib bones protecting the intestine and then free the filet below the backbone all the way to the tail. Cut it free at the base of the tail. Now you have a filet entirely free of bones and no scaling was required. Flip over and filet the other side.

as well as made into a pudding or a salad or chopped into bass fingers. Because of the fine texture of their flesh and the firmness when properly handled and prepared, striped bass can be used as *the* fish in almost any of your favorite seafood recipes. They mix well with your imagination and it is difficult to do a bass in by improper cooking.

Broiled Striped Bass

This recipe is adapted from an old Alabama recipe for red snapper. But because striped bass are also an Alabama fish the same preparation has often been used and has proved to be a delightful method for the preparation of stripers.

ALABAMA STRIPER DELIGHT

The striped bass is fileted and then the pieces basted with fresh orange juice, sprinkled with soy sauce, and then broiled to a tender, juicy perfection. Try this one if you want some elegant but easy dining enjoyment.

2 pounds bass filets, fresh if possible	1 tablespoon soy sauce
1/3 cup orange juice	1 teaspoon salt
1/4 cup butter or margarine, melted	Dash pepper

Cut the filets into serving-size portions. Combine the ingredients and mix thoroughly. Put the fish, skin side up if it has been scaled, into a well greased broiler pan and brush filets with the sauce. Broil about 3 inches from source of heat for 4 to 5 minutes. Turn carefully and brush with sauce. Broil 4 to 5 minutes longer, basting occasionally, until the fish flakes easily when tested with a fork. This should serve about six.

Baked Striped Bass

Prepare the bass for baking by scaling and removing the fins and viscera. The head and tail are often left on when a bass is to be baked. The cavity of a bass can be filled with whatever stuffing you prefer. Because the striped bass is usually a somewhat dry fish—that is, without a lot of naturally occurring fats or oils—fats or oils must be added. Cut three or four gashes in the side of the fish, depending upon its size, and insert pieces of salt pork. Or, you can substitute strips of bacon that are secured by tying them on with pieces of string. This also helps keep the stuffing inside the cavity.

Brush oil over the skin of the fish and place the bass on its belly, on an oiled baking sheet or pan. Bake in an oven at 450 degrees for the first 15 minutes, then reduce to 350 degrees and allow 45 to 60 minutes baking time for a 5-pound fish. Baste from time to time with some extra pork or bacon fat. Serve with hollandaise or Sauce Allemande.

The baked striped bass, garnished with lemon, cherries,
sweet and white potatoes, and parsley and ready to serve.

BAKED FILETS ORIENT

Take a bass filet and cut into individual servings, each about 1/3 pound in size. Then dip each piece in salted milk and roll in finely sifted bread crumbs. Place the filets in an oiled pan and bake in a hot oven (between 450 and 500 degrees) for ten minutes. Serve with tartare sauce.

BAKED FILETS IN CLAM NECTAR

2 pounds filets	2 tablespoons oil
1/2 cup clam juice	3 tablespoons flour
1 cup cream	4 tablespoons butter
1 cup milk	1 onion, finely minced
1 teaspoon Worcestershire	1 small garlic clove, bruised
sauce	1 tablespoon minced parsley
Salt and paprika	Lemon juice to taste

To the heated oil add the minced onions and garlic, stirring constantly. Allow them to fry but not brown, then place on lid and cook for 10 minutes. Oil a baking pan and put the bass filets in it, sprinkling them with salt, pepper, and lemon juice. Then spread the cooked onions and garlic over the filets. Heat the clam broth, add 1/2 cup of boiling water with 2 tablespoons of butter, and bake the fish at 375 degrees for 20 minutes or until done. Heat the milk, melt the other 2 tablespoons of butter, sift in the flour, and cook together, adding the hot milk, and beat. Then add the seasoning and cream. Lift the fish onto a hot platter, add the liquid under the fish to the sauce, stir in the chopped parsley, pour sauce over the filets, and serve at once.

Poached Striped Bass

Poached striped bass recipes are extremely numerous, and perhaps this is about the best manner of preparation. Poaching often requires added sauces, and some of these are found at the end of this chapter.

LE BASSE BAR DE GASPE

This recipe is the work of Joseph Hyde, a renowned New York City chef. It is an elegant method of preparing and serving striped bass, whether it comes from the Gáspe or Cuttyhunk.

The fish must be fresh (not frozen) for this method. Poaching a large striped bass with its head and tail requires a long poacher with rack, and, of course, a large platter upon which to serve the finished fish. With head and tail intact is the ideal way to cook a striped bass because the water surrounds the unbroken skin and the skin in turn holds in all the juices of the bass. Seawater is the preferred salt water for this poaching technique, or you can make a *court bouillon* (which see), which will also give a fine flavor to the fish.

The vegetables for the *court bouillon* are sliced finely and cooked for 1/2 hour in the fish poacher with the other ingredients except for the vinegar or lemon juice, which is added with the fish. As the bass cooks, the water should be just barely simmered. The poaching time varies in relation to the thickness of the fish, about 15 minutes for every inch of thickness. If the fish is to be served cold, it need cook only 10 minutes to every inch.

The bass must be cooled and refrigerated in the *court bouillon*. This takes a large refrigerator. It can be cooled with ice cubes in a portable cooler, but water must never touch the bass. Cooling the fish in this manner is important because it keeps in the juices. When the fish is very cold, the juices congeal and the meat of the bass will not be dry; instead it will be moist and flavorful. This is a complicated method for the preparation of a striped bass but it makes for delicious eating and an impressive presentation.

POACHED BASS ABERCROMBIE

6 1-pound bass steaks	1 lemon
1 quart water	2 teaspoons salt
1 cup dry white wine	

Bass for this recipe should be steaked—that is, cut at right angles through the backbone. Steaks should be snugly fitted into a deep pan that just contains them rested on their sides. For every quart of water that it takes just to cover the bass, add the juice of one lemon, one cup of dry white wine, and two teaspoons of salt. Simmer the affair for 10 minutes for pieces 2 inches thick. Increase the simmering time 15 minutes for each additional inch of bass.

POACHED FILETS IN CURRY

2 pounds filets	Salt and pepper
1 teaspoon curry powder	1 cup fish stock
3 tablespoons oil	1 cup milk
2 tablespoons butter	1/2 cup cream
3 tablespoons flour	

Place the filets in a shallow pan and cover with boiling *court bouillon*. Bring all to a boil, then allow to simmer for only 15 minutes. Then heat the milk and fish stock. Heat the oil and sift in the flour and curry powder, cook together, then add the milk and fish stock, beating the mixture until smooth. Add butter, a spoonful at a time. Beat in well and then add cream and season to taste. Lift out the poached filets to a platter and pour the curry over them.

POACHED FILET OF BASS A LA CREOLE

2 pounds filets	2 onions, finely minced
2 cups strained tomatoes	1 large or 2 small green
1/4 cup oil	peppers
3 tablespoons flour	1 garlic clove, thinly sliced
2 tablespoons butter	1 tablespoon minced parsley
1 teaspoon chili powder	Salt, paprika, sugar

Poach the filets in a shallow pan in salted water. Heat the oil and put in the onions, green peppers (minced), and garlic. Allow to cook for a few minutes, without browning or burning, then add the tomato and season with salt, paprika, and sugar to taste. Let these simmer together under a lid while the fish is cooking. Melt the butter, add the sifted flour and chili powder, cook together, then add to the tomato mixture, stirring until smooth. Then add the parsley. Place the filets on a platter and pour sauce over them.

Boiled Striped Bass

Scale, clean, and cut off the fins of a striped bass and then place it on the oiled rack of a large kettle, or coil the bass in a large frying basket. Cover the entire fish with well flavored *court bouillon* and bring to a boil. Then remove it from the heat to another burner and simmer until the flesh is ready to separate from the bone, about 6 to 10 minutes to the pound, according to the thickness of the fish. Slip off skin and place the bass on a hot platter with your choice of garnishings. Tomato Salsa and Sauce Supreme are rich sauces for a striped bass.

STRIPED BASS PUDDING

1-1/2 cups boiled striped bass, free from skin and bones	Salt and paprika
	1 teaspoon onion juice
3 eggs, yolk and whites separated	1 teaspoon Worcestershire sauce
1 cup cream	1 pinch nutmeg
1/2 cup cracker crumbs	1 teaspoon lemon juice

Work the boiled bass and butter to a cream. Add the yolks of eggs, cream, and cracker crumbs. Add the seasoning and taste carefully, as the success of this dish is in getting it well flavored. Beat the whites of the eggs very stiff and fold them into the mixture. Pour into a buttered mold and allow a little room for rising or expansion as it cools and sets. Steam for two hours. Place in a warm oven to dry out so that the mold can easily be removed, put on a platter, and garnish.

This pudding may be served hot with a rich sauce, or cold with tartare or Norwegian sauce. It may also be baked in the oven, placing the baking dish in another containing hot water. Bake about 40 minutes and serve with a sauce similar to that used for steamed pudding.

STRIPED BASS SALAD

1 cup boiled flaked bass, free from skin and bones	1 cup finely minced celery
	1 head lettuce
3 tablespoons minced olives	Salt and paprika
Mayonnaise to mix	Lemon juice

Mix the fish, celery, olives, and mayonnaise together, and season with salt and lemon juice. Line a salad bowl with leaves of lettuce. Place the salad in the center and dust with paprika.

Striped Bass Fingers

Still another delicious way to prepare striped bass filets, which happens to be a favorite of my wife's and mine, is as strips or chunks of striped bass fried in butter. Cut the striped bass filets into fingers that are as wide as they are thick and place into a buttered frying pan with just enough butter or margarine so that the fish won't stick. Fry until one side is nicely browned and then turn to complete the other side. Serve hot and eat immediately, with dashes of fresh lemon.

Sauces and Dressings

Striped bass alone make great eating, but the gourmet is well aware that the correct seasonings and sauces can enhance the flavor of a bass and turn it into a delight.

COURT BOUILLON

Court bouillon (French for "quick" or "short sauce") is a broth that can be made quickly and often adds the real flavor to what might be a rather bland adventure when a bass is boiled or poached. Court bouillon has many variations. The simplest form comes from Brittany. It consists of equal parts of milk and water, with some salt. The court bouillon is made in advance of the cooking of the fish and must be boiled for at least 1/2 hour before being added to boiled or poached striped bass. The bass is covered completely and simmered gently until cooked (with a lid on).

The following is a more elaborate recipe for the poaching of a large striped bass (8 to 10 pounds) and can be reduced proportionately for smaller fish.

2 gallons water	1 stalk celery
2 carrots	2 tablespoons peppercorns
4 medium onions	1/2 cup red wine vinegar or
3 tablespoons salt	1/3 cup lemon juice
3 bay leaves	

SAUCE VERTE

This sauce is composed of homemade mayonnaise and a collection of blended herbs. Beat the egg yolks with a whisk or beater (the advantage of a whisk is that you have a hand free to add oil). Add the mustard, vinegar, and a little salt to taste. Beat this together, then add oil in a thin stream, whisking constantly. If the mayonnaise is too thick, a little more vinegar may be added.

MAYONNAISE

3 egg yolks	1 cup peanut oil
1 tablespoon mustard	Dash of cayenne
3 tablespoons red wine vinegar	Salt to taste

HERBS

Herbs can be made up of 1/2 cup parsley branches and either 1/2 cup tarragon leaves or 1/4 cup tarragon leaves and 1/4 cup chervil leaves. Put these in a blender with 1/2 cup of oil and use a wooden spoon to help push the herbs into the blades. This mixture is then added to the mayonnaise.

Index

Note: Page numbers in italics indicate illustrations.

Photo and Art Credits

All photographs and line drawings in this book were taken by the author unless otherwise credited as fallows: Jacket Cover, Wayne Trimm; Pages 20-21, Joseph R. Tomelleri; Page 71, Alice Jane Mansuetti; Page 72, Byron Young, New York State Department of Environmental Conservation; Page 82 Michael Hill, Florida Game and Fresh Water Fish Commission; Page 86, Frank Paruka, U.S. Fish and Wildlife Service; Page 88, Larry Green; Page 122, Kentucky Fish and Game Department; Pages 141 and 143, Joseph R. Tomerelli; Page 142, Pris Martin, Texas Parks and Wildlife Department; Page 235, Charles Cinto; Page 258, Bob Inagro, Suffolk *Sun;* Page 270, Lou Tabory; and all line drawings in Chapter 23 by Steve Goione.